Winchester –
a City in the Making

Archaeological excavations between 2002 and 2007 on the sites of Northgate House, Staple Gardens and the former Winchester Library, Jewry St

by Ben M Ford and Steven Teague
with Edward Biddulph, Alan Hardy and Lisa Brown

with contributions by
*Martin Allen, Alex Bayliss, Paul Booth, Christopher Bronk Ramsey,
Greg Campbell, Wendy Carruthers, Dana Challinor, Gordon Cook, H E M Cool,
John Cotter, John Crowther, Gill Cruise, Philip de Jersey, Anne Dodd, Seren Griffiths,
Mark Hounslow, Andrew K G Jones, Vassil Karloukovski, Hugo Lamdin-Whymark,
Richard Macphail, Peter Marshall, Cath Mortimer, Rebecca Nicholson,
Cynthia Poole, Ruth Shaffrey, David Starley, Lena Strid, Helen Webb*

Illustration and design by
*Sophie Lamb, Magdalena Wachnik, Dan Bashford, Mark Gridley,
Ros Lorimer, Sarah Lucas*

Donated to Winchester University Library by Andrew Corrigan

Oxford Archaeology Monograph No 12
2011

The publication of this volume has been generously funded by Keyhaven Land
(a company in the Merlion Group) and Hampshire County Council, with additional
contributions from Laing Homes Ltd and English Heritage

Published by Oxford Archaeology as part of the Oxford Archaeology Monograph series

Designed by Oxford Archaeology Graphics Office

Reconstruction illustrations by Mark Gridley

Edited by Anne Dodd and Alex Smith

Front cover:
Artist's impression showing the area of the excavated site and the north-west corner of
the late Saxon *burh* during the mid-10th to mid-11th century, by Mark Gridley

ISBN 978-0-904220-64-3

Typeset by Production Line, Oxford
Printed in Great Britain by Information Press, Eynsham, Oxford

Contents

Chapter 1: Introduction *by Ben M Ford*

Chapter 2: Prehistoric and Roman evidence *by Lisa Brown and Edward Biddulph*

Chapter 3: The late Saxon period (*c* 850–1050) *by Steve Teague*

Chapter 4: The Anglo-Norman and later medieval period (*c* 1050–1550)
by Steve Teague and Alan Hardy

Chapter 5: Discussion

Chapter 6: Overview of the scientific dating evidence

*by Seren Griffiths, Alex Bayliss, Ben M Ford, Mark Hounslow, Vassil Karloukovski,
Christopher Bronk Ramsey, Gordon Cook and Peter Marshall*

Chapter 7: Overview of the finds assemblages

Chapter 8: Overview of the environmental evidence

List of Figures

List of Plates

List of Tables

Digital contents

Summary

This volume presents the results of two adjacent, large-scale, archaeological projects that took place sequentially between 2002 and 2007 within the north-west corner of the historic core of the city of Winchester. The two sites, Northgate House on Staple Gardens and Winchester Library on Jewry Street, were located on ESE facing slopes overlooking the Itchen Valley, and it is precisely this topographic position that shaped the earliest settlement of the area and provided the legacy that influenced all subsequent 2600 years of change and development. The majority of the evidence focuses on the 9th to 14th centuries, although significant remains from the Iron Age and Roman periods were also recovered.

The earliest evidence related to successive groups of roundhouses positioned along a slight terrace that followed the contour of the hillside dating to the early and the middle Iron Age. The latter phase was contemporary with a holloway located 50 m down slope, which linked the northern and southern entrances of a large enclosure called Oram's Arbour. The apparent linear nature of this part of the Iron Age settlement, combined with the lack of evidence for contemporary pits and other settlement features, suggests a sustained and organised layout with potential zoning of activities.

After a possible hiatus in activity, part of the Oram's Arbour enclosure was developed into a major Roman town, *Venta Belgarum*. The principal north-south street of the town was located at the eastern edge of the excavation area, and took its alignment from the pre-existing holloway. The street was associated with a substantial stone lined water channel/culvert that appears to represent the urban continuation of the aqueduct located outside the North Gate. Occupation during the early part of the Roman period does not appear to have been intensive, but included the remarkably well-preserved remains of a timber-framed house that had burnt to the ground. In the later Roman period there are indications of greater activity, with timber structures aligned along the principal street. Further upslope a focus of iron working activity developed along a secondary east-west street, and another property at some distance from these yielded a full set of bone weaving tablets from its floor. A significant amount of late Roman finds were recovered from Dark Earth deposits that began to form in the late 4th century, after which there is no evidence of significant occupation until the imposition of tenements in the 9th century.

A lack of modern development along the western frontage on Staple Gardens (Brudene Street) resulted in the very exceptional preservation of nearly 350 years of structural development and property usage for five neighbouring tenements. There is also partial evidence for six other tenements opposite these and a further three from the contemporary parallel street (Snitheling Street) to the west. Therefore, aspects of fourteen different properties were excavated and analysed, and links can be suggested between the archaeological data and contemporary documentary sources.

A unique set of scientific dates was obtained and used to create statistical models, which suggest the urban tenement form commenced along Staple Gardens prior to Alfred's *burh* works in the late 9th century. Nearly 1500 post-Roman small finds were recovered, and for the first time from Winchester, a collection of such significant size is considered with reference to its full archaeological context, documenting details of domestic and artesanal activity and trends. These results combine with a wealth of environmental data that provides information on the occupants' diets, the wider environment and rural practices in agriculture and animal husbandry.

As this part of the city became less intensively used in the 13th century, the Archdeacon of Winchester developed a large residence by amalgamating a number of earlier properties, including a small chapel, to create a 'complex' similar in form to a rural manorial model. A handful of finds from the 14th and 15th centuries confirm documentary sources that state the area was depopulated and given over to 'market gardens' as the town contracted.

Acknowledgements

The excavations at Winchester Discovery Centre and Northgate House, and subsequent publication of this volume, have been generously funded by Keyhaven Land (a company in the Merlion Group) and Hampshire County Council, with additional contributions from Laing Homes Ltd and English Heritage. As the archaeological consultant for the Northgate House site, Gifford were engaged by Hampshire County Council to oversee the programme of post-excavation work that led to this publication. The support from all of these organisations is gratefully acknowledged. Gifford extend their particular thanks to Peter North (Merlion Capital Corporation Group).

Staff from Winchester City Council: Tracy Matthews (Historic Environment Officer – Archaeology), Helen Rees (Curator of Archaeology), Graham Scobie (Heritage Information Officer), Ross Turle (Curator of Recent History and Photographs) and Mark Barden (Museums Graphic Designer).

Staff from Hampshire County Council: Alec Gillies (Assistant Head of Architecture), Martin Hallum (Senior Architect), Alex Chinn (Team Leader - Quantity Surveying), and Stephen Appleby (Senior Archaeologist).

Thanks are due to Tom James and Professor Michael Fulford CBE for their constructive comments on the draft text and also to Professor Martin Biddle and Birthe Kyjølbye-Biddle, Professor Barry Cunliffe, and Domonique de Moulin (English Heritage) for sharing their knowledge and advice on site during the excavations.

A huge debt of thanks is also due for the sterling help received from the Winchester Archaeological Rescue Group (WARG) and other volunteers who collectively gave 1146 hours of their time. These included: Denise Baker, Mavis Blanchard, Brian Botwright, Pat Brockway, Geraldine Buchanan, Janet Cairney, Jan Church, Garrard Cole, Britta Echtle, Jean Edwards, David Gollins, Martin Gregory, Sue Harrington, Vicki Harrison, Wendy Haynes, Chris James, Jo James, Janet Johnston, Jennifer Jones, Arthur King, Prue King, David Lloyd, Gill Lovegrove, Jenny Masters, Joanna Morgan, Ann Murphy, Hannah Murphy, Jaynie Oram, Laura Pearson, Val Pegg, Stephen Priestner, Mrs Priestner, Julia Reeves, Julia Sandison, Valerie Sanguine, Catherine Sanguine, Lucy Seviour, Sarah Seviour, Phillip Smith, Rosemary Smith, Tessa Smith, Elizabeth Thorn, Eric Wadham, Pam Wadham, Mollie White, Eleanor Yates

Cath Mortimer would like to thank Dr J O Tate (National Museums of Scotland) for his help with the XRF analyses.

Paul Booth is indebted to Cathy King for help with identification of a number of problematic coins, and, along with Edward Biddulph, is grateful to Helen Rees for her advice with the Winchester pottery fabric series.

Lena Strid thanks Joanne Cooper (Natural History Museum Tring) for identification of cormorant and grey partridge, Helen Rees (Winchester Museum Service) for access to manuscript chapters, and Wendy Smith for commenting on her text.

Rebecca Nicholson owes a debt of gratitude to Dale Serjeantson, Alison Locker and Sheila Hamilton-Dyer for access to their unpublished reports.

Ben M Ford extends thanks to Damian McKenna (Mansells), Terry Rumford (Davis Langdon), Martin Kirby (Gifford), Jules Passingham (Passingham Scaffolding), Penny Lawrence (Capita Symonds), Frank Hallet (The Safety Consultancy), Trish Bould and Belinda Mitchell (Drawing Spaces), and Vik Martin (Vik Martin Photography).

Lisa Brown would like to thank Helen Rees for advice on regional Iron Age pottery fabrics and Professors John Collis and Barry Cunliffe for useful discussions on oppida.

Last but not least, Steve Teague would like to thank Paul McCulloch.

THE PROJECT TEAMS

Ben M Ford was Senior Project Manager for Oxford Archaeology during all stages of archaeological fieldwork and post-excavation for both projects (with the exception of the evaluation (Gifford) and the initial excavation (Wessex) at Northgate House). Steve Teague undertook most of the post-excavation analysis, with support from Lisa Brown, Edward Biddulph and Alan Hardy. Anne Dodd reviewed and extensively revised the draft text for Chapters 3, 4 and 5. Anne Dodd and Alex Smith edited the publication text.

Phil Emery and Dr Gerry Wait of Giffords acted as Archaeological Consultants for Northgate House, and Phil Emery continued in this role for the production of this volume.

NORTHGATE HOUSE

Wessex Archaeology Team

Project Manager: Paul McCulloch
Project Officer: Gail Wakeham
Excavation Staff: Andy Armstrong, Andrew Baines, David Brown, Laura Cassie, Jonathon Crisp, Kirsten Dinwiddy, Neil Fitzpatrick, Victoria Lambert, Steve Legg, Catherine McHarg, Martin McGonigle, Dave Murdie, Christopher Owen, Ruth Panes, Nicholas Plunkett, Clare Roberts, Andy Sole, and Steven Teague.

Oxford Archaeology Team

Project Officer: Dan Dodds
Supervisors: Robin Bashford, Guy Cockin, Emily Glass, Robert Radford, Dan Sykes, Steve Teague
Excavation Staff: Kirsty Bone, Jane Brant, Abigail Brown, Ralph Brown, Will Clarke, Charlie Correa, Rob Cole, Jon Crisp, Patrick Dresch, Kevan Edinborough, Pascal Eloy, Paul Everill, Jonny Geber, J Gibblin, Martin Greaney, Leo Heatley, R Humphey, F Gibson, Emily Glass, Jacek Grusz-czynski, Anna Komar, Vicky Lambert, Adam Lord, S Lucas, D Mahoney, Jennifer Marchant, Alan Marshall, Bryan Matthews, Rowan McAlley, Martin McGonigle, Lucy Offord, Chris Richarsdon (and his invaluable work as Matrix Coordinator), Chris Swales, Phillippa Puzey-Broomhead, D Reay, Mary Saunders, Robert Tannahill, Julian Thorley, Marc Storey, Nick Pankhurst, Tavis Walker, Kate Weaton, Dan Wheeler, D Whittaker, Justin Wiles, A Witkin, and Kevin Wooldridge.

WINCHESTER DISCOVERY CENTRE

Buildings Team
(WW II *Shelters and Library structure*)

Jon Gill, Andy Miller, Jane Phimester, for their work on the WWII shelters and Simon Underdown for his work on the Library Building.

Evaluation Team

Supervisor: Dan Sykes
Excavation Staff: Ian Cook, Darko Maricevic, Chris Richardson, Dan Wheeler.

Excavation Team

Project Officer: Steve Teague
Supervisors: Robin Bashford, Emily Glass, Nick Pankhurst.
Excavation Staff: Laura Cassie, David Carr, Matt Copley, Claire Davies, Mark Dodd, Jodie Ford, Dawn Irving, Hannah Kennedy, Mike Kershaw, Alan Marshall, Steve Martin, Rowan McAlley, Ross McGauran, Dave McNicolls, Dave Murdy, Mary Nicholls, Phillippa Puzey-Broomhead, Chris Richardson, Guy Salkeld, Mary Saunders, Mark Stedman, Elin Ahlin Sundman, Jeni Thurstan, Dan Watkeys, Dan Wheeler. Jane Brant and Leanne Ellis who so competently supervised all the work by the volunteers.

OTHER OA STAFF

For their contributions behind the scenes and back at the office thank you to Leigh Allen, Robert Bailey, Jane Baldwin, Angela Boyle, Robin Latour, Steve Laurie-Lynch, Mark Littlewood, Olivia Pierpoint, Marta Perez, Simon Palmer, Daniel Poore, Kay Proctor, Nicola Scott, Nick Shepherd, Georgina Slater, Elizabeth Strafford, Duncan Waltham, Graham Walton, Robert Williams.

*The Northgate House
Excavation Team
(February 2005)*

*The Discovery Centre
Excavation Team
(March 2006)*

Chapter 1 Introduction

by Ben M Ford

THE PROJECTS

General introduction to the projects

This book and its accompanying CD-Rom present the results of two adjacent, large-scale, archaeological projects that took place sequentially between 2002 and 2007 within the north-west corner of the historic core of the city of Winchester in Hampshire, central Southern England (Fig. 1.1).

The archaeological works were conducted in response to two separate, unrelated but neighbouring developments. Archaeological works on the site of Northgate House (the former SCATS office), on the west side of the north end of Staple Gardens were conducted between 2002 and May 2005 in advance of the construction of new residential and retail units for Keyhaven Land (Winchester) Holdings Ltd and Laing Homes. Subsequently, excavations and building recording works were carried out between 2005 and 2007 on the opposite side of Staple Gardens at the site of Winchester Lending Library on Jewry Street, where Hampshire County Council proposed a new Cultural Discovery Centre (as it was called at the time but now commonly known, and henceforth referred to, as the Discovery Centre).

The fieldwork, post-excavation and publication were funded principally by Keyhaven Land (Winchester) Holdings Ltd and Hampshire County Council, with a minor contribution from Laing Homes Ltd. Additional financial assistance was provided by English Heritage to complete the research-driven aspects of the scientific dating programme. As the archaeological consultant for the Northgate House site, Gifford were engaged by Hampshire County Council to oversee the programme of post-excavation work that led to this publication.

The archives

Both the Northgate House and the Discovery Centre sites have separate fully integrated written, drawn, photographic, artefactual and ecofactual archives, which will be held by the Winchester Museums Service under Accession Codes; WINCM: AY93 for Northgate House, and WINCM: AY220 for the Discovery Centre. The archives will also contain all the documents presented on the CD-Rom (listed in the contents and discussed below).

For the purposes of the analysis, presentation and discussion in this book the two separate archive data sets were studied as a single comprehensive and integrated archive. To enable the reader to distinguish between the two sites the prefix NH is retained throughout for data from Northgate House and the prefix CC for data from the Discovery Centre.

The structure of the report

The two excavations generated very large datasets of written, drawn and digital records, along with substantial amounts of artefactual and environmental material relating to the pre-Roman, Roman, Saxon, Anglo-Norman, medieval, post-medieval, and modern periods of activity at the sites. For publication, it was decided to present this information using a combination of printed and digital formats.

This printed volume contains an introductory background to the projects, the archaeological description and analysis by period and phase, summaries of all the specialist contributions, and a discussion of the results.

Chapter 1 establishes the background and location of the projects. The geology and topography section positions the sites within the landscape, and the historical and archaeological summaries provide the context, as it is currently understood, for human activity in the locality through time. The background to the projects gives a summary of the nature of the development and the archaeological response. Chapter 1 also summarises the research aims that guided the analysis. The last section outlines the approach to dating and phasing that was taken during analysis, and presents short written summaries of the project phases supported by simplified illustrations for each phase, and a land-use diagram.

Chapters 2, 3 and 4 contain descriptions of the phases of the archaeological sequence by period. The prehistoric and Roman periods are covered in Chapter 2, the late Saxon period in Chapter 3, and the Anglo-Norman and later medieval periods in Chapter 4. The descriptions are enhanced by reference to pertinent finds and environmental information and are supported by detailed illustrations. Chapter 5 summarises and discusses the results from each period incorporating stratigraphic, documentary, scientific dating, artefactual and ecofactual evidence to explore a number of themes. Chapter 6 presents the results of the archaeomagnetic and radiocarbon dating programmes and the

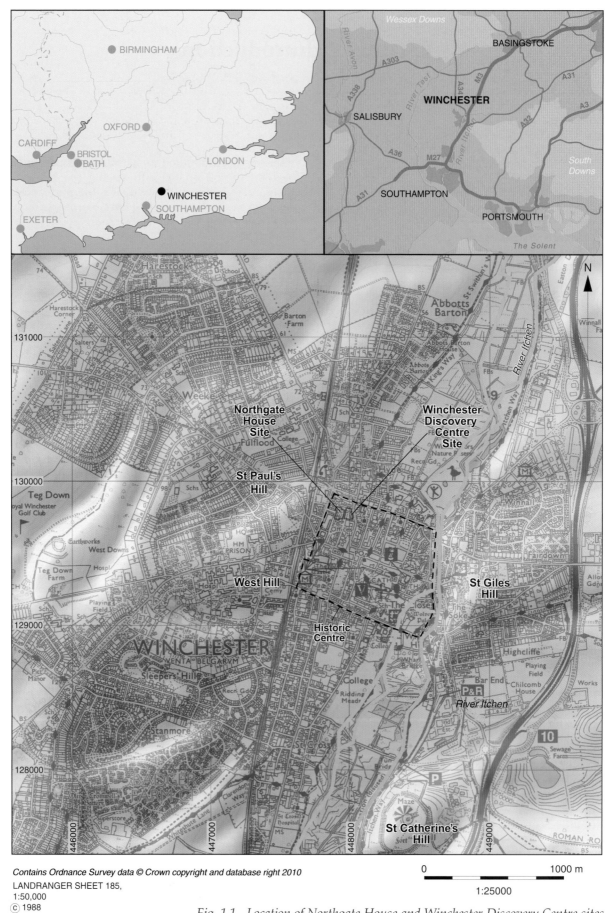

Fig. 1.1 Location of Northgate House and Winchester Discovery Centre sites

report on the Bayesian statistical model developed for the site. Shortened versions of the specialist artefactual and environmental reports appear in Chapters 7 and 8, together with full finds illustrations and a selection of the most significant tables.

The CD-Rom accompanying this volume contains a number of documents relating to the projects; these are arranged as follows:

- Part 1: contains a description of the mitigation methodologies for both Northgate House and the Winchester Discovery Centre, along with the pre-analysis post-excavation Assessment Reports (Teague and Ford 2006, and Teague 2006 respectively) and the Revised Research Design (OA 2007a) that formed the basis for the analysis in this volume.

- Part 2: presents digital copies of the client reports for two Building Recording Projects that were undertaken as a result of the construction of the Discovery Centre. The first covers the WWII shelters (OA 2006) below the carpark of the former Winchester Library and the second covers the former Winchester Library structure itself (OA 2007b).

- Part 3: contains each specialist analysis report in full (referenced to in the print text as *Digital Sections 1 to 19*), including methodologies, catalogues, tables, diagrams, plates and figures. See contents list for details.

- Part 4: is a Photographic Gallery that contains additional selected images of the works.

LOCATION

The Northgate House development site is centred on NGR SU 479 297 and covers an area of 4562 m² (Fig. 1.2), within which 1821 m² was archaeologically investigated. It is bounded on its western upslope side by retaining walls that define the backs of a number of properties that front onto the northern end of Tower Street and on its eastern downslope side by Staple Gardens. The northern boundary of the development site is partly defined by the crooked corner of Tower Street to the north-west, and to the north-east by the southern boundary of Nos 21/22 Staple Gardens and by Northgate Place at the corner of Tower Street and Staple Gardens. The southern boundary of the site is defined by Staple Chambers, a 1960s office block. Immediately prior to the archaeological works the site had been occupied by three derelict buildings: Northgate House, a large 1960s office block set in the middle of the plot, No. 19 Staple Gardens, a late Victorian detached property to its south, and Documation House, a smaller 1960s office block to its north. All three were set back from Staple Gardens and separated by gardens, carparking areas and access roads. The western end of each building had been slightly terraced into the ground and the eastern ends slightly raised on their

foundations to allow for the extant north-east facing slope of the site, which falls from 54.4 m aOD along its western side down to Staple Gardens which slopes down northwards from 51.5 m to 50.3 m aOD.

The Winchester Discovery Centre site is centred on NGR SU 480 297 and measured 3695 m² (Fig 1.2) within which an area of 976 m² was archaeologically investigated. This site is bounded to the west by a long, tall wall that retains Staple Gardens, to the east by Jewry Street, to the north by Tower Street, and to the south by the neighbouring properties of Nos 19–20A Jewry Street (excavated by Wessex Archaeology in 2006) and the Night Shelter on Staple Gardens. The entire site is defined by the curtilage of the former Library, which fronts onto Jewry Street, and is a listed Grade II* building reflecting its architectural history as the former Corn Exchange and Market House designed by local architect Owen Browne Carter in 1836 and completed in 1838 in the Classical style (Freeman 1991, 3–4). Immediately prior to redevelopment the Library was surrounded by a tarmac surfaced carparking area, with a public convenience in the north-east corner, an electricity sub-station in the north-west corner and a small derelict retail kiosk on the Jewry Street frontage in the south-east corner.

The site had a gentle downwards slope to the east and north-east. From a high point in the south-west corner at 49.4 m aOD it slopes down to Jewry Street, which is relatively level, at 46.6 m aOD, as it passes the front of the Library, and down to 48.7 m aOD in its north-west corner. Below the surface of the carpark were two large Second World War air-raid shelter complexes, which consisted of interconnected lengths of 'corridors' arranged in a rectilinear format to fit the available space. The site had evidently been terraced, to varying degrees, into the hillside along the full length of its western side and most of its northern side. This probably occurred during the construction of the Corn Exchange. The design of the Corn Exchange takes account of the resultant slope, with its internal floor broadly level with the external ground level to its west but with the main eastern entrance to this level reached by a set of grand steps from Jewry Street. An indication of the former topography and depth of deposits that had been removed to create the terrace can be gained from the slope of Staple Gardens and the downward west to east slope of Tower Street from its junction with Staple Gardens. This can be seen in the different construction materials used in the retaining wall to the west of the site that separates it from Staple Gardens, and is represented as the interface between the lower stone and flint, retaining, element of the wall with dressed flint panels and brickwork of the upper wall element. It is possible that the stonework in the lower element was derived from buildings that had existed on the site prior to the construction of the Corn Exchange.

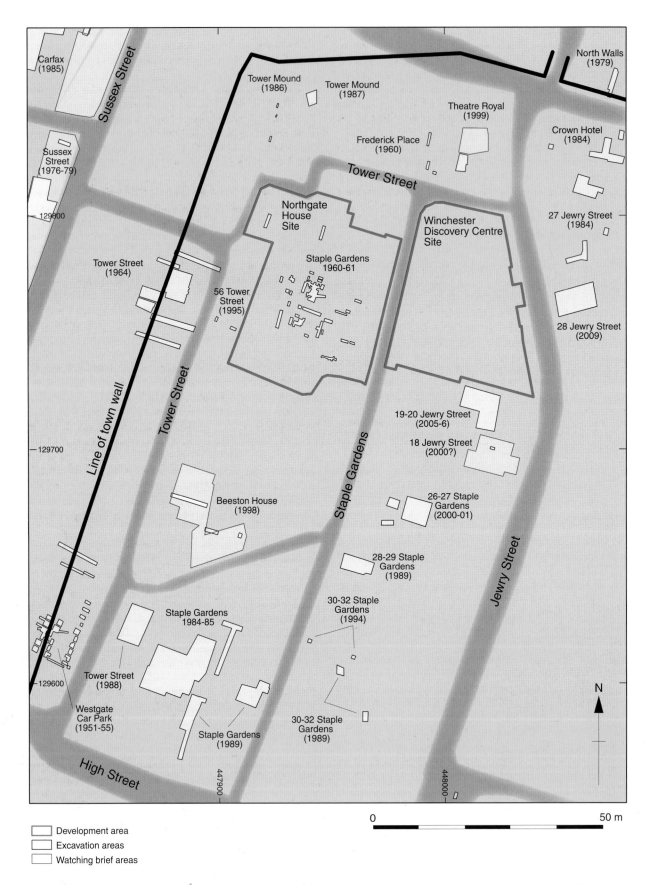

Carfax
(1985)

Sussex Street

North Walls
(1979)

Tower Mound
(1986)

Tower Mound
(1987)

Theatre Royal
(1999)

Crown Hotel
(1984)

Sussex
Street
(1976-79)

Frederick Place
(1960)

Tower Street

—129800

27 Jewry Street
(1984)

Northgate
House
Site

Winchester
Discovery Centre
Site

Tower Street
(1964)

Staple Gardens
1960-61

56 Tower
Street
(1995)

28 Jewry Street
(2009)

Tower Street

Line of town wall

—129700

19-20 Jewry Street
(2005-6)

Staple Gardens

18 Jewry Street
(2000?)

Beeston House
(1998)

26-27 Staple
Gardens
(2000-01)

Jewry Street

28-29 Staple
Gardens
(1989)

30-32 Staple
Gardens
(1994)

—129600

Staple Gardens
1984-85

Tower Street
(1988)

N

Westgate
Car Park
(1951-55)

Staple Gardens
(1989)

30-32 Staple
Gardens
(1989)

High Street

447900

448000

0   50 m

Development area

Excavation areas

Watching brief areas

Fig. 1.2 Location of the Northgate House and Winchester Discovery Centre development sites and other previously excavated sites in the north-west corner of Winchester

GEOLOGY AND TOPOGRAPHY

The City of Winchester sits at the western end of the South Downs, a linear band of chalk downland that extends eastwards through Hampshire and Sussex to Beachy Head and the Seven Sisters on the south coast (Fig. 1.1). This distinctive downland landscape has been formed over millions of years. The Upper Chalk bedrock that was laid down in the seabeds of the Cretaceous Epoch was subsequently folded and pushed upwards creating an incline (known locally as the 'Winchester incline') that is clearly seen in the slanting strata exposed by the Twyford Down cutting for the M3 motorway to the south-east of the city. The upper part of this incline was severely eroded by the actions of advancing and retreating ice sheets during the Pleistocene glaciations, during which time deposits of Clay-with-Flints and Sarsen stones were probably deposited. When the last Ice Age came to an end, a process that took place between 10–20,000 years ago, the retreating glaciers created huge flows of melt-water which carved their way through the area changing the landscape, shaping the hills and valleys, and depositing coarse gravel beds in the valley floors. During the Holocene these flows diminished and were transformed into slower-flowing rivers that laid down finer gravels, sands and silts within the valleys, and it was within these deposits that the rivers of the area, including the River Itchen, settled to meander and seasonally flood, as they do to this day. The geology of the area has been mapped by the British Geological Survey (BGS, Sheet E299).

The resultant local landscape, therefore, is one of undulating hills broken by river valleys, sometimes with steep sides, which are characteristically drained by rivers running from the north-east to the south-west. The rivers themselves are fed by rainfall runoff from the hillsides forming a series of streams that gather in size until reaching the valley floor and the Itchen itself. These would have flowed along smaller gullies and undulations, between which were spurs of higher ground, giving a corrugated rolling effect to the appearance of the hillsides. Winchester itself nestles on the gentle south-east lower slopes at the eastern end of such a spur, known today as St Paul's Hill and West Hill. This promontory in combination with the similar but more dominant St Giles Hill opposite creates a narrowing in the Itchen Valley (Figs 1.1 and 1.3 and Plate 1.1). Within the valley floor at this location there is evidence for at least one large island (Zant 1993, fig. 4) formed of calcareous *tufa* deposits.

The detailed underlying topography of the historic city has been masked by over 2000 years of human occupation, but the general picture is still visible in the townscape today, as the view from St Giles Hill over the city shows (Plate 1.2). The historic city is split into two distinct topographic zones, its western half lying on the broadly east-facing slopes of St Paul's Hill, and its eastern half covering the valley floor of the River Itchen (Fig. 1.3). Over the last 2000 years the valley floor has been reclaimed and raised and the various channels of the Itchen have

Plate 1.1   View over the Itchen Valley and Winchester looking northwards from St Catherine's Hill

Plate 1.2   View over Winchester looking westwards from St Giles Hill

been canalised and diverted, effectively pushing the main course of the river towards the eastern side of the valley. Here, City Bridge leads westwards over the Itchen into the eastern side of the historic city centre and onto the flat expanse of Broadway that leads onto the narrower High Street that travels upslope to the still extant medieval West Gate. These two streets form the city's principal east to west thoroughfare, to both sides of which north-south side lanes and streets can be found. On the valley floor these side streets are level with the Broadway but as the High Street rises it appears that the side streets are set closer together and run along the downhill edges of a series of terraces that accentuate the alignment of the hillside contours. Towards the western end of the High Street, on its north side, the final three side streets run across to the north-west corner of the city where the excavations were located. Jewry Street is the lowest, easterly and largest of these, and forms the principal north-south thoroughfare leading northwards out of the city, with the more minor Staple Gardens and Tower Street running parallel to it, each respectively further upslope (Fig. 1.2). Smaller lanes, such as the east-west section at the end of Tower Street, along with passageways and sets of steps connect these side streets together, and from these the jigsaw of the terraced building plots that front onto them can be glimpsed.

The topographic position of the modern city of Winchester and its surroundings has been favourable for access to a good variety of natural resources relating to the geology and habitats provided by hill and river valley. Its situation, at the narrowing of the valley where the river is divided by islands, provides an advantageous and relatively easy crossing point over the Itchen for east-west inland routes and forms a natural crossroads with routes heading northwards from the south coast. As such, it became a focus for human activity and settlement from small-scale beginnings in the late Bronze Age to the modern city of the early 21st century. This situation and its obvious advantages to human activity have been discussed in previous publications (Zant 1993, 3; Scobie 1995, 4).

THE HISTORICAL AND ARCHAEOLOGICAL SETTING

Background

Over the past 60 years Winchester and its environs have been the subjects of extensive research, into the exceptional surviving documentary evidence, the standing historic buildings and the below-ground archaeological remains. Archaeological work up to the early 1980s has been reviewed by Martin Biddle (1983). This included the rescue work led by Frank Cottrill from 1949–1960, the ambitious research-led urban archaeological projects of the Winchester Excavations Committee and the Winchester Research Unit during the 1960s, which examined 2% of the city's walled area, and the subsequent rescue work of

the Research Unit and the City Museums from 1972, which was mainly focused on the suburbs. In the late 1980s large-scale urban excavations conducted by the Museums Service took place in advance of the construction of The Brooks Shopping Centre.

Since 1990 much archaeological work has been undertaken as part of the local planning process, which has required that new developments take account of the potential archaeological remains that they could potentially destroy, with preservation *in situ* required as a priority, and where this is not possible preservation by excavation and record, supported by the developer. This meant, as with all the previous opportunistic 'rescue type work', that the location and scale of excavations depended on the location and size of new developments rather than sites being targeted specifically for research led excavation. It was also the start of excavation in the town by external archaeological contractors. The documentary resources relating to the settlement, its buildings and topography, trade, and its inhabitants have been comprehensively studied by Derek Keene (1985) and Alexanda Rumble (2003), and the extent of the archaeological research and excavation at Winchester has meant that we now have a considerable body of knowledge relating to the character, date and extent of human activity in the area. As Martin Biddle (1983) has commented, 'It is precisely the long continuation of work in Winchester which is yielding results that are more than superficial sketches of the city's development and changing character'.

The historical and archaeological background relevant to the present excavations is summarised below. The positions of the many archaeological excavations in the north-west corner of the historic core are shown on Figure 1.2, while Figure 1.3 shows the location of many of the other significant sites within the city and its immediate environs. These sites are referred to throughout this volume. Graham Scobie has produced a series of plans that show the current understanding of settlement development from the Iron Age to the medieval period (reproduced in Fig. 1.4). The sequence of landownership in the north-west corner of the city, as derived from the studies of medieval documents by Martin Biddle (1976) and Derek Keene (1985), is shown on Figure 1.5, while Figure 1.6 continues this sequence from the early post-medieval to the modern periods in the form of maps and views. Figure 1.7 establishes the correlation between the modern and medieval street names that will be used throughout this volume.

The pre-Roman period

The area occupied by the modern city of Winchester appears not to have been the focus of intensive activity during the earlier prehistoric period, but the higher downland surrounding the city was occupied from the early Neolithic period onwards. At Winnall Down, on the east side of the River Itchen, an interrupted ring ditch (pit circle) produced Plain Bowl pottery and 4th millennium radiocarbon dates (Fasham 1982). Activity continued during the

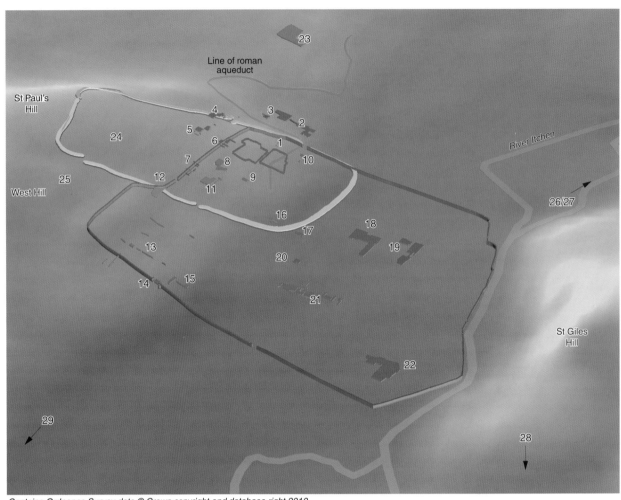

Contains Ordnance Survey data © Crown copyright and database right 2010

1	Frederick Place		15	Henly's Garage
2	Victoria Road		16	St George's Street
3	Eagle Hotel, Swan Lane		17	Mason's Hall, 2 Parchment Street
4	Carfax		18	The Brooks
5	Sussex Street		19	Lower Brook Street
6	Tower Street 1964		20	The Square
7	Westgate Car Park		21	Cathedral Green
8	Beeston House		22	Wolvesey Palace
9	28-29 Staple Gardens		23	Lankhills
10	27 Jewry Street		24	Oram's Arbour 2001-02
11	Staple Gardens 1984-85		25	Mews Lane
12	Castle Yard		26	Winnall II cemetery
13	Lower Barracks		27	Winnall Down/Easton Lane
14	Southgate		28	St Catherine's Hill

Fig. 1.3   Topography of Winchester showing the Iron Age enclosure and the Roman and medieval defensive circuits with the locations of Northgate House and Winchester Discovery Centre sites and other excavations referred to in the text (site locations after WCC UAD)

Fig. 1.4 (opposite page)   The development of Winchester (after Scobie, G, Winchester Museums Service)

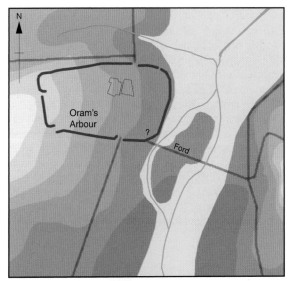

a. The Iron Age enclosure at Oram's Arbour

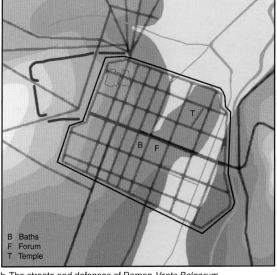

b. The streets and defences of Roman *Venta Belgarum*

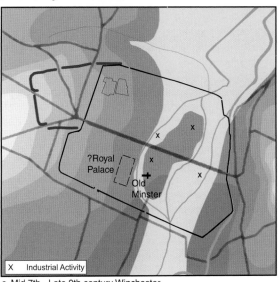

c. Mid 7th - Late 9th century Winchester

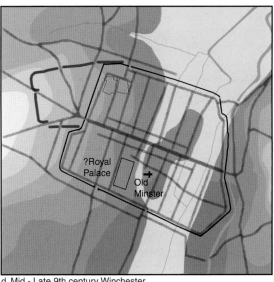

d. Mid - Late 9th century Winchester

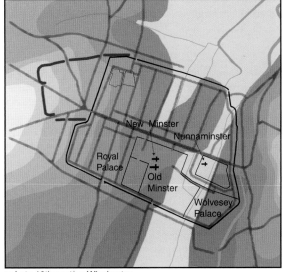

e. Late 10th century Winchester

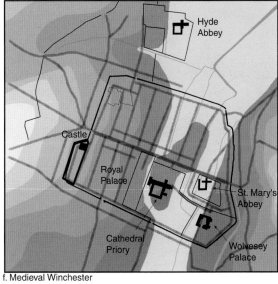

f. Medieval Winchester

0   1000 m

1:20000

middle and late Bronze Age at Winnall Down and at nearby Easton Lane, as attested by farming settlement features and Deverel-Rimbury ceramics (Fasham 1985; Fasham *et al.* 1989). Located both to the west of Winchester, at West Hill, and to the south at Twyford Down, were the remains of Bronze Age settlements and associated burials (James 1997; Stuart and Birkbeck 1936; Walker and Farwell 2000).

Closer to the site of the present excavations, a Bronze Age Beaker was found some 0.5 km away at Mew's Lane and scattered finds of later Neolithic/early Bronze Age flint and pottery have been recorded elsewhere within the city limits (James 1997). Possible post-Deverel-Rimbury sherds from the Westgate Car Park site (Collis 1978, 200) and a late Bronze Age cremation vessel found in Tower Street (Biddle 1965, pl. 48, feature 71) attest to some level of activity during this period, but no structural evidence indicating sustained settlement before *c* 800 BC has been noted in the vicinity of the site. It may be, however, that the lack of recorded earlier prehistoric settlements is a product of the pattern of archaeological investigation rather than a reflection of their genuine absence.

The earliest recognised evidence for settlement and organised farming within the modern city dates to the late Bronze Age/early Iron Age transition (*c* 800–600 BC). Distinctive 8th- to 6th-century pottery was found associated with a hearth excavated close to the present site at George Street (Cunliffe 1964, fig. 12, nos 1 and 2). Slightly later in date were field systems, stock pens, four-post structures and pits representing settlement and mixed agricultural activity, located mostly on the chalk to the west of the present site, including on the eastern slope of St Paul's Hill (Qualmann *et al.* 2004; WUAD No. 1370). The early Iron Age settlement can be put in the context of broadly contemporary sites on higher ground east of the Itchen, including an enclosed settlement at Winnall Down (Fasham 1985) and an unenclosed settlement at St. Catherine's Hill dating from *c* 600 BC (Hawkes *et al.* 1930).

At the current site a settlement with post-built roundhouses, dated to the early Iron Age on ceramic and stratigraphic evidence, was succeeded by a well-dated middle Iron Age settlement, elements of which were also discovered during excavations in the 1960s (Cunliffe 1964). During this time St Catherine's Hill was enclosed by imposing earthworks and the unenclosed settlement on St Paul's Hill underwent a similarly dramatic change with the construction of a bank and ditch enclosing an area of 20 ha, now known as Oram's Arbour (Fig. 1.4a). The line of the defensive circuit has been identified on three sides, along with the positions of western, northern and southern entrances. The eastern side of the enclosure was probably represented by the natural break of slope at the edge of the floodplain (Qualmann 1993, 75), and formalised defences have not yet been discovered—the marshy conditions perhaps rendered these unnecessary. The floodplain was apparently uninhabited during the Iron Age (Zant 1993) and, although evidence for occupation within Oram's Arbour has been recovered at numerous sites (Qualmann *et al.* 2004; see Chapters 2 and 5, Fig. 5.2), the pattern of internal organisation and the precise function of the enclosure have remained elusive. On topographic grounds it could have been designed to control a pre-existing, possibly very ancient, network of trade routes that exploited a ford across the Itchen (Qualmann *et al.*, 2004). Its construction pre-dated the late Iron Age period generally accepted for the emergence of *oppida,* which developed in the wake of pre-conquest Roman trading influence, and its floruit ended during the closing decades of the late Iron Age (Zant 1993, Qualmann 1993), perhaps in response to the ascent of the more conventional *oppidum* of Calleva at Silchester.

The Roman period

The site of the Iron Age Oram's Arbour enclosure was chosen by the Romans to establish the settlement of *Venta Belgarum* (Fig. 1.4b). The settlement was defined by an initial phase of earthen rampart construction, which was erected in the early Flavian period, *c* AD 75 (Biddle 1975a, 110), and may point to the town's status as a *municipium* (Wilson 2006, 30). The site's topographic situation clearly affected the positioning of the new defences, as did the extant remains of the northern earthworks of the Iron Age enclosure, which were in part incorporated into the north-west Roman defences thus maintaining the site's east-west and north-south axis. Notably, the position of the northern entrance remained in the same location as its Iron Age precursor, and a stretch of the northern defensive ditch was recut (Qualmann *et al.* 2004), with the corresponding ramparts probably enhanced. The principal changes were to the southern and western ramparts. The southern rampart was constructed *c* 300 m to the south of the Oram's Arbour earthwork, and the western rampart was sited further down the east facing slopes of St Paul's Hill. This position may have been chosen due to an advantageous break of slope or terrace in the hillside (Qualmann 1993, fig. 4) but it also appears to coincide with the point where the chalk bedrock starts to be overlain by Clay-with-Flint deposits. The river was canalised to the eastern side of the valley floor in the Flavian or Trajanic period, allowing the Romans to overcome the topographic restrictions of the valley floor and reclaim and extend eastwards significantly beyond the higher ground offered by the islands that had thus far been utilised (Wacher 1995, 293; Zant 1993, 50–2). The town was fully enclosed when the earth ramparts were enlarged in the late 2nd century (Qualmann 1993, 73).

The rectilinear pattern of street and *insula* is ubiquitous throughout the Roman Empire; street grids are known at Trier (Germany), Arles (Gaul), Timgad (North Africa), and Silchester (Britain), to name just a few cities (Owens 1992, 121–48). At

Venta Belgarum the grid was influenced by the site topography, and has been relatively accurately predicted by connecting evidence from multiple archaeological observations (WMS, UAD). On the slope of the hillside the north-south streets were orientated with the prevailing contours, and it is notable that these streets were closer together, thus forming smaller insulae, than those in the valley floor. The notable exception to this pattern is the final set of insulae that ran inside the western defences of the town, the northernmost two of which were partially explored by these excavations. On the hillside the pattern may have been established by the end of the 1st century AD (Qualmann 1993, 75), although the principal elements must have been laid down around the same time as the initial earthen defences were being constructed. It is likely that the *insula* and street pattern in the valley floor evolved over a century or so with land reclamation efforts from the late 1st century AD into the late 2nd century (ibid., 76).

Structures in the early Roman town were typically timber-built, but masonry buildings were constructed in time. As expected, the largest public building, the forum basilica (constructed around AD 100), was located in the centre of the town at the modern junction of Middle Brook Street and High Street (Biddle 1964, 203; Biddle and Quirk 1964, 153). A temple was located in the north-east quarter of the town towards Durngate (Biddle 1975b, 298), although more temples undoubtedly existed elsewhere in the town. Few domestic structures are known, but early Roman domestic residences have been excavated inside the south gate (Rees forthcoming) and in The Brooks (Zant 1993, 51). These were replaced in the late Roman period with much more richly-decorated houses, including courtyard houses with painted walls and mosaic flooring (Zant 1993, 83–127). The 2nd and 3rd centuries saw occupation particularly in the eastern and northern suburbs outside the defensive circuit, which was strengthened with a stone wall in the 3rd century (Qualmann 1993, 73). Much of the published evidence for occupation and structural remains comes from excavations in the heart of the settlement, chiefly at The Brooks (Zant 1993), but townhouses are also known from work in the south-east corner of the town at Wolvesey Palace (Biddle 1975b, 321–6), and evidence in the north-west part of the town was recovered from the site of Northgate House in the 1950s and 60s (Cunliffe 1964) and at Frederick Place (Collis 1978). This took the form of timber post-built structures and metalled surfaces with some metalworking activity, and started in the 2nd century, continuing into the later 4th century before being sealed under 'dark earth'. The extra-mural areas inevitably provided space for burial, and extensive cemeteries developed, especially in the late Roman period. Lankhills is one of Winchester's best-studied cemeteries (Clarke 1979; Booth *et al.* 2010), but others are known (Browne *et al.* forthcoming).

The post-Roman: early and middle Saxon periods

The period between the detachment of Britain from western Roman Imperial administration in the early 5th century and the establishment of the bishopric at Winchester in the mid 7th century remains obscure, with fragmentary archaeological evidence that is not closely datable. Several phases of metalling postdating the 360s or 370s were identified from the street to the south of the forum (Biddle 1970, 312–3) and a similar sequence was found on the street leading through the South Gate until it was closed at some point before the early 7th century when access was blocked initially by a ditch and later by a wall (Biddle 1975a, 116–8). Two human burials were found in front of this wall, one of which produced radiocarbon dates of 710±70 (HAR-294) and 660±80 (HAR-364). The Roman cemeteries outside and to the south of the East Gate seem to have been in use no later than the end of the 4th or early 5th centuries (Browne *et al.* forthcoming). The cemetery at Lankhills, outside the north gate, also continued in use at least to the end of the 4th century. Despite recent excavation and a suite of radiocarbon dates (Booth *et al.* 2010) the scale and duration of use into the early 5th century remains uncertain, but were perhaps quite limited (ibid.). A small quantity of Anglo-Saxon 'grass-tempered' pottery has been recovered from 'dark earth' deposits and as residual material in later contexts from with the town. On Lower Brook Street about twenty sherds, from at least three carinated bowls of Germanic type, were found in a late Saxon pit. This material has parallels from Fedderson Wierde in Lower Saxony and is datable to AD 400–50 a time associated with population movements connected with settlements in England (Biddle 1972, 101).

Christianity was established in Wessex around 635 with the conversion of King Cynegils of the Gewisse, followed by the establishment of a bishopric at Dorchester-on-Thames (Biddle 1972, 242), and after 662 the establishment of a second (or a replacement) bishopric in Winchester. At this time or possibly earlier, in 648, Cenwalh of Wessex founded a church, the 'Old Minster', within the former Roman defences near or on the site of the former Forum. This probably served as a royal chapel, and placed Winchester at the centre of the religious life of the king and the kingdom. There are few documentary references to either the church or Winchester until the 9th century, although two 8th-century kings, Cynewulf and Cuthred, possibly descendants of its founder, were buried there (Yorke 1982, 81).

The archaeological evidence for the middle Saxon period is limited but intriguing given the documentary context (Fig. 1.4c). The site of the 7th-century church was excavated after Quirk (1957) accurately predicted its location to the north of the present Cathedral. At Lower Brook Street a small inhumation cemetery seems to have had Christian characteristics with graves orientated on an east-west axis. The grave goods are notably similar to those found in the later 7th-century cemetery at Winnall (Biddle 1975b, 305). One individual was buried with an elaborate necklace comprising three gold-and-garnet pendants, two other gold objects, two silver pendants and 27 silver rings, suggesting that this could be the cemetery of a high-status community. The cemetery was overlain by a rare example of a non-monastic masonry building, possibly two storeys in height. A timber annexe was later added which post-dated a timber-lined well, from which a piece of surviving timber gave a radiocarbon date of 710±60 (HAR-288), recalibrated to 700±70 by Ralph-Michael-Han (Biddle 1975b, 310). Evidence for gold working was found within the building and nearby. The building was later incorporated into the nave of St. Mary's Church on Tanner Street (Lower Brook Street) during the 10th century. Given its pre-urban context, and the associated finds, it seems likely to have been associated with high status settlement, possibly a private estate (Biddle 1972, 244). At The Square (Teague 1989b) excavations revealed a sequence of workshops associated with metalworking, the latest of which was associated with a sceat datable to 720–30 (Zant 1990); these underlay deposits representing the earliest laying out of the street immediately south of the High Street, argued to have been in place before 901 (Biddle 1976, 313–5).

The late Saxon period

It is during the period of sustained Viking threat and attacks throughout the mid-late 9th to the early 10th century that a real change is seen in the character of the occupation at Winchester, with the reintroduction of a truly urban form (Figs 1.4d and e). Although it is generally accepted that this process began in the later 9th century, there has been considerable debate about the precise dates of the re-establishment of the defences, the laying out of the rectilinear street system, and the emergence of urban occupation. Winchester was first listed as a defended *burh* in the Burghal Hidage, an administrative document (which exists in a number of different versions) relating to the obligations for the upkeep and defence of a system of fortifications against the Vikings. The document is currently believed to date from the period 914–19, during the reign of Edward the Elder (899–924), but it describes a system that is believed to have been developed by his father, King Alfred the Great. The network of *burhs* therefore may have been largely implemented during the reign of King Alfred (871–899) (Brooks 1964; Biddle 1975b). Of Winchester specifically, Haslam (2004) suggests a much more precise date of May 878 to August 879, although there is no evidence to support this assertion. However, the West Saxon Charters from the reign of Ethelbald (855–60) indicate the first exaction of the duty of fortress construction, army service, and bridge building, and a 10th-century poem records that a bridge was built over the Itchen

immediately outside the West Gate in 859. This could suggest that the earliest elements of the system pre-date Alfred's reign. Indeed, Yorke has proposed that Winchester was provided with defences in 860, as the result of the substantial Viking raid that it suffered (Yorke 1982, 67). Biddle (1983) notes that specific documentary references indicate that the defences could have been in place by 860, and raises the question of a possible direct relationship between the fortification of Winchester and the decline of the nearby mid-Saxon trading settlement of Hamwic, which had been attacked by the Vikings in 840.

Winchester was one of the very largest *burhs*, with 2400 hides assigned for its maintenance and defence. This figure can be equated with the total length of the circuit of the Roman walls and supports the widely accepted view that the Roman defensive circuit had been repaired, rebuilt or redrafted to protect the *burh*.

On Sussex Street, located outside the north-west corner of the city, excavation of material interpreted as upcast from the defensive ditch contained finds broadly dated to the reign of Alfred (Rees *et al.* 2008, 28). James suggests that the establishment of the streets was a secondary activity to the defensive works and the street system may have been established in stages (James 1997, 40–1), although Biddle and Hill, in an influential paper published in 1971, have argued that a grid of streets formed part of the original design of several of the larger *burhs*. Dating evidence from coins, and other finds retrieved from a limited number of locations, such as Castle Yard (Biddle 1975a) and around Gar St (Biddle 1965; Teague 1989a; Whinney 1989, 11) where the earliest street surfaces along with associated deposits have been encountered, indicate that these were definitely in place by *c* 900 and potentially from the mid 9th century. Elements of the street system are respected by the boundary of New Minster, which was founded in 902. Other evidence indicates a date between 880 and 886, or even perhaps in the decades prior to Alfred's reign (Biddle 1983, 119–21).

A mint was operating by about 896, and around this time a royal official, the town reeve, is first recorded. In 901, New Minster was founded by Edward the Elder as a mausoleum for his father. He also founded Nunnaminster and by 1000, after some enlargement, their precincts occupied a quarter of the walled area. By the Norman Conquest Winchester had been a major ecclesiastical centre and mausoleum for the rulers of Wessex and England for nearly 400 years, and as capital of the Old English kingdom it is estimated to have been the fourth wealthiest English town after London, York, and probably Norwich (Biddle 1976, 469; Keene 1985, 88).

Post-Norman Conquest: The Anglo-Norman and medieval periods

Winchester surrendered without a contest in November 1066, and its annexation allowed William

II of Normandy (William the Bastard) to proceed to capture London. On Christmas Day the following month the Conquerer was crowned William I of England, heralding the start of the Anglo-Norman period. From the 1060s until the early 12th century there was massive rebuilding in the ecclesiastical (south-east) quarter of the city, and in the adjacent royal, south-western quarter a palace and a castle was constructed whose earthworks necessitated the closure and destruction of at least two densely occupied streets (Biddle 1976, 470) (Fig. 1.4f). The city was chosen by William I and his immediate successors for crown-wearing ceremonies at major festivals, and the royal treasury was kept there. During this period of royal petronage, the presence of the court, and the administration associated with the treasury, ensured that Winchester remained at the centre of national life.

The success of Winchester's annual St Giles Fair is also seen as a major contributor to the city's continuing economic prosperity during this time. Biddle and Keene estimate the population of Winchester as in excess of 8000 people by 1148, and the inhabited area of the city was probably at its maximum extent (Biddle 1976, 498). The Anarchy during Stephen's reign (1135–54) brought conflict and disruption to the city in 1139–41 when the royal palace was destroyed and areas of the city were devastated and burnt (James 2007, 76). There is, however, little archaeological evidence for these chronicled events, though excavations on the site of St Mary's Abbey revealed fire damage to the south-western part of its cloister (Scobie and Qualmann 1993). It was probably during this period that a significant amount of aristocratic and official wealth was removed from the city, thus marking the start of Winchester's slow decline in status. As a consequence Winchester did not share the later 12th-century growth of other English cities such as Bristol and by the end of that century may have declined in rank to as low as eighth (Keene 1985, 88). After the accession of Henry II in 1154, the city never again seems to have regained its central role in the government of the kingdom, although it continued to be visited by royalty and in the 13th century it appears to have been a favourite place for Henry III, who was born and christened in the city, to spend Christmas.

The project area from medieval documentary sources

As with London, Winchester is not included in the Domesday Book (compiled in Winchester during 1086) and consequently no detailed records exist concerning the immediate economic and social impact that the Conquest had on Winchester. However, properties under royal ownership in Winchester were surveyed for Henry I around 1110 (Survey I), with notable reference made to details of landholding during the time of Edward the Confessor. The whole city was surveyed again for Bishop Henry of Blois in 1148 (Survey II). These two surveys survive in a single manuscript, known as the Winton Domesday, and give us the earliest and most detailed description of an English (or European) town of this time. A full edition, translation, and analyses of the surveys, drawing on the evidence derived from archaeological excavation and historical research in the city, was published in 1976 (Biddle 1976). Although an invaluable resource, the properties/tenants/owners in these surveys are listed simply as a progression along named streets, and it is not always clear from which direction the listing commenced, therefore they can only be reliably located by the street name they were on, and not where upon that street they fell. However, Biddle has produced a schematic plan of the schedules in Survey II, and suggests the direction in which each street was surveyed (Fig. 1.5a). Although the order of the properties is correct, their size, the direction of travel and the position of properties is not accurate for the streets in the north-west corner of the city (ibid., fig. 4 and 244–8).

Properties from the Survey of 1110 will be referenced with the symbol 'I' and those from the 1148 Survey with 'II'; note that a different property numbering system was utilised for each survey study. The historic documents contain a variety of spellings for the street names, and to assist the reader a consistent terminology, based upon 13th century and later documentation studied by Keene (1985), will be used throughout this volume (see Fig. 1.6). For example, with reference to two of the historic streets that fall within the excavation area, Staple Gardens is first recorded as Bredenstret in Survey I (1110), and appears as Brudenestret in the Survey II (1148) but shall be referred to using the later medieval name of Brudene Street (Keene 1985, 455) throughout this volume. Similarly, modern Tower Street can also be equated with Snithelingastret in Survey I and as Snidelingestret in Survey II, but shall be referred to as Snitheling Street (ibid.).

Although exact positions for individual properties are not reliably discernable the work on Survey II shows that each of the streets in mid 12th-century Winchester had its own well-defined character, with a broad trend for three distinct groupings. Firstly streets that formed the principal routes of communication and trade within and through the city, linking the main gates, but also in the case of Lower Brook Street (Tanner Street) where the passage through the city wall was little more than a postern. High Street/Broad Street that ran between the east and west gates, was the most densely occupied, with the highest property values and the principal market place of the city, clearly representing the heart of the urban community. Streets leading from High Street/Broad Street to the other main gates of the city were the next most densely populated and listed high property values. The second group of streets were less densely inhabited and contained some of the most imposing and desirable residences in the city, these also commanded higher property

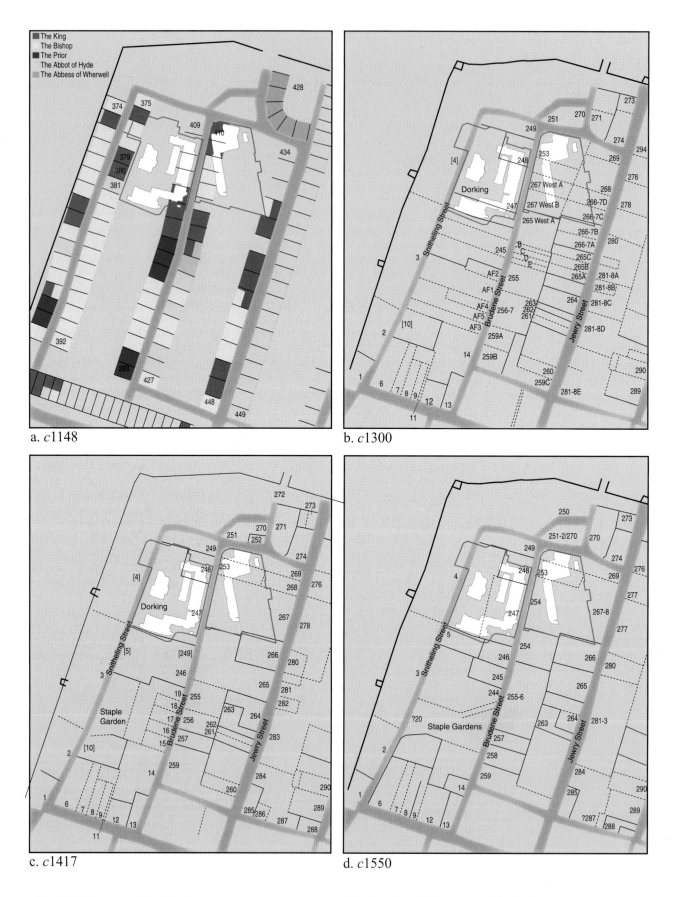

Fig. 1.5 Sequence of medieval tenement arrangements over time (a after Biddle 1976 and b–d after Keene 1985)

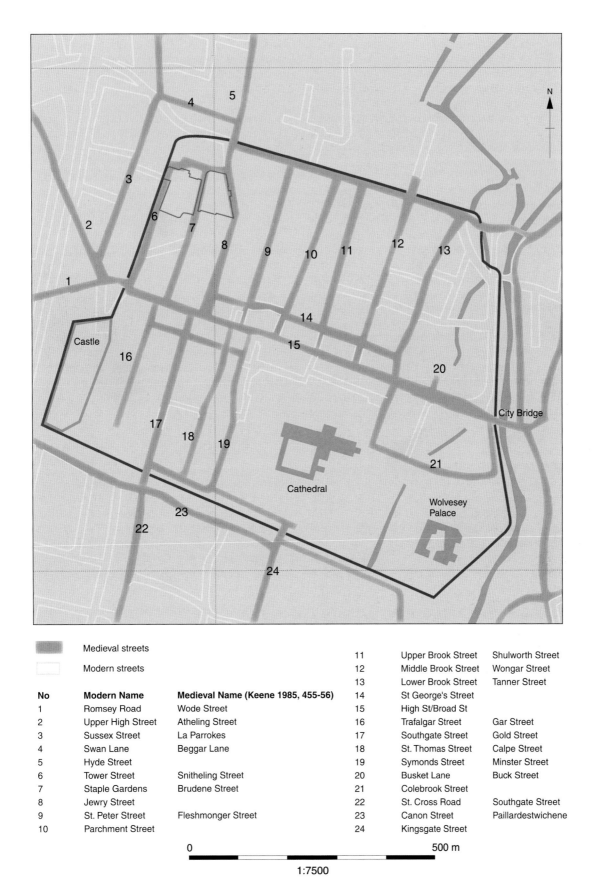

	Medieval streets
	Modern streets

No	Modern Name	Medieval Name (Keene 1985, 455-56)
1	Romsey Road	Wode Street
2	Upper High Street	Atheling Street
3	Sussex Street	La Parrokes
4	Swan Lane	Beggar Lane
5	Hyde Street	
6	Tower Street	Snitheling Street
7	Staple Gardens	Brudene Street
8	Jewry Street	
9	St. Peter Street	Fleshmonger Street
10	Parchment Street	
11	Upper Brook Street	Shulworth Street
12	Middle Brook Street	Wongar Street
13	Lower Brook Street	Tanner Street
14	St George's Street	
15	High St/Broad St	
16	Trafalgar Street	Gar Street
17	Southgate Street	Gold Street
18	St. Thomas Street	Calpe Street
19	Symonds Street	Minster Street
20	Busket Lane	Buck Street
21	Colebrook Street	
22	St. Cross Road	Southgate Street
23	Canon Street	Paillardestwichene
24	Kingsgate Street	

0   500 m

1:7500

Fig. 1.6   Plan of Winchester showing the correlation between the medieval (c 1300) and modern street names used throughout the text (after Keene 1985)

values. St Thomas Street (Calpe Street) is the most striking example of this group of streets, and still contains a fine example of a two-storied hall, constructed in, or more probably well before, the middle of the 12th century. In a third group rents were low and houses were small and closely packed, of which Snitheling Street (with properties at its eastern end falling within the north of the Northgate House and Winchester Discovery Centre excavation areas) is one of the best examples (Biddle 1976, 495–6).

Brudene Street and Snitheling Street appear from the evidence of the surveys to have been populous, but rather different in character. Biddle and Keene have suggested that the combination of high density occupation and relatively high property values of Brudene Steet may mean that its occupants were prosperous people. At the time of Survey I, there is some evidence to suggest that it may have been a street favoured by barons and magnates for occasional visits to the city (Biddle 1976, 387). These included (ibid., 53–57) Herbert the Chamberlain (Royal Treasurer under Henry I) who held Property 152 (I) (ie Property 152 from Survey I (1110)), as well as eleven other properties in the city. Wigod, the Sheriff of Lincoln, held Property 154 (I), and William son of Ansgar, a possible justiciar in Essex, held Property 138 (I). Among the barons, Herbert of St Quentin held Property 149–151 (I), Ralph of Mortemer Property 141–142 (I) and 148 (I) and the Count of Meulan Property 158 (I). Such people would, however, only have been occasional visitors and their properties may well have been sub-let either in whole or in part. By 1148, Biddle and Keene suggest Brudene Street has the appearance of an area perhaps occupied by prosperous tradesmen whereas Snitheling Street, by contrast, was an area of high density occupation and relatively low property values. This could mean it was a street where relatively poor families were living closely together.

The surveys provide some evidence for the occupations and status of property holders in the area, although this is not consistent. There is evidence from both surveys for the presence of possible, probable and definite named moneyers on Snitheling Street including Godric's son at the time of Edward the Confessor (Biddle 1976, 53) and Odo, who may have occupied properties within the site Property 129 (I). The moneyers Chepping, Property 134 (I), and his son Hugh, Property 403 (II), appear to have occupied the same property towards the north of Brudene Street and possibly within the project area at time of the surveys of 1110 and 1148 respectively (ibid., 54 and 98). There is no indication of whether these people worked at their recorded trades on the properties, although the terms in which his tenure is described in the survey suggest that Hugh son of Chepping lived at his property on Brudene Street in 1148. Two smiths are recorded in Snitheling Street in 1110 including Harding in Property 128 (I) who succeeded the tenancy of

Godric's son (ibid., 53). Biddle and Keene's analysis of the evidence from the 1148 Survey (ibid., figs 22 and 23) suggest that cloth workers, building workers, a possible smith, a brewer and victualling trades can be identified in both streets.

Analysis by Derek Keene (1985) of the medieval documents principally from *c* 1200 onwards (but with reference to earlier documents), in conjunction with the comprehensive *Tarrage Roll* survey of 1417, along with post-medieval deeds and topographic evidence (principally Godson's 1750 map and the 1:500 Ordnance Survey published in 1872/3 (surveyed between 1869 and 1871)) enabled a reliable reconstruction of owners, tenants and property boundaries for both the city and its suburbs (ibid., 37–40) over a period of nearly 300 years. The study included a biographical register of over 8000 property holders (most of whom lived in Winchester) and three sequential plans of the city dating to *c* 1300, 1417 and *c* 1550 (ibid., figs 72–4). The property numbers in his work are not related to the earlier Surveys, and will be referred to using simple numbers, eg Property 247.

Keene's work suggests that much of the Northgate House site between Brudene Street and Snitheling Street was located within Property 247, a small part of Property 248 to its north, and a part of Property 245/246 to the south. On the east side of Brudene Street the area of the Discovery Centre excavations fell within two large properties that flanked the street, Property 253, originally bounded to north by the eastwards continuation of Brudene Street (corresponding to the north arm of modern Tower Street), and Property 267 West A and B, whose southern extent corresponded to the existing boundary of the site.

Extracts of the transcripts (Keene 1985, 637–44) relating to these properties, and the sequential plans for the north-west corner of the city, are reproduced below and on Figure 1.5b–d.

West side from south to north

Property 5 and Property 245–6

The land represented by these three entries in the tarrage survey lay between the site acquired by the Austin friars, later the Staple, on the S., 247 on the N., Snitheling Street on the W., and Brudene Street on the E. It appears to have come into single ownership by the late thirteenth or early fourteenth century when the N. part of the land was taken into 247.

In the thirteenth century a tenement belonging to the Silvester family occupied part of the property. This was probably the tenement in Brudene Street which in 1249 Cristina, widow of Robert Sigayn, unsuccessfully claimed as her dower against Edmund Silvester. Andrew Silvester was probably a later owner. Adam de Northampton, citizen and skinner, acquired a substantial property near here in the later thirteenth century. By

1303 Adam and his wife Petronilla enfeoffed Cristina and Catherine, daughters of Adam le Hordier of Southampton, of two properties in Brudene Street: (i) a tenement between the capital tenement of Adam and Petronilla on the S. and the tenement formerly of Andrew Silvester on the N.; and (ii) the moiety of Silvester's tenement, the whole of which lay between the archdeacon's tenement on the N. (247) and the tenement of the donors which had formerly belonged to Joan Girard on the S. Adam de Northampton presumably lived in his capital tenement, and in 1280 was alderman of the ward of Brudene Street. Petronilla was in possession of part of 245-6 as a widow (see 247).

By 1319 the whole property had come into the possession of William de Drokenesford and his wife Catherine. After her husband's death Catherine granted it to John Ace, rector of Brown Candover, who in 1337 sold the tenement and garden here, between the archdeacon's tenement on the N, (247), the tenement of Cristina (surname lost but possibly Starye) on the S. (?AF 2), and Snitheling Street and Brudene Street on the W. and E., to Thomas de Medmenham and his wife Cristina.

De Medmenham's widow Cristina married Richard Wyke, and in (?)1388 they sold the garden 151 feet wide and occupying this site to Robert Crambourne, chaplain. This dimension is too great for the length of Brudene Street frontage later occupied by 245 and 246, and so perhaps applied to the Snitheling Street frontage [see Fig. 1.5c this vol.]. If this was so, a part of the W. end of this property must later have been taken into Staple Garden, which in the sixteenth century was said to lie on the S. and W. of 245.

By 1417 245 had come into the possession of the hospital attached to St. Swithun's Priory and was held by John Somerford, Robert Steward, and others. By 1597 the Dean and Chapter were letting the garden, which comprised 245 and was bounded by Staple Garden on the S. and W., on the same lease as 248 and part of 230 (q.v.). 245 can be traced in later Dean and Chapter records and was sold in 1852.

Property 246 lay between Properties 245 and 247 but is not recorded before the late sixteenth century, when it represented the east part of a garden held by William Burton. Burton purchased 246 from William Bethell. The property may therefore previously have belonged to Hyde Abbey.

The west part of Burton's garden was held on lease from the city for 9s. rent, and is represented by 5. John White leased it from 1569, Humphrey Norton from 1571, and Burton from 1600. 246 lay to the E., a lane (which presumably represented Snitheling Street) to the W., 244 to the S., and 'Hermits ground so called' to the N. The land was sold in 1823[FN11]. In the late sixteenth century the boundary between 5 and 246 was marked by a high bank.

[Footnote 11] *Enfr i, p. 257. In 1571 its dimensions were 40 yards 2 feet 3 inches from E. to W. on the N. side and 41 yards 1 foot 8 inches on the S. side. In 1823 it measured 20 yards from N. to S., and 41 yards from E. to W. By the latter date the lane on the W. had been included within the property: plan, HRO, Box 41 M 67/19 (ii).*

Property 247

Between 245-6 on the S., 248 on the N. and E., Snitheling Street on the W., and Brudene Street on the E. 249 probably also lay on the N.

In the thirteenth century the greater part of the property belonged to the archdeacon of Winchester and was known as Dorking. In 1271 the archdeacon was ordered not to obstruct the public lane called Dorking which he had enclosed. In 1280 John son of Richard Starie was to pay the king 8d. rent for purprestures of a lane apud Dorkynege measuring 60 feet by 16 feet, and of another piece of land there measuring 50 feet by 16 feet.

'In the late thirteenth or early fourteenth century Master Philip of St Austel, archdeacon of Winchester 1285-1304, enlarged the property to the S. By a deed registered in 1303 Petronilla, widow of Adam de Northt', citizen and skinner, granted him the moiety of a garden which had belonged to Agnes Greyshank and lay between the archdeacon's garden on the N. and Petronilla's tenement on the S. The moiety measured 15 and a half yards in width next to the archdeacon's garden and extended from Brudene Street to Snitheling Street.

In 1417 247 was a tenement of the archdeacon called Dorkyng held by Thomas Smale and John Frenshe. John Barbour of Hyde Street was administering the property for the archdeacon in 1412, when William Sequence entered it by force.

In the late sixteenth and early seventeenth centuries the property was a garden held from the archdeacon by William Burton. The garden remained in the possession of the archdeacons of Winchester and its bounds can be reconstructed from leases and sales of that period [FN7].

[Footnote 7] *The dimensions of 247 are recorded in a marginal note in Tarrage 1590. The garden was said to measure 38 and three quarter yards from E. to W. and 64 yards from N. to S. The latter measurement is roughly equal to the frontage of 247 on Brudene Street. The former is no more than two-thirds the distance between Brudene Street and Snitheling Street and cannot easily be reconciled with the evidence that 247 extended the full distance between the two streets. It is possible that the sixteenth-century surveyors were confused by a physical feature in the middle part of the garden, possibly the N. continuation of the bank recorded in association with 245-6.*

Property 248

Between 247 on the S. and W. and 249 on the N.

By his will, proved in 1334, William de Cramburne, citizen, alias William le Lardener, bequeathed the plot of land on this site to his daughter Catherine. In 1335 Catherine granted the plot to Robert of Shaftebury and his wife Juliana, who by 1337 jointly granted it to Walter le Chamberleyn and his wife Maud.

The Cathedral Priory probably then recovered the property, which in 1417 was described as a garden next to the gate of Dorking (247) belonging to the prior and held by John Somerford and John Hall.

In the late sixteenth century the garden was held by John Stephens, alias Stephen Knight, and in 1597 was let with 230 and 245 to John Purdue.

The dimensions in the Dean and Chapter deed of enfranchisement of 1858 enable the bounds of the property to be identified. At that date the rent from the garden was 2s. 9d. and this probably represents the sum due in the sixteenth century.

East side from north to south

Property 253
Probably at the corner of the lane leading from Brudene Street to North Gate, on the E. side of Brudene Street, and between 268-9 on the E. and 267 on the S. Godson shows a boundary which could enclose this property. In the sixteenth century 253 appears to have been bounded by 269 on the N.

By 1304 the tenements of Thomas the chaplain and of Henry de Preslonde lay to the W. of 268. The former was probably the tenement which by 1309 Thomas de Modesfont, chaplain, held from St. John's Hospital, and was probably also the tenement in Brudene Street held by Dom. Thomas of St. Saviour (Salvatoris) from which the hospital had a 4s. rent of assize in 1294. Thomas was thus probably rector of the church of St. Saviour.

Thomas's tenement was probably taken into 267, for later only the property of the de Preslonde family lay to the W. of 268. By 1346 Sibyl de Preslonde held the tenement. In 1352 the Frary and Kalendar had 6d. rent from her tenement next to the lane leading to North Gate, which had been granted, probably in the thirteenth century, by Thomas of St. Margaret. By 1371 the property was described as the garden of Sibyl de Preslonde and in 1376 John Saundres, skinner, was fined for closing the lane running from Brudene Street to Jewry Street next to her former tenement.

In 1398 the garden belonged to Henry atte Swane and by 1410 his tenure had ceased. In 1417 the wife of Richard Fylye held the garden.

In the mid sixteenth century the garden was part of the land attached to the house of William Agulley, whose heirs still held it in 1590; by that date John Gardiner was tenant and in 1604 he held it from William Waller, esquire.

Property 267 West
On the E. side of Brudene Street, probably between 253 on the N. and 265 West on the S. In the early fourteenth century there were two tenements adjacent N. and S. Later in the century the property was absorbed by 267 in Jewry Street.

By 1309 Thomas de Modesfont, chaplain, enfeoffed John le Deveneys of the N. tenement, A, which lay between a tenement which Thomas held of St. John's

Hospital (part of 253?) on the N., a tenement belonging to le Deveneys (the S. part of 267 West) on the S., and 266-7 D on the E. By 1327 le Deveneys enfeoffed William Gabriel and his wife Joan of the S. tenement, B, which was opposite the courtyard (curia) of Dorkyngge (247) and was bounded by the tenement sometime of Nicholas de Eneford (part of 265 West?) on the S.

These two tenements appear subsequently to have been included in 267 (q.v.) in Jewry Street.

The project area from archaeological sources
Excavations in 1960 uncovered the remains of two substantial stone structures; the first a cellar interpreted as having belonged to an 'upper-hall' house, that flanked the second, which consisted of substantial stone foundations for a two-celled structure, interpreted as a 'chapel' or small church, immediately to its north-west (Cunliffe 1964). The internal dimensions of the cellar measured 5 m by 10.4 m (16 ft. 6 ins. by 34 ft. 6 ins.) with evidence for a groined vaulted roof over two approximately square bays. Its walls were generally 1 m wide and rendered with an inch-thick layer of plaster for at least 1.8 m above the chalk and mortar floor. The external north-west corner was built of large greensand blocks tooled with closely set parallel lines reminiscent of the 12th century work at the chapel on St Catherine's Hill, which corresponded in date to pottery recovered from the foundations. In the south-east corner double-thickness stonework possibly indicated the position of an external stair. Evidence for three walls abutting the outside of this structure suggests that it was extended at a later date, possibly in the late 13th or early 14th century. The 'chapel's' foundations consisted of rammed chalk arranged over two chambers. The larger, to the west, interpreted as the nave, measured 4.3 m by 6.1 m internally, with foundations from 1–1.4 m wide, and the smaller, with an internal space a little over 1.8 m square had foundations varying in width from 0.91 m to a very substantial 2 m at its eastern end, perhaps supporting a tower.

Cunliffe (1964, 171–5) postulates that the 12th century structures could be related to the 'mansio' of Drogo (mentioned as being on Brudene Street in Survey II of 1148), with the church being his private foundation of St. Odulf (a Flemish Saint also suggesting Drogos origins), or even having no ecclesiastical function at all. The later structural additions possibly relate to a change of ownership to the Archdeacon of Winchester sometime in the 13th century, being the property referred to in later documents as *Dorkinge*. Biddle (1976, 347 and nn. 2, 4) in a critique of Cunliffe's evidence later argued that revisions to the pottery dating could suggest any date after the 11th century for the stone house, but concurs that both buildings were associated with the tenureship of the Archdeacon of Winchester in the 13th century (the earliest reference to which appears in 1271 when the Archdeacon was ordered not to obstruct the public lane called *Dorking* which he had enclosed (Keene 1985, 641; see above)). It has also been suggested that the chapel, although perhaps originating as a private foundation and clearly indicating the relatively high status of this property, could equate to the parish church of St Marys, *Our Ladye in Burdenstrete* (ibid.).

The post-medieval to modern periods

John Speed's map of Winchester, dated to 1611, shows that the defensive circuit remained a dominant feature in the early 17th century (Fig. 1.7a). Compared to earlier periods, when much of its interior was filled with streets and buildings, by 1611 the town had lost much of its earlier population; the population of Winchester ranged from 8000–11,000 in *c* 1148, 11,625 in *c* 1300, 7–8000 in 1417, 3000–6000 in 1603, and 4000 in 1725 (Biddle 1976; Keene 1985; James 1988). The area towards the north wall, and particularly the north-west corner, is markedly empty, with the area of our site shown with trees, indicating open ground, possibly an orchard (Fig. 1.7a). Buck's view of the city from St Giles Hill in 1736 (Fig. 1.7b), Godsons map of 1750 (Fig. 1.7c), and Thomas Milnes map of 1791 (Fig. 1.7d) show that the density and pattern of settlement within the walls had not changed substantially by the start of the 19th century from that shown by Speed almost 300 years earlier. The area of the present project is shown by Buck to be part of a large plantation occupying the north-west corner of the city up to and beyond the still extant defences, and as open ground by Godson and Milne. Snitheling Street is not shown on any of the 17th and 18th century depictions of the area, suggesting that it had fallen out of use by this time, and there is no trace of any of the buildings of the Archdeacon's residence, suggesting that they had been abandoned and demolished. The parish church of *Our Lady in Burdenstrete*, which is possibly identifiable with the 'chapel' excavated by Cunliffe (see above), was said in a Corporation Petition of 1452, to have been one of the 17 parish churches in Winchester that had fallen down in the previous 80 years

It was perhaps on the initiative of the archdeacons, who remained the most significant landowners in this area until the 19th century, that the area was first put under cultivation. The project area remained under cultivation for several centuries, during which time the city witnessed economic hardship (during the Civil War of the mid 17th century), and then steady economic revival from the late 17th century onwards. This was in part promoted by the decision of King Charles II in 1682 to construct a new palace on the site of the demolished medieval castle. During this period many of the timber-framed buildings shown on Speed's map would have been renovated, or replaced, predominantly in brick and occasionally stone.

During the 19th century the population of Winchester increased dramatically, and the city grew in response to its elevated status as county town of Hampshire and the improved transport connections brought by the arrival of the railways. The Corn Exchange was constructed on Jewry Street between 1836 and 1838, and it was probably at this time that the Winchester Discovery Centre site was terraced and a high brick, flint and stone wall built to retain Staple Gardens and Tower Street. Jewry Street was re-routed to run past the grand frontage of the Corn Exchange, and became the principal route out of the city northwards and to the new railway station (first constructed in 1839). Milner, in 1839, records that the defences in the north-west corner of the city were sold and then levelled, and Tower Street and new property boundaries were marked out and developed (Cunliffe 1964, 62). The terraces on Tower Street, some of which remain today, date from this period. Between Tower Street and Staple Gardens larger walled plots of land were apparent; some of these remained as gardens until as late as the 1960s, while others were developed as large detached Victorian properties. To the north of the Northgate House site, where houses are separated from the street by a high brick and flint wall, there is a small gate with a stone carved with the initials 'J C 1846'. To the south, No. 19 Staple Gardens was constructed between 1872/3 and 1897 in one of the garden plots on the Northgate House site. During this period the cattle market moved to the Corn Exchange. A snapshot of these changes in progress can be seen on the 1872/3 OS map (Fig. 1.7e). By 1883 the land, which had been owned by the Archdeacons for around 700 years, was sold off (Cunliffe 1964, 164).

By the 1950s to 1960s the majority of site was owned by Southern Counties Agricultural Trading Society Ltd (SCATS) (ibid., 163) and in 1961 it constructed a large office building, Northgate House, with a smaller office, Documation House, to its north. These buildings required localised terracing and substantial foundations, which threatened large areas of archaeology. This prompted small-scale rescue excavations carried out by Winchester Museum Services prior to construction (ibid.).

THE ARCHAEOLOGICAL MITIGATION PROCESS

General

The archaeological projects relating to Northgate House and the Winchester Discovery Centre were designed and implemented in accordance with the controls that the Local Planning Authorities (Winchester City Council and Hampshire County Council) have on development in areas under their jurisdiction. These planning principals were laid out in the Department of Environment's Planning and Policy Guidance (PPG) note 16: Archaeology

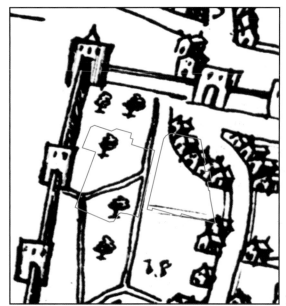

a. John Speeds Map 1611

b. View of the city from St Giles Hill, Buck 1736

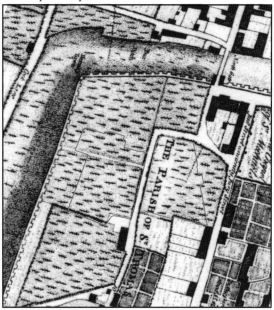

c. Godson Map1750

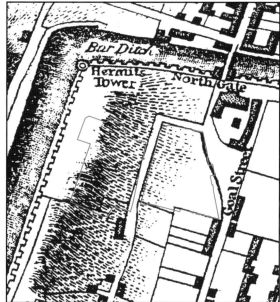

d. Thomas Milne Map 1791

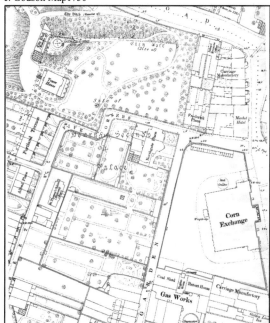

e. 1st Edition 1:500 Ordnance Survey Map, 1873

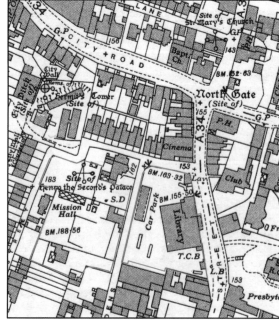

f. 1:1250 Ordnance Survey Map 1935

and Planning (HMSO 1990a), and PPG note 15: Planning and the Historic Environment (HMSO 1990b), along with Policy HE.1 of the Winchester District Local Plan Review (WCC 2001).

The policy guidance requires that the negative effect which development proposals can have upon potential archaeological remains is assessed and mitigated. It emphasises that where possible archaeological remains should be left in place (*preservation in situ*), and where this cannot be achieved then archaeological excavation accompanied by a full photographic, written and drawn record (*preservation by record*) followed by analysis and publication should be required.

In accordance with these requirements, opportunities were actively sought on both projects to allow archaeological deposits to remain undisturbed *in situ*. The impact of the proposed designs upon the archaeological resource was assessed, and some beneficial changes were made to the proposed designs. Subsequently, the archaeological excavations at both sites were specifically tailored to mitigate the impact of each development within the context of a set of pertinent research questions. The result was that a detailed and accurate archaeological archive was generated for all the archaeology that was to be unavoidably destroyed by the developments, with those archaeological deposits that were not destroyed, because they were either below or outside the impacts of the designs, preserved *in situ* for future archaeological study. This approach removed the need for subjective choices to be made about where to excavate. A summary of this process is presented below.

The two development sites (along with the stretch of the Staple Gardens carriageway that divides them) cover an area of 8465 m², which represents about 1.5 % of the total area within the circuit of the Roman and later defences and constitutes a significant portion of the north-west corner of the historic city. Within this larger area 1821m² was archaeologically investigated at the Northgate House site (Evaluation 32 m², Open Area Excavation 1698 m², and Watching Brief 91 m²), and 976m² at the Discovery Centre site (Evaluation trenching 63 m², Open Area Excavation 859 m², and Watching Brief 54 m²).

Figure 1.8 shows the locations of all the archaeological interventions that were carried out at both sites as a result of the mitigation strategies presented above, together with the locations of interventions from the previous excavation work between 1949–1960 (Cunliffe 1964, fig. 57), and the evaluation trenches by Gifford (Gifford 2004b and c) and Oxford Archaeology (OA 2005c). This figure also shows the area along the western side of the Staple Gardens frontage that was only partially excavated, and the area on the Discovery Centre site that had suffered significant horizontal truncation.

The difference between the survival of the archaeological deposits on both sites is represented in cross section on Figure 1.9.

Taken together the archaeological works covered an area of 2798m², or 0.5% of the historic core, and represent the largest excavations in urban Winchester since The Brooks excavations by the Museums Service in 1987–88, which examined 6600 m², equivalent to 1.15% of the historic core.

Site specific strategies

The Northgate House site and the Archaeological Mitigation Strategy

At the Northgate House site the process started in April 2002 when development proposals prompted a Desk Based Assessment that drew together archaeological, documentary and cartographic evidence from the site and its vicinity (Gifford 2004a), and concluded that significant archaeological remains could be present at the site. During May of the same year archaeological fieldwork to assess the physical nature of any such remains was undertaken on the western half of the site with the investigation of four evaluation trenches (Trenches NH1–4; see Fig. 1.8), along with observations made during geo-technical works that consisted of three mechanically excavated pits and three boreholes (Gifford 2004b). A further four evaluation trenches (Trenches NH5–8) were excavated on the eastern half of the site in January 2004 (Gifford 2004c). In combination these works did not recover *in situ* prehistoric evidence, but did encounter probable late–post-Roman Dark Earth along with significant quantities of Roman material that occurred residually within archaeological features that dated from the 10th–13th century. The work concluded that significant archaeological deposits survived largely intact below varying depths of post-medieval 'cultivation' soils, in the areas outside the footprints of the existing buildings, most notably along the Staple Gardens street frontage.

The proposed redevelopment of the Northgate House site consisted of five closely arranged substantial structures or blocks; three of these were arranged along the north, south and east sides of the scheme and formed a U-shape around a smaller fourth block (with a subterranean carpark) located centrally on the western side. The fifth block lay in the north-west corner. Each block was between 3–5 storeys high, and consisted of a large number of small internal spaces that formed multiple separate residential units with a row of retail units at ground floor level along the Staple Gardens frontage. In order to take account of the pronounced slope of the site the blocks had to be terraced into the hillside by

Fig. 1.7 facing page   Location of development sites on the principal historic maps from early post-medieval to the modern period (17th-20th centuries)

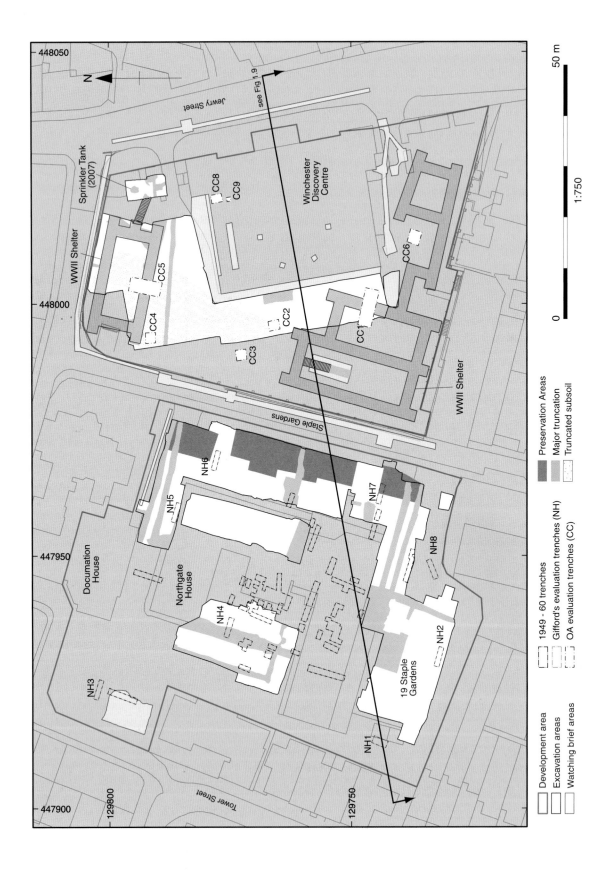

Fig. 1.8   Detailed excavation locations for the Northgate House and Winchester Discovery Centre sites

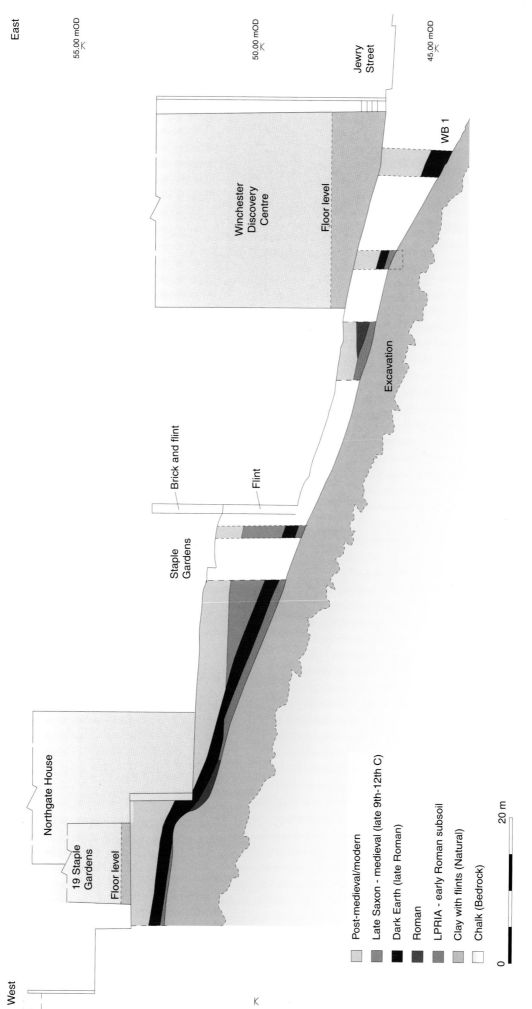

East

55.00 mOD

50.00 mOD

Jewry
Street

45.00 mOD

WB 1

Winchester
Discovery
Centre

Floor level

Excavation

Brick and flint

Flint

Staple
Gardens

Northgate House

19 Staple
Gardens

Floor level

Edge of site

West

Post-medieval/modern

Late Saxon - medieval (late 9th-12th C)

Dark Earth (late Roman)

Roman

LPRIA - early Roman subsoil

Clay with flints (Natural)

Chalk (Bedrock)

0   20 m

Fig. 1.9   Schematic west-east cross-section through the sites showing the survival of the archaeological resource

utilising a series of large steps, each representing a change in the height of the internal floor levels. The scale, mass and height of the proposal, in combination with the highly sub-divided nature of the interior spaces, and the floor level changes, required a heavy and intensive foundation arrangement with the concrete floor slabs strengthened by thicker ground-beams supported on an intensive pattern of concrete piles.

The model of the surviving archaeological deposits gained from the evaluation was compared to the proposed design. It was evident that the need to terrace the blocks into the hillside would impact on the archaeological deposits to different degrees. The entire footprint of the southern and central blocks, and the western halves of the eastern and northern blocks would completely remove all archaeological remains. The eastern half of the eastern block would partially remove remains, and the western half of the northern block and the block in the north-west corner would have a very limited impact. In addition two deep trenches, which would contain all the new services such as electricity, gas, and water, also had a complete impact. Much of the landscaping outside the footprints of these structures would have a limited impact.

An 'Archaeological Mitigation Strategy' was devised by Gifford (2004d; 2005), which broadly proposed full archaeological excavation in areas of complete impact, partial excavation in areas of limited impact and a Watching Brief for the remaining areas.

Part of the archaeological works were completed by Wessex Archaeology (WA 2004), but the majority was undertaken by Oxford Archaeology using methodologies outlined in a Written Scheme of Investigation (OA 2005) to address questions detailed in a Research Design (OA 2004). The areas subject to open area excavation and Watching Brief are shown on Figure 1.8.

The Discovery Centre site and the Archaeological Mitigation Strategy

During February and March 2005 at the Discovery Centre site six evaluation trenches (Trenches CC 1–6) were archaeologically excavated in the car park outside the Library (as it was then), and two geotechnical trenches (Trenches CC 8 and 9) were observed under watching brief inside the building (OA 2005; Fig. 1.8). These identified features dating to the Iron Age, Roman structures, 'Dark Earth' deposits and structures and pits from tenements dating to the Saxon, Anglo-Norman and medieval Periods. The Second World War air raid shelters constructed in 1939 (Pinhorne and Cooper 1998) were fully intact but had truncated all the earlier archaeological remains. Unlike the situation at Northgate House the pre-modern archaeology had also suffered extensive horizontal truncation over most of the western and northern areas of the site.

Here, the survival of the archaeology was restricted to features cut into pre-Roman subsoils and natural deposits, but some horizontal stratigraphy had survived as slumped deposits within negative features. Towards the centre and south-east of the site there had been less truncation and intact Roman and later stratigraphy survived.

The development proposal was for a single L-shaped structure that would be directly connected to the western and northern sides of the existing Library. As with the proposal at the Northgate House site the building design, with regard to its impact upon the ground, was influenced by a number of factors. Its scale and mass had to be sensitive to, and not dominate, the existing Grade II* Library structure, it was therefore designed to be no more than two storeys high. Due to the intended public use of the building the internal spaces were significantly larger than at Northgate House so there were fewer rooms, and fewer load-bearing walls. The existing slope of the site was less pronounced (having already been significantly terraced), but the new internal floor levels had to take account of the Library's existing internal floor levels, which meant that there were fewer changes required in the heights between the proposed floors. The design also needed to minimise, where possible, its impact upon the archaeological resource that had been revealed by the evaluation.

As a consequence the foundations were slighter and less intensive than on the Northgate House development. The larger floor slabs were strengthened by thickened edges and supported on a well-spaced piling array. A small number of foundations were also required to deal with limited works within the former Library structure. The impact of the service corridors that took utilities such as gas, electric, water and sewerage, data cables etc, were minimised by running them, where possible, along the immediate outside of the building's western side. In the north-east corner of the site a subterranean water storage tank was installed. Finally, there were minimal impacts from the external landscaping and hard-standing. There was also a requirement to make-safe and strengthen the existing air raid structures that extended beyond the footprint of the new structure so that they could bear the weight of traffic using the proposed car park. To this end the shelters ageing roof slabs were relaid after the corridors had been filled with free running shingle.

The final design had a broad, shallow and light impact on the existing ground, however this still unavoidably affected the existing archaeological deposits, and elements of the extant air raid shelters.

A mitigation strategy, archaeological methodologies and a research agenda was devised by Oxford Archaeology (OA 2005). Open Area Excavation was chosen for the area affected by the footprint of the new building, the service corridor adjacent to its western edge and the area of the Water Tank.

Generally archaeological remains were not excavated below the levels that would be affected by the construction of the concrete floor slabs. However, features that fell in the positions of the concrete piles were hand-excavated to a safe depth and then hand augered. A number of other features, such as wells, were also mechanically augered. All other impacts from the design were dealt with under an archaeological Watching Brief.

Fieldwork

Historic Building Recording

Historic building recording works were carried on the air raid shelters and on the Grade II* listed Library structure. War period graffiti and notices were photographed, and described. Their height above the floor of the shelters was logged and their individual positions marked on an existing survey of the shelters. Existing surveys of the Library structure were annotated, and a photographic record made to show the details of the building's use that were revealed during the renovation and conversion works.

Open Area Excavation

All overburden was removed by a mechanical excavator under the control of an experienced archaeologist down to the first significant archaeological horizon, or natural geology (whichever was encountered first). The backfills to modern service trenches were also mechanically removed as were foundations from previous buildings, except where their removal would have damaged *in situ* archaeological deposits. On the Discovery Centre site the lengths of air raid shelters that fell within the excavation areas were carefully and systematically dismantled by a mechanical excavator, removing the concrete roof-panels, then the wall-panels, and leaving the floor slab *in situ*. Where possible the surviving graffiti on the wall panels was retained and form part of the site archive.

Archaeological hand excavation then proceeded in stratigraphic order, taking into account areas and features that were to be preserved *in situ*. A single context recording system was followed with all structures, deposits and cuts allocated unique context numbers and described on pro-forma context sheets. All cuts, structures and occupation deposits were photographed and drawn to scale, and all fills and other deposits where not photographed and drawn to scale were sketched on the relevant context pro-forma sheet. All scale drawings and sketches were related to the site grid and levelled to Ordnance Datum. All hand retrieved artefacts were bagged by their relevant context number and small finds were located in 3D. All deposits that contained preserved charred plant remains, and the potential for metalworking residues, were bulk sampled. All hearths that had

not been subject to post-depositional movement were sampled for archaeomagnetic dating by the relevant specialist. Selected areas of 'Dark Earth' deposits were column sampled. Hand and machine augered cores were taken from a selection of exceptionally deep features.

General views of the excavations at Northgate House and Winchester Discovery Centre are shown in Plates 1.3 and 1.4.

Watching Brief

An archaeological Watching Brief was maintained within all areas affected by the new buildings not covered by the open area excavations. Where archaeology was observed, written, drawn and photographic records were made and related to the site grid and Ordnance Datum. Scale, section and plan drawings were made of all the archaeological deposits that were left *in situ* after excavations were completed and can be referred to if and when opportunities for further work arise.

General comment on stratigraphic recording and Harris matrices

Gaining a thorough representation of the stratigraphic sequences was a fundamental aspect of the excavation process. Harris matrices (developed by Harris for use on Biddle's archaeological excavations in Winchester in the 1960s), were initially drawn up by the excavators and their Supervisors, these were unified by the Matrix Supervisor as part of the excavation process. This allowed stratigraphic problems to be resolved with reference to the physical site and the excavation team as an ongoing process during excavation, thus providing the best method for them to reliably reflect the excavated sequence accurately.

General comment on the in-situ preservation of archaeological remains

All archaeological deposits that remained unexcavated were covered with a layer of geotextile, followed by a layer of sand. This was designed to protect them from the subsequent covering of crushed material that then provided a stable surface or 'pile mat' for the process of foundation construction. During this operation no plant was allowed to move over the areas of preserved archaeological remains until the protective layers were put in place (Plate 1.5).

At the Northgate House site, complex occupation deposits relating to structures from the late Saxon and medieval periods were left *in situ* along some of the Staple Gardens frontage; Roman and prehistoric remains in these areas these were also left unexcavated. These are shown as the darker area within the excavation limits for the Northgate House site on Figure 1.8. In the remaining excavation areas shown on Figure 1.8 all archaeological remains of all

Plate 1.3   General view of the excavations at Northgate House

Plate 1.4   General view of excavations at Winchester Discovery Centre

Plate 1.5   View looking north-east showing the process of preservation in situ of deposits along the frontage on the west side of Staple Gardens on the Northgate House site

periods were excavated except for the basal fills of deep pits and wells. At the Discovery Centre the complete excavation of surviving occupation deposits from all periods not contained within cut features was achieved. Partial excavation of deposits within some cut features was achieved. The unexcavated *in situ* archaeology consisted of deep features such as pits, wells and cellars, some of which were augered and explored through small sondages. The phase plans accompanying the archaeological descriptions in Chapters 2, 3 and 4 indicate areas where archaeological remains of the corresponding phase were left unexcavated.

POST-EXCAVATION

The approach to post-excavation and the archives

The client reports that present the results of the two building recording excercises completed on the Winchester Discovery Centre site, the first on the graffiti in the air raid shelters (OA 2006) and the second on the Grade II* former Library building (OA 2007b), are included as Part 2 of the CD-Rom accompanying this volume.

Individual post-excavation assessment reports were produced after the completion of fieldwork at both Northgate House and the Winchester Discovery Centre (Teague and Ford 2006; Teague 2006; see CD-Rom, Part 1). These reviewed the entire archive of records, artefacts, ecofacts and samples for each site and presented an assessment of the potential for further analysis with a project specific Updated Research Design proposal. It was clear from these assessments that there was a compelling case for the analysis and publication of the two sites to be combined. Encouraged by the City Archaeologist this approach was set out in an Updated Project Design (OA 2007c; CD-Rom, Part 1). However, to assist future research, the prefix NH has been retained throughout for data from the Northgate House site and CC for that from the Winchester Discovery Centre site.

The Research Framework

The Updated Project Design (OA 2007) consisted of a series of period-specific research questions designed to explore the results presented in the assessments for each site within the context of the archaeology and historical documentary evidence in the locality and the wider area. It was these questions that guided the analysis for this report. The full set of research questions are presented in Part 1 of the accompanying CD-Rom, with summaries of the principal research aims presented by period below.

The pre-Roman period

The analysis sought to clarify the date, nature and extent of pre-Roman activity in the area and in partic-

ular to explore its relationship with the Iron Age earthwork of Oram's Arbour and nearby settlements.

The Roman period

The analysis sought to clarify the nature and chronology of Roman occupation within the area, and in particular its possible relationship with the pre-existing Iron Age settlement, and evidence for the early development of *Venta Belgarum* within this poorly understood north-west quadrant of the Roman town. Substantial assemblages of finds and craftworking debris would be subject to detailed analysis for evidence of the nature of later Roman occupation and industry in the area. Detailed study would also be undertaken of the morphology and contents of the Dark Earth to add to understanding of its chronology and origin.

The late Saxon period

It was clear that the excavations had recovered exceptional datasets for the late Saxon period. The analysis aimed to clarify the date and nature of the earliest occupation in the area, and the establishment of streets, occupation and tenements. A major programme of scientific dating was integrated into the post-excavation analysis in order to refine the dating of the late Saxon stratigraphy and features, and in particular to try to divide the late Saxon occupation into sub-phases, allowing a better understanding of the early development of the area in the late 9th and earlier 10th centuries. Consideration would be given to the way in which the archaeological data complemented information available from documentary sources, although from the outset it was not anticipated that precise correlations could be achieved.

The programme of analysis was also designed to study development in building forms and functions, and the abundant evidence for varied artisanal or craftworking activity in the area throughout this period. It was also clear that the good survival of animal and fish bone and charred and mineralised plant remains provided an excellent opportunity to study evidence for craftworking, along with diet, economic exploitation of the hinterland of the town, and trade.

The Anglo-Norman and medieval periods

Many of the research aims identified for the late Saxon period were also valid for the Anglo-Norman period, for which a similar large dataset was available. The analysis sought to identify change and development in the project area, in terms of chronology, building and structure types, tenement layouts and the nature of and relationships between domestic and artisanal activity.

For these periods the analysis sought information about the way in which the area changed at this time, in particular for evidence that might support the documentary sources that suggest depopulation and the possible reasons for this. The analysis also sought to extend our understanding of the property of the Archdeacon of Winchester, in terms of its evolution, dating, and its relationship to other tenements in the area.

Dating, phasing and grouping: stratigraphy, artefactual and ecofactual evidence, and scientific dating

The Harris matrices compiled during the on-site excavations were transferred by hand onto Microsoft Excel spreadsheets during the post-excavation assessment stage, and annotated with extensive details relating to context type, stratigraphic groups, dating, and ecofactual sampling information, and thus provided a comprehensive relative chronological framework for all the excavated contexts.

Problems relating to 'residuality' and 'intrusiveness' of artefacts and ecofacts were addressed, using a combination of the stratigraphic sequences represented by the Harris matrices and the datable finds data (such as pottery and small finds). Residuality occurs when material from earlier activity has been redeposited within later contexts and presents a significant challenge for accurately understanding site use over time within urban archaeology.

Principally the problem is contained within each broad Period, ie it is not difficult to recognise Roman artefacts that have been redeposited within features and deposits from post-Roman periods (this occurs for example when multiple pits from different phases intercut each other in the same location), however this is not as easy when earlier late Saxon material is redeposited within later late Saxon deposits. 'Intrusiveness' is where material from later activity has found its way into earlier contexts; this is usually due to human error during the excavation process, or movement/disturbance of the *in-situ* deposits, due to slumping in pits for example. These issues are discussed in detail in the full post-Roman Pottery report (*Digital Section 1.3*), and in the Small Finds report (Chapter 7, and *Digital Section 3*).

A good chronological resolution was considered vital to enable some of the research questions to be addressed. A detailed study of the ceramic assemblages provided a comprehensive relative dating chronology (Chapter 7, and *Digital Section 1*). This was refined by date-ranges acquired through an extensive programme of archaeomagnetic and radiocarbon dating to provide, where possible, an absolute chronological framework (Chapter 6, and *Digital Section 19*). The programme of archaeomagnetic dating carried out during these excavations is quite unique within urban situations in Britain. The

Table 1.1 Periods, site phases and date ranges

Period name	Phase	Applies to	Date range	No of Contexts recorded
Natural	Phase 0	*In situ* natural geology		23
Pre-Roman	Phase 1	All pre-Roman archaeology whose phasing could not be further refined	Prior to *c* AD 43	71
	Phase 1.1	Early Iron Age	*c* 700–400 BC	95
	Phase 1.2	Middle Iron Age	*c* 400–100 BC	35
	Phase1.3	Late Iron Age	*c* 100 BC–AD 43	31
Roman	Phase 2	All Roman archaeology whose phasing could not be further refined	*c* AD 43–400/50	0
	Phase 2.1	Early Roman	*c* AD 43–130/50	161
	Phase 2.2	Mid Roman	*c* AD 130/50–270	73
	Phase 2.3	Late Roman	*c* AD 270–350/75	658
	Phase 2.4	Latest Roman	*c* AD350/75–400/50	75
The post-Roman: early and middle Saxon	Phase 3	All post-Roman archaeology whose phasing could not be further refined	*c* AD 400/50–850	0
Late Saxon	Phase 4	All late Saxon archaeology whose phasing could not be further refined	*c* 850–1050	374
	Phase 4.1	Earlier late Saxon	*c* 850–950	474
	Phase 4.2	Later late Saxon	*c* 950–1050	1142
Anglo-Norman	Phase 5	All Anglo-Norman archaeology	*c* 1050–1225	1842
Medieval	Phase 6	All medieval archaeology	*c* 1225–1550	725
Post-medieval	Phase 7	All post-medieval archaeology	*c* 1550–1800	2
Modern	Phase 8	All modern archaeology	*c* 1800 +	523
Unphased		Contexts that could not be allocated to a Phase		171
Voided		Contexts numbers that were allocated on site but subsequently not used		120
			Total	6568

majority of the archaeomagnetic measurements were taken from *in situ* hearths within structures along the late Saxon Brudene Street West frontage. Complementary radiocarbon samples were chosen from deposits with direct and reliable physical relationships to these hearths, such as ash and charcoal deposits that lay immediately upon the fired surfaces. The stratigraphic sequences and their associated absolute date ranges (along with significant dated historical events) were queried against a number of specific research questions by the use of Bayesian statistical modelling, which resulted in a series of models whose reliability was measurable in terms of associated probabilities (see Chapter 6).

In combination, the stratigraphic sequences, the relative and absolute dating results and the statistical models provided the basis for dividing the evidence from the eight Periods covered by eighteen Phases of activity (Table 1.1).

Grouping

Once issues of phasing and dating were addressed, the grouping of contemporary features and deposits (eg into structures or properties) that had commenced during the excavation process was tested and finalised. The drawn record, consisting of hundreds of individual 'single-context' hand-drawn site plans was digitised into a single visual digital GIS drawing. Plans of contemporary features (along with undated features) could be generated and visual patterns perhaps not obvious during excavation, due to truncation or shear density of features, were then identified and allocated unique group numbers. These groups then formed the basis for further interpretation and analysis.

A detailed methodology for phasing and grouping of the late Saxon and Anglo-Norman periods, where previous studies of the documentary evidence were pertinent in identifying individual properties, is presented at the start of Chapter 3.

SUMMARY OF RESULTS: DEPOSIT SURVIVAL, SITE PHASES AND THE SEQUENCE OF LAND USE

The broad slope of the hillside and the survival of the archaeological deposits across both the Northgate House and Discovery Centre sites are shown on Figure 1.9. The phases of the archaeological sequence are summarised below, and illustrated in a series of simplified plans (Fig. 1.10), and a land-use diagram (Fig. 1.11).

Phase 1: Pre-Roman

It is notable that a lack of pits were found on the site that could be stratigraphically allocated to the pre-Roman Period. A small number of postholes and heavily truncated sections of gullies did not yield any dating evidence and did not form part of any

obvious structural pattern. These probably attest to the presence of roundhouses, as well as four- and six-post structures, which could equally belong to any of the datable pre-Roman phases.

Phase 1.1: Early Iron Age

Occupation at the site started on a limited scale in the early Iron Age with the construction of two, post-built roundhouses situated along the western side of the site (Fig. 1.10a). Traces of a possible third structure were found between the two and produced a fragment of a Greensand saddle quern, a type common during this period in Hampshire.

Phases 1.2 and 1.3: Middle – late Iron Age

Occupation intensified with the replacement of the earlier roundhouses by five middle Iron Age roundhouses represented by truncated lengths of curvilinear drip-gullies associated with burnished flint-tempered 'saucepan pot' ceramics (Fig. 1.10b). Four of the five formed a group aligned on a NNE-SSW axis, a trend indicated in the previous phase, and which clearly took advantage of a relatively level terrace that followed the contour of the hillside. On the same alignment as this group of structures, and approximately 50 m down slope to their east, a shallow linear holloway with a rudimentary surface of flints extended beyond the site limits towards the north entrance of the contemporary ditch and bank enclosure of Oram's Arbour.

The pre-Roman features were sealed by a homogeneous gravelly subsoil that yielded an early Dobunnic coin dated to *c* 40 BC. The holloway contained a similar soil that produced a calibrated radiocarbon date of 40 BC–AD 90 (OxA–16793) from a cattle bone fragment.

Phase 2.1: Early Roman

The alignment of the holloway was re-established a few metres down slope to its east by a ditch (Fig. 1.10c). This was perhaps dug as part of the setting out of the early Roman settlement and although infilled during the last quarter of the 1st century it clearly shared the same alignment as a well-built metalled street surface, which was constructed some 8 m to its east. This street ran beyond the site limits towards the location of the settlement's north entrance (north gate) and therefore represents the settlement's principal NNE-SSW thoroughfare. Running along the western side of the street were the remains of a substantial stone-built water channel; at the southern end of the site the channel turned in a south-easterly direction, across the alignment of the road, presumably at this point in a buried culvert (as it may have been throughout its length). It is probably an extension of the aqueduct known to run up to the area outside the north gate and would have supplied water to the western

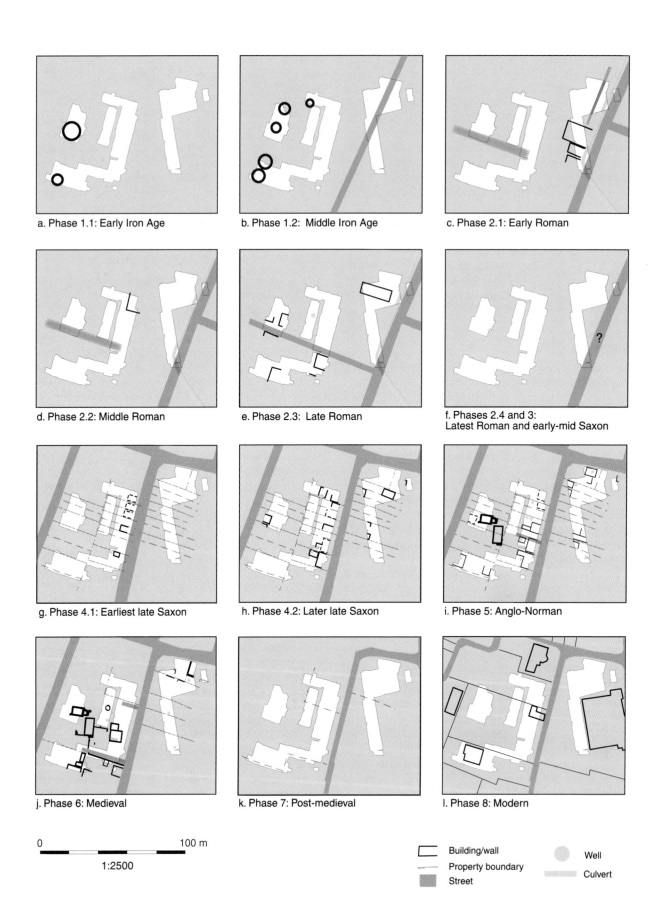

a. Phase 1.1: Early Iron Age

b. Phase 1.2: Middle Iron Age

c. Phase 2.1: Early Roman

d. Phase 2.2: Middle Roman

e. Phase 2.3: Late Roman

f. Phases 2.4 and 3:
Latest Roman and early-mid Saxon

g. Phase 4.1: Earliest late Saxon

h. Phase 4.2: Later late Saxon

i. Phase 5: Anglo-Norman

j. Phase 6: Medieval

k. Phase 7: Post-medieval

l. Phase 8: Modern

0   100 m

1:2500

☐ Building/wall
— Property boundary
▨ Street

● Well

▨ Culvert

Fig. 1.10 *Simplified plans showing the principal site phases*

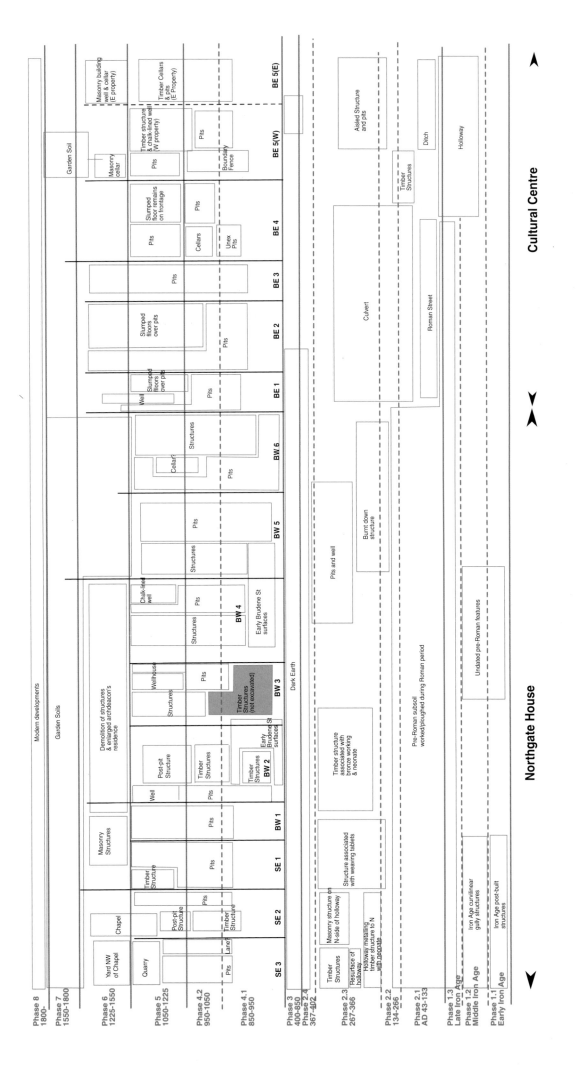

Fig. 1.11   Schematic diagram showing the archaeological evidence for site use over time

slopes of the town. Coin evidence suggests a construction date in the 1st or 2nd century. The very badly truncated remains of up to three timber structures were revealed along the western side of the street.

Phase 2.2: Middle Roman

The evidence suggests that a house was constructed and other activity was taking place away from the principal street (Fig. 1.10d). Towards the south-west part of the site a hearth gave an archaeomagnetic date of 96 BC–AD 130 (WOC), and a nearby neonate burial yielded a radiocarbon date of 1st to 2nd century AD (OxA-16713). Sometime later, perhaps in the first half of the 3rd century, a building with stone foundations was terraced into the slopes in the northern part of the site. The structure, which was only partially excavated, was destroyed by fire, which preserved (as carbonised remains) fairly substantial elements of the timber superstructure. A frame of larger timbers was infilled with wattle and daub that had been internally plastered and painted with orange-brown/red-brown and grey panels, bordered by light grey stripes. The limited dating evidence suggests occupation was probably confined to the 3rd century.

Phase 2.3: Late Roman

The late Roman period saw a noticeable increase in activity and density of settlement in this part of the settlement; the street pattern was extended and new buildings constructed with evidence of varied artisanal activity (Fig. 1.10e). Development extended along a newly metalled street, laid out within the first half of the 4th century on a WNW-ESE alignment and possibly extending as far as the principal thoroughfare to the east (the suggested junction lying just beyond the turn in the culvert). It was flanked on both sides by timber structures, one of which revealed evidence for bronze working. To the south of this new street a building with stone foundations was terraced into the hill slope and yielded a full set of bone weaving tablets. A more substantial structure was built alongside the north-south street using large chalk-packed post-pits, feasibly an aisled building.

Phase 2.4 and 3: Latest Roman and early-mid Saxon

The buildings were abandoned during the second half of the 4th century (Fig. 1.10f). The 'Dark Earth' that formed over the area suggests biological accretion and the deliberate middening of occupation debris from the end of the 4th century. No clear early-mid Saxon evidence was found.

Phase 4.1: Earliest late Saxon

This phase saw the commencement of a sustained period of intensive urban activity probably associated with the establishment of the late Saxon *burh* and Anglo-Saxon town (Fig. 1.10g). A new street (Brudene Street, still surviving as Staple Gardens) was constructed on a NNE-SSW alignment. A number of small timber structures (utilising a sill beam technique), flanked the western side of the street, behind which yards, pits and fence lines were revealed. Together this evidence represented six properties whose boundaries were maintained throughout the later late Saxon and Anglo-Norman Periods where a combination of domestic and artesanal activities including iron working, spinning and dyeing (with madder) took place. Bayesian modelling, based upon a targeted programme of radiocarbon and archaeomagnetic dating, concluded that this activity probably commenced between 840 and 880 (see Chapter 6) and that the properties were established more or less simultaneously.

Phase 4.2: Later late Saxon

There was an increase in the intensity of occupation across the site from the mid 10th century (Fig. 1.10h). The number of structures and their size increased with evidence for encroachment on to the western side of Brudene Street. On one property, a substantial house was constructed with large rectangular-sectioned posts, a new construction technique, that indicates a growing degree of prosperity. Semi-sunken 'cellars' are first noted to the rear of two properties (perhaps indicating a greater requirement for storage facilities), and generally back areas show higher concentrations of pit use. Evidence from the contents of the pits and debris upon internal floors show domestic activity continued but point to a diversification of artesanal activity with bronze, bone and horn working being practised along with a continuation of the dying and iron working activity. Locks and scales appear in the record suggesting trade in rare commodities was taking place with an associated need for added security.

Phase 5: Anglo-Norman

Artesanal activities from the previous phase continued at least during the first part of this phase, however the evidence from some properties appears more domestic in nature (Fig. 1.10i). Indications of increased prosperity are apparent. Wells constructed of chalk ashlar appear on a number of properties, reflecting a focus on controlling a reliable water supply. One property contained a well associated with a very substantial rectangular shaft retained by stone buttressed ashlar chalk walls, and a suggestion of a vaulted roof. Probably towards the end of the 12th century a stone chapel (possibly the parish church of St Mary) and a large stone house were constructed on the site of two properties on Snitheling Street. Another property on this street contained evidence for a furrier. Towards the end of this phase, most of the properties along the western frontage of Brudene Street fell into decline and disuse with pits and wells infilled.

Phase 6: Medieval

During the 13th century the smaller properties that had characterised Brudene Street and Snitheling Street were amalgamated into larger higher status land-holdings (Fig. 1.10j). The residence on Snitheling Street that contained the stone house and chapel was enlarged eastwards encompassing at least three properties that formally occupied the western side of Brudene Street. This property was first documented in 1271 as containing the residence of the ·Archdeacon of Winchester. Additional elements of this property than those revealed in 1960 were recovered, including a possible kitchen, outbuildings, a dovecote, wells, and the boundary wall denoting its southern extent. The properties to the south of this residence were probably enlarged and formed from holdings that formerly fronted onto Snitheling Street and Brudene Street. A range of substantial masonry structures developed on Brudene Street which was probably the residence of Adam de Northampton, a wealthy citizen and skinner, in the later 13th century. On the eastern side of Brudene Street, a substantial stone cellar and a house occupied the northern properties, suggesting occupants of some rank. Evidence from pits from properties to the south of this suggest

that stone buildings also existed along the east side of Brudene Street. By the 15th century, virtually no evidence was found for occupation anywhere on the site.

Phase 7: Post-medieval

Except where it had been removed by later truncation a thick garden soil was noted across the site, corresponding with cartographic depictions by Speed (1610) and Godson (1750) showing that this area of the town was used for horticultural activities (Fig. 1.10k). No features datable to this phase were found.

Phase 8: Modern

The whole of the eastern side of Brudene Street (Staple Gardens) was terraced to provide a relatively flat area for the construction of the Corn Exchange in 1838 (Fig. 1.10l). Staple Gardens was retained by a large wall that defined the western boundary to this development; stonework in this wall may have derived from the remains of former medieval buildings on the site. Two World War II air raid shelter complexes were constructed in the area to the north and west of this structure. A house was constructed on the south side of the Northgate House site during the late 19th century and other parts of the site remained largely open ground until the 1960s.

Chapter 2
Prehistoric and Roman evidence

by Lisa Brown and Edward Biddulph

GEOLOGY AND TOPOGRAPHY

The general geological and topographic setting of Winchester and the area of excavation has been established in Chapter 1. One of the aims of the excavations was to record these aspects in detail to allow a more accurate picture to be established of the area of the site prior to the earliest evidence for human occupation.

The untruncated horizons of the Upper Chalk bedrock and overlying drift geology of Clay-with-Flints were only revealed in profile as a result of the excavation of deep cut features dating from the Roman to post-medieval periods. Investigation of the medieval wells which were cut as vertical shafts into the Upper Chalk bedrock showed that they were all excavated to depths between 34.89 m OD and 43.49 m OD (see Chapter 4), which either demonstrates the presence of perched water table, a spring-line, or they are cisterns collecting water percolating through the rock or redirected rain water.

The interface between the solid chalk bedrock and the drift geology was characteristically irregular and undulating; in places this was quite dramatic with the chalk affected by deep fissures. In all parts of the site the chalk was overlain by Clay-with-Flints deposits, which also filled the deep fissures. This drift geology was a strong orangey-brown coloured silty-clay, which contained over 50% broken angular flints and flint nodules. It varied in thickness but appeared to follow a general trend, being thinner on the upslope western side and thickening further downslope to the east. In one location, at the extreme western side of the site, the Clay-with-Flint deposit contained a single large Sarson stone.

Where untruncated the upper surface of the Clay-with-Flints did not undulate and was overlain by between 0.15 to 0.30 m of a duller orangy-brown sandy-silt with limited flint inclusions, originally representing the pre-Roman subsoil but which had been subsequently subject to cultivation and contained material of early Roman date (see Phase 1.3 below). As a consequence, all pre-Roman activity was found to have been overlain by this soil. Where the soil had been protected by the early Roman north-south street it contained material of largely pre-Roman date. Soil morphology (sample

CCM602; see Macphail and Crowther, Chapter 8) here suggests that it represented slightly phosphate-rich physically disturbed/homogenised possible plough soil, suggesting pre-Roman arable activity. This horizon was present throughout the site apart from along the western half of the Discovery Centre where it had been removed by later terracing. However, enough of the untruncated surface of the Clay-with-Flints survived in order to generate the model of the site's original topography represented in Figure 2.1. It can clearly be seen that the site sloped gradually down from the west (c 52.99 m OD) to east (c 44.69 m OD) at a gradient of 5–6%. There was an indication of several natural terraces, running north-south and broadly corresponding with the Roman street, the modern alignment of Staple Gardens and the western side of the Northgate House site. There was also an indication of a broadly perpendicular east-west undulation within the general slope of the hillside, which started in the south-west part of the Northgate House site and ran eastwards into the southernmost limits of the Discovery Centre site.

THE PREHISTORIC SETTLEMENT (PHASE 1)
by Lisa Brown

Introduction

The NH/CC site lies within the north-east corner of the 20 ha Iron Age enclosure known as Oram's Arbour (Fig. 2.2). The date of the enclosure and the role it played in the development of the modern city of Winchester and surrounding region are still debated. The current evidence suggests a middle Iron Age origin for the earthworks (Qualmann *et al.* 2004) and, although only a small proportion of the enclosure has been excavated, it is now generally agreed that it does not conform in many respects to the traditional model of the *oppidum*, as it has often been described in the past (Collis pers. comm.; Biddle 1990; Cunliffe 1996, 26).

The results of the recent fieldwork and of previous excavations on the plot of land situated between the present day Tower Street and Staple Gardens show that the NH/CC site was occupied by a settlement during the later prehistoric period, from the late Bronze Age/early Iron Age transition through to the late Iron Age. Although

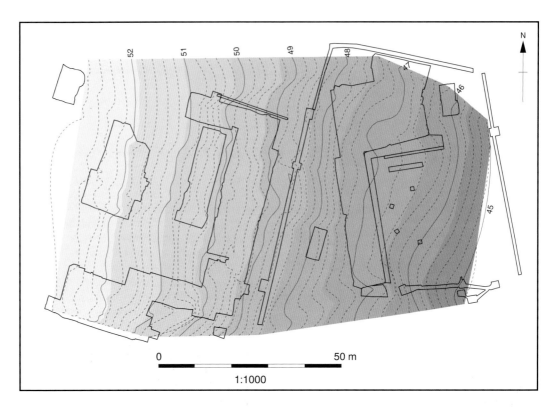

Fig. 2.1 Plan of the natural topography of the site

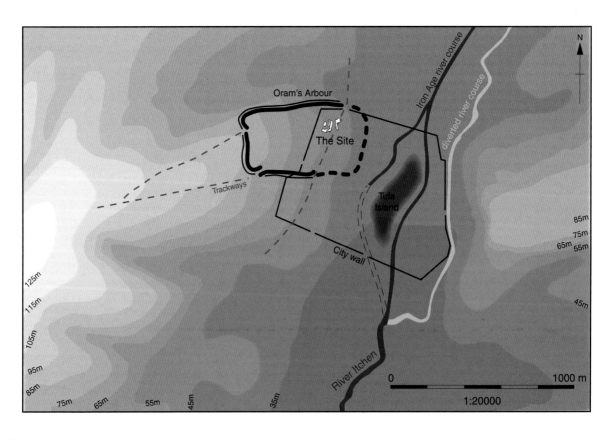

Fig. 2.2 Location of the excavations in relation to Oram's Arbour Iron Age enclosure

Fig. 2.3 Plan of early Iron Age and unphased prehistoric features, Phase 1.1 (c 700–400 BC)

Structure
NH9800

Structure
NH9801

Structure
NH8508

Structure
NH8502

Holloway
CC7000

20 m

1:500

0

N

39

evidence for scattered and sporadic earlier prehistoric activity has been recovered within the modern city, none was found on at this specific site (see Chapter 5).

Several small trenches excavated in 1960–1 within the current project area exposed a number of shallow pits, postholes and gullies cut into the natural gravel and sealed by Roman deposits (Fig. 2.3; Cunliffe 1964; UAD 791). No definite structures were identified but associated pottery corresponded to the decorated variety found at the nearby hillfort of St Catherine's Hill, where it was dated to between 300 and 100 BC (Hawkes *et al.*1930; Cunliffe 2005). Two minor investigations, carried out in 1952 (UAD 789) and in 1959 (UAD 790), also within the project area, produced a few traces of middle Iron Age activity.

Within the *c* 8257 m² development area of the NH/CC site, the excavation trenches formed *c* 2557 m². It is estimated that *c* 412 m² of the prehistoric deposits that could have been expected within this area had either been destroyed by intensive later pitting or lay below the level of archaeological mitigation. The total of undisturbed prehistoric levels available for investigation, therefore, amounted to only *c* 1004 m² (39% of the excavation trenches or 12% of the development area). Most of the surviving prehistoric activity was found in the western half of the NH site, which occupied a level terrace at *c* 52.2 m aOD (Fig. 2.3). However, due to the excavation strategy applied to this part of the site, the trenches did not penetrate the pre-Roman levels along its eastern side. Modern terracing may have removed any early remains along the western part of the CC site, but some traces of prehistoric activity survived further to the east.

As a consequence of the post-Roman destruction to later prehistoric levels and of restricted access dictated by the mitigation strategy, the overview obtained of the nature and pattern of later prehistoric occupation was somewhat limited. Nonetheless, the excavations exposed a number of structural features with associated ceramics that provided convincing evidence for at least two phases of Iron Age settlement activity. Phase 1.1 was represented by at least two post-built roundhouses associated with a few sherds of early Iron Age pottery (Fig. 2.3). A later group of four or five roundhouses (Phase 1.2; see Fig. 2.6), identified only by their eaves drip gullies, produced a somewhat larger assemblage of distinctive middle Iron Age pottery. Features and deposits thought to be contemporary with Iron Age activity, but lacking reliable stratigraphic and artefactual associations, were classified as Phase 1 (prehistoric unphased). These included two concentrations of postholes, which may have represented additional roundhouses or perhaps ancillary structures such as two-, four- or six-post structures.

The absence of genuine pits (as opposed to shallow hollows) within both the early and middle Iron Age settlements cannot be explained purely by the levels of truncation encountered during excavation, since the far less substantial remains of roundhouses survived here. Deep storage pits of the type commonly excavated in southern Britain, and typical of the Iron Age in Hampshire, have been found close to the site, both elsewhere in Winchester and at nearby Iron Age settlement sites such as Winnall Down (Fasham 1985).

A clue to the absence of pits at the NH/CC site no doubt lies in the localised geology (see above). The Iron Age roundhouses were constructed in an area where the Upper Chalk was capped with Clay-with-Flints and gravelly sand, an unsuitable location for digging storage pits. At Downland settlements such as Winnall Down and Easton Lane (Fasham 1985; Fasham *et al.* 1989) and on hilltop sites such as St Catherine's Hill (Hawkes *et al.* 1930) and Danebury (Cunliffe 1984 and 1995), where deep storage pits were common, the chalk lies directly below turfline/topsoil or below relatively thin and sporadic cappings of Clay-with-Flints. In Winchester a 1 m deep early Iron Age pit was recorded at New Road (Qualmann *et al.* 2004, 25) and a middle Iron Age pit at Sussex Street (ibid., 43), both within an area where the chalk spur rises to form St Paul's Hill. These locations lie only 100–150 m to the west of the NH roundhouses, and it would be reasonable to conjecture that the Iron Age inhabitants, who would have been very familiar with the local geology, dug their storage pits in this more suitable zone.

The topography of the area also had some bearing on the siting of a holloway (CC7000) that linked the north and south entrances of Oram's Arbour (Fig. 2.3). This worn track followed the natural line of the contours of St Paul's Hill (Fig. 2.2). It was clearly in use during the Iron Age, and almost certainly had an even earlier origin, predating the construction of the Oram's Arbour earthworks and influencing the arrangement of the early and middle Iron Age structures, and of a later Roman road. The holloway served as the north-south axis of a wide-ranging and probably very ancient network of trade routes linking prehistoric communities for centuries.

Phase 1.1 (*c* 700–400 BC): Early Iron Age roundhouses

During the earliest phase of settlement activity early Iron Age inhabitants constructed at least two post ring-built roundhouses (NH8502 and NH8508) some 60 m to the west of what was probably a pre-existing holloway (CC7000) (Fig. 2.3). The levels of truncation and paucity of artefacts from surrounding features hindered the identification of other settlement features that may have been associated with the roundhouses, but two concentrations of postholes, NH9800 and NH9801 (see below), may disguise poorly-preserved remains of four-post or similar buildings.

Structure NH8502 (Fig. 2.4; Plate 2.1)

Structure NH8502 survived as an arc of eight postholes (NH6167; NH6178; NH6207; NH6223 NH6182; NH6197; NH6180; NH6232) forming the northern side of a single-ring roundhouse estimated to be approximately 8 m in diameter. A south-east facing porched entrance can be inferred from the position of posthole NH5240, forming a pair with NH6232, sited about 1 m beyond the main post ring. The other side of the entrance was not preserved.

Another 12 features enclosed by the post ring could have supported internal divisions or the roof structure. Poorly preserved wide, shallow features, such as NH6212 and NH6225, may have been hearth bases or simple wear hollows produced by continual footfall or scratching animals. Although the precise date of these features and direct association with the structure was uncertain due to the paucity of finds, at least one (NH6195) was cut by the gully of middle Iron Age roundhouse NH8505, and so clearly pre-dated it.

The postholes belonging to Structure NH8502 were 0.3–0.5 m in diameter and survived to a depth of between only 0.05 m and 0.62 m. Their fills were a relatively homogeneous greyish-brown silty clay containing varying amounts of gravel, which distinctly contrasted with the overlying orange-brown subsoil. Four of the postholes, two belonging to the post ring and two internal ones, produced pottery of broadly later prehistoric type (see Brown, Chapter 7). Posthole NH6195 (see above) contained a small sherd of coarse shell-tempered pottery and posthole NH6223, one of the ring posts, produced a sherd of finely made flint-tempered ware, a type

generally dated to the middle Iron Age but in this case possibly intrusive, considering the levels of localised disturbance.

A small, heavily fired brick and a fragment of vitrified furnace lining were found in postholes associated with Structure NH8502 (see Poole, Chapter 7). The furnace lining indicates some level of industrial activity, perhaps bronze-working, within the settlement. The brick may have been simply re-used as post packing, but the practice of deliberate placement of closing deposits within postholes following abandonment of buildings was relatively common in the Hampshire/Wiltshire region during the early Iron Age (Brown 2000).

Charred plant remains from nine features relating to Structure NH8502, including four of the ring postholes, provided evidence that more wheat than barley was being processed, and presumably grown, at the settlement during the early Iron Age. One of the internal postholes (NH6210) near the roundhouse entrance contained a large deposit of black mustard seeds, a native oil seed crop that may have been used for seasoning food.

Some 5 m to the north of Structure NH8502, two shallow hollows (NH6183 and NH6191) were cut by the gully of middle Iron Age roundhouse NH8504 (see below). They were both *c* 1 m across and less than 0.4 m deep, and may have been structural elements of an early Iron Age precursor to the later roundhouse, representing a structure occupying the space between NH8502 and NH8508. Although they contained no pottery, NH6183 produced a fragment of a Greensand saddle quern, a type common during the early Iron Age in Hampshire (Fig. 2.4 Section NH353).

Plate 2.1   Structure NH8502, Phase 1.1, looking south

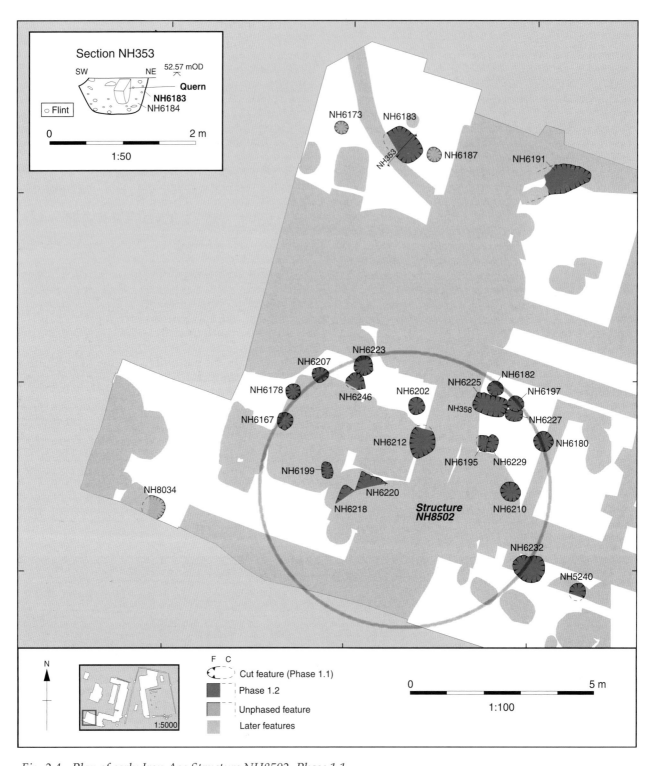

Fig. 2.4   Plan of early Iron Age Structure NH8502, Phase 1.1

Structure NH8508 (Fig. 2.5)

Structure NH8508 was represented by a group of sub-circular features, all probably the truncated bases of postholes. Due to later disturbance it was difficult to trace the full extent of the structure, and the possibility exists that this was a double-ring roundhouse, but equally it may have been a single-ring structure rebuilt at some stage, the second version slightly off-centre from the first. The positioning of the postholes indicated a diameter of about 12 m, much larger than NH8502, but within the recognised range for the early Iron Age. The postholes ranged from 0.63 to 1.15 m across and survived to between 0.25–0.55 m deep, with the exception of NH1614, which was considerably deeper. They were all filled with orange or greyish-brown silty clay with varying quantities of gravel.

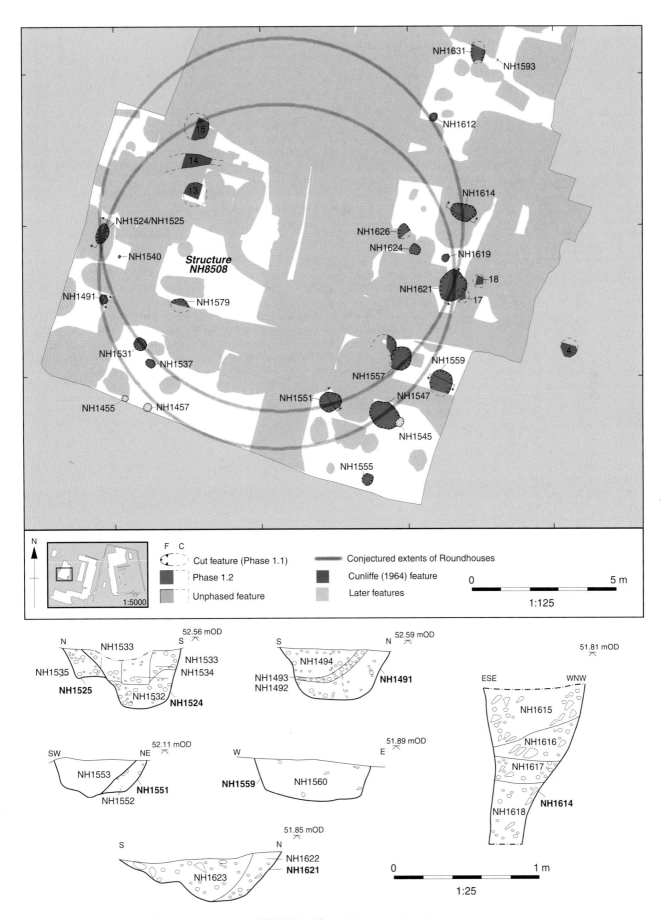

Fig. 2.5   Plan of early Iron Age Structure NH8508, Phase 1.1

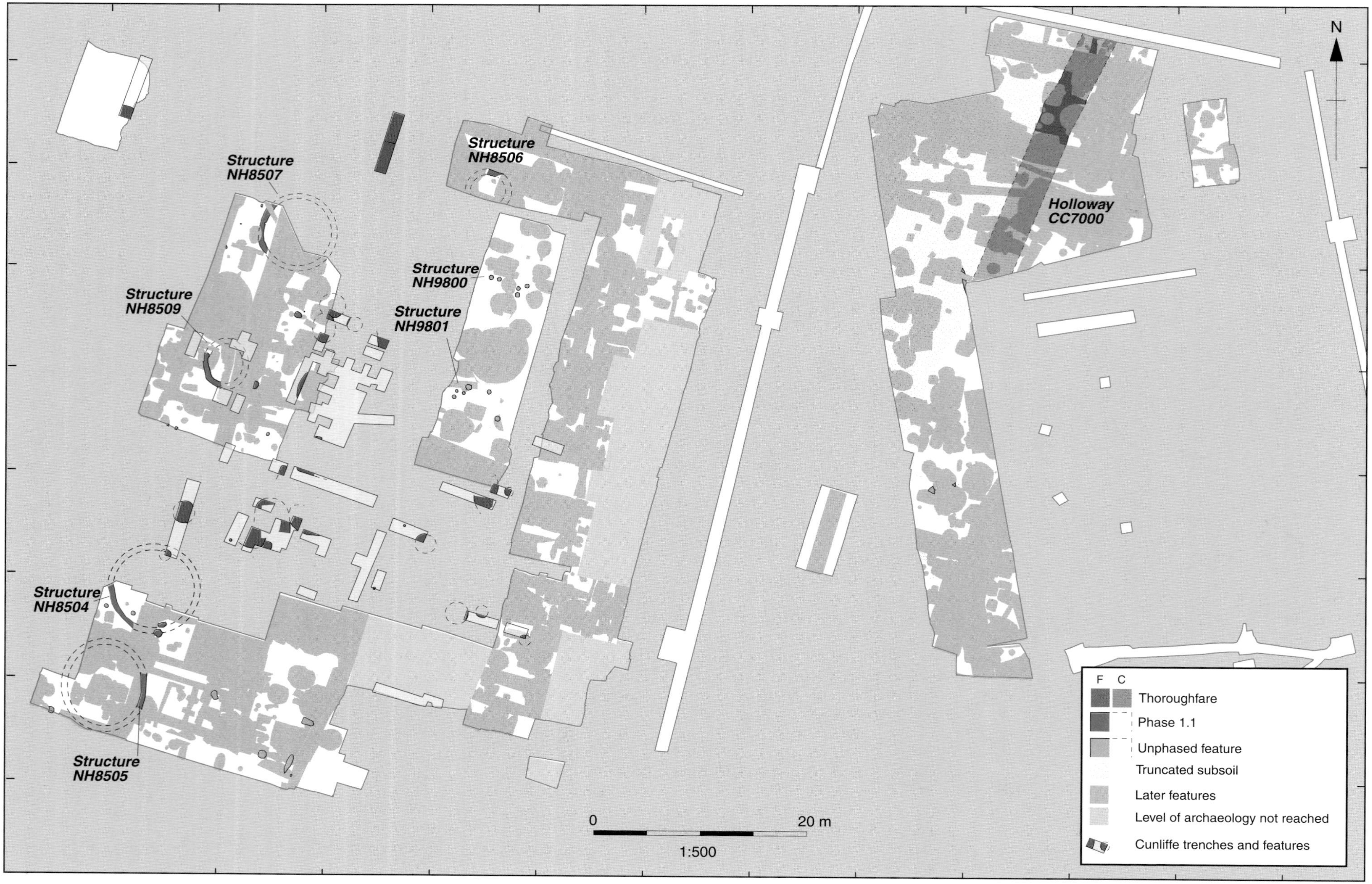

Fig. 2.6 Plan of middle Iron Age and unphased prehistoric features, Phase 1.2 (c 400–100 BC)

Legend:

F C
- Thoroughfare
- Phase 1.1
- Unphased feature
- Truncated subsoil
- Later features
- Level of archaeology not reached
- Cunliffe trenches and features

Labels on plan:
- Holloway CC7000
- Structure NH8506
- Structure NH9800
- Structure NH9801
- Structure NH8507
- Structure NH8509
- Structure NH8504
- Structure NH8505

Scale: 0 — 20 m, 1:500

N

Four roughly equidistant postholes (NH1551, NH1557, NH1621 and NH1614) would have formed the eastern side of a post ring, with postholes NH1612, NH1524/1525; NH1531 and NH1537 completing the circuit. The northern and much of the southern stretch of postholes were lost to later disturbance. Although NH1614 was over 1 m, the profile suggested it was a posthole rather than a pit. Surviving traces of post-pipes in NH1614 and NH1557 indicated upright timbers of at least 0.20 m diameter, suggesting that these were load-bearing elements of a substantial structure. Postholes NH1547 and NH1559, located approximately 1 m outside of the proposed post ring, may have held porch posts.

The possible alternative circuit, second post ring or rebuilt version of roundhouse NH8508 was represented by postholes NH1547, NH1599 and NH1621 on the eastern side of the main circuit, NH1491 (and possibly NH1457) on the south-western side and Cunliffe posthole 15 on the north-western side.

A number of postholes lying within the area described by the posthole circuit/s included small features excavated during the 1960s (Cunliffe 1964) and re-exposed during the current excavations (Fig. 2.5, Cunliffe features 13 and 14). These, along with NH1579, NH1619, NH1624 and NH1626, may have also supported internal structures within the roundhouse.

None of the features relating to this structure, including those reported by Cunliffe (1964), produced any finds apart from a sherd of early Iron Age pottery from NH1621. Samples of charred plants from features NH1524, NH1547, NH1557 and NH1579 produced notably more barley than wheat, particularly posthole NH1524. The barley was mainly hulled but a naked grain suggested that some naked barley was present either as a minor crop or a sporadic variant (see Carruthers, Chapter 8). The presence of chaff fragments indicated that emmer and spelt wheat were being cultivated within the settlement, with spelt as the dominant crop. NH1621 produced a relatively large quantity of charred grain dominated by hulled wheat with some free-threshing wheat, but despite the amount of material, the feature was clearly not a grain storage pit (Fig. 2.5 Section NH1614).

Phase 1.2 (c 400–100 BC): Middle Iron Age roundhouses

Five middle Iron Age roundhouses were represented by severely truncated eaves drip gullies (Fig. 2.6). Four of the five were set in a linear arrangement, occupying a level terrace on the western side of the NH excavations. Again, no associated pits or ancillary structures could be definitely linked to this phase of the settlement.

Structure NH8507

The western curve of a well-preserved curvilinear gully with a projected diameter of *c* 8 m was the only surviving feature relating to roundhouse NH8507 (Fig. 2.6). This U-shaped gully was 0.5 m wide and survived to only 0.13 m deep. The homogeneous fill produced no finds.

Structure NH8509

Structure NH8509 was represented by a discontinuous curvilinear gully that lay within the space previously occupied by occupied by Phase 1.1 roundhouse NH8505 (Fig. 2.6). The gully was 0.45 m wide and 0.15 m deep and its western side had been truncated by later activity. Two small sherds of intrusive Roman pottery and a fragment of ceramic building material were recovered from the fill. A shallow feature (NH1628) to the east of the gully lies in the correct position to have been a south-eastern gully terminal. The primary fill of this feature showed evidence of gradual silting, but upper fill may have been deliberate levelling.

Structure NH8504 (Fig. 2.7)

The southern curve of a penannular gully with a projected diameter of *c* 9 m was probably a drip gully relating to another roundhouse (NH8504). A possible terminus was identified on the eastern side. The gully was 0.4–0.57 m wide and survived to a maximum depth of 0.22 m. The fill was a mid grey silty clay with gravel, which produced a sherd of highly burnished, flint-tempered middle Iron Age pottery. Posthole NH6168, which lay just beyond the south-eastern curve of the gully, may have been a rafter support for a porch. It contained three middle Iron Age sherds, including a fragment of a highly burnished flint-tempered globular jar.

Structure NH8505 (Fig. 2.7)

A short length of a curvilinear gully represented the eastern curve of an eaves drip gully enclosing roundhouse NH8505. The structure was sited only *c* 1 m to the south of NH8504 and was the southernmost of four middle Iron Age roundhouses on the western side of the excavation area. On the basis of the projected diameter of the gully, the roundhouse was probably *c* 8 m or 9 m in diameter. The gully was 0.45–0.5 m wide and 0.14–0.18 m deep, with steep sides and a rounded base. It was filled with greyish brown silty clay with gravel, which produced 11 sherds of burnished flint-tempered pottery, including a 'saucepan pot' rim and 10 fragments of a vessel with burnt organic residue on the inner surface, probably the remains of a meal.

Structure NH8506

A possible fifth roundhouse was represented by a very short length of gully located some 10 m to the north-east of roundhouse NH8507 (Fig. 2.6). Although too little of this feature survived to be certain of its size or function, it was dated to the middle Iron Age on the basis of a burnished, flint-tempered saucepan pot rim found in its fill (NH7607).

Environmental remains from the middle Iron Age structures

Charred plant remains taken from Phase 1.2 gullies NH1633 (Structure NH8507), NH6162 (Structure NH8505), NH6163 (Structure NH8505), NH6189 (Structure NH8504) and NH7610 (Structure NH8506), and from posthole NH6168 (Structure NH8504), were similar to the early Iron Age samples, with mixed domestic waste of mostly wheat, but with relatively abundant barley (see Carruthers, Chapter 8). Chaff and weed seeds were again uncommon, suggesting that processing had taken place away from the immediate area. A

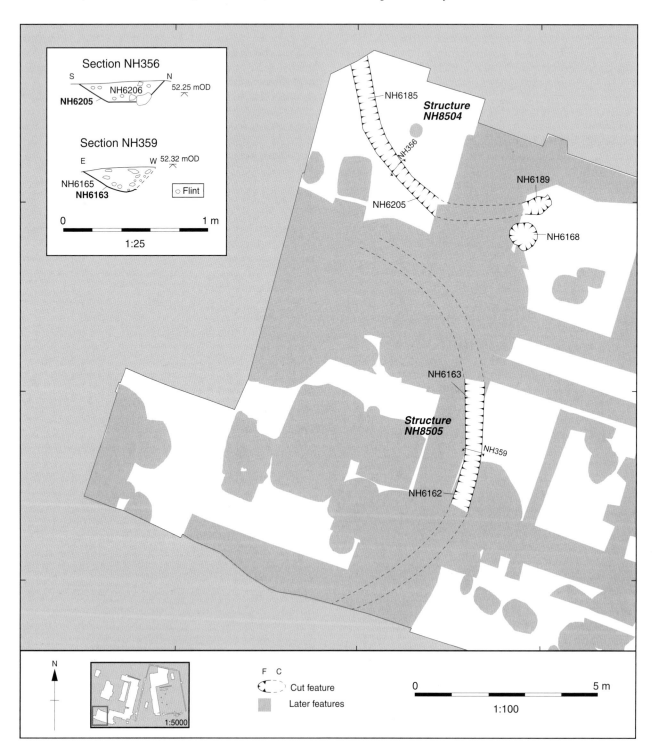

Fig. 2.7 Plan of middle Iron Age Structures NH8504 and NH8505, Phase 1.2

possible sloe stone fragment found in gully NH6162 and a possible Celtic bean from NH1634 provide some limited evidence for elements of the middle Iron Age diet. There was a slight increase in bread-type wheat during this period, a time when oats also made their first significant appearance. The oats may have been weeds rather than cultivated crops even at this late date, although there is evidence from contemporary sites that they were grown for fodder.

Holloway CC7000

The Iron Age roundhouses were constructed on a NE-SW alignment corresponding to that of a shallow linear holloway running *c* 50 m to the east (Figs 2.6 and 2.8). This worn prehistoric track was 3.5 m wide and survived to 0.15 m deep. It was exposed for a length of 11.3 m at the north end of CC site (Fig. 2.8) but modern terracing had removed all

evidence of it in the southern part of the trench. What appears to be the northern continuation of holloway CC7000 (and the later Roman road) was found during excavations at Victoria Road, some 40 m outside of the projected line of Oram's Arbour (Qualmann *et al*. 2004, 47–8). Here, where the track (F856) was much better preserved than at the NH/CC site; it was consistently 5 m wide, with wheel-ruts underlying Roman period metalling.

The eastern side of the trackway was edged with discontinuous patches of flint nodules (CC3409 and CC3374), probably the remnants of an original rudimentary surface (Fig. 2.8, Section CC311). The hollow gradually filled with mixed gravel and soil that resembled the surrounding subsoil, repre-senting a combination of eroded and trampled material deriving from the edges of the track. The surface of the gravelly make-up was overlain by a trampled soil surface incorporating small quantities of occupation material, including burnt flint and a

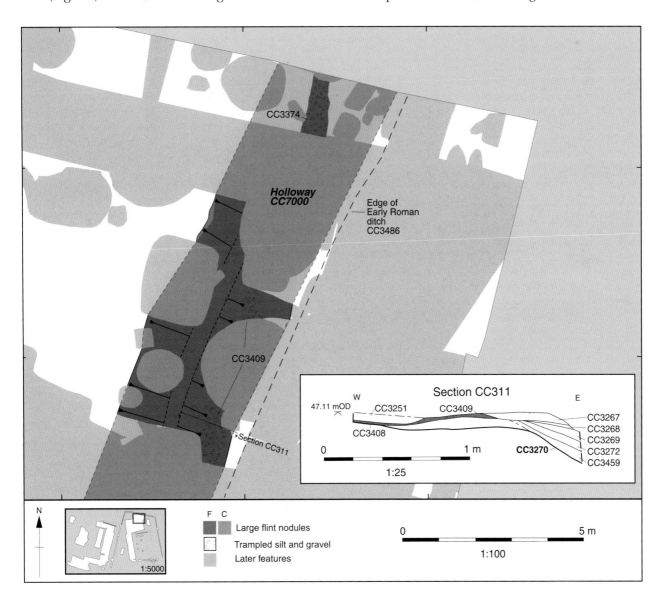

Fig. 2.8   Plan of Holloway CC7000, Phase 1.2

few sherds of flint-tempered prehistoric pottery. A cattle bone fragment recovered from this deposit produced a calibrated radiocarbon date of 40 BC–AD 90 (OxA-16793). A second sample from a sheep/goat tooth produced a calibrated date of AD 260–430 (OxA-16794), but this could have been intrusive from the extensive Roman period activity in the area.

A later Roman street (see below) appears to have mirrored the alignment of the prehistoric trackway, and both routes led to the postulated site of the north gate of the Roman town, which corresponds to the proposed northern entrance into the Iron Age Oram's Arbour enclosure. This ancient orientation was reflected in a V-shaped ditch (CC3486), which flanked the Roman road (Fig. 2.8). A direct association between the prehistoric trackway and the Roman road and ditch seems highly plausible, and suggests that the track, although abandoned prior to the construction of the Roman road, retained a visible presence in the landscape.

Undated features (Phase 1)

Two groups of postholes lay some 10 m to the east of the linear arrangement of Iron Age roundhouses (Fig. 2.6). For convenience sake these have been referred to as Structures NH9800 and NH9801, but it is likely that they were surviving elements of several structures, such as two- or four-posters or fences. The stratigraphic relationship between the postholes and the subsoil (NH8503/CC7001) was not observed during excavation as the posthole fills were similar in composition to the subsoil. None produced dating evidence, with the exception of NH9776, which contained a (probably) intrusive Roman sherd in the top fill.

The five postholes representing Structure NH9800 may have represented a four-post structure, of which one posthole did not survive, and a two-poster. The features were relatively deep at between 0.21 and 0.54 m, with diameters of 0.3–0.42 m, and all were filled with a mid-grey fine silt which contained no finds. Structure NH9801 consisted of six shallow postholes which appeared to follow a curvilinear arrangement, possibly belonging to a small roundhouse, but which, again, may have represented more than one phase and one structure. The postholes were between 0.3–0.5 m in diameter, with surviving depths ranging from only 0.1–0.21 m.

It would be reasonable to suggest that these 'structures' belonged to a zoned alignment of ancillary structures sited between the roundhouses and the holloway, with storage pits located on the western side of the roundhouses.

Phase 1.3 (*c* 100 BC–AD 43): Late Iron Age subsoil

The pre-Roman deposits were sealed by a homogeneous, gravelly subsoil (Phase 1.3; NH8503 and CC7001; not illustrated). Where it was securely sealed by Roman deposits, the subsoil contained no

0   50 mm

1:1

Plate 2.2   Iron Age Dobunnic coin

closely datable material, but elsewhere it included Roman and later artefacts, which had been incorporated during Roman period cultivation and later activity. Three samples taken from this worked soil produced very high concentrations of cereal grains. Bread-type wheat, most of it hulled, was the most common cereal in two of the samples and hulled barley dominated the third (NH1599). Few weed seeds and no chaff fragments were found in this soil, perhaps because they had been destroyed by cultivation, or because the grain found in the samples was processed cereal incorporated in a general mix of burnt household waste used to fertilise the soil. Three corn cockle seeds from two of the samples represent the earliest recorded find on the site for this poisonous plant, and may relate to the bringing in of seed corn from outside the region, probably during the Roman period.

The only pre-Roman coin (SF 1263) recovered from the excavations came from subsoil NH8503 (context NH4390). It was a base silver unit depicting a head on the obverse and a triple-tailed horse and a cock's head on the reverse, a type belonging to the early Dobunnic uninscribed series dated to *c* 40 BC (Plate 2.2 and see de Jersey, Chapter 7). Although the coin was effectively unstratified, its presence here as the first of its type found in Winchester, and occurring some way to the south-east of its currently recognised distribution pattern, is interesting in the context of the role that Oram's Arbour may have served in controlling a complex of far-reaching trade routes from the middle Iron Age and possibly later (see Chapter 5).

THE ROMAN OCCUPATION (PHASE 2)
by Edward Biddulph

Introduction

The excavations reported on here were located in the north-western quarter of the Roman town (Fig. 2.9; see also Fig. 5.3). The north gate utilised the north-east entrance of Oram's Arbour and was located some 100 m north of the excavation area. A street uncovered in the Discovery Centre (CC) area probably led to the gate being identified as the

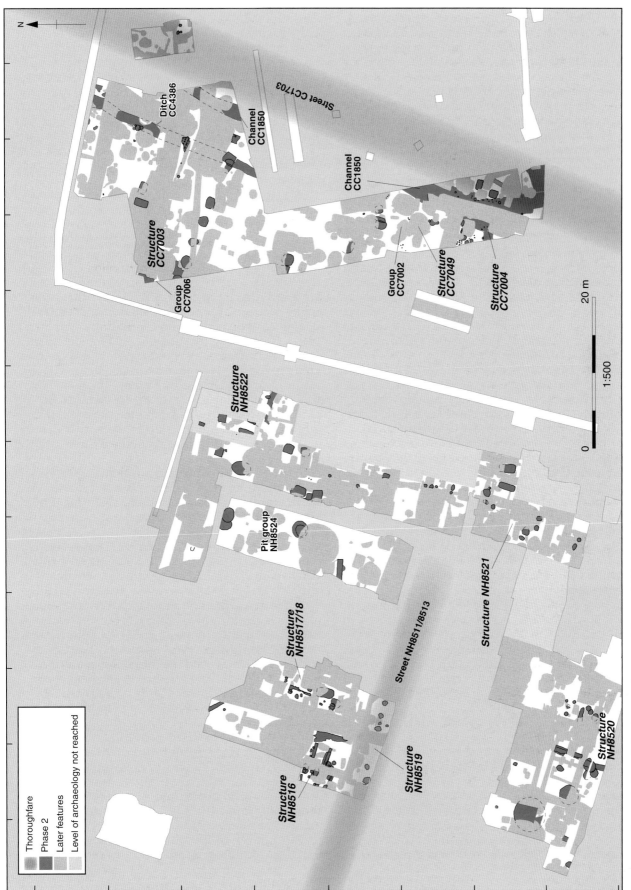

N

UNIVERSITY OF WINCHESTER
LIBRARY

Ditch
CC4386

Street CC1703

Channel
CC1850

Channel
CC1850

**Structure
CC7003**

Group
CC7006

Group
CC7002

**Structure
CC7049**

**Structure
CC7004**

20 m

1:500

0

**Structure
NH8522**

Pit group
NH8524

**Structure
NH8517/18**

Street NH8511/8513

Structure NH8521

**Structure
NH8516**

**Structure
NH8519**

**Structure
NH8520**

Thoroughfare
Phase 2
Later features
Level of archaeology not reached

Fig. 2.9   General plan of the Roman features, Phase 2 (AD 43–400)

principal north-south axis. The character of the early town was to a large extent determined by topography. Development concentrated on the west bank of the Itchen Valley, the streets being terraced into the hillside and orientated with the prevailing contours. The north-west part of the town was more sparsely occupied than areas closer to the centre and its character was distinctly industrial. However, much of the evidence recorded in the fieldwork was the product of domestic occupation and it is likely that the area was given over to both residential and industrial use.

Phase 2.1 (*c* AD 43–130/50): Early Roman structures, street surfaces and a water channel

The north-west quarter of the town saw modest activity from the late Neronian/early Flavian period (Figs 2.9–10). Medieval truncation largely removed walls, foundations and floors of structures, but enough survives to suggest that buildings and yards existed here. These appear to have extended along the street (Street CC1703) leading to the north gate; dating evidence from the road tends towards the late Roman period, but an early Roman ditch (CC3486) aligned with the road may have been associated with it. A flint-lined channel (CC1850) probably carried water through the site.

Three early Roman structures have been tentatively identified. Structure CC7004 survived as hearths, surfaces and occupation layers confined in a small area at the south end of the Discovery Centre site (Fig. 2.10). A silty spread (CC1766), 0.64 m by 0.62 m and 40 mm deep, lay at the base of a sequence of occupation deposits above the prehistoric subsoil (CC1701). The deposit contained the burnt remains of plants and animals—including cattle, pig and probably sheep or goat, and cereal chaff and grain, mainly spelt, but also barley—that contributed to the dietary and other needs of early Roman inhabitants. The deposit was probably dumped to provide a base for a mortar surface (CC1706) laid above it. This was more extensive than CC1766, being 5.65 m long and 1.54 m wide, though it was just as shallow at 80 mm deep. Another part of the surface (CC1735) was seen nearby. This surface almost certainly served as a floor, since hearths were built on top of it. Burnt clay within occupation spread CC1704 provides ephemeral remains of one hearth, while a shallow scoop (CC1734) above deposit CC1735 and containing burnt clay, formed the more tangible remains of another (Fig. 2.11). The latter was replaced by a third hearth (CC1730) suggesting a degree of longevity in terms of occupation. No structural evidence was encountered. Pottery from mortar surface CC1706 gives a *terminus post quem* of AD 60–130 for the laying of the floor; vessel forms included two globular jars (CG) and a platter (JA),

all in grey ware (ZM) (see Biddulph and Booth, Chapter 7). Pottery from CC1766 and CC1735 could only be dated broadly to the Roman period.

A number of features uncovered immediately north of Structure CC7004 may be part of a second structure (Structure CC7049) (Figs 2.10–11). A posthole (CC1863) and stakehole (CC1865) were cut into the prehistoric subsoil. That subsoil could account for the two possibly residual sherds of middle or late Iron Age pottery retrieved from the posthole's single clay-silt fill, although the feature may in fact belong to activity associated with the middle Iron Age settlement. A crushed chalk surface (CC1796–8) was more certain to form part of an early Roman structure. This survived as small patches, the largest measuring 0.45 by 0.42 m. Areas of burnt soil (CC1795/1861) may indicate the presence of hearths. A second phase of flooring is suggested by crushed chalk deposits (CC1859/62) that overlay the burnt soil. Occupation deposits were recorded in the form of sandy silts that sealed the surfaces and burnt areas. These contained small quantities of domestic debris, including amorphous pieces of fired clay, fuel-ash slag, and indeterminate animal bone fragments, but the pottery also recovered proved more useful in terms of dating. A South Gaulish samian Drag. 15/17 platter fragment from CC1780 (an occupation layer that sealed CC1796–8) is likely to have reached the town before AD 80, while a grey ware globular jar (CG, fabric ZMZ) and another South Gaulish samian sherd from below deposit CC1859, generally support a late 1st- or early 2nd-century date for deposition.

A surface or third structure was located at the north end of the Discovery Centre site (Fig. 2.10). Group CC7006 comprised a sequence of surface or occupation deposits. The lowest, a silty soil overlying the natural clay (CC2371), was sealed by redeposited natural (CC2370) followed by a small patch of chalk (CC2369), possibly the remains of a surface. This was followed by a redeposited silty clay natural (CC2193) that may have represented another surface, which was in turn covered by a loamy occupation deposit, CC2158. Pottery and vessel glass from these deposits placed the sequence in the second half of the 1st century AD. Soil CC2371 contained a grey ware globular jar (CH, ZM), a bead-rimmed jar in an oxidised fabric (CG, YM), and South Gaulish samian ware (TSA). Redeposited natural (CC2370) contained a butt-beaker in a fine oxidised ware (EA, fabric NFA) and a grey ware platter (JC, fabric ZM) and globular jar (CH, fabric ZFZ), giving a *terminus post quem* of *c* AD 55–70/80. A South Gaulish samian Drag. 18 platter and Alice Holt/Farnham-type bead-rimmed jars (CG)—supported by glass jug fragments—provide a date after AD 60 for levelling layer CC2193, while pottery from loam CC2158, including South Gaulish samian ware

Fig. 2.10 (facing page) Plan of Street CC1703, channel CC1850 and Structures CC7002, CC7004, CC7006 and CC7049, Phase 2.1 (c AD 43–130/50)

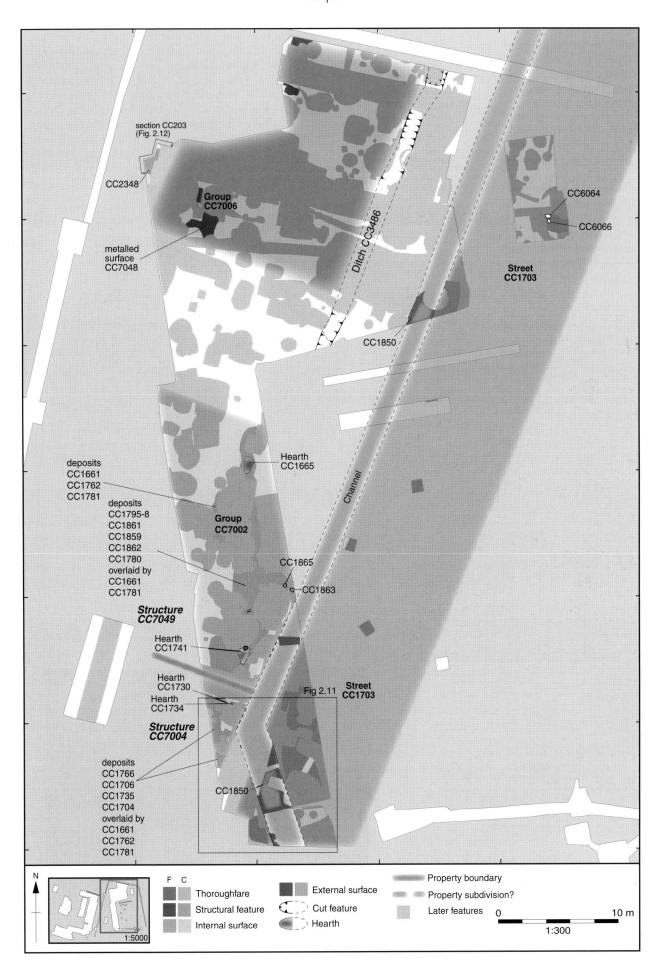

section CC203
(Fig. 2.12)

CC2348

**Group
CC7006**

metalled
surface
CC7048

CC6064

CC6066

**Street
CC1703**

Ditch CC3486

CC1850

deposits
CC1661
CC1762
CC1781

deposits
CC1795-8
CC1861
CC1859
CC1862
CC1780
overlaid by
CC1661
CC1781

Hearth
CC1665

**Group
CC7002**

Channel

CC1865

CC1863

*Structure
CC7049*

Hearth
CC1741

Hearth
CC1730

Hearth
CC1734

Fig 2.11

**Street
CC1703**

*Structure
CC7004*

deposits
CC1766
CC1706
CC1735
CC1704
overlaid by
CC1661
CC1762
CC1781

CC1850

N

1:5000

F	C			

Thoroughfare

Structural feature

Internal surface

External surface

Cut feature

Hearth

Property boundary

Property subdivision?

Later features

0   10 m

1:300

platters (forms 18 and 29), dated to *c* AD 75/90 or later. There were no structural elements apart from surfaces; a fragment of clay render may have derived from the wall of a building, but it was found in CC2370 and seems unlikely to have belonged to the structure that CC7006 may represent.

A pit (CC2348) was dug through the sequence (Figs 2.10 and 2.12). Its fills, comprising redeposited natural or chalk rubble, contained dating evidence that gave a late 1st-century or early 2nd-century date for the feature and the group as a whole. Another metalled surface (CC7048) lay directly over the natural clay (Fig. 2.10). It was composed of tightly packed rounded pebbles supporting a thin mortar-like surface. The lack of subsoil below suggests that it may have been set originally within a terrace or holloway, all trace of which was truncated by modern levelling. No dating evidence was recovered.

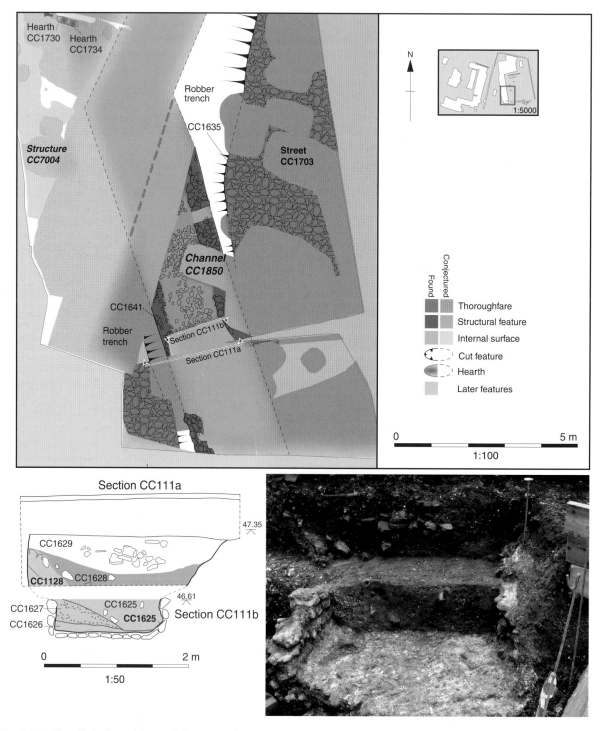

Fig. 2.11 Detailed plan of Street CC1703 and channel CC1850, Phase 2.1

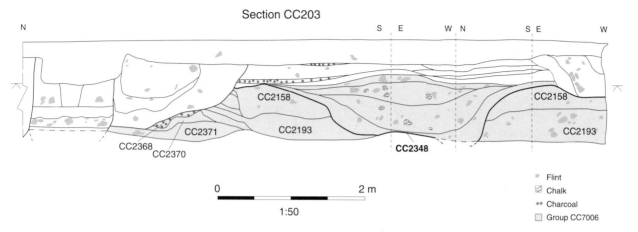

Fig. 2.12 Section showing deposits and features associated with Group CC7006 (surface or occupation deposits), Phase 2.1

A structure or surface (Group CC7002)—it is not clear whether it represented external or internal space—was uncovered towards the southern end of the excavation area (Fig. 2.10). This survived in patches, but stratigraphic relationships were clear enough to indicate that the surface overlay parts of Structures CC7004 and CC7049 and therefore appeared to be a later feature. Two areas of chalk and mortar cobbling were recorded at the lowest part of the sequence of deposits. The largest, 0.12 m thick and extending some 3.8 m by 3 m, lay above a hearth belonging to Structure CC7004. Redeposited natural or silty occupation soil sealed the cobbling, and was subsequently covered by more chalk surfacing or clay silt layers representing repairs or levelling. Dating evidence places the earliest phases of this surface close to the period in which Structures CC7004 and CC7049 were occupied. Pottery from the first phase of the surface (CC1661) included a fine grey ware butt-beaker (EA, fabric ZF) and provides a *terminus post quem* for laying of the surface of *c* AD 55–70. A silty layer (CC1762) trampled into surface Group CC7002 contained a fragment of a South Gaulish samian Drag. 29 bowl that dated to *c* AD 70–85. This early Flavian chronology overlaps with the dating produced by the underlying structures, suggesting that the structures were occupied for a short time only, perhaps little more than ten years, or that they briefly continued in use in some form when the surface was laid. Fire-reddened sandy silt (CC1781) later in the stratigraphic sequence and dated by pottery to AD 70–130 suggests industrial activity when viewed with the relatively large quantities of iron slag, hearth fragments, smithing hearth bottom fragments and cinders recovered from layer CC1762. That said, not all of this, or indeed any of it, need belong to the hearth, since a mixed assemblage of domestic material, including pottery, animal bones (some with butchery marks), vessel glass, and charred plant remains, was found with the industrial evidence, and must have been dumped there, possibly being derived from a number of house-holds and structures. Other hearths were recorded in this part of the site. Hearth CC1665 gave an archaeomagnetic date of AD 30–120. An area of fire-reddened soil (CC1741) further south probably represented another hearth.

The surfaces were supplemented by a number of postholes and stakeholes. These formed no coherent pattern, but nevertheless must have contributed to buildings. The features were invariably cut into the natural deposits and so can be placed early in the stratigraphic sequence.

A metalled surface (Street CC1703) represented the continuation of a street identified during previous excavations to the south of the site (Fig. 2.11; Plates 2.3 and 2.4). The surfaces uncovered at the north and south ends of the Discovery Centre excavations, and during observations of new foundation pads for the refurbished centre, were found to match the NE-SW alignment of the previously-recorded elements exactly. The first phase of metalling comprised a layer (CC1724) of compacted flint and rounded pebbles terraced into the eastern-facing slope (Fig. 2.11 Section CC117). It was reasonably level—the surface was recorded at a height of 46.6 m aOD near its northern end and 47.13 m aOD at the south. The most extensive part of the surface was 2 m wide, but, based on remnants from its east and west sides, the street's full width approached 8 m. Surfaces were on average 90 mm thick. The street was carefully made; an area of metalling at the south end of the site had a foundation of mortar and small flints and was cambered on its western edge. The earliest phases cannot be dated with certainty—no useful dating evidence was recovered from the earliest surfaces—but its long stratigraphic sequence and its relationship with ditch CC3486 (see below) suggest that it was laid during the later 1st century AD. The street did not replace its precursor, Iron Age Holloway CC3049 10 m to the west, but was laid mainly onto the prehistoric subsoil (CC1701) or natural clay, while another remnant sealed early Roman postholes (CC6064 and CC6066; see Fig. 2.10). The Iron Age trackway and

Plate 2.3   Street surface CC1703 in background (marked by ranging poles) and channel CC1850 in foreground, with retained baulk of robber-cut fill in between, looking east

the Roman street more or less shared orientation, though the former diverged slightly from the alignment to meet the north-east entrance (later the Roman north gate) of the Iron Age enclosure.

A channel (Channel CC1850) bordered the western edge of the street (Fig. 2.11 Sections CC111a–b; Plate 2.3). The channel was fragmentary, as much of the masonry had been robbed. It was seen, however, in three segments which indicates a total length of at least 35 m along the street. The channel comprised a steep-sided construction cut 2.5 m wide that was dug through the natural deposits. The sides of the cut were faced with at least three courses of roughly-worked flint nodules bonded by a hard buff lime mortar, which were best preserved at the southern part of the channel (Fig. 2.11, Section CC111b). The flint facing created a

Plate 2.4   Section through multiple surfaces of Street CC1703, overlying buried soil and natural gravel, looking north-east

straight-sided slot measuring 1.2 m wide and 0.5 m deep, also lined with flint nodules. Heights obtained along the base of the channel suggest a very gentle fall from north (on average 46.28 m OD) to south (46.17 m aOD). The height of the channel sides was, on excavation, found to be slightly lower than the street surface. The channel, extending for about 10 m along a NE-SW direction, turned eastwards to cut across the street. It is uncertain precisely how movement was maintained along the street at this point, but if it were covered then brick and mortar were used (see Poole and Shaffrey, Chapter 7) to form a culvert. Dating evidence was sparse, but overall an early or middle Roman date is favoured. Its relationship with the road and a coin from the base of channel segment CC1667 points to 1st- or 2nd-century AD construction. An alternative view is that the channel was a much later construction—3rd or 4th century—and that it cut a street that had long ceased to be maintained. In this scenario, the channel was open or provided with a relatively makeshift covering. On balance, though, an earlier chronology is preferred.

The prevailing orientation was preserved in a ditch that flanked the road *c* 6.2 m to the west. The ditch (CC3486), cut into the natural soil, was recorded at the northern end of the Discovery Centre site (Fig. 2.10). It was V-shaped and measured up to 1.5 m wide and 0.70 m deep. The feature was traced for some 24 m from the northern part of the site, but was discontinuous, having been severely truncated by later activity. The ditch generally contained two fills along its length, usually sandy or clay silt but occasionally including chalky material. Dating the feature is a little problematic in that it bordered the western edge of the prehistoric trackway and would appear to be associated with it. However, all pottery recovered from its fills suggests that the ditch was filled during the last third of the 1st century AD. Four grey ware platters recovered from the lower fill of segment CC3270 point to a date after AD 70 for initial deposition. A larger assemblage from the upper, charcoal-rich, fill included a *terra nigra* carinated bowl, grey ware bead-rimmed jars and a North Gaulish white ware butt-beaker. Early Roman pottery was also recovered from an upper fill of segment CC3458. If not established before AD 43, the ditch was certainly dug within a matter of years after the conquest, possibly marking out the road's alignment before it was surfaced to serve as a drainage ditch.

Phase 2.2 (*c* AD 130/50–270): Mid Roman domestic and industrial occupation

Occupation continued into the middle Roman period and expanded west (Fig. 2.13). The collection of pits and postholes in the Discovery Centre area assigned to this phase give a rather fragmented picture of activity here, but nevertheless relate to structures and domestic or industrial occupation.

Four pits were excavated, which were variable in size, but generally contained silty clay fills that occasionally included domestic material. Pit CC1688, 1.1 m wide and 1.2 m deep, contained pottery, prismatic bottle glass, and animal bone fragments from a range of species. Pottery from the lower of the two fills included pieces from a bead-rimmed dish, poppyhead beaker and cooking-pot jar, all in grey wares, and a south Gaulish amphora that dated deposition to the mid 2nd century. Another pit (CC3347), cut into earlier ditch CC3486 (see above), was also filled with domestic material, and, at the bottom, a rather green silty fill that suggested an initial cesspit function. It was 1.3 m by 1.2 m across and 0.5 m deep and contained animal bone fragments and pottery in its upper fills. The ceramic material gives a 2nd-century date for filling; pottery from the upper fill suggests that the pit continued to receive material in the final quarter of that century.

More coherent evidence was seen in the Northgate House area (Fig. 2.13). A stone structure (Structure NH8522), terraced into the slope, was located in the north-eastern corner of the excavation area (Fig. 2.14). The building lay mainly below the impact level of the Northgate House development and was only partially exposed during fieldwork. The outline was fragmentary, but elements of its southern and possibly western sides were recorded. The southern wall was defined by a mortar and chalk footing (NH2641), at least 3 m long (it extended beyond the excavation area) and 0.5 m wide. A flint and mortar footing (NH7548) almost 1 m long and 0.5 m wide may have formed the building's western side. A 1 m square structure (NH7647) of unbonded flint and chalk rubble within the putative structure may have been a post-pad or similar, or part of an internal wall. Floor surfaces were not reached, although the remains of a yellow-grey sand and mortar floor surface (NH2664) in the southern part of the building, which survived higher up in the sequence, were recorded.

Plate 2.5 Burnt layer from Structure NH8522 showing in situ *wall plaster, Phase 2.2*

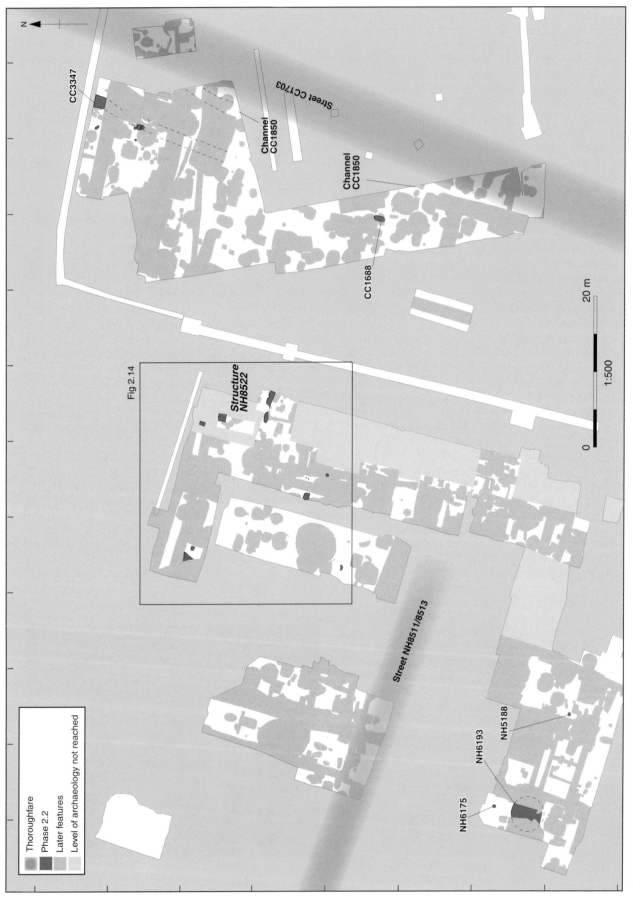

N

CC3347

Street CC1703

Channel
CC1850

Channel
CC1850

CC1688

Fig 2.14

Structure
NH8522

Street NH8511/8513

NH5188

NH6193

NH6175

20 m

1:500

0

Thoroughfare
Phase 2.2
Later features
Level of archaeology not reached

Fig. 2.13 Plan of middle Roman features, Phase 2.2 (c AD 130/50–270)

Given its limited excavation, there was little dating evidence from the structure itself. A grey ware fragment from footing NH2641 dated after AD 100, while pottery from a silt layer below NH7647 dated from the 3rd century. The structure was destroyed by fire, preserving fragments of timbers from the superstructure (Fig. 2.15; Plates 2.5-6). Painted plaster recorded in between and over the burnt timbers indicates that the fragments belonged to a section of a wall. The surviving elements comprised three or four vertical members spaced about 0.2 m apart. Diagonal timbers—four were recorded—were positioned at an angle of 45° to the

vertical timbers and appeared to form a lattice, though may have served as braces. At least one diagonal timber was connected to a vertical by means of a clenched iron nail and apparently an oblique halving. More studs were seen further along the diagonals. Structural nails were collected from other destruction deposits and it is likely that nails were used throughout to fasten the timbers. Regularly-spaced horizontal rows of charcoal fragments may record rods woven between the larger uprights. Daub collected amongst the burnt wood was almost certainly used to infill the wall. Accompanying plaster fragments indicate that the

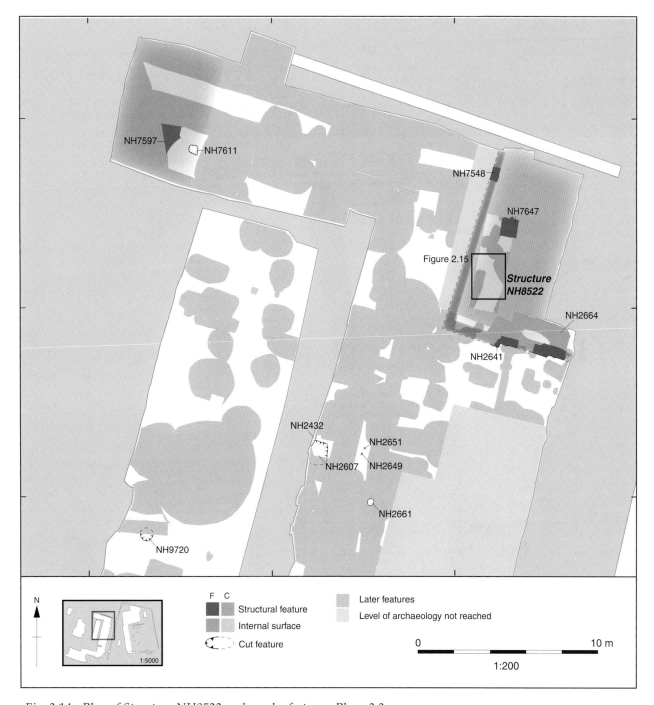

Fig. 2.14 Plan of Structure NH8522 and nearby features, Phase 2.2

Plate 2.6   Burnt timbers from Structure NH8522, Phase 2.2, looking west

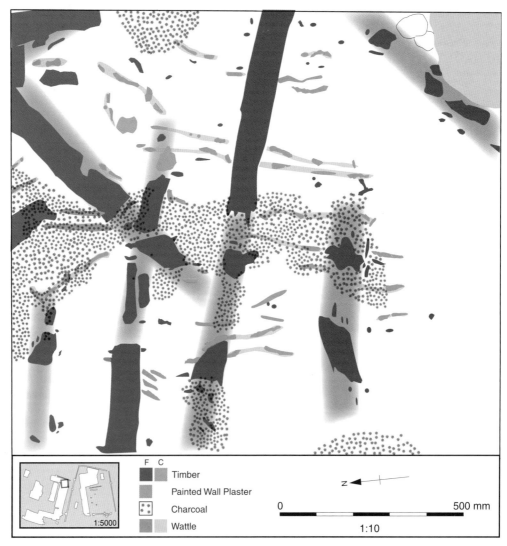

F	C	
		Timber
		Painted Wall Plaster
***	***	Charcoal
		Wattle

1:5000

z

0   500 mm

1:10

Fig. 2.15   Plan of Structure NH8522: detail of collapsed burnt timbers, Phase 2.2

wall was plastered and painted; the range of colours recorded points to a scheme incorporating orange- and red-brown and grey panels bordered by light grey stripes. Layers of ash, charcoal and building material—probably representing the remains of the collapsed structure and deliberate dumps— contained pottery dated after AD 250. Given the dating evidence, occupation was probably confined to the 3rd century, perhaps spanning little more than 50 years.

Another trace of a wall, an unmortared flint foundation, 1.4 m wide and 0.25 m deep (NH7597), was detected 18 m west of Structure NH8522 (Fig. 2.14). No dating evidence was retrieved, but like Structure NH8522, it was sealed by a dump that contained pottery, including grog-tempered ware (fabric SG) and a bag-beaker with scale decoration (Fulford 1975a, 58), with a date range of *c* AD 270–330. A number of pits, postholes and stakeholes were located to the south and west of Structure NH8522, although given the level of truncation it is impossible to be certain about what they repre- sented. Little material was recovered, but pit NH2607 and posthole NH9720 were cut by Phase 2.3 pits (Fig. 2.14). Feature NH7611, possibly a posthole or pit and next to wall NH7597, contained pottery— including a fragment from a Central Gaulish samian cup—consistent with a 2nd-century date.

A neonate burial (NH6175) was recorded in the extreme south-west of the excavated area (see Fig. 2.13). A radiocarbon determination obtained from the skeleton gave a 1st- to 2nd-century AD date (cal AD 30–210; OxA-16713). Shallow pit NH6193, just to the south of the burial, can also be assigned to this phase on the basis of pottery recovered from it. Hearth NH5188 offers a further indication of Phase 2.2 activity in this area. The hearth was uncovered as a spread of burnt soil that was cut by Phase 2.3 postholes (NH5228, NH5230, NH5232 and NH5236) that formed part of Structure NH8520 (see below). Archaeomagnetic dating from NH5188 gave a date of 96 BC–AD 130 (WOC).

Phase 2.3 (*c* AD 270–350/75): Late Roman structures and a street

The late Roman period saw increased development of the site as new buildings were erected, especially in the Northgate House site (Fig. 2.16). Here, devel- opment extended along a new street, which was laid out and metalled in this phase (Street NH8511; Figs 2.16 and 2.17). Too little of the metalling survived to confirm the street's orientation, but we cannot assume that it extended NW-SE to meet Street CC1703 at right angles, not least because it appears to have replaced an older (and potentially irregu- larly-coursed) holloway. Instead of the expected dome-like profile (*agger*), allowing surface water to drain to the sides, the street surface gently sloped downwards so that its sides were higher than its centre (Fig. 2.18; Plate 2.7). The street's width approached 6 m, while the metalling—well-

compacted flint gravel in a clay matrix—was on average 80 mm thick. The gravel surface was laid after AD 300. It sealed Iron Age gully NH1519 (Fig. 2.18), from which intrusive 2nd- to 4th-century pottery was collected. Silty clay deposits (NH1440 and 1486), probably dumped as levelling and sealed by the metalling, contained 4th-century pottery, including a grey ware, funnel-necked, globular beaker (Fulford 1975a, 89, 92) and black-burnished cooking bowls and jars (types CK and HB, fabric ZMA). During the course of its use, the street surface was trampled and disturbed, causing deposits of silt and gravel (Group NH8512 comprising NH1415, NH1377, NH1371 and NH1263) to accumulate (Fig. 2.18). This sequence was covered with a surface of relatively coarse flint nodules and occasional rammed chalk 80 mm thick (Street NH8513) as the street was re-metalled (Figs 2.17B and 2.18). The surface was narrower than the first; a flat-bottomed gully (NH1431) that cut through the earlier metalling defined the northern edge of the second phase and probably served as a drain (shown in Fig. 2.18). Like Group NH8512, trampled deposits and silts (Group NH8515, comprising NH1269 and NH1250), on average 90 mm thick, accumulated above the later surface. Coins and pottery were collected from these layers, but overall deposition could be dated no more precisely than 4th century.

Buildings were erected on both sides of the street. Structure NH8518 fronted on to the street's north side during its first phase (Fig. 2.17A). Little of the building survived, preserved only as a sequence of floors and a number of possibly related postholes. A layer of mortar (NH1539), containing charred cereal remains, and animal bone fragments, was first in sequence and levelled the area ready for construc- tion. Another mortar deposit (NH1175), 70 mm thick, was laid above this—the two separated by a thin deposit of silty clay—though the loose nature of the mortar suggested that this was a foundation for a floor, rather than the floor itself. Pottery from the silty clay layer included grog-tempered ware (fabric SG) dated from AD 270 onwards; a larger assem- blage from the overlying mortar was of similar date. Postholes, which cut into the mortar, held timbers that presumably formed part of the structure; the postholes were relatively wide at 0.44 m, but shallow at 0.11 m. It is impossible to determine quite how they were incorporated into the building. Postholes NH1510 and NH1464 were surrounded by mortar NH1175, suggesting that they marked an internal division. Further excavation revealed the small grave of an infant (NH1527) cut into the mortar layer. In common with many neonate burials (Philpott 1991, 97–102), the burial was made within the building and possibly underneath the floor- boards. Fragments of pottery deposited with the grave's backfill dated to the 3rd or 4th centuries.

Timber Structure NH8518 was replaced by masonry Structure NH8517 (Fig. 2.17B; Plate 2.8). The building was defined by two walls made of un- bonded flint up to 0.4 m wide and surviving to a

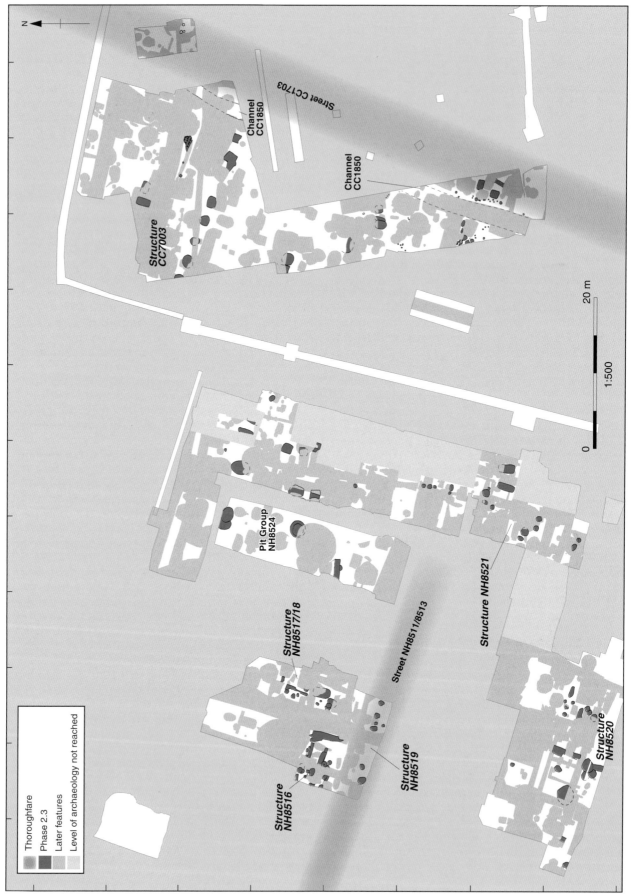

Fig. 2.16   Plan of late Roman features, Phase 2.3 (c AD 270–350/75)

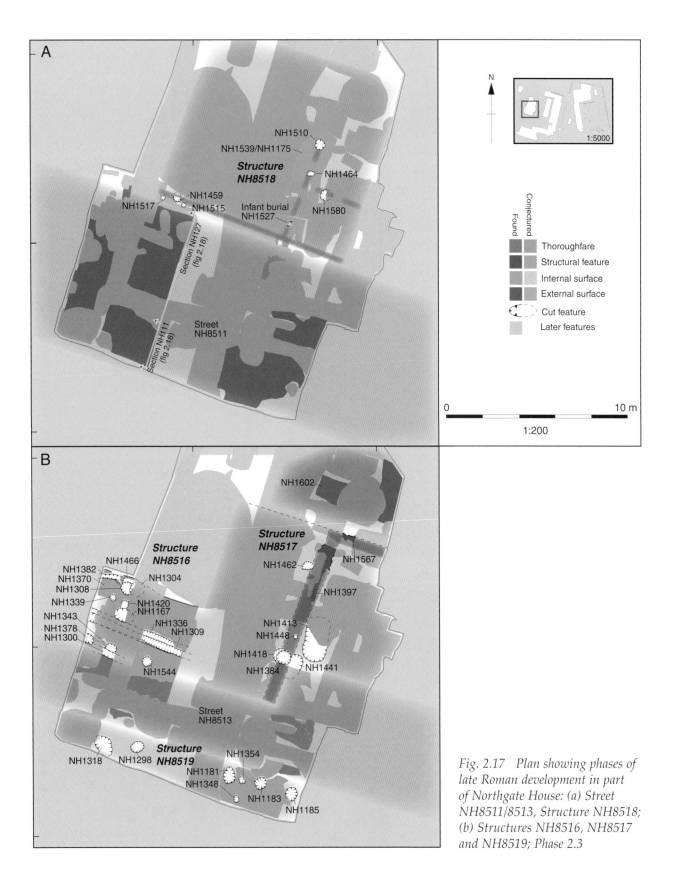

Fig. 2.17 *Plan showing phases of late Roman development in part of Northgate House: (a) Street NH8511/8513, Structure NH8518; (b) Structures NH8516, NH8517 and NH8519; Phase 2.3*

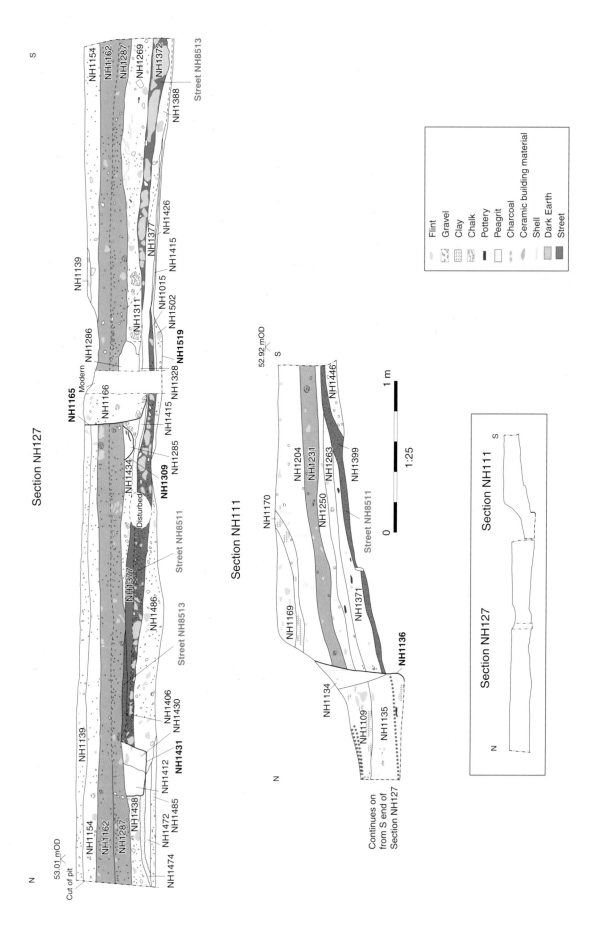

Fig. 2.18   Sections through Street NH8511/8513, Phase 2.3

Plate 2.7   Street surface NH8511, Phase 2.3, looking north-east

Plate 2.8   Structure NH8517, wall NH1397, Phase 2.3, looking east

height of 0.15 m (NH1397 and NH1567). The extent of this structure is unclear, but a shallow pit or posthole (NH1441) filled with large flint nodules, possibly packing for a post, could represent the position of its south side or equally mark the end of the north side of Structure NH8516 (see below). An extensive spread of gravel (NH1602) to the north of NH8517/8 was probably an external yard. Soil accumulating on the surface contained grog-tempered pottery (fabric SG) dated to AD 270–400.

The re-metalling of the street in the 4th century saw a change to the appearance of the street frontage as Structure NH8516 was erected along its north side (Fig. 2.17B). The post-built structure was cut into a deposit of silty clay that accumulated over the remains of the abandoned Structure NH8517/8; pottery from the deposit—some 60 sherds that included New Forest colour-coated ware, grog-tempered ware and black-burnished ware (fabrics TR, SG and ZMA respectively)—dated from AD 270 onwards. The south side of NH8516 was defined by a row of large postholes (NH1378, NH1343 and NH1544), which measured on average 0.5 m wide and 0.6 m deep. There were a number of postholes to the north of these. The outermost feature, NH1466, seems most likely to have held an external post given its size—0.7 m wide and 0.7 m deep. Internal features were restricted to two small postholes (NH1339 and NH1420), which may have marked an internal division, and the remains of a chalk surface (NH1370) up to 1 m thick, which partially overlaid the second-phase street metalling. Fired clay collected from the chalk floor was part of an oven, though whether it belonged to the building is in some doubt since it was found with long-discarded pottery and animal bone fragments. Some repair or rebuilding work was carried out some time after initial construction. A slot for a baseplate (NH1382) located along the north side of the building was dug into the edge of surface NH1370, while the postholes were cut by other postholes (NH1308, NH1304, NH1167), suggesting that the posts had been replaced. This second phase of construction cannot be dated precisely, as pottery from the later features was broadly dated to the late Roman period only. An east-west aligned shallow gully (NH1300), which cut the edge of a posthole along the southern side of the building and so appeared to post-date the building, may have served as a street-side drain. More drainage was provided by gully NH1336 (re-cut by NH1309), which extended through the centre of the now presumably abandoned structure (Fig. 2.17B). A silty clay layer (NH1287; Fig. 2.18) subsequently accumulated over the remains of the building and the drainage gullies. Pottery recovered from it suggested that this episode occurred before the end of the Roman period.

The south side of the street also saw development. Postholes revealed the position of timber-built Structure NH8519 that encroached on to the second phase of street metalling, or rather the silty deposits

that had accumulated above it (Fig. 2.17B). The building's north side was defined by five large postholes (NH1318, NH1298, NH1181, NH1183, NH1185) averaging 0.77 m wide by 0.46 m deep and giving the structure a length of over 10 m. These cut into a spread of chalk and flint nodules that may represent part of the street surface. All the postholes were packed with chalk and flint nodules that must have held substantial, load-bearing posts. Two other postholes (NH1354 and NH1348), slighter at 0.36 wide by 0.25 m, projected at right angles from the alignment of the larger postholes and appeared to form an internal division, creating at least two rooms. No surfaces or floors were recorded. Dating evidence from the postholes confirmed a late Roman date offered by the stratigraphy. The structure was probably abandoned by the mid–late 4th century; the latest coin (AE4) from the thick deposits of Dark Earth covering the structure dated to AD 350–364.

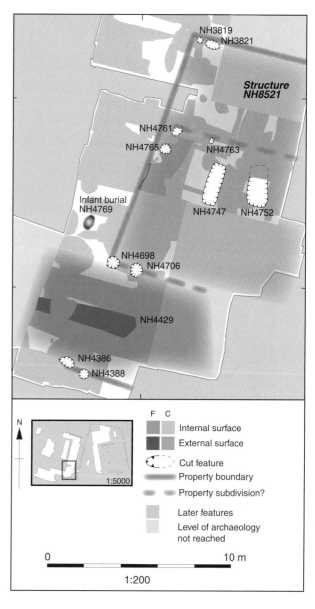

Fig. 2.19 Plan of Structure NH8521, Phase 2.3

If assumed to follow a NW-SE alignment to connect with Street CC1703 at right angles, then Street NH8511/8513 would have met Structure NH8521, which stood across it and was located close to the edge of a shallow terrace to the east (Figs 2.16 and 2.19). This possible structure was defined by two parallel rows of postholes. An alternative interpretation is that the rows represent successive phases of fence line, although, with a mean diameter of 0.6 m and depth of 0.3 m, the postholes were sufficiently substantial to serve a structural function. Nevertheless, the two rows are difficult to reconstruct as a building. Postholes NH3819/3821 and NH4386 may have marked the known limits of the west side of a structure, while postholes NH4763, NH4706 and NH4388 formed east-west alignments marking internal divisions, which continued into the area not investigated below Saxon levels. However, if a chalk, flint and gravel surface (NH4429) separating postholes NH4698 and NH4386 was external, then postholes NH4386 and NH4388 may define the edge of a second building to the south of Structure NH8521. In any case, pits NH4747 and NH4752 were internal features. Quite how NH4747 would have been incorporated into the predominantly timber structure is uncertain; the feature measured 2.2 m long by 0.61 m wide and 0.21 m deep and contained a hard chalk rubble and mortar fill. A patch of mortar seen within the building may be the remains of a floor. Pottery, for example grog-tempered ware recovered from pit NH4747, points to a date for deposition after AD 270. Occupation after AD 300 is suggested by an AE2 coin of Constantius or Constantine dated AD 300–307, which was found in a dark silty clay soil (NH4754) into which pit 4752 was cut, while loam soil (NH4742) that accumulated above the mortar floor produced New Forest colour-coated ware (fabric TR) and grog-tempered ware (fabric SG) dated more broadly to the 4th century. A grave containing a neonatal burial (NH4769) that was uncovered to the west of the north-south posthole rows may have been associated with the building, though was presumably an external feature. Late Roman pottery was recovered from its backfill.

The location of Structures NH8519 and NH8521 have implications for the dating and use of Street NH8511/8513. Both phases of street metalling can be placed with the first half of the 4th century, but the route that the street followed must have been earlier if a holloway preceded it. Structure NH8516 was contemporary with the second phase of metalled road, as NH8517 may also have been. However, by the time Structures NH8519 and NH8521 were erected, they encroached onto the

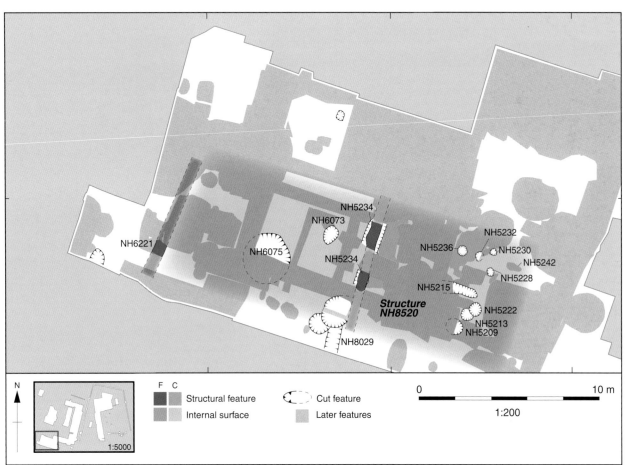

Fig. 2.20   Plan of Structure NH8520, Phase 2.3

street, or blocked its course, suggesting that the street had ceased to be used and maintained by the middle of the 4th century.

Structure NH8520 was located some 30 m south of the street (Figs 2.16 and 2.20). It was stone-built, though a number of postholes suggests that it had timber elements. Masonry NH5234 was the best-surviving wall. It marked the edge of a shallow terrace and was set within a trench 0.6 m wide by 0.1 m deep and comprised a single course, 0.3 m deep, of chalk and flint rubble. The NE-SW aligned wall, cut by later features, extended for a length of 3.8 m. Gully NH8029, 0.8 m wide by 0.08 m deep, was on the same alignment and may have been a wall trench, although no masonry was recovered. The remains of another wall (NH6221) were recorded 10 m further west. The clay-bonded flint foundation measured up to 0.75 m wide and 0.2 m deep and was set within a marginally larger wall slot.

A group of pits and postholes was uncovered some 5 m east of wall NH5234. Postholes NH5228,

NH5230, NH5232 and NH5236 averaged 0.46 m in diameter by 0.2 m wide; three of them were aligned reasonably well, perhaps contributing to the side of a structure with the fourth potentially forming a corner. However, this is somewhat speculative given the potential loss of associated features from later truncation and disturbance. An east-west aligned gully (NH5215) immediately south of the postholes was similarly difficult to place, although it is possible that it carried a wall. Pits NH5213, NH5209 and NH5222, south of the gully, were small, on average 0.81 m in diameter and 0.44 m deep, though they had probably been truncated.

A mortar surface (NH5242) up to 0.4 m thick, laid above a gravel make-up deposit 0.05 m thick, was recorded at the east end of the structure, cut by the postholes. A rich assemblage of finds was recovered from the floor, including five weaving tablets. Pottery collected from walls NH5234 and NH6221 and the floor deposits, including grog-tempered ware, New Forest colour-coated ware and a parchment ware bowl (fabrics SG, TR and UMP respec-

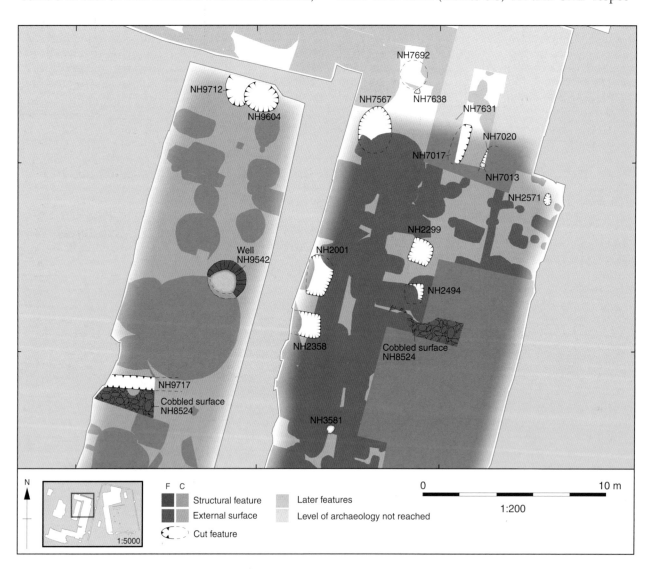

Fig. 2.21 Plan of Pit Group NH8524 and nearby features, Phase 2.3

tively), gives a late Roman date for construction. Fourth-century occupation is suggested by three of the pits (if associated with the use of the building), which were filled after AD 300. The structure was abandoned after AD 350; Dark Earth sealing the entire structure contained pottery, including imported 'marbled' ware (*céramique à l'éponge*) and an Oxford colour-coated ware stamped carinated bowl, that dated to the second half of the 4th century.

An area to the north-east of Structures NH8517 and NH8518 was reserved for communal activities. Pits were dug to receive household rubbish, a probable well provided water, and a surface defined a yard (NH8524; Figs 2.16 and 2.21). The pits measured on average 1.7 m in diameter and at least 1.3 m deep (not all pits were fully excavated). Some were cesspits (for example NH2299, NH2358, NH2494), containing multiple fills of green-grey silt sealed by charcoal from hearths, but the features were also rich in domestic rubbish, particularly pottery and animal bone. Well NH9542 was 2.05 m in diameter and over 1.8 m deep. Identification of the feature was uncertain as its base and the water-table were not reached, but the shaft was lined with bonded chalk and flint rubble behind a facing of chalk-blocks, which strongly suggests an open well. The lower fill of the feature was a silty clay with chalk and flint derived from the lining. The upper fill was similar to the Dark Earth that sealed the feature.

The yard surface (NH8524), 0.29 m thick, comprised a flint deposit over gravel bedding. Dating evidence places the group as a whole into the late Roman period, and some features more precisely to the second or third quarter of the 4th century. Pottery (187 sherds) from the bottom fill and a coin (AE3) from the top fill suggested that pit NH2001 filled between the second and third quarters of the 4th century or later. The latest coin (an AE4 of Constans or Constantius) in the top fill of pit NH2299 dated to AD 335–341, while pottery from an upper fill of pit NH2358 dated from the mid 4th century.

At the Discovery Centre site there was development along Street CC1703 during the late Roman period (Fig. 2.16). Structure CC7003 at the north end of the site was a timber building set at right angles to the street (Fig. 2.22; Plates 2.9 and 10). Its southern side was defined by a row of large post-pads. The features measured on average 1.3 m in diameter and 0.4 m deep and some were filled at their bases with thick deposits of chalk on which the undoubtedly substantial posts stood (the depth of the features varied quite considerably, with some being defined mainly by the chalk layer). Once the posts had been erected, the deeper postholes were packed with more chalk. Just one posthole was recorded on the building's north side (CC3279). Others, presumably little more than hard pads on top of the ground surface, were completely lost to later truncation. Like those on the south side,

posthole CC3279 was large, having a diameter of 1.45 m and depth of 0.2 m. It was similarly filled with a hard chalk pad. The area marked out by the postholes measured some 20 m long by 7 m wide. It may have represented the nave of an aisled building, with the roof extending beyond the posts. However, there is no hint of the wall slots or further postholes required for the external walls, even along the south side where the later truncation was less severe, and so the postholes appear to define the outline of the structure. Posthole CC3318 cut pit CC3330, which contained a large pottery assemblage dated to the final quarter of the 3rd century, while fragments of a grey ware globular beaker recovered from the post-pad of posthole CC2030 support a date after AD 270 for construction. Occupation was sufficiently prolonged for the building to require repairs; posthole CC3316 cut CC3318 perhaps as the original post was reset or replaced. Pits (eg CC7047) were located around the structure and may have been associated with it, probably serving as rubbish pits; all contained relatively large quantities of pottery, animal bone, shell, and in one case iron nails. The pottery suggested that one pit had filled by *c* AD 380. The others did not begin to receive material until the 4th century and may have been open up to that date.

Groups of stakeholes beneath post-pads CC3279 and CC3432 at the eastern end of the building seem unusual. Three rows orientated NW-SE were seen below the former, while two parallel rows orientated NE-SW were recorded below the latter. If projected, the rows would have met at 90°. The alignments were not shown to continue beyond the limits of the structure, nor were they associated with other postholes. The stakes below CC3279 (Plate 2.10) were driven into a clay silt layer that accumulated during Phase 2.1, while those below CC3432 cut into the silty sand fill of a Phase 2.1 ditch. The function of the stakes was no doubt identical to that of the harder metalled surface underneath some of the building's other post-pads—to provide a solid foundation for the posts in areas of relatively soft soil. A similar measure, albeit belonging to the medieval phase, was recorded during excavation at The Brooks; stakes there had been driven into alluvium of the flood-plain and overlain by chalk walls (S Teague, pers. comm.).

Further groups of stakeholes were recorded in the southern part of the Discovery Centre area (Fig. 2.23). These did not form coherent plans, but were presumably related to roadside structures or represented temporary constructions. Stakehole Group CC1849 was associated with a robber trench whose fill contained a coin (AE2) dated AD 320–324, while Stakehole Group CC1662 was cut into a surface belonging to Phase 2.1 Structure CC7002 and sealed by Dark Earth. The dating of Stakehole Group CC1599, cut into the natural soil and sealed by post-Roman deposits, is rather looser, but given its proximity to the other groups, a late Roman date may also be appropriate. Pits and a hearth may have associated with the stakeholes. The brick- and tile-built hearth (CC1567) was set into the prehistoric subsoil. The burnt soil around the tile was archaeomagnetically dated to 96 BC–AD 25 (JSB1572), but pottery collected from the feature, including a New Forest colour-coated ware and a grog-tempered ware cooking jar (fabrics TR and SG), better placed it in the late Roman period. In addition, the tile used was in a

fabric that was unlikely to have been of early Roman date. The pits (CC1048, CC1414, CC1510, CC1513, CC1556, CC1586, CC1588), circular or square in plan, were generally located to the south of the stakehole groups. None contained material that suggested function, but their dimensions—the square features were on average 1.16 m by 0.36 m, while the round pits measured 0.79 m by 0.5 m—were within the range encompassed by larger postholes (for example from Structure

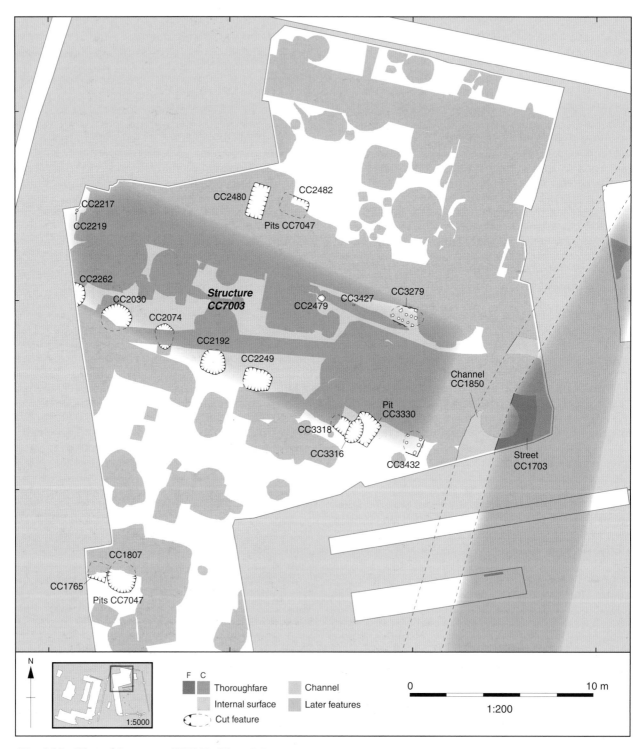

Fig. 2.22   Plan of Structure CC7003, Phase 2.3

Plate 2.9   Chalk-filled post-pads of Structure CC7003, looking south-east

Plate 2.10   Stakeholes of Structure CC7003, Phase 2.3, looking north-west

CC7003). A structural function cannot be dismissed, but as the features were truncated, it seems more reasonable to regard them as pits. The latest pottery recovered from the features dated after AD 250.

Evidence that Street CC1703 continued to be used as a thoroughfare into the late Roman period is provided by a wheel rut (CC1698), which cut into the uppermost street surface of flint and gravel. Two pits, CC1439 and CC1694, were subsequently cut into the street surface and mark a period when the street ceased to be maintained (Fig. 2.23). The pits were below the thick horizon of 'Dark Earth' (see below) that covered the area when it was abandoned, which suggests that they were among the latest features of Phase 2.3 and that they were dug relatively soon after the street was no longer used. Pottery recovered from pit CC1439 included

69

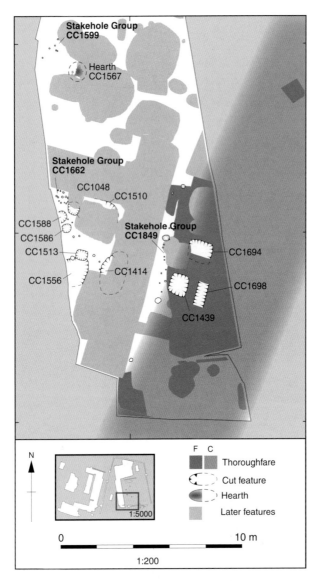

Fig. 2.23 Plan of pits and stakeholes in the eastern part of the Discovery Centre, Phase 2.3

New Forest colour-coated ware (fabric TR) and grog-tempered ware (fabric SG), while Oxford red colour-coated ware (fabric TO/TOR) and New Forest parchment ware (fabric UFN) were collected from pit CC1694. The groups suggest that the pits were filled, and the street abandoned, in the late 3rd or 4th century or later.

Phase 2.4 (c AD 350/75–400/50): Latest Roman Dark Earth

The landscape changed significantly from the late 4th century when structures were abandoned, became derelict or were steadily robbed of useful building material. A thick layer of dark, compact, soil—'Dark Earth'—accumulated over the remnants of the Phase 2.3 occupation (Fig. 2.24). The soil was consistent across the excavated areas. In the Discovery Centre site the silty clay deposit was on average 0.2 m thick, although in places the soil was

as little as 0.06 m and as much as 0.5 m thick, no doubt depending on the extent of later truncation. The silty clay soil across the Northgate House site accumulated to a similar average thickness of 0.17 m. The latest coins from the Dark Earth included an AE3 dated AD 378–383 and at least two AE4 coins dated to AD 388–402, while the latest Roman pottery supports a date for deposition from the late 4th century onwards, potentially extending into the 5th century.

The soil was rich in artefacts and organic traces of occupation, and these provide information about how the deposits formed. Charred cereals (recovered from six samples), relatively well preserved and comprising a high proportion of burnt bread-type wheats and low proportion of fodder-type crops, suggested a domestic origin (see Carruthers, Chapter 8). The condition of almost all the animal bone from Phase 2.4 deposits was graded as fair to good (see Strid, Chapter 8). Dark Earth soils were also subjected to microstratigraphic investigation, including micromorphology and chemical and pollen analyses (see Macphail and Crowther, Chapter 8). The sampled deposits (NH4412 and NH5059) were dumped soils containing ash, dung and domestic waste, which were subsequently biologically worked through the growth and decay of vegetation and the action of worms and other creatures. Dark Earth also contained some of the largest pottery groups from the entire site, with almost 3000 sherds collected in total (see Biddulph and Booth, Chapter 7). The assemblage comprised a standard range of 4th-century forms and fabrics and included some of the latest products that emerged from the New Forest and Oxford industries. The condition of the pottery was generally good, with each fragment weighing on average 17 g, equal to the overall site mean, while the proportion of pottery certain to be residual (that is, dated earlier than the date of deposition) was very low at around 4% by sherd count.

The formation of Dark Earth is a well-known late Roman and early post-Roman urban phenomenon. The Dark Earth of Winchester's north-west quadrant is similar to the Dark Earths of, for example, London, York, Carlisle and other parts of Winchester, which generally consisted of homogeneous soil that accumulated through roots and worm action and the dumping of mixed cultural material and human waste (Watson 1998, 103; Macphail 1981, 321–2; Zant 2009, 363–9; Zant 1993, 154–5). The activities which caused the soil to form in these cases is not precisely known, but stratigraphic, artefactual and micromorphological analyses appear to rule out cultivation and garden activity and instead lead to the combination of biological accretion and the deliberate middening of occupation debris (Zant 2009, 368–9). The evidence from the Dark Earth of the Discovery Centre is consistent with this profile; indeed the micromorphological evidence (see Macphail and Crowther, Chapter 8), with its signature of ash, faecal matter and poor pollen preservation denoting earlier-formed soils, points strongly towards

Fig. 2.24 Plan showing extent of 'Dark Earth', Phase 2.4 (c AD 350/75–400/50)

it. The condition and chronological coherence of the pottery assemblage suggests that the middens were frequently dumped, then sealed in fairly rapid succession by new waste deposits. This explanation for the origin of Dark Earth is supported by evidence from The Brooks. The excavators dismissed the possibility of cultivation on the basis of the recovery of large, well-preserved animal bone and pottery fragments from the site's Dark Earth and the lack of evidence for disturbance and truncation (Zant 1993, 155). The shared characteristics between the sites suggest that the Dark Earth accumulated for the same reasons. Buildings may have been abandoned, but occupation of a sort that enjoyed new supplies of pottery, heat and light from hearths, and livestock for meat, clothing and dairy products, must have continued. No structures belonging to this phase were detected, although the rural, rather than urban, character of the occupation (see Macphail and Crowther, Chapter 8) suggests a relatively sparse population.

Chapter 3
The late Saxon period (*c* 850–1050)

by Steve Teague

THE INHERITED LANDSCAPE (PHASE 3)

The latter part of the Roman period (Phase 2.4; *c* AD 350/75–400/50) saw the accumulation of 'Dark Earth' over all the latest discernible occupation horizons, although the nature of its formation, despite intensive study, still remains far from certain (see Chapters 2 and 5). Where it survived on the site it was usually described as a single homogeneous deposit and found to be up to 0.5 m thick sealing all evidence of Roman occupation and was directly overlain by mid-9th century deposits (see Phase 4.1 below). There was no evidence for deposits datable between the end of its accumulation and the earliest late Saxon deposits found on the site. In order to maintain a contiguous sequence of phasing this intervening phase has been allocated to Phase 3.

Modern terracing had removed nearly all traces of the Dark Earth from the Discovery Centre site and had also affected its upper levels within the central area of the Northgate House site (for extent of Dark Earth see Chapter 2, Fig. 2.24). Alongside the west frontage of Brudene Street its upper surface was found to directly underlie the earliest street surfaces and flanking occupation levels, datable to the 9th century or later. Similarly alongside Snitheling Street, where late Saxon occupation levels survived, these directly overlay its surface. The lack of any recognisable intermediate deposits suggests either that they had been deliberately removed during the re-occupation of the site in the mid 9th century or that the 'Dark Earth' continued to accumulate up to this time. Where its upper levels survived within Property BW 2 (see Section NH271, Fig. 3.3 below), little evidence for preparation work such as terracing for structures was found and its thickness was largely consistent, following the topography that was in place during the Roman period. Its surface across the Northgate House site was represented by a gentle but consistent slope from west to east, from *c* 52.8 m to *c* 49.00 m OD, with little evidence for the possible terracing identified from the Roman period.

It is probable that the new inhabitants of the mid 9th century inherited an overgrown site devoid—in this area at least—of any visible evidence for its Roman occupiers. Presumably vegetation clearance would have been necessary before the laying out of streets or buildings. If vegetation burning was utilised, however, no stratigraphically early charcoal-rich deposits that could be interpreted as such were found. If the upper levels such as turf/topsoil had also been removed, then any clearance horizons would also have been removed, perhaps together with ephemeral evidence of earlier (post-Roman) activity.

It has been noted (see Biddulph, Chapter 2) that the late Roman pottery groups recovered from the Dark Earth deposits were usually large, in relatively good condition, and contained little obviously residual material from the underlying levels. This suggests contemporary middening rather than cultivation during the late Roman (and later) period, and a similar conclusion was reached by micromorphological analysis of the soil (see Macphail and Crowther, Chapter 8).

The few sherds of late Saxon (and occasionally later) pottery found in the Dark Earth are most likely to be intrusive given their rather uneven distribution across the site and the high levels of pit digging in the late Saxon period (Table 3.1). In areas where pit digging was less intense, such as the area excavated within the northern half of Property BW 2 (see below), no post-Roman pottery was contained within the assemblage of 75 (1.4 kg) sherds. A single sherd (weighing 4 g) of early-middle Anglo-Saxon organic-tempered pottery (see Cotter, Chapter 7) was recovered from Dark Earth remnants that survived close to the north-east corner of the Discovery Centre site and may

Table 3.1: *Intrusive post-Roman pottery within Dark Earth deposits on Northgate House*

Area	No of Sherds			% Post-Roman
	Pre-Roman	Roman	Post-Roman	
Wessex central area	1	947	18	1.9%
Brudene Street Frontage	2	426	16	3.6%
SW area	1	427	12	2.7%
Total	4	1800	46	2.5%

suggest some contemporaneity with the deposit. However, no other contemporary finds, residual or otherwise, were identified from the site. Its find spot, some 9–15 m west of the Roman north-south street that led to the North Gate, may be of some significance.

A single sceat fragment, possibly of mid to late 8th-century date (see Allen, Chapter 7), was the only middle Saxon find on the site. It was found in a Anglo-Norman pit in association with the fragmentary remains of a penny of Athelstan (924–939) suggesting the objects were originally intended for re-use and were probably brought in to the site together.

THE LATE SAXON PERIOD (PHASE 4)

Phasing methodology

Contexts throughout the site were grouped hierarchically according to their relationship with other closely related stratigraphic units (pit group, structural evidence, yard area etc.) and then allocated a spatial location identifier according to the property in which they occur (eg Property BW 2; see below). Where the evidence survived, and also where the extent of excavation allowed, some attempt was made to describe the structural development of buildings in terms of their function and status through the incorporation of the finds and environmental evidence in their description. A similar approach was adopted with the description of the pits to their rear, the vast majority of which were not

bottomed by hand-excavation. Often no direct stratigraphic link could be made with the structures, though where possible comparisons between material found in pits and within buildings have been used to suggest associations (eg metalworking evidence).

Contexts allocated to the late Saxon period (Phase 4, 850–1050) were phased on the basis of their stratigraphic position and the dating of associated pottery (Table 3.2). Analysis of the pottery (see Cotter, Chapter 7) identified two dominant late Saxon fabrics, chalk-tempered ware (MBX) and chalk and flint-tempered ware (MAV). The former occurs throughout the late Saxon period but is often the only pottery present in stratigraphically early contexts, while the latter occurs alongside chalk-tempered pottery in stratigraphically later contexts. The introduction of glazed Winchester ware (MWW) and other wheel-thrown finewares such as the later type of Michelmersh-type ware (MMU and MZM) is traditionally thought to be broadly contemporary and dates from *c* 950–1050 (see Cotter, Chapter 7). Although their occurrence is relatively rare in the assemblage, these wares are often associated with contexts that also contain chalk and flint-tempered ware (MAV) suggesting some contemporaneity.

Based upon this model for the ceramic phases, the contexts on the stratigraphic matrix were phased according to presence or absence of flint-tempered ware (MAV) and wheel-thrown and finewares and were grouped into two sub-phases (4.1 and 4.2) with due regard to their stratigraphic position. No detailed sub-phasing was attempted for those areas of the site that were not subject to detailed excavation, or where detailed cataloguing of the pottery was not undertaken. Of the 1953 contexts that were allocated to the late Saxon phase, a total of 1606 (or 82.2%) could be sub-phased.

The phasing was supplemented by a programme of scientific dating that comprised on-site archaeo-

Table 3.2: Phasing allocation for Phase 4

Phase	Date	Pottery fabrics present	No of contexts	%
4	c 850–1050	No detailed catalogue	347	17.8%
4.1	c 850–950	MBX MDL MSH	474	24.3%
4.2	c 950–1050	MAB MAQ MAV MBN MBX MDL MFGY MBEAU MMU MPIN MSV MWW MZM WWX	1132	57.9%
Total			1953	100.0%

Table 3.3: Archaeomagnetic dated hearths phased to the late Saxon period (Phase 4)

Context	Hearth Ref	Phase	Calibrated date (95% confidence)
NH1276	SG1-8	4.2	975-1102
NH2156	WOA	4.1	580-1125
NH2391	WOD	4.1	800-1125
NH3506	WOJ	4.1	436-1175
NH3576	WOL	4.1	498-1148
NH3680	WON	4.2	914-1121
NH4261	WOE	4.2	979-1165
NH4523	WOK	4.1	1065-1245
NH4692	WOM	4.1	880-1093
NH4733	WOO	4.1	559-1084
NH7513	WOI2	4	498-1125
NH7522	WOI1	4	559-1084

Table 3.4: Radiocarbon and Bayesian dating from late Saxon phased contexts (Phase 4)

Context	Lab. No.	Phase	C14 Calibrated date (95% confidence)	Posterior density estimate (95% probability)
NH2156	SUERC-13908	4.1	900–1040	900–1010
NH2156	OxA-17174	4.1	780–980	780–980
NH2391	SUERC-13914	4.1	770–970	840–950
NH2391	OxA-17137	4.1	690–890	840–900 (86%) or 920–950 (9%)
NH2424	SUERC-13915	4.1	880–1020	880–980
NH2424	OxA-17179	4.1	870–980	880–970
NH3175	SUERC-19286	4.2	770–990	940–1000
NH3175	SUERC-19285	4.2	670–890	680–880
NH3260	SUERC-19284	4.2	890–1030	930–990
NH3260	SUERC-19280	4.2	880–1020	920–990
NH3494	OxA-17181	4.1	780–970	910–970
NH3494	SUERC-13917	4.1	880–1020	900–970
NH3578	OxA-17172	4.1	770–940	770–900
NH3578	SUERC-13906	4.1	890–1020	890–950
NH3587	OxA-17173	4.1	780–970	830–940
NH3587	SUERC-13907	4.1	730–970	830–940
NH3664	SUERC-13910	4.2	900–1030	890–1010
NH3664	OxA-17178	4.2	780–980	780–790 (1%) or 810–980 (94%)
NH4379	SUERC-19288	4.2	900–1030	940–1010
NH4379	SUERC-19287	4.2	880–1020	930–1000
NH4394	OxA-17184	4.2	780–970	910–980
NH4394	SUERC-13919	4.2	880–1020	900–980
NH4507	SUERC-13920	4.1	780–1010	890–960
NH4580	OxA-17183	4.1	780–960	860–950
NH4580	SUERC-13918	4.1	830–1010	880–950
NH4697	SUERC-13909	4.1	780–990	770–920
NH4697	OxA-17177	4.1	770–940	770–890

magnetic dating of 18 hearths and a subsequent programme of targeted radiocarbon dating that was confined to the western frontage of Brudene Street (Tables 3.3 and 3.4). These results and the limited coin dating evidence formed the basis of Bayesian modelling that was used to test the validity of the dating of these sub-phases (see Chapter 6). With rare exceptions (Hearth WOK and radiocarbon sample SUERC-19285) the scientific dating results are in broad agreement with the phase dates that were established through the ceramic dating. All calibrated archaeomagnetic and radiocarbon dates are quoted at the 95% confidence level.

The organisation of the description: streets and properties

The location of the trenches and the overall distribution of the late Saxon features is shown on Figures 3.1 and 3.2. The trenches are shown here in relation to the late Saxon street layout as currently understood from documentary and archaeological sources. This corresponds closely, although not precisely, to the modern street layout of the area (see Chapter 1, Fig. 1.6). The excavations confirmed that modern Staple Gardens does indeed follow the line of its late Saxon predecessor, known by the 12th century as Brudene Street. On the west side of the

excavations, the suggested line of the most westerly late Saxon street, known by the 12th century as Snitheling Street, is based on Keene's analysis (1985, figs 72–4). He concluded that Snitheling Street lay to the east of the line of modern Tower Street. It is likely that the original east edge of Snitheling Street is still marked in the modern topography of the area by the high retaining wall that defines the rear of properties fronting onto the east side of Tower Street. This wall marked the western edge of the present development site (see Chapter 1, Fig. 1.6). It retains a 1.9 m high terrace to the west, and if Keene's analysis is right, late Saxon Snitheling Street would have occupied the eastern edge of this terrace.

Brudene Street may have occupied a similar position at a terrace edge, since there is a high retaining wall between its eastern side and the Discovery Centre site, with a drop in ground level in site of *c* 1.9 m. However the origins of this terrace are unclear since recent terracing on the west side of the Discovery Centre site has removed nearly all but the earliest Roman levels alongside this frontage. A third street corresponding to the northern arm of modern Tower Street (flanked by the northern edge of the Discovery Centre site) appears to have been in existence by 1300 (Keene 1985, fig. 72). It may have originated as a lane along the south side of the

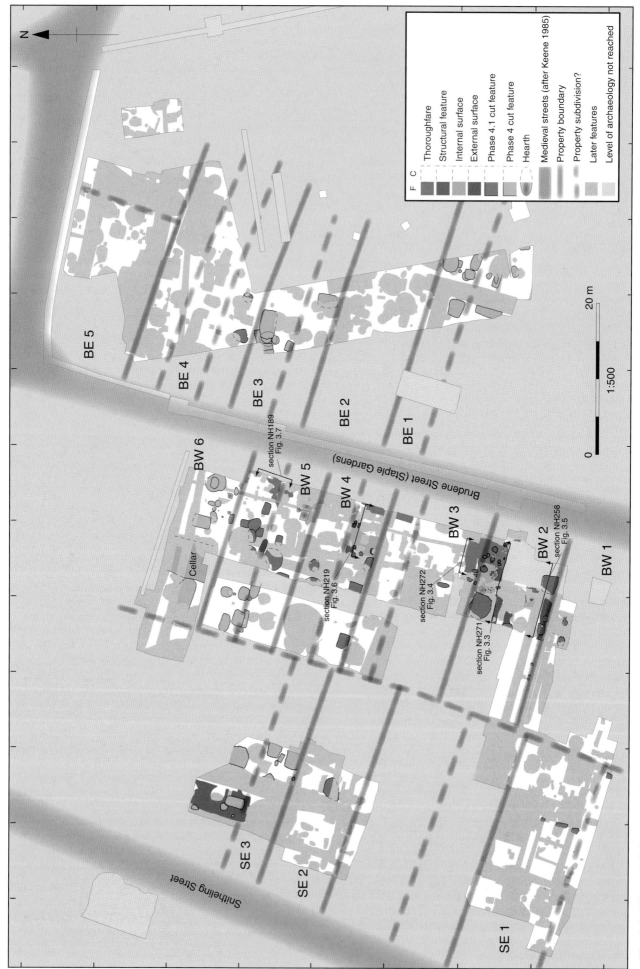

Fig. 3.1 Plan of all features, Phase 4.1 (c 850–950)

Legend:
- F C
- Thoroughfare
- Structural feature
- Internal surface
- External surface
- Phase 4.1 cut feature
- Phase 4 cut feature
- Hearth
- Medieval streets (after Keene 1985)
- Property boundary
- Property subdivision?
- Later features
- Level of archaeology not reached

BE 5
BE 4
BE 3
BE 2
BE 1

BW 6
BW 5
BW 4
BW 3
BW 2
BW 1

Cellar

section NH189
Fig. 3.7

section NH219
Fig. 3.6

section NH272
Fig. 3.4

section NH271
Fig. 3.3

section NH258
Fig. 3.5

Brudene Street (Staple Gardens)

SE 3
SE 2
SE 1

Snitheling Street

N

0   1:500   20 m

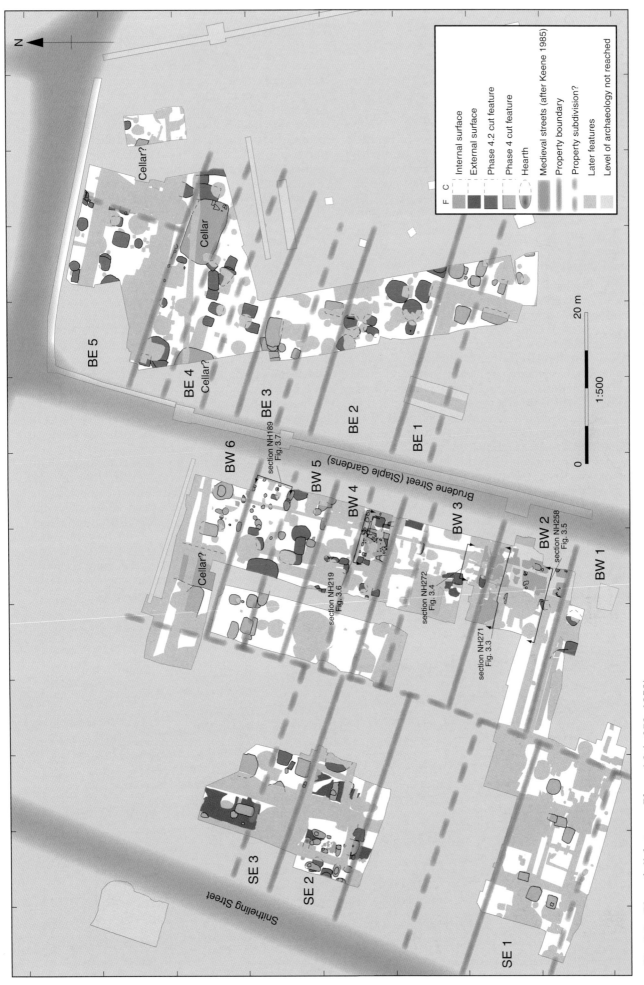

Fig. 3.2 Plan of all features, Phase 4.2 (c 950–1050)

Legend:

F C

Internal surface
External surface
Phase 4.2 cut feature
Phase 4 cut feature
Hearth
Medieval streets (after Keene 1985)
Property boundary
Property subdivision?
Later features
Level of archaeology not reached

0   1:500   20 m

N

Labels on plan:

Snitheling Street
Brudene Street (Staple Gardens)

SE 1
SE 2
SE 3

BW 1
BW 2
BW 3
BW 4
BW 5
BW 6

BE 1
BE 2
BE 3
BE 4
BE 5

Cellar?
Cellar
Cellar?
Cellar?

section NH189
Fig. 3.7
section NH219
Fig. 3.6
section NH272
Fig. 3.4
section NH271
Fig. 3.3
section NH258
Fig. 3.5

parish church of St Saviour that is first recorded in 1172, and may have existed in the mid 11th century (Keene 1985, 643), but ultimately it led to the North Gate.

No part of Snitheling Street was seen in the present excavations, but early surfaces of Brudene Street were recorded and are described below. The archaeological results are presented here in relation to the late Saxon street layout, on the east and west frontages of Brudene Street (Properties BE 1–5, BW 1–6), and on the east frontage of Snitheling Street (Properties SE 1–3).

Property boundaries

During the later medieval period the area of the present excavations appears to have been all but abandoned for occupation, and was largely turned over to gardens and orchards until 19th-century redevelopment (see Chapter 1). As a result, little evidence of late Saxon and medieval property boundaries survives either in early maps and plans, or in the modern topography of the area. On the Northgate House site the only evidence for boundaries that survived into the later medieval and post-medieval period were the 13th-century and later boundaries of the Archdeacon of Winchester's property, which may be depicted by Godson's 1750 Map of Winchester (see Chapter 1, Fig. 1.7c).

Given the lack of documentary evidence, the reconstruction of the bounds of the late Saxon and early medieval properties that we propose here was achieved almost wholly on the archaeological evidence alone. The basis on which individual property boundaries were identified is set out in Table 3.5. The lack of later medieval and post-medieval occupation on the site meant that there

were few long-lived boundary features such as stone walls. Only two such boundaries were found on the site. Both relate to later medieval masonry structures but their origins could be shown to date from the late Saxon period. A substantial wall footing (see Chapter 4, Phase 6) probably marked the south boundary of the Archdeacon's residence in the 13th to 14th centuries and lay *c* 1 m north of the boundary predicted (albeit tentatively) by analysis of the documentary evidence (Keene 1985, fig. 72 Property 247). This replaced an earlier fence that was abutted to the north by structures and pits of late Saxon and early medieval date (see Property BW 2 below and Chapter 4). Similarly, on the east side of Brudene Street the south side of a medieval cellar and adjoining boundary wall (see Chapter 4, Property BE 5) corresponded closely with the south boundary of Property 269 (Keene 1985, figs 72–4), a boundary that could also be shown by the archaeological evidence to have originated during the late Saxon period. In a few cases, late Saxon and Anglo-Norman boundaries were indicated by the presence of fencelines.

During excavations at The Brooks in 1987–8 (Scobie forthcoming; see Chapter 5), the evidence of pit grouping and building extents was used to identify individual properties and property boundaries. This was found to correlate closely with property boundaries shown on maps of the area up to and including the 1st Edition Ordnance Survey plan. This methodology has been adopted for the present project. On the east side of Brudene Street, Keene locates the boundaries of several later medieval properties (1985, figs 72–4 Properties 267 West B, 267 West A, 253 and 269) and there is a fairly good correlation with the archaeological evidence (particularly towards the north), which suggests

Table 3.5: Evidence for property boundaries

| Property | Archaeological Evidence | | | | Keene Tenement No |
	Phase 4.1	Phase 4.2	Phase 5	Phase 6	(1985, Figures 72–74)
BE 1	PC (N)	PC(N)	F(N)	267 West B	
BE 2		PC(N), PC(S)	PC(N)	F(S), PC(N)	267 West A
BE 3	PC(S), PC(N)		PC(S), PC(N)	PC (S)	Unnumbered plot between 267 West A and 253 (Fig. 72)
BE 4		PC(S)/F(N),BR(N)	PC(S), PC,BR (N)	PC(N)	253
BE 5 (W)		F(E), PC (E), F(S)	PC(E)	BR,BW(S), PC(E)	269(S)
BE 5 (E)		F(W)	PC(C)	BR(W), PC (S)	269 (S)
BW 1	F(N)	PC (N)	See BW 2(S)	BW (N)	245/246
BW 2	F, PC(S), BR,PC (N)	BR (N and S)	BR (N and S)	BW (S)	247
BW 3	See BW 2(N), BW 4(S)	See BW 2(N), BW 4(S)	BR (N and S), PC(N)		
BW 4	BR,PC(S), see BW5(S)	BR,PC(S), PC (N)	BR (S), PC (N)		
BW 5	BR(S),BR(N)	BR(S),BR(N)	PC (S)		247/248
BW 6	BR,PC (S)		PC (S)		248
SE 1			BR, PC(S), PC (N)		245/246 (Fig. 72)
SE 2		BR(S), (PC), F?(N)	BR?(S)		247
SE 3	PC (S)				

Key to boundary Evidence: PC: Pit Cluster F: Fence-line BR: Extent of building remains BW: Boundary wall

five properties (BE 1–5). On the west side of Brudene Street the archaeological evidence suggests at least six properties (BW 1–6). The evidence for the Snitheling Street frontage suggests at least three properties (SE 1–3) and a further two (SE A–B) can be construed from the evidence of Cunliffe's excavations (1964).

During analysis it became clear that evidence from some of the properties suggested a more complex pattern, and that some of the proposed properties may have been subdivided into two or more. For example the arrangement of the pit clustering within Property BE 4 suggests the property could be subdivided equally into three separate plots of 1 perch. Similarly the pit clustering within Property BW 4 suggests that this property could be subdivided into two plots measuring 1.0 and 1.1 perches. Elsewhere along this frontage the evidence is less convincing, partially as a result of the lack of excavation within the Properties BW 2 and BW 3. However, where possible subdivisions were identified, pits and any structural elements contained within them were allocated separate stratigraphic group numbers in order to allow for the comparison of differences in the socio-economic evidence.

The configuration of the excavations did not allow the opportunity to investigate the boundaries that defined the rear of the properties and most are likely to have fallen outside the area of the investigations. It is likely that these were originally demarcated by fences rather than more substantial features such as ditches. Documentary evidence (Keene 1985) and the study of the modern topography suggest that the boundaries between the rear of the properties on Brudene Street and Snitheling Street corresponds closely to the extant modern boundaries, particular in the southern part of the site. To the rear of Properties BW 1/2 this corresponds closely to the apparent northwards return of the Archdeacon's wall and the west wall of the adjacent medieval Structure NH8536 within Property BW 1 (see Chapter 4), a boundary apparently respected by earlier pits within the adjacent Property SE 1 (see below). The position of the boundaries to the rear of the properties on the east side of Brudene Street remains uncertain but documentary evidence (Keene 1985) and Godson's map of 1750 suggests that the boundaries lay immediately to the east of the excavations (see Chapter 1, Figs 1.5 and 1.7c).

THE EARLY SURFACES OF BRUDENE STREET

The street surfaces were recorded in section at numerous locations along the west edge of Staple Gardens, illustrated here in Figures 3.3 to 3.7 (see Figs 3.1–2 for location of street sections). Within Properties BW 2 and BW 3 a 5 m length of frontage was fully excavated exposing a thick sequence of hard gravel surfaces that was confined alongside

the eastern edge of the excavated area (Fig. 3.3). By the end of Phase 4.1 it had become completely covered or encroached on by floor levels pertaining to structures. Here three major sequences of metalling and associated silting were identified, the earliest (Street NH8644; see Fig. 3.3) was abutted by (and therefore pre-dated) the earliest structural evidence within Property BW 2 (see Property BW 2, Phase 4.1, Structure NH8625 below). The second metalling (Street NH8607; see Figs 3.3–4) pre-dated the construction of Structure NH8526, though the structure may have been contemporary with the third metalling (Street NH8609; see Figs 3.3–4). Subsequently Structure NH8529 (Property BW 2, Phase 4.1) and its successor Structure NH8530, the latter of pre-Conquest origin, both postdated the latest visible surfaces of the street, by which time it had been totally encroached upon within the excavated area.

The first phase of Street NH8644 (NH4702) directly overlay the surface of the Dark Earth at a point where it had slumped into a slight and extant underlying terrace, at approximately 0.2 m below the level towards the west (see Fig. 3.3). It comprised a single course of tightly packed small flint cobbles that extended for *c* 3 m from the eastern limit of the excavation. It was directly overlain by a second surface (NH4701) of fine angular flint gravel, the lack of occupation silts between them implying that the second surface was laid soon afterwards. The second surface had become very worn and was overlain by a thick accumulation of trampled green-stained grey silt (NH4700) that also overlay the postholes of Structure NH8625 suggesting that it had ceased to be used (see Property BW 2 structures below). The silt contained sherds of pottery with a flinty reduced brick-earthy fabric and chalk-tempered pottery (fabric MBX) with simple undeveloped rims—forms that may indicate a mid–late 9th-century date. Repairs of chalk gravel and chalk were followed by a further accumulation of green-stained silts (NH4595= NH4697) that produced a considerable quantity of animal bone presumably deposited by the occupiers of adjacent structures. Radiocarbon samples from silt NH4697 produced calibrated dates of 770–940 (OxA-17177) and 780–990 (SUERC-13909), recalibrated by Bayesian modelling to 770–890 and 770–920, suggesting a date prior to 920 (see Table 3.4). The silts also produced a bone spindlewhorl datable to the 10th to 11th centuries (SF Cat no. 172) and a few sherds of madder-stained pottery implying dyeing and weaving were undertaken close by.

The second phase of street (Street NH8607) comprised two surfaces of well-compacted orange gravel (NH4690 and NH4685), each up to 0.12 m thick, the latter supporting a hard surface of tightly packed, rounded flint pebbles (see Figs 3.3–4). The earlier surface pre-dated the second structure on the BW 2 frontage (Structure NH8526), though the second surface was contemporary with its use. It

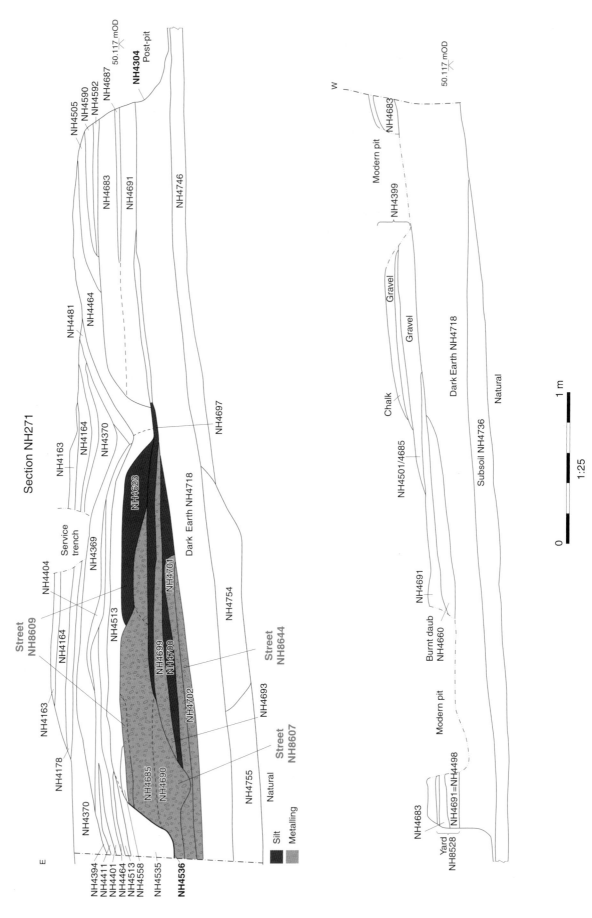

Fig. 3.3   Section through Brudene Street and showing adjacent occupation levels in Property BW 2, Phases 4.1 and 4.2

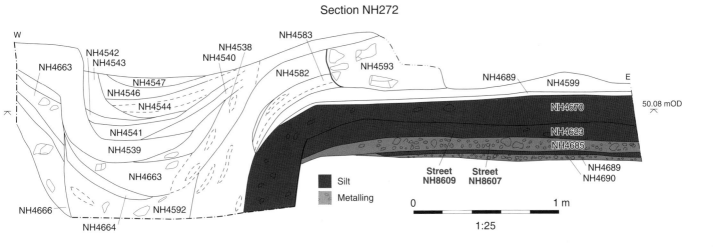

Section NH272

Fig. 3.4   Brudene Street surfaces (Phase 4.1) and slumping Anglo-Norman deposits exposed on the south side of Property BW 3

extended *c* 2 m further west than the first phase of street (Street NH8644), implying that the street had been widened at this point. A clayey silt (NH4689) that developed over the first surface (Fig. 3.4) contained a large quantity of chalk-tempered pottery (Fabric MBX) and a sherd of late Saxon sandy ware (Fabric MSH) suggesting a date before 950 (see Cotter, Chapter 7).

The latest visible phase of street (Street NH8609; see Figs 3.3–4) was contemporary with the use of Structure NH8526, seeming to dog-leg around its north side (within adjacent Property BW 3), and was completely encroached on by its successor, Structure NH8529 (see below). It comprised two well-compacted, coarse angular gravel surfaces (NH4684 and NH4644, not on section), each 0.05–0.10 m thick. These surfaces had become very worn and uneven, perhaps as a consequence of use by horse and cart. The earliest surface (NH4684) was overlain by thick trampled greenish silt (NH4623) that contained a large quantity of animal bone and some smithing debris, possibly associated with the nearby structure. The relatively high frequency of dog gnawing on the bones suggests that this rubbish was left to fester in the street. The pottery was predominantly chalk-tempered ware (Fabric MBX), with sherds of late Saxon Sandy ware (Fabric MSH) implying a date before the mid 10th century, despite the presence of two sherds of more flinty ware, tentatively identified as fabric MAV (*c* 950–1050). The later surface showed evidence of repairs (NH4559) with chalk and gravel and was similarly overlain by thick rubbish-rich silts (NH4670).

Within the unexcavated area, close to the boundary with Property BW 1, a succession of compacted gravel surfaces overlain by thick occupation silts were recorded within the sides of a service trench (see Fig. 3.5). The earliest surface (NH4247), directly overlying the Dark Earth

(NH4248), comprised a hard matrix of flint pebbles that was overlain by a second surface of pebbles in a hard reddish clay matrix (NH4246). These surfaces are reminiscent of the earliest phase of street that was excavated further north (see Street NH8644 above), and pre-dated the earliest floors in this area. They therefore probably represent the equivalent surfaces of Brudene Street. A thick silt (NH4244) overlay these surfaces, above which was evidence of later metalling (NH4243).

Within Property BW 4 and pre-dating the earliest structure (Structure NH8566) was a succession of flint surfaces recorded within a beam trench (Street 8565; Fig. 3.6). Like those seen in Property BW 2, they extended *c* 5 m from the east side of the excavation, the earliest surface (NH3730) resting directly upon the surface of Dark Earth (NH3398) that appeared to have been terraced. Two further surfaces (NH3725 and NH3627) directly overlay the earliest surface, the later of them (NH3627) comprising compacted orange gravel up to 0.25 m thick. A small quantity of chalk tempered pottery (Fabric MBX) was found associated with these surfaces. A similar sequence of unexcavated gravel surfaces were recorded within a sewer trench that cut the south side of the property (not illustrated)— the latest of which was overlain by a thick dark grey brown clayey silt (NH3587) that contained much animal bone suggestive of dumping onto a street. Two samples for radiocarbon dating produced consistent calibrated dates of 780–970 (OxA-17173) and 730–970 (SUERC-13907), refined by Bayesian modelling to 830–940. Such dates are comparable to the latest visible gravelled surfaces found within Property BW 2 suggesting that encroachments by structures onto the street within the excavated area had similarly been completed by the mid part of the 10th century.

Further metalling (Street NH8587) was recorded on the east edge of Property BW 5 to the north (seen

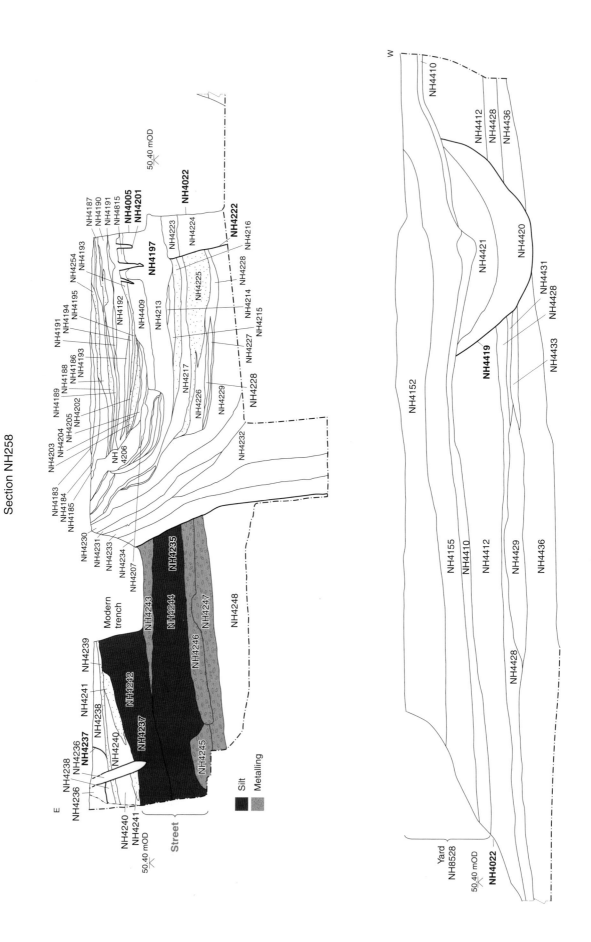

Fig. 3.5   Saxon Brudene street surfaces (unexcavated) and overlying Anglo-Norman floors exposed on the south side of Property BW 2 (slumping into Phase 4.1 cesspit NH4235)

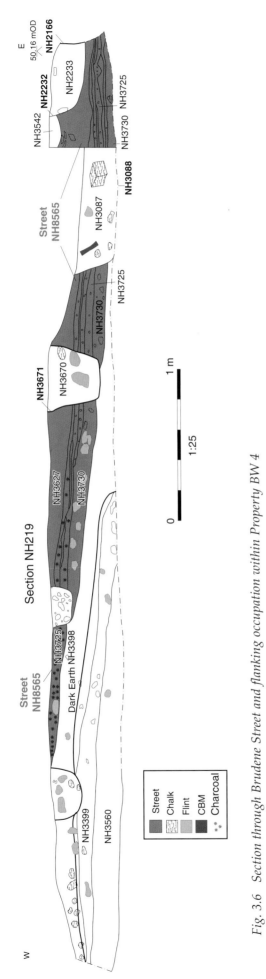

Fig. 3.6   Section through Brudene Street and flanking occupation within Property BW 4

in Figure 3.7), to the south of floor surfaces associated with Structure NH8586. As in Property BW 4, the street surfaces survived where they occupied a terraced area within the Dark Earth (NH2034 and NH2054). The earliest surface (NH2724) comprised a thin spread of redeposited natural gravel, 0.05 m thick, overlain by a thick clay silt (NH2712). This was in turn overlain by a further dump of redeposited natural gravel (NH2333) that was up to 0.4 m thick, which seems to have acted as bedding for overlying tightly packed cobbled surface NH2137 that formed a hard solid surface. Unlike the earlier surface (NH2724), it extended up to 3.3 m west into the excavated area. No similar street surface deposits were seen beneath the floor levels of Structure NH8586. This could mean that the structure had encroached onto the street by this point, or that the cobbled surface in fact represented a lane or passage to the south of the building, rather than part of the street. The only dating from the sequence came from a thick greyish brown clayey silt (NH2213) overlying cobbles NH2137 (not shown on section), which produced sherds of late Saxon chalk tempered ware (Fabric MBX). A small single sherd of flinty ware, possible fabric MAQ (*c* 1000–1250), if correctly identified and not intrusive, could suggest a date late within this period.

BRUDENE STREET EAST

Property BE 1 (Fig. 3.8)

Phase 4 pits

The pits within this property formed two clusters, separated by a strip of *c* 1.2 m that was devoid of features. The larger group (Pit Group CC7056), located to the north, comprised six pits that cut through the latest surviving surfaces of the Roman street (Street CC1703; see Chapter 2) implying that the thoroughfare had ceased to function by this date. The southern group (Pit Group CC7058) comprised 5 pits, similarly located largely cutting through the Roman street.

Pit Group CC7056 was characterised by regular rectangular pits. Most were not bottomed, although the largest (CC1100) was augered and found to be 2 m in depth, the basal 0.42 m of fill comprising loosely compact soft green black (cess-like) sandy silt (see Macphail and Crowther, Chapter 8). The vertical and unweathered sides of the pit suggest that it was originally timber-lined or otherwise protected from the elements. Two smaller pits (CC1469 and CC1427), aligned with its southern side, may also have functioned as cesspits, the latter containing mineralised faecal bran. The large vertical-sided circular pit CC1153, 2.1 m in diameter, could have been a well, although at its excavated depth of 0.8 m it contained domestic refuse and possible cess. A small quantity of ironworking debris including slag, furnace fragments and hammerscale was found within pits CC1208 and

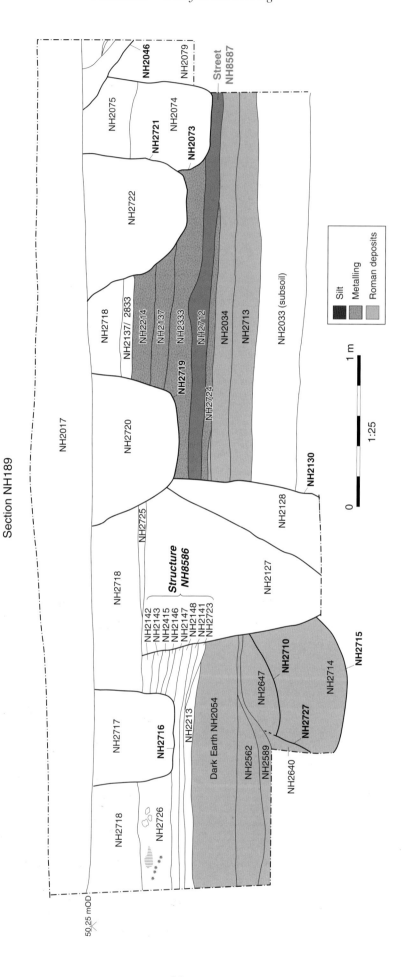

Fig. 3.7   Section through floors pertaining to Structure NH8586 (Property BW 5) and later deposits

CC1427, indicating that smithing was being undertaken in the immediate vicinity, presumably within structures located towards the west. Possible copper-alloy slag from pit CC1100 suggests the production of more elaborate items and a copper alloy mount with traces of gilding was also found within the pit (SF Cat no. 341; see Chapter 7, Fig. 7.31).

The southern group (Pit Group CC7058) contained five pits. The largest, rectangular pit CC1010, measured 3.7 m across and was excavated to a depth of 1.24 m. It contained a rich and diverse assemblage of animal and fish remains, with cessy fills including mineralised faecal remains. The pit also contained ash and charcoal-rich tips containing iron slag, hammerscale flakes and cinder, suggesting sweepings from a nearby smithy. Smaller rectangular pit CC1346, although containing some cess-like fills, produced predominantly iron metalworking waste, including much slag and a large part of a smithing hearth bottom. The remaining three pits within this group were shallow and of indeterminate purpose, although they contained some domestic refuse.

Property BE 2 (Figs 3.8–9; Plate 3.1)

Phase 4.2 pits

Three groups of pits were identified within Property BE 2. Pit Group CC7007, consisting of five pits, was located within the southern half of the property. Pit Group CC7013 comprised two pits located against the proposed northern boundary of

the property. Sequences of floor deposits from later structures that had slumped into two of the pits in these groups are described separately under Group CC7009 and Group CC7014 below. Pit Group CC7012 comprised at least three pits that were not excavated because of time constraints, and are not described any further.

Within Pit Group CC7007, only pit CC1339 was excavated to its base, the remainder being excavated only to mitigation level. Three of the pits were rectangular in plan (CC1397, CC1522 and CC1339) and, with circular pit CC1234, may have lain along a boundary with the property to the south. Pit CC1522 contained cess-like fills at its excavated depth, and an equal-armed balance (SF Cat no. 211; see Chapter 7 Fig. 7.27) and a padlock key (SF Cat no. 303) were recovered from its upper backfill. These objects are datable to the 10th to 13th century, and are indicative of the weighing and storage of precious items nearby. Pits CC1397 and CC1339 probably also served as cesspits; the former presumably contained decayed organic material within its lower unexcavated fills, since its upper excavated fills comprised a sequence of severely slumped compacted chalk deposits (Group CC7009 below). It is possible that circular pit CC1234 may have served as a well although this was not tested by augering. The sixth pit (CC1392) was set back immediately to north of the others, implying that it may represent the latest pit to be dug. A small quantity of iron smithing debris was recovered from pits CC1234, CC1339 and CC1392.

To the north, Pit Group CC7013 represented the earliest pits identified alongside the presumed

Plate 3.1   Floor group CC7014, slumped into pit CC1352, Property BE 2, Phase 4.2, looking east

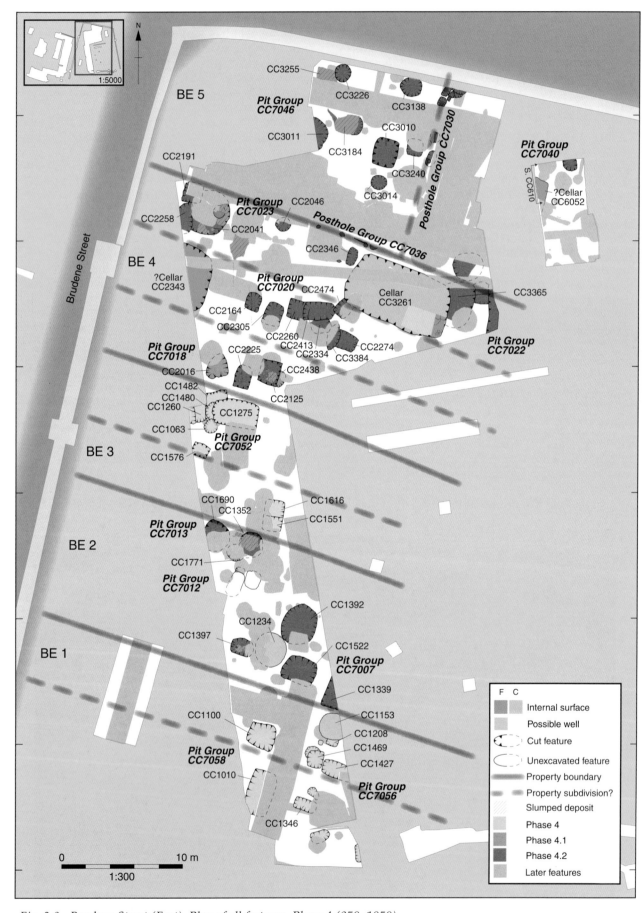

1:5000

CC3255

BE 5

**Pit Group
CC7046**

CC3226

CC3138

CC3011

CC3010

Posthole Group CC7030

**Pit Group
CC7040**

CC3184

CC3014

CC3240

S. CC610

?Cellar
CC6052

CC2191

CC2258

**Pit Group
CC7023**

CC2046

CC2041

Posthole Group CC7036

CC2346

BE 4

?Cellar
CC2343

**Pit Group
CC7020**

CC2474

Cellar
CC3261

CC3365

CC2164

CC2305

CC2260

CC2413

CC2334

CC2274

CC3384

**Pit Group
CC7022**

**Pit Group
CC7018**

CC2225

CC2016

CC2438

CC2125

CC1482
CC1480
CC1260

CC1275

CC1063

**Pit Group
CC7052**

BE 3

CC1576

CC1690

CC1616

CC1352

CC1551

**Pit Group
CC7013**

BE 2

CC1771

**Pit Group
CC7012**

CC1392

CC1234

CC1397

CC1522

**Pit Group
CC7007**

BE 1

CC1339

CC1153

CC1100

CC1208

CC1469

CC1427

**Pit Group
CC7058**

CC1010

**Pit Group
CC7056**

CC1346

Brudene Street

F C

Internal surface

Possible well

Cut feature

Unexcavated feature

Property boundary

Property subdivision?

Slumped deposit

Phase 4

Phase 4.1

Phase 4.2

Later features

0   10 m

1:300

Fig. 3.8   Brudene Street (East), Plan of all features, Phase 4 (850–1050)

boundary with Property BE 3 within an area possible occupied by a structure later in the phase (Fig. 3.9). It comprised three pits, two of which (CC1771 and CC1690) had been largely removed by later pitting. The third (CC1352) contained possible slumped floors to its excavated depth and is discussed below (Group CC7014).

Phase 4.2 structural evidence

Slumping into two of the pits were a succession of possible floor deposits, suggesting that structures had occupied the area soon after the infilling of the pits. Group CC7014 represented the upper fills of pit CC1352, located adjacent to the northern

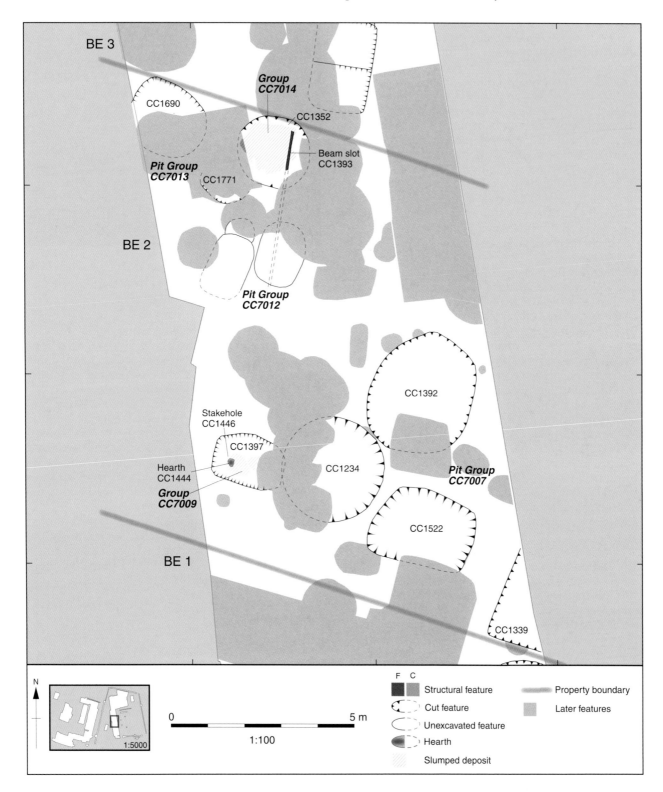

Fig. 3.9 Plan showing slumped floor groups CC7009 and CC7014 within Property BE 2, Phase 4.2

boundary of the property, and Group CC7009 those within pit CC1397 against the southern boundary.

Group CC7014 (Fig. 3.9; Plate 3.1)

The excavated fills of pit CC1352 comprised a sequence of interleaved deposits of thick compacted chalk and firm charcoal or ash-rich silts (Group CC7014), the earliest of which had slumped almost vertically from the top of the pit to its excavated level of 1 m. Given the nature of this sequence it is likely the deposits postdate the filling of the pit and derived from overlying occupation deposits that had sunk into a deep hollow formed as a consequence of the decay of underlying soft organic fills located below the excavated levels of the pit. Within the sequence was a straight narrow flat-bottomed slot (CC1393) that crossed the pit from north to south for a length of 1.24 m. It measured 0.09 m in width and 0.07 m in depth and appeared to have delimited the eastern extent of the possible floor deposits. It would have been too narrow to have held a beam for an external wall, so perhaps it supported an internal panel screen.

Micromorphological analysis of the deposits suggests that they represented coarse and fine fragmented floor deposits derived from domestic kitchen waste (see Macphail and Crowther, Chapter 8, thin sections CCM130B and CCM130A). The charcoal deposits contained a rich and diverse selection of animal and fish remains confirming the micromorphological analysis that they represented sweepings from a nearby domestic hearth within a kitchen. The presence of hammerscale implies that iron smithing was also being undertaken close by. The deposits also produced several closely datable objects including a riveted bone mount (SF Cat no. 313; mid 10th–late 11th century), a bone spindle whorl (SF Cat no. 168; 10th–11th century) and most notably an elaborately decorated bone spatula (SF Cat no. 189; late 10th–early 11th century; see Chapter 7, Fig. 7.26). The spatula has a very distinctive style of figurative incised decoration, which featured an acanthus or flower-like motif.

Group CC7009 (Plate 3.2)

The earliest excavated fills of pit CC1397 comprised a succession of three thick and compacted chalk surfaces interleaved with thin loose spreads of clean brown-grey silts. These generally contained few finds, apart from CC1531 which contained some sherds of MAV ware indicating a date after the mid 10th century. The latest chalk floor was cut by stakehole CC1446 providing further evidence for the structural nature of these deposits. Overlying these levels was a well-laid surface of yellowish mortar (CC1437) with a heavily scorched area (CC1444) on its southern side, indicating the position of a hearth. This was overlain by a thin charcoal-rich silt containing a high concentration of both flake and spherical hammerscale, which would imply *in situ* iron smithing. An abundance of charred hazelnut shells (representing the sole evidence for fruit and

Plate 3.2   Floor CC1437 (Group CC7009) with scorched area (?hearth) slumped into pit CC1397, Property BE 2, Phase 4.2, looking west

nuts) suggests the shells were used as fuel for smithing and metalworking (see Carruthers, Chapter 8). Re-flooring with compacted chalk followed, overlain by a thick succession of mostly charcoal-rich silts and ash that contained further hammerscale, a smithing hearth bottom and possible smithing slag. This appears to have represented a sustained period of activity since several sherds of post-Conquest pottery were associated with the latest levels. An abundance and wide variety of animal and fish remains also suggests that food was being prepared/consumed within the immediate area.

The floors were similar to those slumped into pit CC1352 (Group CC7014) located some 7 m to the north, and could form part of similar structures, possibly associated with cooking and craftworking within backyard areas.

Property BE 3 (Fig. 3.8)

Phase 4 pits

At total of nine pits have been allocated to the late Saxon period, although it was not possible to subdivide these between Phases 4.1 and 4.2. Six of the pits (Pit Group CC7052) formed an intercutting sequence against the proposed northern boundary of the property, with a further two pits located close to the proposed southern boundary, and one roughly centrally located between them. There was a notable lack of evidence for any pits to the east of Pit Group CC7052, which persists into

Phase 5 (see Chapter 4), suggesting the possibility that a *c* 2 m wide strip here may have been set aside for access.

The pits of Pit Group CC7052 appear to have been cut sequentially from west to east. These pits were characteristically rectangular in shape, becoming larger over time. The original function of the pits is uncertain, although pit CC1482 was augered and found to be 2.74 m deep with organic cess-like rich brown silt near its base. All these pits could have served as successive cesspits, although only the upper backfills were excavated, containing domestic refuse. The earliest pit, CC1260, contained a fairly diverse selection of animal bone and a possible bronze stylus tip (SF Cat no. 219). Shallow circular pit CC1063, which cut the southern edge of this pit, contained furnace mould and crucible fragments and a 10th- to 11th-century bone lucet (SF Cat no. 292) that may have been used for textile working.

Pit CC1576 probably also originally functioned as a cesspit. At its excavated depth of 1.45 m it contained stained compacted chalk that could have acted as a seal for underlying cess before the pit was used for rubbish disposal. The upper fill of the pit contained a particularly rich and diverse assemblage of animal, fish and marine shell deposits. The presence of deer and a variety of sea fish (including sea bream, plaice, thornback and mackerel) implies that the occupants enjoyed a wide variety of food. A bone spatula could offer further evidence for the perhaps higher status of the occupants.

Rectangular pits CC1616 and CC1551, located close to the southern boundary of the property, may have served a different purpose from those situated to the north. These pits were bottomed at 0.85 m and 0.9 m respectively and were filled with sequences of interleaved dumps of burnt clay and charcoal-rich silts indicative of an industrial process. Neither pit contained any slag or other metalworking debris, but pit CC1551 produced some fragments of vitrified hearth-lining implying that some process that required a high temperature was being undertaken. This pit also produced a bone eyed weaving implement (SF Cat no. 178) datable to the 11th to mid 12th century.

Property BE 4 (Figs 3.8, 3.10–11; Plates 3.3–4)

Phase 4.2 pits

Pit Group CC 7018

A group of four pits (Pit Group CC 7018) were located near to the southern boundary of Property BE 4 (Fig. 3.8). Rectangular pits CC2225 and CC2125 were probably cesspits, but pits CC2438 and CC2016 were somewhat irregular and shallow, and their function is not clear. Rectangular, straight sided pit CC2225 (Plate 3.3) measured 1.78 by 1.4 m in plan and was fully excavated to its base, reached at a depth of 1.5 m.

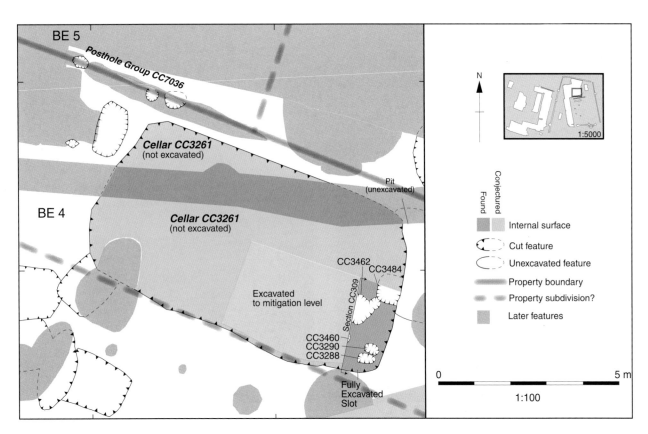

Fig. 3.10   Plan of cellar CC3261 (Property BE 4), Phase 4.2

Its basal fills contained cess-rich silts with one fill (CC2449) consisting of over 90% faecal concretions. The presence of frog and toad remains within bottom fill CC2458 suggests that the pit was left open at least long enough for these creatures to fall into it. The cess also contained a rich assemblage of diet indicators including cherry, plum, celtic beans, fish (predominantly herring and eel) and herbs/spices (including garlic, mustard seed and hedge parsley). The notable presence of opium poppy seeds suggests the alleviation of pain or perhaps the spicing-up of a monotonous diet (see Carruthers, Chapter 8). The pit also contained hammerscale and a bone spindlewhorl (SF Cat no. 170) indicating that smithing and spinning were undertaken by the occupants. Butchered horse bones were also present; such meat was probably for feeding dogs since horse meat was not normally eaten in late Saxon England (see Strid, Chapter 8). Adjacent pit CC2125 was of similar dimensions but was not bottomed at 0.7 m (mitigation level), but presumably also represented a cesspit. Hammerscale and several iron blades/knifes (SF Cat no. 276,

269) add to the evidence for smithing in the vicinity. The pit also contained sherds of pottery stained with purple madder and an eyed weaving implement (SF Cat no. 180 dated 11th to mid 12th century), providing evidence for textile working.

Pit Group CC7023

A number of pits attributed to Phase 4.2 (CC2258, CC2191, CC2041, CC2046, CC2346) were identified along the northern boundary of the property, although they had been heavily truncated by construction of a Second World War air raid shelter here (Fig. 3.8). Three formed an intercutting cluster. The earliest of this group was pit CC2191, which was much truncated, small and rectangular. It was not fully excavated but probably represents a cesspit. A bone (possibly ivory) pin-beater of 5th- to 10th-century date (SF Cat no. 174), used to adjust the weft whilst weaving, was recovered from the pit. Sub-circular pit CC2041 cut its east side, and measured about 3.3 m across. Although not fully excavated, its underlying fills were presumably soft and organic (cess?) to account for the considerable slumping of

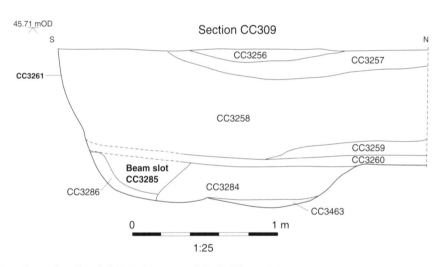

Fig. 3.11   Section through cellar CC3261 (Property BE 4), Phase 4.2

Plate 3.3   Cess pit CC2225, Property BE 4, Phase 4.2, looking west

Plate 3.4   Cellar CC3261, as excavated, Property BE 4, Phase 4.2, looking west

overlying floor deposits (see Group CC7024, below). The latest pit, a much truncated ?rectangular pit (CC2258) was shallow, at 0.82 m depth, with well-preserved cess at its base (CC2259). This cess layer contained a diverse selection of fish remains, predominantly eel, but including other freshwater fish (gudgeon, carp, trout) and a small selection of marine fish (ray, herring). Also notable were a selection of pulses including field bean, peas and other legumes. Pit CC2046 to the east was circular, with a diameter of 1.2 m, and could have served as a well, perhaps the forerunner to the elaborate chalk-lined well later located immediately to its west (see Phase 5 below). A brown-stained silt against its edges may have represented evidence for a timber-lining, although this could not be determined at the depth excavated.

Immediately to the south was a much larger, rectangular pit CC2343. Although only partially exposed, it measured *c* 5 m across, its excavated fills comprising a homogeneous mid-grey soil, possibly indicative of rapid infilling. Augering of its unexcavated fills revealed its total depth to be 2 m, with its basal fill comprising laminated deposits of moderately compacted chalk suggesting trampled floor deposits. On the basis of the observed dimensions of this feature, and the nature of its fills, it is suggested that it was a cellar pit.

Pit Group CC7020

This group represented seven square/ rectangular pits, all measuring 1.2–1.4 m across (Fig. 3.8). They were located centrally and towards the east of Property BE 4 in an area that remained essentially unexcavated below a maximum depth of 0.3–0.6 m. No geoarchaeological probing was available since there was no further impact from the development below the levels excavated. Consequently only general suggestions can be made concerning their likely function and distribution, although several contained artefactual and environmental evidence worth commenting on. Four of the pits (CC2260, CC2413, CC2334, CC2474) were stratigraphically earlier than cellar CC3261 (see below) and these formed a 'linear' cluster, the latest (CC2474) located to the east. It is conceivable that western outliers (CC2305, CC2164) were dug before the cluster to their east. Pit CC2413 contained two large fragments of smithing hearth bottoms and sherds of rare late Saxon wheel-thrown pottery, North French greyware (875–1000)—the only sherd found on the site (Fabric MFGY; see Cotter, Chapter 7)—and Portchester Ware (925–1050; Fabric MBN; see Cotter, Chapter 7). Many of the pits contained green-stained fills implying that most served as cesspits although only pit CC2164 was excavated to a sufficient depth to provide a rich enough sample for analysis, confirming the presence of mineralised faecal concretions (with bran). The pit was also particularly rich in fish remains, largely eels, but including herring, mackerel and ray. Sloe (or cherries), celtic field beans and peas were also being consumed. Pit CC3384 (possibly one of the latest) produced a key for a mounted lock (SF Cat no. 307) that compares with similar examples found in mid 11th- to mid 13th-century contexts elsewhere at Winchester (Goodall in Biddle 1990, 1028 nos. 3781–85, fig. 327). However, the pottery from the pit would suggest a pre-Conquest date. Perhaps significantly, a barrel padlock (SF Cat no. 305; see Chapter 7, Fig. 7.30) of 10th- to 11th-century date was found with adjoining Phase 5 pit CC2373 (see below), although this had cut into earlier late Saxon pit CC2474 and is possibly residual from it.

Pit Group CC7022

A group of three pits to the east of cellar CC3261 (see below) were left unexcavated, as their upper levels remained below mitigation level (Fig. 3.8). All three are presumed to be post-Roman in date since they cut Roman Street CC1703 (see Chapter 2). One of the pits (CC3365) was also cut by cellar CC3261.

Structural evidence—Cellar CC3261
(Figs 3.10–11; Plate 3.4)

Located towards the rear of the property was a large rectangular pit that measured 8.5 by 4.6 m in plan, its longer northern edge flush against the boundary with Property BE 5. Its south-west edge appeared to have clipped but otherwise respected the latest pit that formed part of the largely unexcavated Pit Group CC7020 (see above). All but the very upper part of its fills lay below mitigation level but they appeared to comprise two main episodes of infilling, probably in rapid succession. The earlier comprised dumps of chalk that were deposited from its west side, followed by dumps of fairly homogeneous loamy soil. Its (surviving) depth of 1.2 m was revealed by the excavation of a slot along its east side, against its south-east corner (Fig. 3.11). Several shallow postholes measuring less than 0.05 m depth were found cutting the base of the feature and are interpreted as bracing posts that may have held horizontal timbers lining its east side. Two of the postholes (CC3288 and CC3290) formed a pair and were located on its south-east corner while a third was located 1.1 m along the eastern edge. There was evidence for a possible beam void (CC3285) along its southern side but this could not be established with any certainty within the limited area excavated. No trampled deposits that could be attributed to floor deposits were identified although thin and loose ashy silt that overlay the base may have been derived from timber planking above or alternatively from the dismantling of the structure.

Property BE 5 (Figs 3.8, 3.12; Plate 3.5)

Phase 4.2 boundaries

Property BE 5 contained clear evidence for an early boundary (Posthole Groups CC7036, CC7030). Posthole Group CC7036 comprised a straight line of four circular postholes that had diameters of between 0.3 and 0.6 m and varied in depth from 0.08 to 0.35 m. It is probable, given the degree of truncation that has occurred, that they were originally significantly deeper. All were filled with a similar greyish brown silty clay, and two also contained sherds of late Saxon chalk and flint-tempered ware (fabric MAV) suggesting a date after *c* 950. They may have represented a timber precursor to boundary wall CC7337 (see Phase 6, Chapter 4), since they directly underlay its foundations and followed its alignment exactly.

However, the postholes did not extend eastwards beyond the north-west corner of possible cellar CC3261 (see above), implying a degree of contemporaneity with the structure. To the west, the boundary was truncated, but otherwise respected, by the construction of the south wall of cellar CC7044 (see Phase 5, Chapter 4). Also, if projected westwards, it would be respected by Pit Group CC7023 (Property BE 4, Phase 4.2) and medieval well CC2039 (Property BE 4, Phase 5) to its south.

At right-angles to Posthole Group CC7036 was a second line of postholes (Posthole Group 7030) that were cut (but otherwise respected) by Phase 6 pit CC3220 to the west and similarly by the west wall of medieval structure CC7038 to the east (see Phase 6, Chapter 4). They also apparently delimited the eastern extent of Phase 4.2 Pit Group CC7046 (see below), implying that Property BE 5 may have been sub-divided in two tenements at an early date (hereafter BE 5 (W) and BE 5 (E)). An eastwards return of the boundary was suggested by the presence of two early postholes on the line of the demolished brick and flint wall that until recently delimited the present street frontage. Here, two very truncated postholes were seen beneath the wall during its reduction to foundation level. The

postholes of Posthole Group 7030 were fairly large, up to 1.1 m across, and were presumably originally significantly deeper than their surviving depths of 0.1–0.3 m, given the degree of truncation that had occurred in the area. As such, they seem too substantial for simple fence posts, and it is possible that they formed part of the wall of a structure located within proposed Property BE 5(E). The postholes at the street frontage were replaced on at least one occasion, implying some longevity of this structure/boundary. Due to subsequent disturbances it not clear whether the postholes originally extended southwards to meet the boundary (Posthole Group CC7036) between Properties BE 4 and BE 5. However, later structures in this area (Phase 5 pit CC3322 and Phase 6 well CC3077) appear to respect this alignment, arguably occupying a position immediately inside the south-western corner of Property BE 5 (E).

Phase 4.2 Property BE 5 (W)

Pit Group CC7046

The earliest phase of pitting comprised nine largely discrete rectangular or circular pits. Several of the pits (CC3010, CC3184, CC3226 and CC3138) contained structural evidence datable to Phase 5 (see CC3031–35, Chapter 4, Phase 5) slumped within their upper fills, indicating that they pre-date structures identified within the area. Two circular pits (CC3138, CC3226) measuring respectively 1.8 m and 1.3 m in diameter flanked the existing frontage of Tower Street, presumably the northern boundary (and contemporary street frontage?) of the property. Pit CC3138 was augered and found to be 2.7 m in depth. It contained a thick chalky, compact dark grey brown silt clay at its base

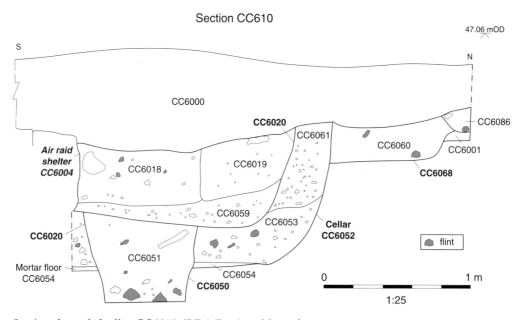

Fig. 3.12   Section through ?cellar CC6052 (BE 5 East) and later features

overlain by further apparent episodes of rapid infilling with well-consolidated clays and chalk. The lack of organic deposits seems to preclude its use as a cesspit and given that its depth was significantly above the known water-table, it could not have served as a well. It is possible that pit CC3226 served a similar purpose though its earliest excavated fill comprised a ?capping of burnt clay, possibly derived from a process that utilised considerable heat. Similarly circular pit CC3014, (bottomed at a depth of 0.6 m) seems to have been used for a purpose other than rubbish disposal given the lack of such material from its fills. It is likely that rectangular pits CC3010 and CC3184 contained soft organic fills below their excavated levels to account for the considerable slumpage of overlying occupation/consolidation deposits that had occurred. The earliest excavated fills of both pits contained much domestic refuse, including butchered horse bones and a smithing hearth bottom from pit CC3184. Rectangular pit CC3011 (partially exposed) to the west, and truncated pit CC3240 adjacent to the eastern boundary, may also have originated as cesspits before their final use as rubbish pits.

Structural Evidence

Evidence for possible occupation surfaces within proposed Property BE 5 (W) survived slumped into pit CC3184 (Group CC7035). The earliest

comprised compacted chalk (CC3128) over which was a dark brown clay silt, followed by a succession of compacted chalk or gravels interleaved with grey silts. These deposits overlay the latest fills of the pit, comprising compact chalk rubble and gravelly silt, possibly capping the pit, and therefore cannot have been used to seal underlying cess or other pungent organic matter. Their laminated nature suggests a prolonged period of accumulation implying that they may represent surfaces, occupation and make-up levels associated with an overlying structure. A possible pine marten bone, a species valued for their fur, which was reserved for the aristocracy during the medieval period, was recovered from one such deposit. Also recovered was a copper alloy pin, possibly used for an annular brooch or buckle, and dated from the later 12th to 15th centuries. However, such a date does not correspond with the ceramic dating (predominantly fabric MAV with some Winchester ware), which implies a pre-Conquest date. Further occupation deposits survived slumped over pits to the south and may represent later extensions to the structure to which these deposits pertain (Phase 5, Groups CC7031–34).

Phase 4.2 Property BE 5 (E)

Only two features attributable to the pre-Conquest period were found within Property BE 5 (E), both

Plate 3.5   ?Cellar pit CC6052 showing floor CC6054 on its base, Property BE 5 (E), Phase 4.2, looking west

confined to the north-west corner of the sprinkler tank excavation (Pit Group CC7040). Vertical sided pit CC6052 was partially exposed, but probably rectangular, and was bottomed at a depth of 1.1 m (Fig. 3.12; Plate 3.5). Its base contained a thin and compact mid-light brown/beige chalky mortar (layer CC6054 on Fig. 3.12) that probably represented a floor, over which was homogeneous loamy soil, indicative of rapid infilling. Although too little of this feature was exposed to allow detailed interpretation, it may have been part of a cellar, and is comparable in depth to cellar CC3261 within adjacent Property BE 4 (see above), although it lacked any evidence for timber lining. A shallow pit of uncertain function was located to its northeast.

BRUDENE STREET WEST

Property BW 1

Phase 4.1 yard and pits

Little of the area of this property was available for investigation (Fig. 3.13), and it had been extensively disturbed by later activity (see Fig. 3.14 below). The earliest evidence comprised a thick spread of redeposited natural gravel (NH4371) that had been laid directly over the surface of the Dark Earth. It was seen in two small exposures within Property BW 1, but appeared similar to and broadly contemporary with the gravel yard found within adjacent Property BW 2 (NH8528), although the evidence for the stratigraphic relationship between them had been removed by a modern trench. The area exposed was too small to warrant further interpre-

tation, suffice to say that it probably represented an exterior yard to the rear of a structure that flanked Brudene Street to the east. A small pit (NH4364) filled with loose gravelly silt and a possible posthole appear to have been associated. Subsequently a thick deposit of dark silty clay containing sherds of madder-stained pottery accumulated over surface NH4371 before a second surface of thick gravel was laid. This was in turn cut by a small and shallow pit (NH4287) containing domestic rubbish.

Phase 4.2 pits

The area seems to have remained open and set aside for the digging of pits, presumably serving the occupants of structures to the east (see Figs 3.14 and 3.16 below). The largest was shallow rectangular pit NH4345 (Fig. 4.16), partially exposed against the limit of excavation, which contained a rounded vertical-sided shaft lined with rammed chalk, suggesting that it may have served as a well (see Section, Fig, 3.5 above). Its excavated fills comprised gravel-rich silts and grey silty loams, indicative of rapid infilling. Pit or well NH4345 cut a vertical-sided circular(?) pit NH4289, that lay largely outside the excavated area (Fig. 3.16), but may also have served as a well. It was seemingly rapidly infilled with alternating dumps of gravel and grey silt to the depth excavated. It also contained hammerscale and burnt hazelnut shells, indicative of smithing activity. A third pit, NH4278 (Fig. 3.16), with similar fills, contained many burnt hazelnut fragments and a disc brooch (SF Cat no. 121; see Chapter 7, Fig. 7.24) datable to the 10th century.

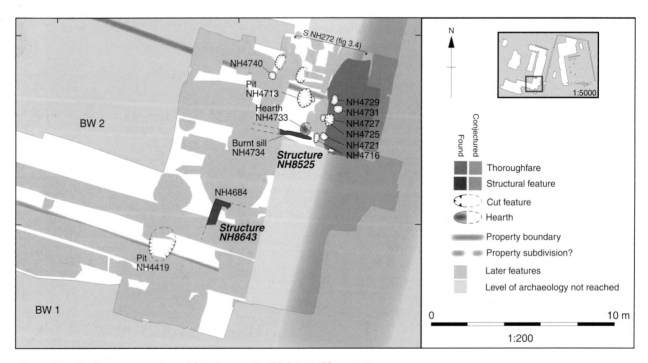

Fig. 3.13   Earliest occupation within Properties BW 1–2, Phase 4.1

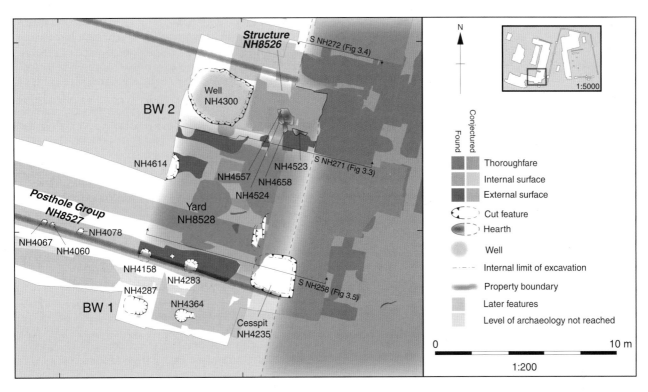

Fig. 3.14   Plan of Structure NH8526 and contemporary features (Property BW 2), Phase 4.1

Property BW 2

Phase 4.1 structural evidence (Figs 3.13–15; Fig. 3.3; Plate 3.6)

Relationship between Structures on Property BW 2 and Brudene Street

The earliest post-Roman activity, directly overlying Dark Earth deposits, comprised a number of postholes and deposits associated with burnt daub implying the existence of one or more structures (Structure NH8525) (Fig. 3.13). The relationship between these postholes, successive structures in this location, and successive surfaces of the street to the east, is key to understanding the chronology of the development of the project area in the late Saxon period. The postholes of Structure NH8525 respected the earliest street surfaces and the silts that built up over the top of them (Street NH8644 on Fig. 3.3). This demonstrates that they were in contemporary use, and (arguably) that Structure NH8525 was constructed after the establishment and earliest metalling of Brudene Street. Subsequently Structure NH8525 went out of use and its postholes were sealed by further layers of gravel street surfacing and silt build-up (Street NH8607 on Fig. 3.3). The location of these surfaces suggests that the street had been widened slightly to the west. A second structure, Structure NH8526 (Fig. 3.14), was constructed over the western edge of Street NH8607, thus encroaching slightly on the line of the widened street. The street was subsequently resurfaced again (Street NH8609 on Fig. 3.3) and Structure NH8526 appeared to respect the west edge of this latest resurfacing, which implies a slight narrowing of Brudene Street again. Street NH8609 was the latest street surface seen in the excavations. The third successive building on the property, Structure NH8529 (Fig. 3.15), subsequently encroached significantly on Brudene Street, extending some 3 m eastwards across the street frontage line associated with Structure NH8526.

Structure NH8525 (Fig. 3.13)

A double line of postholes spaced *c* 1 m apart followed the western edge of the street but did not extent beyond the boundary with Property BW 3, suggesting that it was in existence by this time. A further posthole (NH4740) formed an approximate right-angle to their west, on an alignment close to that of the later boundary between the two properties. The north-south alignment of posts may represent two phases of construction, with the earlier represented by oval postholes NH4716, NH4725 and NH4729, measuring 0.36–0.55 m across with depths of 0.17–0.32 m. The later postholes (NH4721, NH4727, NH4731) to their east were more rounded and substantial with diameters of 0.43–0.59 m and depths of 0.26–0.55 m. All were filled with soils containing flecks of burnt daub, but otherwise almost indistinguishable from the Dark Earth that they cut. None contained dating evidence apart from residual Roman pottery and coins (common throughout the Dark Earth) but they included large brick/tile fragments used for packing.

Plate 3.6   Structure NH8525 showing burnt ?sill-beam NH4734 and hearth NH4733 with postholes forming part of its east wall, Property BW 2, Phase 4.1, looking east

Perpendicular to the southern limit of the postholes was a thin linear spread of dark grey 'ash' (NH4734) containing fired clay fragments, possibly representing the impression of a burnt sill-beam (Plate 3.6). It was *c* 0.21 m wide, surviving for a length of 1.76 m, and suggests that the structure had been subjected to a fierce fire. Immediately to its north a small circular spread of burnt clay that directly overlay the Dark Earth indicates the presence of a hearth (NH4733). An archaeomagnetic sample (WOO) taken from the hearth produced a date of 559–1084. Approximately 1 m further to the north was a small, shallow rectangular pit (NH4713) measuring 0.8 by 0.3 m in area and 0.25 m deep, 'lined' with a compact green-stained sandy silt that contained a high concentration of flake hammerscale. This offers convincing *in situ* evidence that secondary smithing was undertaken within the structure, possibly adjacent to its north wall. The pit was backfilled with redeposited Dark Earth that contained fragments of an oven wall, some with the remains of thick white (burnt grey) lime wash on its interior surface and many with interwoven wattle impressions. This possibly represents the remains of a discarded ?domestic oven perhaps used for baking bread, since charred bread-type grain was present within the pit.

Structure NH8643 (Fig. 3.13)

Located some 5 m to the south-west of Structure NH8525 was further evidence for an early structure that, like Structure NH8525, may also have been destroyed by fire. The rather fragmentary remains directly overlay the Dark Earth, and were probably largely cleared when overlying gravel Yard NH8528 (see below) was constructed. A short length of a possible earth-fast sill (NH4686) was discernible and represented by a thin linear spread of burnt clay aligned parallel with Brudene Street. There was a possible return to the east at its north end implying that it may have represented the north-west corner of the structure. Partially overlying the possible sill but otherwise confined to its east (internal?) side was a dump of fired clay fragments totalling over 8.2 kg in weight (NH4660 and NH4661; not shown on plan) that formed a significant part of a nearby demolished oven, similar in nature to the fragments found within adjacent Structure NH8525. No evidence for flooring was found, though a thin spread of greenish grey silt was recorded below the demolished oven remains. This contained a large fragment of smithing hearth bottom and a significant quantity of iron slag and is perhaps associated with smithing activity that was undertaken within Structure NH8525.

Pit NH4419 (see section on Fig. 3.5 above), was probably contemporary with Structure NH8643, since both predated the earliest surfaces of an overlying gravel yard (Yard NH8528). This pit was roughly circular, measuring 1.44 m in diameter and 0.7 m in depth. It contained a dark silty, slightly organic basal fill with cess patches and had been backfilled with redeposited Dark Earth. Given its proximity to the structure it could have served as a latrine. The pit pre-dated the boundary fence between Properties BW1 and BW 2 (Posthole Group NH8527), suggesting either that the boundary was not in existence at this time or that it lay further to the south.

Structure NH8526 (Fig. 3.14; Plate 3.7)

Rectangular Structure NH8526, probably timber-built, was identified flanking and contemporary with the latest (visible) metallings on the western edge of Brudene Street (Street NH8609). It had seemingly encroached onto the western edge of the earlier street surfaces (Street NH8607) that had overlain the eastern part of earlier Structure NH8525, implying that the earlier structure had been cleared and the area remained open for a period of time. Charcoal from the silting on the earlier Street NH8607 produced calibrated radiocarbon dates of 770–940 and 780–990 (OxA-17177 and SUERC-13909). Bayesian modelling has refined these dates to 770–890 and 770–920 respectively (see Chapter 6). No elements of the walls or frame of the structure survived, and its extent was delimited by the survival of its floor deposits. The walls were probably constructed on earthfast sill-beams, since the northern, eastern and western extents of the floor deposits were often sharply defined, the northern floor limits corresponding closely with the proposed line of the boundary with Property BW 3. The structure seems to have extended no more than 3.8 m back from the street frontage and measured up to 2.9 m wide, its southern extent apparently delimited by a slight encroachment onto the gravel yard to its south (see Yard NH8528 below).

Its earlier floor (NH4692) comprised compact clay that had been baked hard by intense heat and may have represented a working surface for some industrial process that required a high temperature. Archaeomagmetic sampling (WOM) produced a date of 880–1093. A thin layer of yellow-grey silt above (NH4687) was relatively devoid of charcoal and lacked any evidence for industrial activity (eg hammerscale) though it contained a small quantity of cinder, animal bone and fish remains indicative of domestic activity. Above, a new floor (NH4682) was laid, comprising compacted chalk with a thickness of 0.15 m, suggesting a major refurbishment of the structure. Several large fragments of smithing hearth bottoms and large lumps of iron slag were recovered from the basal level of the floor and had perhaps been used as hardcore. It is unclear whether this material had been brought in from elsewhere or was derived from activity associated with the underlying burnt floor NH4692. A small clay hearth (NH4658) was located near the centre of the inferred south wall. The evidence from the associated thin occupation silts and charcoal spreads suggests that the floor of the structure was kept relatively clean, perhaps indicating a domestic rather than an industrial function. However, one deposit (NH4556) contained

a large quantity of charred hazelnut shells (384 fragments) that might have been collected as kindling for smithing hearths and kilns (see Carruthers, Chapter 8). A second larger clay hearth (NH4557) was associated with a charcoal spread (NH4580) that produced calibrated radiocarbon dates of 780–960 (OxA 17183) and 830–1100 (SUERC-13918). Bayesian modelling refined these dates to 860–950 and 880–950. A Phase 4.1 date is supported by a rather limited pottery assemblage comprising chalk-tempered ware (Fabric MBX).

The structure was then re-floored with compacted chalk (NH4527), which had become heavily worn through use. Further clay hearths (NH4523 and NH4524) were added towards the south wall of the structure and the former was archaeomagnetically dated to 1065–1245 (WOK). This date is considered unreliable since an overlying hearth NH4261 (see Structure NH8529 below) produced a more consistent date of 979–1165 (WOE). This is reinforced by a radiocarbon sample from charcoal spread NH4507 that overlay the hearths, which gave a calibrated date of 780–1010 (SUERC-13920), enhanced by Bayesian modelling to 890–960. This date is in agreement with pottery from occupation silt NH4526 that also overlay the floor, which contained abundant late Saxon chalk-tempered ware (Fabric MBX) and fresh sherds of

Plate 3.7   The latest surface of Brudene Street (Street NH8609) with the chalk floor of Structure NH8526 to its west. (The floor deposits of later Structure NH8529 can be seen overlying the street on the top left-hand corner), Property BW 2, Phase 4.1, looking south-west

late Saxon sandy ware (Fabric MSH), which is conventionally dated to before *c* 950. A small quantity of iron slag was recovered from occupation silt NH4526, but the lack of other evidence for industrial activity suggests that Structure 8526 had a primarily domestic function.

Yard NH8528 (Figs 3.14–15)

An extensive area of gravelled yard (Yard NH8528) was located to the south/south-west of Structure NH8526 and overlay Structures NH8525 and NH8643 (Figs 3.3 and 3.5). The surfaces survived as isolated islands between later pits and disturbances although they were shown to abut the inferred south wall of Structure NH8526. Their southern extent was probably delimited by a line of later postholes (see Posthole Group NH8527 below) that may have defined the southern limit of the property at this time. However, a modern service trench had destroyed the relationship with gravel surfaces (eg NH4371) found within Property BW 1, so it was not possible to establish if the two areas represent the same yard or not, although both were stratigraphically early. At least two surfaces were extant. The earlier (NH4410, Fig. 3.5 and NH4691, Fig. 3.3) comprised fine well-compacted orange gravel *c* 0.1 m thick. The later (NH4152, Fig. 3.5 and NH4683, Fig. 3.3) was more substantial, measuring up to 0.2 m thick and comprising well-compacted angular gravel with occasional larger flint nodules. In the area adjacent to Structure NH8526, the second surface was overlain by trampled silts (NH4592; see section on Fig. 3.3). This contained much animal bone (mainly cattle, pig, sheep/goat), some fish remains (including eel and herring) and a large part of a chalk-tempered spouted pitcher (see Chapter 7, Fig. 7.13, no. 81), presumably dumped from the nearby structure.

Fence Line (Posthole Group NH8527)

Cutting the southern extent of the second surface of Yard NH8528 were postholes NH4283 and NH4158, aligned at right-angles to the street (Figs 3.14–15). Three further postholes (NH4078, NH4060 and NH4067) located further west followed this line exactly, suggesting contemporaneity. This alignment could be traced for a length of nearly 9 m and, if projected 3 m eastwards, would correspond with the southern edge of cesspit NH4235. Postholes NH4158 and NH4283 were more substantial than the others, measuring 0.6 and 0.8 m in diameter respectively; both were 0.35 m deep. The postholes to west were generally smaller measuring 0.3–0.62 m, although they were of similar depth. They lay less than 1 m north of Wall NH4068, which probably delimited the boundary with Property BW 1 during the 13th–14th centuries (see Chapter 4), and could therefore mark a precursor to it.

Structure NH8529 (Fig. 3.15)

Structure NH8526 appears to have been enlarged by at least 3.1 m to the east, forming Structure NH8529 and thus encroaching significantly onto the surfaces of Brudene Street (see Fig. 3.3) implying that the street had been narrowed at this point. The structure also appears to have been enlarged northwards across the boundary with Property BW 3 by about 1 m and to the south across Yard NH8528, although its western extent seems to have remained unchanged. As with its predecessor it was probably constructed on sill-beams, although these were not identifiable during excavation. The extent of the building was represented by the extent of the floors which were particularly sharply defined along its western and northern sides. A short length of an otherwise truncated shallow slot (NH4536; see section in Fig. 3.3) may have defined its eastern side and had been cut into the underlying street surface. It contained a small circular posthole (NH4537). Overall, the structure may have measured 7.3 m from the street frontage and at least 4.5 m in width, although the southern extent of the floor deposits was not seen as the floors lay below mitigation level.

The structure had a thin floor of compacted chalk (NH4505=4513), measuring no thicker than 0.06 m, that showed evidence for heavy wear (see Fig. 3.3). No major repairs of the floor seem to have occurred, apart from patching with mortar, gravel and chalk. A succession of small baked-clay hearths was recorded within the southern half of the structure. One of the earliest (NH4457), located adjacent to the west wall, may have been delimited by a rectangular arrangement of stakeholes possibly supporting a cauldron or similar cooking vessel. Certainly the associated charcoal sweepings produced no evidence for industrial activity. In contrast, hearth NH4491 was associated with spreads of charcoal and trampled silts that contained evidence for metalworking including flake hammerscale (NH4481) and fragments of crucible, some with copper droplets adhering (contiguous layers NH4464, NH4403, NH4411; see Fig. 3.3). It is possible that the ubiquitous small fragments of fired clay found in these deposits could be from moulds used for the manufacture of small copper (alloy) objects. The pottery associated with the structure at this point comprised predominantly late Saxon chalk-tempered (MBX) ware with some sandy ware (MSH) implying a date prior to 950. A few sherds of the pottery were stained with madder-dye, and another sherd had a hole pierced through it, possibly for use as a spindlewhorl. This suggests that dyeing and spinning were also undertaken within the structure.

The latest hearth (NH4261) was more substantial. It measured 1.2 m across, and the clay (0.2 m thick) had been baked hard throughout, providing a particularly suitable sample for archaeomagnetic dating (WOE). This gave a date range of 979–1165 for its final firing. A charcoal sweeping (NH4394) associated with the hearth produced radiocarbon dates of 780–970 (OxA-17184) and 880–1020 (SUERC-13919), recalibrated by Bayesian modelling

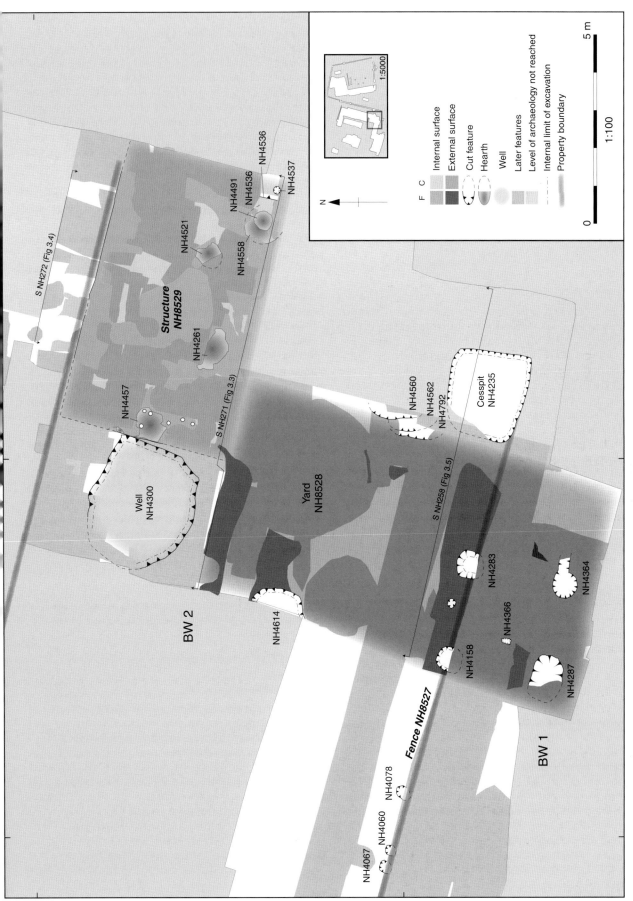

Fig. 3.15   Plan of Structure NH8529 (Property BW 2) and features in Property BW 1, Phase 4.1

to 910–980 and 900–980 respectively. The presence of a sherd of late Saxon wheel-thrown sandy ware (Fabric MZM) in a make-up deposit immediately underlying charcoal NH4401 would suggest that Structure NH8529 continued to be occupied to shortly after 950. Fragments from at least two crucibles (see Chapter 7, Fig. 7.14, no. 88) were recovered from charcoal NH4394 suggesting that the hearth could reach temperatures sufficient to melt the copper. Fragments of a Roman copper-alloy earring (SF Cat no. 30) from the charcoal may have represented metal scrap intended for reworking. The relatively wide range of remains of animals and birds (including domestic fowl, sheep/goat and pig) and fish (mainly herring, but including trout, eel, plaice, cod and flat-fishes) indicate the inhabitants had access to a fairly diverse range of foodstuffs.

Phase 4.1 pits

Six pits were attributable to Phase 4.1 and are there-fore broadly contemporary with the structures described above, although it was not generally possible to associate the pits stratigraphically with individual structures. Of these, pit NH4419 has been described above (Fig. 3.13), as there was good evidence that it was contemporary with the earliest structures on this property (Structures NH8525 and NH8643).

Well NH4300 (Fig. 3.14) was located immediately adjacent to the west wall of Structure NH8526 and its successor NH8529 but was sealed by the floors of its westward extension, Structure NH8530 (see below). The pit was rectangular with straight vertical edges and measured 3.1 m by 2.55 m in area. Owing to the considerable subsidence of the overlying floors of later Structure NH8530 it was not possible to investigate its fills below its upper-most deposit of loose orange gravel (NH4362); this was similar to the gravel used to construct Yard NH8528 and suggests a reversion of the area to yard use. Geoarchaeological investigation located the base of the feature at 43.49 m OD (*c* 6.8 m below the surface), a level 0.57 m above the base of nearby chalk-lined well NH4019 (see Property BW 2 – Phase 5 below), suggesting that it was probably a well. Its basal levels comprised three similar fills of (cessy) dark brown silt, each 0.15–0.4 m thick, separated by voids 0.8 m in depth probably formed as a result of the considerable decay and shrinkage of organic content, suggesting its final use as a cesspit. The primary silt (NH4679) contained fish bones and cereal pollen that had presumably passed through the gut of the inhabitants, the latter implying that individual(s) had been near an arable field or in an area of cereal processing when the pollen was swallowed. The other taxa present suggest the presence or utilisation of heathland (heather), possibly for flavouring a drink, meadow grassland or rough grassland (black knapweed, thistle and grass), possibly for animal fodder or

bedding that was discarded into the cesspit, and woodland (pine). The latter was probably some distance from the site (Vaughan-Williams *et al.* 2005).

Cesspit NH4235 was located within the largely unexcavated area to the south of Structures NH8526 and NH8529 (Figs 3.14–15), although part of its southern side was excavated after overlying levels associated with Structures NH8538 and NH8539 (see BW 2, Phases 4.2/5 below) had been sampled for soil morphology. Although its northern extent was not revealed, evidence from the considerable degree of slumping from the overlying floors suggests that the pit was square and measured *c* 2.3 m across; an excavated sondage revealed its depth to be *c* 1.85 m. Its basal levels (see Fig. 3.5 NH 4233–35) comprised cessy grey silts that contained a significant assemblage (2.5 kg) of chalk-tempered ware (fabric MBX), largely from heavily sooted jars that had probably been used for cooking. The pit was also fairly rich in fish bone, with identifiable bones being predominantly from herring, though other fish (flat-fishes, trout and eel) were also present. It is not clear whether the pit was associ-ated with Structures NH8526 and NH8529 or with a structure occupying the frontage to their south that was not seen because this area was not excavated. Flake hammerscale and a small quantity of iron slag also recovered from the pit suggests secondary smithing was undertaken close by, perhaps associ-ated with similar activity that was identified within the earlier levels of Structure NH8529.

Pit segment NH4614 (Figs 3.14–15) lay largely outside the excavated area though it was apparently sealed by Yard NH8528 since its upper fills consisted of slumped orange gravel from the yard surface. The pit probably served as a cesspit though its lower fills remained unexcavated. Similar inter-secting pits (NH4560, NH4562, NH4792; Fig. 3.15), located immediately to the north of cesspit NH4235, lay mainly below mitigation levels—though their presence suggests that this area was set aside for disposal of waste over a sustained period of time.

Phase 4.2 structural evidence (Fig. 3.16; Plate 3.8)

Structure NH8530

The latest surviving phase of structure within the property appears to have maintained a similar sill-beam construction (in its original form) to its prede-cessors (Structures NH8526 and NH8529). It was enlarged to the west over earlier well NH4300 (Phase 4.1) and appeared (at least at its latest state) to occupy the whole frontage of the property, although only the later floors of the central part were exposed within the mitigation area. However a 1.2 m wide 'island' of stratigraphy (see Group NH8538 below) exposed on either side of service trenches was investigated at its southern extent where floor deposits had slumped into cesspit NH4235 (see Phase 4.1 pits, above). The structure may have been

L-shaped in plan with its eastern arm (or frontage) measuring at least 11.2 m in length and 5.6 m at its maximum exposed depth to the east. The western extent of this arm coincidentally corresponded with the western limit of the mitigated area since this represented the extent of the floor deposits at this point, abutted by a compact area of gravel (NH4405; see Phase 5, Chapter 4), probably an exterior yard surface containing a chalk-lined well. Due to later disturbance and the similarity of the floors it was not certain whether the west arm was an integral part of the structure or represented a separate structure in itself. Posthole NH4495 may have defined its south wall given that floor deposits did not extend beyond it, suggesting that this arm was 3.5 m in width. The northern extent of the structure corresponded closely to earlier Structure NH8526 suggesting that the 'encroachment' on to Property BW 3 by its successor (Structure NH8529) had been reversed.

The structure was floored throughout by compacted chalk (NH4370; see section on Fig. 3.3) up to 0.12 m thick. Its western arm had been similarly floored with thick compacted chalk (NH4086) that had extended over and slumped considerably into well NH4300 (Plate 3.8). The soft underlying ground at this point had been recognised by the constructors since thick dumps of compacted gravels and clays underlay the floor in an attempt to stabilise the area, implying that a relatively short period had passed since the pit was filled. A thin charcoal-rich grey silt (4369) overlay the floor, associated with a small fired clay hearth (NH4317) or possibly with other hearths located within the unexcavated area to the south. This was

devoid of any industrial evidence but contained much fish bone, almost exclusively herring, and a large quantity (343 fragments) of charred hazelnut shells (see below).

The floor within the northern part of the east arm of the structure was repaired several times before being levelled with mid grey brown clay to support a re-flooring with chalk (NH4277). This levelling deposit (NH4164) contained a rich assemblage of animal bone including a possible deer bone, which would imply a potentially luxury element to the diet. The pottery was dominated by chalk-tempered ware (Fabric MBX) but with sherds of Portchester ware (MBN), Michelmersh ware (MMU) and late Saxon Sandy ware (MSH) suggesting a pre-Conquest date. The structure was provided with a further floor of thick chalk (NH4126=NH4384) representing the final or latest surviving significant floor of the structure, exposed across its full area (but unexcavated within the mitigation area). This floor was supported by thick make-up of brown mottled clay that contained two small sherds of pottery possibly attributable to the post-Conquest period (Fabric MBK; c 1050–1150), although sherds of Winchester ware were also present (see Chapter 7, Fig. 7.17, no. 133). The Fabric MBK sherds may have been intrusive, since subsequent repairs to level the floor (NH4381) located towards the south of the structure produced pre-Conquest Winchester ware and a possible late Saxon import (see Chapter 7, Fig. 7.17, no. 142), although a pre-Conquest origin of this fabric cannot be discounted (see Cotter, Chapter 7). Furthermore, two samples from an overlying spread of charcoal (NH4379) were radiocarbon dated

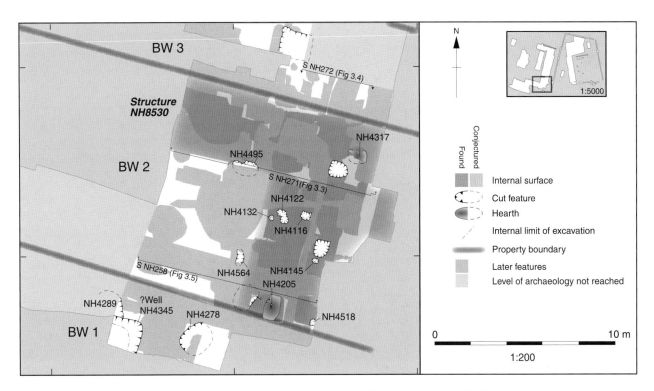

Fig. 3.16   Plan of Structure NH8530 and contemporary features (Properties BW 1–2), Phase 4.2

(SUERC-19287, SUERC-1928) producing consistent calibrated dates of 880–1020 and 900–1030 respectively. Bayesian modelling has refined these dates to 930–1000 and 940–1010. The surviving evidence suggests that the structure continued to have a predominantly domestic function; two bone spindlewhorls (SF Cat nos 160–1) were recovered from intercutting postholes NH4145/4147 and one (SF Cat no. 163) from earlier make-up NH4322.

The floors at the south end of the structure appear to have been part of a kitchen area since they comprised a prolonged accumulation of charcoal-rich silts associated with a succession of chalk floors and hearths, investigated by a small sondage (see section, Fig. 3.5). The earliest floor comprised well compacted chalk (NH4229), 0.2 m thick, that supported spreads of burnt sandy clay that had probably been disturbed from a nearby hearth. Above was a charcoal spread (NH4226) that was rich in burnt hazelnut shells (482 shells) and contained garlic mustard seeds used to flavour food. It is suggested that roasting makes the nuts last longer in storage, it makes them more digestible, and enables them to be ground into flour. The presence of a charred flax seed suggests that oil may have been extracted or that flax was used for medicinal purposes, since black nightshade seeds were also present in some quantity. Black nightshade is thought to have been used externally to relieve inflammation, and flax seeds are known for their laxative properties (see Carruthers, Chapter 8).

The internal and domestic nature of the occupation is further emphasised by the soil micromorphology analysis, which identified these as chalk floors intercalated with trampled ash, charcoal and fine burned bone-rich microlayered deposits of near-domestic hearth (kitchen) origin, and burned brickearth clay and silts (loess) of hearth origin (see Macphail and Crowther, Chapter 8, samples NHM253D-E). A group of stakeholes associated with a subsequent floor (NH4225) may have formed part of a structure associated with hearth NH4205. Thick charcoal deposits (NH4217 and NH4221) above contained a rich assemblage of fish remains including herring, cod, whiting, eel and scad. Several further episodes of chalk refloorings followed, probably in an attempt to level up the underlying soft ground, associated with further clay hearths constructed on top of hearth NH4205. Soil micromorphology analyis identified these as trampled floor deposits mainly composed of hearth rakeout including much burned food waste (bone and eggshells), but also burned coprolitic/latrine and stabling waste (ibid., NHM253F). The only evidence for industrial activity was found with charcoal deposit NH4212 where a small quantity of flake hammerscale was found suggesting that limited secondary smithing was being undertaken close by. The area continued to serve as a kitchen into the post-Conquest period (see Phase 5 below).

Plate 3.8   Floors of the western extension of Structure NH8530 slumping into earlier ?well NH4300, Property BW 2, Phase 4.2, looking north-east

Phase 4.2 pits

The area to the west of Structure NH8530 would appear to have been external since a small surviving patch of gravelled yard (NH4405) was recorded with deposits of Phase 5 (see below). Only shallow pit NH4564 could be attributed to Phase 4.2 (Fig. 3.16), although it is possible that Phase 5 ?cesspit NH4339 may also originally date to this phase since only its upper fills were excavated, and showed a high degree of slumpage.

Property BW 3

Phase 4.1 structural evidence (Fig. 3.17)

Levels pertaining to Phase 4.1 lay below mitigation levels over the majority of the excavated frontage of Property BW 3 except for a 2.2 m wide strip adjacent to the boundary with Property BW 2, and partially within ground beams (for the new development) towards the north. Two postholes, NH4549 and NH4736, and two small stakeholes were identified close to the suggested line of the boundary with Property BW 2 to the south and may have represented a fence. No other evidence for structures was found within the excavated area alongside the boundary with Property BW 2 and this area appears to have remained open during this period. This is supported by the presence of an early but unexcavated pit that cut the western edge of the original alignment of Brudene Street over which floors pertaining to Phase 5 had severely slumped (see Chapter 4). Similarly, where contemporary levels were exposed within beamslots to the north these appear to represent surfaces that were possibly associated with the edge of Brudene Street or external areas to its west (see above). It seems unlikely that the property was unoccupied during Phase 4.1, and any associated structures must have been located within the unexcavated areas.

Phase 4.1 pits

Only one pit (NH3721) could be assigned to this phase; it was sealed by occupation layers associated with the subsequent Phase 4.2 structure on the site, Structure NH8556 (see below). The pit was ovoid, measuring 1.6 by 0.58 m across and 0.7 m in depth, with straight vertical sides apart from its north end which sloped in. Given its rather restricted size, it

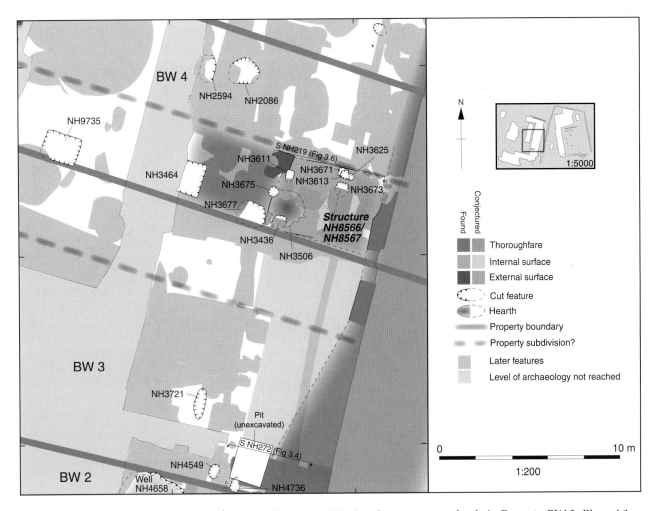

Fig. 3.17   Plan of Structures NH8566/NH8567 (Property BW 4) and contemporary levels in Property BW 3, Phase 4.1

may have had a structural purpose although no evidence for a post was found within its homogeneous fill of firm dark orange-brown silty clay. Although later activity may have removed much of the evidence, there was a complete absence of pre-Conquest pits within the relatively undisturbed area towards the north of the property. This may support the view that this area remained open for access from an early date (eg as a lane) or was set aside for other use.

Phase 4.2 Structure NH8556 (Fig. 3.18; Plate 3.9)

As with Phase 4.1, evidence for structural remains along the frontage lay largely below mitigation level although slightly more evidence was recorded from the beam slots for the new structure. Immediately to the west of the unexcavated area, towards the south of the property, was a succession of hearths and floors probably from within a structure for which no other evidence was seen (Structure NH8556), and probably associated with metalworking. This structure would have measured at least 2.9 m north-south, corresponding to the extent of its surviving surfaces, and continued eastwards beyond the excavated area. Its earliest levels comprised a large hearth (NH3680) constructed with a fired clay pad measuring 2.3 by 1.6 m and up to 0.1 m thick that directly overlay the Dark Earth. The hearth was archaeomagnetically dated (WON) to 914–1121 and was contemporary with an adjacent rectangular pit (NH3806) that contained similar fire-hardened clay at its base (NH3782; see Plate 3.9). The pit measured at least 1.5 by 1.2 m and was 0.64 m deep and may have served to contain a fire of considerable heat. Numerous charred hazelnut fragments recovered from the pit may have comprised fuel for smithing and metalworking. Charcoal spreads (NH3679 and NH3669) associated with the use of the hearths produced metalworking evidence, the former flake and spherical hammerscale indicating hot iron working, while the latter produced crucible fragments showing that copper alloys were being melted and cast. Further hearths were added, associated with compacted scorched chalk surfaces and charcoal spreads, and pit NH3806 continued in use as a fire pit. However, there was little further metalworking evidence, and the presence of animal and fish remains indicates the hearths may have been used to cook food. One charcoal spread associated with flint-tempered pottery (Fabric MAV) produced a calibrated radiocarbon date of 900–1030

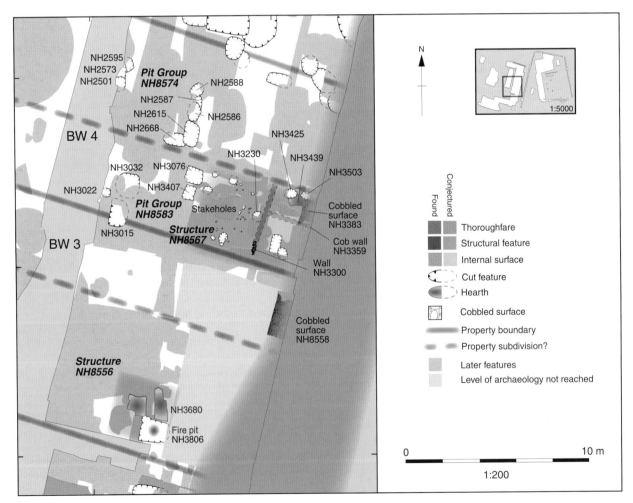

Fig. 3.18   Properties BW 3 and BW 4, Phase 4.2

Plate 3.9   Fire pit NH3806 within Structure NH8556, Property BW 3, Phase 4.2, looking east

(SUERC-13910), refined by Bayesian modelling to 890–1010. Several sherds of madder-stained pottery were found throughout these levels indicating that textile dyeing was undertaken.

Exterior Area

Phase 4.2 levels within the frontage area were reached within the small area of a modern beamslot located in the north-east corner of the property, and comprised apparent external surfaces (Group NH8558; Fig. 3.18) either pertaining to Brudene Street or to a yard/lane leading off the street (see Property BW 3 Phase 5, Chapter 4). The earliest surface exposed comprised a rather worn and uneven area of compacted chalk with traces of flint pebbles adhering overlain by greenish-brown clay silt. Further surfaces of gravel and chalk were laid and overlain by well-trampled greenish-grey silts containing domestic refuse. A large fragment of a smithing hearth bottom and iron slag was also recovered implying that metalworking was undertaken close by.

Property BW 4

Phase 4.1 structural evidence (Fig. 3.17; Plate 3.10)

Structure NH8566

To the north of Property BW 3, the excavations were more substantially affected by the truncation of late Saxon levels, as a result of the site's position on the south-eastwards sloping hillside. Within Property BW 4 evidence for the earliest structures only survived within the southern part of the excavated area. In addition, because of the effects of the underlying west-east slope, the level of the late Saxon archaeology also fell from west to east across the site. This resulted in two phases of late Saxon activity lying above impact level, and therefore being excavated, in the west, whereas on the east side only the later Saxon activity lay above impact level, and earlier deposits remained unexcavated. The exception to this was at the very eastern edge of the excavated area, where deeper excavation of beamslots allowed the recording of these underlying layers. Here, structural deposits were seen to overlie gravel metalling probably representing early surfaces of Brudene Street (Street NH8565; see section on Fig. 3.6). At the south edge of the property a modern pipe trench had destroyed all evidence for the relationship between Property BW 4 and BW 3 to the south.

The earliest evidence from Property BW 4 suggests the presence of a structure towards the street frontage (Structure NH8566), with a yard behind. The structure was represented only by surviving floor and occupation surfaces, which were clearly stratigraphically earlier than the postholes associated with the rebuild (Structure NH8567; see below). This suggests that the structure was of sill-beam construction. It extended at least 4.1 m north-south and 5.8 m east-west and encroached eastwards by at least 3 m upon the earlier street surfaces. Its earliest floor was of thin and rather worn compacted chalk (NH3723), exposed in a modern ground beam trench to the north. Towards the south the floor comprised a pink/cream 'mortar' suggesting that there was a subdivision within the structure. A charcoal-rich silt (NH3720) above the floor to the north produced flake hammerscale, but little slag, implying secondary smithing being undertaken within this part of the structure. A wide range of animal bone (cattle, pig, sheep) and fish remains (including plaice, mackerel and herring) suggests that food was also being prepared and consumed. This activity may have been associated with a fired clay hearth located towards the south (NH3576) that has been archaeomagnetically dated to 498–1148 (WOL). A subsequent chalk floor (NH3575) overlay the hearth and supported charcoal-rich silts that were presumably derived from a nearby hearth that was not seen within the excavated area. Among these, charcoal deposit NH3578 produced calibrated radiocarbon dates of 770–940 (OxA-17172) and 890–950 (SUER-C13906), reduced by Bayesian modelling to 770–900 and 890–950. The latest floor (NH3506) comprised compacted yellowish clay up to 0.1 m thick that had been extensively scorched red by intensive heating (Plate 3.10), especially at its northern extent where archaeomagnetic sampling (WOJ) produced a date of 436–1175. Although a small quantity of hammerscale was present within an associated occupation deposit (NH3504) there was no other evidence for industrial activity. The

Plate 3.10   Scorched floor NH3506 (Structure NH8566), Property BW 4, Phase 4.1, looking south (see Fig. 3.17)

hearth probably served a predominantly domestic function and this is supported by charcoal sweepings NH3494 that contained a wide variety of wood taxa including oak, hazel, hawthorn group, ash and field maple (see Challinor, Chapter 8). Also present were fish bone (mainly herring but also eel, trout and flat fish) and a small, fairly diverse animal bone assemblage. A date for this final floor and hearth in the first half of the 10th century is suggested by radiocarbon samples (OxA-17181 and SUERC -13917) that produced calibrated dates of 780–970 and 880–1020 respectively, reduced by Bayesian modelling to 910–70 and 900–70.

Structure NH8567

Structure NH8566 appears to have been re-built or remodelled using postholes rather than sills, to form Structure NH8567, which encroached slightly further eastwards over earlier metallings of Brudene Street (Street NH8565; see section Fig. 3.6). Its western side appears to have been defined originally by rectangular postholes NH3611, NH3675 and NH3436 since these coincided with a division between floor deposits to the east and a probable gravelled yard surface (NH3674) to the west. Similarly, the floor deposits did not extend north beyond postholes NH3671, NH3613, NH3625, and those pertaining to the structure during Phase 4.2 (see NH3425 and NH350; Fig. 3.18). The southern extent of the structure had been truncated by a modern service trench though it is possible that it was defined by the position of later posthole

NH3277 (see Phase 4.2 below). The structure probably measured about 4.2 m in width and extended at least 6.1 m from the street frontage. An internal posthole (NH3673) may have subdivided the structure into two roughly equal bays, as seems to have been the case in Phase 4.2, though unfortunately the floor deposits within the eastern bay lay largely below the level of excavation.

The west bay was predominantly floored with thin compacted chalk that had become heavily worn and was replaced on at least two occasions, the latter in use after 950 judging by the presence of Winchester ware pottery from occupation above it. Although there was little recovered from the floors to suggest anything other than domestic occupation, posthole NH3625 contained a significant quantity of flake and spherical hammerscale as well as many fragments of iron including plate and nails. This would strongly imply that, despite evidence to the contrary from the floors, smithing activity had taken place in the area.

Phase 1 pits

Three pits attributable to Phase 4.1 were located along the proposed boundary with Property BW 3, their alignment corresponding with the surviving southern extent of Structures NH8566 and NH8567. Two of the pits (NH3464 and NH9735) were rectangular with vertical straight sides and measured 2 m and 1.8 m in length respectively, the former at least 1.8 m in depth. A truncated pit (NH3677) located close to the western extent of Structure NH8566 but pre-dating its construction was of a similar form. Though none were bottomed they may have served as cesspits before their final use for the disposal of domestic refuse. The unweathered and vertical sides of pit NH3464 suggest either that it did not remain open for any length of time or that it was originally timber-lined or enclosed. The pit contained a considerable quantity of animal bone, largely cattle and sheep/goat but also a small quantity of fowl and horse. The pit also contained sherds of madder-stained pottery from two or three vessels suggesting dyeing was undertaken close by. Similar pottery was present in make-up deposits (NH3387) of Phase 4.2 and may have been residual from Phase 4.1.

Towards the north were two heavily truncated pits (NH2594, NH2086). Pit NH2594 contained large fragments of smithing hearth bottoms and sawn off and shaved bone-working waste in its basal fill, that may be associated with similar activity identified within Structures NH8566 and NH8567. This pit contained much animal bone including a sizeable quantity of horse bones, a meat that was not normally eaten during this period and therefore probably fed to dogs belonging to the occupants. Also present in the pit were the remains of a deer, perhaps indicative of a more refined diet. Adjacent but much truncated pit NH2086 served as a cesspit and contained cess-rich deposits for its whole depth of 1 m, including mineralised bran and much bread-type free-threshing wheat grain.

Phase 4.2 Structure NH8567 (Fig. 3.18; Plate 3.11)

Structure NH8567 (see Phase 4.1) continued in use in its previous state through Phase 4.2 as a two-bayed structure, though most of the excavated

evidence was obtained from its west bay. Postholes continued to be replaced along its north wall (NH3503, NH3425) in the same line as the Phase 4.1 structure but extended eastwards to the limit of the excavation suggesting, together with the presence of floors in this area, that the building had further encroached onto the street by this time. The position of posthole NH3230, although largely unexcavated, suggests the partition wall between the two bays was maintained. The floors within the west bay continued to be of compacted chalk, repaired or replaced on several occasions and each associated with charcoal-rich occupation silts presumably derived from a nearby hearth or oven. An approximately rectangular arrangement of stakeholes around an otherwise truncated area in the centre of the west bay may have marked the position of such a hearth. The presence of Winchester ware (Fabric MWW) from an early makeup deposit NH3384 would suggest a date after the mid 10th century. Radiocarbon dates obtained from debris associated with later floors produced calibrated dates of 890–1030 (SUERC-19284) from occupation deposit NH3260 and 770–980 (SUERC-19286) from subsequent occupation spread NH3175. Bayesian modelling has reduced the date ranges to 930–980 and 940–1000, which suggest occupation remained within the second half of the 10th century.

The earliest exposed floor level (NH3542) within the east bay comprised compacted chalk, its surface lying approximately 0.2 m below the level of the earliest floor within the west bay. This could be a reflection of the topography of the underlying Brudene Street whose surfaces occurred at a lower level than the flanking structures and perhaps prevented run-off from the street. A subsequent area of scorched clay (NH3439) located close to the north of the structure and associated with floor repairs

Plate 3.11   'Cob' partition wall NH3359 within Structure NH8567, Property BW 4, Phase 4.2, looking east

indicated the position of a hearth. Two further floors of compacted chalk (NH3376), 0.1 m thick, were subsequently laid, supported by a thick make-up of clay and gravel containing much animal bone, oyster shell and several sherds of madder-stained pottery, possibly to raise the area to the level of the west bay. At this point the east bay may have been partitioned by the addition of a partition wall (NH3359) that was constructed directly on top of floor NH3374. It was constructed with yellowish 'mortar' in a brown silty clay reminiscent of a cob wall (Plate 3.11) and measured 0.15 m in width, surviving for a height of 0.25 m above the floor. It did not extend further than 0.27 m into excavated area and delimited a surface of coarse and tightly packed flint cobbles to the north (NH3383) suggesting an external surface perhaps leading off from the street. A short stub of 'wall' (NH3300) of similar width, comprising unmortared chalk rubble, may have been contemporary and corresponded with the division between the east and west bays of the structure.

Evidence of smithing, predominantly flake hammerscale, was found throughout the sequence within the west bay suggesting that the structure continued to be used for secondary smithing. A small amount of bone-working waste was also recovered, including a possible unfinished spindle-whorl from occupation layer NH3168 suggesting a more diverse range of activities. The floors of the west bay were also rich in fish remains throughout, predominantly herring, though the remains of eel, whiting, mackerel, sea bream, garfish, trout, plaice and other flat fishes show that the occupants prepared and consumed a diverse selection of sea and freshwater fish.

Phase 4.2 pits

Two distinct groups of pits were recognised, Pit Group NH8583 located to the rear of Structure NH8567 and a larger Pit Group NH8574 that was situated to their north and possibly flanking the west side of an otherwise unseen structure. Pit Group NH8583 comprised four rectangular or square pits, all measuring 0.96–1.2 in length and 0.5–1.15 m in depth. Little was obtained from their fills to indicate their original purpose although all were seemingly rapidly backfilled with domestic refuse and redeposited natural. Pit Group NH8574 comprised eight pits of similar size and shape to Pit Group NH8583; none was deeper than 1.4 m, and most were considerably shallower. Several of the pits showed evidence of weathering deposits implying that they had remained open for an appreciable period of time though the general low density of domestic waste or other organic material contained within them seems to preclude their primary function as cess or refuse pits. Given their rectangular arrangement it is possible that they may have represented post-pits forming part of a substantial timber structure but no evidence was obtained to support this.

Property BW 5

Phase 4.1 structural evidence (Fig. 3.19)

Evidence for structures from this and later phases comprised mainly postholes and other cut features located towards the frontage area. Horizontal layers such as floors survived only within the extreme southern end of the area and within a small lower-lying area close to the north end. Given the degree of later truncation sufficient evidence survived to suggest two separate structures (NH8585 and NH8586) occupying the frontage from the outset and throughout the pre-Conquest period.

Structure NH8585

Structure NH8585 was located adjacent to the proposed boundary with Property BW 4 and comprised a small area of chalk flooring and occupation silts associated with two phases of hearths. No structural features were found, implying that it was of sill-beam construction. The earlier hearth (NH2391) was fairly large, measuring 2.05 m across, comprising fired clay set in a shallow pit. This represented the earliest occupation above the Dark Earth and was archaeo-magnetically dated to 800–1125 (WOD). Samples from the hearth also produced calibrated radio-carbon dates of 690–890 (OxA-17137) and 770–970 (SUERC-13914). Bayesian modelling has refined these dates to 840–900 and 840–950 respectively which could imply a date in the second half of the 9th century for the use of the hearth. Two nearby stakeholes (NH2427 and NH2429) appeared to be associated and perhaps represent part of structure to support a cauldron or similar cooking vessel. The structure may have been remodelled, perhaps after a period of disuse, since the hearth had become levelled with a mid-brown clay silt (NH2292) which contained a smithing hearth bottom and a horseshoe (SF Cat no. 225) datable to the 9th or 10th century. The silt levelling layer supported a compact chalk surface NH2282 representing the earliest discernible floor surface within the structure. A charcoal lens below gave calibrated radiocarbon dates of 870–980 (OxA-17179) and 880–1020 (SUERC-13915), refined by Bayesian modelling to 880–970 and 880–980 respectively. Cutting into the floor and contained within a small shallow pit was a small fired clay hearth, NH2156, that was located immediately to the north of earlier hearth NH2391. The hearth (WOA) gave an archaeomagnetic date of 580–1125 and charred plant remains from its matrix produced calibrated radiocarbon dates of 780–980 (OxA-17174) and 900–1040 (SUERC-13908), refined by Bayesian modelling to 780–980 and 900–1010 respectively. It was not clear whether the hearth was associated with this structure or its successor, Structure NH8589 (see Phase 4.2), although a date around the mid 10th century seems likely.

Structure NH8586

Overlying the possible Brudene Street surfaces (Street NH8587; see section Fig. 3.7), Structure NH8586 comprised a succession of four compacted chalk floors, each measuring 0.03–0.05 m thick, and associated occupation deposits that survived in a small area along the east side of the excavated area and adjacent to the boundary with Property BW 6. No other structural elements were present, suggesting a sill-beam construction—though their southern extent corresponded with that of later post-built Structure NH8590 (see Phase 4.2). Little was obtained from the floors to indicate the use of the structure although a sherd of madder-stained pottery recovered from occupation above the earliest floor suggests dyeing was undertaken.

Phase 4.1 pits

Given the spatial arrangement of the pits within Property BW 5, they have been grouped with either southern Structure NH8585 or northern Structure NH8586. The upper fills of some of the pits contained pottery dating after 950, suggesting that they were used over a considerable time or that they represented later accumulation over the top of the pits after their fills had settled. Where appropriate these upper fills will be discussed in Phase 4.2.

The southern group

Pit Group NH8591: A possible boundary was represented by two postholes (NH9628, NH 9571) and three narrow and elongated pits (NH9626, NH9550 and NH2700). These were aligned with the northern edge of the succeeding post-built Structure NH8589 (Phase 4.2), but they could also have been associated with the earlier Structure NH8585. Pit NH2700 was 0.8 m wide and had steep sides (75–85°) with a concave base at a depth of 0.83 m, and extended for length of at least 1.6 m. Its lower fills comprised weathered natural implying that it remained open before it was rapidly infilled. Pits NH9550 and NH9626 were of similar profile, the full length of NH9626 visible at 2.7 m, and each contained weathered deposits at their base. If the earlier postholes delineated a boundary then the pits could represent a more substantial replacement, though no evidence was forthcoming for any post-pipes. Alternatively their size suggests they could have formed part of a more substantial structure.

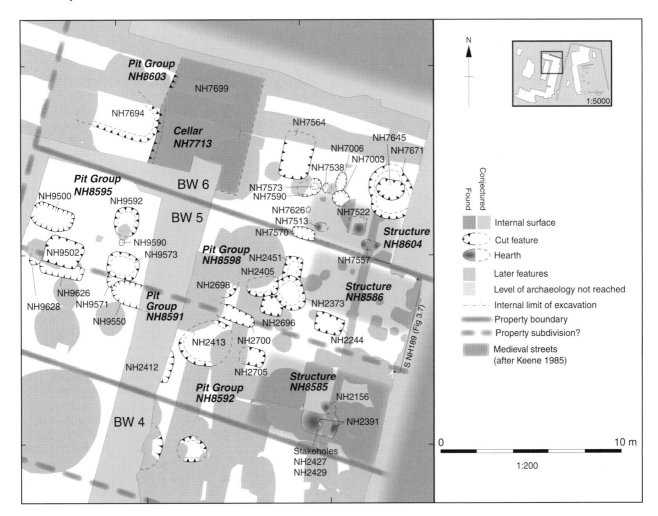

Fig. 3.19   Plan of Structures NH8585 and NH8586 (Properties BW 5 and BW 6), Phase 4.1/4

Pit Group NH8592: Three pits located immediately to the west of Structure NH8585 are considered broadly contemporary with the structure. The largest, vertical sided pit NH2413, was possibly circular and measured *c* 2.7 m across with a depth of at least 2.7 m (although it was not excavated to its base). Its vertical and unweathered sides suggest that it was originally protected by a timber lining suggesting a possible use as a well rather than cesspit since its fills did not show any marked degree of slumpage caused by the decay of underlying organic matter. However, it served finally for the disposal of domestic refuse, and contained a large amount of cattle, sheep and pig bones. Sub-rectangular pits NH2412 and NH2705 were no deeper than 1.4 m, the former containing a large animal bone assemblage similar to that within adjacent pit NH2413.

The northern group

Two discrete pit clusters were identified to the west of Structure NH8586, both of which included pits in a distinct west-east alignment parallel to Pit Group NH8591. The east group (Pit Group NH8598) comprised six pits, three of which were intercutting. The west group (Pit Group NH8595), located towards the rear of the property, were excavated rapidly; these pits did not contain closely datable finds and can only be assigned to the general late Saxon Phase 4.

Pit Group NH8598: This comprised four sub-rectangular cesspits, three of which formed an intercutting cluster (NH2451, NH2373, NH2405) with a fourth pit, NH2244, located *c* 1 m to their east, suggesting that this area had been set aside for toilet use for a considerable period. The earliest of the cluster (NH2451) measured 1.48 m by 1 m in plan and its base was revealed at depth of 2.3 m. At its base were thick deposits of cess-rich silts that contained mineralised faecal concretions of bran with numerous fly pupae, suggesting that the contents had been exposed sufficiently to allow infestation by insects. Also contained within the cess were seeds of cherry/sloe, apple and a possible imported fig, the latter suggesting that the occupants at this time enjoyed a wide variety of fruit. The presence of straw could suggest that it was used as toilet paper or to dampen smells (see Carruthers, Chapter 8). The cess also contained a significant quantity of flaked hammerscale presumably representing sweepings from a nearby hearth or floor where smithing had being undertaken. Also obtained from the pit was a possible heckle tooth from a comb used to remove the fibrous core and impurities from flax, prior to weaving into linen. Interestingly, a charred fragment of possible cultivated flax was also present in the cess. The next pit in the sequence, NH2373, was slightly larger at 1.9 m across but shallower at 2.1 m and was presumably dug after the infilling of the earlier pit, though its north edge sloped in, as if to avoid disturbing its lower fills. It also contained a sequence of cess-rich

deposits that contained rushes, possibly used as toilet paper. Pit NH2244 was similar in size to pit NH2451 and contained a thin greenish grey cessy silt at its base, at a somewhat shallower depth of 0.58 m. The pit presumably lay outside the building on the street frontage, which like its successor (Phase 4.2, Structure NH8590), lay immediately to its north.

Pit Group NH8595: Pit Group NH8595 comprised four pits, two of which abutted Pit Group NH8591 to the south; the other two, located immediately to their north, were therefore presumably dug subsequently. The rectangular pits closest to the boundary (NH9502 and NH9573) measured 2 m and 1.75 m in length respectively and were not bottomed at 1.8 and 1.6 m, though both were probably used as cesspits as there were green cessy silts adhering to their sides. Pit NH9500 was of similar size but shallower, with its base at 1.34 m. It contained no cess and had been rapidly filled with dumps of homogeneous dark soil containing refuse and an appreciable quantity of iron slag. The fourth pit (NH9592), potentially the latest, was sub-circular and contained cessy fills at its excavated depth of 1.6 m.

Phase 4.2 structural evidence (Fig. 3.20; Plate 3.12)

The frontage continued to be occupied by two separate structures, Structures NH8589 and NH8590, replacing Phase 4.1 Structures NH8585 and NH8586 respectively. No *in situ* horizontal deposits had survived later levelling, though a sequence of probable occupation deposits were found slumped into earlier cesspits close to their western sides. These often contained pottery significantly later than the underlying pit fills, and are discussed with the associated structure groups below.

Structure NH8589

Structure NH8589 was defined by a rectangular arrangement of small oval pits that may have supported timber uprights for a substantial timber structure measuring *c* 6.1 m in width and extending from the frontage for a length of at least 7 m. The north side corresponded to the line of Pit Group NH8591 and the south side to the extent of the floors of earlier Structure NH8585. The structure extended over cesspit NH2076 (see pits below) implying that the earlier structure did not extend this far north. The pits were of similar size, all measuring between 0.8–1.2 m across and most were between 0.35–0.45 m in depth, containing single fills of firm dark grey-brown silty clay. No evidence for post-pipes was found, suggesting that the posts had been removed after the dismantling of the structure before the pits were deliberately infilled. Several of the posts had been replaced on at least one occasion, possibly resulting in the narrowing of the structure, suggesting that it had stood for a significant period of time. The remains of floor and occupation surfaces were found slumped over possible Roman pit NH2497, located partially under the west side of the structure, but extended westwards beyond it. A thick sequence of alternating deposits (Group NH2322, Plate 3.12) comprising at least nine compacted chalk surfaces and overlying occupation deposits may represent interior floors that have otherwise been truncated. It is possible that they were floors that formed part of an otherwise undefined west bay of the structure or perhaps they were levelling for an external area around an entrance way. The latter view would seem to be reinforced by soil micromorphology that suggests that these layers were deposited under wet conditions and represent 'domestic space waste disposal of floor and hearth debris, cereal pollen of probable cess origin, where grass pollen likely from floor coverings' (see McPhail and Crowther, Chapter 8, thin section NHM187B).

Structure NH8590

Approximately 1 m north of Structure NH8589 was a second cluster of postholes that formed no coherent plan though an approximately rectangular arrangement could be suggested. The postholes were smaller than the adjacent structure, mainly oval in shape and mostly measuring 0.32–0.56 m across. It is possible that they represent a later phase of Structure NH8586 (see above) since the eastern postholes cut its latest surviving floor. Several showed evidence for post-pipes, one with a diameter of *c* 0.15 m, implying a fairly insubstantial structure.

Phase 4.2 pits

Pit NH2076 was located within the east end of Structure NH8589 but apparently pre-dated its construction since it was cut by a posthole of the north wall. If so, it could have been contemporary with its predecessor Structure NH8585 (see above), which may not actually have extended this far north. The pit was sub-circular measuring *c* 1.9 m across and was excavated to a depth of 1.3 m, which revealed soft greenish brown sandy silt suggesting the pit had been used to dispose of cess. Two of the Phase 4.1 cesspits, located immediately behind Structure NH8590, were apparently re-cut and re-used. Pit NH2451 was emptied of its contents to a depth of 1 m and its base lined with crushed chalk to form pit NH2520. A thin layer of charcoal and hearth debris overlay the crushed chalk lining, possibly to neutralise the odour of the cessy silt that subsequently overlay it. The pit was sealed by a further dump of crushed chalk, and was then used for the disposal of domestic refuse including a sherd of madder-stained pottery. Adjacent pit NH2405 was similarly emptied to depth of 0.9 m to form a new cesspit, pit NH2531. It too was finally sealed by laminated chalk and charcoal before being rapidly infilled.

A very large pit centrally located within Property BW 5, pit NH2237, which measured 4.4 m across, may have served as a well, though no evidence was

Plate 3.12   Floor group NH2322 (Structure NH8589) slumped into earlier pit NH2497, Property BW 5, Phase 4.2, looking south

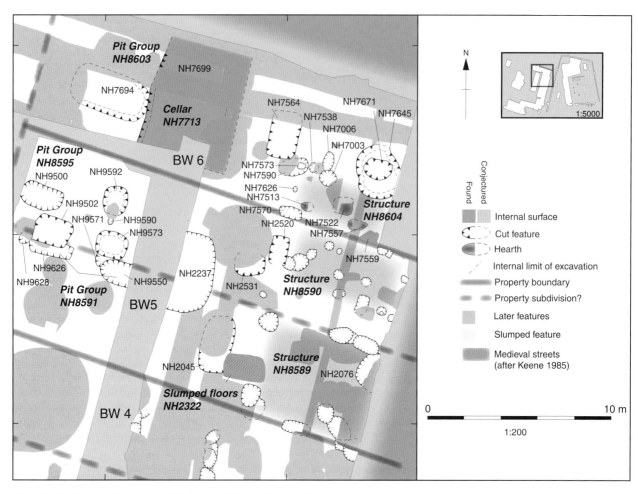

Fig. 3.20   Plan of Properties BW 5 and BW 6, Phase 4.2/4

found for a lining at its excavated depth of 2 m. Its location immediately adjacent to later well NH2495 (see Phase 5) could imply that it was replaced by the more elaborate chalk-lined, post-Conquest, example. The presence of sandy flint-tempered pottery (fabric MAQ; dated *c* 1000–1250) and a riveted bone mount datable to the mid 10th to late 11th centuries (SF Cat no. 322) suggest an 11th-century century date, and the upper fills contained post-Conquest pottery (see Phase 5). Whatever its purpose it was eventually rapidly filled with domestic refuse including considerable quantities of animal bone that predominantly comprised cattle, with lesser amounts of sheep/goat, pig and occasional fowl. Fish remains were mostly of herring, with occasional salmon, scad and flat fishes. Sherds of Winchester ware within the lower excavated fills may suggest the inhabitants had access to more refined tableware (see Chapter 7, Fig. 7.16, no. 131 and Fig. 7.17, no. 134). Flake hammer-scale from ash dumps, presumably sweepings from nearby hearths/floors, indicate that secondary smithing was undertaken close by. Indeed nearby Phase 4.1 pit NH2373, that may have been levelled around this time, contained large fragments of smithing hearth bottoms.

Property BW 6

Phase 4 Structure NH8604 (Fig. 3.20)

Later truncation had effectively removed all horizontal stratigraphy down to the surface of the Dark Earth and the only surviving evidence for structures along the frontage comprised several hearths, a scatter of small pits and a remnant of possible floor and occupation deposits. Two hearths (NH7513 and NH7522) comprised irregular areas of burnt clay that apparently directly overlay the Dark Earth, archaeomagnetically dated to 498–1125 (WOI2) and 559–1084 (WOI1) respectively. Given their stratigraphic position, they are the earliest surviving evidence for structural activity within the property, though closer dating was not possible. A third hearth (NH7557=7559) was contained in a shallow oval pit, measuring 1 m across, that had been lined with burnt clay after a thin layer of ash had been deposited within it. The ash was rich in flake hammerscale implying that secondary smithing was undertaken close by and perhaps derived from sweepings from a floor associated with the structure. A thin patchy spread of charcoal (NH7589) located immediately adjacent to the hearth also contained a significant quantity of flake hammerscale suggesting some degree of contemporaneity. However, this deposit also included spherical hammerscale suggesting that hot working was also undertaken, feasibly associated with one or more of the hearths.

The southern extent of charcoal spread NH7589 was sharply delimited and perhaps corresponded to the edge of a sill beam that defined the extent of the structure. This aligned with flat-bottomed pit NH7570 which, at its shallow depth of 0.17 m, may have represented an otherwise truncated beam-slot; pit NH7570 also corresponds to the northern extent of Property BW 5. Two postholes (NH7626 and NH7573) were aligned at right angles to its north, perhaps representing the line of its west wall. The lack of further postholes to the north could suggest that posthole NH7573 and posthole NH7538, located a short distance to its east, represent the line of the north wall.

Phase 4 pits

Most of the associated pits were subject to only limited investigation. Pits NH7645/7671 were located towards the street frontage and possibly respected the northern extent of the structure. Only the upper 0.5 m of their fills were investigated and these comprised dumps of compacted chalk, redeposited natural, charcoal and Roman building rubble that probably represented consolidation after their final use, especially if the structure had later extended over them. Madder-stained pottery and antler waste offer evidence for dyeing and bone/antler working, material that could have been dumped from the adjacent structure. Rectangular pit NH7564, though essentially unexcavated, is similar to contemporary pits elsewhere on the site and given its location, immediately to the rear of the structure, could have served as a cesspit. Pit NH7694, located towards the west of the property, contained brownish organic fills that produced domestic refuse and presumably was dug as a cess or rubbish pit.

Rectangular pit NH7713/NH7699 must have served a different function, possibly a cellar, on account of its large size. It measured at least 4.9 m across (north-south) but could not have extended beyond the boundary with Property BW 5 since it was absent from the area to the north of pits NH2337 and NH9592. Similarly, it measured at least 4.6 m east-west. The pit is assumed to have been of considerable depth since its fills (as exposed along sides of two modern service trenches) were sharply inclined to almost vertical throughout its length, and had been tipped from its western edge. Where observed the edges of the pit were sharp and vertical implying that they had been protected from the elements by a lining. A small sondage that was excavated close to its east edge revealed burnt 'timber plates' (NH7665) that survived as charcoal, offering evidence for

surviving *in situ* timber lining. Whatever its function, its fills, which included compacted chalk and redeposited natural gravel, were suggestive of rapid infilling and consolidation.

SNITHELING STREET

Property SE 1 (Fig. 3.21)

The evidence for occupation within Property SE 1, especially during Phase 4.1, was comparatively slight. This could result from truncation of late Saxon levels across the area, as here the post-medieval garden soils generally directly overlay the Dark Earth. The only features that were recognised were those cut into the Dark Earth. However, there seemed to be a lower density of pitting here than elsewhere. Two pit clusters were determinable, separated by large areas of apparent open space where no evidence for other activity survived. It is possible that these areas were occupied by structures whose flimsy construction (eg sill-beam) left no trace in the archaeological record. A case in point is the area between the 'linear' arrangement of Pit Group NH8619 situated to the west and Pit Group NH8611 located *c* 6 m to the east. The area between was free of pitting, a situation that continued into the post-Conquest period.

Phase 4.1 pits

The few features that could be tentatively attributed to this phase comprised rather truncated and poorly dated small shallow pits of uncertain function, forming the earliest features within Pit Group NH8611 (see Phase 4.2 below) together with isolated pit NH8064. Those within Pit Group NH8611 appeared to form a north-south alignment (NH5191, NH5089 and posthole NH5200) suggesting that they may have delimited a division or boundary. Only isolated pit NH8064, located to the south-east, was of note. Given its location, it may have belonged to an adjacent property to the south of Property SE 1, the boundary of which became more evident during Phase 5. Pit NH8064 is similar to the early rectangular cesspits found elsewhere on the site. It measured at least 0.84 m across and had soft organic fills to its excavated depth that contained much domestic waste. The presence of late Saxon sandy ware (Fabric MSH) within its fills would suggest a date no later than the mid 10th century. Several of the pottery sherds were stained with madder implying that dyeing of cloth was undertaken at this time

Phase 4.2 pits

Pit Group NH8619 comprised three small rectangular cesspits (NH6158, NH6231 and NH6138) measuring 1.6–2 m in length and 1.1–1.4 m in width. All the pits had straight vertical sides that showed little evidence for weathering; two were 2

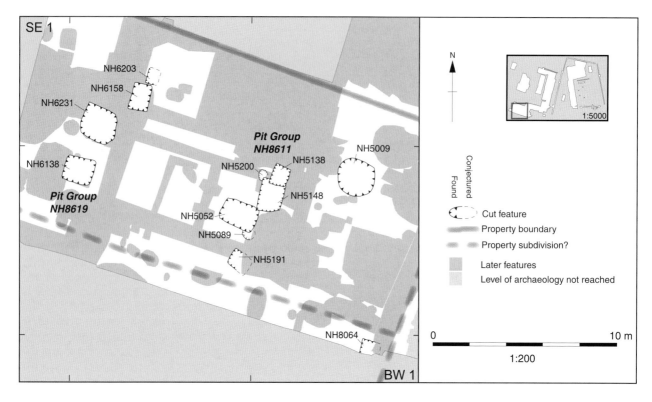

Fig. 3.21   Plan of Property SE 1, Phase 4.2

m deep and the third (NH6158) was somewhat shallower at 1.1 m. All contained dark brown organic silts at their base, and the two deeper pits were rich in mineralised remains including faecal bran and fly pupae and remains of apple, pear, sloe/cherry, Celtic bean, peas and other legumes. These pits also produced evidence for more luxurious, imported foodstuffs and spice, including a possible peach stone from pit NH6231 and a fennel mericarp from pit NH6138 suggesting the occupants enjoyed a more refined diet, indicative of higher status. The fennel may have served a medicinal use since the pit also contained a significant quantity of opium poppy seeds, used to relieve pain, though both could also have been used to flavour food. Shallower pit NH6158 showed evidence for a timber lining since it contained a narrow slot 0.075 m deep around the edges of its base, possibly to support timber planks that were presumably held by horizontal bracing. Whatever the original function of the pit, the timbers were removed before the pit was used to dispose of cess and rubbish that included a considerable quantity of madder-stained pottery. Several different vessels were represented, and further madder-stained sherds were present in pit NH6138, implying that dyeing formed a important aspect of the lives of the occupants of the property. The presence of a cultivated flax seed within pit NH6158 suggests that linen may have been manufactured on site prior to dyeing, though flax seeds are also known for their laxative properties. Some operations required heating or boiling and portable earthenware vessels such as cooking pots could have been used for this.

Pit Group NH8611 similarly comprised three small rectangular pits (NH5138, NH5148 and NH5052). The deepest, vertical-sided pit NH5052, measured 1.82 m by 1.17 m in plan but was excavated only to a depth of 1.55 m. It had been rapidly infilled with domestic refuse that included lenses of cessy silts and given its similarity to the pits to the west may have also served as a cesspit. The pit contained a broken horseshoe of 10th- to 11th-century date, hammerscale and sherds of madder-stained pottery, the latter possibly derived from the same activity as found in timber-lined pit NH6158 to the west. Pit NH5148 and NH5138 were of similar size but only 1 m and 1.1 m deep respectively. Both contained a single homogeneous fill of dark loamy soil that contained domestic refuse.

Circular pit NH5009 located to the east could not have functioned as a well given its depth of 1.1 m, but it had evidently remained open long enough for a thin weathering deposit to accumulate above its base. As with pits in Pit Group NH8611 it was thereafter rapidly infilled with dark loamy soil and dumps of domestic refuse that included a considerable quantity of oyster shells. The basal fill of the pit contained fresh sherds of chalk-tempered ware implying a pre-Conquest date, though the presence of flinty (fabric MAB; dated *c* 1000–1250) and sandy wares (fabric MAQ; dated 1000–1250) in the backfill could imply an 11th-century date, the latter having a fine sandy fabric similar to post-Conquest fabric MBK.

114

Property SE 2 (Fig. 3.22; Plates 3.13–14)

Phase 4.2 structural evidence

Early activity

Hearth NH1277 represented the earliest evidence for occupation and was located towards the north of the property. It comprised a small oval pit measuring 0.83 m across and 0.14 m deep, lined with clay scorched red through intense heat. No associated surfaces were found suggesting that it may have represented a sporadic external activity, perhaps relating to metalworking since a small amount of iron slag was found in its backfill. A rough surface (Yard NH1161) comprising coarse flint nodules and large fragments of Roman tile that partially overlay the disused hearth may have represented a working surface relating to the same activity. A clean yellowish brown silty clay (NH1154) subsequently accumulated over much of the area, indicative of a period of inactivity and perhaps represented a developed turf line.

Structure NH8624 (Plate 3.13)

The earliest clear evidence for structures was found towards the west of the excavated area, presumed to be closer to the frontage of Snitheling Street. All that survived later levelling was a thin and patchy floor of compacted chalk that overlay the possible turf horizon NH1154 (Plate 3.13). The southern extent was fairly sharply defined and, to a lesser degree, its eastern and north limits, though later truncation had probably removed all traces of the floor near to the western edge of the excavation. The surviving areas of floor suggest a structure that measured at least 2 m across (north-south) by at least 1.9 m east-west. The lack of structural features would suggest that it was constructed on earth-fast sills that had left no evidence in the archaeological record. A patch of burnt clay (NH1151) located against the proposed north wall of the structure probably represented the remains of a hearth, but nothing else was found to indicate the function of the structure.

Structure NH8642

Further fragmentary structural evidence was found some 3 m to the south of Structure NH8624, possibly occupying a property to the south. A north-south 'linear' pad of re-used Roman flat tiles (NH1211), laid flat onto the surface of the Dark Earth, may have acted as a foundation pad or baseplate for a sill. No contemporary levels survived to its west, though abutting its east side was a mid yellowish brown silt (NH1204). This may have represented an exterior accumulation and contained pottery (fabric MAQ) probably attributable to the 11th century. This was overlain by a thin and patchy gravelly clay (NH1170) that may have represented a rudimentary, possibly external surface. Finally, a 0.12 m thick accumulation of grey-brown silt clay (NH1169) developed over the surface, abutting the possible foundation pad NH1211, suggesting the structure was still standing.

Plate 3.13   Chalk floor of Structure NH8624, Property SE 2, Phase 4.2, looking north

Fragments of oven wall including a wedge-shaped piece of oven furniture, possibly a prop, suggest domestic activity; otherwise no other evidence was found. These levels were cut by post-pit NH1136 that defined the south wall of Structure NH8622 but sealed posthole NH1247 that corresponded to the northern extent of pad NH1211. Since this posthole apparently coincided with the northern extent of the Structure NH8642 and the southern extent of later Structure NH8622, it may have represented part of a boundary. The position of Phase 5 pit NH1005 (see Chapter 4) against the southern side of this proposed boundary would offer further evidence for this.

Structure NH8622 (Plate 3.14)

Cutting into the surviving deposits of Structures NH8624 and NH8642 was a rectangular arrangement of small pits, some with impressions of large posts at their bases, which formed a substantial timber structure. This could have been part of a building fronting onto Snitheling Street to the west. The north wall is represented by pits NH1156, NH1119 and NH1087, and the south wall by pits NH1223, NH1201 and NH1136. The structure may have extended further eastwards since pit NH1149, located 4.8 m to the east, was similar in character. The structure formed by the main group of postpits was square within the excavated area and measured

Plate 3.14   Post-pit NH1117 (Structure NH8622), Property SE 2, Phase 4.2, looking east

c 5.1 m in width (from the centre of the posts). If this formed part of a building with a gable end fronting onto Snitheling Street it could have measured 10.2 m in length. The configuration of the posts was not entirely symmetrical or fully understood, although the following arrangement can be suggested. The north-east and south-east corners were represented by pairs of posts (NH1119/NH1087 and NH1136), the post-impressions set 1.2–1.3 m apart, the latter contained within a single post-pit. The posts within the northern wall, judging by the evidence of the post impressions at the base of the pits, were round with diameters measuring between 0.4–0.5 m. Here the posts were each set in the northern end of elongated oval pits measuring 1.5–2 m in length and up to 0.9 m wide with their depths varying from 0.83 to 1.39 m. All three post-pits of the north wall had concentrations of large flint nodules at their north end, presumably as packing around the posts, though there was no evidence for post-pipes, suggesting that the posts had been deliberately removed. The gradient of the southern side of each pit was shallower than the other sides, perhaps to assist with easing the heavy post into the pit. The posts of the south wall, apart from the south-east corner, did not correspond symmetrically with their counterparts on the north wall and were set in smaller and shallower pits, although the surviving evidence suggests they held posts of a similar size.

There were three similar pits contained internally within the rectangular arrangement (NH1117, NH1212 and NH1082) whose function is difficult to ascertain, though given their size they presumably had a load-bearing function, perhaps to support a staircase at the east end of the structure (Plate 3.14). Later levelling had removed all evidence for floors apart from a spread of compact chalk that overlay post-pit NH1156 and patchy brown clay that similarly overlay post-pit NH1119, both of which abutted the position of their respective post-pipes.

Dating for the construction of the structure is problematic given that the fills of the post-pits probably date from its dismantling. Only a single sherd of coarse grained sandy pottery could be dated to after the Conquest; otherwise the presence of Winchester ware and other late Saxon wheel-thrown sandy wares suggests a mid 10th- to mid 11th-century date. It is notable that one post-pit (NH1156) contained a fragment of worked Quarr stone, possibly a wall fragment, a stone which was used quite extensively in ecclesiastical building in Anglo-Norman Winchester, including the cathedral, but becomes rare after the later 12th century as the quarry on the Isle of Wight was worked out.

Phase 4.2 pits

Pit Group NH8533 comprised four pits that were clustered within the footprint of Structure NH8622. Pit NH1152 was probably rectangular and 0.99 m deep, and was cut by post-pit NH1156 and therefore

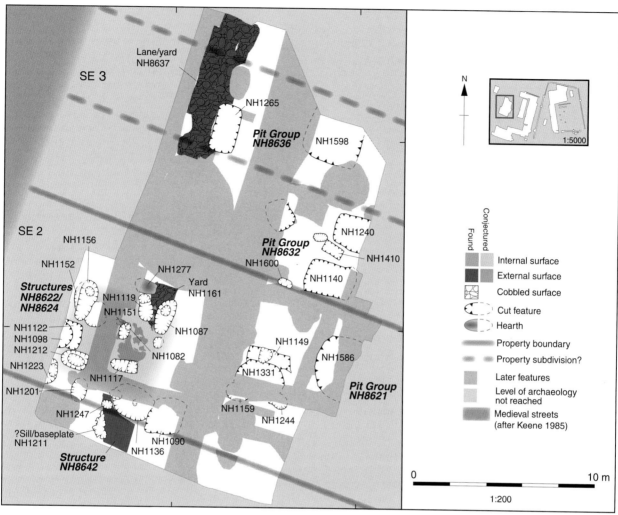

Fig. 3.22   Properties SE 2 and SE 3, Phase 4.2/4

pre-dated the construction of Structure NH8622. It had been rapidly infilled with brown clay and soil containing chalk-tempered ware (Fabric MBX) with flint tempered ware (Fabric MAV) implying a date after the mid 10th century. Intercutting pits NH1098 and NH1122 may also be contemporary; the earlier pit (NH1122) was circular, measuring 1.5 m in diameter and 0.78 m in depth. It appears to have been left open for a sufficient period of time to allow for a thick accumulation of weathered material on its base. Nothing was contained within the pits to indicate their function though the presence of a madder-stained pottery sherd in pit NH1152 would suggest dyeing was undertaken in the vicinity.

Five pits (Pit Group NH8621) located to the east of Structure NH8624 are likely to have been contemporary with its use or its successor, Structure NH8622. Four of the pits (NH1586, NH1331, NH1159 and NH1244) were cut by the footings of the chapel excavated here by Barry Cunliffe in 1960 (see Phase 5) and pit NH1586 was partially investigated during those excavations (Cunliffe 1964, fig. 58, Pit M6), though details and its finds were not published. It was probably circular, measuring c 3 m across, and had been rapidly infilled with thick alternating

deposits of compacted clay and dark soil to its excavated depth of 0.95 m. Its use as a well cannot be precluded, and if so, the dating evidence suggests that it had gone out of use prior to the Conquest since one fill (NH1589) contained a large part of a spouted pitcher in a chalk and flint fabric that had a simple undeveloped rim type, indicative of a mid 10th- to mid 11th-century date. Adjacent pit NH1331 was circular and of a similar diameter to pit NH1586 and excavated to a depth of 0.93 m. The nature of its earliest fills suggests that it had been left open to allow significant erosion of its sides before being rapidly filled with dumps of redeposited natural and dark soil, fills similar to those found within pit NH1586. The pit contained domestic refuse including chalk-tempered ware and late Saxon sandy wares (Fabrics MBX and MSH) implying a date prior to 950, though the presence of small sherds of flintier MAV ware could also imply a later date. Two further pits located immediately to its south had been largely removed by the footings of the chapel though shallow pit NH1159 contained a greenish fill suggesting it had been used to depose of cess. The fifth pit NH1090 apparently clipped the eastern edge of post-pit NH1136 that formed part of Structure

NH8622 and seemingly post-dated its construction. It was probably circular measuring in excess of 1.68 m in diameter and excavated to a depth of 1.12 m. Its earliest excavated fill comprised compact chalk rubble, possibly deposited to cap the pit, followed by a succession of slumped deposits that were probably laid for consolidation. Evidence from the earliest of these consolidation layers suggests a pre-conquest date but included coarse grained sandy ware (Fabric MAQ) which is datable to *c* 1000–1250.

Post-pit NH1149 cut pit NH1331. The function of this post-pit is unclear. It was similar to the post-pits and postholes that formed Structure NH8622 but there is no further evidence to suggest whether it was associated with Structure NH8622 or not. It is possible that it was associated with the construction of the medieval chapel (see Chapter 4).

Property SE 3 (Fig. 3.22)

Phase 4 boundary evidence

The earliest surviving evidence for the boundary between Property SE 3 and Property SE 2 to the south is probably posthole NH1600. It corresponded to the southern extent of Pit Group NH8632 and also to the northern extent of the medieval chapel. During Phase 5 (Chapter 4) a short row of postholes/small pits (Phase 5 Pit Group NH8631) probably demarcated a property subdivision on the line proposed here, although it is not certain if the property was subdivided in this way during Phase 4. However, the later post-row does appear to correspond to the northern extent of Pit Group NH8632. The distance between the two lines of postholes measured *c* 5.5 yards or 1 perch, corresponding to the general width of properties seen elsewhere. Any evidence for structures to the west would have been removed by a large quarry pit NH1034 (Phase 5, Chapter 4) and by later levelling to its north.

Phase 4 pits

Pit Group NH8632

Three vertical-sided rectangular pits were excavated in a row towards the east of the area. The southernmost pit (NH1140) was cut by the footings of the medieval chapel and measured 2 m by at least 1.8 m and was excavated to depth of 1 m. Its northeast corner was cut by a feature that can be equated with pit M5 from the 1960 excavations (Cunliffe 1964, fig 58). The pit contained thick and fairly compact gravel-rich clayey soils suggestive of rapid infilling and consolidation, the soil perhaps derived from the cutting of the adjacent pit NH1240. This was probably undertaken after the mid 10th century since a lamp-bowl in flinty fabric MAV was recovered from one fill. The fills contained a large fragment of smithing hearth bottom and fragments of furnace lining with thickly vitrified surfaces indicative of intense heat. The presence of iron slag including fragments with fayalitic runs would suggest that both smelting and smithing were undertaken probably from a workshop nearby on the property, presumably located to the west. Adjacent pit NH1240 was of similar dimensions and was excavated to a depth of 0.95 m. Its lowest excavated fills probably date to the pre-Conquest period and comprised soft dark brown sticky clays rich in domestic refuse including animal bone and oyster shells. In contrast its upper fills were compact and gravel-rich representing final filling and consolidation and possibly date to the 11th or 12th century (see Phase 5).

Small rectangular pit NH1410 was 'sandwiched' between pits NH1140 and NH1240, its positioning suggesting that it may postdate both. The pit was straight-sided, measured 0.95 by 0.5 m and 0.55 m deep, and may have served a structural purpose given that its upper fills contained large flint and chalk nodules, perhaps packing around a post that had subsequently been removed.

Pit group NH8636

Two rectangular pits were located to the north of postulated boundary with Property SE 3. The earlier (NH1265) measured 2.6 by 1.3 m and was positioned flush against the line of the boundary, apparently respecting the eastern edge of a possible lane/yard NH8637 (see below). It was filled with mid grey-brown silty clay to its excavated level of 0.53 m and contained domestic rubbish including cattle, sheep/goat and pig bones. A small quantity of iron slag suggests nearby metalworking. The second pit (NH1598) was comparable in size and form to the large squarish pits to the south (Pit Group NH8632) though its excavated fills contained pottery suggesting a post-Conquest date for its filling (see Phase 5). The pit was hand-excavated to a depth of 1.55 m and thereafter by machine, which revealed its total depth to be 4.55 m, a depth considered too shallow for the pit to have served as a well. The basal fill of the pit comprised thin sticky mid-dark grey silty clay, a sample of which was retrieved from the machine bucket for analysis. This contained a small quantity of largely indeterminate charred cereal grains and several fragments of hazelnut shells, but lacked any evidence for mineralised remains. Also present was a quantity of flake and spherical hammerscale that presumably originated from the sweepings of nearby smithing. Above were deposits of re-deposited natural gravel perhaps derived from weathering of the open pit. The subsequent fills comprised greenish organic silts, representing its use for the disposal of cess. This also contained a significant amount of hammerscale and a quantity of waste derived from bone-working suggesting a variety of trades were undertaken on the property. The cessy fills were subsequently capped by a thick deposit of clay before its subsequent use as a rubbish pit (see Chapter 4).

Phase 4 Yard or Lane NH8637

A strip alongside the western part of the property appears to have been open throughout the late Saxon period and also remained devoid of pits throughout the medieval period. A thin sequence of deposits survived to suggest the area may have been used to provide access, possibly forming part of a lane leading from the north. Curiously the late Roman Dark Earth, extant elsewhere (if not previously removed by modern levelling) was absent and late Saxon levels resided directly upon the truncated and thin remains of the early Roman subsoil, suggesting that the prevailing east-west slope had been terraced to provide a level platform. The earliest level comprised an extensive thin and clean dark brown silty clay (NH1356) sealing two small and very shallow pits that contained a small quantity of late Saxon chalk-tempered pottery. A metalled surface (NH1327) comprising closely packed small rounded pebbles (20–50 mm in diameter) was laid and abutted the western extent of silty clay NH1356. It was aligned approximately SW-NE and measured a maximum 1.6 m in width, extending for a distance of least 7.6 m cross the full width of the property. The surface was compact and well worn and showed evidence of repair with larger and more angular flints. A patchy and thin dark brown silty clay (NH1302) that contained animal bone and iron slag fragments was allowed to develop over the surface, before a second surface of gravel and coarse flints was laid (NH1289), which extended further west than the earlier surface, itself allowed to become very worn. Further patchy repairs comprising gravel and coarse flints followed, though much of this evidence may have been removed by modern truncation. A large fragment of smithing hearth bottom was recovered from repair NH1259, apparently utilised as part of the metalling but perhaps originally derived from ?contemporary smithing activity identified within Property SE 3 (see Pit Group NH8632).

The need for a lane here is somewhat puzzling given that Keene (1985, figs 72–4) places Snitheling Street some 7 m to the west at this point. If it led from the north arm of this street, which Keene suggests lies *c* 40 m to the north of the excavated area, then this would have bisected several properties. It is unlikely that it represented an early alignment of the street itself since no trace of it was found within Property SE 1 and indeed it may not have extended into the adjacent property, this area having been destroyed by the excavation of large Anglo-Norman pit NH1034. It seems that the most likely explanation is that it represented a 'private' lane leading from a point from the western arm of Snitheling Street to access the area behind structures that occupied the area to its east.

Chapter 4
The Anglo-Norman and later medieval period
(c 1050–1550)

by Steve Teague with Alan Hardy

INTRODUCTION

Contexts allocated to the medieval period have been subdivided into two broad phases:

Phase 5 c 1050–1225

Phase 6 c 1225–1550

The contexts were phased in accordance with their stratigraphic position and in conjunction with the fabric analysis of the pottery (see Cotter, Chapter 7), and to a much lesser extent with other associated datable objects such as glazed tiles and small finds. Surprisingly, closely datable objects such as medieval coins and tokens were completely absent from the assemblage. Two hearths and an oven were archaeomagnetically dated and charcoal spreads with three associated contexts were also radiocarbon dated. As indicated in Chapter 3 the difficulties in closely dating many of the Saxo-Norman pottery fabrics on the cusp of the Conquest is a common feature on many sites in Winchester and elsewhere in other contemporary urban centres (eg Southampton, Brown 2002), especially since many of the coarse late Saxon wares (that form the bulk of assemblages) are known to have been used well into the post-Conquest period. This is compounded by the high degree of residuality of late Saxon pottery (and other contemporary finds; see Cool, Chapter 7) that has undoubtedly occurred, particularly in the areas of dense pitting, a problem compounded higher up in the stratigraphic sequence. The increasing diversity of fabrics is a feature of the later stratigraphic sequences, which include the introduction of coarse grained sandy ware (eg fabric MAQ), probably during the 11th century. However, those contexts lacking the more diagnostic Anglo-Norman fabrics such as the scratch-marked sandy wares (Fabric MBK and MOE), Newbury-type ware (MTE) and the glazed Tripod pitchers (MAD), have been, with due regard to their stratigraphic position, allocated to the late Saxon Phase 4.2. The introduction of early South Hampshire red ware (MNG) that occurs towards the end of the Anglo-Norman sequence allowed for some contexts to be dated to the late 12th–early 13th century, though its rather patchy occurrence did not allow the allocation of a separate sub-phase.

The situation is clearer regarding the high medieval period (Phase 6) where there is better understanding of the dating and chronology of the more abundant glazed pottery. However the unglazed sandy ware (MDF), which occurs throughout the late 11th to mid 14th centuries, presented the same problems as in Phase 5 and phasing was achieved in a similar manner to the methodology described for that phase. Though not all the later medieval pottery was analysed in detail it is abundantly clear that there was a sharp decline in activity on the site by the 15th century (and probably by the early or mid 14th century) attesting to the depopulation of the area that is known to have occurred (Keene 1985). Indeed the site produced only a single sherd of pottery that could be attributable to the 15th century (late medieval red ware MGR). Similarly there were only nine sherds (from three contexts) that were attributable to a date after the mid 14th century, and all were from the top fills of deep pits and a well of medieval date.

As for the late Saxon period, the results are described here in relation to the contemporary street layout and property divisions that were established on the basis of archaeological and limited documentary evidence. The evidence for these is described at the beginning of Chapter 3. As before, the description for Phase 5 features begins on the east side of Brudene Street (Properties BE 1–5), followed by the west side of Brudene Street (Properties BW 1–6) and the east side of Snitheling Street (Properties SE 1–3). The same sequence is followed for Phase 6, although by this time properties on the west side of Brudene Street and on the east side of Snitheling Street appear to have been amalgamated and are described together where appropriate.

Calibrated archaeomagnetic and radiocarbon dates are quoted at the 95% confidence level.

THE ANGLO-NORMAN PERIOD (PHASE 5)

A general plan of all features of in Phase 5 (c 1050–1225) is shown on Figure 4.1.

N

Cellar?

Well

Well

BE 5

BE 4

BE 3

BE 2

BE 1

Well

Brudene Street

BW 6

BW 5

Well

Wells?

BW 4

BW 3

BW 2

Well

BW 1

Well

Wellhouse

Chapel

Quarry pit?

House

SE 3

SE 2

Snitheling Street

SE 1

Well

Structural feature
Internal surface
External surface
Slumped deposit
Medieval streets (after Keene 1985)
Property boundary
Property subdivision?
Later features
Level of archaeology not reached

F C

0   20 m

1:500

Fig. 4.1   Plan of all features, Phase 5

122

BRUDENE STREET EAST

Property BE 1 (Fig. 4.2; Plate 4.1)

Structural Group CC7057

Slumping into Phase 4 cesspit CC1100 was a succession of floor-like deposits and structural features that had survived later truncation. Given that they were *c* 19 m from the street, they presumably formed part of a structure that was set back from the frontage. The earliest comprised thick compacted chalk that represented an attempt to form a secure base for the overlying floor of thin light orangey brown 'mortar'. Small circular posthole CC1253 (0.15 m in diameter and 0.16 m deep) was associated with the floor and conceivably could have formed an early structural element of the building since it was sealed by subsequent floors of similar mortar or compacted clay. Late in the sequence the posthole was replaced by more substantial square installation (CC1220) measuring 0.6 m across and 0.74 m deep possibly to provide more substantial support for the structure over the underlying soft ground. Little was found to indicate the use of the structure though an exceptional assemblage of seafood shell including 372 periwinkles, 27 mussel and 13 oyster shells was recovered from an occupation deposit/

dump in the upper part of the sequence (CC1096; see Campbell, Chapter 8). This deposit also produced 3 fiddle key nails (SF Cat no. 236) that were used for horseshoes from the 11th to the 13th centuries and could indicate a use of the structure as a stable or that such a structure was located nearby.

Pits

The density of pitting was significantly lower than in the preceding period and was confined to the east of the excavated area implying that the area to the west was used for other purposes such as structures (see above). Two groups of pits were apparent, located towards the north and south sides of the property, possibly reflecting the proposed subdivision that may have occurred during Phase 4 (see Chapter 3).

Pit Group CC7055 comprised three small circular pits that measured 0.8–1.2 m in diameter, and 0.25–0.63 m in depth. The deepest pit (CC1147) contained a thin deposit of a green-stained silt at its base, before being rapidly infilled, suggesting it had been used as a cesspit, possibly serving the inhabitants of Structure CC7057 that stood immediately to its west.

Chalk-lined well CC1128 (Plate 4.1) was located to the south of the property and possibly adjacent to

Plate 4.1   Well CC1128, Property BE 1, Phase 5, looking north

its boundary. The lining was set off-centre within a large sub-square pit possibly allowing for a working area to the west. Alternatively the pit may have represented a timber-lined predecessor to the well, but this could not be established at the depth excavated. If the well originally had a timber lining all evidence of it would have been removed during the construction of the later well. It had presumably been constructed by laying a number of courses and then backfilling with soil around them before repeating the process until completed. The well shaft was near circular with a diameter of 1.8 m and up to four courses of ashlar chalk were exposed at the depth excavated. The lime mortar bonding of each course was concentrated away from the interior face, possibly to prevent contamination of water by the mortar. Possible lime-scale staining on the north interior face of the well suggests that access to it was from this side, the staining probably deriving from overflow of the bucket. Augering revealed that the base of the well lay at 34.89 m OD or 12.4 m below its highest surviving point, although the water-table was not reached. The base of the well contained 0.2 m thick fine-grained but otherwise sterile light clay, probably deposited at the base of the feature from suspension within an open water body implying that the water-table at the time was higher. Above, the deposits were characteristic of rapid infilling and comprised well-compacted chalk and chalky soils containing 12th- to 13th-century pottery, implying the well had a relatively short period of use.

Immediately to the south of well CC1128 was small circular pit CC5011 whose function could not be established at the depth excavated. However, like CC1128, it had been levelled with chalk rubble to its excavated depth of 0.42 m.

Property BE 2 (Fig. 4.2)

Structural evidence

A group of small pits or postholes (Structure CC7008) located towards the south of the property may have represented the truncated remains of a timber structure that was sited towards the rear of the property and possibly an extension eastwards of proposed pre-Conquest Structure CC7009 (see Chapter 3, Property BE 2 above). Four of the pits or postholes (CC1668, CC1386, CC1403 and CC1176) formed an approximate line that ran perpendicular to the street, their close spacing suggesting a load bearing function rather than a fence. The features were oval or circular, measuring 0.6–0.97 m across and varying in depth from 0.12 to 0.54 m, although they had been truncated and would originally have been significantly deeper (perhaps more than 0.5 m). Truncation may also have removed all evidence of further such pits to the west. No post-pipes were evident though a fifth pit (CC1509), located immediately to their north, contained a rectangular post-impression *c* 0.5 m across at its north end. A sixth pit

(CC1548) located adjacent to the boundary with Property BE 1 may also have been associated. Although contemporary floor levels had been removed by later terracing, the upper levels of late Saxon pits CC1392 and CC1522 (see Chapter 3) contained thick deposits of compacted chalk that may have represented slumped levels associated with the postulated structure. Similarly the upper levels of late Saxon pit CC1397 included a compact chalk fill associated with Anglo-Norman pottery suggesting that the proposed pre-Conquest structure CC7009 continued in use (see Chapter 3). These deposits contained a smithing hearth, indicating that the structure continued to be utilised for smithing.

Pits

Two groups of pits were apparent, to either side of the possible subdivision of the property recognised in the previous phase (see Chapter 3).

The southern group (Pit Group CC7011) comprised a tight cluster of four intercutting pits that flanked the north side of possible Structure CC7008, none of which were bottomed at mitigation level. The earliest pit (CC1466), which may have been circular, had been backfilled with chalk rubble in which a horseshoe (SF Cat no. 231) datable to the mid 11th to 12th century was found. The latest pits, CC1241 and CC1457, were vertically sided and circular, measuring 1.1 m and 1.4 m in diameter respectively, and therefore may have served a similar purpose. The latter pit was augered which revealed its base to be below 44.17 m OD (or over 3.2 m deep), a depth that may suggest that it functioned as a well. The earliest fill reached comprised cess-like soft green-grey clay from which a coprolite was recovered, indicating that it may later have served as a cesspit. Its upper fills comprised mortar and chalk rubble, presumably derived from a nearby masonry-built structure, before being capped by compacted chalk. The pit contained a madder-stained sherd of Newbury B-style ware offering evidence that dyeing was undertaken here during the Anglo-Norman period.

The northern group (Pit Group CC7017) included a large circular pit (CC1640) measuring 2.85 m in diameter that was bottomed by auger at a depth of 2.1 m, so could not have served as a well. No evidence for its initial use was found and the pit appears to have been rapidly backfilled with soil and domestic refuse that included cat and dog bones. Two small shallow pits, one (CC1506) containing abundant oyster shells, probably represented subsequent use of the area for the disposal of rubbish.

Property BE 3 (Fig. 4.2)

Structural evidence

The degree of truncation that had occurred within this area of site had removed any traces of structures that may have occupied the intervening space between Pit Group CC7050 (see below) and the street frontage, a distance of approximately 11 m. Only within pit CC1190, a small part of which was exposed against the western edge of the excavation, was there evidence for surviving occupation levels. These comprised a succession of layers of compacted chalk or redeposited natural clay/gravel interleaved with dark occupation deposits that could conceivably have represented floors that formed part of a structure. The presence of mortar rubble (CC1189) suggests the presence of a structure containing masonry elements and therefore fairly substantial. Upper levels of pit CC1168 contained a succession of three compact chalk fills that may

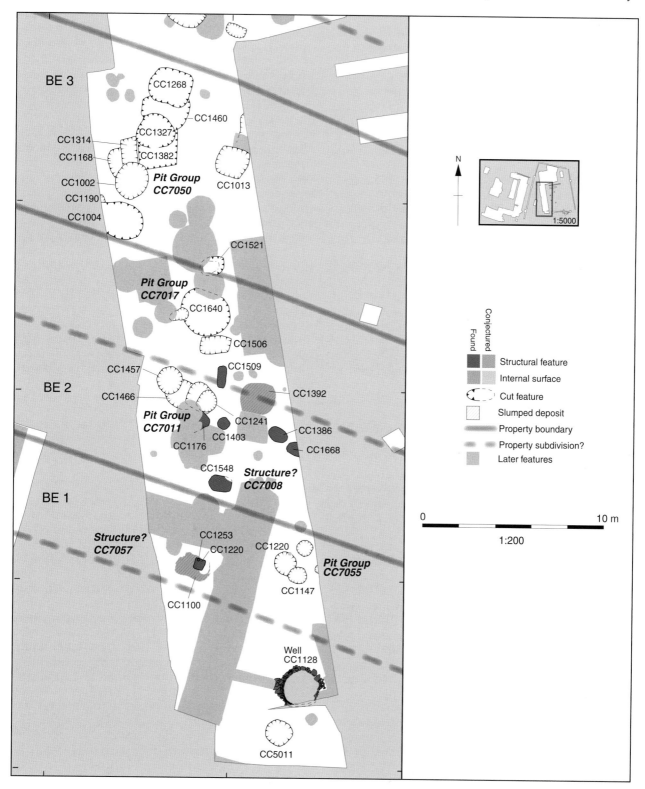

Fig. 4.2   Properties BE 1–3, Phase 5

have post-dated the filling of the pit and possibly represented the foundation of floors. The earliest was cut by a posthole (CC1195; not shown on plan) that been removed subsequent to the laying of the later 'surfaces', supporting the interpretation that they pertain to structural remains.

Pits

Unlike the adjacent Properties BE 2 and BE 4, the density of pitting showed a marked increase from that of the preceding period and is dominated by a SW-NE linear arrangement of nine intercutting pits (Pit Group CC7050) suggesting an intense and sustained period of activity. The spatial layout of the pits suggests that the subdivision suggested for the property in the pre-Conquest period did not extend into the Anglo-Norman period. The sharp delimitation on their sides suggests that space was at a premium and perhaps the area to their west was set aside for structures (see above). As previously noted (see Chapter 3), the area to the south-east was relatively free of pits, which suggests it may have been set aside for other use, or for access.

All the pits of Pit Group CC7050 were excavated to mitigation level (at 1.1–1.2 m depth) and were largely rapidly infilled, the rather similar nature of their levelling deposits often making the identification of the correct chronological sequence difficult at the depths excavated. None of the pits corresponded with the pile positions of the new building and as a result they were not subject to augering in an attempt to establish their function and depth. Given the degree of slumping encountered in some of the pits it is possible the earliest pits may have originated in Phase 4 even though their excavated fills contained post-Conquest pottery. These pits (CC1190, CC1168, CC1314 and CC1460), largely removed by later pits, were mostly rectangular, and two of them contained fills that may be interpreted as slumped floor and occupation deposits (see above). The subsequent four pits (CC1004, CC1002, CC1327, CC1268) formed a straight line and unlike the earlier pits, most were circular and of a similar size, measuring 2–2.5 m across. All contained domestic rubbish before being rapidly infilled with well-consolidated redeposited natural chalk or clay/gravel. The northernmost pit CC1268 was effectively the re-excavation of late Saxon pit CC1275 (see Chapter 3) and unlike the other pits showed no evidence for consolidated filling.

The pits were particularly rich in animal remains, mainly cattle and lesser quantities of pig and sheep, the earlier pits being notable also for the presence of goose, duck and other fowl. Fish, grain, seeds and other indicators of diet were not present, however, probably due to the fact that any cess-rich deposits would have been at lower depths and were thus not available for investigation. However, appreciable quantities of herring were recovered from a cessy fill of pit CC1268 as well as a large quantity of oyster and mussel shells. Evidence for horn working was found in pit CC1268 and adjacent pit CC1327, the former also containing hammerscale suggesting that smithing was undertaken close by. Possible evidence for weaving included an eyed bone pin from pit CC1004 (SF Cat no. 179) datable to the 11th–mid 12th century.

Three further pits were identified to the east of Pit Group CC7050. Only one (CC1013) was exposed or survived to any great extent. Pit CC1013 was square and vertical sided, measuring 1.8 m across and was partly excavated, to a depth of 1.1 m. Unlike the pits to the west it appeared to have been left to fill over a period of time with dumps of domestic refuse though its original purpose remains uncertain. This pit and pit fragment CC1521, located adjacent to the postulated south boundary of the property, appear to have been filled late in the Anglo-Norman period, probably during the late 12th to early 13th century. Pit CC1013 was notable for containing a sherd from an un-sooted (unused?) chimney pot rim that had an elliptical or deformed aperture (see Chapter 7, Fig. 7.9, no. 18). A further sherd of possible chimney pot was found in pit CC1521 (see Chapter 7, Fig. 7.12, no. 53). Such chimney pots are thought to date from as early as the late 12th century and suggest the presence of buildings of middling to higher status (see Cotter, Chapter 7), the deformed sherd possibly representing a reject during the construction of the building it had been intended to adorn. The presence of a floor tile and a possible roof tile from pit CC1013 offers further evidence for the substantial nature of the building that was presumably located towards the street frontage.

Property BE 4 (Fig. 4.3; Plates 4.2–4.4)

Structural evidence

Structure CC7024

The north-west area of the property, west of well CC2039 (see below), which had been occupied by pits during the preceding Phase 4 (see Chapter 3), seems to have been used for structures, indicated by surviving levels which had subsided into earlier features. Successive layers of compacted chalk and thin occupation silts had slumped into late Saxon pit CC2041, and probably represented occupation over a protracted period of time, the earliest possibly of pre-Conquest date. The later floors consisted of mortar, one (CC2113) comprising yellowish-buff chalky mortar that had slumped severely, leaving fractured terraces of floor at various levels, but otherwise surviving intact (Plate 4.2). Towards its north side, at a point immediately adjacent to the projected south wall of cellar CC7044 (see Property BE 5 Phase 6, below), chalk rubble blocks and a fragment of wall render were found within the mortar, indicating it was nearing a walled edge. Thin occupation silts and charcoal

Plate 4.2   Mortar floor (Structure CC7024) collapsing into pit CC2041, Property BE 4, Phase 5, looking south-west

Plate 4.3   Well CC2039, Property BE 4, Phase 5, looking north-west

spreads above the floors contained a small quantity of flake hammerscale suggesting intermittent secondary smithing; otherwise occupation appears to have been domestic. A complete barrel padlock of 10th- or 11th-century date was recovered from a dark brown make-up level over the earliest floor, suggesting the need for security. Compacted mortar (CC2181) containing large flint nodules was found slumped into earlier features immediately to the north-west. It may have represented the remnants of a wall, and it corresponded with the westward projection of the south wall of later cellar CC7044 (Phase 6).

Structure CC7025

Further possible slumped floors or internal consolidation levels were found filling the upper levels of pre-Conquest pit CC2343, possibly a cellar, located 5 m to the south of Structure CC7024. The possible floors comprised thick hard orange/brown chalky clay or chalk of different character to those found to the north, suggesting they were either not contemporary or pertained to a separate structure. They were cut by a line of circular postholes (CC2011, CC2271 and CC2278) that may have formed a late element of the structure, suggesting timber construction and perhaps delimiting its eastern extent some 6.5 m from the street frontage. The little evidence that was recovered suggests a domestic function.

Well CC2039

Abutting the boundary with Property BE 5 and located immediately to the east of Structure CC7024 was an elaborately built well (CC2039) (Plate 4.3). Though no direct dating was obtained for its construction, it pre-dated the construction of cellar CC7044 (Property BE 5; See Phase 6 below) to the north and it chalk ashlar construction is suggestive of a 12th-century date. Its chalk block lining was formed of curved blocks with regular level courses and staggered perp joints; the highly quality of its construction was such that no mortar was required for the joints. The chalk blocks on its north side had been removed by the foundation of the south wall of the cellar but did not overlap the inner edge of the well lining. It is possible that the cellar wall may have replaced the lining at this point and the well continued to function, since the backfill of the well apparently abutted both the wall and lining at the level excavated. The chalk lining of its north-west face was pitted, possibly as the result of damage by the bucket that may been retrieved from this point of the well, presumably by the occupants of the adjacent building. The shaft of the well was slightly elliptical, measuring 2.1 m at its widest point and, unlike contemporary well CC1128 (Property BE 1), had been built flush within a circular construction pit. The base of the well was determined by a borehole which revealed its depth to have been 9 m below its highest surviving point at 38.66 m OD. The borehole revealed that, like all the wells on site,

it was dry and contained a thin, sterile, well-compacted clay at its base. This probably represented initial backfill, before the remainder of the well was rapidly infilled with dumps of redeposited natural clay and chalk. Alternatively it may have acted to prevent the water from seeping back into the porous underlying natural chalk. Its earliest excavated levels suggest that it may have been infilled during the 13th–14th centuries though a large quantity of 18th- to 19th-century tile was recovered from its uppermost fill, possibly accumulated as a result of subsidence.

Pits

The density of pitting attributable to the Anglo-Norman period showed a marked decline from the preceding period. All were fairly scattered and confined within an area located towards the rear of the property, some 12–20 m from the street frontage.

Pit Group CC7019 comprised three pits arranged in a line adjacent to the southern boundary of the property but back *c* 1 m to the north compared to the pits of the preceding period. Pits CC2002 (Plate 4.4) and CC2043 were both circular and of similar diameter, 2 m and 1.9 m respectively. The bases of both were found by auger which revealed that pit CC2002 was substantially deeper at 4.4 m (42.96 m OD) than pit CC2043 whose depth was 2.6 m. The base of the deeper pit lay 4.3 m above the base of nearby chalk-lined well CC2039 (38.66 m OD), a depth that suggests this pit was unlikely to have served as a well. Augering revealed that pit C2002 contained a 1.9 m thick deposit of soft, green-stained sand-silt cessy deposit at its base suggesting it was used as a cesspit. Both pits contained a significant quantity of domestic refuse in their upper fills. The relative scarcity of diagnostic post-Conquest pottery in pit CC2002 suggests that it had been used and infilled prior to the use of pit CC2039, probably early in the Anglo-Norman period. This may be borne out by a riveted mount (SF Cat no. 318) found

Plate 4.4 Cess pit CC2002, Property BE 4, Phase 5, looking north

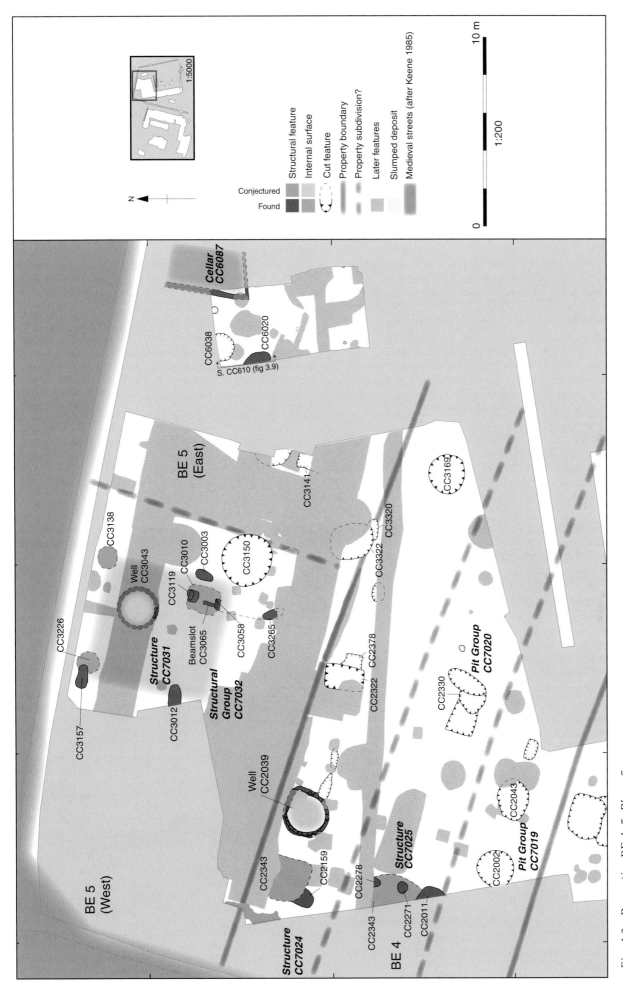

Fig. 4.3 Properties BE 4–5, Phase 5

close to the top of the pit that is datable to the mid 10th -late 11th centuries. Both pits contained parts of locks, indicating a need for security: a barrel padlock bolt from pit CC2043 (SF Cat no. 308) and a curved bar that formed part of a lock fitting from pit CC2002 (SF Cat no. 306). Evidence for trade was found in pit CC2002 where part of an equal-arm balance (SF Cat no. 320) was recovered. This could have been used for weighing items such as coin, luxury spices or even precious metals.

The presence of sawn horn cores (goat and deer) in both pits, and mould fragments (including a fragment with an inverted pattern for a metal decorative fitting) from pit CC2043, suggests that the manufacture of bone and non-ferrous objects was also undertaken on the property. Much of the food waste from both pits was predominantly cattle, with pig and sheep present in lesser quantities. Pit CC2002 was notable for butchered badger bones; perhaps the fur had been used to make brushes. Fish remains were present within cess-rich dumps and included predominantly herring and eel, though small quantities of salmon, trout, mackerel, cod and ray were also found.

Pit Group CC7020, located towards the centre of the property, represented the continuation from the Phase 4 pits in this area and similarly remained unexcavated below a depth of *c* 0.15 m. The upper fills probably represented the consolidation of pits datable to the pre-Conquest period (see Chapter 3). Pit CC2330 contained layers of compacted clay and chalk, interleaved with thin charcoal-rich silts that may have represented floor levels that had sunk into the pit. The charcoal was rich in flake and spherical hammerscale suggesting that it formed part of the floor of a smithy that would have occupied this central part of the property. It also contained a rich assemblage of fish remains, predominantly herring and eel, though more exotic fish such as Dover Sole and Conger Eel were also represented (see discussion in Chapter 5).

Circular pit CC3169, located towards the east of the property, was similar in diameter to the pits of Pit Group CC7020 and remained unbottomed at 1.7 m. The nature of its fills, comprising dumps of gravel and chalk rich soils, suggests the pit was rapidly filled, the green staining on its sides indicating that it had been used as a cesspit. The pit was notable for containing two sherds of contemporary madder-stained Newbury B ware indicating that dyeing was being undertaken on the property.

Pits CC2322 and CC2378 abutted the boundary with Property BE 5 and contained compacted chalk and mortar fills that had slumped to the excavated depth of the pits. This material may have been deposited to strengthen the foundation level for wall CC2315 (see Phase 6 below). However, it likely that these pits are of Phase 5 (or possibly Phase 4) date and may have contained soft organic material such as cess within the unexcavated lower levels.

Property BE 5

BE 5 West 'Property' (Fig. 4.3, Plate 4.5)

A post-built timber structure (Structure CC7031) was found that flanked the street to the north of the property and may have represented a successor to, or a remodelled version of, the proposed structure of the preceding phase (see Structure CC7035, Chapter 3). As with the preceding phase, floor levels only survived the later terracing where they had slumped into earlier pits. One such group (Structure CC7032) contained a well-preserved sequence of floors and structural features which may represent a southwards extension of the structure.

Structure CC7031

A rectangular arrangement of large postholes probably formed part of a timber-built structure or structures alongside the frontage of the north arm of Brudene Street. The western postholes (CC3012 and CC3157) were aligned at right-angles to the street, their substantial nature suggesting that they supported uprights for an exterior wall. Posthole CC3157, possibly the north-west corner of the structure, was contained within a rounded rectangular pit measuring 1.28 m in length and 0.44 m deep; a square(?) post, *c* 0.4 m wide, was visible as a slight impression at the base of its east end. Posthole CC3012, which cut into Phase 4.2 pit CC3011, was of similar size and contained clear evidence of a post-pipe at its west end; it could have represented the south-west corner. Posthole CC3003 was a similar size and shape and could conceivably have represented its south-east corner though no corresponding posthole was found to mark the north-east corner; this could have been removed by later truncation. If the postholes form part of the same structure, then a rectangular arrangement can be suggested measuring 6.6 by 5.2 m, the substantial nature of the postholes suggesting the structure had more than

Plate 4.5   Floors and features of structural group CC7032 slumped into pit CC3010, Property BE 5 (W), Phase 5, looking north-east

one storey. Any associated floor deposits were removed by later levelling of the site though compact chalk surfaces 'capping' pits CC3226 and CC3138, situated on the north side of the structure, may have represented surviving floor or associated levels.

Well-preserved occupation levels and structural elements (Structure CC7032) possibly pertaining to a southwards extension to the building were found collapsed into Phase 4.2 pit CC3010 close to its south-east corner. This comprised a succession of compacted chalk floors supporting thin occupation deposits often rich in charcoal suggesting the presence of a nearby hearth. The floors were divided by a shallow beamslot 0.16 m wide (CC3065; Plate 4.5) aligned with two postholes at each end (CC3119 and CC3058) that presumably represented timber uprights that fitted into the ground-sill. The northern post (CC3119) had been replaced on at least one occasion (CC3056) probably as the result of the severe subsidence. It is possible that shallow posthole CC3265 on the same alignment represents a continuation southwards of this timber wall. Evidence from the floors would suggest a largely domestic function though a small quantity of flaked hammerscale was recovered suggesting occasional secondary smithing. The floors were particularly rich in fish remains, including a wide variety of sea fish such as herring, plaice, sea bream, sea bass, cod, haddock, and conger eel, and with freshwater fish represented solely by eels. This suggests the preparation or consumption of such foodstuffs within the structure. Also present was a significant quantity of barley and oat grain, present in equal quantities, suggesting that a maslin or mixed crop called 'dredge' had been grown. Although dredge was often used as animal fodder (see Carruthers, Chapter 8), it was also used in medieval beer production (Unger 2004, 143). A higher proportion than normal of rye, an important component in medieval beer, would add further evidence that brewing was being undertaken within the structure.

Pits

The contemporary pits within the west property comprised a single pit (CC3150) and well CC3043, the former of which abutted the line of the pre-Conquest boundary NH7030 (see Chapter 3) suggesting it had continued in use. It may also have been contemporary with Structure CC7032 that lay immediately to its west. The vertical-sided pit measured 2.8 m in diameter, its base reached by augering at 42.53 m (4.9 m depth), a level nearly 4 m above the base of adjacent wells CC3043 and CC2039. The pit may have served as a cesspit, as in the similar pits found in the adjacent Property BE 4, though no evidence was found during the augering, which suggested that the pit had been rapidly filled with homogeneous mid grey-brown silty clay.

Well CC3043 had been largely destroyed by an air raid shelter though some evidence for its construction survived. It had been built with dressed ashlar

chalk blocks, similar in style to well CC2039 within Property BE 4. It showed diagonal tooling marks on its lowest two visible courses, which is indicative of an Anglo-Norman rather than a later medieval date. Otherwise no dating evidence was found. Unlike well CC2039, it had been built free-standing within a circular pit with packing backfill of compacted chalk surrounding the block lining. It is likely that the internal diameter of the well shaft measured *c* 1.5 m, somewhat smaller than its counterpart whose diameter was 2.1 m. A borehole revealed that the level of its base was identical to CC2039 (at 38.69 m OD) suggesting both wells sourced the same aquifer and possibly that they had been dug around the same time.

BE 5 East 'Property' (Fig. 4.3, Plate 4.6)

Structural evidence

In the extreme north-east area of the site part of rectangular timber-lined pit (CC6087) was exposed that may have represented a shallow cellar or undercroft for an overlying structure. Unfortunately only its south-west corner was exposed although it was set at right-angles to the street to the north and measured at least 2.2 m across, its rear side set back some 7 m from the frontage. Its base lay at a depth of 0.45 m though given the degree of truncation that had occurred in this area, its original depth was

Plate 4.6 'Cellar' CC6087, showing slot for timber lining on its west side, Property BE 5 (E), Phase 5, looking north

probably significantly more. A sharply defined flat-bottomed slot, 0.42 m in width, had been cut in its base alongside its western and southern edges and probably marked the position of timber planking that would have lined its sides (Plate 4.6). The slot was filled with a homogeneous loose grey silt in marked contrast to the backfill of the pit, suggesting that the timbers were left to decay rather than removed. No evidence for upright posts was found, though any post that may have marked its south-west corner would have been removed by a modern pit. Thin trampled grey silty clays (CC6071 and CC6082) containing domestic refuse, including Newbury B-style ware, would imply that the natural gravelly clay acted as a floor. The structure was subsequently re-floored with thick yellowish-buff chalky mortar (CC6069) that was supported on a

base of compacted clay (CC6070), the former heavily worn through use.

A large post-pit (CC6020) that cut through the infilled, possible late Saxon cellar CC6052 (see Chapter 3) may have formed part of the east wall of a later structure to the west, perhaps forming its south-east corner.

Pits

The pits within this part of the property were confined to the south-west suggesting the area to the east and north-west was occupied by structures or used for other purposes. Three of the pits were circular; one (CC3322) was cut by Phase 6 well CC3077 and had been rapidly filled with chalk rubble; it could conceivably have represented a precursor to it. Pit CC6038, measuring *c* 1.5 m in

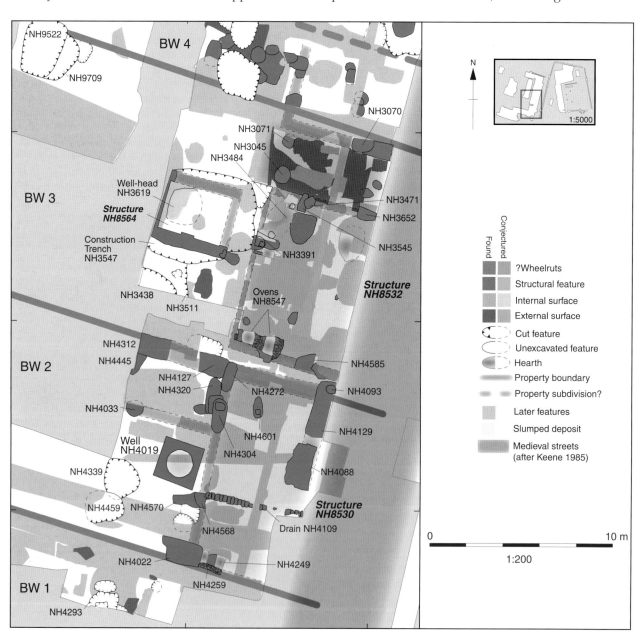

Fig. 4.4 Properties BW 1–3, Phase 5

diameter, contained domestic refuse and was bottomed by machine at a depth of 1.2 m. Partially exposed rectangular pit CC3141 had green-stained edges and presumably served as a cesspit, though its lower levels lay below mitigation. It was backfilled with domestic refuse that contained sea fish including conger eel, cod, halibut, and flat fishes.

BRUDENE STREET WEST

Property BW 1 (Fig. 4.4)

As with the preceding period only a small area to the rear of the property was available for investigation, the area to the street frontage being either below mitigation level or outside the excavations. The area continued to be set aside for the digging of pits, largely within a zone that had not previously been used. The pits recorded were mostly either shallow or their extents lay largely beyond the limits of excavation. Only rectangular pit NH4293 was of note and contained ashy fills, probably sweepings from nearby smithing activity since they contained flake hammerscale and iron slag. The presence of several burnt bones, scarce elsewhere on the site, perhaps indicates higher status activity since charring of bones indicates roasting, a relatively fuel demanding and labour intensive cooking method (see Strid, Chapter 8; see also Property SE 1, Pit Group NH8612 below).

Property BW 2 (Fig. 4.4, Plates 4.7–9)

Structure NH8530

The late Saxon L-shaped structure (NH8530) that occupied the full frontage of the property during Phase 4.2 (see Chapter 3, Fig. 3.16) continued to be occupied, though contemporary occupation levels did not survive except where they had slumped into a late Saxon pit located alongside its southern extent. At some point the sill-beams had been replaced by substantial post-pits that appeared to follow the same footprint as the earlier phase. The date of this remodelling is uncertain since many of the post-pit fills derived from the robbing/removal of the posts; however, none contained pottery later than the early 13th century, suggesting that the building had been demolished by this time. In form and construction technique the structure is characteristic of early medieval houses (see discussion, Chapter 5) dating from the late 10th century onwards and is similar to Structure NH8622 that occupied Property SE 2 (see Chapter 3, Fig. 3.22).

The structure was defined by a number of small elongated pits along the western side (NH4272 (Plate 4.7), NH4304, NH4568/NH4570 and NH4022). Their alignment corresponded with the west wall of the sill-built late Saxon structure, the limits of the northernmost and southernmost pits corresponding to the north and south property boundaries. Pits NH4272 and NH4304 were of similar size and depth

measuring 1.6 m and 1.75 m in length and 0.62 m and 0.69 m in depth respectively. Pit NH4304 contained a slight rectangular depression measuring 0.47 m by 0.6 m at its north end that probably marked the position of the post, though no post-pipe was evident. Pit NH4570 was aligned at right-angles to the pits to the north, possibly influenced by the site of well NH4019 which may have been in position at this time. A later pit (NH4568), contained within its east end may have marked the position of a post as this would have formed a straight alignment with post-pits NH4272 and N4303 to its north. Evidence for an intermediate post-pit between NH4570 and NH4304 may have been removed by the robbing pit for the well. The south-west corner of the structure appears to have been marked by pit NH4022; although this had been heavily disturbed by later activity a post impression was identified at its east end, in alignment with the west wall of the structure. A notable quantity of large flints was found within the pit that may have represented disturbed remains of packing around the post.

Substantial posthole NH4093 may have marked the position of the north-east corner of the structure and hence the position of the street frontage at this time. It measured 0.43 m in diameter and was filled with a loose brown silt, possibly the decayed remains of the post, which contained an iron arrowhead of 9th- to 11th-century date (SF Cat no. 371; see

Plate 4.7   Post-pit NH4272 forming north wall of Structure NH8530, Property BW 2, Phase 5, looking north-east

Chapter 7, Fig. 7.32). The posthole was located within the north end of earlier pit NH4129 which may have been associated since its base corresponded to the base of the posthole, at a depth of 0.62 m. A similar pit (NH4088) lay immediately to its south, on the alignment of the projected east wall of the structure, though it remained unexcavated since it lay below mitigation level. Post-pit NH4601, within the interior of the structure, was smaller and contained an impression of a squarish post at its south end measuring *c* 0.28 m in width. Although this post is smaller than the others it is still sufficient in size to have had a substantial load-bearing function and could have formed a roof support rather than part of a partition wall.

The structure appears to have maintained a west wing or annexe at its north end, which was reconstructed in a similar manner to the main part of the building. Its south wall may have been defined by pit NH4033 which was positioned perpendicular to pit NH4304 within the main west wall. The north wall may have been delimited by pit NH4445, which corresponded to pit NH4033 on the south wall and contained the remains of an apparent post-pipe at its north end that extended throughout its depth of 1 m. The constraints of the excavation edge did not allow the shape of the post to be revealed, but it must have measured at least 0.51 m across, comparable in size to the other posts of the building. The pit had been backfilled with compacted gravel, probably to add more support for the post since it cut into the soft fills of a late Saxon cesspit. This post may have been set in a shallow flat linear trench (NH4312) that seems to have defined the north wall of the structure. A similar trench (NH4127) lay on the same alignment to the east, and may have been associated with post-pit NH4272. Both trenches measured 1 m across and

Plate 4.8   Slumped remains of oven NH4249 at south end of Structure NH8530, Property BW 2, Phase 5, looking south-east

were filled with compact gravel-rich soil suggesting that they may have acted as the baseplate for a massive sill-beam into which the upright posts fitted. The length of the sill as estimated by the distance between the posts was at least 5.4 m. The purpose of post-pit NH4320, located close to the west edge of the west wing, is difficult to ascertain but it could have supported an internal structure such as a staircase since the structure was substantial enough to have had at least two storeys.

The area at the southern end of the structure continued (as in the preceding period) to be used for cooking as evidenced by well-preserved floor deposits and structural features that had survived slumped heavily into the soft fills of underlying late Saxon pits (see Chapter 3). A major phase of re-construction seems to have occurred that was possibly contemporary with the re-build of Structure NH8530. A short length of an east-west wall (NH4259) coincided with the line of the south wall of the structure and may have formed the back part of one or more oven structures. It comprised chalk and flint rubble measuring 0.25 m in width, bonded by loose sandy beige mortar and had a render of brown clay on its south (?exterior) face. A compact surface of fired red chalk and clay may have represented the internal area within an oven immediately to its north. Several episodes of re-flooring of scorched chalk or clay followed, each associated with charcoal rich silts derived from the use of ovens. The oven was later remodelled with the addition of a short length of masonry (NH4249) (Plate 4.8) that abutted the north side of wall NH4259 comprising flints bonded with beige creamy mortar. This may have represented the west wall of an oven whose internal area lay to its north since the clay floor abutting its east side was hard fired red by intense heat whereas to its west the clay floor showed no evidence for heating.

The diverse range of animal bone recovered, including cattle, pig, sheep, fowl, pigeon and other birds, suggests that food was being prepared and cooked, the presence of burnt bones of larger mammals suggesting large joints were also being roasted. The domestic nature of these deposits was confirmed by the soil micromorphology, which showed that charcoal-rich occupation layer NH4192 comprised finely to broadly layered trampled floor deposits originating from kitchen hearth rake out rich in charcoal, with ash and burned food residues (see Macphail and Crowther, Chapter 8). Additionally the presence of dung residues within charcoal rake out NH4186 suggests that, if not trampled in from outside, the dung may have come from fuel used in the ovens. Part of a perforated curfew (a fire cover), showing heavy internal sooting, indicates a concern for fire prevention. A vessel of Newbury B-style ware (see Chapter 7, Fig. 7.15, no. 115) was recovered from close to the upper level of the sequence and is datable to no later than the early 13th century.

Immediately to the north of the kitchen area were the remains of a chalk-lined drain (NH4109) that ran east-west across Structure NH8530 towards the south side of well NH4019 (see below), its western extent apparently corresponding with the line of the west wall of Structure NH8530. Only its base survived, comprising chalk slabs cut into rectangles measuring approximately 0.3 m by 0.25 m, each of equal thickness of 0.1 m, laid flat, tightly packed and without mortar bonding on a thin bedding of puddled chalk. Rubble that overlay it contained similar broken chalk slabs that probably derived from its side lining, and perhaps from any covering slabs. Below the rubble was a thin deposit of gravel and sand that may have derived from the use of the drain. The date of the drain is uncertain though it must have been cut from a level above that of the latest surviving floor level of Structure NH8530 and so could feasibly have post-dated its use, though its apparent terminus at the line of its west wall would seemingly preclude this. If the drain had extended beyond the west wall of Structure NH8530 it must have pre-dated robbing of well NH4019 during the 13th or 14th centuries. An unabraded sherd from a Winchester ware pitcher was found within its foundation bedding, possibly disturbed from underlying floors but in any case dating the construction of the drain to no earlier than the late 10th to late 11th century. If contemporary with Structure NH8530 it may have served the needs of the kitchen, or alternatively if later, may have formed part of the Archdeacon's property, possibly serving as a drain for an access lane leading off Brudene Street (see discussion, Chapter 5).

Pits

The area south-west of Structure NH8530 continued to be used for disposal of rubbish, though a large part of this area was set aside for the construction of well NH4019 (see below). Vertical sided pit NH4339 was sub-circular, measuring 2.1 m across, and remained unbottomed at a depth of 2 m. The pit appears to have been rapidly filled with dumps of gravel, chalk and refuse rather than through the gradual accumulation of rubbish, implying that it may originally have served as a cesspit. Its earliest fill contained a large rim sherd/body sherd of coarse grained sandy ware (Fabric MOE) indicating the pit had been filled between the late 11th and early 13th century, the presence of early South Hampshire red ware (Fabric MNG) recovered from the fills above suggesting a date in the latter part of this range. The pit also contained a complete bolt from a medieval barrel padlock (SF Cat no. 297; see Chapter 7, Fig. 7.29), similar examples of which have been found in 11th-century contexts elsewhere in Winchester (see Cool, Chapter 7). A fragment of bone, sawn and polished on one side, suggests that bone objects were being manufactured. The upper levels of the pit contained compacted orange gravel supported by rammed chalk. This suggests that the area was later re-utilised as a yard. Alternatively it may be related to consolidation of an entrance into the archdeacon's property that was later constructed in this area (see discussion, Chapter 5). A second slightly smaller, shallow pit (NH4459) containing domestic refuse apparently cut its south edge and had also been levelled with compacted orange gravel.

Chalk-lined well NH4019 (Plate 4.9) occupied a position immediately to the rear of the southern arm of Structure NH8530, though later robbing had destroyed any stratigraphic relationship between the two. Its construction was unusual compared to the other wells on the site as it had been constructed within a square pit measuring 2.2 m across, within which a circular shaft of chalk blocks was constructed. As construction proceeded, clean chalk was packed in behind the chalk blocks in order to help consolidation, the chalk possibly having been tipped in from the south side of the pit. The need for a square construction trench is difficult to understand and it is possible that it represented an existing open pit, perhaps a timber precursor to the well. The shaft measured 1.48 m in diameter and predominantly consisted of large, rectangular roughly hewn blocks although some had been shaped in an ashlar fashion. A borehole

revealed that the base of the well lay at 41.27 m OD (a depth of 9.5 m) and contained a 0.56 m thick light grey clayey silt at its base. The presence of fine-grained sediment may indicate deposition of mineral matter from suspension within an open water body. No dating was obtained for the construction of the well, although analogy with the other chalk-lined wells on the site and its position with regard to Structure NH8530 would imply a date around the 12th century. The well appears to have been rapidly infilled with rubble and robbed of its upper courses prior to final levelling by the 13th or 14th centuries.

Property BW 3 (Fig. 4.4; Plates 4.10–14)

Compared to the late Saxon period, much of the frontage area was subject to full excavation and only the earliest deposits pertaining to this phase lay below mitigation levels. A deep accumulation of floor levels along most of the frontage pertain to one or more timber structures (Structure NH8532). The area to its north appears to have remained open and may have represented an access route (or lane) leading off the street (see below). An elaborately built well-house (Structure NH8564) also occupied a position immediately to the west of the structure.

Plate 4.9   Well NH4019, Property BW 2, Phase 5, looking south-east

Structure NH8532 (Plates 4.10–11)

The lack of structural features suggests this building in its earliest visible phase had been constructed on earth-fast timber sills, though there was no positive evidence to prove this. However, the floor levels were delimited to the west by a line of pits associated with a later and more substantial timber phase of the structure. The extent of the floors to the north was fairly sharply defined and corresponded approximately with the north side of well-house Structure NH8564. Similarly their southern extent was clearly defined by the boundary with Property BW 2, which remained essentially unchanged from the late Saxon period. As such the structure may have occupied a frontage of *c* 9.1 m and is estimated to have extended *c* 6.1 m from the street frontage. From the outset the structure appears to have been subdivided into two bays, as there was a clear dividing line between the floors in the northern and southern parts of the building. The line of this division corresponded closely to the inside face of the south wall of well-house Structure NH8564, the apparent lack of a dividing ground sill or other structural evidence suggesting an internal screen. The two bays thus formed were of unequal length, with the south bay measuring 5.3 m in width compared to 3.8 m for the north bay.

The floors of the north bay comprised thick compacted chalk, the earliest levels of which remained unexcavated and below mitigation level. The northern extent of their earliest levels seems to have been delimited by east-west slot NH3652 that may have represented part of a beam-slot, although it remained undefined towards the west. The slot had a slightly concave bottom and measured 0.6 m in width and 0.3 m in depth and was filled with sandy gravel. Its concave base and gravelly fill suggest that it did not serve as a beam-slot, and it could have been a drain for rain run-off onto the exterior area or possible lane to its north (see below). The floor of the north bay had been replaced with chalk on at least one occasion, with intervening thick make-up levels of orange gravelly clay and thick greenish or charcoal rich occupation silts. Evidence from the floors would suggest predominantly domestic occupation, with a fairly diverse range of food waste that included Brent goose, duck, fowl and red deer, the latter, if being consumed, indicating the occupants enjoyed a more refined diet. However, this diversity was not reflected in the fish remains, which comprised predominantly herring and eel.

Sooty occupation layer NH3617 contained significant quantities of burnt cereal grains and hazelnut shells. The hazelnut shells could have been used as fuel for a nearby hearth, though no such contemporary features were found at the levels excavated. The burnt cereals included a preponderance of oats and barley that could also have been used for the brewing of ale. Soil micromorphological analysis undertaken in the north-west of the room (see Macphail and Crowther, Chapter 8; Thin sections NHM226A-B) revealed evidence of strongly burned mineral material from hearths or furnaces and possible industrial evidence. However, there was no other evidence of industrial activity, so perhaps this

Plate 4.10   Floor levels of Structure NH8532, near to mitigation level, Property BW 3, Phase 5, looking south-west

Plate 4.11   Unexcavated floor deposits slumping into underlying pit NH3017 within the northern part of Structure NH8532, Property BW 3, Phase 5 and earlier, looking west

Plate 4.12   Oven NH8547 Property BW 3, Phase 5, looking south-east

material was brought by trample from elsewhere. The floors within the south bay similarly consisted of thick compacted chalk overlain by charcoal-rich silts that also contained evidence suggesting a predominantly domestic use of the area. However, finds of three spindlewhorls from three contiguous floor deposits at south end of the room suggest that this area could have been associated with spinning. Two of the whorls were made of chalk (see Shaffrey, Chapter 7) and the third (SF Cat no. 164) from the latest floor was made from bone and is datable to the 10th–11th centuries. Also found within these deposits was a short length of copper alloy rod (SF no. 1296; not in catalogue) with a rounded end that may have originated as casting waste and perhaps derived from the possible metalworking activity identified from the northern bay of the structure.

The north bay may have seen a change of use since a number of clay hearths were subsequently added against the west wall of the room. The surface of the chalk floor area towards the east wall had also been scorched red, presumably by intense heat. One hearth (NH3484) was archaeomagnetically dated to 1195–1267 (hearth WOH). The hearths were seemingly associated with a thick and well-preserved sequence of chalk floors, ash and charcoal-rich occupation deposits that subsided into an underlying pit (NH3017) within the central area of the room (Plate 4.11). As a consequence most of these deposits occurred below mitigation levels and thus remained unexcavated—though the evidence obtained from the upper levels suggests domestic occupation.

Possibly at same time masonry built ovens (NH8547) were added to the south end of the southern bay. Two adjacent horseshoe-shaped ovens were formed of a single build comprising roughly faced flints bonded by pale yellow sandy lime mortar with a shared integral floor of hardened chalk. The opening of the east oven measured 1 m in depth and was 0.56 m in width whilst the west oven was wider at 0.92 m. The ovens had been built free-standing upon the underlying floor and with their openings facing northwards. The southern wall of the oven appears to have been an integral part of the building since it contained a step that may have been used to accommodate a sill beam for its southern wall (Plate 4.12). Although the ovens had been demolished to near floor level and partially robbed, the central wall appeared to overhang slightly at its northern end suggesting the start of a springer (the lowest voussoir on each side of an arch, where the vertical support for the arch terminates and the curve of the arch begins). The west wall of the oven showed evidence for repair that effectively narrowed its opening to 0.69 m. The rebuild contained a fragment of re-used and squared Quarr stone, a type of stone also used in the construction of the well-house. The floor of the west oven had been resurfaced on several occasions with chalk, the penultimate floor (NH4430) producing an archaeomagnetic date of 477–1175 (WOF). The area

around the front of the oven contained a series of thick spreads of laminated charcoal that derived from sweepings out from the use of the ovens. Those in front of the east oven were contained within a deep hollow that had formed from subsidence into an underlying late Saxon pit. Charcoal (NH4458) from the earliest spread in front of and within the west oven produced a radiocarbon date of 1020–1210 (SUERC-13916), which was reduced by Bayesian modelling to 1020–1090. Charcoal (NH4373) from the latest use of the west oven produced a radiocarbon date of 1030–1220 (SUERC-13904), reduced by Bayesian modelling to 1050–1230 implying that the ovens had ceased to be used by the end of the early 13th century. As with the north room, evidence from the use of these ovens suggests a domestic function. The charcoal sweepings contained charred bread wheat, suggesting the ovens were used for the baking of bread. The animal and fish remains were similar to those found within the north bay and included goose, snipe and pigeon, along with fish remains composed predominantly of herring with small quantities of grey mullet and cod.

Well-house Structure NH8564 (Plates 4.13–14)

Situated *c* 2 m to the rear of Structure NH8532 was a large, rectangular and elaborately constructed masonry-lined shaft that may have served as a well-house since it enclosed and was apparently contemporary with a well, located on its base. The internal faces of its north and south walls were in alignment with the corresponding extents of the northern room of Structure NH8532, implying that it formed a contemporary and closely associated feature. Its south side clipped the edge of pit NH3511 whose upper levels contained Anglo-Norman sandy wares including a sherd of late Saxon/early medieval chalk tempered ware (Fabric MAV) and Newbury B ware reminiscent of Norman wares from Canterbury and London. The lack of more diagnostic wares such as Tripod pitchers and developed forms could suggest a date early within the Anglo-Norman period, perhaps prior to the mid 12th century.

The west and south walls were well preserved and survived up to the top of the shaft whilst its north and east walls had seemingly collapsed completely into the shaft. Full excavation of the feature was not possible, though a sondage excavated against its west wall revealed that the base of the shaft (natural chalk) lay at a depth of *c* 4 m, which corresponded with the base of the lining. The lining, measuring 0.61–0.72 m in width, comprised chalk rubble bonded by yellow sandy mortar that been dressed internally with rectangular ashlar chalk blocks, cut to a consistent size of *c* 0.3 m by 0.2 m by 0.18 m. The internal area of the shaft, according to the extent of the lining, measured 2.55 by 3.55 m. A gap behind the south wall, probably formed as a result of collapsing sides of the shaft pit during its excavation, had

Plate 4.13   'Well-house' NH8564, Property BW 3, Phase 5, looking south-west

been filled with packed chalk and mortar. There were two rows of square putlog holes, each *c* 0.12 m across, on its south wall (and presumably corresponding holes on its north wall) that would have held temporary platforms in order to aid the construction of the walls. Located centrally along and bonded into the south wall was a short protruding buttress that had been faced with Quarr limestone (utilised rarely after the 12th century) in a similar manner to the lining. The facing on the buttress was absent from the upper five surviving courses of the wall though a protruding wedge-shaped stone fragment survived on its west face (corresponding to the second course) that was similar to voussoir blocks used for the start of a springers for a vaulted arch. This suggests that the structure supported a substantial roof and certainly the unweathered condition of the walls would suggest that it was protected from the elements.

At the base of the excavated sondage, part of a pit was exposed, the upper levels of which, at least, were filled with rubble derived from the collapse of the walls. The pit (NH3619), though rather irregular within the small area exposed, may have been circular—possibly 1.9 m in diameter—and if so, was contained within the west side of the shaft. A geoarchaeological borehole revealed that its base lay at

depth of 8.89 m (37.70 m OD) below the floor of the shaft, the depth suggesting that it represented the well-head. The basal fill comprised a thin deposit of orangey-brown silty clay that contained mineralised faecal material including strawberry and legume seeds, suggesting that cess had been deposited in the well after it had gone out of use (Vaughan-Williams *et al.*, 2005). As no evidence for a lining was found, perhaps timber was used or the hard surrounding natural chalk may have provided sufficient support for the sides. The position of the well-head, close to the west, north and south walls of the shaft, would imply that access down to it must have been from the east (from Structure NH8532) and presumably by means of steep steps or a ladder. However the east side of the shaft was left largely unexcavated to any depth, and no evidence was definitely recorded for the existence of such steps.

The structure and the well-head appear to have been filled with rubble derived from the north and east walls of the well-house. The complete absence of the north wall apart from its basal course would imply that it had been deliberately pushed in; perhaps the west and south walls were retained to ensure stability of the sides in order to prevent subsidence of extant structures in this area. The rubble contained complete blocks derived from the lining

Plate 4.14 'Well-house' NH8564, detail of south wall showing buttress and infill, Property BW 3, Phase 5, looking east

and possible elements of an arch suggesting little effort had been made in reusing the material. The structure appears to have been rapidly filled with well-consolidated soil and re-deposited natural that contained Anglo-Norman pottery. One fill (NH3286) contained a large part of a Tripod pitcher, a sherd of imported northern French ware and a flanged roof tile fragment, all suggestive of a date during the second half of the 12th century. Furthermore the presence of small quantities of early South Hampshire red ware (fabric MNG) could suggest a late 12th- or early 13th-century date for its infilling.

Exterior areas

The lack of distinct floor deposits within the area to the north of Structure NH8532 suggests that this area remained open and would presumably have led to the street to the east. The earliest levels of this area lay below mitigation though thick spreads of flint gravel were exposed within a ground beam at the east end and similar deposits were also partially exposed towards the higher area to the west. These may have represented exterior surfaces, and they supported thick accumulations of trampled dark grey clay and dumps of domestic refuse, offering further evidence for their exterior nature. Two parallel and rather irregular shallow trenches, spaced *c* 1.6 m apart and filled with compact stony grey-brown silty clay, may have represented ruts from a cart. It is probable that this area represented access leading from the street to the rear of the Structure NH8532, which otherwise occupied the whole of the frontage area. The abundance of general domestic rubbish contained within the deposits suggests such material may have been deposited from the building or by the occupants of the adjacent Property BW 4. One such dump (NH3098) included the remains of a domestic oven found with a large quantity of charred hazelnut shells. The fragments contained well-preserved

interwoven wattle impressions. The oven was probably removed during renovation works and may have feasibly originally occupied a position within the northern bay of Structure NH8532, possibly against its east wall, an area where the floor had been heavily scorched.

A group of pits and small features were clustered in the north-west corner of the property. These were sectioned by machine and little useful dating and other material evidence was recovered to determine their purpose. Pits NH9522 and NH9709 were in excess of 2 m deep and are similar in form to cesspits elsewhere on the site. It is possible that these features belong with the reorganised layout of Phase 6, along with well NH9530/9630 (see below).

The south-west part of Property BW 3, south of well-house Structure NH3547, seems to have been set aside as a yard. The yard comprised a very compact layer of flints and pebbles within a clay matrix (0.08 m thick) that had been coloured red by intense heat. It is probably at this time that a large rectangular pit (NH3511), possibly of late Saxon origin, had been levelled since its excavated fills comprised thick dumps of gravel and chalk. Cutting the yard was a large circular pit NH3438 that may have measured up to 3.1 m in diameter and was excavated to a depth of 1.14 m. Its fills comprised dumps of mortar, gravel and domestic refuse that had been tipped in from its northern side and probably represented its final levelling. The refuse contained the remains of deer, including some identified as roe deer, food often associated with high status individuals in the Norman period (Sykes 2006b, 168). A charcoal-rich dump (NH3415) also produced a selection of sea fish including cod, plaice, thornback and other flatfishes. The presence of a significant quantity of charred bread wheat remains also found within this dump suggests that bread ovens lay nearby, probably within the south end of Structure NH8532 (see above). The area to the west of these pits may also have been utilised for waste disposal as several otherwise undated circular pits were found during the 1960s excavations (Cunliffe 1964, Pits M10-12 and M18). These pre-dated the 13th- to 14th-century eastern extension of the Archdeacon's house and therefore may be attributable to the Anglo-Norman phase, although no further dating evidence was published.

Property BW 4 (Fig. 4.5)

The intensity and pattern of occupation within this property was maintained into the Anglo-Norman period. The northern part of the property continued to be used for the digging of pits over a sustained period of time whereas Structure NH8566 within the southern part seems to have continued in use and was possibly enlarged to the west. The complete lack of contemporary pits in the south-west corner of the property suggests this area was set aside for other uses though no other evidence of this survived.

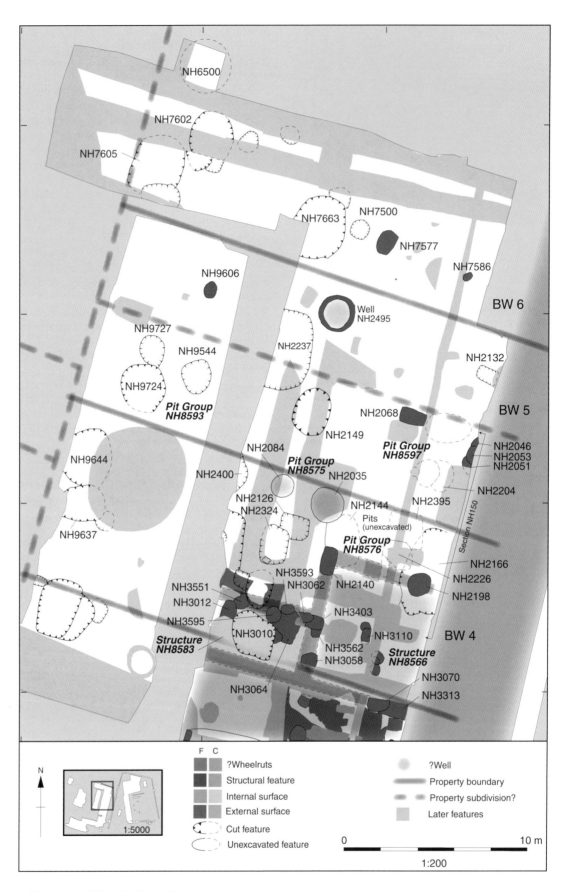

Fig. 4.5   Properties BW 4–6, Phase 5

Structure NH8566

Contemporary post-Conquest floor and occupation levels pertaining to Structure NH8566 did not survive though elements associated with the rebuild of its west and south walls and other internal features indicate its continued use. The rebuild seemingly utilised much larger posts which were set in elongated, rectangular post-pits, those on the west wall (NH3058 and NH3562) following the line of the earlier build whereas the southern wall may have been built further south (NH3313 and NH3070), slightly intruding onto the possible access 'lane' that ran along the north side of Property BW 3 (see above). The line of the north wall is uncertain unless represented by shallow pits NH2140 and NH2198, the latter containing large flint nodules that could have represented post-packing. Pits NH3058 and NH3562 within the west wall were of similar depth, measuring 0.78 m and 0.81 m respectively, the north side of pit NH3058 sloping perhaps to aid the insertion of the post that presumably was located at its south end (removed by a modern sewer trench). The pits contained large flint nodules and chalk blocks that may have been used as packing around the post. Pit NH3313, within the south wall of the structure, measured 0.76 m in depth and could have been integral with sub-rectangular pit NH3070 that was contained within its west end, possibly marking the position of the post. This pit was cut deeper at 1.1 m and measured 1.2 m across; this is too large to represent a post-pipe so may represent its removal. A number of mainly shallow postholes located internally within the structure may have marked divisions or working areas. Shallow pit NH3110 contained charcoal-rich silt that contained much flake hammerscale suggesting that, if contemporary with the structure, secondary smithing activity had been undertaken within it. It is possible that the upper levels of 'pit' NH2166, comprising interleaved thick spreads of compacted chalk and clay with grey silts associated with Anglo-Norman pottery, represented trampled levels—perhaps floors associated with the structure. The upper levels (NH2174) contained copper alloy debris and spill and flake hammerscale implying *in situ* evidence for copper working and secondary smithing.

Structure NH8583

An arrangement of small pits or postholes to the west of Structure NH8566 suggests that it may have been extended westwards over the area formerly set aside for pits in the late Saxon period. Pits NH3403, NH3062, NH3593, NH3595, NH3551 and NH3012 formed an approximate straight line perpendicular to the west wall of Structure NH8566. Most were shallow and rounded, measuring less than 0.2 m in depth, though pit NH3403, that could have defined its north-east corner, appeared to have represented a substantial post-pit similar to those used for the

rebuild of Structure NH8566. It was rectangular and measured 1.05 in length and 0.72 in width and was 1.31 m in depth suggesting it held a large post that supported a substantial load. No post-pipe was recorded but it contained a number of large flint nodules. A similar pit (NH3012), though shallower at 0.5 m, may have defined the north-west corner of the structure, and if so it measured *c* 5 m across. Its south wall had been removed by a modern sewer trench but presumably extended no further than the south wall of structure NH8566. No internal deposits survived though a shallow hollow (NH3604) within its east side may have represented the remains of a contemporary trodden surface; otherwise no evidence for its use was found. The structure appears to have gone out of use after a relatively short period since a large chalk-rubble filled pit (NH3010), containing Anglo-Norman pottery (if not residual), cut into its western side.

Exterior area

The area to the north of Structures NH8566 and NH8583 was set aside for the digging of pits that seem to have extended the whole length of the property. The pits were on the whole considerably larger than those that occupied the area during the late Saxon period and their increased density suggests more intense occupation. Two groups of pits were determinable, Pit Group NH8576 that comprised largely rectangular pits, the majority of which were to the north of the buildings, and Pit Group NH8575, which comprised circular pits closer to the proposed west and south boundaries of the property. The circular pits may have been later, since two of them cut rectangular pits pertaining to Pit Group NH8576. A strip measuring *c* 1.5 m located immediately to the north of Structure NH8583 was surfaced with thick angular gravel suggesting this area was maintained for access.

Pit Group NH8576

The pits in this group were rectangular and measured between 1.6 and 3.1 m in width. The only exception was a large, irregular pit-like feature (NH2166) in the north-east corner of the property, which measured *c* 4.8 m across. The excavated fills of this feature suggest that it represents slumping or levelling over one or more unexcavated pits below, rather than being a single pit itself. Pit NH2126 was bottomed at 1.34 m and contained a thin layer of decayed cess at its base suggesting that it represented a cleaned out cesspit. This also contained crucible fragments and copper alloy waste, the former with residues of copper alloys suggesting the manufacture of small bronze objects. The pit remained open long enough to allow for the weathering of its sides. It was eventually filled with refuse that contained a bone spindlewhorl (SF Cat no. 167) and a chalk spindle-whorl (see Shaffrey, Chapter 7) together with madder-stained sherds of Anglo-Norman pottery (including Newbury B-style fabric MTE dated *c* 1050–1200) suggesting that spinning and dyeing of yarn was being undertaken. Other notable finds included an iron flesh-hook (SF Cat no. 192) used for extracting meat from cauldrons. Adjacent pit NH2324/NH2184, which cut the southern edge of pit NH2126, probably originally served a similar purpose, though it was not bottomed at 1.9 m. It contained cessy fills at its excavated depth, whose decay had resulted in a marked degree of subsidence of its upper levels (NH2184). These fills also contained crucible fragments of a similar nature to pit NH2126 and madder-stained sherds of coarse grained sandy ware (Fabric MAQ dated *c* 1000–1250) suggesting that the manufacture of copper alloy objects and dyeing continued over a sustained period of time. It is possible that a folded piece of copper alloy sheet and fragments of iron that were also found may have represented items originally intended for the manufacture of metal objects. The pit was levelled and capped with burnt clay and chalk, and contained pottery datable to the late 12th or early 13th centuries. The pits to the west were rapidly excavated but appear by their shape and size to be broadly contemporary with those to the east, implying that the bulk of the northern half of the property was reserved for the digging of these types of pits. One pit (NH9644) was at least 1.74 m deep and contained cessy fills, domestic refuse and a half-finished boned object, possibly the start of a skate.

Pit Group NH8575

The north side of pits NH2084, NH2035 and NH2400 form a straight line, probably reflecting the boundary between Properties BW 4 and BW 5 first established during the late Saxon period, which continued to be maintained though perhaps with a slight encroachment to the north. Pits NH2084 and NH2035 formed almost perfect circles, measuring 1.2 m and 1.8 m in diameter respectively, both having straight vertical sides with little evidence for weathering, suggesting they were originally lined. Probing revealed that NH2084 was at least 3 m deep suggesting that it could have served as a well (Plate 4.15). There was a narrow void between the fills and the pit edge suggesting this was once occupied by a timber lining that had subsequently decayed *in situ*. The pit had been rapidly filled with ashy and cessy fills that contained industrial debris including crucible fragments and flake hammerscale. The former had residues containing copper, zinc and lead indicating small bronze/brass objects were being cast and the latter were probably sweepings from secondary smithing undertaken nearby. An iron strap and bar that were also found could also represent waste from such metalworking activity. A sheep bone fragment showed evidence for marrow draining and the bone may have been waste from bone working. The upper levels of pit NH2084 were capped with large flints and

Plate 4.15 Pit NH2084, showing rubble and compacted chalk capping, Property BW 4, Phase 5, looking north

compacted chalk that contained large fragments of a Tripod Pitcher (Fabric MAD dated *c* 1050–1225) and small quantities of Laverstock ware (Fabric MNX dated *c* 1230–1350) suggesting a filling date during the early-mid 13th century. The presence of a medieval ridge tile, an Anglo-Norman peg-tile and a rounded block of possible Paludina limestone (assuming it is not residual Roman) suggests that a substantial structure stood nearby, the latter was almost exclusively used for churches. Adjacent pit NH2035 may also have served as a well but voids in its fill forced the abandonment of its excavation at a depth of 0.83 m. Its compacted chalk and clay fills suggest it was deliberately capped. Amongst the finds from this feature were an iron bell clapper (SF Cat no. 374; see Chapter 7, Fig. 7.32) and a copper dress pin with a glass head of 11th- to 12th-century date (SF Cat no. 131; see Chapter 7, Fig. 7.24). Given that the bell was found close to the chapel on Property SE 2 it is tempting to suggest it may have been used in some religious ceremonial function; however, it might simply represent a product of the smithy that seems to have existed within Property BW 4 (see Cool, Chapter 7). Too little of pit NH2400 was investigated to suggest its function though pottery from its upper fills of chalk rubble suggest that, as with the other pits, it was levelled during the late 12th or early 13th centuries.

Property BW 5 (Fig. 4.5)

Structural evidence

Little evidence for buildings within the property was found, though horizontal levels pertaining to floors or other internal deposits may have been removed by later truncation. The presence of pits and the construction of a chalk-lined well (see below) towards the west of the property would imply that structures occupied the frontage. It is possible that late Saxon Structures NH8589 and NH8590 (see Chapter 3) continued in use without major structural alteration that left any coherent archaeological trace (but see Pit Group NH8597 below). However, the presence of shallow pits within the frontage area inside the southern half of the property would suggest that Structure NH8589 had been demolished during this period and conversely the lack of contemporary pits to the north would imply that Structure NH8590 continued in use. The lack of pits within the north-west quadrant of the property and the presence of substantial posthole NH9606 could imply that this space was also occupied by a structure. The posthole was oval and measured 0.9 m across and 0.62 m in depth and contained a post-pipe measuring 0.4 m across implying a substantial timber upright. No other postholes were identified in the area and it probably survived later truncation because it had been dug deeper into the fills of an earlier pit that may subsequently have subsided.

Pits

The intensity of pit digging showed a significant decline compared to the preceding period and was, with the exception of well NH2495, confined to the southern half of the property. Two main groups were represented, Pit Group NH8593 located towards the west and comprising large circular pits, and Pit Group NH8597 consisting of small shallow pits to the east. In addition the upper levels of late Saxon pit NH2237 contained a long sequence of fills suggesting either that it remained partially open, or more likely, that there had been several episodes of consolidation over underlying subsiding fills, the latest datable to the late 12th or early 13th centuries. These contained dumps of ashy waste that contained predominantly flake hammerscale derived from secondary smithing activity undertaken close-by. A large amount of domestic refuse was also dumped that included notable quantities of horse and roe deer.

Pit Group NH8593

This was represented by four large circular or sub-circular pits, all confined to the south of the

proposed late Saxon property subdivision, Pit Group NH8591 (see Chapter 3), which may imply that the possible division within the property remained extant into the Anglo-Norman period. Three of the pits were clustered towards the west in an area previously not utilised for the digging of pits. These were largely mechanically excavated and limited evidence for their use and precise date was recovered. Pit NH9544 measured 1.7 m in diameter and was bottomed at 1.57 m, its fills containing domestic refuse including a notable quantity of horse remains, although there was no evidence for the disposal of cess. The largest pit (NH9724) was probably the latest, and measured 1.7 m in diameter and over 1.8 m in depth. It is unlikely to have served as a well since its sides showed evidence of considerable weathering implying that it had not been lined and had been open for an appreciable period of time. Its lower fills comprised rather homogeneous dark fills containing largely domestic refuse, though a significant quantity of undiagnostic iron slag also present suggests waste from iron working. The pit was eventually capped with compacted mortar-rich rubble and crushed ceramic rubble that seemingly represent a deliberate attempt to stabilise the area of the pit. Little useful dating was recovered, though the nature of its upper fills suggests that they were derived from construction debris associated with a nearby (medieval) masonry-built structure. Pit NH2149 was located within a previously dense area of pitting towards the west, apparently a re-cut of late Saxon pit NH2045 (see Chapter 3). The pit was sub-circular, with straight vertical sides and measured 2.3 m across and at least 2.4 m in depth. It was filled largely with a homogeneous and loose mortar-rich clay silt indicating that it had been rapidly filled and had possibly been a well, though there was no evidence for a lining. It contained South Hampshire red ware and other pottery that suggests a late 12th- to early 13th-century date, and this is supported by the presence of a horseshoe fragment (SF Cat no. 228), a type datable to the 12th–13th century. The pit also contained a large part of a smithing hearth bottom and hammerscale probably dumped from nearby smithing activity and it is conceivable that the horseshoe may have been a product of such activity—perhaps discarded as a waster. The presence of worked squared Quarr stone, a stone used predominantly before the 13th century (Tatton-Brown 1980, 213–15 and see discussion in Chapter 5), and fragments of mortar wall plaster further testify to the presence of substantial structures nearby at the time of the filling of the pit. Like pit NH9724, its uppermost levels comprised compacted mortar rubble that formed part of a levelling process—the similarity of the deposits with those capping pit NH9724 suggesting they were deposited at the same time.

Pit Group NH8597

Located towards the south-east of the property, the function of this group of small, mainly shallow or unexcavated pits is uncertain. Most contained fairly consistent fills of mid-dark grey-brown sandy silts loams, one (NH2068) containing a horseshoe fragment (SF Cat no. 227) datable to the late 11th–13th centuries. Most were poorly dated though three pre-dated medieval pit NH2007 (see Phase 6 below). Only pit NH2068 was of note, being trapezoid in shape with a concave end and rather deep (0.68 m) for its size; it resembled the narrow elongated pits that formed part of possible late Saxon boundary, Pit Group NH8591 (see Chapter 3). However, it was off-set to the south of this boundary and it may have formed a later element of the north wall of late Saxon Structure NH8591, though no evidence for a post or associated packing was recorded. Similarly, one or more of inter-cutting pit fragments NH2046, NH2053, and NH2051 (see section in Fig. 4.16 below) may also have represented late elements of the east wall of the structure.

Well NH2495

Chalk-lined well NH2495 was located adjacent to the boundary with Property BW 6 within an area formerly set aside for the digging of cess and other pits. It was constructed free-standing within a circular pit measuring 3.4 m in diameter, the intervening space between the cut and the chalk lining packed with redeposited natural and disturbed fills of the earlier pits and containing sherds of 11th–12th-century Tripod Pitcher ware. The lining was constructed with rectangular chalk blocks *c* 0.3 m in length and *c* 0.2 m in width, that had been cut to fit the curvature of the well shaft which measured 1.5 m in diameter. No mortar bonding was apparently used and the face showed an ashlar like appearance, though many of the exposed blocks were heavily pitted through weathering, and the south side had collapsed altogether. 'Limescale' staining on the northern face may have been derived from the lifting of the bucket and associated spills. A geoarchaeological borehole revealed that the base of the well lay at 39.38 m OD or *c* 10.5 m below the surviving surface. No waterlogged deposits were revealed at its base

Plate 4.16   Chalk lined pit or well NH7602, Property BW 6, Phase 5, looking north

and the well was seemingly rapidly backfilled with flint-rich clay mixed with blocky chalk rubble. Its uppermost fill, presumably representing its final levelling, contained a sherd from an imported Paffrath-type ladle and other contemporary pottery suggesting an early 13th-century date. Also contained within the fill were many slate fragments, a medieval floor tile and a large block of Quarr stone. The latter came from a pointed corner of an architectural stone block, probably from a buttress, and had slightly splayed tooling of classic Norman type. It could conceivably have originated from the buttress that formed part of the lining of well-house Structure NH3547 (see Property BW 3 above).

Property BW 6 (Fig. 4.5; Plate 4.16)

Structural evidence

It is probable, given the lack of pits within the eastern half of the property, that this space was set aside for structures. Any floors or associated levels pertaining to such structures had been removed by later terracing and it is assumed that late Saxon Structure NH8605 (see Chapter 3), only tentatively identified, continued in use without any major modifications, or that any subsequent structures were not substantial enough to leave any trace. It is possible that shallow posthole NH7577 represented a modification of its west wall, while a mortar filled posthole, NH7586, gives some hints on the use of floor material. A shallow ovoid pit, NH7500, may have been closely associated with the structure since it contained charcoal-rich sandy clay that was rich in hammerscale. The pit also contained many fish and marine shell remains, particularly herring and periwinkles, but including an appreciable quantity of other marine fish including plaice/right-eyed flat-fishes, turbot, conger, thornback and dace that suggest the preparation and consumption of food in the immediate vicinity. A diverse assemblage of animal remains came from the pit, including fowl such as duck, goose and other birds. Amphibian remains such as toads suggest that the pit had been left open to the elements. The presence of madder-stained sherds of Newbury-B style pottery (Fabric MTE dated *c* 1050–1200) suggests that dyeing was also undertaken within the property during the 11th–12th centuries. The possible late Saxon cellar (NH8503; see Chapter 3) may have continued in use into the post-Conquest period given the lack of pits cutting its infilling, though it is equally possible that the area was left open for use as a yard given the well-consolidated nature of its fills. Eventually possible well NH7633 (see below) cut through its eastern side.

Pits

The density of pitting seems to have increased into the post-Conquest period implying that the occupation levels within the property intensified. They were confined toward the rear half of the property implying that the area adjacent to the frontage was occupied by structures. The pits formed a cluster that may have reflected the western extent of the property, possibly marked by pits NH7605 and NH6500 given the apparent absence of further pits to their west. In contrast to the earlier pits, most were circular, with the largest pits (NH7602, NH7605 and NH7663) all of a similar size and measuring between 2.6 m and 2.9 m in diameter. The fills of the most easterly and largest pit (NH7663) were in marked contrast to those of the other pits, comprising thick dumps of compacted gravel and chalk to its deepest excavated extent of 1 m. The presence of unglazed medieval sandy wares suggests a date between the mid 12th and 13th centuries, slightly later than the other pits. The pit would have been situated immediately to the rear of any structures that presumably lay to its east and may have originally served as a well, though no evidence for a lining was found at the level excavated. Its rapid infilling with well-consolidated material seems to have been a deliberate and well-managed attempt to provide level and stable ground.

Pit NH7605, given its location immediately to the rear of late Saxon pit NH7694 (see Chapter 3), occupied the last available space along the southern boundary of the property and therefore was probably dug sequentially after NH7694. It was excavated to a depth of 1 m and contained domestic rubbish. Its upper levels contained waste from a hearth and much undiagnostic iron slag, presumably from iron-working on the property. Adjacent pit NH7602 (=NH7693) was probably the next pit dug and was excavated to a depth of 1.6 m. The lower levels of the pit sides had been 'lined' with compacted chalk (Plate 4.15), though it is unclear whether this was deliberate or the result of severe subsidence of the unexcavated underlying fills. If the latter is the case then it simply represented capping to seal off pungent odours from organic material such as cess that had subsequently decayed and subsided. The pit was levelled with dumps of cess-stained soils containing much domestic refuse and a notably large quantity of horn-cores, presumably waste after the removal of the sheath during horn working. It is probable that pit NH6500, given the degree of subsidence of its fill, served a similar purpose before being used as a rubbish pit.

SNITHELING STREET

Property SE 1: West side (Fig. 4.6)

Pits pre-dating Structure NH8618

Rectangular pit NH6107 formed an almost perfect 2:1 rectangle measuring 4 m by 2 m with straight, vertical sides and 1.67 m in depth, its regular nature and the lack of weathering of its sides suggesting that had originally been timber-lined. Its earliest fills comprised thick dumps of redeposited natural clay with lenses of dark brown organic silts suggesting these represented rapid infilling after it ceased to have been used for its original purpose. They contained domestic refuse and Anglo-Norman coarse sandy wares suggesting a date prior to the mid 12th century. Its upper fills contained a significant quantity of horn-cores suggesting waste from nearby horn-working. In the absence of evidence for its use for some industrial purpose, the pit may have served as a small timber-lined cellar—perhaps given its depth, as a cold storage pit. If so, it may have been sited close to, or possibly attached to, a structure, though its fillings apparently pre-dated Structure NH8618 (see below). A shallow pit (NH6112) located adjacent to its south side may have been integral to the possible cellar, possibly representing some form of access, though too little survived to establish this with any certainty. Similarly, rather irregular and shallow pit NH6070, located immediately to the west of NH6112, may also have been associated although it appeared to truncate the south-west corner of pit NH6107. Its base sloped sharply downwards towards the east towards a point alongside the southern edge of the possible cellar and it may have formed part of a ramped access. A further shallow rectangular pit (NH6047) lay to its south, and contained refuse including bone from a roe deer.

Oval pit NH6034 was somewhat larger, measuring 4.15 m across, and appears to have been rapidly filled with a sequence of mainly dark grey silty clays to its excavated depth of 1.2 m before being capped with compacted redeposited natural clay. It contained a moderate quantity of domestic refuse including Tripod Pitcher ware (Fabric MAD, dated 1050–1225) suggestive of a date prior to the mid 13th century. It is feasible given its size that it originally served as a well but this could not be determined at the depth excavated.

Structure NH8618

An arrangement of small pits and postholes located towards the west of the property formed part of a rectangular structure that may have flanked the street frontage to the west. A straight line of small pits (NH6001, NH6095, NH6117, NH6066) represented the east wall of the structure. The pits were roughly oval, with concave sides and bases, varying in size from 0.74–1.74 m across and 0.1–0.7 m in depth. Pits NH6117 and NH6066 contained evidence for circular post-pipes measuring 0.2 m and 0.34 m in diameter respectively. The post-pipes were spaced *c* 2.1 m apart and if this distance was projected southwards then it would correspond with the position of the other postholes. The northern extent of the structure may have been delimited by pits NH6152 and NH6071, although any evidence for the north-east corner of the building would have been removed by a modern foundation trench. Similarly, its southern extent was probably delimited by pits NH6135 and NH8055, the base of the former containing compacted chalk rubble possibly acting as a pad for the post. If the interpretation of this arrangement is correct then the width of the structure would have been *c* 8.5 m and if its length is projected westwards to the postulated street frontage, it may been 12–13 m in length. Internal posthole NH6012, located centrally along its longitudinal axis, may have been part of a line of uprights that would have supported the roof.

No evidence of flooring survived, though thin spreads of trampled silt located within its footprint may have been associated. These contained domestic refuse and one also produced a copper alloy buckle plate fragment datable to the 12th–15th centuries (SF Cat no. 140). Similarly, compacted clay filling a shallow hollow formed over earlier pits may have formed part of a floor level. A shallow pit (NH6126), located against the north wall, contained burnt clays set on a bed of yellowish cream mortar and probably represented a hearth. Given the lack of evidence to the contrary, apart from a small

quantity of hammerscale in pit NH8055, it is assumed that this was a domestic dwelling.

Pits associated with Structure NH8618

Apparently contained within the structure was a chalk-lined well (NH6146), although only the very eastern edge of its lining lay within the excavated area. It was constructed with rectangular chalk blocks bonded with cream mortar that had been built free-standing within a circular pit. The void between the wall and the pit edge had been filled with compact redeposited natural gravel and clay that contained sherds of mid 11th- to mid 12th-century Newbury B ware. Its subsequent robbing had removed any stratigraphic relationships with Structure NH8618, though if it was associated, this would imply that this part of the structure represented an enclosed well-house. After robbing, the well was levelled with compacted redeposited natural gravel and chalk containing early and medieval sandy wares attributable to the late 12th to early 13th centuries.

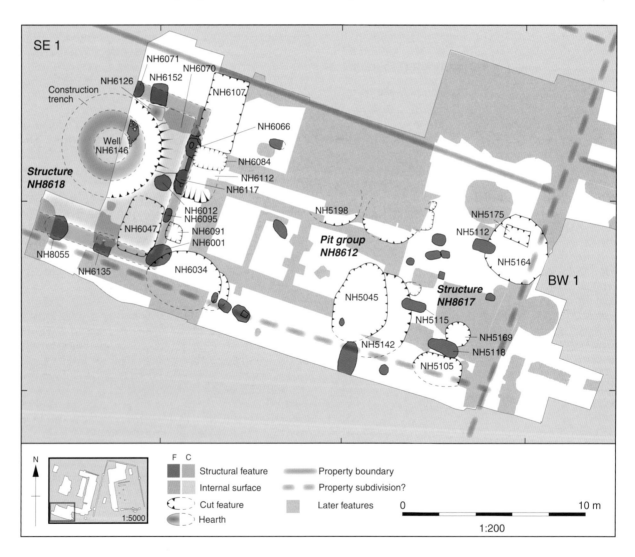

Fig. 4.6   Property SE 1, Phase 5

Abutting the line of the east wall of the structure were two small cesspits that may have been contemporary with its use, perhaps given their position serving upper storey garderobes. Rectangular and vertical sided pit NH6084 measured 1.8 by 1.2 m and was 0.7 m in depth and contained thick deposits of greenish-brown sandy silt indicative of cess; it was capped with loose chalk and charcoal presumably to seal in the odours. A possible sherd of South Hampshire Red ware was recovered from the cess suggesting that the pit was in use from the late 12th or 13th centuries. Square pit NH6091 was of a similar depth and also contained a thick, organic, brown, silty clay and had been capped with compacted clay. The pit was notable for containing bones from a roe deer (see pit NH6047 above) and from a juvenile cat, the latter, given its age, possibly to be associated with the evidence for fur-industry animals identified within contemporary pits at the east end of the property (see Pit Group NH8612 below).

Property SE 1: East side (Fig. 4.6; Plate 4.17)

Structure HN8617

Evidence for a possible timber structure or structures was found at the east end of the property defined by a scatter of postholes and small shallow pits, several of which cut into the backfilled rubbish pits in the area. No coherent plan could be established though it was noted that several of the larger pits located towards the south contained post impressions and were reminiscent of post-pits that formed part of substantial structures elsewhere on the site (see Property SE 2, Chapter 3). It is possible that the south part of the structure represented a timber phase of medieval masonry-founded structure NH8615 as one post-pit was overlain by wall NH5104 (see Phase 6 below).

Pit Group NH8612

The density of pitting increased during the Anglo-Norman period, the pits becoming substantially larger and occupying the whole area, though they did not extend any further west than the late Saxon pits leaving a gap *c* 5 m wide between these pits and the pits associated with Structure NH8618 to the west.

Only three of the pits (NH5169, NH5164 and NH5175) were sufficiently excavated to allow some insight into their original use. Pit NH5169 was of particular interest since it contained a rich assemblage of finds giving insights into the status, diet and occupation of the inhabitants of the property. It was almost perfectly circular measuring 1.35 m in diameter and survived to a depth of 1.45 m, with very straight and vertical sides and a flat base that indicated it had been protected from the elements, though its rather small diameter makes it unlikely that it had been lined. The pit contained dumps of kitchen waste and ash assumed to have come from

Plate 4.17   Pit NH5045, Property SE 1, Phase 5, looking north

domestic ovens and hearths. Most notably the pit contained several foot/lower leg bones of squirrel, fox, polecat/ferret and stoat, suggesting furrier activity, rare evidence from an archaeological site. Furs from squirrels and mustelids formed a very extensive trade in early medieval Europe. The foot bones were often left on the pelts, and were later removed by furriers at their final destination (see Strid, Chapter 8). Also present were partially articulated remains of several juvenile cats, some showing evidence for skinning marks on the skulls and mandibles implying that their fur was also utilised.

The pit was rich in a variety of fish remains, predominantly herring, but including other marine fish such as garfish, cod, whiting, ling, flounder, plaice, mackerel and a bone from a sturgeon. The latter is a fish normally associated with individuals of higher status and was designated as a royal fish in the reign of Edward II (1307–27). The unusually high proportion of burnt bones, indicative of roasting, could also be an indicator of higher status as this is a relatively fuel demanding and labour intensive cooking method. The pit contained a large quantity of Anglo-Norman fine sandy ware (Fabric MBK), a form that is thought to date mainly up to the middle of the 12th century (see Cotter, Chapter 7). The upper levels of the pit also contained medieval sandy ware (MDF) and a few sherds of Early South Hampshire red ware (MNG) that could imply that it was levelled during the late 12th or early 13th century.

Large circular pit NH5164, measuring 3.4 m in diameter, was initially assumed originally to have been a well due to the appearance of a large and deep void during the excavation of its upper levels. However, mechanical excavation revealed its depth to have been *c* 1.8 m with cess-stained silts noted against its sides and along its base, the shrinkage of which may have accounted for the void. The pit appears to have been rapidly filled with mid grey silty clay, the upper levels of which contained a large quantity of domestic refuse including Anglo-Norman fine sandy wares (MBK), suggesting a date before 1150. It is possible that much of this material had accumulated over the pit after its infilling since a small amount of pottery recovered from its lower levels during machining included a large part of a chalk-tempered storage jar in fabric MBX that would imply a date no later than the 11th century and a pre-Conquest date cannot therefore be ruled out. A significant period of time must have elapsed before a second cesspit (NH5175) was dug into its upper fills. This pit was small and rectangular, measuring 1.2 by 0.9 m across and 0.64 m deep, its size and shape similar to pit NH6084 located within the western part of the property. A fine deposit of green/brown cess at its base contained a few mineralised fruit seeds and stones that included a grape pip, an imported fruit usually consumed by occupants of higher status. Interestingly, the upper fill of the pit also contained the remains from at least at least three juvenile cats and a fox metatarsal, suggesting waste from a furrier, similar to pit NH5169, situated 5 m to the south. Like pit NH5169, it also contained a wide variety of sea fish remains including sea bream and scad and was probably levelled during the late 12th or early 13th centuries.

Large oval pit NH5045 (Plate 4.17), in excess of 1.9 m in depth, had been rapidly filled with homogeneous dark soil that contained a horseshoe datable to the late 11th–13th century, the pottery suggesting a date prior to the mid 12th century. It is possible that shallow pit NH5142, flanking its east side, may have allowed access into it, otherwise its function is uncertain. Pit NH5105 contained an equal-armed balance (SF Cat no. 216) and a large part of a smithing hearth bottom, the former suggesting the accurate weighing of valuable items was required. The pits to the north-west were too fragmentary to warrant further comment apart from pit NH5198, which contained a high percentage of burnt bone and charred meadow hay suggesting bedding or fodder for animals. Further evidence for furrier activity was also found, including remains of a ferret and a small mammal showing cut marks around the area of the foot, perhaps an attempt to remove the paw.

Properties SE 2 and SE 3 (Figs 4.7–8; Plates 4.18–19)

Within the broad time span of Phase 5 (*c* 1050–1225) this area of the site saw a significant change in character. Two substantial stone-built structures

located towards the rear of Property SE 2 and the adjacent (unexcavated) property to the south seem to have formed the original core of what was to become a spacious urban residence, identifiable in the 13th century as that of the Archdeacon of Winchester. Both structures were first partially exposed in a series of small trenches by Cunliffe in 1960 (Fig. 4.7) and interpreted by him as a two-celled chapel and the cellar of a stone house, both of which he considered to be of late 12th-century date. The stone house lay outside the area of the excavations that form the subject of the present report, but the western cell of Cunliffe's chapel, and the area immediately surrounding it, were re-examined. The west end of the chapel had been

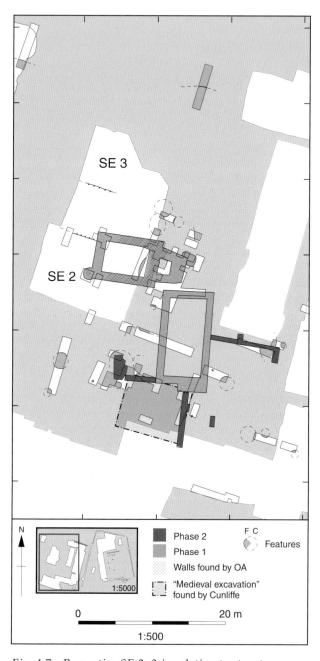

Fig. 4.7 Properties SE 2–3 in relation to structures found in Cunliffe's excavation

destroyed by the foundations of Northgate House, the SCATS office building built on the site after Cunliffe's 1960 excavation, and this has caused problems in understanding the relationship between the construction of the chapel and other features in the vicinity. Nevertheless, the present excavations have added valuable new information regarding the context within which these developments took place. The interpretation and dating of these buildings are discussed in Chapter 5 in the light of the additional evidence from the present excavations, but for the sake of clarity here we will continue to refer to them as the chapel and the stone house.

Property SE 2: The chapel (Structure NH8629)

Relationship to earlier features

During Phase 4.2 a substantial earth-fast timber post structure (NH8622) occupied the western part of the excavated area of Property SE 2 (see Chapter 3; Fig. 4.8). This building seems not to have survived long into Phase 5, since the pottery from

the fills of its post-pits was of markedly late Saxon character, including Winchester ware (Fabric MWW dated *c* 950–1100) and other late Saxon wheel-thrown sandy wares. One pit produced sherds in coarse grained sandy fabric MAQ (dated *c* 1000–1250). Only a single sherd of exclusively post-Conquest pottery was present and this, together with a fragment of worked Quarr stone, is considered likely to be intrusive. Quarr stone is known to have been used in the construction of the stone house, but it is not known whether it was used in the construction of the chapel.

A number of pits to the east of Structure NH8622 were contemporary with its use. Four of these pits (NH1586, NH1331, NH1159 and NH1244, described in Chapter 3 above) were cut by the footings of the chapel. The pottery recovered from these pits dates them to the pre-Conquest period, but cannot shed any further light on the date of the construction of the chapel.

A single pit in this area, NH1005, located immediately south of Structure NH8622, is datable to Phase 5. This pit clipped the south side of one of the post-pits of the south wall of Structure NH8622. It was

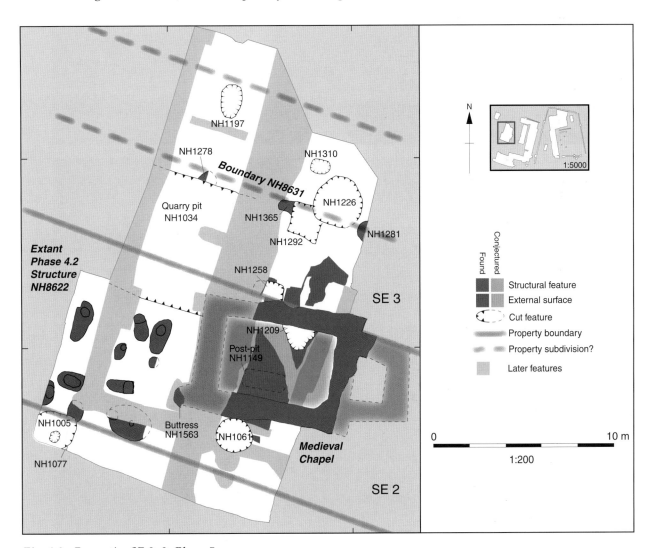

Fig. 4.8   Properties SE 2–3, Phase 5

sub-rectangular, measuring approximately 2 m by 1.9 m in plan, and was excavated to a depth of 1.06 m. At this depth the sides of the pit were somewhat irregular as a result of weathering, and this was reflected in the nature of its earliest fills, exposed against its edges, which comprised redeposited natural and lenses of silting. The pit had been levelled with dumps of domestic refuse that contained metalworking debris including a small quantity of crucible fragments, smithing slag, vitrified furnace fragments and hammerscale. The

crucible fragments (NH1022) contained traces of quaternary copper alloy, the size of the fragments suggesting that small decorative objects were being manufactured (see Mortimer, Chapter 7). The pit contained predominantly Anglo-Norman pottery including Newbury B-style ware (Fabric MTE dated 1050–1200) and Tripod pitchers (Fabric MAD dated *c* 1050–1225), although the presence of Early South Hampshire red ware (*c* 1175–1250) suggests that it was finally filled at a relatively late stage within Phase 5 (*c* 1175–1200?).

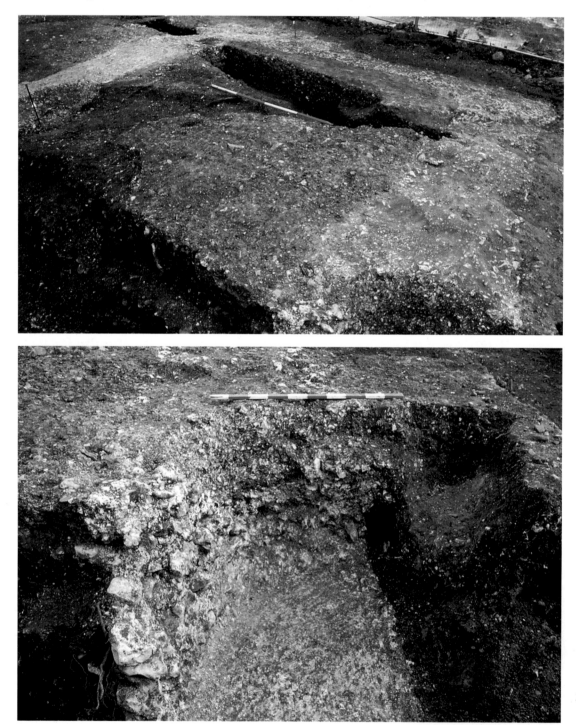

Plate 4.18   Chalk footings of 'Chapel' NH8629, Property SE 2, Phase 5, looking west and north-east

Structural and associated evidence

The exposed footings of the chapel (NH1066) within construction cut NH1067 defined a two-cell building, orientated west-east. The footings were of chalk rubble contained within an outer and inner face of rough chalk blocks compacted into and abutting the continuous vertically sided construction trench (see Plate 4.18). The foundations of the north, south and west wall of the western cell were 1.1 m wide, with its eastern wall 1.6 m wide; to the east was the smaller cell whose north and south walls were 1.1–1.3 m wide, and whose eastern wall was exceptionally wide at 1.9 m. The depth of the footings was observed to be 0.8 m in a single location only, which was provided by the re-excavation of a trench from the 1960 excavation.

The western cell measured 6.1 m by 4 m internally. At its south-western corner a buttress footing was exposed (NH1563), presumably added to counter subsidence over the soft fill of an earlier feature. The eastern cell extended from the east wall of the western cell, and was trapezoidal in shape, enclosing a small area of 1.7 m by 2.4 m. A small earlier pit under its north-eastern corner had been filled with rammed chalk, again presumably to counter subsidence.

A sequence of layers was revealed in the interior of the western cell. Whether any of these layers can be correlated with layers observed outside the footprint of the chapel remains unclear. Within the footprint of the chapel the sequence of layers was recorded as beginning with the infilling or levelling (NH1257) of Phase 4.2 pit NH1331, followed by a laminated layer of silty clay (NH1192). A similar layer (NH1226) was identified against the northern footing trench. Cut into layer NH1192, and cutting pit NH1331, was a large oval feature (NH1149), probably a post-pit, which was itself backfilled and sealed by subsequent layers in the sequence, suggesting that the post within this post-pit had stood for only a relatively short time. (The similarity between this post-pit and the post-pits of Structure NH8622 was noted in Chapter 3, above. There is, however, insufficient evidence to determine whether the post is more likely to have been associated with the late Saxon building or with a phase of construction of the chapel itself.) The internal layer sequence within the western cell of the chapel footprint continued with two clay layers (NH1138 and NH1128), followed by a shallow spread of pinkish mortar (NH1129), the latter possibly a residue from plastering of the interior. A more robust layer of gravel and flint (NH1105) may represent the make up for a floor surface; this was followed by another silty clay layer (NH1085) and a further layer of gravel and silty clay (NH1062). This, the highest surviving deposit, contained a fragment of a copper alloy figurine (SF Cat no. 373; see Chapter 7, Fig. 7.32) and could have formed the base for a solid floor of tiles or flagstones that were presumably salvaged for reuse elsewhere when the building was eventually demolished.

The pottery from these layers is of post-Conquest date, including the common local fine sandy ware fabric MBK (predominantly datable *c* 1050–1150) and the flint-tempered Newbury B-style ware, fabric MTE (*c* 1050–1200).

Pit NH1209 was identified inside the footprint of the chapel, against the footings of the north wall. It was not visible on the outside of the wall. It is unclear whether the pit was earlier than the chapel and cut by the footings, or whether it had been excavated against the north wall. It was at least 1.09 m in depth and appeared to have been rapidly backfilled with dark soil that contained domestic refuse (including oven fragments and fragments of animal bone) and Newbury B-style pottery. Shallow pit NH1258 was located against the north side of the north wall. Its function is unclear and it may have been a post-pit associated with earlier activity in the area. Pit NH1061 was located almost flush against the outer edge of the footings of the south wall, although no stratigraphic relationship between the two survived. It was circular, vertical-sided and measured 1.5 m in diameter, and its base was not reached at its excavated depth of 1.43 m. Its straight and unweathered sides could imply that it had once been lined and served as a well, although there was no further evidence to support this. Its relationship to the chapel remains unclear, although at the excavated depth its fills comprised predominantly chalk, flint rubble and lime mortar, well-consolidated in its upper levels. It also contained a significant amount of Anglo-Norman pottery, including Newbury B-style ware and fine sandy wares. The upper layers of this pit could attest to deliberate backfilling to consolidate an earlier feature (and are similar to deposits observed elsewhere) in preparation for construction, and therefore seem likely to be contemporary with the building of the chapel.

The stone house

The stone house, excavated by Cunliffe in 1960, lay outside the area of the present excavations, and the following description is based on his published report (see Fig. 4.7).

In close proximity to the chapel footprint was the footprint and cellar of a rectangular hall, defined by the footings, which comprised roughly coursed chalk blocks and flint nodules in a cream mortar bond, set within a construction pit. At the northern end of the building the cellar wall survived virtually to the level of the estimated contemporary ground surface, measuring 10.4 m by 5.1 m, and the outer surface of the structure was seen to be faced with Greensand blocks tooled with fine parallel lines. The possible location for the springing of the cellar vault was identified in the north-west corner of the cellar at a height of approximately 1.8 m from the cellar floor. The cellar floor itself comprised a layer of puddled chalk over a sporadic layer of mortar (the latter presumably spillage from the cellar's initial rendering).

The average width of the cellar footings at ground level was 1 m, although in the south-eastern corner the footing was 1.9 m wide. This was interpreted by Cunliffe as the likely base of an external staircase, set against the gable end of the hall. Cunliffe noted that such external stairs were typically—but not invariably—set against the long side of the building. Their situation in this instance may relate to the available room within the property.

Some evidence possibly pertaining to the superstructure of the hall was recovered from the cellar infill. The angles of two coping stones, both of Quarr stone, allowed Cunliffe to estimate the roof pitch at 55°, consistent with the use of a heavy roof covering like stone slates, of which several fragments were found. The presence of Quarr stone, and the date-range of its use in this region is significant, and is considered further in Chapter 5.

Associated features

Cunliffe noted (1964, 170), but did not closely investigate, a 'six foot deep medieval excavation'—a large deep pit measuring at least 6.7 m by 5.5 m that abutted the south-west corner of the hall, and was sealed by the later structural additions (its approximate location and size are indicated on Fig. 4.7). He did not suggest a function for this feature, but in the light of the existence of the quarry pit directly adjacent to the chapel (see below, Property SE 3), it is reasonable to suggest that this 'excavation' might have been a similar quarry dug to extract chalk for the construction of the hall.

Cunliffe noted that occupation layers contemporary with the house had suffered truncation, and no other features or deposits could be confidently associated with its early life. In the scatter of trenches he dug across the site, a total of 25 'medieval' pits were recorded, although only the few directly related to the structures were detailed in the published report. As to the 'isolated' pits, away from the buildings, only the pottery groups 'of interest' were published. These produced pottery generally dating to the late 12th century or earlier, suggesting that, once the hall was built, the area around it was maintained as a clear yard surface, free from pitting.

Definitive artefactual dating evidence for the hall itself is lacking, although some conclusions can be drawn from its relationship to the chapel, its architectural characteristics, and its historical context (such as exists). These aspects are discussed further in Chapter 5.

Property SE 3 (Fig. 4.8; Plate 4.19)

Quarry pit NH1034

Immediately to the north-west of the chapel footprint was a very large steep-sided pit (NH1034) that occupied most of the western excavated area allocated to Property SE 3 in this phase. The north edge of pit NH1034 lay just to the south of a possible boundary line (Boundary NH8631) marked by three small, evenly spaced pits or postholes (NH1278, NH1365 and NH1281). If it is accepted that a property boundary was marked in the late Saxon period by the south edge of pit NH1140 (see Chapter 3), then the south edge of pit NH1034 clearly encroached significantly onto the north side of Property SE 2. The relationship between pit NH1034 and the chapel footings could not be determined, as this end of the chapel had been destroyed after Cunliffe's 1960 excavation by the footings for Northgate House. The same modern footings had also removed evidence for the original west and east extents of pit NH1034, although the east edge presumably lay within the area of the modern footings as the pit was not seen in the excavated area to their east. To the west, the modern footings formed the limit of the excavated area and it is not known whether the pit extended further in this direction.

Pit NH1034 was largely excavated by machine (Plate 4.19), the mechanical excavation ceasing at a depth of 2.25 m. Although the base of the pit was not reached, it had clearly been cut into the underlying chalk. The edges of the pit appeared to be vertical and unweathered as if it had not been open long, or had originally been lined, although no further evidence for timber or stone lining was seen. The vertical, rectilinear edges of the pit suggest that it might originally have been a cellar, although its considerable depth suggests that it was ultimately used for quarrying chalk. The earliest fill reached, visible against the northern and southern edges, comprised a thick deposit of compacted chalky mid grey clay loam that extended up to the top of the pit. Subsequent fills included domestic refuse and cessy silts. Finds were not generally retained from the mechanically excavated fills, although a large part of an Anglo-Norman cooking pot in a coarse sandy fabric was recovered. The fills of this feature appear to have continued to slump and subside, creating a large hollow that may have been used for dumping for a considerable time. Eventually, a large quantity of decayed mortar and flint (NH1041), possibly demolition from a nearby building, was tipped into the pit from the south, and sealed the layers of cess and refuse. This was overlain by a layer of clean chalk (NH1040), a layer of silty clay with flint and flecks of charcoal (NH1039/NH1045), a further layer of chalk (NH1036) and a further dump of silty loam (NH1035) which produced sherds of 13th- to 14th-century pottery. The final deposit in the sequence was a sandy mortar, the bedding for a cobbled surface (NH1026), which survived in a slight depression. This suggests that a concerted attempt finally to stabilise and consolidate the hollow was made some time during the occupancy of the Archdeacon of Winchester as part of the laying out of an external surface.

The relationship between this large feature and the adjacent chapel is not easy to understand. It seems more likely than not that pit NH1034 was

Plate 4.19   Possible quarry pit NH1034 (mechanically excavated), Property SE 2, Phase 5, looking south-east

used to quarry chalk for the chapel foundations. A pre-existing deep feature such as a disused cellar on the adjacent tenement to the north offering relatively easy access to the underlying chalk, might help to explain the uneasy juxtaposition of the quarry and the chapel. The builder of the chapel presumably held Property SE 2, and possibly the tenement to the south, but the fact that the chapel appears to respect a boundary with Property SE 3 to the north suggests that its builder did not have the right to encroach significantly onto this land. If the builder of the chapel did not hold Property SE 3, then it is easier to understand why he tolerated (or was unable to prevent) the dumping of cess and refuse in the backfilled quarry. We may assume that he accessed his chapel from the south-west, either through Property SE 2 or through the property to the south. The large quantity of decayed mortar and flint that was eventually tipped into pit NH1034 to seal the layers of refuse was in fact tipped from the south, and it is plausible that this was associated with a repair of the west end of the chapel, perhaps at the same time that a buttress was added to the south-west corner. We may imagine that more substantial repairs would have been required at the north-west corner, built over the edge of the subsiding quarry pit.

Other pits

The density of pitting within the excavated area of the property appears have been much reduced in contrast to the late Saxon period. Cunliffe's 1960 excavation to the east of the area of the present investigations also revealed only a limited number of pits of medieval date (1964, fig. 58 pits M1–M5). Large rectangular late Saxon pit NH1598 appears to have remained in use, and this relatively long period of use may explain the evidence for collapse of its sides. The presence of Anglo-Norman coarse

sandy wares, together with the absence of pottery such as Newbury B-style ware and Tripod pitchers, could indicate a date within the early part of the period. The pit contained many dumps of domestic refuse and much evidence for industrial activity, most notably smithing. Smithing hearth bottoms, hammerscale, smithing slag, vitrified furnace fragments and fayalitic runs suggest that the property contained a smithy, which seems to have existed on the property since the pre-Conquest period. The pit also contained a notable quantity of bone- and horn-working waste. Several fragments of bone had small holes drilled into them, and the sheaths had been removed from the horns. It is tempting to suggest that this activity could be related and perhaps objects of composite materials such as bone-handled knives were being manufactured on the site.

Square pit NH1292 measured 1.6 m across and was rather shallow, at 0.82 m. At its base was loose brown clay that contained domestic refuse and a large part of a Newbury B-style ware cooking pot. The pit was apparently rapidly backfilled with homogeneous grey-brown silty clay. This fill produced a large rim and shoulder sherd from an Anglo-Norman sandy ware jar (see Chapter 7, Fig. 7.15, no. 105) or cooking pot that was presumably contemporary with the filling of the pit, though a worn fragment of a medieval floor tile was also recovered and is possibly intrusive. Circular pit NH1226 abutted the line of Boundary NH8631 and clipped the north side of pit NH1292. It measured 2.6 m in diameter and was bottomed by machine at a depth of 2.6 m. The pit seems to have served as a rubbish pit and had remained open for a significant period of time judging by the weathering of its sides and the episodes of silting and the dumping of domestic refuse that included sherds from Tripod pitchers. The pit appears to have remained partially open until its filling during the 13th or14th centuries (see Phase 6, below). Isolated oval pit NH1197 was located immediately to the north of late Saxon pit NH1265 and adjacent to possible lane or yard NH8637 (see Chapter 3). Only the upper 0.79 m of it fills were investigated, revealing that it had been rapidly filled with homogeneous grey-brown silty clay containing domestic refuse including sherds of coarse sandy Anglo-Norman pottery and Winchester ware—the latter suggesting a later 11th-century date.

THE MEDIEVAL PERIOD (PHASE 6)

Features of Phase 6 (1225–1550) are described beginning with Brudene Street East (BE 1–5). The properties on the west side of Brudene Street and the east side of Snitheling Street, which were combined in this period, are then described, beginning with the amalgamated Properties BW 1/SE 1, followed by Properties BW 2 to BW 4/5, which had been incorporated into a single large property focused on the chapel and stone house in Property SE 2.

BRUDENE STREET EAST

Property BE 1 (Fig. 4.9)

Little evidence for activity was found within the property and what there is cannot be dated with any certainty to after 1300, although it is unclear whether this reflects a genuine lack of occupation or the effects of modern terracing of the site. Chalk-lined well CC1128 (see Phase 5 above) appears to have been filled and levelled during the early part of this period and no other features that could be interpreted as wells were found within the area excavated. It is possible that Posthole Group NH7054 defined the northern extent of the property during part of this period, although this would represent a 2.2 m encroachment northwards into Property BE 2.

Two pits were located towards the north of this property. Small pit CC1014 measured 0.94 m across and 0.86 m in depth and may have served as a cesspit since it contained cessy silt at its base. Its location is of note since it would have been positioned within or close to possible Phase 5 Structure NH7057, and it close association could suggest its continued use, though no further evidence for the continuity of this structure was seen. Rapidly filled pit CC1011 may have served a similar purpose though this could not be determined at the depth excavated.

Property BE 2 (Fig. 4.9; Plate 4.20)

In contrast to the adjacent property the density of pitting with Property BE 2 appears to have been maintained. Two distinct pit clusters were evident, Pit Group CC7011 located towards the southern side of the property and Group CC7015 located to the north.

Pit Group CC7011 was located immediately south of the Phase 5 pits (see Phase 5, Pit Group CC7001 above), an area perhaps formerly occupied by Phase 5 Structure CC7008. Four of the pits (CC1008, CC1198, CC1167, CC1159) formed a tight intercutting cluster of mainly small vertical-sided rectangular pits, none of which were bottomed at the excavated depth of *c* 1.2 m, and thus their original functions are difficult to determine. Most of the pits contained single rubble-rich fills containing relatively small amounts of domestic refuse suggesting rapid infilling rather than any prolonged use for the disposal of rubbish, at least at the depths excavated. Their confinement within such a small area suggests the presence of structures nearby, probably to the west. The repeated digging of pits in the same spot could suggest this area was set aside for latrines (feasibly within Structure CC7008) that were continuously emptied and re-dug, although there was no direct evidence of this. A fifth, squarish, pit (CC1298), located immediately to their east, cut across the wall line of Structure CC7008 and must therefore post-date its demolition. It had been rapidly filled with dumps of chalk rubble and domestic refuse to the depth excavated (1.2 m). Spot-dating of the pottery suggests that it was filled later than the pits to its west, possibly in the 14th century. The presence of medieval roofing tiles suggests a fairly substantial structure stood on the property, and further fragments of tile were also present within the pits to the west. A sherd of potash glass was also recovered from the pit, suggesting the inhabitants had access to glass vessels, items normally associated with those of higher status.

Pit Group CC7015 occupied an area previously devoid of pits close to the boundary with Property BE 3 and to the west of the earlier Anglo-Norman pits. Sub-rectangular pit CC1860, the earliest of three pits in the north-west area, was in marked contrast

Plate 4.20   Flint-lined cess-pit CC1518, Property BE 2, Phase 6

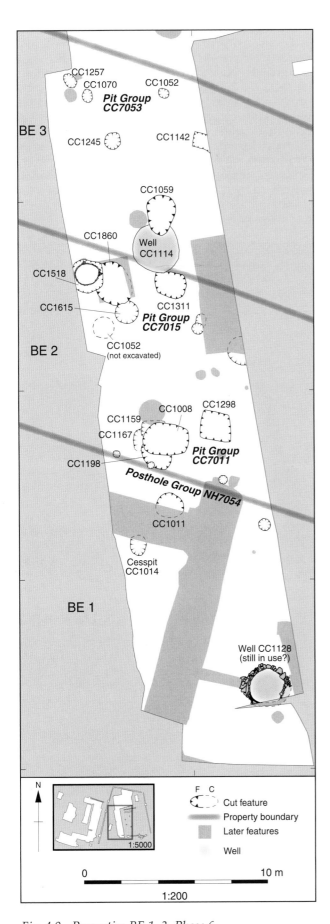

Fig. 4.9   Properties BE 1–3, Phase 6

to the later small circular pits in the area. It appears to have been rapidly filled with dark grey-brown clay-silt that contained domestic refuse and 13th- to 14th-century pottery to its excavated depth of 1.2 m. It was 'clipped' but otherwise respected by circular pits CC1615 and CC1518, both of which also contained pottery datable to 1200–1400. Pit CC1518 was notable for being lined with mortared flint and chalk rubble, its inner faced comprising roughly knapped flint nodules (Plate 4.20), and its internal diameter measuring 1.1 m. Geoarchaeological coring revealed the base of the pit at 43.96 m (*c* 3.4 depth), a level too shallow for it to served as a well. Its base lay at a depth of 5.3 m above the base of the wells found in Properties BE 4 and BE 5 and nearly 9 m above the base of well in Property BE 1 (see Phase 5 above). Its basal levels comprised loose, dark green-grey, charcoal-rich cess/clay silt from which two coprolites were recovered and although they contained no parasite evidence, they are probably human in origin (see Jones, Chapter 8). Such evidence points to the feature's use as a cesspit, maybe attached to or within a structure, the remains of which did not survive but which may have been located to the west. Its upper (hand-excavated) fill comprised chalk rubble that contained a selection of medieval ceramic tiles, predominantly peg-tiles but also including floor tile fragments, and roofing slate; these were presumably derived from the demolition of a nearby structure. Medieval roofing tiles and a limestone floor tile found within the upper fills of pit CC1311 further attest to the presence of a substantial building nearby. A sherd from a Saintonge poly-chrome jug, datable to 1280–1350 and rarely found in Winchester (see Cotter, Chapter 7), would offer further evidence that the occupants had access to fine imported goods.

Property BE 3 (Fig. 4.9)

The intensity of pitting that had occurred within this property during the preceding phase (see Phase 5 above) had all but ceased, possibly before 1300. Pit CC1114 located immediately adjacent to the boundary with Property BE 2 probably served as a well since geoarchaeological coring revealed its base at 39.88 m OD (*c* 7.4 m in depth), a level less than 1 m above the base of the chalk-lined wells in Properties BE 4 and BE 5 (see Phase 5 above). The coring also revealed that its base was lined with a deposit of stiff orange clay that may have acted as lining to prevent seepage of water through the chalk, although it was not possible to show whether the sides were lined in a similar manner. No evidence was found for a well-lining in its upper levels, though its straight and unweathered sides may originally have been protected by a timber lining. It is possible that the well was eventually disused but remained open since a 0.66 m thick deposit of very dark grey/black silt had accumu-lated over the base. Eventually it was deliberately infilled with chalk rubble and soil before finally being given a capping of hard chalky mortar. Its upper fills produced pottery and an equal-armed balance (SF Cat no. 212; see Chapter 7, Fig. 7.27) that suggests a date no later than the 13th century for its final filling, which could imply that the well had been in use for some time beforehand and possibly during Phase 5. Sufficient time must have elapsed for pit CC1059 to have clipped its north side before its final filling by the end of the 14th century.

Circular pit CC1245 cut into the western 'alignment' of pits (see Phase 5, Pit Group CC7050 above). The pit had a small diameter (0.92 m) in relation to its depth (below its excavated level of 1.1 m). Its earliest fill comprised a rich dump of domestic refuse that contained a large quantity and variety of fish remains, predominantly herring and eel, but also a diverse selection of marine species including sea breams, plaice, cod, sea bass, conger, whiting, garfish, thorn-back and mackerel. The fill also produced a bone mount with openwork design (SF Cat no. 200; see Chapter 7, Fig. 7.26), a characteristic of more expensive caskets, and its association with the rich fish remains is indicative of more well-to-do occupation (see Cool, Chapter 7). The pottery evidence suggests a 13th-century date and this is supported by the presence of part of a copper alloy sewing pin (SF Cat no. 133), a form that is thought to date to no earlier than the 13th century. Despite

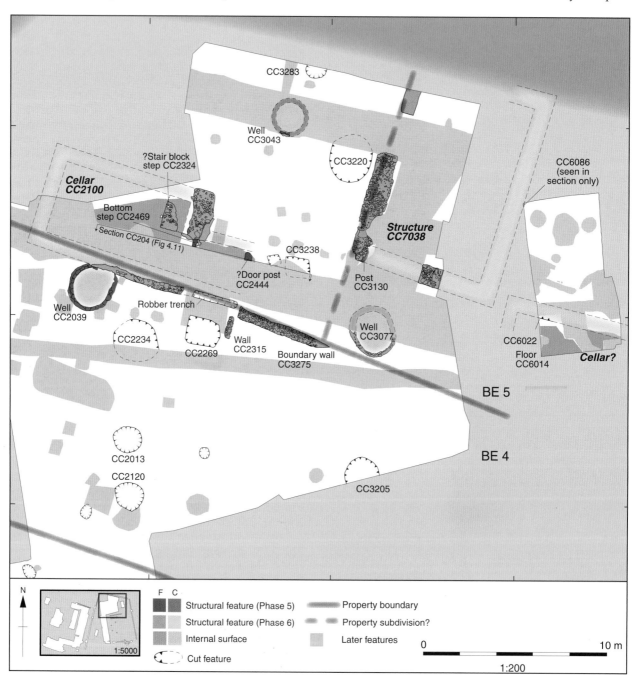

Fig. 4.10   Properties BE 4–5, Phase 6

cutting through the soft fills of earlier pits, its sides were unweathered, implying that it had been enclosed internally since its small size would seemingly preclude lining. If so, it may originally have served as a latrine attached to or within a structure and was later utilised for the disposal of rubbish before being capped with compact chalk and gravel.

In the northern part of the property there were a few small, shallow, circular pits (Pit Group CC7053) some of which could have been postholes; however, they did not form any coherent arrangement.

Property BE 4 (Fig. 4.10)

The low density of pitting that was apparent during Phase 5 seemingly continued into at least the early part of Phase 6, although these pits were only excavated to depths of 0.32–0.55 m, and it is possible that at least some of them were originally of Phase 5 date, but finally levelled during the 13th or 14th centuries. The pits to the south (CC2120, CC2013 and CC3205), like those in Phase 5, were all circular and of similar size, all measuring 1.5 to 1.8 m in diameter and presumably serving similar purposes. Only pit CC2120 was bottomed, at 0.80 m, revealing fills comprising dumps of both domestic and industrial material, similar in nature to fills of the pits of the preceding phase. The pit clipped but otherwise respected the north side of Phase 5 pit CC2043 (see above) suggesting its filling remained visible or least remained in the memory of the pit diggers. Pottery from the pit suggests a 13th-century date for its use. The pit contained dumps of charcoal-rich silts at its base that contained small quantities of hammerscale, iron slag and vitrified furnace fragments suggesting that smithing was undertaken close-by. The presence of sawn-off goat horn-cores suggests that bone objects continued to be manufactured, possibly (given the evidence for iron-working) composite bone/iron tools. The pit was also used for the dumping of domestic refuse that contained a variety of marine fish remains, plum, sloe/cherry and mineralised bran, the later probably derived from human faecal waste.

Pit CC2013 located immediately to its north contained a similar variety of fills, although given the degree of their slumpage, the pit was presumably considerably deeper than its excavated depth of 0.55 m. This suggests that the earlier unexcavated fills had subsided because they contained organic material such as cess, and the earliest excavated fills comprised compacted chalk and clay that were possibly intended to seal off the odours from the underlying fills. Like adjacent pit CC2120, it contained small quantities of hammerscale and sawn-off goat horn-cores.

Pit CC2269, located close to the boundary with Property BE 5, represented the latest of a group of small intercutting rectangular pits, possibly cesspits given its size, though this could not be established at the depth excavated. It appeared to have been rapidly filled with mortar-rich chalk and clay rubble, presumably derived from nearby masonry structures.

Immediately to the east of pit CC2269 was a short length of a north-south aligned wall-footing (CC2315) that had survived the modern terracing of the site because it had subsided into an adjacent and earlier pit. The wall, measuring 0.37 m in width, comprised a single course of flint nodules, some of which had been roughly cut to size, bonded by a lime mortar. It had been founded upon a bed of compacted chalk, perhaps in an attempt to firm up its foundation over the underlying soft ground. The wall ran perpendicular to the 'boundary' wall between Properties BE 4 and BE 5 and perhaps formed part of a lean-to structure, feasibly surrounding pit CC2269, if so suggesting a covered latrine pit.

Property BE 5 (Figs 4.10-11; Plates 4.21-3)

The apparent sub-division of the property, in place by Phase 4.2 (950–1050; see above), seems to have continued into the 13th and 14th centuries. The boundary between the two subdivisions was delineated by the west wall of Structure CC7038. The boundary with Property BE 4 to the south was defined by the southern wall of Cellar CC2100, the construction of which had encroached some 0.5 m southwards into the adjacent property. To the east of the cellar the boundary was marked by wall foundation CC3275, which abutted the south-east corner of the cellar entrance (see below). The foundation, measuring 0.52 m in width and up to 0.11 m in depth, comprised flint nodules and chalk rubble mortar, bounded by a pale yellowish lime mortar. Its eastern extent corresponded with the projected line of the west wall of Structure CC7038 which would suggest that it belonged to the western sub-division of the property rather than the adjacent Property BE 4. Given its fairly substantial nature, it may have represented a high wall or it could have belonged to a structure that adjoined the entrance of Cellar CC2100, the remains of which did not otherwise survive.

Property BE 5 (West)

Cellar Structure CC2100 (Figs 4.10–11; Plate 4.21)

The remains of a stone-built cellar (Cellar CC2100) were excavated at the rear of the property. It had cut into and removed the chalk blocks from the north side of Phase 5 well CC2039 (see Phase 5, Property BE 4 above), although it is possible that the well continued in use and that the wall of the cellar acted as lining at this point. The structure had been heavily robbed and a large part of it had been removed by a Second World War air raid shelter; however, enough survived to suggest it had once formed part of a building of some substance. The cellar was rectangular and measured externally 5.7 m north-south and at least 6.6 m east-west. It had been cut to a depth of 1.5 m below the level of natural but, allowing for the modern terracing of the site, its original depth may have been around 2 m below the contemporary ground level. It was flanked on its east side by an entrance, possibly within a porch.

The cellar walls were constructed of chalk rubble and flint bonded with yellow sand mortar and were probably originally dressed internally with quality ashlar blocks or other equally valuable masonry since all traces had been robbed away; the area of robbing was still visible on the inside faces of the east and north walls. The walls were probably built directly upon the natural chalk on the base of the cellar cut, though where the east wall intercepted the soft fills of underlying Roman pits around the entrance the foundations were cut deeper and thickened to a width of 1.4 m; elsewhere the walls were probably considerably narrower. To the east, all but the north side of the cellar entrance had been destroyed, although robber trench CC2384 probably marked the south side. However, the trench, at 0.23 m depth, was too shallow to have been the south wall of the entrance way, although it may have served as a boundary wall with Property BE 4, or alternatively it might have been associated with the wall (CC2315) that surrounded cesspit CC2269. Posthole CC2444 may mark the position of the north post of a doorway leading into the cellar. There was probably a masonry wall on the north side of the entrance, though robbing had removed all evidence for it; its position is implied by a *c* 0.6 m gap between the cellar cut and its floor levels.

The earliest floor level of the cellar comprised a soft mid whitish-yellow mortar that may have acted as a bedding layer for a stone or tiled floor rather than the floor level itself, though no evidence for such a floor remained. The entranceway appears to have been stepped (see Fig 4.11) presumably utilising a hard stone, since a flat limestone slab (CC2469) survived at the position of the threshold (bottom step) with the cellar. A possible stair block (CC2324) was built directly over the mortar though it is unclear whether this was an original feature of the cellar or was added subsequently. It survived as a rectangular stub of masonry, the south side of which was aligned with the north side of the entranceway. It presumably original abutted onto the face of the east and north walls of the cellar, as later robbing of their facing stones cut across its north and east sides.

The cellar appears to have undergone a refurbishment that involved the raising of its floor level, the demolition of the possible stair block and the remodelling of the entranceway. The floor level within the cellar was raised by 0.3 m by the dumping of soil and rubble (CC2212) that contained 13th-century pottery, before a new floor of hard light whitish yellow sandy mortar (CC2206) was laid. A similar sequence occurred within the entranceway, which resulted in the removal of the steps and their replacement with a ramp whose

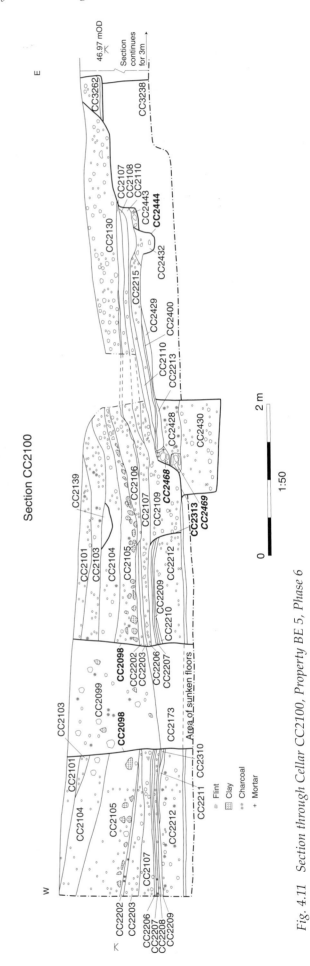

Section CC2100

Fig. 4.11 Section through Cellar CC2100, Property BE 5, Phase 6

Plate 4.21 Cellar CC2100, Property BE 5 (W), Phase 6 looking north-east

base was flush with the new floor of the cellar. The lack of occupation silts above the mortar suggests that a stone floor had been laid, perhaps re-used from the earlier floor.

After the thorough robbing of the wall facing, the east wall was reduced to near floor level, whereas the south wall survived to its full height, possibly retained as the boundary with Property BE 4. The cellar appears to have been deliberately filled by the end of the 14th century with dumps of mortar and chalk rubble devoid of any usable building material, suggesting such material had been removed for use elsewhere. A few fragments of fine-grained sandstone, dressed limestone and ceramic floor and roofing tiles are the only surviving evidence for the material that must have adorned a building of this status.

Pits

Three pits were possibly contemporary with the use of the cellar. All were located close to the east side of possible Phase 5 Structure CC7031, suggesting that it might have continued in use or that the area it occupied was utilised for other purposes. The largest, circular pit CC3220 measured 2.2 m in diameter, and lay immediately adjacent to a similar Phase 5 pit, CC3150 (see above). It was excavated to a depth of 0.61 m, and its earliest excavated fill comprised domestic rubbish including large sherds of medieval sandy ware (Fabric MDF) and Laverstock-type ware (Fabric MNX) that would suggest a date range of 1225–1350. The pit was levelled with fills of rubble that contained fragments of wall render and an architectural chalk fragment that presumably adorned the nearby structures.

Circular pit CC3283, measuring 1.18 m across, lay close to the street frontage to the north and was fully excavated to a depth of 0.61 m. The basal levels contained thick charcoal-rich silts and domestic rubbish with flake hammerscale and at least 29 broken iron nails of various sizes, perhaps wasters from their manufacture on the site. The fill was exceptionally rich in a diverse range of both fresh-water and marine fish, including carp, eel, perch, trout, pike, herring, cod, sea bream, Dover sole and turbot, the latter a fish perhaps suggestive of a more refined diet.

Rectangular pit CC3238 measured 1.35 m across and at least 0.95 m in depth and may have served a different function. Its location in front of the entrance into Cellar CC2100 suggests that it was not contemporary with its use but it appears to have been rapidly filled about the time of the cellar's construction since it contained a medieval crested ridge roof tile and a sherd of high medieval pottery.

Property BE 5 (East)

Structure CC7038 (Fig. 4.10; Plate 4.22)

The substantial chalk footings of a masonry-founded building, probably a house, survived within the eastern part of the property. Only its west and south wall lay within the excavated area; the north wall presumably lay alongside the street frontage immediately to the north of the site. Its east wall probably lay outside the excavated area, though a small fragment of mortared chalk and flint (CC6086) revealed on the north-west corner of the sprinkler tank excavations might have been its outside edge. Assuming the suggested extent of the structure is correct then it measured externally 8.4 m in width and extended at least 10 m from the street frontage. The majority of the structure had been removed by the air-raid shelter and all internal levels had been removed by modern terracing.

The walls (1.1 m thick) comprised mainly roughly hewn chalk blocks/rubble but incorporated the occasional large fragment of re-used Roman brick, all bonded by yellow-brown lime mortar. Both survived within a foundation trench measuring a maximum depth of 0.33 m though given the degree of modern terracing that had occurred, the foundations were presumably substantially deeper. The south-west corner of the structure overlay a shallow square 'posthole'

(CC3130) measuring 0.6 m across and 0.25 m deep that had also been filled with mortared chalk rubble, presumably at the time the foundation was built. Given that it occurred at the base of the (truncated) foundation trench it probably originally represented a substantial post that had been removed immediately prior to the construction of the wall. It is possible that this may have formed part of a timber precursor to the masonry building, though no other corresponding postholes were found. The west wall of the structure clipped the eastern lip of Phase 5 pit CC3150. The upper levels of this pit contained mortar and chalk rubble with abundant roofing slate fragments, which could have derived from the building of Structure CC7038. The deposits also contained a large quantity of medieval pottery including South Hampshire red wares and medieval sandy ware (Fabrics MMI and MDF) suggesting the building had been constructed between 1225 and 1350.

To the south-east of the structure was a 0.25 m-thick deposit (CC6014) of firm light yellowish-brown lime mortar of medieval date that directly overlay the remains of the north-south Roman street or the underlying subsoil. As such it may represent the floor of a shallow cellar, measuring at least 4.4 m across, that had cut through the Roman street and its overlying levels and had itself been largely removed by modern terracing. What survived suggests that its northern extent corresponded with an eastwards projection of the southern wall of Structure CC7038. The only evidence for a wall in this position came from slight traces of a shallow trench (CC6022) that may have marked its position. The mortar overlay a thin trampled silt that contained sherds of high medieval whiteware (Fabric MMH) and Northern French green-glazed white ware (Fabric MNV) suggesting a date of 1225–1300. Notwithstanding the degree of modern terracing, it is unlikely that this was ever a full-depth cellar and it perhaps formed part of an undercroft below a building.

Plate 4.23   Well CC3077, Property BE 5 (E), Phase 6, looking south

Plate 4.22   West wall of Structure CC7038, Property BE 5 (E), Phase 6, looking south

To the south of the south-west corner of Structure CC7038 and abutting the line of the boundary with Property BE 4 were the remains of chalk-lined well CC3077 (Plate 4.23). Unlike the fine ashlar of the Phase 5 wells within Properties BE 4–5, this was constructed more crudely and utilised random un-coursed and roughly hewn chalk blocks (with occasional coarsely knapped flint modules) bonded by light yellowish-brown silty mortar. A geological borehole revealed its base at 41.70 m OD (a depth of *c* 5.1 m), a level 3 m above the base of the earlier wells implying that it either sourced a separate aquifer or that its construction was not completed. The well had been backfilled throughout largely by soft mid-dark grey silt clays, the earliest of which contained slate fragments. Its upper fill comprised more compact gravel/silt with chalk and flint rubble suggesting a deliberate capping. The top fill also produced a small fragment of 18th- to 19th-century roofing tile, probably intrusive; otherwise the pottery evidence suggests a mid 13th- to 14th-century date.

BRUDENE STREET WEST AND SNITHELING STREET

Later development of the stone house/hall
(Fig. 4.12)

Cunliffe recovered no evidence from the cellar under the stone house relating to any major structural modifications to the hall itself during its lifetime. However, he identified other structures that suggest the development of a more elaborate residence in the late 13th/ early 14th century.

The principal addition to the hall was an extension, built of flint in mortar, attached to the west side of the southern half of the hall. The partially exposed footings of this, which were up to 1.2 m deep, extended 5.8 m to the west before turning north for 3.2 m. The end of this structure overlay a large open pit which had been backfilled with building rubbish and consolidated with chalk blocks round the edges. Pottery from the pit suggested a late 13th/early 14th century date for the construction of the extension. Cunliffe (1964) suggested that the likely function of this extension was a garderobe tower, serving an upper floor private chamber. Two further walls were found to the east and south of the hall, which Cunliffe interpreted as later than the western additions, possibly of 14th-century date since they lay over a thin scatter of slates which he suggests were derived from damage to roofs during a storm that, according to documentary sources, badly damaged certain roofs in Winchester in 1314.

Properties BW 1 and SE 1 (Fig. 4.13; Plate 4.24)

Property BW 1 was subject to only limited investigation because much of it lay outside the area impacted by the new construction scheme. Only a few pits datable to Phase 5 were seen within the excavated area, but it is clear that a range of substantial masonry structures occupied the property during Phase 6. These extended to the western limit of Property BW 1, where they appear to be closely related to similar structures at the very east end of Property SE 1. Although no definitive evidence for the boundary between these two properties was seen in previous phases, it seems very likely that the structures of Phase 6 extended across its line, and therefore that the two properties had been combined. This would be consistent with the documentary evidence (see Chapter 1 and Chapter 5), which suggests that by the late medieval period Properties BW 1 and SE 1 formed a single tenement. During Phase 5, a post-built structure that was possibly a well-house had stood on Property SE 1, probably located behind a substantial street-frontage house (see above). To the rear were numerous pits, some containing large quantities of remains of fur animals, and postholes from a possible structure or structures of indeterminate form. Pottery dating suggests that the latest use and the levelling/backfilling of the well and pits occurred during the late 12th or early 13th centuries. The buildings assigned to Phase 6 are broadly dated to the 13th and 14th centuries on the basis of the presence of 13th- to 14th-century pottery, and of roofing materials such as slate and crested ridge tile, in their demolition rubble. Structures seen on Property SE 1 in this phase were restricted to the area adjacent to Property BW 1; the remainder of the excavated area was essentially devoid of features or deposits of later medieval date and may have been left open.

Structure NH8535 (Plate 4.24)

A small trench close to Brudene Street revealed the latest levels of a substantial masonry structure (Structure NH8535) that is likely to have extended to the street frontage. The area was recorded in plan but no further excavation was undertaken, since its levels were not impacted by the new development. The remains of Structure NH8535 comprised a length of a north-south wall (NH9037) parallel to and *c* 6 m from the existing street frontage. It was constructed with chalk rubble bonded by a yellowish-brown mortar. Its thickness would imply it represented an exterior wall, an interpretation supported by the fact that a dark loamy soil containing slate fragments abutted its western side. The facing stones that would have adorned its sides had probably been robbed but this could not be ascertained at the level excavated. A second less substantial and apparently later wall (NH9038) adjoined its east side, possibly a blocking of a door since an ashlar quoin still marked its junction with the earlier wall. The floor layers were not exposed, and within the north room these lay below a substantial spread of slate fragments that presumably represented the collapsed roof. The only dating

Plate 4.24   Unexcavated Structure NH8535, Property BW 1, Phase 6, looking south

evidence recovered were fragments of crested ridge tiles suggesting that the building was in use during the 13th to 14th centuries.

Structure NH8536

A second substantial masonry structure was located against the postulated former rear boundary of Property BW 1. Part of the north-west corner of the structure was exposed and rapidly recorded, and had apparently been constructed in two phases. The earlier wall (NH8049) comprised a north-south foundation, 1.15 m wide, constructed with mortared chalk rubble; the lack of evidence for any facing suggests that it lay below the contemporary ground level. This was abutted by east-west wall NH9043, 0.62–0.76 m wide, that was constructed mainly of flint rubble bonded by a light yellowish-brown chalky mortar upon a slightly off-set foundation of coarse mortared chalk rubble. Its north face was lined with knapped flints above the level of its foundation, suggesting an exterior face. An opening

(doorway) on the north wall, 0.96 m wide, had a dressed stone block surviving on one side that may have allowed access to flint-lined well NH9047 (unexcavated) that was located immediately to the north-west. No evidence for the date or function of the structure was found though mortar rubble and slate fragments contained within it suggest it is datable to the late 12th century or later.

Structure NH8615

Fragmentary remains of a further stone-founded structure were found to the west of Structure NH8536 in Property SE 1, post-dating possible timber Structure NH8617 (see Phase 5 above). It comprised a length of a heavily robbed east-west wall (NH5043) that was aligned with the west wall of Structure NH8536, but appears to have formed a separate structure. This would suggest that it was a westwards extension to the same range, implying encroachment into the eastern part of Property SE 1. No evidence for a return was found but given its shallow depth, this probably did not survive. Floor levels to its south implied that it represented part of the wall of a structure that largely lay to the south of the excavated area. Later a large, shallow rectangular pit that evidently represented the remains of a shallow cellar or undercroft (Cellar NH5050; see below) was attached to its north side.

Wall NH5043 had been robbed of its stone (presumably re-used stone such as flint) and survived as a discontinuous shallow trench measuring 0.1–0.4 m in depth, containing traces of

mortar at its base. However, a small fragment of shallow wall foundation, 0.64 m thick, did survive, comprising predominantly large flint nodules bonded by a hard pale brown chalky mortar. A thin and compacted spread of light buff chalky mortar respecting the south side of the wall was probably an internal floor. It overlay Phase 5 pit NH5105 that had been levelled with mid brown clay acting as the base of the floor within this area. This contained south-east Wiltshire ware (Fabric MADW) datable to the late 11th to mid 13th

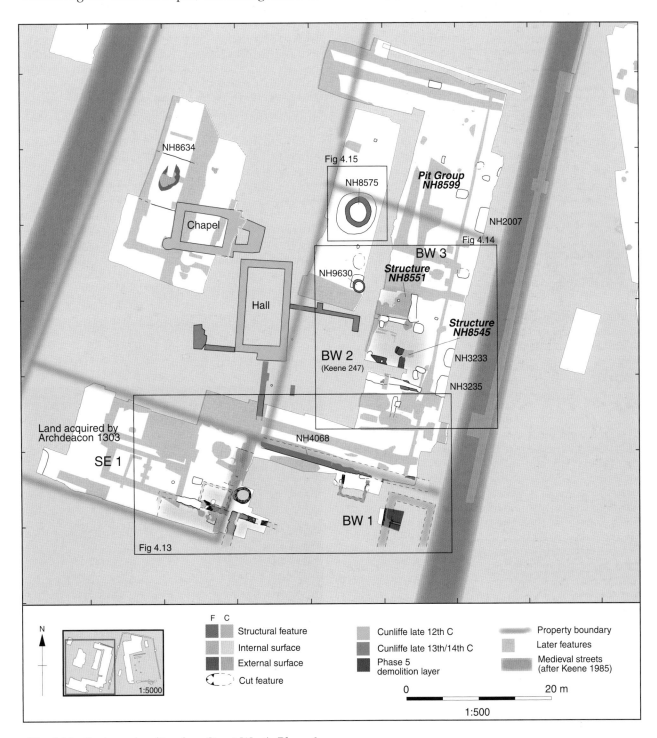

Fig. 4.12   Feature plan (Brudene Street West), Phase 6

centuries. The presence of medieval sandy ware (Fabric MDF) and a small sherd of Hampshire whiteware (Fabric MHH, early 13th to 14th century) could suggest an early to mid 13th-century date for the construction of the structure. The lack of any discernible occupation debris above the floor would suggest either that it was kept clean or that it supported a stone/tile floor.

Cellar NH5050

The construction of shallow Cellar NH5050 involved the partial levelling of wall NH5043 of Structure NH8615 in order to provide access into it from the adjacent structure. It comprised a rectangular pit measuring 2.8 m by at least 3.2 m, and was dug to a depth of *c* 0.63 m below the floor level of Structure NH8615. A fragment of chalk and flint wall bonded by pale brown sandy mortar survived on its southern side, and was probably the only remnant of an original stone lining. The natural gravel may have formed the floor, since it was overlain by thin trampled grey silt and patchy spreads of re-deposited natural clay. Part of a crushed glazed jug of 13th- or 14th-century date was found within these deposits, perhaps suggesting storage of wine, otherwise no evidence was found for the function of the cellar. At the time of construction of Cellar NH5050, Structure NH8615 was re-floored with pale orange-brown mortar that survived within the area of the proposed entrance into the cellar. The cellar was eventually levelled with mortar and chalk rubble and dumps of stone roofing slate, that were presumably derived from the demolition of the cellar and adjacent Structure NH8615; the associated pottery was of 14th- to 15th-century date.

Structure NH8616

To the north of Cellar NH5050 and Structure NH8536 were the fragmentary remains of chalk and mortar floors and a hearth that survived over Phase 5 pits NH5164 and NH5175. No evidence for the nature of the walls of the structure survived but it may have been a detached building, possibly a kitchen, since it contained a fragment of a plinth or oven wall (NH5157). The surface of the mortar floor in the area of NH5157 had been baked hard by intense heat. The limited dating evidence suggests that the structure was in use during the 13th–14th centuries.

Structure NH8537

The north-east part of the property, adjacent to Property BW 2, formerly set aside for pits, was levelled with dumps of gravel and mortar-rich soils, probably in preparation for construction in the area. A substantial boundary wall (NH4068; see below) was built, dividing Properties BW 1 and BW 2. A narrow chalk and flint foundation (NH4100) was probably part of an auxiliary lean-to

structure built against the south side of this boundary wall. No other corresponding walls were found, unless shallow trench NH4170, located 2.9 m to east, represented the remains of a robbed-out wall.

Property BW 2 (Figs 4.13–14; Plate 4.25)

During Phase 5, a large L-shaped building stood on Property BW 2. This building, which originated in the late Saxon period, had been reconstructed using large timber posts during the Anglo-Norman period. To the rear of the building was a chalk-lined well. Pottery from the fills of the post-pits suggests that the building was dismantled by the early 13th century at the latest, and the well (NH4019) was deliberately infilled, robbed of its upper courses, and levelled with gravelly clay and chalk containing Laverstock-type ware (Fabric MNX dated *c* 1230–1350) and medieval sandy ware (Fabric MDF dated *c* 1150–1350) suggesting a date range of 1230–1350. A cesspit (NH4339) had been rapidly filled with dumps of gravel, chalk and refuse containing sherds of Early South Hampshire red ware, which is datable to the period 1175–1250. Following the demolition of the Anglo-Norman structures, the property appears to have been left largely empty, and the presence of layers of compacted gravel and rammed chalk in the upper levels of the disused Phase 5 pits suggests that a gravelled external surface was laid down.

Wall NH4068 (Plate 4.25)

The southern boundary of Property BW 2 in this phase was clearly defined by wall NH4068 (Fig.

Plate 4.25   Boundary wall foundation NH4068, Phase 6, Property BW 2, looking east

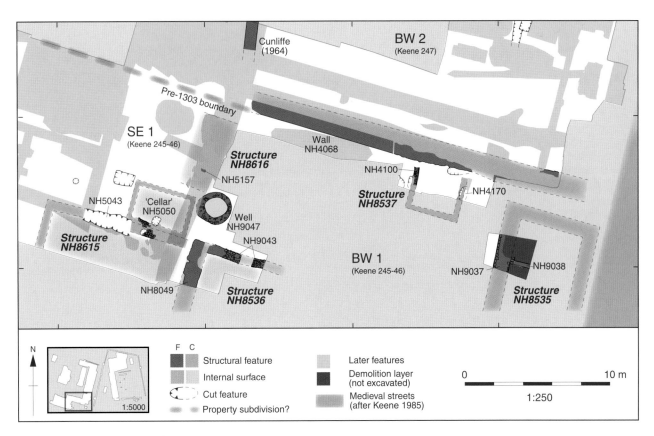

Fig. 4.13   Property BW 1/SE 1, Phase 6

4.13; Plate 4.25). This survived as a 21 m-long mortared chalk and flint rubble footing, measuring (where not truncated) 0.75 m wide by 0.5 m deep. As the north side of the wall was cut away by a modern service trench, its original width is likely to have been greater, perhaps up to a maximum of 1.5 m. As preparation for the wall's construction the ground had been levelled over subsided Phase 4 and 5 features within Property BW 1, with dumps of chalky silty sand (NH4167). The upper fills of Phase 5 pits NH4293 and NH4176 that pre-dated the wall contained similar material from which fragments of South Hampshire red ware pottery (Fabric MNG and MMI, dated *c* 1225–1400) were recovered. The abundance of Newbury-style ware (if not residual) and fragments of medieval sandy ware (Fabric MDF) could suggest a date early during this range, perhaps sometime around the early to mid 13th century. Although the full width of the wall was not seen, it appears to have encroached slightly onto Property BW 1 to the south.

A substantial linear feature (NH4045; Fig. 4.14) along the line of the northern boundary of Property BW 2 was probably related to a building constructed on Property BW 3 to the north and is described below. Two further shallow features were identified to the south (short linear feature NH4036 cutting a square pit NH4032). Either or both could have been stratigraphically of this phase but their function was not clear.

Property BW 3 (Fig 4.14; Plate 4.26)

During Phase 5, Property BW 3 had contained a timber house occupying the southern two thirds of its street frontage, with an open area, possibly a lane or passage, to the north, and an elaborate well-house to the rear. Charcoal from the latest use of an oven on the south side of the house gave a radio-carbon date of 1050–1230, and pottery associated with the demolition of the well-house and the infilling of the well included small quantities of Early South Hampshire red ware, datable to the period 1175–1250. This suggests that the Phase 5 structures had been demolished by the early to mid 13th century at the latest.

Structures NH8551 and NH8545

The succeeding structures on the property, largely represented by robber trenches, appear to have been the last structural elements in the medieval sequence in this area. Their alignment is slightly different from Phase 5 structures fronting Brudene Street, being slightly more north-south oriented, and they are set well back from the street frontage. As a group they appear to be associated with the stone house identified by Cunliffe to the west (see above and Fig. 4.12). Although they had suffered considerably from modern truncation and distur-bance, there are reasonable grounds to interpret them as a kitchen and small annexe, both related to the hall complex to the west.

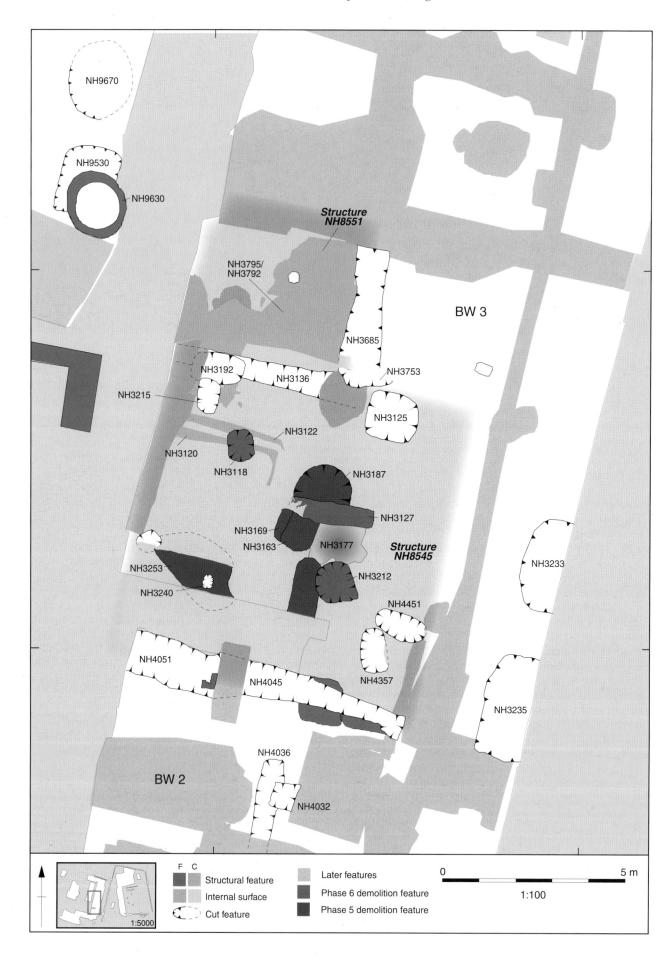

NH9670

NH9530

NH9630

Structure NH8551

NH3795/ NH3792

BW 3

NH3685

NH3192

NH3136

NH3753

NH3215

NH3122

NH3125

NH3120

NH3118

NH3187

NH3127

NH3169

NH3163

NH3177

Structure NH8545

NH3233

NH3253

NH3212

NH3240

NH4451

NH4051

NH4045

NH4357

NH3235

NH4036

BW 2

NH4032

F   C

Structural feature

Internal surface

Cut feature

Later features

Phase 6 demolition feature

Phase 5 demolition feature

0

5 m

1:100

1:5000

The south-east corner of part of Structure NH8551 is represented by shallow robber trenches NH3685, NH3753 and NH3136, bordering a sequence of chalk and clay floor surfaces (NH3795/NH3792). Trench NH3685 was 3.15 m long by up to 1.1 m wide. Trench NH3136 survived to a length of 3.3 m, averaging 0.6 m wide. Later activity truncated the junction of the two features. Just south of the western end of robber trench NH3136 were two pits (NH3215 and NH3192), which may have been the settings for posts contemporary with the walls.

Small patches of a similar chalk floor were found to the south of these features, suggesting that the building continued to the south (as Structure NH8545), and robber trench NH3136 may therefore have been a partition wall. Two shallow linear features containing degraded daub (NH3120 and NH3122) may indicate the type of wall fabric used in the construction of the superstructure of this building. A sub-rectangular shallow pit (NH3125) may be an internal feature of the building, for instance a post-setting, although its function is unclear, and no stratigraphic relationship with other Phase 6 features was recorded. It was filled with a mix of silty clay and chalk rubble, and produced 12th- to mid 13th-century pottery.

To the south-east of pit NH3125, an area of fired clay was revealed (NH3177), the latest surviving burnt surface in the area. No oven structure was evident, and the burning on the surface was relatively slight, so it may well have been the site of a brazier, or a platform hearth, rather than the hearth itself.

At the south end of Property BW 3 was a substantial linear feature (NH4045/NH4051), possibly representing a beamslot oriented west-east and measuring 8.9 m long, 0.9 m wide and 0.4 m deep. The trench cut through the fill of the robbed out Phase 5 oven structure (NH4136), filled with mortared chalk and flint rubble (NH4135). A small pit or post setting to the north (NH4451) may have been associated, along with a slighter feature (NH4357).

To the north of the possible beamslot, the surviving part of a large Phase 5 pit (NH3253) was identified, filled with a single fill of clay, possibly representing consolidation of a feature prior to the insetting of a posthole (NH3240) which may be part of a structure within the building.

To the east, partly revealed at the edge of the site, were two substantial pits (NH3233 and NH3235). Neither was completely excavated, but both contained quantities of late medieval pottery, roof tile, worked stone fragments and animal bone, along with an assemblage of small finds. Pit NH3233 produced a very long copper alloy sewing pin (SF Cat no. 132), and pit NH3235 produced a late 13th-century knife blade and handle (SF Cat no. 256; see Chapter 7, Fig. 7.29), along with a bar

Fig. 4.14 (facing page) Property BW 2/BW 3, Phase 6

mount (SF Cat no. 147) and a stud fastener (SF Cat no. 335) of similar date. Also recovered from the fill was a fragment of a late 3rd- to 5th-century copper alloy bracelet (SF Cat no. 13) and a small quantity of slag, which might suggest some limited craft activity here, although it is most likely to be residual material from Phase 4 or 5.

Well NH9630 (Plate 4.26)

To the north and west of the buildings of Phase 6 was well NH9630. The well was defined by a circular shaft lined with chalk blocks, set within a construction cut. The top of the cut was truncated, destroying its immediate stratigraphic context so its construction date can only be inferred from the dating evidence from the excavated fills of the well shaft, and its position in the line of the possible Phase 5 lane leading back from Brudene Street.

The construction cut (NH9530) was restricted to the north side of the whole feature. In the south side the well-lining had been built directly against the natural. The lining itself was exposed (by excavation of the well backfill), to a depth of 2.2 m from ground level. Against the natural the exposed lining was 0.2 m thick, and on the north side it averaged 0.3 m thick. The resultant circular lined shaft was up to 1.26 m in diameter.

The lower exposed courses of the lining were of finely finished chalk blocks, with a slightly curving

Plate 4.26 Well NH9630, Property BW 3, Phase 6, looking north-west

face, averaging 310 mm by 200 mm by 200 mm. It was clear that the upper courses of the original lining of the well had collapsed or had been robbed, and were later rebuilt. The two or three rebuilt courses above were mortared rough unfinished chalk blocks, set within a construction cut backed by crushed chalk. Overlying these, the rebuilt lining comprised crudely mortared large flint nodules and chalk rubble.

The shaft fill was investigated by a borehole, and at a depth of 10 m the bottom of the well was not reached. Early fills of the sequence revealed fragments of stone roofing slate, suggesting a medieval infilling. No artefactual dating was recovered from any part of the structure of the well, although the latest pottery contained within its fills was Tudor Green ware, datable to *c* 1400–1550. A fresh rim sherd from a glazed jug in a pink quartz Hampshire ware (Fabric MMG dated 1225–1400) could imply a date in the ?early 15th century. The date of construction of the well therefore remains somewhat problematic, as wells lined with chalk blocks were constructed on numerous properties during Phase 5. It seems unlikely, however, that it would have been necessary to dig a second well while elaborately constructed well-house Structure NH3547 was still in use, and this may argue for a date of construction contemporary with the Phase 6 structures on the property, for which it would have provided a convenient water supply. The well appears also to have been located on the line of the proposed lane or passage on the north side of Property BW 3, and the implications of this are discussed in Chapter 5, below. The late date of the pottery in its final fills, and the evidence for a phase of repair, suggests that this well may have continued in use until the 15th or 16th century.

To the north of well NH9630 was a 1.7 m wide steep sided pit (NH9670) cut through Phase 4 charcoal spread NH9633, and measuring 0.6 m deep with a fill predominantly of chalk and flint rubble. The pit may represent the re-filling of an earlier pit, part of the consolidation/landscaping of the area.

Properties BW 4 and BW 5 (Figs 4.12, 4.15; Plate 4.27)

During Phase 5, the southern part of Property BW 4 had been occupied by an L-shaped building of timber post construction, while the northern half had been used for the digging of pits. Finds from the upper levels of Phase 5 pit NH2084 included large fragments of a tripod pitcher (which would be datable up to *c* 1225) along with sherds of Laverstock ware (Fabric MNX), datable from *c* 1230–1350, and fragments of roof tile. A number of Phase 5 pits on Property BW 5 had been backfilled with building debris and pottery of late 12th- to 13th-century date, including Early South Hampshire red ware, datable to the period 1175–1250. During Phase 6 a large circular pit/shaft

Plate 4.27 (below) Pit/shaft Structure NH8575, Property BW 4, Phase 6, looking south

Structure NH8575 was built towards the west end of Property BW 4; the function of this feature is considered in Chapter 5, below. A scatter of pits was recorded to the north and east.

Pit/shaft Structure NH8575 (Fig. 4.15; Plate 4.27)

The group comprised a single large sub-circular pit (NH9531) measuring up to 6.2 m in diameter, and

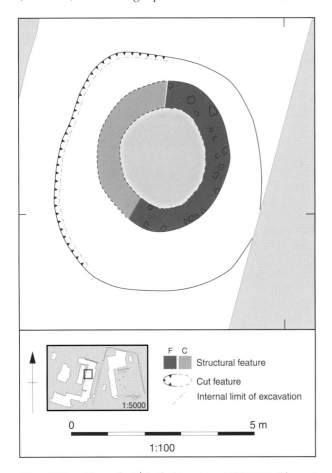

Fig. 4.15   Plan of pit/shaft Structure NH8575, Phase 6

excavated (but not bottomed) to a depth of 1.4 m. Within it was a sub-circular shaft (NH9533) built of chalk rubble with occasional flint nodules (see Plate 4.27). The digging of pit NH9351 had cut into the southern side of Phase 2.3 stone well NH9542, which had probably led to the slight distortion in the northern part of shaft NH9533, as it was modified to accommodate the remains of the earlier feature.

The shaft's greatest diameter was 4.2 m external, and 2.73 m internal (north-south). The space within the pit outside the shaft was infilled with several mixed dumped layers of chalk, gravel and silty clay. Lenses of mortar within this sequence suggest that the gap between the pit edge and the chalk and flint shaft was filled progressively as the shaft was built up. Fragments of 11th- to 12th-century pottery were recovered from the upper backfill of the construction pit.

The stone shaft NH9533 was backfilled with a single deposit (NH9534) of brown clayey silt, containing sherds of 11th- to 15th-century pottery. There appeared to be no other elements to this structure and no obvious evidence to indicate the character of any superstructure that may have existed over or around it. A single posthole (NH9568) was located 1.5 m to the south of pit NH9531, although there is nothing to suggest that it was related. The initial interpretation of this feature was a well. However, for a number of reasons this interpretation is open to question and is considered further in Chapter 5.

Pit Group NH8599 (Figs 4.12, 4.16)

A loose grouping of pits lay in the north-eastern part of the area, within the bounds of Properties BW 4 and BW 5. A single large subrectangular pit NH2007 was identified against the eastern baulk of the site, measuring 3.1 m north-south and surviving to a depth of 0.9 m (Fig. 4.16). Its primary fill (NH2066) was cessy, and overlain by a sequence of dumped deposits, starting with a thin charcoal layer

Section NH150

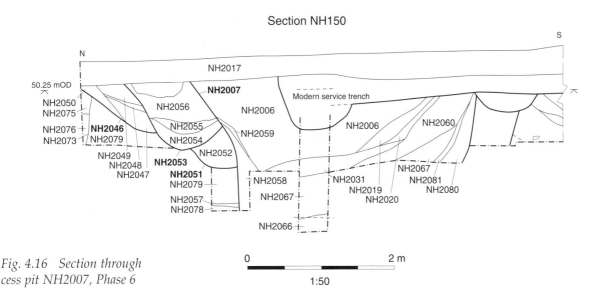

Fig. 4.16   Section through cess pit NH2007, Phase 6

(NH2081), which may represent an attempt to seal the noxious layer beneath. Sherds of 13th- to 15th-century pottery were present in the upper fills, and the dating evidence from the uppermost fill (NH2006) suggests a final infilling well before the end of the 16th century.

The other pits of this group were of a variety of shapes and sizes, and could not readily be ascribed any function. They contained pottery of 12th to 14th century date, along with a copper alloy scale pan (SF Cat no. 215; see Chapter 7, Fig. 7.27), dated to between the 10th and 13th centuries, from pit NH2100.

POST-MEDIEVAL DEVELOPMENT OF THE SITE (PHASE 7–8)

Phase 7 (*c* 1550–1800)

Where it survived, the latest medieval features and levels of Phase 6 were sealed by a thick and homogenous accumulation of dark brownish-grey 'garden' soil that was in turn overlain by features and layers of 19th-century or later date. It was not subject to detailed recording and was removed with modern levels during the initial machine stripping of the site.

On the Northgate House site, the soil survival was intermittent, with landscaping for the construction of No. 19 Staple Gardens and Northgate House in the 19th–20th centuries having removed much of it. Towards the south-west of the excavated area the soil lay directly over late Saxon levels of Property SE 2 (see Chapter 3) and further south directly over the late Roman Dark Earth (see Chapter 2). Where it survived alongside the western frontage of Staple Gardens it was 0.45 m thick and directly overlay the floors of Phase 4.1 Structure NH8586 and the Phase 6 pits that cut into them.

On the Discovery Centre site, terracing for the construction of the modern car park had removed all evidence for the 'garden' soil within the main excavated area. However, during the watching brief a thick accumulation of mid-dark grey-brown silty clay loam was observed within new foundation trenches within the Discovery Centre, lying directly below the existing floor of the building. In addition, an evaluation trench (see Chapter 1, Fig 1.8, Trench CC6) and observations during the excavation of a new drainage channel on the south side of the building revealed thick garden soils, since these areas seem to have been less truncated during the

19th–20th centuries. Within the evaluation trench the soil comprised friable, mid grey-brown clay silt, up to 0.48 m thick, and sealed pits of 9th–12th century date. Further to the east and alongside the pavement on Jewry Street, similar thick garden soils were recorded directly below the modern street levels. Though no useful dating was obtained, it appears to have accumulated after the latest discernible medieval activity on the site, which alongside the western frontage of Brudene Street was after the 14th–15th centuries.

Phase 8 (*c* 1800–present)

Given the complete lack of archaeological evidence to suggest otherwise, the Northgate House site remained largely open and unoccupied until the 19th century. Between 1873 and 1897 a house (formerly 19 Staple Gardens) was constructed on its southern side within the area that was previously occupied by Property SE 1; this house was demolished shortly before the commencement of excavations. The remaining part of the site remained open until 1961, when a large office block that housed the headquarters of SCATS was constructed in the centre of the site (Northgate House). A number of drains, services and footings pertaining to the use of these buildings were revealed.

Similarly no evidence for post-medieval occupation on the Discovery Centre site was found pre-dating the construction of the existing structure (formerly the Corn Exchange) in 1838. The only feature of note from this period was a rectangular brick-lined shaft that that was partially revealed against the west wall of the 19th-century building; otherwise the evidence suggests that the area remained open. This structure is depicted on the 1:500 Ordnance Survey map of 1873 (see Chapter 1, Fig. 1.7e) and is marked as a weigh bridge. During refurbishment of the existing building a number of original architectural features were revealed and a full report can be found in the site archive. In 1939 a number of underground air-raid shelters were constructed on the site which until the refurbishment and extension of the building in 2006 remained open below the surface of the car park. Prior to their infilling during the course of the new works a full photographic survey was undertaken, the results of which are in the site archive. Parts of two of the shelters were revealed along the northern and southern ends of the excavated area (see Chapter 1, Fig. 1.8).

Chapter 5
Discussion

THE PREHISTORIC EVIDENCE *by Lisa Brown*

The early prehistoric setting

The Iron Age settlement was established within a landscape with a rich history of human activity. No palaeolithic sites have been identified in the Winchester area, but finds of hand-axes and other material attest to activity of that period, probably concentrated on the river gravels at the base of the Itchen Valley. Although there is evidence for extensive Mesolithic occupation in south-east Hampshire (Draper 1966), little material of that date has been recovered close to the site. A lack of earlier Neolithic sites, apart from long barrows, is a feature of Hampshire archaeology, but the apparent absence of causewayed enclosures, henge monuments and other Neolithic constructions may reflect the intense pressure during the Iron Age and Roman periods to convert land to agricultural use, possibly resulting in the clearance of earlier monuments (Fasham 1980).

The best evidence for Neolithic occupation close to the current site has come from the chalk spur of Winnall Down overlooking the Itchen Valley, across the river from Winchester. Neolithic sites discovered during construction of the M3 motorway across the ancient chalk downland of Twyford Down include an interrupted ring ditch of uncertain function radiocarbon dated to 4690±90BP (Walker and Farwell 2000). A pit found close to the ring ditch provided evidence for high quality flint-working at around 2470–2040 cal BC (Pearson and Stuiver 1986). A curvilinear alignment of postholes in the same general area included two deep cone-shaped pits of possible ritual function. One contained a crouched inhumation accompanied by barbed-and-tanged arrowheads (Fasham *et. al.* 1989). Residual early Neolithic pottery was found in sufficient quantity at nearby Easton Lane, just to the south of the Winnall Down sites, to indicate localised activity in this location (ibid., 142).

Bronze Age occupation evidence is relatively abundant in the Winchester area. Some 245 round barrows have been identified in the vicinity and post-built houses and pits indicate that occupation continued at Winnall Down during the middle Bronze Age (Fasham 1985). Evidence of activity spanning the entire Bronze Age was also identified at Easton Lane (Fasham *et al.* 1989). At West Hill, south-west of the modern city (James 1997), and at Twyford Down to the south-east, evidence of both settlement and burial activity dating from the end of the early Bronze Age has been recovered (Stuart and Birkbeck 1936; Walker and Farwell 2000).

In general terms, however, the available evidence indicates that occupation within the area described by the modern city of Winchester was limited and perhaps sporadic during the earlier prehistoric period. The sparse scatter of Neolithic and Bronze Age features and flint, stone tools and pottery, including a Beaker found at Mew's Lane some *c* 500 m from the site (Beaumont James 1997), suggest that associated activity was peripheral to as yet undiscovered occupation foci, probably located on the higher ground surrounding the city.

The later prehistoric setting

Late Bronze Age–early Iron Age Winchester

Winchester and its environs undoubtedly possess natural geographical advantages that form a favourable position both as a crossing point of the River Itchen and as a location for settlement (Fig. 5.1). Although relatively little is known about the social and economic development of this location during the prehistoric period, it is clear that by the early Iron Age the lower terrace of the spur of chalk downland on the western side of the Itchen was occupied by an apparently unenclosed settlement. This western slope of the modern day St Paul's Hill, in the heart of city, was also chosen later in the Iron Age for the construction of the massive Oram's Arbour enclosure. The origin and development of the Roman and later town of Winchester may be directly linked to early Iron Age occupation of the Itchen Valley and surrounding downland. However, an apparent hiatus between late Iron Age settlement activity within the modern city and the establishment of the Roman town has yet to be firmly bridged by the archaeological evidence.

Late Bronze Age activity in the vicinity of Winchester is verified by finds of Deverel-Rimbury pottery at Winnall Down. The earlier settlement at this site continued as a cluster of at least four post-built houses associated with loomweights and querns, a rare example for central Hampshire of a late Bronze Age farming community (Fasham 1985, 126). Possible evidence for late Bronze Age occupation closer to the site comes from Staple Gardens, where a group of coarse flint-tempered pottery was recovered from a small pit or posthole (UAD 1195).

Residual late Bronze Age pottery found during excavations at the Westgate Car Park Site (Collis 1978, 200), resembled a late Bronze Age cremation vessel found in Tower Street (Biddle 1965, Pl. 48, feature 71). Other urns, since lost and therefore of unverified date, are reported to have been found also near St James Lane (UAD 380) and on St. Giles Hill (UAD 1698).

The transition from the late Bronze Age to the Iron Age is characterised in this part of Wessex by a marked development of hillfort construction and/or elaboration, a proliferation of 'celtic' field systems, many of which had earlier origins, and a proliferation of (mainly) enclosed farmsteads. The likely role of the early-middle Iron Age settlement at the Discovery Centre/Northgate site must be viewed within this wider context.

Several hillforts or hilltop settlements were constructed within 10 km or so of the current site at least as early as the Iron Age, but most have been examined only by geophysical survey at most (Fig. 5.1). Oliver's Battery (Farmer 2000) and Merdon Castle (Cole 1994) lie 3 km and *c* 7 km respectively to the south-west of the Discovery Centre/ Northgate site and Norsebury Ring 10 km to the north (Payne *et al.* 2006). These monuments are of uncertain date and their primary function unclear. Only St. Catherine's Hill, sited some 2 km south of the city, has been excavated (Hawkes *et. al.* 1930). The limited excavation produced evidence of occupation from around 600 BC predating the enclosure of the hilltop in the middle Iron Age.

Slightly further afield, the comprehensively excavated Danebury hillfort occupies a high position above the Test Valley some 18 km north-west of the site, and the somewhat inaptly named Old Winchester Hill lies located almost 14 km to the south-east of Winchester near West Meon. Most of these hilltop sites would have been visible from long distances away, and so may have served as territorial landmarks or 'landmark enclosures' within the complex Wessex Iron Age landscape (Hamilton and Manley 1997; Payne *et al.* 2006).

The evidence for early Iron Age activity within the Winchester region has largely been recovered through excavation rather than stray finds or casual observation (UAD Section 3.2, 1). As for the earlier prehistoric period, however, much of the best evidence was recorded in the course of the M3 road workings across Twyford Down and, in particular, at Winnall Down. The early Iron Age enclosed (Phase 3) settlement discovered at this site was comprehensively excavated and remains to date the best-defined of such sites for the period (Fasham 1985). However, recent excavations at an apparently extensive middle Iron Age settlement site at Bereweeke Fields (UAD 942) to the north-west of Winchester produced early Iron Age furrowed bowl pottery, albeit residual in later features, indicating an early origin for the site (Fig. 5.1).

Traces of activity dating to the late Bronze Age/early Iron Age transition (*c* 800–600 BC) within the modern city are largely limited to pottery scatters and partially exposed features. A residual

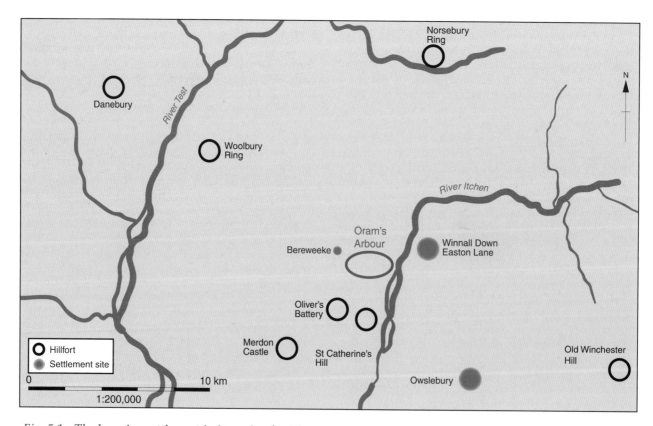

Fig. 5.1   The Iron Age settlement in its regional setting

8th–7th century BC type furrowed bowl fragment was found in a Roman deposit at Staple Gardens (Holmes *et al.* 2004, 57–9), and furrowed bowls resembling examples dated to the 8th–6th centuries at Potterne (Gingell and Morris 2000, 150) were found associated with a hearth in George Street, some 200 m or so from the current site (Cunliffe 1964, fig. 12, nos 1 and 2).

A scatter of excavated sites testifies to permanent settlement and agricultural occupation on the east-facing slope of St. Paul's Hill in Winchester from at least the 6th century BC onwards (Fig. 5.2). Although possible to date, the character and extent of the settlements are not fully understood due to the piecemeal evidence-gathering. It seems, however, that the inhabitants were engaged in a

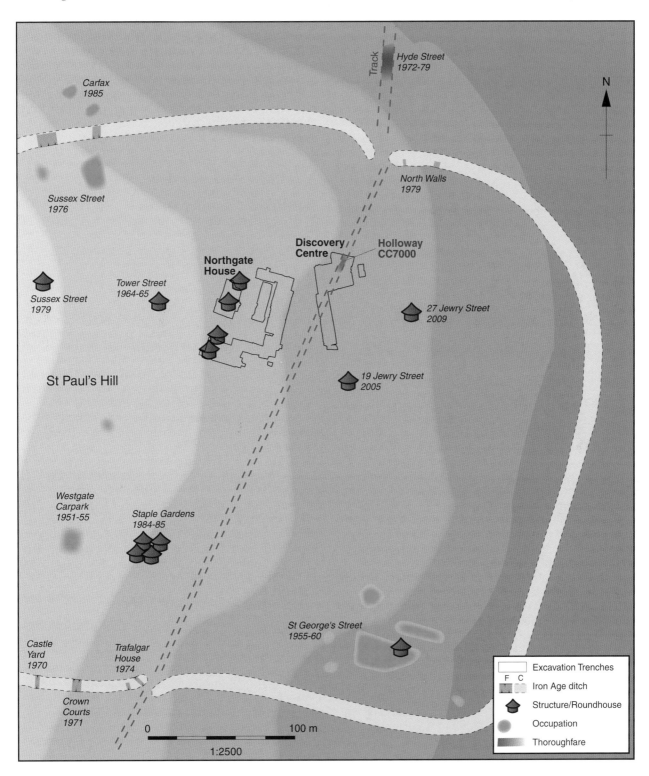

Fig. 5.2 The Iron Age settlement in its local setting

mixed agricultural regime. A postulated grain-parching oven discovered at Staple Gardens in 1984–5, a short distance to the south of the Discovery Centre/Northgate site, was observed to predate a series of middle Iron Age roundhouses (Qualmann *et al.* 2004, 12). Evidence of early Iron Age agricultural activity was found some 100 m to the north-west of the site, where a complex of field boundaries and four-post structures, along with an early Iron Age pit and the base of a developed soil, were exposed in trenches at New Road and Carfax, close to the modern railway station. Two more early Iron Age storage pits, dated by finds of pottery, were found at Victoria Road, adjacent to the northern entrance of the later Oram's Arbour. The remains of another early Iron Age field system associated with stakehole alignments defining livestock pens was recorded at Crowder Terrace on the western side of the railway line, 0.5 km to the south-west of the Discovery Centre/Northgate House site. Buried Iron Age plough soils exposed at North Walls (UAD 1209) and Station Road (UAD 1370) indicate that the field systems were fairly extensive.

The Discovery Centre/Northgate House early Iron Age settlement

The two post-built roundhouses (Structures NH8502 and NH8508) were reasonably well-dated to the early Iron Age on the basis of a few pottery sherds, and by their stratigraphic relationship with later Structures NH8505 and NH8509, which were securely dated on the basis of distinctive middle Iron Age pottery from their gully fills. It is also clear that features previously excavated on this site by Cunliffe (1964) belonged to the same Iron Age settlement, but to which phase of occupation is unclear as only middle Iron Age sherds are described in the report on this site (Cunliffe 1964, 176). Spatially, his feature 15 (0.61 m across and 0.23 m deep) could represent a ring posthole of Structure NH8508 (see Chapter 2, Fig. 2.5), but it contained no dating evidence.

The surviving early Iron Age features, even considered in conjunction with Cunliffe's findings, provide only limited evidence for the layout and organisation of the settlement during this period. It seems likely, but not certain, that the settlement was aligned and contemporary with an early phase of Holloway CC7000, but this was also poorly dated. The early Iron Age domestic focus may have been largely confined to the western side of the holloway, as no clear evidence of pre-middle Iron Age round-houses have been identified to date on the other side. The relationship between roundhouse Structures NH8502 and NH8508 and the undated structures represented by Posthole Groups NH9800 and NH9801 is uncertain, as their precise date and form could not be ascertained

The early Iron Age settlement sat within an apparently extensive agricultural field system, extending at least as far northwards as the Carfax

and North Walls and westwards beyond the modern railway station as far as Crowder Terrace. Within the agricultural complex were possible fenced animal enclosures and a small number at least of grain storage pits. The parching ovens identified at Staple Gardens and St George's Street testify to grain processing within the early Iron Age community.

At Winnall Down to the east during this period storage pits were far less common than four-post structures, and it may be that NH9800 and NH9801 supported similar structures. This pattern is not consistent for all farming communities of the period, however. At Houghton Down (Stockbridge) near Danebury, early Iron Age roundhouses and pits were found in close proximity (Cunliffe and Poole 2008), but this settlement was located entirely on chalk where the selection of pit positions was not dependent on avoiding lesser subsoils, as was the case at Winchester.

Middle–late Iron Age Winchester

Oram's Arbour

Sometime between *c* 300 and 100 BC an area of about 20 ha of previously unenclosed settlement on the downland spur was enclosed by a bank and ditch of defensive proportions (see artist's reconstruction in Plate 5.1). Sited at an intersection of several pre-existing routeways across the Iron Age landscape, and at a crossing point of the River Itchen, the Oram's Arbour enclosure would have marked a strategic point within an important prehistoric communications and trade network (see Figs 2.2 and 5.2). The enclosing of the Winchester settlement broadly corresponds to the floruit of the nearby unenclosed middle Iron Age Phase 4 settlement at Winnall Down (Fasham 1985, 18–30).

The enclosure exhibits some features of the late Iron Age '*oppidum*' class of earthworks, especially its size and location, but recent consideration of the evidence favours an origin somewhere in the middle Iron Age (Qualmann *et al.* 2004, 87), with abandonment or at least decline in the decades preceding the Claudian invasion, at a time when the *oppidum* of *Calleva* at Silchester, the tribal centre of the Atrebates, was thriving. Although Oram's Arbour does not clearly qualify as an *oppidum* (Collis pers. comm.) several factors distinguish it from the hillforts and other contemporary enclosed sites in the Wessex region. It occupies a highly strategic position overlooking a major river ford and crossroads. The specific morphology of the enclosure exploits natural landscape features, including the floodplain on the eastern side and a break of slope on the northern and western sides. This position would undoubtedly have been ideal for controlling or at least encouraging access to the site from approach routes in all directions (Qualmann *et al.* 2004, 91). The find at the Discovery Centre/Northgate site

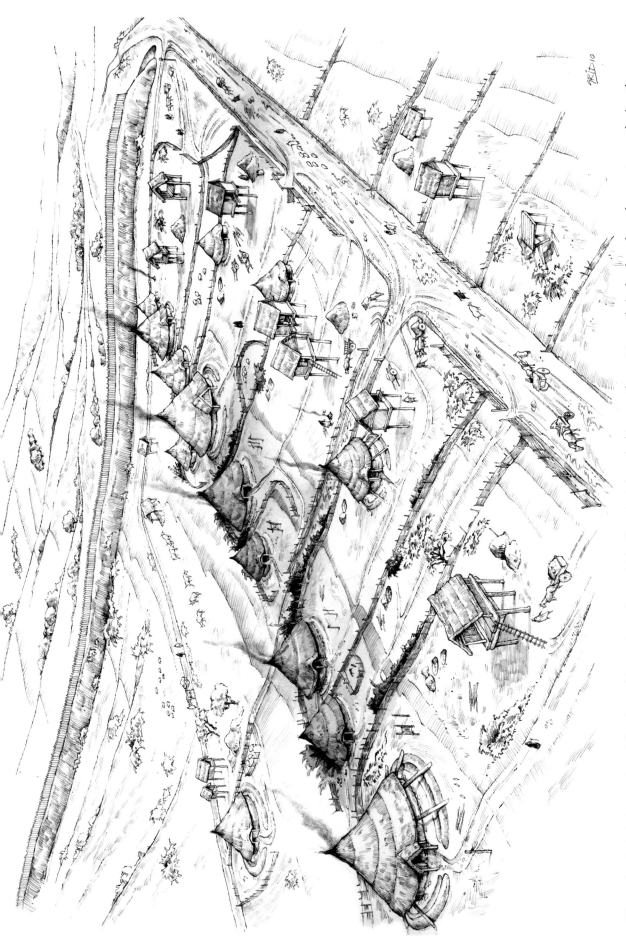

Plate 5.1   Artist's impression of the site and its environs from within Oram's Arbour looking north-west towards its bank and northern entrance during the 5th to 1st century BC, Phases 1.2–1.3: middle to late Iron Age

(albeit unstratified) of an exotic Dobunnic coin of *c* 40 BC (see Chapter 2, Plate 2.2) must also be taken into account with the other evidence when considering the role of the enclosure.

Qualmann has offered a possible model for the role of the enclosure within the wider middle Iron Age landscape of hillforts and low-lying settlements. He postulates that Oram's Arbour, sited centrally within the 'St Catherine's Hill-Worthy Down' ceramic style zone, may been created by the inhabitants of this area to exploit trade routes that were emerging as a result of increasing contact with the Roman world (Qualmann *et al.* 2004, 92–3). The site would have been more easily accessible than St Catherine's Hill, lying on a valley slope rather than a hilltop and dominating the north-south route from the south coast up the Itchen Valley. Although not particularly rich in exotic materials, evidence of coastal trade in the form of sea fish and briquetage have been recovered, along with native and exotic coins (Biddle 1983, 108). A small collection of Dressel 1 amphorae has also been collected from the enclosure and from sites nearby, including Owslebury (Collis 1970).

Evidence of middle Iron Age activity within Oram's Arbour is reasonably abundant, but it has rarely been possible to link specific finds and settlement features to the occupation and use of the enclosure itself, except where stratigraphic relationships with the earthworks were clear. The enclosure earthworks were not designed to incorporate the entire early Iron Age agricultural system, as the northern and southern ditches excluded, and indeed bisected, the field blocks at Carfax and at Crowder Terrace (Fig. 5.2). This could lend weight to the argument for a short period of abandonment of the settlement at the end of the early Iron Age (Qualmann *et. al.* 2004).

Observations and small scale excavations from the 19th century onwards have allowed the construction of a clearer picture of the configuration, if not necessarily the function, of the Oram's Arbour enclosure. By 1955 the northern and southern ditches of the enclosure had been recorded (Collis 1978, 245–255) and in 1966–7 the western entrance was identified (Biddle 1967, 254; 1968, 251). Finally, an inturned southern entrance was exposed during a salvage excavation at Trafalgar Street in 1974 (Biddle, 1975, 8; Qualmann *et al.* 2004, 8, 84) and by the late 1970s the entire circuit of the enclosure had been tentatively identified (Collis 1978), although the precise line of the eastern side remains unclear. Collaborative investigations by the Winchester Museums Service and King Alfred's College, Winchester in 2001–2 clarified the nature of the earthworks and of areas of the interior of the enclosure.

The combined evidence shows that Oram's Arbour was defined by a ditch surviving between 4 m and 11 m wide and up to 4.6 m deep (Thorpe and Whinney 2001). The eastern earthworks appear to have been constructed by enhancing the natural

valley-side terrace (Qualmann *et al.* 2004, 84-5). The holloway (CC7000) ran between the north-east and south-east entrances of the enclosure.

Traces of middle and late Iron Age activity, including roundhouses, postholes and pottery, have been found during excavations at numerous sites within the enclosed area, including at Tower Street, Staple Gardens and Westgate Street (Cunliffe 1964; UAD 893 Biddle 1965, 234–5; Collis 1978, 186–197; Fig. 5.2). A transect of the Roman wall in 1960 produced further indications of contemporary activity (Cunliffe 1964, 58–62; UAD 793). A probable roundhouse was also recorded at Castle Yard in 1930–31 (Qualmann *et al.* 2004).

By the middle Iron Age, the earlier settlement excavated at the Discovery Centre/Northgate site had clearly expanded to the east of the holloway. The discovery near Jewry Street Library of late Iron Age activity was recorded in the Hampshire Observer in 1939 (Qualmann *et al.* 2004, 82), and recent excavations at 19 Jewry Street have uncovered more middle-late roundhouses on the eastern side of holloway CC7000 (WA 2008, 6) (Fig. 5.2). These features were sealed in places by a Roman-period chalk surface and elsewhere by a late Iron Age/early Roman soil horizon. Further excavations at 27 Jewry street in 2009 revealed the location of another probable roundhouse (Steve Teague pers. comm.).

There remains a lack of closely datable evidence from Winchester for the period between the immediate pre-Roman Iron Age and the establishment of the *civitas* capital at about AD 75, although recent fieldwork has enhanced the archaeological record (Qualmann 1991; Qualmann *et al.* 2004; Thorpe and Whinney 2001; Whinney 1994).

The Discovery Centre/Northgate House middle-late Iron Age settlement

The middle Iron Age settlement lay within the eastern sector of Oram's Arbour, later occupied by the north-west corner of the Roman walled town. Some idea of the settlement arrangement can be gleaned from the surviving evidence. Of the five roundhouses (Structures NH8504, NH8505, NH8506, NH8507 and NH8509) defined by gullies that superseded the early Iron Age buildings, four lay in a linear arrangement following the alignment of holloway CC7000. The roundhouses identified in Staple Gardens in 1984–5 (Qualmann *et. al.* 2004) may have continued the alignment southwards. The less well defined Structure NH8506 was possibly one of a second row of houses that occupied the unexcavated and/or disturbed area running southwards from it, but this is entirely speculative. Whether the roundhouses in Jewry Street on the opposite side of the holloway were part of the same settlement is unclear, and these, in any case, were dated somewhat later, but on limited ceramic evidence.

Little in the way of contemporary agricultural activity has been identified within the earthworks and the main field systems may have been located beyond their limits. There were no storage pits in the vicinity of the structures, but a separation between domestic space and agricultural and storage space may have been a feature of the settlement, and the higher chalk a short distance to the west of the roundhouses would have been a more suitable position for features intended for grain storage. In fact, middle Iron Age pits were found in the western part of Oram's Arbour during the course of small scale excavation (Qualmann *et. al.* 2004, 82–5 and fig. 36). At the Phase 4 unenclosed middle Iron Age settlement at Winnall Down, there was a clear spatial arrangement wherein the roundhouses occupied the western area of the settlement and were separated by about 20 m from a relatively orderly range of pits, the two elements divided by a blank area, presumably a thoroughfare (Fasham 1985, fig. 15).

The domestic economy continued to be based on agriculture during the middle and late Iron Age. The charred plant evidence from the Phase 1.2 deposits indicated a slight increase in the cultivation of bread wheat (spelt/emmer) over barley during this time, suggesting that there was a change in the arable regime and in the local diet. However, an examination of the later prehistoric animal assemblage, which was dominated by sheep/goat and cattle, with some pig throughout the later prehistoric and early Roman period, failed to reflect a transition from a mutton dominated diet in the early Iron Age to one that favoured beef and pork, as has been cited as a feature of increased Roman influence (see Strid, Chapter 8). This small piece of evidence may have wider implications for the development of the later prehistoric settlement economy at Winchester but may merely corroborate the argument for a hiatus between the late Iron Age occupation of Oram's Arbour and the surrounding landscape and the establishment of the *civitas* capital at Winchester.

Conclusions

The results of the Discovery Centre/Northgate House site excavations have contributed significant evidence for the later prehistory of Winchester. Taken together with the results of piecemeal excavation and observations elsewhere within the modern city and in the surrounding area, the Iron Age settlement features add to the growing body of evidence that can help to establish the nature, sequence and changing status of the rural agrarian community that preceded the establishment of the Roman town. Topographic location was clearly a significant factor in influencing the evolution of the ancient trackway network that must subsequently have determined the orientation and arrangement of several phases of settlement during the early and middle Iron Age, and the construction of the somewhat anomalous Oram's Arbour enclosure. Whether there was a significant hiatus in activity in the late pre-Roman Iron Age period is a question that relies on the recovery of yet more archaeological evidence.

THE ROMAN TOWN by *Edward Biddulph*

Origins and the pattern of development

Roman Winchester was established in the late 1st century AD. The enclosure at Oram's Arbour was partly covered by the town, although earthworks were of sufficient preservation to be incorporated into Roman defences. The earthwork rampart was erected in the late Neronian-early Flavian period; coin evidence suggests AD 75 (Biddle 1975a, 110), although Wilson (2006, 12) speculates on a date closer to AD 100.

The Discovery Centre/Northgate House site occupied part of the north-west quarter of the Roman town (Fig. 5.3). The earliest Roman-period pottery recovered from the area of excavation included a *terra nigra* bowl, a South Gaulish samian platter (Drag. 15/17), and a North Gaulish white ware butt-beaker, which were in use after *c* AD 50 though likely to have been deposited before *c* AD 80 (see Biddulph and Booth, Chapter 7). Oram's Arbour, the Iron Age enclosure, had an indirect influence on the development of the Discovery Centre/Northgate site. The location of its north-east entrance subsequently marked the entrance of the Roman town's north gate, and it is thought that late 1st-century Street CC1703, which shared the orientation of the Iron Age holloway (CC7000), led to the north gate. Ditch CC3486 also extended along the line of the holloway. Apart from this, there is little evidence for continuity between the Iron Age activity and earliest Roman phase at the Discovery Centre site. Potentially occupation of the middle Iron Age structures extended to the mid 1st century AD, since globular jars of the sort recovered from Structures NH8505 and NH8506 (see Chapter 7, Fig. 7.1, nos 4 and 6) have long date ranges that continue beyond AD 43 (see Brown, Chapter 7). Furthermore, the rudimentary surface along the edge of the Iron Age holloway (CC7000) contained a cattle bone that was radiocarbon dated to 40 BC–AD 90 (OxA-16793). The shared orientation of the Iron Age holloway and the early Roman street and ditch has been noted, although the alignment may simply be a coincidence determined by the topography. Even assuming that the latest Iron Age activity dated up to the mid 1st century AD, the subsoil (NH8503 and CC7001) that covered the abandoned Iron Age features marks a break in domestic occupation of the area between the Iron Age and Roman period. The horizon, above which all earliest Roman features were placed, had the environmental signature of a ploughsoil (see Macphail and Crowther, Chapter 8 and *Digital Section 17*); charred corn cockle seeds suggest that the soil formed, or continued to form, after AD 43 (see Carruthers, Chapter 8).

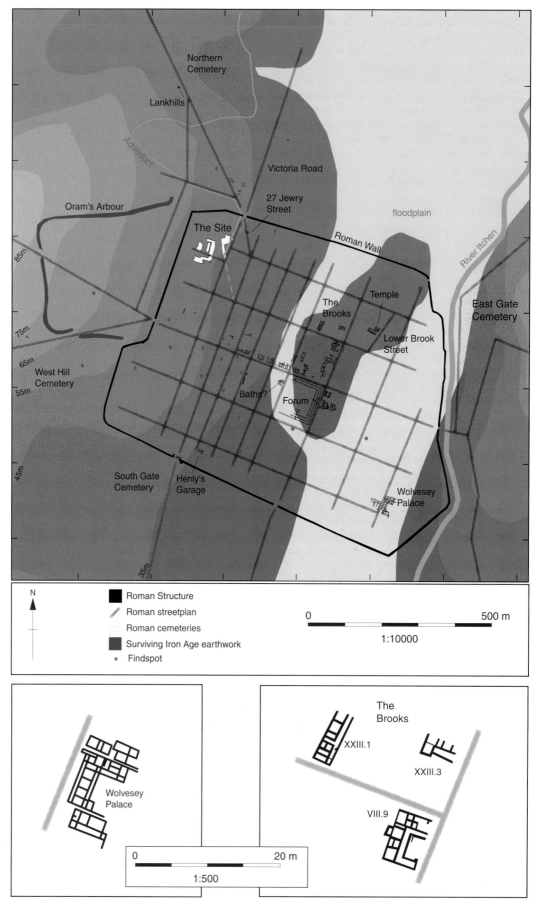

Fig. 5.3 Roman Winchester

Topography had a significant bearing on the development of the Discovery Centre/Northgate site. The site was situated on the south-east facing slope of the Itchen Valley (Qualmann 1993, fig. 4), and the street pattern reflected this. The earliest metalled street (Street CC1703) was orientated NE-SW, parallel with the river and aligned with the contours of the slope. The evidence is patchy, but judging by the orientation of posthole alignments and wall segments, structures fronting on to the street extended from it at right-angles. It is reasonable to suppose, too, that Street CC1703 dictated the alignment of the second street, NH8511/8513, which we assume extended NW-SE to meet Street CC1703 and mark the second side of the *insula* (the western and northern sides presumably being formed by the town walls). This is not confirmed by the excavated evidence, though, and in any case the street pattern in this quarter of the town need not have been so regular. Information relating to the dating of Street CC1703 adds little to the chronology of the street grid, which was established within the final quarter of the 1st century AD (Wacher 1995, 293), presumably coincident with the erection of the earthen ramparts. No dating evidence was recovered from the earliest deposits associated with Street CC1703. However, the fills of ditch CC3486, which may have served as a roadside drainage channel, contained some of the earliest Roman-period pottery, including the *terra nigra* bowl and white ware butt-beaker mentioned above. It is also instructive that the first metalled surface was laid on the Iron Age subsoil. Street NH8511/8513 was metalled in the 4th century (gravel levelling below the surface contained 4th-century pottery), but probably replaced an earlier holloway. Amounting to little more than a track, this was shaped by the inhabitants of the town and its course may well have developed organically to reflect the short-cuts and meanderings of daily use.

Structures NH8519 and NH8521 perhaps never encroached on the metalled street, but instead were built alongside a street that wound its way around properties. Generally, though, the pattern uncovered in the north-west quarter of the town adds to the view that topography affected the development of the town as a whole. At The Brooks, situated on the floodplain of the River Itchen (Fig. 5.3), early Roman occupation was focused on the eastern part of the site, which sat on an island of tufa (Zant 1993, 46). Drainage and consolidation in the later 2nd century enabled the lower-lying western part of The Brooks to be occupied. Rees notes (forthcoming) that expansion into the eastern suburbs was restricted by a steep chalk slope, while the hillside rising from the Itchen meant that the western suburbs remained relatively sparsely occupied.

The evidence relating to a military presence in the town during the 1st century is almost non-existent (Wacher 1995, 291). Ditches reputedly of military character below Flavian structures in Lower Brook Street could offer a location for a fort, but, as Zant (1993, 50) points out, unless the installation was a very minor post, the fort would have extended into the lowest-lying area of the floodplain, which was unavailable for occupation until the late 2nd century. Evidence from the Discovery Centre/Northgate House site included nothing of military character, at least not dating to the early Roman period. A copper alloy strap-mount from a Dark Earth deposit and a bow-brooch from Structure NH8518 could have been used by military personnel, perhaps serving in a unit engaged in policing duties, but in any case belong to the later 2nd and 3rd centuries (see Cool, Chapter 7). Still, the argument for a military or at least a state involvement in the early development of the town is not entirely lost given the date of the ramparts and the possible circumstances in which they were built; Wilson (2006, 30) suggests that the ramparts denote municipal status on a par with Verulamium.

Nature of occupation

Traces of three buildings dating to the later 1st century were found. There may have been more structures, but the medieval truncation makes it impossible to gauge the density of occupation. In any case, a yard surface (Group CC7002), immediately north of Structure CC7049, indicates that there were open areas. The marginal aspect to the location of buildings extends to their use. That the yard was a scene of industrial activity is clear from the soil reddened by burning and the remains of hearths, and is also well supported by a large quantity of material relating to metalworking recovered from a layer of trampled soil. Fragments of smithing hearth bottoms, hearth linings, and cinders provide unequivocal evidence for iron smithing (see Starley, Chapter 7); this on its own cannot confirm that the yard was the place of this activity and indeed the evidence may simply represent dumped material. However, hammerscale—a particularly useful indicator of location, typically being deposited very close to where it was produced—was recovered from pits associated with the yard surface. Whether smiths occupied any of the nearby structures is uncertain, although a small amount of fuel-ash slag from Structure CC7049 may identify this as a workshop that opened onto the yard.

Maltsters or brewers may also have been active in the north-west part of the town during the later 1st century AD. Deposit CC1766 within Phase 2.1 Structure CC7004 contained relatively abundant sprouted grains of spelt wheat, collapsed grains and detached embryos that indicate waste from malting (see Carruthers, *Digital Section 15*). In the late Roman period, malting would typically be carried out in a corn-drier and permit two of the essential stages to occur—germination to promote sprouting and heating to arrest it (Reynolds and Langley 1979). Such structures were not common in Roman Britain during the 1st and 2nd centuries. Instead, the grain was steeped in water-filled tanks or lined pits to allow it to germinate before being removed and spread out on the floor of a warm, dimly-lit barn to continue the process (Dineley 2004, 2–3). The grain was then parched over hearths to arrest germination, or alternatively the maltsters rolled hot stones over it (ibid., 4). The excavation at the Discovery Centre site uncovered the sorts of features that an early Roman maltster might have utilised—chalk or mortar surfaces as malting floors, buildings as malthouses, hearths for parching, and a channel supplying water—but attributing them to malting specifically is problematic.

Little survived of the earliest structures in the Northgate House site, which dated to the 2nd century AD and survived as odd postholes and pits. Industrial debris, such as hammerscale, fuel ash slag, and hearth lining fragments from one pit (CC1688), suggests that smiths worked here. The building of Structure NH8522 in the first half of the 3rd century heralded a change in the use of the area. Its masonry footings, painted walls, possible paved floor, and a range of ceramic continental-style tablewares points to relatively high-status domestic occupation, although hammerscale retrieved from an associated pit suggests that ironworking continued nearby. Given the depth and condition of a well-worn holloway, the north-west quarter of the town saw a reasonable flow of traffic during this time. It was replaced by a metalled street (Street NH8511/8513) after AD 300, and this appears to have encouraged further building work, or was a product of increased structural activity. The buildings erected after AD 250 may have been principally domestic or were used for craft or industrial activity that left no trace (see artist's reconstruction in Plate 5.2). No ironworking evidence was recovered within the structures or from associated features, although smithing may have continued in this area during the 4th century (a small quantity of hammerscale was recovered from Pit Group NH8524) and expanded eastwards into the Discovery Centre site, as attested by 12 kg of slag, smithing hearth bottoms and hammerscale from pit CC1688. A waste glass fragment or moile, intrusive in a prehistoric subsoil, adds to evidence for glass-blowing in Winchester, although such activity is unlikely to have taken place at the Discovery Centre/Northgate House site, as the amount of waste is too low (see Cool, Chapter 7).

Towards the middle of the 4th century, Street NH8511/8513 was re-surfaced. This proved an optimistic measure and soon afterwards maintenance ceased, allowing soil deposits to accumulate and structures to encroach. Structure NH8521 was erected across the street and it is possible that access through the area was by means of an irregular track which snaked around the buildings. Vitrified hearth linings and oven wall recovered from the structure may identify it as a workshop. Structure NH8520, probably contemporary with NH8521, was also potentially a workshop, though used for weaving. The discovery here of weaving tablets may help us to place the *procurator gynaecii, Ventensis* (weaving-works' manager), mentioned in the *Notitia Dignitatum*, in Winchester, rather than Caistor-by-Norwich or Caerwent (Wacher 1995, 299). The marginal location of the Northgate House site makes it ideal for cloth-manufacture and unsocial activities like fulling, but whether this area supported the large industry implied by the post of procurator is uncertain. Cool (Chapter 7) reminds us that weaving tablets were more appropriately used in a domestic, rather than industrial, setting, and that the amount of textile working equipment from Winchester is very low. All buildings were probably abandoned by the late 4th century. Trenches cut across the channel flanking Street CC1703 to remove the structural material are perhaps suggestive of more extensive robbing, but in any case the landscape was sufficiently denuded to allow Dark Earth to form.

The low-status, artisanal character of the site is reflected in the diet of its inhabitants. Apart from malting, spelt was used, along with bread-type wheat, for everyday consumption. The charred remains suggest that the hulled cereals were cleaned and ground in the home on a subsistence level (see Carruthers, Chapter 8). Barley, oats and rye were grown, but used mainly for fodder. Evidence of diet was also collected from cess pit NH8521 in the form of peas and sloes or cherries, and charred shells from other features suggests that hazelnuts were foraged and consumed regularly. Together the evidence points to a diet with a low-status, rural character.

This is supported by the animal bone assemblage, which recorded a diet largely based on beef, lamb or mutton, and pork, supplemented by chicken and game. The assemblage was limited and there were relatively few individuals that could be aged and sexed. However, the data that are available suggest that most cattle were reared for meat. Cows did provide milk, but this was mainly the role of sheep and goats. Pigs provided meat and fat only and inevitably this led to an assemblage dominated by boars (see Strid, Chapter 8). This profile is consistent with urban sites in Roman Britain and may owe something to the influence of the military diet, which gives a similar profile. Dobney (2001, 36–7) contrasts the military and urban pattern with the Mediterranean diet, which, judging by recipes in *Apicius* and other ancient sources, was based around pork to a much greater extent. Winchester's location meant that fish inevitably contributed to the diet. Salmon, trout, eels and flounder—all represented at Winchester—are freshwater fish that may have swum in local rivers and streams. Herrings, sea bream and flatfish were imported presumably from nearby coastal waters, though perhaps arrived as preserved products (see Nicholson, Chapter 8). These were accompanied by oysters, mussels and periwinkles (see Campbell, Chapter 8). The animal bone suggests that some of Winchester's inhabitants enjoyed a distinctly north-west European diet, but while the ingredients were not, on the whole, exotic, they were used in continental ways. In the kitchen,

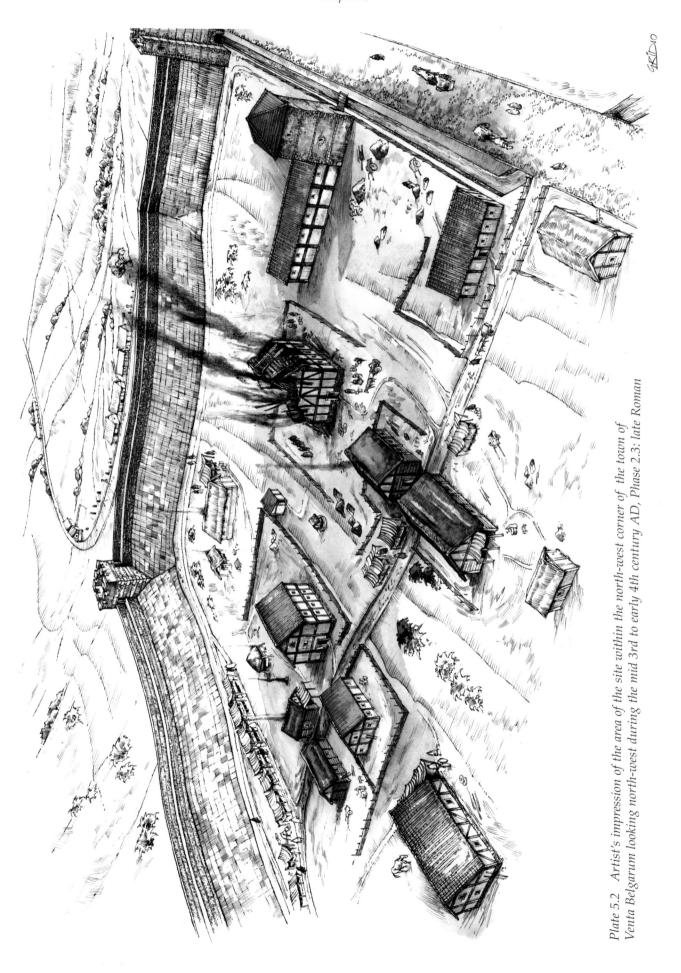

Plate 5.2 Artist's impression of the area of the site within the north-west corner of the town of
Venta Belgarum looking north-west during the mid 3rd to early 4th century AD, Phase 2.3: late Roman

mortaria—items specified in *Apicius*—were used for mixing and grinding ingredients, and dishes for cooking on the hot ashes of the gridiron. In the dining room, an assortment of dishes, flagons, and beakers, some imported from Gaul or made in Britain in imitation of continental styles, were placed on the dining table.

The site's low status contrasts with the higher-status occupation in other parts of the Roman town. Comparison of pottery assemblages from the Discovery Centre/Northgate House site and Victoria Road outside the north wall along the road leading out of the north gate (see Fig. 5.3) suggests that residents of the northern suburbs had better access to imported tablewares and were higher placed in social or wealth terms, at least during the 2nd and 3rd centuries (Rees forthcoming). The 1st and 2nd-century structures (*insula* VIII) at The Brooks in the central part of the Roman town (Fig. 5.3) were timber-built, like those at the Discovery Centre/Northgate House site, but possibly included a winged or courtyard house (Zant 1993, 51), which was almost certainly domestic. The contrast was starker in the late 2nd century when large private houses were built. Structures VII.10 and XXIII.1 at The Brooks were built to a double corridor plan; the latter incorporated elaborate mosaics (Zant 1993, 79). Further development took place in the 4th century. Building VIII.9 acquired mosaics, while a hypocaust was inserted into building XXIII.3 (Zant 1993, 83-127). A masonry town house built in the later 2nd century was uncovered at Henly's Garage inside the south wall (Rees forthcoming). The Wolvesey Palace site in the south-east corner of the town similarly developed from an area of street-front timber structures in the early-Flavian period into masonry buildings in the later Roman period. Building 2, which replaced an earlier timber structure in the mid Roman period, was a relatively grand town house with a courtyard, a well, veranda, and series of rooms extending off a corridor (Fig. 5.3). Another building had a tessellated floor (Biddle 1975b, 321–26).

We know little about what the buildings looked like above ground and how they were decorated internally. Fragments of ceramic building material and worked stone point generally to the use of limestone slabs and ceramic tiles for roofs and floors, but none was found *in situ* and, being often found in deposits laid after the identified structures were abandoned, need not have derived from those buildings. Poole and Shaffrey (Chapter 7), suggesting that much of the material arrived from elsewhere, note a higher than usual proportion of ceramic brick (most often used in ovens) and a conversely low proportion of roofing and flooring tile, a profile associated more with rural than urban sites, and in strong contrast to the relatively larger and more varied assemblage from The Brooks site, where town-houses were uncovered (Zant 1993).

There are, however, traces of evidence that give some impression of appearance. Structure NH8522 provides more clues than most buildings, since a fire that led to its abandonment also helped to preserve important structural elements. Removal of demolition layer NH2589 revealed in the soil the charcoal stain of burnt timbers. The stain retained the structural form of the timbers, which almost certainly formed part of a wall panel that collapsed during the fire. This had been left in place and was eventually covered in soil. A block of wall plaster recorded on top of a burnt timber suggests that the entire surface of the panel was plastered, and consequently the beams would have remained unseen by the building's occupants. The *in situ* plaster was painted red, but fragments with an orange wash and a grey-striped motif were collected from the demolition deposit, pointing to a colourful decorative scheme overall (see Chapter 2, Fig. 2.15 and Plate 2.5). There are further clues to the building's appearance. The chalk and mortar footings that define the southern side of the building may have supported timber walls, while a slightly burnt limestone slab from chalk layer NH2646 possibly paved a floor within the building. An unpainted clay fragment with an impression of a lath or rod from demolition layer NH2589 could have formed part of the ceiling.

The evidence for the appearance of other buildings was sparser still. Structure NH8516 was a timber-framed building presumably walled with daub. Limestone slab fragments from two of the building's postholes were undoubtedly structural and, recovered from upper fills associated with abandonment, were probably from the building itself. However, it is uncertain whether they formed part of the roof or floor (either on top of or additional to a chalk surface).

Structure NH8519 also yielded evidence of flooring, but in this case a worn sandstone tessera and three limestone slab fragments found in the packing fills of two postholes are much less likely to have been used inside the building and instead relate to a structure that had been re-floored or abandoned when NH8519 was erected. The arrangement of postholes and postpads of Structure CC7003, dating from *c* AD 270 to the later 4th century, suggests that it was an aisled building, but the paucity of evidence for external walls points more strongly to a simple hall-type structure. Good parallels are known at Beddington villa, Surrey. Two late Roman buildings *c* 18 m by 7 m were defined by post-pits, or occasional post-pads, up to 1.5 m in diameter. Like Structure CC7003, there was no evidence of aisles, although the report authors did not regard the provision of aisles as impossible (Howell 2005, 32–5). A wattle-and-daub filling in between the posts of Structure CC7003 is suspected, but the small amount of daub assigned to the structure is not sufficient to settle the matter. Hall-houses have been regarded as domestic structures or industrial or craft buildings. A byre for livestock is another obvious possibility, although J T Smith (1997, 45) considers the necessary evidence, such as drains or space, to be limited generally. A piece of marble wall veneer from a pit associated with Structure CC7003 need not have belonged to the building and may well have been deposited casually with waste drawn from a variety of sources. However, it can be grouped with other imported marble fragments found on the site that nevertheless point to buildings in the area that approached the luxury of the town-houses at The Brooks.

Returning to the building's function, fired clay with wattle impressions recovered from an upper fill of one of the building's postholes formed part of an oven dome, potentially giving the building a working, rather than domestic, role, for example as a bakery. Grain storage was important too. A deposit of bread-type wheat recovered from a late Roman midden associated with street surface NH8512 reminds us that large amounts of processed grain was a requisite for feeding the town's inhabitants; the wheat showed signs of insect damage and presumably had been burnt in order to eliminate storehouse pests (see Carruthers, Chapter 8). If the building was not associated with grain storage or baking, then an industrial use is an alternative possibility. The scale of the metalworking, and possibly weaving too, may have been significant, and a large hall provided well-needed space for working, storage and administration. The appearance of a large rural-type building in an urban setting cannot be regarded as completely unexpected. At Silchester, an aisled building constructed in the 2nd century contained the remains of hearths from which evidence of metalworking was recovered, allowing the excavators to describe it as a work hall (Clarke and Fulford 2002, 139–41).

The aqueduct

The conduit that extended along the edge of Street CC1703 offers tantalising support for the course of an aqueduct proposed by P J Fasham and R J B Whinney (1991). A watching brief at Woodham's Farm in the Itchen Valley uncovered a steep-sided and flat-bottomed channel up to 2.7 m wide. The observation that the feature followed the contours of the Fulflood valley, the presence within its water-lain fills of aquatic, open-land and wetland molluscs, and its similarity in terms of shape with the Dorchester aqueduct led Fasham and Whinney to interpret the channel as a section of an aqueduct servicing Winchester (ibid., 5–10). A source in an area of springs near Itchen Stoke is a possibility. The channel, if continuing a gentle downhill course along the side of the valley, would wind its way around Headbourne Worthy before arriving at the north gate in the north-west quarter of the Roman town, giving a total length of 23.75 km. K E Qualmann (1991, 11) suggested that deep deposits of silty clay uncovered at Andover Road immediately outside the north gate may mark the location of a reservoir or cistern, which could feed pipes and channels allowing water to be distributed to different parts of the town. Fasham and Whinney

(1991, 8) put the height of the putative cistern at 47.72 m aOD. Potentially, channel CC1850 observed along the western edge of the street can be connected with such a cistern. Its profile, similar to that of the Woodham's Farm channel, and mortared flint lining make it ideal for carrying water, while the levels obtained along the base of the channel were appropriately lower than the level at the north gate and suggested a gentle fall to the south.

There is a difficulty, however, with identifying the channel with the aqueduct. How the channel was constructed is problematic. It is likely to have been covered if it was to avoid receiving the run-off from the street surface or casually-dumped waste material, and was almost certainly covered where it crossed the street itself. Unfortunately, the archaeological evidence is equivocal on the matter. We know that the channel was lined with a hard flint mortar surface, but what part, if any, the mass of ceramic building material found within the fill of the channel played is open to question. None was found *in situ*, but instead recovered from the backfill of a robber trench and the overlying Dark Earth. Bricks and flat tiles that could have covered the channel, or formed supports for a cover, were found in significant quantity, but roof tiles and flue-tiles were also collected, albeit in smaller quantity, indicating that the bricks were dumped as part of a mixed deposit of material potentially derived from elsewhere. Evidence of use that some bricks exhibited also pointed to other structures; burnt tiles, for example, could have been incorporated into a hypocaust, although it is possible that water flowing through the channel was responsible for the heavy abrasion seen on the underside of some flat tiles.

A street-side timber-lined channel from The Brooks may help with the interpretation here. The construction cut was substantial (the first phase was over 4 m wide and 2 m deep), but the wooden channel inserted into it was, at 2 m wide, only marginally wider than channel CC1850 (Zant 1993, fig. 23). The channel extended east-west to ultimately issue into the Itchen or a smaller stream and was dug to drain the land around and reclaim the floodplain (Zant 1993, 52). Its location surely means that channel CC1850 cannot have helped with land reclamation, but its construction (and no doubt regular maintenance and cleaning), like that of The Brooks channel, suggests an equally significant function. That said, street-side ditches designed to take rainwater run-off from the street surface were at times substantial depending on the size of the street. Ermin Street extending through Cirencester was at least 5 m wide and 1.5 m thick (though this included multiple episodes of resurfacing). The ditch flanking the street was a concave-profiled feature measuring 2.5 m wide (Havard and Watts 2008, 35). The side-ditches associated with another part of Ermin Street were on average 2 m wide and 0.5 m deep (Evans 2008, 42). Still, the use of a mortared flint lining, even without tiled facing or capping, represents a work of engineering that must take the function of channel CC1850 beyond that of an ordinary street ditch. That it served as some form of aqueduct seems most likely, but how it related, if at all, with the leat that approached the north gate, or whether it was covered, is difficult to resolve on present evidence.

From urban to sub-urban

The buildings of the final phase of occupation in Winchester's north-west quarter were abandoned during the second half of the 4th century. Dating from pottery and coinage suggests that the process of structural abandonment spanned the period from about AD 340, when the last in the series of pits cut in the Northgate House area was filled, to AD 380 or later when Dark Earth was accumulating over the late Roman properties. The events of the intervening years are difficult to establish, but some clues are provided by the structural remains, which generally point to a period of deconstruction and robbing. Most of the postholes that define Structure NH8519 exhibited evidence of postpipes, indicating that the posts had rotted *in situ* and possibly that the building decayed and collapsed as disrepair and the elements took their toll. Such evidence appears to be exceptional, however, since the posts belonging to Structures NH8520 and NH8521 were almost certainly removed deliberately. The evidence lies with the character of the posthole fills. The postholes of both Structures NH8520 and NH8521 were filled with a single deposit, or occasionally a second and final fill. In these cases, the posts either sat on the base of the posthole and were packed with a single deposit or rested on a deposit of usually stonier material that formed a pad, and were then stabilised with packing. When the posts were removed, the packing fills collapsed into the void. This contrasts with the postholes of Structure NH8519, where the packing fill retained the shape of the post, which survived as a soil stain. We should note that all postholes undoubtedly suffered from later truncation and may therefore lack upper fills, but the differences between the postholes of Structure NH8519 on the one hand and Structures NH8520/NH8521 on the other are sufficiently marked to suggest contrasting treatment. That materials were removed from the site is shown more clearly by channel NH1850, or rather the trenches cut either side of the channel. Robbing of the channel and some of the structures was, it seems, a systematic operation.

If the picture that emerges of demolition, rather than gradual decay, is tentative, being based on limited evidence, it is nonetheless consistent with that from other parts of the town. A similar phase of demolition was recorded at The Brooks. Building VIII.9 (Fig. 5.3) was demolished by the third quarter of the 4th century, while others continued into the final quarter (Zant 1993, 152). Evidence for this phase comes from scatters of building material around the structures. Such spreads were largely

missing from the Discovery Centre/Northgate House site, but this may be because the buildings were mainly timber-built. Zant makes a similar observation with regard to The Brooks. *Insula* VIII had relatively little demolition material associated with it compared with *insula* XXIII, but its masonry features were limited to footings and roofing (Zant 1993, 133). The town house at Henly's Garage was poorly maintained during the second half of the 4th century, and it too succumbed to robbing (Rees, forthcoming).

The second half of the 4th century was clearly a period of upheaval, as buildings were taken down, the materials removed in some cases, and remaining upstanding structures levelled. But while the formal structures of town life were being dismantled, occupation of some sort continued; after all, there must have been people around to carry out the demolition. Structures associated with this occupation are hard to detect, presumably because they comprised temporary wooden buildings that left few remains. Evidence possibly relating to such structures was identified within the rubble at The Brooks; rough surfaces and hearths were recorded overlying the demolition deposits of building VIII.1, but the nature of this occupation—domestic, industrial or both—could not be determined by the excavators (Zant 1993, 154). Stakeholes and an oven seen at the southern end of the Discovery Centre area may relate to a similar period of post-urban occupation, but these features were dated broadly and cut into the prehistoric subsoil, and it was therefore not possible to assign the features to a period of less formal occupation. Floor surfaces and postholes cut into a levelling deposit covering Structure NH8522, destroyed by fire in the 3rd century, may similarly be dated to the late Roman period, but again do not necessarily belong to the Roman town's final phase.

The final decades of the 4th century or the early years of the 5th century saw the accumulation of Dark Earth. Brian Yule (1990; 2005, 80) attributes the formation of Dark Earth in late Roman London to 'reworking', but, largely ruling out cultivation and dumping, suggests that it led to a truncation horizon

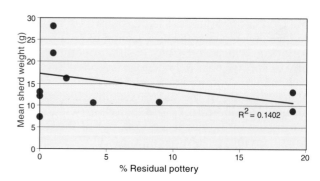

Fig. 5.4 Dark Earth pottery: scattergram showing relationship between the percentage of residual pottery by sherd count and mean sherd weight

which sealed chronologically varied stratigraphy. We can see that process to some extent at the Discovery Centre/Northgate House site, since some Dark Earth deposits meet levels pre-dating the late Roman period; the interfaces separating the Dark Earth and underlying deposits seem as varied as they are in London (Yule 1990). But it is worth reviewing the character of the soil from Winchester. Micromorphological analysis records biological reworking, an aspect shared by London Dark Earth, but also lenses of material, for example charcoal, that point to middening and occupation (see Macphail and Crowther, Chapter 8). Pottery groups recovered from Dark Earth deposits were usually large, in relatively good condition, and contained little obviously residual material. Admittedly, where the soil covered much earlier horizons, the proportion of residual pottery increased (19% by sherd count above a Phase 2.1 level, compared with, say, 1% over a Phase 2.3 horizon), but otherwise the assemblages had no obvious reference to the underlying deposits and could not have been brought up from below. The conclusion must be that the material had been cleared from dumps of occupation waste and redeposited above the demolished late Roman buildings and pockets of earlier stratigraphy.

Once the soils were laid, it can be argued that they were subject to reworking. This could have been responsible for bringing up some material from underlying layers. While the levels of residuality offer some support for this, assuming that redeposition can lead to further fragmentation of material, there is surprisingly no strong correlation between the percentage of residual pottery and the size of sherds. Regression analysis (Shennan 1997, 141) comparing mean sherd weight and residuality percentage values (Fig. 5.5) indicates that just 14% of the variation in one variable is explained by variation in the other. In other words, the residual pottery could well have derived from elsewhere and may have accompanied the midden material. Whatever form the reworking took, it potentially continued into the 5th century or later, although only a single sherd of early to mid Saxon pottery was recovered from the Dark Earth during the present excavations (see below). At The Brooks, however, 10th-century pottery was recovered from upper parts of the Dark Earth (Zant 1993, 156; Biddle and Kjølbye-Biddle 2007, 194).

THE ANGLO-SAXON BURH, AND THE ANGLO-NORMAN AND LATER MEDIEVAL CITY: OVERVIEW AND DISCUSSION OF THE EVIDENCE *by Steve Teague*

Early and mid Saxon Winchester

The date and circumstances of the re-establishment of Saxon Winchester as an urban centre are key research questions that have been pursued by archaeologists in the city over the past 50 years. Apart from a single sherd of early to mid Saxon

pottery no evidence (either finds or structural) was found for occupation in the area of the present excavations between the late Roman period and the mid to late 9th century, the time at which the Anglo-Saxon *burh* was established. The nature of the Dark Earth that built up in the area after it ceased to be occupied in the late Roman period is reviewed by Biddulph (above), and the implication is that the area saw little or no activity of any kind after the early years of the 5th century. The earliest evidence for the post-Roman use of the city still derives largely from Martin Biddle's excavations at Lower Brook Street (1975b, 295–338; 1975c). Biddle has suggested that by the second half of the 7th century the south-east quarter of the old Roman town housed both the Old Minster with an associated residence for the bishop and his community, and a royal palace close by. A small number of private estates may have existed in the vicinity (Biddle 1975c, 126) but occupation was evidently very limited in extent and in no sense urban. Part of what may have been one of these proposed estates, excavated by Biddle at Lower Brook Street, consisted of a small late 7th-century cemetery with a richly furnished female burial. This was succeeded in the 8th and 9th centuries by a sequence of three buildings, two of which were built in stone and reused elements of a nearby ruined Roman workshop. Evidence for gold working was found in association with the latest of the buildings, which Biddle suggested could have been a secure two-storey structure for the storage, assay and working of precious metals. The presence of other potential early enclosures has been proposed on documentary grounds at Coitebury, in the north-east sector of the Roman walled area, at Wolvesey (Wulf's Isle), at the New Minster, and the area bounded by Colebrook Street that was given as an endowment to the Nunnaminster (James 1997, 40). Despite large-scale excavations at The Brooks, located less than 100 m to the west of Biddle's site, no further evidence for contemporary occupation was found (Scobie *et al.* 1991). However, nearby at The Square, the remains of timber workshops were found (Teague 1989b) that pre-dated a street known to have defined the northern extent of the New Minster, established in or shortly after 901 (Biddle 1976, 313–5). One of the structures produced a sceat, provisionally dated to 720–30 (Zant 1990).

The creation of the *burh*

The creation of the *burh*, which is reviewed in Chapter 1 above, is believed to have involved the reinstatement of the Roman defences and the laying out of a grid pattern of new streets (see artist's reconstruction in Plate 5.3). The defences lay outside the area investigated as part of the present project, but new evidence was recovered for the date at which the streets were laid out here, and for the establishment of occupied tenements along their frontages.

Plate 5.3 Artist's impression from the south-east showing the area of the site and the north-west corner of the late Saxon burh during the mid-10th to mid 11th century, Phase 4.2: later late Saxon

The streets

The streets of Winchester have long been regarded as an integral element of the original design of the late Saxon *burh* (see Chapter 1, above). Opportunities to test this by archaeological excavation and dating remain rare, since the street pattern has remained essentially unchanged and the late Saxon levels are rarely accessible beneath the city's modern road system. The survey of 1110 (Survey I) provides both the earliest and at the same time the largest group of street-names available from any English town before the 13th century (Biddle 1976, 231), two of them in the area of the present excavations: Brudene Street (presently Staple Gardens) and Snitheling Street (a precursor to Tower Street). The only significant changes that are known to have been made to the late Saxon street system occurred during the mid 10th century, when the monastic precincts were enlarged, and around a century later during the construction of the Norman castle (Biddle 1975c, 127), both of which resulted in the closure of a number of streets.

Evidence for an early date for Winchester's streets has been recovered archaeologically at a number of sites. During excavations at Castle Yard, two hitherto unknown streets were identified below the earthworks of Winchester Castle (attributable to *c* 1067), both of which had been repaired on up to eight or nine occasions resulting in a total depth of over 1.5 m of mud and metalling prior to the construction of the castle. A radiocarbon date of 880±60 (HAR 295), recalibrated to 902±60 was obtained on material from the lowest surface, and an iron stirrup of Wheeler's Type C of 10th- or 11th-century date was found in the cobbling of the fourth surface of the north-south street (Biddle 1975d, 27). Excavation across Gar Street (closed during the 19th century) revealed six superimposed streets of flint and gravel that were separated by black earth (Biddle 1965). The first street produced no closely datable material, although a silver penny of the later years of Edward the Elder (899–924) was found under the second; the third and subsequent streets were dated from the 11th to the 16th centuries and later. A coin of Alfred was recovered from levels associated with a workshop adjacent to Gar Street during excavations at the Lower Barracks (Teague 1989a); during recent excavations at 28 Jewry Street, a second coin of Alfred, struck by the moneyer Lulla between 875 and 880, has been found within the earliest levels of a structure alongside the Saxon precursor to Jewry Street (Paul McCulloch, Wessex Archaeology, pers. comm.). At Henly's Garage 'early-type pre-850' pottery was found in a pit associated with loomweights, and suggests some form of domestic occupation dating to *c* 850 or earlier (Rees *et al*. 2008, 393–4).

During the present excavations at Northgate House, it became clear that late Saxon Snitheling Street lay beyond the area of the archaeological investigations. However, the earliest surfaces of Brudene Street were seen in numerous locations along the Northgate House frontage of Staple Gardens (see Chapter 3, Figs 3.3–6). The best sequence was seen at the east edge of Properties BW 2 and BW 3 (Fig. 3.3, section NH271). Here, the earliest surfaces (NH4701–2) directly overlay the Dark Earth and consisted of a single layer of tightly packed small flint cobbles (NH4702), which probably formed the base for a directly overlying surface of fine angular flint gravel (NH4701). This surface had become very worn, and was overlain by a thick accumulation of trampled green-stained silt (NH4700) from which sherds of pottery with simple undeveloped rims in the early chalk-tempered fabric MBX were recovered. This pottery is likely to be of mid to late 9th-century date (see Cotter, Chapter 7). The surface was repaired with chalk and gravel, and further silts accumulated above. The presence of animal bone, madder-stained sherds of pottery and a spindlewhorl in these silts provides evidence that domestic occupation had been established nearby by this time, and evidence was recovered for early contemporary structures respecting the street line on Property BW 2. Charcoal from the silts was radiocarbon dated to 770–940 (OxA-17177) and 780–990 (SUERC-13909). Bayesian modelling (see Chapter 6) has further refined these dates to 770–890 and 770–920 respectively, and if the earlier dates are taken to be reliable, this would suggest that the street had been in use for a significant period of time before 890, or at least that it had been subject to heavy wear.

A second phase of resurfacing (Street NH8607) comprised two layers of well-compacted, thick orange gravel, the later layer supporting a surface of tightly packed, rounded flint pebbles. The first of these layers appeared to extend some 2 m further west than the earlier surfaces, over the structures on Property BW 2, suggesting that the street had been widened. However, the west edge of the street was subsequently encroached upon by buildings (see Property BW 2, Chapter 3) and narrowed again by some 3 m on its west side. The latest phase of street surfaces (Street NH8609), datable to before 950, consisted of two well-compacted coarse angular gravel surfaces (NH4684 and NH4644), which had become very rutted and uneven, suggesting that the street continued to be heavily used.

Taking into account further dates derived from within adjacent buildings, the Bayesian model provides an estimate for the start of Saxon occupation here in the period 810–890, with a high probability that this occurred after 840 but before the 880s (se Chapter 6). This is comparable to the evidence found at Castle Yard, where the first three street surfaces could feasibly be dated to the second half of the 9th century. However, the dating derived from the present excavations suggests that the street grid was first laid out earlier than the conventional model suggests, early in Alfred's reign (871–899), or before, rather than during the 880s or later.

Analysis of documentary evidence suggests that the streets of late Saxon Winchester were significantly wider than their modern counterparts and were encroached upon by properties from an early date, and probably by the late 11th century (Keene 1985, 48–50). Keene has suggested that the side streets (*horbes rues* or blind streets that lead off the High Street) were originally 12.2–15.25 m (between forty and fifty feet) in width (ibid.). There has been little opportunity to test such theories archaeologically, though small-scale excavations close to the west side of Upper Brook Street (Shulworth Street) revealed a succession of street surfaces ranging in date from the 12th to the 15th century that were up to 4.5 m wider than the existing street (Webster and Cherry 1979, 265). Excavations on the site of the former Masons Hall on Parchment Street revealed substantial encroachment by 12th-century structures over earlier flint metallings alongside the south side of St George's Street, suggesting that the present 'dog-leg' on this part of this street had its origins by the 1100s (Teague 1991). On the south side of the High Street, a substantial encroachment onto the medieval street by predecessors of the buildings that form 'The Pentice' was probably in progress by the 11th–12th centuries (James and Roberts 2000, 187). The existing width of Staple Gardens/Brudene Street within the area of the site is c 5.5–6 m, although it is now clear that it was originally substantially wider, at least on its western side. Here, the evidence, particularly within Property BW 2, shows that the earliest levels of the street extended c 5 m west of its present line (see Chapter 3, Fig. 3.3). Any evidence for the original extent of its eastern side has been removed by later terracing on the Discovery Centre site, though thick metalling directly overlying Dark Earth was observed within a service trench cut along the eastern edge to the existing street, implying that the street had originally extended this far east from an early date. If a similar degree of encroachment occurred along its eastern side, then the street may originally have measured 15–15.5 m in width. However, this does not take into account the topographical difficulties for such an encroachment from properties on the east side of the street, given the inherent west-east slope. The contemporary levels on the east side of the street are unknown though there is an appreciable drop (c 1.5 m) between the level of the underlying natural found in the service trench and the truncated level found along the western edge of the Discovery Centre excavations. Any structures that would have lined its east side would have been terraced into the slope such that the street would have effectively occupied a raised terrace. Evidence for this raised terrace has been found during excavations on the east side of Staple Gardens at 28-29 Staple Gardens (Teague 1990, 6–8) and at 31 Staple Gardens (Nenk *et al.* 1995, 220) both of which contained well-preserved late Saxon levels. On the former site, a trench located 3 m east of the existing frontage showed that late Saxon levels occurred at 1.9 m below the level of the extant pavement, and late Saxon levels occurred at a similar depth on the latter site. Though the contemporary level of the

street is not known at these points it seems unlikely that a subsequent accumulation of 1.9 m of medieval and later deposits has occurred over the late Saxon street.

Land apportionment and tenement formation

By the time of the survey of 1148, and probably by c 1057, most of the tenements in Winchester fell within the one of the seven great fiefs of the king, the bishop, the Cathedral Priory, Hyde Abbey and the nunneries of St Mary's of Winchester, Wherwell and Romsey (Biddle 1976, 341, 349, 456 and fig. 19; Keene 1985, 184). The way in which these tenements appear in the survey of 1148, disposed as blocks of adjacent small properties under a single lordship throughout the city and the suburbs, suggests that they may preserve the outline of earlier larger holdings that had subsequently been subdivided (Biddle 1976, 452). Neither the nature nor the date of origin of such early large holdings is known (ibid., 341), although it is suggested that they could have been in some way comparable to (or belonged to) rural estates, with the lord having associated rights of territorial jurisdiction and sometimes a private church (ibid., 341, 452). In considering the way in which such a system might have operated from the earliest years of the *burh*, Biddle and Keene (ibid., 340–4) speculated that once the street system was established, the frontages and lands behind them might have been parcelled out to individual lay and ecclesiastical lords in large blocks of perhaps the order of 0.2–0.4 ha in size. They might then have been provided by their owners with a principal dwelling and a private church, and could have provided temporary accommodation for people and their livestock from the neighbouring estates of the lord in times of trouble (ibid., 453–4). Within the area of the present excavations, the 1148 survey shows small contiguous blocks of properties under the ownership of the king (410–411, 403–405, 379–380), the bishop (412–414) and the reeves of Worthy (406–409) (Fig. 5.5).

Biddle and Keene review evidence for the process of subdivision of the proposed early large holdings and note that this was clearly underway in Winchester in the 10th and 11th centuries (Biddle 1976, 343) and parts of the High Street may even have been crowded by c 901 (ibid., 314, 454). The increasing evidence from archaeological excavation suggests, however, that the creation of small tenements fronting onto the streets occurred at an even earlier stage in the city's development, at least in some areas. The earliest structures seen in the present excavations were two small buildings towards the street frontage of Property BW 2, which were contemporary with the first surfacing of Brudene Street. Subsequently, the buildings appear to have burnt down and the street was widened westwards over the early building line. This was possibly associated with a hiatus in occupation. The next structure to be built on Property BW 2, Structure

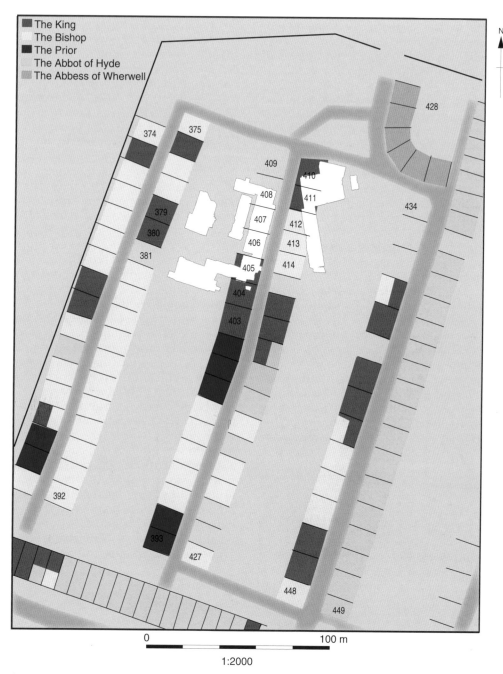

The King
The Bishop
The Prior
The Abbot of Hyde
The Abbess of Wherwell

Fig. 5.5   Land ownership in 1148 of the tenements in the region of Brudene Street and Snitheling Street (after Biddle 1976, fig. 19)

NH8526, encroached some 3 m eastwards over the street, establishing a new street edge that was respected by the subsequent surface. On Properties BW 4 and BW 5 the earliest structures also encroached onto the western edge of the street, suggesting that they might be contemporary with Structure NH8562. The radiocarbon dating estimate derived from Bayesian modelling for these properties suggests a high probability that this all happened before the end of the 9th century (see Chapter 6).

These structures are discussed in more detail below, but it is worth noting here that the early buildings are all of a similar size, located on the street frontage, with evidence for gravelled yards on Properties BW 2 and BW 4, and evidence for boundaries on all three properties. Moreover, the associated finds and environmental evidence suggests predominantly domestic occupation at all three, with some evidence for craft working. In itself, this does not prove the laying out of a sequence of small, long, narrow tenements for rent, as the structures described above could equally have formed street-frontage elements of larger properties. However, it is notable that, once established, the pattern of buildings on these properties remained remarkably consistent through subsequent phases of reconstruction, and by the later 10th and early 11th centuries there is clear evidence for sequences of contiguous tenements with buildings on the street frontages, and sometimes behind, and rows of backyard pits and wells (see Chapter 3, Fig. 3.2).

Excavations at The Brooks during 1987–88 revealed substantial lengths of the late Saxon and medieval frontages of Upper and Middle Brook Street (Sildwortenstret and Wunegrestret), and provide important evidence for the early development of properties, although the excavations remain currently unpublished (Scobie forthcoming). The distribution of the very numerous pits on the site during the late Saxon and Anglo-Norman periods has shown that distinct regularly apportioned properties were in existence from the outset. On the Middle Brook Street frontage the distribution pattern of the pits suggests that a standard width of between 10.5–11 m (approximately 2 perches, poles or 11 English yards) was used here (Fig. 5.6). The boundary lines inferred from these distributions appeared, significantly, to be respected by all late Saxon features. The boundaries were found to remain unchanged throughout the medieval period, although several properties were amalgamated into single larger tenements towards the end of the period. The same property divisions remained unchanged until the later 19th century and can be accurately tied to the 1st Edition OS map of the area. Further afield, during excavations around Cheapside in London, similar conclusions were

reached concerning the alignment of pits from as early as the late 9th century into the 11th (Schofield and Vince 2003, 80) and particularly the regular spacing of cess pits along the boundaries at intervals of 5 m or so (one perch). Excavations at 28–29 Staple Gardens (Teague 1989) revealed the well-preserved remains of two properties, each containing a house, whose boundaries were shown to have remained unchanged from the outset of occupation during the late Saxon period through to the post-Conquest period.

Following Scobie's methodology, the distribution of pits was used to suggest the location of property boundaries for the present excavations, along with other evidence such as the extent of structures and (in a few cases) clear fence lines. Here, as on Scobie's site, the widths of the proposed properties show a marked consistency in size (Table 5.1), most forming near whole multiples of perches (equivalent to $5\frac{1}{2}$ English yards or 5 m), with two perches being the most common width, though there are two properties on the east side of Brudene Street that measured three perches. Assuming that two perches was used as a standard measurement, then eight of the properties have widths that have an accuracy of at least 95% (or within 0.1 m of a perch) offering compelling evidence that a standard system of measurement was being deployed. The most notable anomaly is Property BW 3, which measured 2.8 perches in width, although if the lane that may have occupied its north side is taken into consideration (measuring *c* 4.2 m in width or *c* 0.8 perches) then a width of 2 perches can be suggested. Other anomalies could be explained by early encroachments (for example in Property SE 1) and/or by uncertainties in the determination of these boundaries (for example Property BE 2). The degree of uniformity of width of the properties and the use of a standard measurement

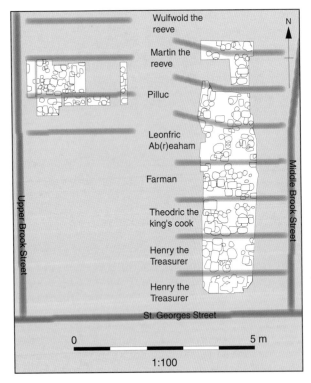

Fig. 5.6 Saxon-Norman properties at The Brooks, Winchester with conjectural correlations with occupants named in survey of Edward the Confessor (c 1057) (after G Scobie, Winchester Museums Service)

Table 5.1 Widths of properties

Property		Width of property	
	Metres	Yards	Perches (5.5 yards)
BE 1	9.5?	10.4?	1.9?
BE 2	11.4	12.4	2.3
BE 3	10.2	11.2	2.0
BE 4	15.2	16.6	3.0
BE 5	15.2	16.6	3.0
BW 1	?	?	?
BW 2	10.5	11.5	2.1
BW 3	13.9	15.2	2.8
BW 4	9.5	10.4	1.9
BW 5	10.5	11.5	2.1
BW 6	?	?	?
SE 1	11.4?	12.4?	2.3?
SE 2	9.6	10.5	1.9
SE A	10.1	11.1	2.1
SE B	8.8	9.6	1.8
SE 3	10.3	11.2	2.0

implies a highly planned and organised layout, which seems more likely to have originated from a central authority than from a gradual subdivision of early large properties for which no positive evidence was seen in the present excavations.

Within Winchester, therefore, as elsewhere, it seems increasingly likely that small, regularly sized tenements aligned on the street frontages were an early, if not an original, feature of the city layout. The very earliest evidence from Property BW 2 suggests that there may have been a hiatus in the development of Brudene Street, and the appearance of buildings encroaching onto the west side of the street may represent a second phase of development, although still probably datable to the later 9th century, after an interruption and reorganisation.

Biddle and Keene (Biddle 1976) have noted that the streets leading to the gates were the first to be built up, and the evidence from the present excavations clearly supports their conclusion that parts of the city were densely built up by the middle of the 10th century.

Concordance with the surveys of 1110 and 1148

Neither of the two early surveys of Winchester (Surveys I and II) gives sufficient information about the order, size or location of properties in Snitheling Street and Brudene Street to allow any of them to be identified with any degree of certainty within the site. Both streets were of approximately equal length at around 120–125 m, though it is not known

Table 5.2: Concordance of Surveys I and II within the area of the site (after Biddle 1976)

Survey I (c 1100)		Survey II (1148)	
No	Entry	No	Entry
Brudenestret (East) (North-South)			
131	The tenement of Brunstan paid 30d and the customs TRE. Now Arnulf Burdin and Ulf owe the same	410 (BE 5 East?)	Ulf's land pays the king 15d
		411 (BE 5 west)	Reginald of Sees pays the king 15d
		412 (BE 4)	Silvestor pays the bishop 30d from the land of the barons
		413 (BE 3)	William of Caen pays the bishop 30d from land of the barons
		414 (BE 2/1?)	The daughter of Henry's son Thurstin pays the bishop 4s from the land of the barons. She again pays the bishop 2s from the land of the barons & receives 4s in rents. And on another tenement she has her servants & chattles
Brudenestret (West) (South-North)			
134	Peter Paid 10d and the customs TRE. Now Cheping (a moneyer) son of Alvera owes the same	(BW 1) 403	Hugh (a moneyer) son of Chepping pays the king for his kitchen 4d. and has from it his living-accommodation(?) quit; and Hugh receives from it 5s
132	Eustace paid 8d and the customs TRE. Now Godwin Withmunding owes the same.	404 (BW 2)	Osmoth pays the king 8d
133	Odo Ticchemann's son held a land which was free except for Watch TRE, and from royal demesne 8 pennyworth of land. Now his son William owes the same	405 (BW 3)	The sons of William son of Odo pays the king 8d
		406 (BW 4)	Pain (son of) Picard pays the reeves of Worthy 24s (sic) and receives from the land 5s
		407 (BW5)	William the palmer ought to pay the same reeves 25d; but the land is waste
		408 (BW 6)	Wazo the clerk pays the reeves (of Worthy) 25d
Snidelingestret (East) (North - South)			
		378 (SE 3)	Hoppecole pays the bishop 3s
128	Godric King's son (possibly a moneyer) paid 4d and the customs TRE. Now Harding the blacksmith owes the same	379 (SE 2)	Harding the blacksmith's son holds 1 land of the king worth 4d quit in return for his services and receives 18d. And from the same land Roger the painter receives 4s. 6d; and from the same land Harding the brewer recieves 2s
129	Anod Stud paid 6d and the customs TRE. Now Odo the monyer owers the same	380	Richard Son of Odo pays the King 6d and receives 2s
		381	Drew Blond pays Hugh de Hahela 6d for 1 land which Hugh holds quit
		382 (SE 1)	Richard the painter pays the bishop 12d from the land of the barons and receives 2s

whether they originally extended further north and up to the city defences (Collis 1978, 165). Analysis of the evidence from the survey of 1148 (Biddle 1976, table 26) suggests a possible total of 35 properties on each street frontage and although a complete listing is not available from the survey of 1110 (as only the king's properties are recorded) this may not have been very different.

Using Biddle and Keene's conclusions (Biddle 1976) concerning the sequence of the survey of 1148, and assuming an average size for the properties surveyed, then on spatial considerations alone Table 5.2 lists those properties that may fall within the bounds of the site and tentatively attempts to corre-late them with the excavated properties. An attempt to correlate the properties with the king's properties from the survey of 1110 has also been made where continuity of tenancies has been identified (after Biddle 1976). However, if Brudene Street and Snitheling Street originally extended up to the city defences there could be room for a margin of error of up to three properties.

Houses and occupants

The development of buildings

Up to 48 buildings or structures were recognised on the site, of which 7 can be allocated to Phase 4.1 (*c* 850–950), 12 to Phase 4.2 (*c* 950–1050), 10 to Phase 5 (*c* 1050–1225) and 10 to Phase 6 (after *c* 1225). Although not a complete record, these provide a good sample of changing building styles in the area over time. The structures of the late Saxon phases were without exception built of timber as were the majority from the Anglo-Norman Phase 5, although wells with chalk-block linings, and stone ovens, were present on some properties at this time. The chapel and stone house that belonged to the Archdeacon of Winchester by the 13th century were the first structures to be built entirely of stone in the area, and were probably constructed during the 12th century. Much more widespread construction of stone houses with tiled roofs, chimney pots and tiled floors is evident from the late 12th or early 13th century. In Phase 6 (after *c* 1225), most of the excavated buildings were of stone. The construction of masonry houses in the 13th century is generally reflected elsewhere in the city, though the poor continued to live in timber buildings such those at Tanner Street (Biddle 1976, 348). This would suggest that the substantial stone structures that were found in Properties BW 1 and BE 5, like those within the Archdeacon's residence, belong to inhabitants of higher status.

The buildings can be divided into two types; principal structures largely located on the street frontage; and ancillary structures located to the rear of the properties. Due to truncation of deposits that often occurred to the rear of the properties, ancillary structures are poorly represented, and in some cases, the presence of a building was indicated only by floor deposits that had slumped into the upper fills of earlier pits. Consequently these structures are only found within Phase 4.2 or later levels.

Principal structures

The earliest structures on the site were found along the west frontage of Brudene Street, and appeared to be confined to the area immediately adjacent to the street. The best surviving examples were found within Properties BW 2 and BW 4, which contained well-preserved floor levels and were also subject to greater excavation. Within Property BW 2, the earliest structure (Structure NH8525) was built before the westward extension of Brudene Street and constructed with a double-line of closely spaced postholes along its east side and a possible sill along-side its south wall, a method of construction not paralleled elsewhere on the site. However, building with paired uprights seems to reflect a tradition that dates back to the 6th–8th centuries as evident at Cowdery's Down, West Stow and Mucking (James 1999, fig. 4.9). After its apparent destruction by fire, it was replaced by the more typical type of timber structure found on the site, Structure NH8526, constructed on surface-based sill-beams whose presence was sometimes identified as shallow, flat-based slots formed by internal and external deposits abutting the ground beam. A similar sequence of structural remains was found at 28–29 Staple Gardens where the earliest structures, of possible mid-late 9th-century date, utilised a close post-built technique and were succeeded by structures utilising sill beams measuring some 4.5 m in length (Teague 1990). Interestingly, here this earliest struc-ture had also been destroyed by fire. These early buildings appear to be small rectangular structures aligned at right-angles to the street, the earliest structure within Property BW 4 (Structure NH8566) measuring 4.1 m in width and at least 5.8 m in length and Structure NH8568 within Property BW 2 at least 3.8 m by 2.9 m. The structures were enlarged by the end of Phase 4.1 especially eastwards and encroaching onto the street, although their rear limits remained unchanged.

No evidence for the upper wall construction of the structures survived, though at The Brooks paral-lels were drawn with the woodworking traditions seen in the timbers within Anglo-Norman timber-lined pits that were well preserved in the anaerobic conditions on the site (Scobie forthcoming). In these pits, rectangular or wedge-shaped oaken base plates were laid on the level base against two or more sides of the pit. The corner posts and upright members were formed of less substantial rectan-gular or wedge-shaped timbers sharpened to a point, and driven through slots cut through the base plates at the corners and at regular intervals along the sides. The upper lining of the pits did not survive *in situ*, but collapsed timbers suggest that the lining was tied together by a top plate to form a rigid box structure. The width of the beamslots

(0.2–0.3 m) of the ground beam based buildings found on the site compared well with that of the base plates in the timber-lined pits (Scobie forthcoming). It is assumed that the infilling of wall panels comprised wattle and daub, although unless it was burnt, daub would eventually decay to an unrecognisable state. A similar process would also occur with cob infilled walls, though curiously part of one such filling survived within Phase 4.2 Structure NH8566 (Property BW 4).

For the same reasons the nature of the roofing materials used is unknown, though at 28–29 Staple Gardens charred remains of possible thatch were found on the floor of a burnt building of possible late 9th-century date (Teague 1990). At Lower Brook Street waterlogged conditions allowed for the preservation of oak roof shingles from houses dating from the 10th century to the early 13th century and this is suggested to be the usual roofing material for private houses, though thatch may have been used for small houses and outbuildings (Keene 1990a, 320).

During Phase 4.2 (*c* 950–1050) a number of developments can be seen. The building on Property BW 2 seems to have developed into an L-shaped plan, occupying the whole of the street frontage, and with a rear wing on its northern side; an early instance of a layout that is generally more characteristic of later tenements. This layout was maintained on the property into Phase 5, and another L-shaped building was also constructed during Phase 5 on Property BW 4. A number of cellars are also seen in this phase. At least one of these (Property BE 4, pit CC2343) was found towards the street frontage, although its full extent was not revealed within the excavated area. However, it seems likely that it was of similar dimensions to the cellar on the property immediately to the north, and if so it would have extended to the street frontage, measuring some 7.5 m by 5 m in plan and 2 m deep. Other cellars of this phase were found set back from the street frontages and are considered further below.

This period was also marked by the introduction of structures built with large rectangular-sectioned posts (0.4–0.6 m) set into the ends of deep elongated pits. Structures of this type are best illustrated by Phase 4.2 Structure NH8622 within Property SE 2 and Structure NH8630 within Property BW 2. This technique continued to be used into the Anglo-Norman period, and was seen in the present excavations in Phase 5 buildings Structure NH8566 within Property BW 4 and Structure CC7031 within Property BE 5. This more substantial building technique has been associated with houses of higher rank in 11th- and 12th-century Winchester (Biddle 1976, 345–8) and may have come into use as early as the end of the 10th century (Keene 1985, 171). Certainly there is a growing body of archaeological evidence for these structures, such as Houses VI and VII at Tanner Street (Biddle 1965, 248–9, fig. 3), Building B.9 at The Brooks (Scobie forthcoming) and more recently a structure within the northern

suburb at Swan Lane (Teague 1998b). It is suggested that the wall panels of such structures comprised interlocking quarter-cut planks with grooves along the wider edge, a methodology commonly used in contemporary structures in northern Europe (Keene 1985, 171). The substantial nature of such structures suggests that they could easily have supported more than one storey, the size of the timbers employed implying a considerable expenditure of wood. Presumably such structures would have a greater life-span than the earlier and less substantial structures.

The first buildings entirely of stone to be constructed in the area were the stone chapel and house of what became the Archdeacon of Winchester's residence. The construction of these buildings is not closely datable but both seem more likely to have been built in the 12th century than not, the chapel perhaps earlier than the house. Stone houses were also constructed on Property BW 1 (amalgamated with Property SE 1) and on the east frontage of Brudene Street, although most of these fell outside the scope of the present excavations. These appear at the very end of Phase 5 and the beginning of Phase 6, and the best dating evidence for their construction comes from the latest fills of the postholes and pits associated with the preceding occupation of Phase 5. In most cases this can be dated by pottery to the period *c* 1175–1250. The substantial stone building CC7038 on the street frontage of Property BE 5 East had an internal length of *c* 9.6 m (if the street frontage is assumed to not have altered since its construction), which is comparable to the Archdeacon's house, and it appears to have been slightly wider at *c* 6.1 m (*c* 20 ft), suggesting that this too may have been a building of considerable pretensions.

Evidence elsewhere in the city shows that throughout the medieval period the majority of private houses of low to middling status nevertheless continued to be constructed mainly with timber, and increasingly timber-framed, with the sills supported upon a low (dwarf) wall of flint and chalk rubble (Keene 1985, 171).

Internal features

The floors of the earlier buildings on the site were of compacted chalk, and these were frequently recorded where they had survived subsided into the settling fills of earlier pits. In Phase 6 structures such as the stone cellar CC2100 on Property BE5 West and Structure NH8615 on Property BW 1/SE 1, bedding layers were recorded that probably formed the base for floors of stone flags or ceramic tiles. Often, thick accumulations of domestic and industrial debris were allowed to build up over the floors before they were eventually covered with new floors. Analysis of the plant remains from floor occupation deposits within the late Saxon structures on Properties BW 2 and BW 4 showed that most contained small quantities of mineralised seeds suggesting that faecal or midden material had been spread or trampled around the structures. Micromorphological analysis also revealed trampled coprolitic bone and dung (stabling waste) from Phase 4.2 and Phase 5 floor deposits within Properties BW 2 and BW 3. Given their likely filthy state at this time, this material was probably trampled in from the back yards and adjacent street. It is difficult to establish from the plant remains whether any of the charred grains present represent straw floor coverings. The most suitable would have been barley straw, though this was also used as animal fodder (see Carruthers, Chapter 8). Small quantities of hulled barley grain were present on the floors of structures on Properties BW 2–4, possibly surviving only by accidental contact with hearths. By far the highest levels come from a slumped Phase 5 floor deposit within Property BE 5, though it is possible this material may have been derived from malting for the brewing of ale.

Hearths were present within most of the late Saxon buildings along the west side of Brudene Street, sometimes represented by scorched areas on the floors themselves, and sometimes by shallow pits. As far as can be ascertained, hearths were most commonly located close to or against walls of the structures rather than being centrally placed. During Phase 5 the hearths within kitchen areas of the structures within Properties BW 2 and BW 3 were replaced by stone built ovens. In both these properties the ovens were placed against the south wall of the structure, with evidence for a narrow wall possibly acting as a 'fire-break' at the front of an oven in Property BW 2. Stakeholes around some of the hearths may represent the position of associated structures to suspend cooking vessels or spits over the fires. Some of the hearths were associated with debris from metalworking, but others were clearly domestic in function with only food remains present in rakeout deposits. The division of internal space for different functions is clear in a number of properties. On Property BW 2, the south end of Structure NH8530 appears to have been used as a kitchen, a function that it retained into Phase 5. Clear subdivision of space was also evident in Structure NH8567 on Property BW 4 in Phase 4.2, possibly to separate working areas from living quarters. Postholes inside the substantial Structure NH8622 on Property SE 2 in Phase 4.2 and Structure NH8530 on Property BW 2 in Phase 5 may have been the supports for staircases.

Ancillary structures

Two main types of structures were recognised: those which are interpreted as cellars, and outbuildings that enclosed wells and possibly latrines or served as workshops, stables or kitchens.

Cellars

Cellars appeared during Phase 4.2, the largest and deepest occurring within Properties BE 4 (CC3260)

and BW 6 (NH7713). These features are characterised by their regular rectangular plan and stood out as being considerably larger than the other pits on the site, measuring 8.5 m and at least 4.9 m in length respectively. Both were set well back from the street frontages and were unattached to the principal structures on the property. Unfortunately the limited excavation undertaken on both does not provide much information about their form, though cellar CC3260 did show evidence for a timber lining constructed of horizontal planks retained by timber uprights. This is a form of construction well known from elsewhere, and particularly from the very well-preserved late 10th-century examples in Coppergate, York (Munby 1985, fig 68); a similar example was found to the rear of a late Saxon house excavated at 28–29 Staple Gardens (Teague 1990). Assuming that the contemporary ground level was at least 0.3 m above that which survived, the original depth of cellar CC3260 may have been 1.5 m or more, enough to allow full headroom. It was not possible to ascertain whether these cellars contained structures above them, though evidence elsewhere in London and Chester suggests the presence of an upper storey (Richards 1991, 61). It has been suggested that cellars developed in the second half of the 10th century as a response to the revival of trade and growth in English towns (ibid.). They met the growing need for secure storage of stock and could also have provided cool conditions for foodstuffs. The concentration of padlocks and keys found within Property BE 4 during Phases 4.2 and 5 supports the view that there was an increased need for security here at this time. A similar cellar excavated on the High Street at Oxford contained imported pottery in its backfill and was interpreted as perhaps the property of a merchant (Mellor 2003, 340). In this context it is interesting to note that one of the very few sherds of imported French pottery found in the present excavations was associated with Property BE 4 in this phase.

The heavily disturbed and robbed Phase 6 stone-built cellar (CC2100) found in Property BE 5 may be a direct successor to the timber counterpart found in Property BE 4, its dressed wall perhaps reflecting an increase of wealth of the occupants or at least reflecting the latest styles. Certainly in plan, and allowing for the thickness of its walls, it would be similar in size to the earlier example, although somewhat deeper at *c* 2 m but presumably serving a similar purpose. It too was set back from the street although the example from Property BE 5, given its location, may have formed a subterranean part of a larger structure flanking the north-east corner of Brudene Street. Goods were brought in by means of an external entrance on its east side, probably from the street to the north, without the need to access the main house. In some ways this arrangement has parallels with the vaulted undercrofts of medieval merchant houses in Southampton that often had external spur walls enclosing stairs that led down

Table 5.4: Quantities and shapes of pits over time

Phase	4		5		6		All Phases	
	All	>1.5 m	All	>1.5 m	All	>1.5 m	All	>1.5 m
Circular	76	31	96	51	31	15	198	97
	44.2%	36.0%	56.1%	63.0%	52.5%	55.6%	50.5%	50.0%
Rectangular	89	52	68	29	25	12	178	89
	51.7%	60.5%	39.8%	35.8%	42.4%	44.4%	45.3%	47.9%
Unknown	7	3	7	1	3	0	17	4
	4.1%	3.7%	4.1%	1.2%	5.1%	0.0%	4.2%	2.1%
Total	168	82	166	77	59	27	402	194

original purpose of numerous pits could not be established as only their later fills were investigated. However, some general conclusions can be drawn regarding their size, shape and possible function over the main phases of the site. The pits have been subdivided into rectangular and circular types. Table 5.4 shows that rectangular pits slightly predominated (51.7%) during the pre-Conquest phases, especially pits that were greater than 1.5 m across (60.5%). However, during the post-Conquest phases circular pits began to dominate (56.1%), especially those whose diameters were greater than 1.5 m (63%). By Phase 6 the use of circular pits began to decrease though they still predominated over the rectangular pits. It is unclear whether this reflects a trend seen elsewhere in the city, since published evidence of other large-scale sites with intensive pitting is still awaited. A brief inspection of the numerous late Saxon and medieval pits found during the excavations at the French Quarter, Southampton (Brown and Hardy forthcoming) could suggest a similar preference for circular pits in the post-Conquest period.

The distribution of pits in each property is difficult to assess since they were dug over a long period of time. However, some general conclusions can be suggested about their clustering and spatial relationships with structures and property boundaries. As we might expect, most pits were confined to the rear of the principal structure on the property, although in a few cases pits were seen at the street frontage (see for example Properties BW 2, BW 3, BE 4 in Phase 4; Property BW 4 in Phase 5). Phase 6 pits towards the street frontage of Properties BW 3 and BW 5 were probably by this time concealed behind the wall enclosing the Archdeacon's residence.

Within some properties strips of land remained free of pitting (and apparently structures) throughout Phases 4–6 and may indicate access routes or lanes, the best examples of which can be found on the north side of Property BW 3 and within Properties BE 3 and BE 4. The reduction in evidence for pits in Phase 6, at least on the west side of Brudene Street and Snitheling Street, is probably to be related to the reorganisation of the area at the time into fewer and larger properties, and the decline in absolute numbers of people living there.

Pits continued to be dug in the back yards of properties facing onto the east side of Brudene Street in this phase.

Undoubtedly most of the pits were used to dispose of domestic, industrial and craft waste, or at least this was their ultimate function. It is possible that some of the pits that were not augered may originally have served as wells, such as the line of Phase 5 circular pits that abutted the northern boundary of Property BW 4. Some of the larger pits may have been used to quarry chalk for flooring, well linings and wall footings, and it seems likely that the very large pit NH1034 (Property SE 3) generated the chalk for the footings of the Archdeacon's chapel, given its close proximity. Some of the small and usually rectangular or nearly square pits seem originally to have served as cess pits since their basal levels were found to contain cessy silts often rich in mineralised faecal remains containing bran, fruits seeds, pulses and fly pupae. A typical example was Phase 4.2 pit CC2458 (Property BE 4) which measured 1.8 by 1.4 m in plan, and was 1.5 m deep as found (but possibly 2 m deep originally). These pits tended to cluster close to the principal structures (for example, in Properties BW 4 and BW 5). Three cess pits clearly abutted the east wall of Phase 5 Structure NH8618 (Property SE 1) in a way that suggests they might have been associated with upper storey garderobes (see Chapter 4).

The clustering of cess pits suggests that areas were purposely set aside for latrines over sustained periods of time, the number of pits dug suggesting that they were not cleaned out. Dumps of cess often also appeared as secondary fills in other pits, sometimes adhering to their sides, which may represent more casual disposal, for example from night-pans. The latest cess pits (Phase 6) all occurred within properties on the east side of Brudene Street. This period saw the introduction of stone-lined cess-pits though only one example was found on the site, within Property BE 2 (CC1518). Unlike other well-known examples of stone-lined latrines within the city (Teague 1991; Scobie *et al.* 1991) and Southampton (Brown and Hardy forthcoming), this was smaller, circular and significantly deeper at 3.4 m (perhaps originally around 4 m allowing for the terracing). It would seem unlikely that such a pit could be emptied easily, so perhaps it acted (like the other cess pits on the site) as a septic tank, holding the waste to allow the liquid to leech away through porous chalk on its (presumably unlined) lower levels, while the solids gradually settled on its base (Newman 2001, 139). It is not possible to establish whether this served a latrine attached to the principal structure, though given its proximity to the street frontage and the effort undertaken in its construction, this would seem likely.

Industry and craft

The evidence from early street names indicates that Winchester had developed as a centre of manufacture and trade by the late 10th century. The street of tanners (Tænnerestret, later Tanner Street and now Lower Brook Street) is recorded in 990, and the streets of shield-makers (Scyldwyrthtana, later Shulworth Street and now Upper Brook Street) and of the butchers (Flæscmangere, later Fleshmonger Street and now St Peter Street) in 996 (Biddle 1976, 427). The Winchester Mint, ranked fourth in the country, had six moneyers working in Winchester in 925–35, and may have had as many as fourteen by 1050–53 (ibid., 396). The archaeological evidence recovered from Winchester (much of it unpublished) certainly reflects the wealth and diversity of trades practised in the late Saxon and medieval city and its suburbs (Biddle 1990; Rees *et al.* 2008). Winchester is particularly rich in archaeological evidence for metalworking industries, and for the manufacture and working of textiles and leather, the latter focused in the low-lying north-east part of the town, an area that has easy access to large quantities of water.

The present excavations recovered evidence principally for iron working, elements of cloth production (dyeing, spinning and, to a lesser extent, weaving), and bone and antler working. There was also evidence for horn working, copper alloy working and the fur trade. Figure 5.7 shows that many of the properties were used for two or more of these activities, with an increasing diversity of the evidence into Phase 5 when most of the evidence for bone and horn working appears. The evidence falls off sharply in Phase 6, and this is probably to be associated with the depopulation and changing character of occupation of the area at this time.

Iron working

Evidence for iron working on the site was widespread in the late Saxon period and continued throughout the Anglo-Norman period, though by Phase 6 (after *c* 1225) most or all of the material is likely to have been occurring residually. Nevertheless the overall quantities on the site are not large compared to the other published sites within Winchester. The site at Henly's Garage, for example, produced 82 kg of slag from 9th- to 12th-century working surfaces and hearths within a relatively small area (Rees *et al.* 2008, table 37 and 356–7), compared with only 36 kg from the present site. A single evaluation trench at the Lower Barracks that sampled deposits pertaining to a late Saxon smithy produced about 42 kg of slag (Winchester Museum Service – Site Archive LB 89). Indeed if the weight of the material is divided by the number of contexts that produced it, the difference is much more marked, with an average of 2.28 kg from Henly's Garage against only 0.15 kg from the present site. This is very similar to the relatively low quantities found at sites within the suburbs, such as Victoria Road, which recorded an average of 0.20 kg, and Chester Road, with an average of 0.19 kg (Rees *et al.* 2008).

Evidence for smithing occurs from the outset within four of the properties (BW 2, BW 4–6) along the west side of Brudene Street. Here, much of this evidence occurred within internal occupation deposits, usually charcoal-rich silts, rich in hammerscale, and associated with structures on the street frontages. On the east side of Brudene Street, despite the truncation of most of the structural evidence within the properties, enough evidence survived from the sweepings of debris into pits to suggest pre-Conquest smithing within Properties BE 2, BE 4 and BE 5. There is also relatively strong evidence for iron working in Property SE 3. The presence of hammerscale is often taken as a sign of *in situ* smithing activity, and if all these properties were functioning as smithies this would suggest a very intensive zone of activity. Given the relatively modest quantities of smithing debris recovered, however, this seems rather unlikely. Analysis of floor deposits (see this chapter, above, 'Internal features') showed that these contained foul matter and stabling waste that had probably been accidentally incorporated from the street and yards outside, and it is possible that smithing waste was also moved around in this way. In other cases, it might be suggested that smithing debris was the result of the manufacture of composite objects such as knives and combs, or discrete episodes of iron working, perhaps during building works, or resulting from a smith's visit to re-shoe horses or mend carts or tools on individual properties.

Some of the most extensive and consistent evidence for smithing came from Properties BW 2, BW 4 and BW 5 where hammerscale and smithing hearth bottoms were recovered from within the structures as well as from pits to their rear. The process of blacksmithing involves heating pieces of iron or steel until the metal becomes soft enough to be shaped with hand tools, typically a hammer and chisel. Within the earliest structure in Property BW 2 (Phase 4.1 – Structure NH8525) a small shallow pit (NH4713) contained a rich concentration of hammerscale. The pit had probably remained open for some time in order for the hammerscale to accumulate on its sides and it is perhaps significant

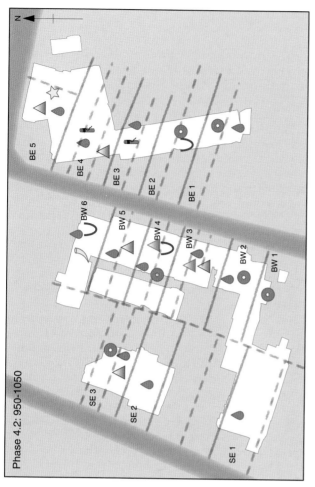

Phase 4.2: 950-1050

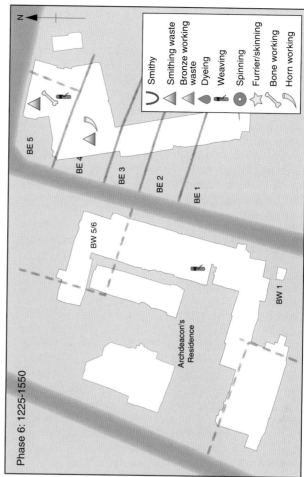

Phase 6: 1225-1550

Archdeacon's Residence

Smithy
Smithing waste
Bronze working waste
Dyeing
Weaving
Spinning
Furrier/skinning
Bone working
Horn working

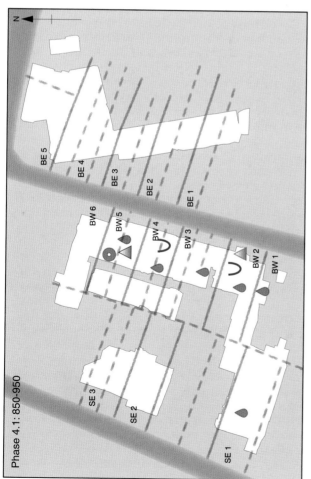

Phase 4.1: 850-950

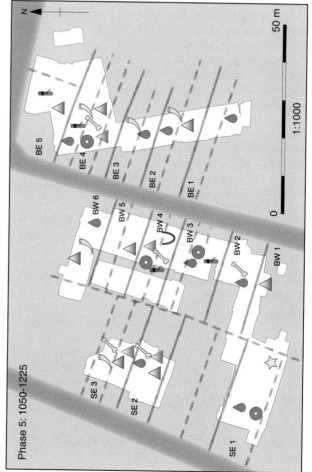

Phase 5: 1050-1225

0   1:1000   50 m

Fig. 5.7   Concordance of industrial and craft activity on the properties through time

201

that it was located near to a hearth (see Chapter 3, Fig. 3.13, NH4733). It is possible that the pit may have been used for quenching, its apparent lining having served to contain the water. Smithing hearth bottoms were found within all three properties, those within BW 4 and BW 5 discarded within pits to the rear of the structures. However within Property BW 2, three complete examples were found used as make-up for the floor of the second structure on the property (Phase 4.1, Structure NH8526) and they may have come from the demolished remains of its predecessor (Structure NH8525). A fourth example was found within the demolished remains of Structure NH8643—apparently a separate building behind Structure NH8526. Within Phase 4.1 Structure NH8595 in Property BW 5, a smithing hearth bottom was found associated with a hearth.

There was less evidence for possible structural remains associated with iron working. Although the forge (hearth) could be at ground level (within a pit), it would have been easier to work if built to waist level (see Starley, Chapter 7) and in these circumstances remains would not normally survive in the ground. It is possible that fragments of vitrified furnace lining that were found in some of the pits of these properties derived from discarded furnaces, though the amounts recovered were relatively small and those found during Phase 5 contexts are more likely to be residual. However, a fragment with possible tuyere hole (for blowing air into the hearth) was found in association with the smithing hearth bottoms within Structure NH8526 (Property BW 2). Areas of scorched floors such as floor 3056 found within Phase 4.1 Structure NH8566 (Property BW 4) and its Phase 4.2 successor (Structure NH8567) could indicate the position of raised furnaces. The use of such furnaces would have required access to good quality charcoal in order to reach the high temperatures required to heat the metal. The possible quenching pit found within Phase 4.1 Structure NH8525 produced an assemblage dominated by oak, a species notable for producing high quality charcoal that can be used for fuel to obtain such high temperatures (see Challinor, Chapter 8). Carruthers (see Chapter 8) suggests that the very numerous charred hazelnut shells found in some of the hearth rakeout samples could suggest that they were used as kindling for smithing hearths and kilns. However, analysis of the data showed no association between contexts with high levels of charred hazelnut shells and contexts with hammerscale within the properties under discussion. Only within a slumped deposit within Property BE 2 on the east side of Brudene Street did high levels of charred nutshells occur with smithing debris, although even here the nutshells could simply have been food waste since appreciable quantities of fish remains and animal bone were also present.

Evidence for smiths' tools was very limited, although part of a tanged punch (SF Cat No. 274,

Fig. 7.29) commonly used by blacksmiths for finishing was found within a Phase 4.2 pit to the rear of Structure NH8567 within Property BW 4, a pit that also produced a smithing hearth bottom. There were many more examples of tools for finishing and sharpening, 28 of which were recovered from the post-Roman phases of the site. Although many of these may have been for domestic use, the fragments of rotating whetstones that were present on the site came from Properties BW 2–4 and suggest the presence of a smith's workshop (see Shaffrey, Chapter 7). Rotating whetstones (or grindstones) were operated by crank handles, as shown in the Carolingian Utrecht Psalter of the mid 9th century (McNeil 1990, 389). Two of the fragments from the present site were quite thin and may have been used for sharpening small blades.

Two 'postholes', one of which apparently formed part of the north wall of Structure NH8567 (Property BW 4, Phase 4.1) and a second within the area of Structure NH8586 (Property BW 5, Phase 4.1), were both rich in hammerscale. The former also contained ten nail shank fragments and iron debris, the latter including a knife and horseshoe fragments. Starley suggests (see Chapter 7) that they may represent footings for anvil blocks, which later became filled with debris from the workshop floor. However, it is also possible, given the number of iron objects found in them, that these were in fact small pits used to store scrap material for re-use.

The blacksmith is likely to have been employed in the manufacture or repair of objects such as knives, tools, nails and horseshoes, with their manufacture requiring a stock of iron bars, rods or worn-out implements to be re-worked into new objects (Clarke 1984, 163). If such items were being made on the site (rather than simply being sharpened by the blacksmith), and given that smelting of iron was not being undertaken, we could expect to find evidence for stock items or for the recycling of iron objects. Significantly a high number of iron bars were obtained from Property BW 4, all within Phase 5 pits, which could conceivably represent raw material brought in for the production of small items such as knives and nails. Property BW 4 also contained relatively high numbers of knives and bladed tools (see Cool, Chapter 7). Similarly, in the case of iron nails, Property BW 4 produced the largest number of these objects on site during Phases 4.2 and 5 when the evidence for smithing was most prevalent, whereas Property BW 2 produced the most during Phase 4.1 (5 out of 7 on site) when smithing was most evident in this property (see Cool, *Digital Section 3*, Table 15). Horseshoes were concentrated within Properties BW 5 and BE 4 during Phases 4.1 and 5, three in contexts that also contained high levels of smithing debris, and it is tempting to suggest that these represented waste from re-shoeing of horses that was undertaken by the smith within the property. It may also be significant that these properties were located towards the north of the site, relatively close to the lane that led to the North Gate. Perhaps these smiths were shoeing horses for travellers while they otherwise conducted their business elsewhere in the town.

Non-ferrous metalworking

In contrast to the iron smithing evidence, there is only limited evidence for non-ferrous metalworking on the site, comprising a handful of crucible fragments and a small amount of copper alloy debris. This seems to derive from the small-scale production of small bronze or brass objects, since no evidence was identified for the working of precious metals (see Mortimer, Chapter 7 and Macphail, Chapter 8). This is in contrast to the abundant evidence for silver working found during Martin Biddle's excavations in Winchester at the Assize Courts, Lower Brook St, Cathedral Green and Wolvesey Palace (Biddle 1990, 85) and more recently at the southern end of Staple Gardens (Winchester Museums Service archive SG 84–85) and at St Peter Street (Teague 2002).

The bulk of the evidence for the crucibles was confined to, and fairly evenly spread between, Properties BW 2 and BW 4, though such activity only occurred within Structure NH8529 (Property BW 2) during its use in Phases 4.1 and 4.2 and from Phase 5 pits within Property BW 4. The activity within Property BW 4 occurred alongside the evidence for iron working, which had commenced here as early as Phase 4.1. A few fragments of iron slag with copper alloy corrosion were found within Property BW 4 suggesting the use of copper alloys in the production process, perhaps for brazing, coating or inlaying (see Starley, Chapter 7). Fragments of bronze sheet and a bent fragment of a possible box mount found in contemporary contexts within the property may have originated as stock to be melted down for use in this process. On the east side of Brudene Street within Property BE 4, Phase 5 pits produced a small quantity of crucible fragments and several fragments of two-piece moulds, which were probably used to cast a decorative object or fitting (see Poole, Chapter 7).

Taken together, the evidence would suggest some diversification during Phase 5 within Property BW 4 and probably Property BE 4, since previously (particularly within Property BW 4) only iron working had been undertaken. However, within Property BW 2 iron working appears to have been superseded at an earlier date by the manufacture of copper alloy objects and had apparently ceased by Phase 5.

Dyeing, spinning and weaving

About 300 sherds (2%) of the late Saxon and Anglo-Norman pottery assemblage had been stained purplish-red or reddish-brown internally (Table 5.5), probably as a result of contact with boiling solutions that contained the purple-red plant dye

madder (*Rubia tinctorum*) (see Cotter, Chapter 7). No analysis of the staining was undertaken for the present assemblage, but the presence of madder has been confirmed by chemical testing of similar sherds from The Brooks in Winchester (Walton Rogers 1996). The *c* 300 sherds from the present excavations probably represent the largest quantity of madder-stained pottery recovered from a single archaeological site in England. Madder-stained pottery has not been reported from other published excavations in Winchester (Cunliffe 1964; Collis 1978), although these mainly deal with small-scale excavations within the suburbs of the city. However, given that substantial assemblages of post-Roman pottery remain unpublished from sites within the walls, it is not currently possible to assess how widespread this activity was in Winchester. Recent excavations at 26–27 Staple Gardens did not identify any stained pottery from an assemblage comprising *c* 900 sherds of late Saxon and Anglo-Norman pottery (Vince and Steane 2008, 147–61) so perhaps this may suggest that the practice was not widespread along Brudene Street. No evidence was found for the cultivated remains of the plant on the site and therefore it is likely that the dye arrived ready processed, and possibly imported; the merchants of Saint Denis, Paris, had established a trade in the dye by the 9th century, although there is some evidence for its cultivation in England by the 10th century (Wild 1988, 60). Dyer's greenweed, *Genista tinctoria*, was probably present among waterlogged plant remains in a late 10th- to 11th-century pit at The Brooks (Carrott *et al.* 1996, 4) though the authors suggest this could have been brought in incidentally with cut grassland vegetation. The dye-pots at the present site were apparently re-used medium to large cooking pots since deposits such as limescale, evidence of their former use, were sometimes visible under the staining.

Most of the properties contained some evidence for dye-pots, though the material tended to occur in small quantities across a wide number of contexts, the highest quantities occurring within Properties SE 1, BW 3, BW 4 and BE 4 (see Table 5.5 and Fig. 5.8). Dyeing was occurring from the outset since a significant quantity (27%) of the sherds came from contexts attributable to Phase 4.1, which cannot have been redeposited. Some 73% of the madder pot assemblage comprised the ubiquitous chalk-tempered pots that occur throughout the late Saxon period and into Phase 5. It is difficult to assess levels of redeposition among the material occurring in Phases 4.2 and 5, but the presence of madder-stained sherds in ceramic wares that appear for the first time in Phases 4.2 and 5 confirms that the dyeing activity continued into these phases (for example, Fabrics MAV and MAD respectively). There were no examples of madder-stained pottery in fabrics of later medieval (Phase 6) date.

By far the largest assemblage came from Snitheling Street Property SE 1, from the infill of Phase 4.2 pit (possible cellar) NH6158, which

Table 5.5: Concordance of dyeing, spinning and weaving evidence

Property	Phase 4.1 Madder Sherds	Spindle Whorls	Weaving implement	Phase 4.2 Madder Sherds	Spindle Whorls	Weaving implement	Phase 5 Madder Sherds	Spindle Whorls	Weaving implement	Phase 6 Madder Sherds	Spindle Whorls	Weaving implement
BE 1	*			*	(1)							
BE 2				1(0)	1		1(1)			*		
BE 3	*			*		2	*			*		
BE 4				22(19)	2	2	6(2)	1	1			
BE 5								1				1
BW 1	2(2)			1(1)			2(0)			1(0)		
BW 2	10(10)	1		3(1)	3		4(0)	1		1(0)		
BW 3	1(1)			4(1)			26(11)	2	1	8(0)		1
BW 4	23(23)			12(0)	2		22(3)	2	2			
BW 5	2(2)			7(0)			2(0)					
BW 6	*			*			*					
SE 1	5(5)			88(6)			14(0)	1				
SE 2				3(2)			17(0)					
SE 3	*			*	(1)		*					
Totals	55(55)	1	0	141(30)	8	4	94(19)	7	5	10(0)	0	2

Note: * Pottery no catalogued but noted during assessment (numbers in brackets: quantity of sherds of fabrics new to that phase)

produced a total of 80 madder-stained sherds derived from at least a dozen vessels, which may suggest a single clearance episode from dyeing activity close-by. Some of these particularly well-preserved pot sherds showed staining around the brim of their rims suggesting that the pots had been filled full of the dye. One vessel also had evidence of iron working debris under its base, suggesting that both activities had been taking place simultaneously in the vicinity. Similar evidence came from Property BW 4, where iron working evidence was present within Structure NH8566 and madder-stained pot sherds were recovered from the contemporary (Phase 4.1) pit, NH3464. On the east side of Brudene Street a large part of a dye pot was found in a charcoal-rich dump (hearth sweepings?) within a Phase 4.2 pit (CC2135) on Property BE 4.

Given the lack of evidence otherwise on the site it must be assumed that dyeing was undertaken on a small scale, especially given the difficulties of access to the large quantities of water and heat that would have been required to operate large dyeing vats. The process of dyeing can occur at any stage between the spinning and the finished cloth, but it would seem more likely that the process was undertaken before weaving, and involved the dyeing of a hank of yarn that could easily be accommodated within a domestic cooking pot (Rogers 1999).

Other stages of cloth production were also carried out within the excavated area. A possible iron heckle tooth and iron comb teeth, used for the preparation of wool prior to spinning, were found in late Saxon pits within Properties BW 3 and BW 4, and a total of 19 spindlewhorls of bone or stone were recovered from the site as a whole and offer convincing evidence for the spinning of wool. It

may be significant that higher numbers of these occurred within Properties BE 4, BW 2 and BW 4, which also contained some of the larger assemblages of madder-stained pottery, suggesting both activities may have been occurring concurrently. Within Property BW 2 the spindlewhorls were found on the floor of Structure NH8529 (Phase 4.1) and within fills of internal features of its Phase 4.2 successor (Structure NH8530), though by then they may have been occurring residually. The earlier structure also contained madder-stained pottery on its floor levels, which suggests that yarn was spun and then dyed there. It interesting to note that there was a group of tightly spaced stakeholes within the structure against its west wall that could have formed part of a rack used to dry the dyed yarn.

A rubbish dump in pit NH2126, within Property BW 4, contained two madder-stained sherds from a post-Conquest pot found in association with a spindlewhorl, offering evidence for the continuation of spinning and dyeing on this property in Phase 5. Post-Conquest madder-stained pottery and spindlewhorls also occurred in Properties BW 3 and BE 4. It is perhaps significant that no spindlewhorls were found in Phase 6 contexts, at a time that corresponds with the gradual introduction of the spinning wheel by the 14th century, if not before (Whitney 2004, 122, Clarke 1984, 131); however, this could also simply reflect the depopulation and changing use of the area at the time.

Evidence for weaving is largely confined to Properties BW 2, BW 4 and BE 4, the same properties where there is association of spinning and dyeing. In common with published evidence from elsewhere within the city (Keene 1990, 203–6), there is a notable absence of the weights that were used

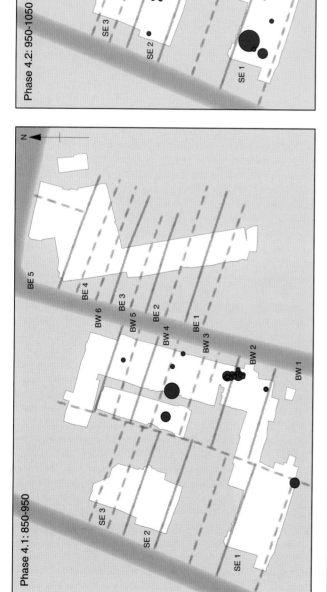

Phase 4.2: 950-1050

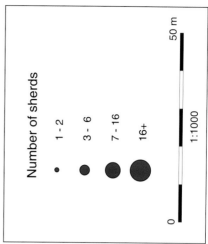

Number of sheds

Number of sherds

1 - 2 •
3 - 6 ●
7 - 16 ●
16+ ●

0   1:1000   50 m

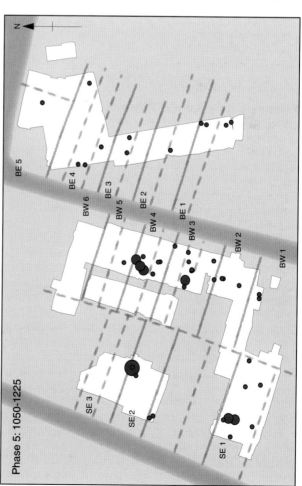

Phase 4.1: 850-950

Phase 5: 1050-1225

Fig. 5.8 Distribution of madder-stained pottery

for the early medieval upright warp-weighted looms. At Back Street, located within St Cross, a row of doughnut-shaped fired clay loomweights that had fallen from an upright loom were found within a structure of 11th- to 12th-century date, suggesting that such looms persisted into the post-Conquest period (Hedges 1978). It possible that the fragmented remains of such items were not recognised by the excavators or remain unidentified among the amorphous fragments of the fired-clay assemblage on this site. However, a pin beater (SF Cat No. 174), used to adjust the weft whilst weaving on an upright warp-weighted loom, was found in a Phase 4.2 context within Property BE 4. It has been suggested that the paucity of evidence in the city for the warp-weighted loom is a reflection of the introduction during the mid to late Saxon period of the upright two-beam loom; picker-cum-beaters, used for such looms, have been found in pre-Conquest contexts (Keene 1990, 204). On the present site the only stratified picker-cum-beater was found in a posthole associated with Phase 5 Structure NH8573 within Property BW 4, though it is likely that the object was occurring residually from a pre-Conquest context.

A single tenterhook found within Property BW 5 (Phase 5), used to stretch lengths of cloth after it had been fulled to allow even drying, offers only very limited evidence that finishing of cloth was undertaken on the site, though such items are difficult to recognise given the poor quality of the preservation of the ironwork on the site (see Cool, *Digital Section 3*).

Skinning and furriering

The identification of 745 bones of cat, fox, squirrel, ferret/polecat, stoat and other small mammals from a single late 12th- to early 13th-century pit (NH5169) on the east side of Property SE 1 (Phase 5) offers convincing evidence of a furrier/skinner within the property during the later part of Phase 5. The remains of the small mammals consisted entirely of the lower legs and feet suggesting that skinning was undertaken elsewhere, as the feet were usually removed from the pelt at its final destination (see Strid, Chapter 8). However, the cat remains comprised semi-articulated skeletons of at least 10 individuals aged 8.5–11.5 months, one of which showed typical skinning cut marks on the frontal bone of its skull and on its mandible. At Victoria Road, in the northern suburb of Winchester, the remains of at least 50 cats, a few with skinning marks, were found in 14th- to 15th-century pits, and half had died before the age of 11 months. It is suggested, on account of their similar age at death, that cats were purposely reared in spring before being killed at the onset of the following winter when the fur was in prime condition, and presumably at the time of greatest demand (Serjeantson and Rees 2009, 178). The pit also contained the bones of neonatal lambs/kids with higher than

expected representation of metapodials. None showed evidence for skinning, but an association with cat bones has been noted elsewhere in medieval Winchester and within other medieval towns and suggests that the lamb skins were used to make garments on the site. It is possible that the furs and lamb skins were used to make entire small garments such as hoods, or to provide robes with fur linings or trimmings, work that was occasionally commissioned by tailors (Keene 1985, 286). Garments made or decorated with the coarse furs such as cat fur or budge (from lamb) were typically worn by the lower orders of society whilst those using finer furs such as fox and squirrel were reserved for the lesser nobility and middle classes (Emberley 1998, 47). The very fine furs of martens and ermine generally adorned princely or court garments and it is interesting to note that a possible pine marten bone was found in a Phase 4.2 pit within the west part of Property BE 5.

Bone and horn working

Low-level evidence from the site of sawn bone waste suggests that the manufacture of objects from bone was undertaken on a small scale in most properties, perhaps as a sideline to the other activities (see Strid, Chapter 8). Indeed the absence of major workshop activity, as denoted by substantial deposits of waste material from the various stages of manufacture, mirrors the lack of such evidence from the medieval suburbs (Rees *et al.* 2008, 360–3). The work may have complemented the other crafts since a drilled femur head, probably an unfinished spindlewhorl (see Cool, Chapter 7), was found on the floor of Phase 4.2 Structure NH8569 in Property BW 4, at a time when spinning seems to have been undertaken there (see Table 5.5). The raw material for the small-scale production of such items was at hand in the domestic refuse that was generated on the properties.

The outer sheath of the horn was of value to Saxon and medieval craftsman since it could easily be bent and moulded and made into various commodities such as knife handles, buttons, combs and spoons. The casing was removed from the core by boiling, or alternatively the horn was allowed to decay to such an extent that the sheath could easily be twisted off. Only the horn-core waste survived on the present site. Given that there is no firm evidence that butchery was undertaken on the site it must be assumed that the horns had been bought in, perhaps from butchers in Fleshmonger Street (originally Parchment Street but later allocated to St Peter Street), or cut off from hides and skins delivered to the tanners and tawyers, the former residing on Tanner Street (Lower Brook Street) (Serjeantson and Rees 2009, 176). Evidence for horn working derived almost entirely from Phase 5, and horn cores were found in appreciable quantities in pits within adjacent Properties BE 3 (CC1268) and BE 4 (CC2035, CC2043), and within Property SE 3

(NH1598) (see Strid, Chapter 8). Property SE 3 offers the best evidence that bone working had been undertaken on any scale, since the same pit also produced 589 fragments of large mammal ribs, many with their inner faces smoothed, and some with holes drilled down their mid-line for iron rivets. The purpose of these bone mounts is not fully understood (see Cool, Chapter 7) though Biddle has argued (1990, 678–83) that they represented strengthening plates for double sided horn combs. Certainly there is a clear association between these mounts and horn-cores within this pit. It also contained significant quantities of smithing waste, which might conceivably derive from the manufacturing of small iron rivets for the making of composite combs on this property.

Economic status and trade

The finds and environmental assemblages were analysed in detail for indicators of the economic and social status of the inhabitants of the area (Table 5.6). However, there were few clear trends and results were not necessarily consistent between different assemblages. At a general level most assemblages were consistent with low to middle status occupation, but differences between properties do emerge in the detail of the more unusual elements. This is considered further below, but overall Property SE 1 is the most conspicuous, with some evidence for a more varied and elaborate diet during Phase 5 and the largest group of glazed tripod pitcher ware pottery. Some of the more unusual items found in the excavations were recovered from this property, including a stylus, two balances of a type that may have been used for weighing coin, part of an elaborate casket fitting and French pottery. The other conspicuous group of properties are those on the east side of Brudene Street. Here all the other examples of balances and French pottery occurred together within Properties BE 2–4, all but one in contexts of Phases 4.2 and 5, and in association with other rare finds types from the site—a decorated bone spatula from BE 2 and a stylus and casket mount from BE 3. Property BE 4 included a cellared structure in Phase 4.2 and more than half of all the locks and keys found in the excavations. Although these differences are not reflected in any of the other assemblages, they may be indicative of inhabitants whose trading activities were becoming both wider and increasingly profitable.

Animal bone assemblages were dominated by sheep/goat, cattle and pig, with very low quantities of game and wild fowl. There was no clear evidence for status differences between properties in terms of the meat component of the diet, although more beef may have been consumed at late Saxon Property BW 5 and Anglo-Norman Property BW 4 than elsewhere (see Strid, *Digital Section 11*). Property BW 3 contained the largest diversity of bird species, including woodcock, which could suggest higher status (Ticehurst 1923, 33). Although burnt bone was generally scarce, a higher than average quantity (7% of the assemblage) came from the Anglo-Norman phase of Property SE 1, and

Table 5.6: Status indicators

Phase/ Property	4.1	4.2	5	6
BE 1				P (Imp.)
BE 2		W, L/K, P (imp.)	P (imp.)	Pot (imp.), BM (Roof & b floor tile)
BE 3		SF (dec. Spatula and stylus)	SF (vessel glass), BM (Chimney pot, AN flanged roof, floor tile)	W, BM (Chimney pot, stone latrine)
BE 4		LK (4), SF (?Ivory pin beater), P (imp)	LK (2), W, B (Ashlar well)	
BE 5		LK (1)	B (Ashlar well), P (imp.)	P, P (imp.), B, BM (dec. floor tiles)
BW 1				B
BW 2		M	L/K	
BW 3			M, B, L/K(2), P (Imp.)	P; B (roof tiles, dec. floor tile), SF (Chess piece),
BW 4		P	M, L/K (2), P (Imp.)	B (roof tiles)
BW 5	PR(fig?)	M, P	SF (Cu stylus), L/K	
BW 6				
SE 1		PR (fennel)	M*, F, PR (grape, peach), SF (Casket fitting), W(2), P (Imp.), B (Purbeck marble slab)	SF (silver brooch pin)
SE 2		B	SF (Figurine), B	B
SE 3				

Key

Fish F   Cereal/fruit PR   Meat M   Pot P   Finds SF   Building material BM   Building B   Locks/Keys L/K   Weighing W

suggests differences in the preparation of meat. In comparison to stewing, roasting is expensive in terms of fuel and labour and can be seen as a sign of increased wealth (Woolgar *et al.* 2006, 70).

The plant remains (see Carruthers, Chapter 8) provide an interesting insight into possible dietary differences that may be related to status and to changing tastes. The late Saxon cess pit samples produced significant quantities of pulses, suggesting that cheap, protein-rich peas and beans formed a major component of the daily diet at the time. Samples from Anglo-Norman cess pits, however, suggest that there was a decline in the consumption of pulses in the post-Conquest period. In the light of the evidence for roasted meat noted above, it is interesting that Property SE 1 also produced seeds of grape and fennel, and a possible peach stone, suggesting that its inhabitants had access to imported fruit and flavourings, and were less dependent on cheap pulses, which were present in only comparatively low concentrations. In general the staple diet is likely to have been bland, and the main possible flavourings identified were seeds of mustard, carrot and poppy.

Fish consumption (see Nicholson, Chapter 8) appears to follow a similar pattern within all the properties, with herring and eel making up 60% and 30% respectively of the Phase 4.2 recorded assemblage. A variety of other fish were also present but evidently only as a minor and occasional component of the diet. The composition of the assemblages from the present site is similar to that of the contemporary assemblages found within the suburbs of Winchester. The increasing quantity and diversity of marine fish consumed reflects the national trend, which saw a marked expansion in sea fishing around the year 1000. Amongst the Anglo-Norman (Phase 5) assemblages the proportion of herring increased to 80%, while eel declined to only 6.5% and was overtaken amongst the numbers of identified bones by flat fishes, particularly plaice/flouder/dab. The assemblage is very similar to that from the recent excavations at Southampton, and Southampton was probably the primary source of fish for Winchester. The consumption of shellfish seems to have increased in the Anglo-Norman period, with mussels and periwinkles becoming particularly popular, whereas oysters had predominated in the late Saxon assemblages (see Campbell, Chapter 8). The only notable fish was a sturgeon scute that was found with late 12th- to early 13th-century pottery, near the bottom of Phase 5 pit NH5169 on Property SE 1, a very expensive fish only available to the most affluent. This adds to the evidence noted above for a higher status diet on this property than elsewhere on the site. Elsewhere in Winchester sturgeon has been found in a monastic context (St Mary's Abbey, located within the monastic south-east corner of city) and from a 13th- to 14th-century house in the western suburb during excavations on Sussex Street (Serjeantson and Rees 2009, 180).

The Phase 4 and Phase 5 pottery assemblages (see Cotter, Chapter 7) were dominated by functional vessels for cooking and storage in coarse local wares that provide no evidence for differences in social status. Tablewares such as bowls, cups and dishes are rare in the assemblage and many households may have used wooden tableware, such as the examples found at Lower Brook Street (Keene 1990c, 959–65), which date from the 10th up to the 13th centuries. The introduction of relatively small amounts of brightly glazed Winchester Ware during the second half of the 10th century, occurring as jugs or spouted pitchers, would have been in stark contrast to the dull pottery that previously dominated the household. Winchester Ware seems to have been made locally but in imitation of the exotic North French yellow glazed ware that was imported into Southampton and London (see Cotter, Chapter 7). Glazed wares tended to be used for tablewares, mainly jugs for the serving of wine and other beverages, and it is generally accepted that there is a connection in the medieval period between glazed wares, increased prosperity and social drinking. However, all properties apart from BW 6 contained some evidence for this ware, suggesting it was used by most households, but perhaps on special occasions rather than on a day to day basis. The distribution of its successor, tripod pitcher ware, introduced during the early part of Phase 5, suggests that these large glazed pitchers and jugs were more abundant on the properties on the west side of Brudene Street, and at Property SE 1, and less well represented on the east side of Brudene Street. Taken at face value this could suggest that the properties on Brudene Street West were more prosperous, but this is not obviously reflected in other assemblages. In broad terms, on the basis of the pottery evidence, it can be suggested either that there were no marked differences in social and economic status between the different properties, or that the pottery assemblages (particularly those of the late Saxon and Anglo-Norman periods) are not a very sensitive reflector of these.

Pottery from Phase 6 was not subject to the same level of analysis as it was not all recorded in detail. It is notable, however, that high glazed ware sherd counts were recorded for Properties BW 3 and BE 5. The sherds from Property BW3 were mostly from the backfill of the Phase 5 stone well-house, and were presumably deposited in the well after it had gone out of use, at a time when the property had been incorporated into the residence of the Archdeacon of Winchester. A more exotic assemblage recovered from his infilled cellar included a sherd from a 15th-century Valencian bowl (Cunliffe 1964, 144). The highest glazed ware sherd count for any phase was from the stone cellar and stone-lined well of Phase 6 Property BE 5, which John Cotter comments may indicate wealthy occupants (see Chapter 7). Most of the scant imported pottery came from the properties on the east side of Brudene Street, and in Phase 6 high quality imported pottery was found (albeit in very small quantities) at Property BE 5 and Property BE 2, including a sherd of polychrome Saintonge ware from south-west France that was probably imported into Southampton. This could suggest that the occupants had a comparatively wide range of contacts and were perhaps traders or merchants. A substantial house excavated on The Brooks that belonged to wealthy wool merchant John de Tyting between 1299–1312 (Scobie *et al.* 1988, 40–5) also produced jugs of Saintonge ware.

The distribution of ceramic oil lamps (see Cotter, Chapter 7) may have some bearing on the activities and wealth of the occupants, although again the evidence is inconclusive. Most date from the 10th to 12th century, at a time when most domestic lighting was probably in the form of rush lamps. The possession of such ceramic lamps could be seen either as an indication of slightly greater wealth or as an accessory to activities such as textile working or writing. During Phases 4.2 and 5 Properties BW 4, BW 5 and BE 4 had the greatest concentration of lamps at a time when spinning, bone working and copper alloy working (perhaps inlaying objects) were being undertaken, activities that require good lighting especially during the dark winter months. Conversely, where there was little or no evidence for craft activities, for example within Properties BW 2 and BW 3 during Phase 5, there were few lamps. The same conclusion was reached at Lower Brook Street where a high incidence of lamps from two medieval houses was interpreted as the use of these buildings for light industry, requiring long hours of indoor work (Barclay and Biddle 1990, 986).

Status is also reflected by the buildings that the occupants lived in, and here the differences become more apparent, especially during Phases 5 and 6. The late Saxon structures were of timber throughout the period, comprising small mainly single-room buildings used both for domestic occupation and as workshops. The enlargement of such structures (for example, in Properties BW 2 and BW 3) during Phase 4.2 could reflect increased stability and prosperity. The appearance of cellared structures (Properties BE 4, BE 5, SE 1 (?) and BW 6 (?)), allowing for the secure storage of considerable quantities of valuable stock or personal possessions, may also be a sign of expanding trade and increasing prosperity, and a growing need for security may also be reflected in the unusually high numbers of locks and keys that were found on the site (see Cool, Chapter 7). Significantly nearly half of the 14 items were found within Property BE 4 during Phase 4.2 at a time when a large cellar had been built to the rear of the property.

Cool also draws attention to the number of balances that were found on the site and suggests that they may have been used for checking the weight of coin. Single examples occurred in Properties BE 2 and BE 4 in Phase 4.2, two in Phase 5 contexts within Property SE 1 and one (possibly residually) from a Phase 6 context within Property BE 3. Most of the handful of imported pottery from the site came from the properties where balances were found: late Saxon Beauvais-type ware (Fabric MBEAU; *c* 900–1100) from north-east France (Phase 4.2, Property BE 2), early medieval Pingsdorf-type ware (Fabric MPIN; *c* 925–1250) from the Middle Rhine (Phase 5, Property BE 3), North French grey ware (Fabric MFGY; *c* 875–1000) (Phase 5, Property BE 4) and Normandy gritty ware (Fabric MFI; *c* 1070–1250) (Phase 5 Property SE 1). Taken together the evidence could suggest the presence of traders or merchants here. Certainly these properties (particularly BE 3 and SE 1) contained some of the few higher status personal objects found in the excavations, notably the decorated bone spatula from Property BE 2 (SF Cat No. 189, Phase 4.2; Fig. 7.26) and the casket mounts found in Phase 5 contexts within Properties BE 3 and SE 1. Part of a copper stylus of late Saxon type (SF Cat. No. 218; Fig. 7.27) came from a pit on Property BE 3, suggesting writing on waxed tablets was undertaken. Two further Saxon styli were recovered from the site, one residually in a Phase 5 pit within Property BW 5 and the other intrusively within the subsoil on Property SE 1.

By the end of the 13th century (Phase 6) the structural evidence shows that substantial residences occupied a number of the proprieties (BW 1/SE 1, BE 5 and the Archdeacon's residence combining BW 2–5 and SE 2–3). Unfortunately very little of these properties fell within the area of detailed excavation of the present project, and information about them therefore remains limited. Finds of a 12th- to 14th-century chess piece from a robber trench within Property BW 3 and a silver brooch pin from Property SE 1 (both contained within the Archdeacon's residence during this time) provide a hint of higher status. Elsewhere the evidence from the present excavations is only indirect, but other masonry buildings appear to have been constructed on Properties BE 2 and BE 3, from perhaps late Phase 5 onwards. Pits on Property BE 2 in this phase contained mortar and chalk rubble in their upper fills, while the upper fills of pits within Property BE3 contained fragments of building materials such as chimney pot, floor tiles and Anglo-Norman flanged roofing tiles.

The project area from the 13th century

Winchester probably remained stable in terms of its size and population between the first half of the 12th century and the early 14th century (Keene 1985, 93). However, there is a general impression (ibid., 142–3) of a shift away from the higher western side of the city towards the low-lying eastern part over this period. This could reflect an increase in the numbers of people engaged in the trades relying on the water resources of this part of the city. Snitheling Street was one of the more densely populated parts of the city in 1148 (according to Survey II) with 35 properties, but it appears to have been virtually deserted by around 1300 when only four are known (ibid., 148 table 3).

During the course of the 14th century Winchester underwent a marked contraction (ibid., 93) and Keene comments that the streets of the north-west quarter suffered considerable depopulation during this time. In the project area, there was a significant reduction in the number of properties in Brudene Street, although the decline of Brudene Street was slower than that of Snitheling Street. There were 35 properties in Brudene Street in 1148, 26 in 1300, 15 in 1417 and 13 in 1550 (ibid., 148, table 3), though the tarrage survey of 1417 lists only one house and three cottages—the remainder comprising gardens and a croft—testament to the depopulation of this area of the city. This contrasts with the contiguous Shulworth Street, Wongar Street and Tanner Street, located in the heart of the industrial east side, where the numbers of properties grew in the period 1148–*c* 1300 and where there appears to have been much less depopulation by *c* 1500 (ibid.).

The 13th and early 14th centuries

These changes were very marked in the evidence from the present excavations, even allowing for the probable truncation of later medieval levels in parts of the site. By the late 12th to early 13th century it is clear that the earlier pattern of rows of narrow plots occupied by the timber houses of artisans and traders was breaking down. Most of the excavated tenements along the west side of Brudene Street and the east side of Snitheling Street were subsequently amalgamated and incorporated into the spacious urban estate of the Archdeacon of Winchester. To the south, Properties BW 1 and SE 1 were amalgamated and substantial stone buildings were constructed on the newly enlarged plot; stone houses with tiled roofs, chimneys and tiled floors were constructed on the east side of Brudene Street, and on the northernmost excavated plot the surviving remains of a substantial stone cellar and a stone house suggest that these may also have been buildings of considerable pretensions. The development of the Archdeacon's residence is considered in more detail below.

Although this change of use is apparent in documentary evidence, the archaeological results are key to understanding exactly when this process began, and how it proceeded. The excavated evidence suggests that the decline of the Phase 5 Anglo-Norman tenements is broadly datable to the period *c* 1175–1250, since sherds of Early South Hampshire red ware are a characteristic component of the backfills of the associated pits and postholes. A make-up layer in the top of Anglo-Norman pit NH5105 on Property SE 1, probably consolidation associated with the construction of the Phase 6 buildings above, contained five sherds from tripod pitchers in South-east Wiltshire coarseware (MADW), datable up to 1250, along with single sherds of sandy ware MDF (probably 1150–1350) and high medieval glazed white ware MMH, which appears *c* 1225. This would be consistent with a date

around the second quarter of the 13th century for the construction of these buildings, and by implication the amalgamation of Properties BW 1 and SE 1 into a single tenement facing Brudene Street. Similar evidence comes from Property BW 4, where the upper fills of Phase 5 pit NH2084 contained large fragments of tripod pitcher (fabric MAD; *c* 1050–1225) together with sherds of Laverstock type anthropomorphic jug (Fabric MNX; *c* 1230–1350).

Although several of the Anglo-Norman tenements were incorporated into the Archdeacon's residence, the evidence for a prosperous tenement with numerous masonry buildings on the amalgamated Property BW 1/SE 1, and the new buildings on the east side of the street, suggests that the 13th century was not a time of decay and decline in the project area, but rather a phase of redevelopment which saw the construction of fewer, but larger and more elaborate properties. There is, nevertheless, a clear sense that properties were being reorientated towards Brudene Street, which is consistent with the evidence that there was a much more rapid decline along Snitheling Street to the west.

From the 13th century much more documentary evidence is available to help to identify some of the people who held these properties. Documentary information that relates to the area of the excavations from the 13th to the 17th centuries is summarised in Chapter 1 and a proposed correlation with the excavated tenements is shown in Figure 1.5 (after Keene 1985, 637–41). This initially seemed to suggest that by 1303 the area of Property BW 1 had been incorporated into the Archdeacon's residence, and was identifiable with a property formerly owned by Agnes Greyshank. At this time it extended from Brudene Street to Snitheling Street and lay between the Archdeacon's property on the north and Petronilla's (widow of Adam de Northampton) property to the south. However, this seems to be at odds with archaeological evidence which suggests that the boundary wall that defined the southern extent of the Archdeacon's residence had been constructed about this time but lay to the north of Property BW 1 (see Chapter 4). Therefore it seems more likely that Agnes Greyshank's property was actually Property BW 2, since it is located to the north of the wall. The substantial structural remains that were revealed within Properties BW 1 and SE 1 may therefore have formed part of the capital tenement of Adam de Northampton and his wife Petronilla (see Chapter 1). It is interesting to note that beforehand and by 1249 this tenement was inhabited by the Silvester family whose ancestors appear to have been moneyers, including Hugh Silvestre who in 1248 was a moneyer at the Winchester Mint (Keene 1985, 1347). The name can be traced back to the survey of 1148 (Siluester), which lists two occurrences on Brudene Street (Biddle 1976, 172) though neither of these appear to have been connected to any of properties on the site.

There is no clear archaeological evidence for the amalgamation or enlargement of the properties on the east side of Brudene Street in the 13th century or later. Documentary research suggests, however, that Properties BE 4 and BE 5 were one property by 1300 (see Chapter 1, Fig. 1.5b, Property 253) and by 1417 Properties BE 1–3 formed the rear part of a single property that fronted Jewry Street (see Fig. 1.5c, Property 267). However, the archaeological evidence suggests that Property BE 5 remained a separate entity at least until the construction of the substantial cellared building (CC2100) within its western part sometime in the 13th century, as this building appeared to be abutted by the wall that had formed the boundary with Property BE 4 to the south since at least the period 950–1050 (Phase 4.2). This elaborate but heavily robbed cellar, possibly originally dressed with expensive stone and with a stone or tiled floor, must have been part of a property of some pretension. Such elaborate cellars have been excavated elsewhere in Winchester, for example the 13th- to 14th-century cellar found at the former Masons Hall, 2 Parchment Street that belonged to a wealthy wool merchant (Teague 1991). Property BE 5 was located opposite the parish church of St Saviour, which was situated across the lane that defined the north side of the property. Documentary research (see Chapter 1; Keene 1985, 643) suggests that Thomas de Modesfont, chaplain, who was probably the rector of the nearby church, held part of a property here by 1304 (property 253, which can be equated with the excavated Properties BE 4–5). It would seem reasonable to assume that he resided adjacent to his church, though it is not clear that a priest would have needed the elaborate cellar (possibly used to store wine or other valuable merchandise), so perhaps he occupied the house to the east which would have been directly opposite the site of the church. It is of note that a second tenant is also listed in the same entry, Henry de Preslonde (ibid.), who might therefore have occupied the west part of Property BE 5.

The project area after the early 14th century

The 13th-century redevelopment of the area was, in the event, to prove short-lived. The excavations recovered almost no material datable after the late 13th or 14th centuries. Indeed, apart from 19th-century material, only three sherds of pottery (Tudor green ware, *c* 1375–1500) need date to later than the 14th century. By the late medieval period, the properties on the west side of Brudene Street, including the Archdeacon's residence, appear largely to have been abandoned, and documentary evidence suggests that the area was used for gardens and orchards (see Chapter 1; Keene 1985, 640–2). The pottery associated with demolition rubble and the final fills of pits on the Phase 6 properties here suggests that this change of use happened no later than *c* 1350–1450. On the east side of Brudene Street the abandonment is best represented by the robbing and infilling of the cellar, CC2100, within Property BE 5, which had

happened before the end of the 14th century. A thick dark loamy soil survived over its upper levels suggesting that the area remained open as garden and this would correspond with the description of what may have been this property in 1371 as the garden of Sibyl de Preslonde (see Chapter 1; Keene 1985, property 253). Evidence from the pits within Property BE 2 suggests that occupation did not continue later than the 14th century. The lack of later pits, if not evidence for complete abandonment, does at least suggest a marked change of use within this part of the property. By the end of the 14th century it probably formed the rear (garden?) of a large property fronting Jewry Street to the east (Keene 1985, Property 267). The lack of Phase 6 pits within Property BE 1 and the infilling of well CC1128, possibly as early as the early 13th century, might also be consistent with amalgamation and reorientation, if not with complete abandonment.

THE RESIDENCE OF THE ARCHDEACON OF WINCHESTER *by Alan Hardy*

Taken together, the evidence of Cunliffe's excavations in 1960 and the present excavations along the west side of Brudene Street suggest that numerous tenements in the area were amalgamated to form a single large property that is identifiable in the 13th century as the residence of the Archdeacon of Winchester. The proposed final layout of this property is shown in Figure 5.9 and an artist's reconstruction is shown in Plate 5.4.

A summary of Cunliffe's structural interpretation

The footings defining the groundplans of two distinct buildings were identified by Cunliffe, one interpreted as a church or chapel, and the other (the cellar of) a hall building. Part of a short wing was found abutting the west side of the south end of the hall, and was interpreted as a garderobe tower. In addition, two later walls were partially revealed, one extending to the east and one to the south of the hall, and one short length of possible wall was found to the south-east of the hall. With the exception of the west end of the church/chapel none of the structural remains revealed by Cunliffe were re-examined in the present project.

The chapel

The present project revealed the footings of the west end of the chapel, and confirmed the building footprint as determined by Cunliffe. The archaeological evidence recovered by both Cunliffe and the present project found no dating evidence from within the fabric of the footings. However, pottery from the layers inside the chapel footprint and from a number of associated pits includes fine sandy ware fabric MBK (1050–1150) and Newbury B-style ware (1050–1200). Although not closely datable, this is clearly an Anglo-Norman assemblage. The

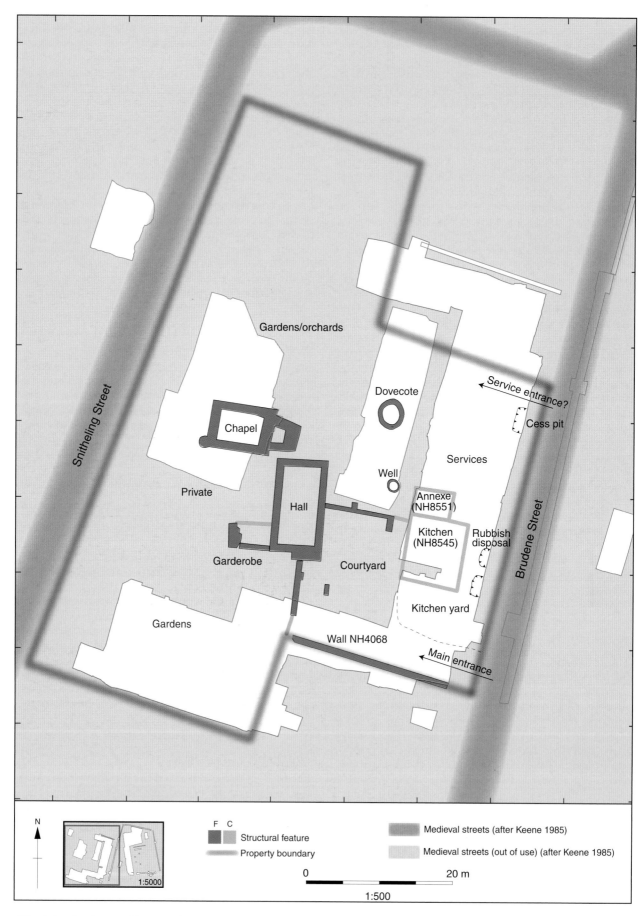

Fig. 5.9 Conjectural layout of the Archdeacon's residence at the end of the 13th century

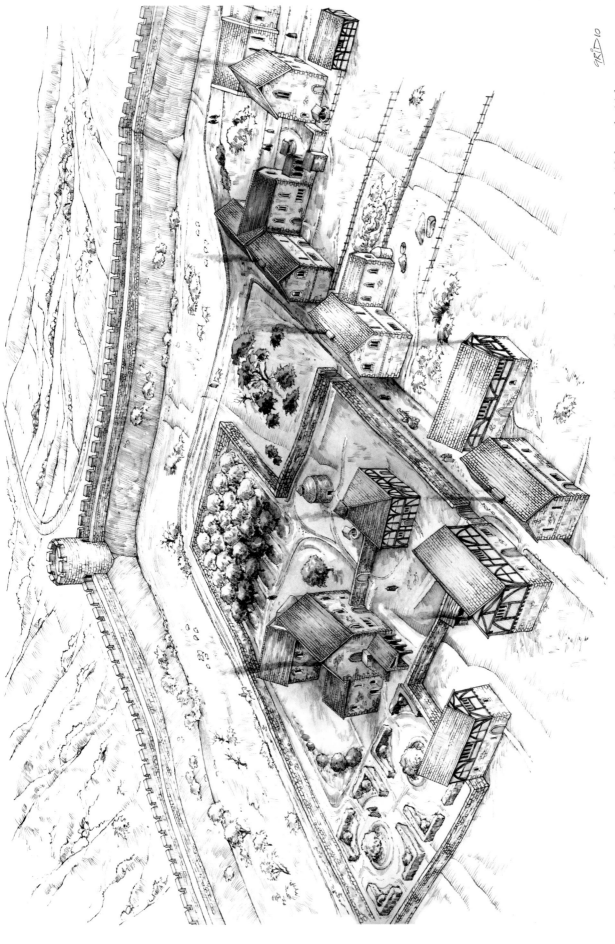

Plate 5.4 Artist's impression from the south-east showing the Archdeacon of Winchester's residence and Brudene Street during the late 13th–early 14th century, Phase 6: medieval

presence of sherds in fabric MBK and the absence of wares introduced in the later 12th and 13th century would support a tentative dating for the construction of the chapel perhaps in the early to mid 12th century, although a late 11th-century date cannot be ruled out on the evidence available. It is not clear whether the chapel and the stone house were built at the same time; it is possible that the chapel was originally built to accompany a principal residence towards the Snitheling Street frontage of the unexcavated area to the south of Property SE 2. What is reasonably clear, however, is that it was not contemporary with the imposing timber-built Structure NH 8622 excavated to its west, since the pottery from the backfilled postholes and pits associated with Structure NH 8622 is entirely late Saxon in character, and suggests that the structure had been demolished before Anglo-Norman ceramics came into general use. There was no evidence in the area of the chapel to suggest that an earlier church had been built here.

The small size of the structure (as judged from its footings) is notable, as is the apparent lack of any subsequent structural modification or enlargement (or at least such as would affect the groundplan). Keene notes the typically modest size of some of the parish churches in Winchester, at least in their original phase (1985, 126). Figure 5.10 shows the groundplan of the chapel alongside those of other parish churches in Winchester in the 11th–12th centuries. The church of St Mary in Tanner Street is of a comparable size, but clearly more substantial, and the churches of St Peter in Macellis and St Pancras were clearly more developed. Keene suggests that the small size of the chapel under investigation may reflect its private foundation, and certainly its very close proximity to the hall could be seen as supporting this contention. The width of the foundations of the smaller cell of the church/chapel as revealed by Cunliffe led him to suggest that they might have supported a tower (1964, 170). Equally, however, these foundations could have supported an apsidal end similar to those seen at St Peter in Macellis or St Mary Tanner St, and this possibility is illustrated in the reconstruction of this period (see Plate 5.4).

The linking of the chapel and the hall as two parts of a single enterprise is in keeping with a trend of the late Saxon period. Blair's survey of the late Anglo-Saxon church in England concludes that individual seigneurial initiative was much more common, especially in the context of the new urban courts ('*hagae*') belonging to the many established rural manors in the region (Blair 2005, 402–3). Furthermore there was no distinctive urban church architectural style at this time, except where space constrictions dictated, and a conventional one- or two-cell plan was the norm (ibid.). Identification of the builder and early owner of the property is problematic, and is considered further below.

The chapel becomes a church?

If the chapel did for a time serve as a parish church, the apparent absence of any associated burials, either within the building or close by, is noteworthy. However, while this could be seen as support for the option that the building was a private chapel and not a church, the absence of a dedicated burial ground seems to have been common in the 12th and 13th centuries for the parish churches in Winchester. Until the 14th century the Cathedral restricted the parish churches' rights to burial (Keene 1985, 107–8). In some cases practical considerations played a part; some churches had no room for a burial ground until the depopulation of the late medieval period provided space in adjacent empty tenements.

Whether it ever became the parish church, as Keene and Biddle suggest (Biddle 1976), and if so for how long, is still unclear, and the archaeological evidence can currently add little new information. It is interesting to note, however, that the lane or passage identified along the north side of Property BW 3 could have provided access to the chapel from Brudene Street (see Chapter 4, Fig. 4.1). Keene notes the survival of meandering lanes that originated as *ad hoc* means of access from the nearest street through the tenements to the churches, which were often set back from the frontages (1985, 51). This passage originated in the late Saxon period, when there is no reason to propose the existence of a church or chapel in this location, but it could have become a means of

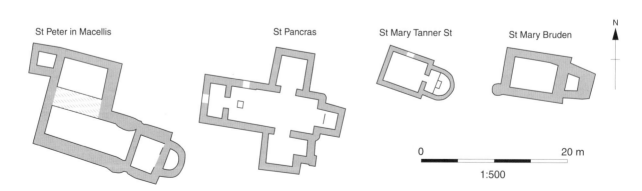

Fig. 5.10   Contemporary 11th to 12th century church footprints in Winchester

access to the chapel for the people of Brudene Street during the 12th century. No physical evidence of a lane or road surface was found in the immediate vicinity of the chapel, although a small area of cobbling was seen to the north.

If this did in fact change from being the private chapel of the builder and occupier of the hall to being the parish church of St Mary, Keene suggests that it remained as such 'for most of its life' (1985, 641). However, other churches within the city, such as St Mary in Tanner Street, or St Pancras, show a steady sequence of structural change and enlargement, responding (presumably) to the increasing parish populations, at least through the 12th and into the 13th centuries. There is no sign that this chapel was ever enlarged in this way, and documentary evidence suggests that it had fallen down or been demolished by the middle of the 15th century. In the context of a decline in population in the area underway from the later 12th century onwards, there may perhaps never have been any need to enlarge the chapel to cater for a growing congregation. The evidence that the Archdeacon enclosed his property during the 13th century and obstructed a public lane in the area might equally suggest an attempt to discourage public access to the church through his land, and a reversion of the chapel to essentially private use.

The hall

The remains of the cellared hall excavated by Cunliffe, along with its later structural additions, did not come within the perimeter of the trench outline of the current project. We are still, therefore, entirely dependent upon the original published description and interpretation of the structural evidence. In summary, Cunliffe interpreted the building as a two storey house of 'the upper-hall type', comprising a vaulted cellar, with a compacted chalk floor some 2 m below contemporary ground level. His interpretation that the enlarged footing at

the south-east end of the building represented an external staircase implies, according to Keene's discussion (1976, 347 n.), the possibility of two above-ground storeys, which Cunliffe did not consider in his excavation report. A possible parallel can be seen in the form of the manor house at Boothby Pagnell in Lincolnshire, built at the beginning of the 13th century, which has a simple vaulted cellar below an open hall, with a solar at one end (Fig. 5.11; also Wood 1965, fig. 6).

Faulkner's model (1958) of the self-contained building consisting of a first-floor hall over a basement clearly formed the basis for Cunliffe's interpretation, and was the accepted model for English medieval houses of status. However, the wealth of archaeological data made available in succeeding decades has warranted a re-examination of this model. It is worth, therefore, reconsidering the hall that Cunliffe found, in the light of these developments. By examining the archaeological evidence in association with documentary references and the contemporary terminology used to describe properties, Blair (1993) has argued that what was seen as the two-storied 'hall' *'aula'* was actually typically the chamber block *'camera'* associated with a separate open hall, an arrangement with its origins in late Saxon manorial houses such as Goltho. Particularly in ecclesiastical properties, these buildings might be arranged to form a courtyard, perhaps echoing the claustral arrangement of monasteries (ibid. 10–11). Examples cited by Blair include the alien priory at Grove in Bedfordshire; this originated as a plain hall with a possible partitioned end, and a separate chamber block, later converted to a chapel. A third structure was rebuilt as a replacement (but still separate) chamber block (ibid., 7; Fig. 5.11) .

If this was the case with the Archdeacon's residence, and Cunliffe's hall is in fact the chamber block only, then it could indeed have been a single storey over a cellar. In which case the enlarged footing at the southern end could not be a staircase

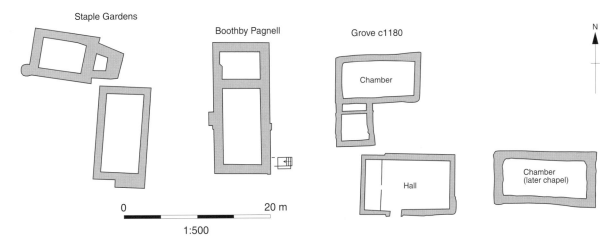

Fig. 5.11 The footprints of the hall and chapel at Staple Gardens compared to those at Boothby Pagnell, Lincolnshire, and Grove, Bedfordshire

and perhaps was no more than some sort of buttress. So is there any evidence—from his excavations or the present ones—of a separate hall on the property, which might add support to Blair's model in this instance? A hall in Blair's model need not be as substantial a building as the chamber (1993, 8), and its footprint need not necessarily be defined by equally substantial footings. While there is fragmentary but reasonably convincing evidence for a probable timber-framed building to the east of the residence, in the form of beam slots, remnants of a clay floor surface, and an internal hearth base, the putative structure seems better characterised as a service range, incorporating a square kitchen and an annexe, with two large rubbish pits close by.

It is just possible that the later walls Cunliffe found to the south and east of the hall represent parts of later buildings. Both of the footings were shallow and only 0.5 m to 0.75 m wide—much less substantial than the hall or chapel footings. Following Blair's argument, either could represent one side of a timber-framed hall set on plinth stone footings, of which no further trace has survived. However, the easterly wall meets the hall at an oblique angle, and the southerly wall meets the hall at the point where the putative staircase (or buttress) ascends. The small length of footing exposed to the east may represent a parallel wall, but it is only 3.6 m away, too close to represent the opposite wall of a hall, although some sort of gallery might be a possibility. Taken as a whole, however, Cunliffe's evidence does not provide strong evidence for a large hall in addition to the two he identified—the rectangular hall and the chapel.

While Cunliffe's excavation area was modest, and the present project, though more extensive, was still limited in area and depth of investigation, on balance it seems more likely that Cunliffe's original interpretation (with Keene's modification in regard to the number of storeys) was correct. The flint wall with expanded foundations added to the south-west corner of the hall building was interpreted by Cunliffe as probably a garderobe (1964, 168). The size of this addition (at approximately 8 by 5 m) is too large for this sole function, but it is possible that a garderobe over the backfilled pit at the west end was joined to the main building by a wardrobe. Similar interpretations have been suggested for added structures at Penhallam, Cornwall (Beresford 1974, 106, and fig 27) and the manor of the Barentin family at Chalgrove, Oxon (Page *et al.* 2005, 161–2 and fig. 2.3).

Possible support for Cunliffe's original interpretation (and Keene's elaboration of it) may lie both in the relatively constrained size of the building plot and the depth of the watertable. For the plot to accommodate both the dwelling and the chapel, the hall and chamber and cellar would be better combined in one three-storey structure. The low groundwater meant that there would be little risk from groundwater flooding in constructing a full-depth cellar.

The extent and layout of the original property

While the present project has revealed significant evidence of the surroundings of the chapel and hall, there are still many unanswered questions surrounding the early life of this property. The relationship between the chapel and the hall is significant. The chapel was, unsurprisingly, orientated west-east. The alignment of the hall was clearly dictated by that of the chapel, the effect being to achieve a courtyard between them. The fact that there is very little gap between the two suggests a desire to create a 'private' space. No physical evidence was found of boundaries to the property within which these two buildings were constructed, but setting the two building footprints within the conjectural tenement boundaries of Phase 4 and 5 (see Chapter 4, Fig. 4.1), suggests that the property was a composite of SE 2 and the unexcavated property to the south. If the quarry pits for the buildings were also part of the same property, this would incorporate Property SE 3 as well.

Biddle and Keene suggested that the evidence of the 1110 Survey (Survey I) might mean that Brudene Street was favoured by magnates and barons for occasional visits to the city (Biddle 1976, 387), although their analysis of the later survey indicates this character may have become influenced by incoming traders and craftsmen. In contrast, they see Snitheling Street as the backwater it topographically was, a street of low rents and high population density.

Cunliffe argued that the juxtaposition of the two buildings implied that the original 'front' of the property was to the west, onto Snitheling Street. His documentary research suggested a possible tenant cited in the 1148 survey—one Drogo (Drew), who held a 'messuage there and servants and chattels'. The survey's description at least suggests a substantial property. However, Keene and Biddle argued (1985) that this entry related to a property fronting onto Brudene Street, not Snitheling Street. They suggested that the buildings could possibly be associated with tenements 379, 380 and 381 (see Fig. 5.5 above), of which the first two belonged to the king, and whose entries are as follows in the 1148 survey:

379 Harding the blacksmith's son holds 1 land of the king worth 4d quit in return for his services and receives 18d. And from the same land Roger the painter receives 4s. 6d; and from the same land Harding the brewer receives 2s

380 Richard Son of Odo pays the King 6d and receives 2s

381 Drew Blond pays Hugh *de Hahela* 6d for 1 land which Hugh holds quit

Is Cunliffe's conclusion about the orientation of the property in its original guise correct? Unfortunately the current excavations did not add any useful information to the issue. The 'back' of the property, or eastern boundary is (in Cunliffe's scenario) conjectured to be congruent with the south-east corner of the hall. No physical trace of a boundary was found, which is not necessarily conclusive, but there is no clear documentary evidence to suggest that, in the early/mid 12th century, there were any single properties extending from Brudene Street right through to Snitheling Street, in the area of investigation. Even if the evidence cannot put a name or occupation to the builder of the hall and chapel, they were clearly of some considerable status, which stands in sharp contrast to the view espoused by Biddle and Keene (Biddle 1976, 387) that by the mid 12th century Snitheling Street was an area of a high density of population and low property values.

Phase 6: The later development of the residence

The 'service range' (Structure NH8545/NH8551)

The most problematic structure by far was Structure NH8545/NH8551, the successor to the elaborate Phase 5 tenement in Property BW 3. This was the only part of the Brudene Street frontage to see continuous activity running through Phase 6 until at least late in the 14th century, and, although the stratigraphic sequence was badly disturbed by later wall foundations and generally truncated by post-medieval and modern levelling, the possible remains of a timber framed building or buildings were identified. On the basis of the structural evidence, its spatial relationship to the hall to the west, and the proximity of the well (NH9530) and two contemporary rubbish pits (NH3233 and NH 3235), it is suggested to be a service range. It appeared to be in the form of two cells; the southern one (Structure NH8545) is suggested to be approximately square, measuring 8 m across, with the northern cell (Structure NH8551) a smaller square annexe, possibly around 5 m across (Fig. 5.9).

The small annexe displayed a sequence of chalk and clay floor surfaces, and the larger cell contained the latest stratigraphic evidence of burning located in the area. The surface of this was archaeomagnetically dated to 1046–1227 (WOB), and by radiocarbon to 1430–1470 (OxA–17175). The disparity between the two dates is clear. It is considered that, given the stratigraphic position of the context, the archaeomagnetic date is likely to be suspect, and has probably been affected by subsidence (see Chapter 6).

The presence of a large free-standing kitchen would be consistent with the residence requirements and layout. Its construction in wood, rather than stone, would encourage the siting of the principal cooking area in the centre of the building, to minimise fire risk. The clay surface found within Structure NH8545 was burnt, but not excessively so, and showed no evidence that there had ever been a brick or stone superstructure on it, or incorporated

within it. This may suggest that a metal brazier stood at this spot. By their very nature timber-framed kitchens will be less robust in the archaeological record than those built of stone or brick, but comparable constructions have been identified. For instance, at Northolt Manor, Middlesex, the early 14th-century kitchen was a square timber-framed building with a central hearth (Hurst, 1961, 214–5 and fig. 61).

Structure NH8575, the 'dovecote'

The function of this chalk-block lined pit feature is not at all clear from the evidence revealed (Fig. 5.9; see also Chapter 4, Fig. 4.15 and Plate 4.26). There is little—beyond its circular shape—to support the excavator's provisional interpretation that it was a well. The internal diameter is much larger than any other well on the site, and the stone lining is much more substantial than would seem to be required; it was surely intended to support a substantial superstructure. Furthermore the chalk and flint lining is unfaced, in contrast to all the other wells (especially the contemporary well just a few metres to the south). Given that it was a structure within the grounds of the Archdeacon's residence, one would expect a reasonable level of finish to any visible stone structure. Although the base of the pit was not reached, there was no evidence from the pit fill, or surrounding deposits, for the pit having a craft or industrial use, and no staining or apparent residue on the lining itself.

A circular, vertically sided pit, lined with chalk rubble and flint was identified in Property BE 2, on the eastern side of Brudene Street, and interpreted, from the coprolites and cessy material found in its fills, to be a purpose built cess pit—the earliest stone-built cess pit found on the site. Though broadly contemporary, it is suggested that Structure NH8575 was unnecessarily large to be a cess pit—nearly three times the diameter of CC1518—and much more substantial.

A similar feature, of a broadly contemporary date, was fully revealed during excavations at The Brooks, in the north-east corner of the medieval city, in 1987–8 (Scobie *et al.* 1991). It was slightly larger in diameter (3.1 m internally) and fully excavated to a depth of 3 m, revealing a shallow round pit in the centre of the flat base. The tentative interpretation at the time was that the structure was the base of a dovecote (ibid., 52–4); this interpretation has been confirmed and elaborated, with the conclusion that the below-ground shaft acted as a receptacle for pigeon droppings, and the central pit in its base was the setting for the potence (the revolving scaffold enabling access to all the nestboxes which would have lined the above-ground circular superstructure (G. Scobie pers. comm.)). This interpretation is supported by a documentary reference to a dovecote on the site in 1400, and the absence of any other structural candidate of that period found during the excavation.

Dovecotes were very much emblems of status and wealth; apart from the doves providing a useful food resource, dove dung was valued as a potent fertiliser (Thirsk 1967, 168). The major problem with the interpretation of this circular structure as a dovecote is the subterranean aspect. The floor of a dovecote is typically at ground level or above. Archaeological evidence for dovecotes having a 'sunken' floor is very rare. In 1989, excavations along part of the medieval city walls in Southampton revealed a circular free-standing dovecote, dating to around 1300, and probably built by the adjacent God's House Hospital (Gaimster *et al.* 1990, 186–7). The floor contained a rectangular stone-lined pit, with surviving traces of a wooden lid, and was thought possibly to be a receptacle for the collection of pigeon droppings, although no residue of droppings was mentioned in the report. In this instance the presence of surviving nest boxes confirms the identity of the structure as a whole, but still leaves uncertainty with regard to the function of the pit. In 1984, excavations in Greyhound Yard, Dorchester, Dorset, revealed the base of a circular dovecote (Woodward *et al.* 1993). The internal floor surface of the structure was the surface of the natural chalk bedrock, which was a little over 0.5 m below contemporary ground level. In the centre of the structure was a circular pit, 1 m wide by 2.5 m deep, interpreted as a collection pit for droppings.

Only one standing example of a dovecote with a sunken floor has been identified, in the late medieval dovecote within the churchyard at Norton sub Hamdon, in Somerset. The (modern) internal floor is approximately 0.5 m below the external ground surface (McCann and McCann 2004). In this instance one wonders if the discrepancy in levels has more to do with the accretion of graveyard soil outside as any design element inside.

The examples cited above at Dorchester and Southampton were definitely dovecotes—each had surviving nesting boxes. The example in the Archdeacon's residence revealed none (and neither, it should be remembered, did the example in Brook Street). In conclusion therefore, the identification of Structure NH8575 as a dovecote remains somewhat qualified, and the purpose of the surviving sunken element of it remains unclear.

Well NH9630

The well to the south of the possible dovecote shows, in its original construction and finish, the attention to detail and quality that would be expected in the context of the high status property owner (Fig. 5.9; see also Chapter 4, Fig. 4.14 and Plate 4.25). The fact that the construction trench only extends around the northern half of the feature is interesting, a characteristic not shared with the construction cuts of any of the other wells on the other tenements of the site. This is probably an indicator of the firmness of the ground into which the well was dug, and the absence of recent disturbance of the area, the site being on the

putative line of the Phase 5 lane leading off Brudene Street (see above).

The layout of the Phase 6 residence

The fragmentary nature of both the present investigations and those of Cunliffe, coupled with the degree of truncation and disturbance of the whole area, mean that the layout of the property of the Archdeacon is still far from clear, but some consideration of the way the residence may have functioned is warranted (Fig. 5.9).

The enlarged property now had a frontage on Brudene Street, and the layout of the hall and associated structures suggest that it now faced east. While the original hall footings cannot in themselves indicate a 'volte face' of the building, the later additions to the range, and the disposition of the other buildings and structures lend weight to the possibility. If, as seems most likely, the additional wing attached to the south end of the hall incorporated a garderobe, it would be reasonable to expect that to be sited away from the 'public' face of the building. Similarly, with the demise of Snitheling Street, it would be odd in these circumstances to retain a western orientation of the property. It would be much more likely now to present the residence to the east, with (presumably) a main entrance somewhere along the eastern boundary. The substantial boundary wall identified along the southern edge of the residence gives some indication of the likely scale of a boundary wall running along Brudene Street. No trace of it was found in the excavation, so it must have lain immediately to the east. However, the watching brief on the service trench excavated approximately 6 m to the east revealed a consistent deposit of stone and mortar demolition material lying over the medieval street surfaces; this could represent the demolished wall.

Access to the residence

Following the acquisition of the properties along the Brudene Street frontage and the establishment of the Archdeacon's residence in the early 13th century, the possible lane surfaces in the northern half of Property BW 3 were covered by floor surfaces and beamslots relating to the Phase 6 buildings. In addition, a chalk-block lined well (NH9630), also possibly of 13th-century date, was constructed, again on the conjectural line of the original lane (see above). If the original lane was blocked, where was the main entrance to the residence?

Most of the frontage contains, at sporadic intervals along its length, features post-dating the clearance of the Phase 5 tenements and pre-dating the final abandonment of the residence. Only the area of Property BW 2, alongside the southern boundary wall of the residence, is apparently devoid of open or 'active' Phase 6 features, and so could, on that basis, have been the site of a putative entranceway (Fig. 5.9). A 2 m deep Phase 5 cess pit (NH4339) displayed what might be seen as an excessive sequence of five capping layers of gravel and chalk (see Chapter 4, Fig. 4.4). However, this effort makes sense if it is seen as part of the consolidation of the entranceway into the residence. Interestingly, the truncated base of a west-east aligned stone-lined drain (NH4109), surviving to a length of 5.6 m, extended from close to the southern edge of the Phase 5 well NH4019 towards the frontage to the east, and may have been associated with the putative entranceway. Some support from documentary sources can also be suggested, as Property BE1 (Keene's property 267 West; 1985, 644) is referred to in the early 14th century as being opposite the *curia* (courtyard) of *Dorkyngge* (the contemporary name of the Archdeacon's residence).

Could there have been another entranceway to the residence, possibly a service entrance? Keene noted the discrepancy in the stated measurements of the residence property (as recorded in the Tarrage of 1590) and the actual measurements. This discrepancy can be explained in two ways. Firstly the cited orientation of the measurements assumed (whether by accident or convenience) that the line of Brudene Street represented the west-east axis of the property. Secondly, the cited measurement along this axis—of 38¾ yards (35.4 m)—fits if allowance is made for the width of a track of approximately 5 m.

Keene cites an order in 1271 for the Archdeacon not to obstruct the public lane called *Dorking* which he had enclosed (1985, 641). The description of the lane as 'public' suggests it was not part of the Archdeacon's property. A later description of the property to the north (Keene's no. 248; Property BW 5/6) describes it as being 'a garden next to the gate of Dorking'. The gate would, presumably, give onto a lane or entranceway. The width of such a lane, especially if was by the 14th century effectively just an entrance way leading into the residence, need not have been wider than a cart width. As a comparison Keene cites the record of a private cart gate in the rear of property 474 (1985, 791), situated on Tanner Street, measuring 9ft 6in (2.95 m) wide.

A possible location for such an entrance would be hard by the boundary to property 248, to the north. A lane or track here could have skirted around the north side of the possible dovecote (Structure 8575), and also have given access to the service area to the south. It is possibly not a coincidence that Godson's map of 1750 (see Chapter 1, Fig. 1.7c), which shows the site as gardens and completely cleared of all buildings, still indicates, by dotted lines, a track or pathway heading westwards from Brudene Street towards the city wall, approximately along what would have been the northern boundary of the residence.

The updated design of the residence

The acquisition of the tenements along Brudene Street and the reorientation of the residence is indicative of a design that was taking advantage of

an enhanced space, and applying the rationale of a layout more usually seen in rural manors of this period. Much of the early analysis of urban high status houses, for instance by Pantin (1962–3), focused on the development of medieval building plans in the context of tightly packed tenements with a shortage of space. As Schofield and Vince have pointed out (2003, 87), where resources and space permitted, the design parameters of a rural manor, where the space around the central hall is a key part of its design, were readily adapted to an urban situation. This was of course much more likely to be the case if the occupier (as in the case of the Archdeacon) was not a manufacturer or seller of goods or commodities and was not obliged to use the space for shops, workshops, or warehousing.

So in this instance it is pertinent to compare the layout of the Archdeacon's residence with that of a contemporary high status secular property, for instance that in Upper Brook Street, which by the late 13th century was a complex arrangement of interconnected rooms and buildings, the property of a wealthy wool merchant John de Tytyng, leaving almost no open space except a small back yard (Scobie *et al.* 1991, fig. 34; James 2007, fig. 4). Within this restricted space was accommodated a street-side shop front, warehousing, private rooms, public rooms, a kitchen, latrines, workshops and well, all in an area of less than 30 m by 40 m.

The material culture of the residence

There is sound archaeological and documentary evidence that the density of occupation and the intensity of activity in the area was beginning to decline during Phase 5. That during Phase 6, or between the late 13th and the 15th centuries, it declined to the point where occupation effectively ceased altogether to the west of Brudene Street, is evident. But during the period when the area was the Archdeacon's residence, the material evidence would arguably give a similar impression in many ways. There would be a much smaller population, principally a household staff, occasional guests, and the Archdeacon himself. The number of rubbish pits or cess pits that could be confidently ascribed to this period was very low. Three substantial ones were located along the eastern edge of the site (Fig. 5.9), supporting the conclusion that the Phase 5 building frontage onto Brudene Street had been cleared. The most northerly pit (NH2007) appeared to have served originally as a cess pit or latrine, later being used as a general rubbish pit, with successive dumps of material.

Although residual pottery from these three pits was unsurprisingly evident, a high proportion of 13th- and 14th-century material was present, commensurate with the lifespan of the residence. The proximity of the southern two of these pits to the proposed kitchen and annexe could be seen as supporting its interpretation as a detached service range. A number of medieval roof tiles were recovered from their fills, possibly indicative of the building's roof. A possible glazed costrel (flask) from this site and a ceramic cistern for ale-brewing also point both to wine or ale consumption and a degree of self-sufficiency in that regard, as do a couple of small sherds from a Tudor Green ware cup (*c* 1375–1500)—the latest type of medieval pottery recovered from the site.

The animal bone assemblage in this phase shows reduced slaughter-age patterns and a high percentage of lambs on the site, perhaps indicative of high status consumption. No samples were retrieved of fish remains from the residence, and across the whole site there was some indication of a decline in the consumption of shellfish generally, but a single dump of 38 oyster shells in Phase 6 pit fill NH3236 (of pit NH3235) suggests occasional feasting.

The characterisation of this area as part of a high-status residence can be seen as much in the quantities and types of material *not* present on site at this time. A scarcity of rubbish pits, and a scarcity of accumulated occupation layers such as would be expected in an 'active' urban environment, means also a lack of small finds of metal, bone or stone. There was no evidence of on-site craft or industrial work. The two smithing hearth bottoms from Phase 6 contexts in Property BW 2 are almost certainly residual material from earlier activity.

To the west of the Brudene Street frontage only a few of the isolated pits encountered in Cunliffe's excavations were investigated, in particular where they related directly to the exposed foundations of the chapel or hall. Those that were sample-excavated produced generally 11th- or 12th-century material. In the present excavation there were very few contemporary pits outside the proximity of the service range (Structure NH8545/NH8551). This would be consistent with the function of the whole property.

The abandonment of the residence and the clearance of the site

The archaeological evidence suggests that the tenement may have been abandoned as the residence of the Archdeacon in the first half of the 14th century. Although it is likely that the property continued to be occupied by tenants, the quantities of 14th- and 15th-century pottery recovered are low, suggesting that the property was never intensively used from then on.

The documentary sources offer some support to the archaeology. In a reference dated to 1417 (see Chapter 1; Keene 1985, 641), the tenement (called *Dorkynge*) is stated as belonging to the Archdeacon and held by Thomas Smaile (vintner and chamberlain) and John Frenshe (butcher and mayor); from this it might be inferred that at that time the buildings may still have been standing, although by the late 16th and 17th centuries the site is only referred to as gardens. There is no known documentary evidence to explain the reasons for the abandonment of the residence. The area seems to have become progressively depopulated for both demographic and commercial reasons. A residence that was becoming increasingly isolated from the ecclesiastical and secular centre of activity, now retreating back to the High Street and the Cathedral precinct, may no longer have been appropriate for a leading member of the clergy. His status could not be satisfactorily maintained while he resided in what had become a deserted backwater of the city, used increasingly as a convenient wool storage area, and a general rubbish dump. The modern name for the area 'Staple Gardens' originates in the establishment of the Winchester Staple on this site in 1326, for the storage and marketing of wool (Keene 1985, 472). The land assigned to this role had been confiscated from the Austin Friars by the king (after pressure from the bishop). However, by the late 14th century, the changing pattern of the wool trade reduced the importance of the Winchester Staple, and the land became a rubbish dump, and was later rented out piecemeal as gardens (ibid.,72–3).

Post-medieval activity

No archaeological features of the post-medieval period were discovered, which is consistent with Speed's depiction of the city in 1611, showing the area as totally devoid of any building (see Chapter 1, Fig. 1.7a). Godson's map of 1750 shows that by the 18th century the whole area had been put down to cultivation, and this is supported by the absence of significant deposits of domestic or craft debris of the post-medieval period. However, it is worth noting the possible west-east track marked by Godson crossing the northern part of what would have been the residence grounds. In an area otherwise denoted on the map as a uniform expanse of gardens and orchards, this track may possibly be a relic of the putative gateway into Dorking (Keene 1985, 641), as discussed above.

The Archdeacon's residence: overview and conclusions

Cunliffe's excavation, although limited in extent, revealed the remains of the groundplan of two buildings in some detail, and Biddle and Keene's documentary analysis (Biddle 1976) provided a plausible historical context within which to set these structures. The present investigation, also limited in extent (albeit in different ways) has broadened that context and allowed the buildings to be considered as elements within a whole property.

While some conclusions can be drawn, setting the archaeology in the documentary context, there are still some fundamental uncertainties. It is principally because of its role as the residence of a high church official (rather than, for example, a merchant or tradesman) that the material evidence is so slight. Nevertheless, a plausible narrative for the residence can be reconstructed, still speculative in parts, but generally consistent with both the archaeological evidence and the documentary history.

In summation, it is suggested that, sometime between the late 11th and mid 12th century a person of some considerable wealth held or acquired the two or three tenements north of Property SE 1, and built a stone chapel along the east side of Snitheling Street. Sometime during the 12th century the chapel became the parish church of St Mary Brudene Street and may have been accessed via the lane or passage leading across the north end of Property BW 3 from Brudene Street. Whether the chapel was built at the same time as the hall, or whether the hall was a later addition, remains unclear on the basis of the archaeological evidence.

By or during the 13th century the property passed to the Archdeacon of Winchester. Whether the Archdeacon acquired the hall and chapel with the property or whether he built them remains unclear from the archaeological evidence. A number of tenements fronting Brudene Street were acquired, probably during the early 13th century, and incorporated into the Archdeacon's property. The old frontage was cleared, and replaced with a new service block, serving the hall, which was re-ordered to face to the east. Lands to the south and north of the hall / chapel were cleared and set down to gardens; a final territorial acquisition was the western part of the tenement of Petronilla, widow of Adam de Northampton (Keene 1985, 641), to the south of the residence, which augmented the gardens. In addition to the wardrobe / garderobe block added to the west side of the hall, two boundary walls led from the hall to the east and south defining the more expansive estate, and defining the private, public and service areas of the property.

Sometime in the first half of the 15th century the residence was finally abandoned, although it may well not have served as the Archdeacon's residence for some time. The archaeological record suggests the last domestic activity occurred around the third decade of the 15th century, about the same time (according to the evidence from Cunliffe's excavation) as the demolition of the hall and the chapel. Indeed, the only reference to the church of 'Our Ladye in Burdenestrete' (St Mary) comes from 1452, citing it as one of the 17 parish churches of Winchester to have fallen down in the previous eighty years (Keene 1985, 641).

From the mid 15th century the residence grounds were leased out as gardens or intramural pasture. With the possible exception of the rebuilding of the well (NH9630), no further development or building took place on the site until the 19th century.

CONCLUSIONS *by Steve Teague*

The date of the establishment of the burh

The present excavations revealed no new evidence for the period between the decline of the Roman city and the establishment of the late Anglo-Saxon *burh*. Although it is clear that there was occupation of some kind in the city in the mid Saxon period (see this chapter, above), this did not extend to the north-western corner of the walled area. Here, at least on the western frontage of Brudene Street, the stratigraphic evidence suggests that the establishment of occupation was broadly contemporary with the laying out of the late Saxon street itself. A substantial programme of scientific dating formed part of the excavation strategy in this area in order to refine the dating of the occupation sequence, and particularly its start. Bayesian modelling was used on dates obtained from five adjacent properties (BW 2–6) that included 32 radiocarbon dates (17 from the earliest phase, Phase 4.1) and incorporated archaeomagnetic dating from 14 hearths (7 from Phase 4.1) (see Chapter 6). The model predicted that occupation within Properties BW 2, BW 4 and BW 5 began during the second half of the 9th century, with an 86.3% probability that occupation commenced before 880 and an 87.1% probability for a date after 842, when there may have been a Viking raid at Hamwic (although see Morton 1992, 76 for the arguments against this). However, it was not possible to establish whether these properties were established before or after the documented Viking raid on Winchester in 860 (the probability that they existed before 860 is 41.1%, or only after 860 is 58.9%). The model also suggested that occupation of Properties BW 2, BW 4 and BW 5 commenced more or less contemporaneously and that the earliest inhabitants of these properties probably knew each other.

The model therefore suggests that the laying out of Brudene Street and the establishment of occupation in the area is most likely to date to the period between *c* 842 and 880, which would challenge the conventional view that urbanisation of Winchester was prompted by the establishment of the *burh* by Alfred during the 880s. An earlier date for the establishment of the streets would be supported by the thickness of the occupation sequences of late Saxon date found at the Northgate House site, and at others within the city (eg 28–29 Staple Gardens, Castle Yard, the Lower Barracks and Henly's Garage) which can reach over 1 m in depth (see this chapter, above, 'The streets'). References to 'fortress work' first begin to appear regularly in West Saxon charters from the reign of Aethelbald (855–60) (James 1997, 41; Yorke 1984, 67), and it is possible that the refurbishment of the Roman defences and the laying out of the street grid began shortly after or even prompted the Viking attack on Winchester in 860 that is recorded in the Anglo-Saxon Chronicle. This also corresponds closely to the traditional date for the re-bridging by St Swithun of the Itchen outside the east gate around 859, which would have had a positive impact on the trade and economy of the city (Biddle 1976, 271–2; James 1997, 44).

There is some evidence (Chapter 3 and this chapter, above, 'Land apportionment and tenement formation') that the initial laying out of Brudene Street for occupation may have suffered a temporary setback; the first buildings here, on Property BW 2, burnt down and were not immediately replaced. However, this hiatus seems to have been followed by a phase of determined redevelopment to a new building line, with the construction of at least three, and probably all six, of the properties excavated on the west side of Brudene Street before the end of the 9th century. Although less evidence survived, it is likely that this also happened on the east side of the road. If so, the area may have been quite densely populated from an early date.

This is supported by results from excavations undertaken at the south end of Staple Gardens in 1984–85 and 1989, which revealed part of a cemetery that comprised at least 282 inhumations (from an estimated original total of 2000–3000 individuals) in close proximity to the presumed site of the medieval parish church of St Paul. This densely occupied cemetery included a sequence of 15 intercutting burials. A programme of radiocarbon dating and Bayesian modelling suggests that the cemetery originated before the end of Alfred's reign, and that it was probably in use over the period *c* 850–975, and perhaps a decade or two longer at either end (Helen Rees pers. comm., *ex inf* Alex Bayliss). The cemetery appeared to have been delimited by Brudene Street to its east and had gone out of use when a street representing a western extension of St George's Street was laid out over it, which itself had gone out of use by the end of the 12th century (Kipling and Scobie 1990). It seems reasonable to assume that individuals living on Brudene Street had been buried here, although there is currently no evidence for the contemporary church. Keene suggests that the medieval parish church of St Paul was located in this area, where 'great quantities of human bones' were found in the 19th century (1985, 467–8 and fig. 52). The church is first recorded in 1256, but had been amalgamated with the church of St Peter Whitbread along the High Street to the east possibly by the early 15th century.

Winchester and Hamwic

The origins of such a large early population invite some speculation. The coincidence of Winchester's reappearance as an urban centre and Hamwic's disappearance as a trading centre and royal mint by the later 9th century has often been remarked upon (eg Biddle 1993, 119–26; Morton 1992, 75–7; Andrews 1997, 255–6). There is no actual archaeological evidence that the Vikings caused widespread disruption to Hamwic itself (Morton 1992, 76–6; Andrews 1997, 256), but it was clearly vulnerable, and the fact that it could not be readily defended may have contributed to a decision to transfer its key administrative functions to the relative security of Winchester. Whether this also involved moving Hamwic's inhabitants to Winchester is unclear, but Winchester clearly experienced a significant influx of population in the later 9th century, and the first new inhabitants of Brudene Street seem to have been essentially artisans, involved in iron working and the spinning and dyeing of yarn.

However, there is not much evidence in finds assemblages for direct links between Hamwic and Winchester (Biddle 1990; Rees 2008; Serjeantson and Rees 2009), although there are typological similarities between the main coarseware pottery traditions, which are represented at both Hamwic and at Winchester by chalk-tempered wares. The clay for both traditions was probably sourced from the same Reading Beds outcrop immediately south of the chalk escarpment. It is just feasible that some Hamwic potters moved closer to Winchester around this date and continued production, though this needs further investigation by scientific analysis (see Cotter, Chapter 7). The very low levels of imported pottery found at Winchester are in marked contrast to both Hamwic (Brisbane 1998) and the late Saxon and later phases of recent excavations at the French Quarter in Southampton (Brown D H, forthcoming). This is not in itself, however, an argument against the presence in Winchester of former inhabitants of the trading settlement at Hamwic. Low levels of both coin finds and imported pottery generally in southern England for the 9th and 10th century are thought to reflect a sluggish regional economy and a decline in overseas trade; by contrast 10th-century towns in the Danelaw, such as York and Chester, provide evidence for intensifying industry and trade. Grenville Astill has suggested that this could reflect a reorientation in trade away from the traditional southern English contacts with the Low Countries and the Rhineland to the northern English contacts with the Scandinavian kingdoms across the North and Irish seas (2000, 37). Morton also usefully reminds us that from *c* 825 onwards the West Saxon kings had access to the ports of south-east England (1992, 77) including, from the 880s, London itself. A general resurgence in trade in southern England is evident from the 970s onwards, and is mirrored archaeologically by the growth of new ports such as Southampton and Bristol; while late Saxon Winchester must have benefited from its proximity to Southampton (the source, for example, of much of the fish consumed in the city), it never seems to have taken on Hamwic's function as a port of trade. Whatever the connection between Hamwic's demise and Winchester's renewal, by the early 10th century Winchester replaced Hamwic as the administrative centre of Hampshire, with a mint rated fourth in the country and with a thriving population.

Late Saxon occupation in Brudene Street and Snitheling Street

The formation from the outset of regular narrow properties, at least alongside the frontages of Brudene Street, suggests a high degree of centralised planning. There was no evidence in the present excavations to suggest that the properties had been created by the subdivision of larger properties or urban estates, and if this did take place it must have happened at a very early stage. Indeed on other excavations where such early property boundaries have been recognised (for example at The Brooks and 28–29 Staple Gardens) the evidence would similarly imply that such narrow properties were in existence from the start. The impression of early planned development is reinforced by the apparent use of standard measurements based on whole multiples of poles or perches ($16^{1}/_{2}$ feet/$5^{1}/_{2}$ yards) for the width of the 14 properties identified along the frontages of Brudene Street and Snitheling Street and on the 10 Anglo-Saxon properties excavated at The Brooks (see this chapter, above, 'Land apportionment and tenement formation'). Philip Crummy has previously noted the regularity of the layout of the streets of Colchester, London and Winchester, which he demonstrated made use of the 4-pole unit (Crummy 1979, 149–64).

In those properties where evidence was obtained, the earliest occupants seem for the most part to have been craftworkers occupying small lightly built timber structures located adjacent to the street frontage that served both as homes and workshops. These rectangular structures were constructed either using small shallow earthfast posts or using surface-based beams against which the floors of beaten chalk accumulated. The most widespread evidence in these early properties was for small-scale blacksmithing (Properties BW 2, BW 4–5), probably for the manufacture or repair of everyday objects or tools and the shoeing of horses. The scale and nature of this activity is comparable to the evidence found within the late Saxon suburbs of the city in which the level of expertise was perhaps quite basic (Rees *et al.* 2008, 399). In most of the properties smithing waste was found in conjunction with evidence for spinning and dyeing of wool, again apparently practised on a small scale. The dyeing of wool with the reddish-purple dye madder could have been for private use within the household, but it seems possible that it could also have been a more organised industry, with the spun and dyed yarn being sold on to weavers or tailors. The dye seems to have been readily available, suggesting its production or supply nearby. The survey of 1148 lists three individuals described as a *Waranchier* who occupied properties in the western and eastern suburbs of the city (Biddle 1976, 430, table 48). Von Feilitzen suggested that this Old French name referred to 'one who manufactures, or dyes in, madder' (Biddle 1976, 217; Crowfoot *et al.* 2006, 200), which suggests it could refer to traders of

madder as well. The evidence from the present excavations shows that this craft had been established in the city from the later 9th century. Perhaps the association of purple with the church and the rapidly growing monastic quarter of the city would have provided a ready market for such dyed yarn.

Over time, evidence for larger, more elaborate and more diverse buildings suggests growing stability and prosperity in the area as the late Saxon period progressed, with the enlargement of houses and the appearance of the first substantial post-pit buildings. This is accompanied by some evidence for a shift in emphasis in the activities of the inhabitants, although craftworking clearly persisted in this area throughout the late Saxon period. However, the decline in evidence for metalworking at the enlarged Properties BW 2 and BW 3, and the appearance of cellars for the storage of goods and merchandise at Properties SE 1, BE 4, BE 5 and BW 6, suggests that some of the inhabitants at least may have been trading on a larger scale than their late 9th-century predecessors, and their activities may have been diversifying.

The Anglo-Norman period

The Norman Conquest appears to have had little immediate impact on the area of the present excavations, by comparison with other parts of the city. Within the south-western quadrant of the city the construction of the castle, which commenced within months of the surrender of the city in November 1066, saw the destruction of a whole street and the houses that stood alongside it, and the construction of a new extramural street (Biddle 1976, 470). By contrast, there is little evidence for disruption along Brudene Street; no properties appear to have been abandoned or amalgamated, and several new buildings in the substantial post-pit tradition were constructed (Properties BW 2, BW 4 and BE 5). Property BW 2 may have become largely residential by this time, but metalworking continued at Properties BW 4 and BE 4, where there is evidence for the use of copper alloys in brazing, coating or inlaying, and for the manufacture of small decorative objects or fittings. It is also clear that the spinning and dyeing of yarn continued in the area in the Anglo-Norman period. Three Anglo-Norman properties (BE 3, BE 4 and SE 3) produced evidence of horn working in this period; by contrast there had been little evidence for horn or bone working in the area in the pre-Conquest period. Supplies of horn and bone would have been readily available from the butchers within the city, several of whom were concentrated on the High Street close to the West Gate by 1148 (Biddle 1976, 437).

The only hint of the widespread social and economic disruption that followed the Conquest comes from Property SE 2 on Snitheling Street, where the substantial late Saxon post-pit building was subsequently demolished. The pottery associated with the fills of the post-pits was entirely late

Saxon in character, which suggests that the building was dismantled before Anglo-Norman ceramics came into general use, and a date around the time of the Conquest is therefore a strong possibility.

More tangible evidence of Norman impact can be found in the use of chalk-lined wells that were introduced in many of the properties, reinstating a method of construction that seems to have been lost in the city since Roman times. Prior to the Conquest very few properties produced any definitive evidence for wells; if they were present on the site they probably remained unidentified within the mass of partially excavated pits and all were probably timber-lined. Alternatively water may have been brought in by water carriers, and it is interesting to note that the survey of 1110 records that Alwin (the) Wet-Monger (a seller of water?) held a property in Brudene Street before the Conquest (Biddle 1976, 55, 429).

Some of the wells, especially the large well found in Property BE 4 and the elaborately constructed 'well-house' within Property BW 3, were particularly ostentatious in the use of finely dressed chalk ashlar, work that presumably required the services of skilled masons at some appreciable cost. Chalk-lined wells are a common feature of other late 11th- to 12th-century sites in Winchester, though the finer examples are often associated with wealthier residences, such as the example found at The Brooks identified as belonging to Roger the Vintner (a wine merchant listed in the survey of 1148) adjacent to a finely constructed chalk-ashlar cellar (Scobie *et al.* 1991, 54–7).

By the late 12th or early 13th century there is evidence for a wealthy household associated with the fur trade on Property SE 1 (see this chapter, above, 'Economic status and trade'). The 1148 survey records three individuals called 'parmentarius' in Snitheling Street, which is usually translated as 'tailor' (Biddle 1976, 203 and table 48). Keene (1985, 285) has noted that skinners ('pelliparii'), who dealt in fur, were the most numerous craftsmen in 14th-century Winchester but no record of 'pelliparii' exists in the 12th-century surveys, when demand for skins and furs had probably reached its peak. However the largest group of tradesmen recorded in the 1148 survey are listed as 'parmentarius', a term that is not current in the later medieval documentation, and some of these at least may also have been associated with the fur trade. Given the uncertainties of the precise direction of the 1148 survey within this part of the city (Biddle 1976, fig. 4) it would be unwise to suggest any correlation with any named 'parmentarius', though one (Robert) may have occupied a property located towards the north of the street (Biddle 1976, 96 and fig. 23). The association of the area with skinning is later noted by Keene (1985, Properties 245–46) when Adam de Northampton, citizen and skinner, acquired a substantial property on Brudene Street during the later 13th century that may be identifiable (in part at least) as Property BW 1 (see above).

By this time the documentary evidence suggests that the property may already have extended to Snitheling Street, incorporating Property SE 1. It would seem that the apparent increase in prosperity noted in this property began prior to the occupancy of Adam de Northampton.

The 13th century onwards

In the late 12th and early 13th century the area of the excavations saw a major change in the character of occupation. A new phase of redevelopment saw the construction of fewer, but larger and more elaborate properties, replacing the smaller properties that once occupied these frontages (see this chapter, above, 'The project area from the 13th century'). This suggests that the decrease in occupation evident in the documentary record was not associated with decline in the status and character of the area at this time, but rather the reverse. Buildings of good quality stonework with tiled roofs and floors were being constructed within the project area and the earlier tenements were being amalgamated to create more spacious properties. The largest of these belonged to the Archdeacon of Winchester (see this chapter, above, 'The residence of the Archdeacon of Winchester'); the amalgamated Properties BW 1 and SE 1 may have been in the hands of the wealthy skinner Adam de Northampton in the later 13th century (see above), and the stone cellar that was built on Property BE 5 may have been the property of a substantial merchant. Biddle and Keene (Biddle 1976) have suggested that there was a general shift in population from the west of the city towards the heart of the industrial east side where much better water resources were available. The lack of evidence for craft working in the excavated properties by this time would be consistent with the abandonment of the area by artisans, and this may have provided the opportunities for the acquisition and amalgamation of vacant properties by a smaller number of wealthier occupants. It is equally possible, however, that the acquisition of tenements by wealthy people with a view to creating larger properties could in itself have encouraged this process.

In the event, this was to prove a relatively short-lived development, and the depopulation of the area is evident from the later 14th century onwards in both the documentary and the archaeological record. Although no longer inhabited, however, the land did not remain unproductive during the 15th and 16th centuries as there was significant increase in the extent of orchards and later the cultivation of hops became important, even close to the High Street (Keene 1985, 153). In essence many parts of the city, especially north of the High Street, resembled an agricultural landscape and this is best illustrated on the depictions of the city by Speed (1611) and later by Godson (1750) (see Chapter 1, Fig. 1.7). Not until the coming of the railway during the 19th century did the project area again see redevelopment.

Chapter 6
Overview of the Scientific Dating Evidence

by Seren Griffiths, Alex Bayliss, Ben Ford, Mark Hounslow, Vassil Karloukovski,
Christopher Bronk Ramsey, Gordon Cook and Peter Marshall

INTRODUCTION

Two chronometric techniques were employed to provide a scientific chronology for Winchester Discovery Centre (CC) and Northgate House (NH). Full details of the radiocarbon and archaeomagnetic sampling and laboratory processing are outlined in the digital report (*Digital Section 19*).

The recovery of a large number of undisturbed *in situ* fired hearths throughout the Saxon sequence from the Northgate House site offered the potential to provide a precise chronology for the site, addressing a series of specific research objectives:

- Did settlement on the site begin before the mid AD 880s (the date derived from Burghal Hidage for the foundation of the Alfredian *burh*)?

- How did the street pattern develop? Were the properties deliberately laid out at one time or did they spread organically from a central core?

- When did occupation of the Saxon properties on the site cease? Did it continue after AD 1066?

- Is it possible to refine the chronologies of the ceramics recovered from the sites?

The radiocarbon dating programme also contributes to these objectives, but was principally designed to test the accuracy of the existing archaeomagnetic calibration data for Britain (Clark *et al.* 1988). These dates would also provide additional calibration data for archaeomagnetic directions in this period.

The results of these measurements were calibrated using the archaeomagnetic calibration and radiocarbon calibration curves. The calibrated radiocarbon results and archaeomagnetic results are shown in Tables 6.1–3 and Figs 6.1–2. The ranges in Table 6.2 have been calculated according to the maximum intercept method (Stuiver and Reimer 1986); all other ranges are derived from the probability method (Stuiver and Reimer 1993). Those ranges printed in italics in the text and tables are *posterior density estimates*, derived from the mathematical modelling described below.

Table 6.1: List of the hearths sampled for archaeomagnetic dating from Northgate House.
N= number of samples per hearth.

	Hearth	Feature No	N	Dimensions
1.	WOA	2156	10	~0.15m thick, 0.6 x 0.45m
2.	WOB	3177	9	~0.10m thick, 1.0 x 1.0m
3.	WOC	5188	8	~0.20m thick, 1.0 x 0.7m
4.	WOD	2391	10	0.02–0.10m thick. Consists
				of two parts: 0.5 x 1.0m
				and 1.0 x 1.0m
5.	WOE	4261	8	0.02–0.10m thick, 1.0 x 0.6m
6.	WOF	4430	9	~0.05m thick, 1.0 x 1.3m
7.	WOG	3462	9	~0.03m thick, 3.0 x 0.8m
8.	WOH	3484	8	~0.05m thick. 0.7 x 0.5m
9.	WOI	7513	3	~0.04m thick, 0.5 x 0.2m
		7511	6	~0.07m thick, 0.5 x 0.8m
10.	WOJ	3506	8	0.03–0.10m thick, 1.25 x 1.50m
11.	WOK	4523	9	~0.05m thick, 0.25 x 0.80m
12.	WOL	3576	10	~0.05m thick, 1.0 x 1.4m
13.	WOM	4692	9	~0.04m thick, 1.3 x 1.8m
14.	WON	3680	9	0.02–0.05m thick, 0.8 x 1.0m
15.	WOO	4733	9	0.03–0.04m thick, 0.6 x 0.6m
16.	WOP	3780	9	0.03–0.05m thick, 0.3 x 1.2m

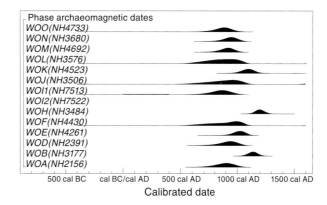

Fig. 6.1   Saxon archaeomagnetic dates from Northgate House, Winchester, calibrated by the probability method (Stuiver and Reimer 1993) using the calibration curve of Zananiri et al. *(2007); distributions have been truncated on the basis of archaeological information to exclude possible dates before 400 BC or after AD 1500*

Table 6.2: Radiocarbon determinations from Northgate House, Winchester

Context & Posterior density Sample Number	Laboratory Number	Material and context	Radiocarbon Age (BP)	δ13C (‰)	Weighted mean (BP)	range (95% confidence)	Calibrated date estimate (95% probability)
<234>(NH3587)A	OxA-17173	charcoal, Betula sp., from an occupation horizon within property BW4	1153±25	-25.7		cal AD 780–970	cal AD 830–940
<234>(NH3587)B	SUERC-13907	charcoal, Salix/Populus sp., from the same context as OxA-17173	1175±35	-26.8		cal AD 730–970	cal AD 830–940
<232>(NH3578)A	OxA-17172	hazelnut shell from a lens of charcoal associated with the firing of hearth (3576)	1181±27	-26.2		cal AD 770–940	cal AD 770–900
<232>(NH3578)B	SUERC-13906	grain, Triticum sp. from the same context as OxA-17172	1065±35	-22.9		cal AD 890–1020	cal AD 890–950
<225>(NH3494)A	OxA-17181	charcoal, Corylus sp., from a occupation layer rich in charred plant remains	1138±24	-25.8	1151±18	cal AD 780–970	cal AD 910–970
<225>(NH3494)A	OxA-17182	replicate of OxA-17182	1166±25	-25.4	(T'=0.7; T'(5%) =3.8 O=1; Ward and Wilson 1978)		
<225>(NH3494)B	SUERC-13917	charcoal, Pomoideae, from the same context as OxA-17181–2	1105±35	-25.9		cal AD 880–1020	cal AD 900–970
<174>(NH2391)A	OxA-17137	grain, Avena sp., from a layer of in situ burning within hearth (2391)	1213±27	-23.0		cal AD 690–890	cal AD 840–900 (86%) or 920–950 (9%)
<174 >(NH2391)B	SUERC-13914	grain, Avena sp., from the same context as OxA-17137	1165±35	-25.3		cal AD 770–970	cal AD 840–950
<177>(NH2424)A	OxA-17179	charcoal, Acer sp., from a layer of charcoal within occupation deposits in property BW4	1130±25	-25.2		cal AD 870–980	cal AD 880–970
<177>(NH2424)B	SUERC-13915	charcoal, Pomoideae, from the same context as OxA-17179	1110±35	-27.9		cal AD 880–1020	cal AD 880–980
<164>(NH2156)A	OxA-17174	charcoal, Pomoideae, from a layer of in situ burning associated with the firing of hearth (2156)	1146±27	-27.3		cal AD 780–980	cal AD 780–980
<164>(NH2156)B	SUERC-13908	charcoal, Salix/Populus, from the same context as OxA-17174	1030±35	-25.3		cal AD 900–1040	cal AD 900–1010
<237>(NH3664)A	OxA-17178	charcoal, Prunus sp., from a layer of in situ burning within property BW3	1140±25	-25.0		cal AD 780–980	cal AD 780–790 (1%) or 810–980 (94%)
<237>(NH3664)B	SUERC-13910	charcoal, Pomoideae, from the same context as OxA-17178	1050±35	-26.2		cal AD 900–1030	cal AD 890–1010
<211>(NH3177)A	OxA-17175	charcoal, Prunus spinosa, from a layer of in situ burnt earth within hearth (3177)	432±24	-25.6		cal AD 1430–1470	cal AD 1420–1490
<550>(NH4697)A	OxA-17177	charcoal, Pomoideae, from a layer of silting forming over the Saxon street surface, sealed below layers of resurfacing	1181±25	-24.8		cal AD 770–940	cal AD 770–890
<550>(NH4697)B	SUERC-13909	charcoal, Corylus sp., from the same context as OxA-17177	1140±35	-25.4		cal AD 780–990	cal AD 770–920
<289>(NH4580)A	OxA-17183	hazelnut shell from a discrete charcoal–rich deposit associated with in situ burning on hearth (4692)	1172±26	-23.1		cal AD 780–960	cal AD 860–950
<289>(NH4580)B	SUERC-13918	hazelnut shell from the same context as OxA-17183	1115±35	-22.7		cal AD 830–1010	cal AD 880–950
<276>(NH4458)A	OxA-17180	grain, Triticum sp., from a discrete area of charred plant remains probably representing rake–out from oven (4485)	1027±25	-21.7		cal AD 980–1030	cal AD 970–1040
<276>(NH4458)B	SUERC-13916	grain, Hordeum sp., from the same context as OxA-17180	915±35	-25.2		cal AD 1020–1210	cal AD 1020–1090
<262>(NH4373)A	OxA-17176	hazelnut shell from an occupation layer above hearth (4430)	1012±25	-24.1		cal AD 990–1030	cal AD 970–1050 (91%) or 1090–1120 (4%)
<262>(NH4373)B	SUERC-13904	grain, Triticum sp, from the same context as OxA-17176	885±35	-20.6		cal AD 1030–1220	cal AD 1050–1230
<285>(NH4507)B	SUERC-13920	grain, Avena sp., from a spread of charred material within an occupation horizon	1120±35	-25.7		cal AD 780–1010	cal AD 890–960

Table 6.2: Radiocarbon determinations from Northgate House, Winchester (continued)

<266>(NH4394)A	OxA–17184	charcoal, Pomoideae, from a discrete charcoal spread associated with *in situ* burning on hearth (4261)	1169±26	-27.0	cal AD 910–980
<266>(NH4394)B	SUERC–13919	charcoal, *Prunus sp.*, from the same context as OxA–17184	1105±35	-25.9	cal AD 900–980
<216>(NH3260)A	SUERC–19280	hazelnut shell, *Corylus avellana*, from occupation horizon (3260)	1105±30	-20.6	cal AD 920–990
<216>(NH3260)B	SUERC–19284	grain, *Avena sativa*, from occupation horizon (3260)	1070±30	-23.9	cal AD 930–990
<208> (NH3175)B	SUERC–19285	grain, *Triticum aestivum*, from occupation horizon (NH3175)	1240±30	-21.0	cal AD 680–880
(NH3175)A	SUERC–19286	bone, unfused fragments of sternum, from medium mammal (probably sheep or goat) from occupation horizon (NH3175)	1145±30	-20.1	cal AD 770–990
(NH4379)A	SUERC–19287	bone, cattle rib from occupation horizon (NH4379)	1110±30	-20.9	cal AD 880–1020
(NH4379)B	SUERC–19288	Bone, cattle carpal, articulated with radius from occupation horizon (NH4379)	1040±30	-21.3	cal AD 900–1030
(NH6176)	OxA–16713	Bone, human – right ulna shaft fragment.	1901±28	-18.6	cal. AD 30–210
(NH6177)A	OxA–16757	Charred bread wheat grain, *Triticum aestivum* from the fill of post-hole (NH6178)	1151±26	-23.4	cal AD 780–980
(NH6177)B	OxA–16758	Charred bread wheat grain, *Triticum aestivum* from the fill of post-hole (NH6178)	1134±26	-21.7	cal AD 820–990
(NH6204)B	OxA–16759	Charred grain, *Triticum aestivum* from from the fill of pit (NH6203)	1177±26	-23.4	cal AD 770–950
(NH6204)A	OxA–16775	Charred grain, *Triticum aestivum* from the fill of pit (NH6203)	1145±55	-20.4	cal AD 720–1020
(CC3251)A	OxA–16793	Bone, large mammal cf. cattle – rib from holloway (CC3408)	1966±27	-21	40 cal. BC – cal. AD 90
(CC3251)B	OxA–16794	Tooth, sheep/goat, from holloway (CC3408)	1669±25	-21.2	cal. AD 260–430

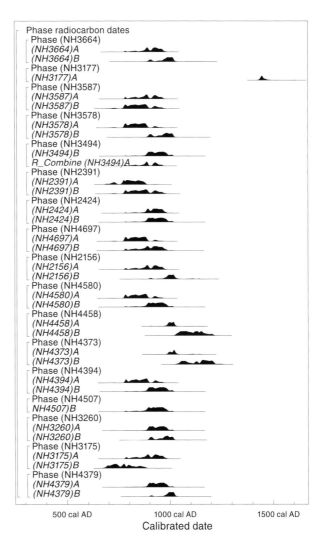

Fig. 6.2   Radiocarbon dates from Northgate House, Winchester, calibrated by the probability method (Stuiver and Reimer 1993) using the calibration curve of Reimer et al. (2004)

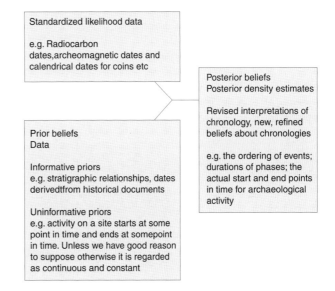

Fig. 6.3   Components of a Bayesian chronological model

Table 6.3: Weighed sample–mean ChRM directions for the hearths from Northgate House, Winchester

($\hat{E}$ = 51.065°Δ N, $\ddot{I}$ = 1.3169° W, SU 47929). *Specimen–mean directions for hearth WOI (features 7513 and 7511). Ns= number of data (samples or specimens), K = Fisher concentration parameter. D=declination, I=inclination, ·95=95% cone of confidence about the mean direction. Directions variation corrected. The 95% confidence intervals for the Northgate hearths are also shown. For hearth WOI the specimen–averaged directions are used.*

| | ChRM [°] | | | | | Class | Calibrated Date |
Hearth	D	I	·95	Ns	K		(95% confidence)
WOA	20.4	69.4	3.8	7	252	C	AD 580–AD 1125
WOB	16.6	60.8	2.8	9	333	C	AD 1117–AD 1229
WOC	352.5	66.8	1.9	8	883	A	96 BC–AD 130
WOD	18.7	68.1	2.8	6	584	B	AD 800–AD 1125
WOE	22.7	64.8	3.3	8	269	C	AD 979–AD 1165
WOF	13.7	67.5	2.1	9	625	A	AD 477–AD 1175
WOH	13.6	58.9	2.4	7	652	A	AD 1195–AD 1267
WOI1	20.2	70.8	4.4	19	59	C	AD 559–AD 1084
WOI2	12.9	70.1	3.4	34	52	C	AD 498–AD 1125
WOJ	14.7	67.8	3.9	6	304	C	AD 436–AD 1175
WOK	18.7	62.4	4.3	6	239	B	AD 1065–AD 1245
WOL	13.6	68.1	2.2	8	613	C	AD 498–AD 1148
WOM	22.4	68.9	2.3	6	839	B	AD 880–AD 1093
WON	23.3	67.8	2.9	9	317	A	AD 914–AD 1121
WOO	19.1	69.8	2.5	8	494	A	AD 559–AD 1084
JSB5991	359.2	67.9	2	9	661	??	150 BC–AD 130
JSB1572	346.3	66	2.4	11	477	??	96 BC–AD 25
SG1–8	30.7	65.9	2.6	6	646	A	AD 975–AD 1102

A Bayesian statistical chronological model was used for the analysis and interpretation of the calibrated archaeomagnetic and radiocarbon results. A Bayesian chronological model consists of three fundamental components—the 'standardised likelihoods' and 'prior information' which are the inputs of the model, and the 'posterior beliefs' which are the output (Fig. 6.3). In this case, the probability distributions of calibrated archaeomagnetic and radiocarbon dates, and calendrical dates derived from coins, form the 'standardised likelihoods'. The 'prior information' consists of the relative dating provided by the stratigraphic sequence and our statistical assumption that activity on the site was continuous (see Bayliss 2007 and Bayliss *et al.* 2007 for further discussion of building chronological models).

THE FOUR SAXON TENEMENTS

Scientific dating is available from four tenements, and four Saxon coins were recovered from the excavations, three of which can be associated with the properties. Two archaeomagnetic dates are available from hearths in Property BW 6 (WOI1 and WOI2), and must date the use of this tenement. These deposits cannot be related by stratigraphy.

Scientific dates are available from three sequential deposits in Property BW 5 (Fig. 6.4). Two statistically consistent radiocarbon measurements are available from two oat grains dated from a layer of *in situ* burning (NH2391) (OxA-17137 and SUERC-13914;

T'=1.2; T'(5%)=3.8; df=1), along with an archaeomagnetic date on the same feature (WOD NH2391). Later than this deposit are two statistically consistent results on fragments of short-life charcoal from a charcoal-rich layer (NH2424) within occupation deposits in the structure (OxA-17179 and SUERC-13915; T'=0.2; T'(5%)=3.8; n=1). Later again is a hearth, dated by archaeomagnetism (WOA NH2156) and by two statistically inconsistent radiocarbon results on short-life charcoal from an *in situ* layer of

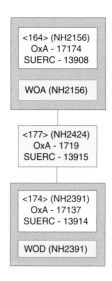

Fig. 6.4 Summary of the relationships between dated deposits in Property BW 5

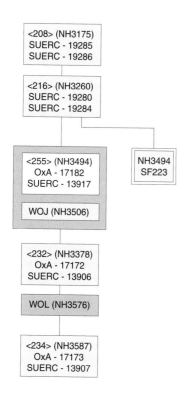

short-life charcoal fragments are available from an occupation horizon (NH3587) (OxA-17173 and SUERC-13907; T'=0.3; T'(5%)=3.8; n=1). These dates are earlier than a hearth, which has been dated by archaeomagnetism (WOL(NH3576)). Later again are two statistically inconsistent radiocarbon results on short-life material from a lens of charcoal associated with firing hearth (NH3578) (OxA-17172 and SUERC-13906; T'=6.9; T'(5%)=3.8; n=1). Again, because of the inconsistency in the radiocarbon results, the earlier of the two charcoal fragments has been interpreted as redeposited and has only been used as a *terminus post quem* for overlying deposits. Later than this is another hearth dated by archaeomagnetism (WOJ(NH3506)). Two statistically consistent measurements on fragments of short-life charcoal from fuel associated with the firing of this hearth (NH3494) (SUERC-13917 and OxA-17181–2; T'=1.4; T'(5%)=3.8; n=1) are also available. Later than this, are two statistically consistent radiocarbon measurements on charred plant remains from occupation horizon (NH3260) (SUERC-19280 and SUERC-19284; T'=0.7; T'(5%)=3.8; n=1). A silver penny of Edgar or Alfred (SF223) from underlying context (NH3466) provides a *terminus post quem* of 871–975 for occupation layer (NH3260). Two statistically inconsistent radiocarbon results (SUERC-19285 and SUERC-19286; T'=5.0; T'(5%)=3.8; n=1), however, have been obtained from another occupation horizon (NH3175), which is stratigraphically later than (NH3260). The earlier of these, SUERC-19285 on a grain of wheat, has been interpreted as residual and has been included in the model only as a *terminus post quem* for the end of the use of Property BW 4.

Fig. 6.5 Summary of the relationships between dated deposits in Property BW 4

burning within the hearth (OxA-17174 and SUERC-13908; T'=6.3; T'=3.8; n=1). Because of this inconsistency, the earlier of these two charcoal fragments has been interpreted as redeposited and therefore incorporated into the Bayesian model only as a *terminus post quem* for the end of the use of this phase of activity in the property.

Scientific dates are available from six sequential deposits in Property BW 4 (Fig. 6.5). Two statistically consistent radiocarbon determinations on

Scientific dates are available from three stratigraphic strings in Property BW 3 (Fig. 6.6). A hearth which has been dated by archaeomagnetism (WON(NH3680)) is earlier than two statistically inconsistent radiocarbon results on short-life

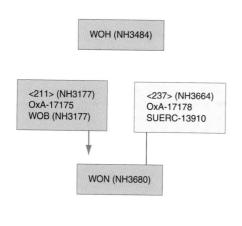

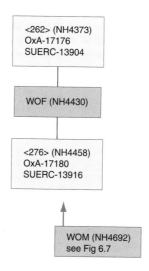

Fig. 6.6 Summary of the relationships between other dated deposits in Property BW 3, (NH4458) is stratigraphically later than hearth (NH4692) in Property BW 2 (see Fig. 6.7)

charcoal fragments from a layer of *in situ* burning within the property (NH3664) (OxA-17178 and SUERC-13910; T'=4.4; T'(5%)=3.8; n=1). Because of the inconsistency in these radiocarbon results, the earlier of the two charcoal fragments has been interpreted as redeposited and has only been used as a *terminus post quem* for overlying deposits. Also later than hearth (WON(NH3680)) is another hearth dated by archaeomagnetism (WOB(NH3177)). A layer of burning within this hearth produced a short-life charcoal fragment which must be intrusive as it dates to the 15th century (OxA-17175). Hearth (WOB(NH3177)) dates to cal 1117–1229 (95% confidence), which is consistent with the associated Phase 6 pottery assemblage. It has been included in the model as a *terminus ante quem* for the end of Phase 4.

The second sequence of dated deposits in Property BW 3 cannot be related to the sequence just described, and contains a series of deposits in Phase 5. For this reason they have only been included in the model as *termini ante quos* for the end of Phase 4. All are comfortably later than hearth (NH4692) in Property BW 2 (see below), which is stratigraphically earlier than (NH4458), a discrete rake-out from oven (NH4485). This produced two statistically inconsistent radiocarbon measurements on cereal grains (OxA-17180 and SUERC-13916; T'=6.7; T'(5%)=3.8; n=1). The earlier of these (OxA-17180) has only been included in the model as a *terminus post quem* for the overlying hearth, which has been dated by archaeomagnetism (WOF(NH4430)). Later than this hearth are two statistically inconsistent radiocarbon measurements on short-life material from an occupation layer (NH4373) (OxA-17176 and SUERC-13904; T'=8.7; T'(5%)=3.8; n=1). The earlier of these may therefore be residual and has only been included in the model as a *terminus post quem* for the end of occupation of Property BW 2.

Hearth WHO(NH3484) has been dated by archaeomagnetism to cal 1195–1267 (95% confidence). This Phase 5 feature is recorded as being stratigraphically earlier than (NH4458) and the rest of the sequence just described. The scientific dates are in poor agreement with this interpretation, as both the archaeomagnetic date from Hearth WOF(NH4430) and the radiocarbon dates from (NH4458) and (NH4373) are earlier than the archaeomagnetic date from WOH(NH3484). Both archaeomagnetic dates in this sequence are Class A and so it is unlikely that either is inaccurate. In these circumstances, it appears that the stratigraphic record may be in error. Examination of the sequence of stratigraphic relationships between (NH3484) and (NH4458) suggests that it may be the relationship of unplanned occupation horizon (NH3486) with floor (NH3667) which has been misinterpreted. This relationship was inferred over a horizontal distance of more than 4 m in an area of heavy slumping, and it appears that similar charcoal rich occupation horizons may have been

conflated. For this reason, we suggest that WOH(NH3484) is not related stratigraphically to the other dated deposits from Property BW 3, and so it has been included in the model simply as a *terminus ante quem* for the end of Phase 4.

Dates are available from 12 deposits that can be stratigraphically related in Property BW 2 (Fig. 6.7). From the base of the sequence, an archaeomagnetic date has been produced on hearth WOO(NH4733). This feature is earlier than hearth (NH4692), which has also been dated by archaeomagnetism (WOM(NH4692)). Two statistically consistent determinations on short-life charcoal from the silting of the Saxon street surface (Street NH4697) (OxA-17177 and SUERC-13909; T'=0.9; T'(5%)=3.8; n=1) provide *termini post quem* for hearth (WOM (NH4692)). The uncertain taphonomy of the dated material means that we have not interpreted these dates as later than hearth (NH4733), even though the street surface itself sealed this hearth (see Fig. 6.7).

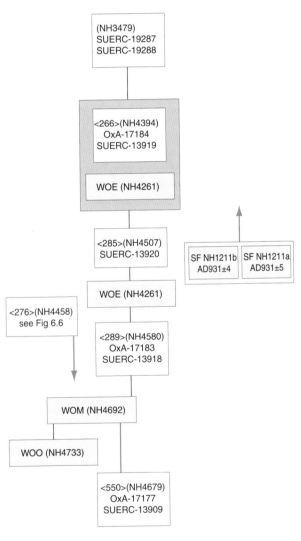

Fig. 6.7 Summary of the relationships between other dated deposits in Property BW 2, hearth (NH4692) is stratigraphically later than (NH4458) in Property BW 3 (see Fig. 6.6)

Two stratigraphic sequences are later than hearth (NH4692). The first sequence begins with two statistically consistent radiocarbon measurements on charred hazelnut shell from a discrete charcoal-rich deposit (NH4580) associated with *in situ* burning of burnt surface (NH4557) (OxA-17183 and SUERC-13918; T'=1.7; T'(5%)=3.8; n=1). Later than deposit (NH4580) is hearth (NH4523), which has produced an archaeomagnetic date (WOK(NH4523)). This produced an anomalously late archaeomagnetic date, both in relation to the stratigraphic sequence and the associated ceramic assemblage. There is evidence in this hearth of possible disturbance, since four of the nine samples show consistent within-sample deviation from the remaining five samples which have tightly grouped specimen directions. It has therefore been excluded from the model. Above this was a charcoal spread within an occupation horizon (NH4507), which produced a single radiocarbon age on a charred oat grain (SUERC-13920). In turn, this is earlier than hearth (NH4261), dated by an archaeomagnetic date (WOE(NH4261)) and two statistically consistent radiocarbon determinations on short-life charcoal from a discrete charcoal spread (NH4394) associated with *in situ* burning from the hearth (OxA-17184 and SUERC-13919; T'=2.1; T'(5%)=3.8; n=1). Later than this are two statistically consistent radiocarbon measurements on animal bone from occupation deposit (NH4379)(SUERC-19287–8; T'=2.7; T'(5%)=3.8; n=1). One of these samples, SUERC-19288, was a cattle carpal which was recovered in articulation with a radius. This sample, at least, cannot be residual. The second sequence contains a series of Phase 5 deposits in Property BW 3, as hearth WOM(NH4692) is stratigraphically earlier than rake-out (NH4458). The sequence above this has been described above (see Fig. 6.6).

Pit (NH4095) cannot be stratigraphically related to those deposits from Property BW 2 that produced scientific dates. It did, however, produce a silver penny of Athelstan (924–939) and an Anglo-Saxon sceat, tentatively assigned to series K and thus probably minted between *c* 720 and 740. These provide *termini post quem* for the end of the use of Property BW 2.

Archaeological interpretation: the site chronology

The overall structure of the chronological model which incorporates this interpretation of the archaeological data as prior information is shown in Fig. 6.8. This treats the phase of activity represented by Phase 4 as a continuous and relatively constant period of occupation. Although in reality the tenements probably continued in use beyond this pottery phase, these deposits frequently have not survived later truncation and had been under-sampled by both the excavation and the dating programme. For this reason, it was decided that a chronological model of this period of use of the site

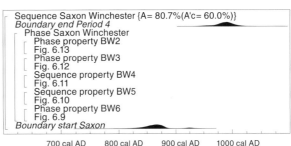

Fig. 6.8   *Overall structure for the chronological model of Phase 4 deposits from Northgate House, Winchester. The component sections of this model are shown in detail in Figures 6.9–6.13.*

The distributions correspond to aspects of the model. For example, the distribution 'start Saxon' is the estimated date when activity on the site began. The large square brackets down the left hand side of these figures along with the OxCal keywords define the overall model exactly.

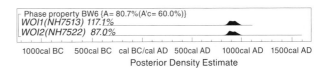

Fig. 6.9   *Probability distributions of dates from Property BW 6 at Northgate House, Winchester. Each distribution represents the relative probability that an event occurred at a particular time. For each of the dates two distributions have been plotted, one in outline, which is the result produced by the scientific evidence alone, and a solid one, which is based on the chronological model used. The 'event' associated with, for example, 'WOI17513Batt', is the last firing of hearth (NH7513).*

Dates followed by a question mark have been calibrated (Stuiver and Reimer 1993), but not included in the chronological model for reasons explained in the text.

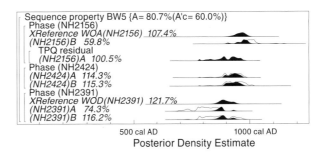

Fig. 6.10   *Probability distributions of dates from Property BW 5 at Northgate House, Winchester. The format is identical to that of Figure 6.9.*

alone was more realistic than that for the full span of the use of the properties. The component section of this model relating to Property BW 6 is shown in Fig. 6.9. Elements relating to Properties BW 5, BW 4, BW 3 and BW 2 are shown in Figs 6.10 to 6.13 respectively. The large square brackets down the left hand side of these figures along with the OxCal chronological command language define the model exactly.

This model has good overall agreement (Aoverall =80.7%, A'c=60.0%; Bronk Ramsey 1995, 429), and suggests that the Saxon occupation of these tenements began in cal 810–890 (88% probability; start Saxon; Fig. 6.8) or cal 910–940 (7% probability) and probably cal 840–890 (68% probability). It is 86.3% probable that these tenements were established before the 880s, which according to the Burghal Hidage, is regarded as the foundation date of the Alfredian *burh*. It is also probable that these properties and the associated street pattern were established after the Viking raid of Hamwic documented in AD 842 (*87.1% probable*). It is not possible to establish whether these properties were established before or after the documented Viking raid of Winchester in AD 860 (the probability that they existed before AD 860 is *41.1%*, or only after AD 860 is *58.9%*).

Properties BW 2, BW 4 and BW 5 appear to have been established in the second half of the 9th century (Fig. 6.14); it is possible that Properties BW 3 and BW 6 were established slightly later, in the

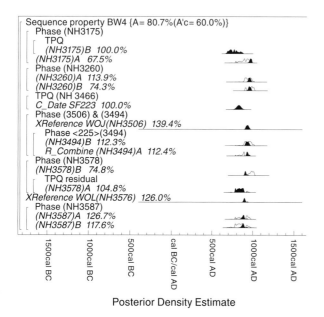

Fig. 6.11 Probability distributions of dates from Property BW 4 at Northgate House, Winchester. The format is identical to that of Figure 6.9.

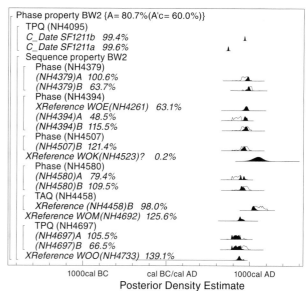

Fig. 6.13 Probability distributions of dates from Property BW 2 at Northgate House, Winchester. The format is identical to that of Figure 6.9.

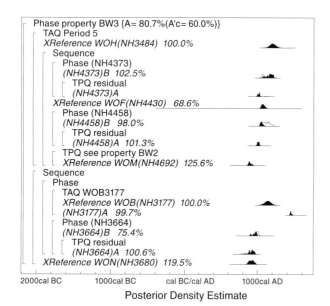

Fig. 6.12 Probability distributions of dates from Property BW 3 at Northgate House, Winchester. The format is identical to that of Figure 6.9.

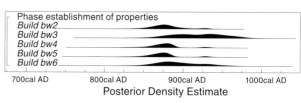

Fig. 6.14 Probability distributions of the first dated events in Properties BW 2, BW 3, BW 4, BW 5, and BW 6 at Northgate House, Winchester, derived from the model defined in Figures 6.8–6.13.

Table 6.4: Posterior density estimates from alternative models of the dating of the site phases

	Model A (contiguous sequence of posterior density estimates derived from the site chronology)	Model B (contiguous sequence of dates)	Archaeological estimate
Start site phase 4.1	cal AD 825–895 (95%)	cal AD 825–895 (74%) or 905–940 (21%)	
	cal AD 855–890 (68%)	cal AD 855–895 (58%) or 915–930 (10%)	AD 850
Transition site phase 4.1–4.2	cal AD 855–965 (95%)	cal AD 890–965 (95%)	AD 950
	cal AD 890–910 (34%) or 925–955 (34%)	cal AD 890–910 (17%) or 925–955 (51%)	
Transition site phase 4.2–5	950–1020 (95%)	cal AD 945–1055 (95%)	AD 1050
	cal AD 975–1010 (68%)	cal AD 975–1025 (68%)	
End site phase 5	cal AD 1060–1305 (95%)	cal AD 1065–1325 (95%)	AD 1225
	cal AD 1125–1245 (68%)	cal AD 1130–1250 (68%)	

first half of the 10th century. However, the earlier parts of the sequences from Properties BW 3 and BW 6 are more poorly dated than those from the other properties. The establishment of Properties BW 2, 4 and 5 might therefore have formed part of a planned development, and it is possible that the other two properties were also established as part of this initial phase. It is possible that the properties could have been built up over a few decades rather than all being established at exactly the same time. Either way, it is likely that the first inhabitants of each tenement knew each other, and that occupation in this place, at this time, was directly related to the development of Brudene Street.

Archaeological interpretation: the ceramic chronologies

The site matrix provides the primary means of presenting change through time derived from stratigraphic relationships. Further to this, ceramic typologies provide means of exploring change through time at the site. Four pottery site phases were established at Winchester Northgate House which have relevance for Saxon chronometric results. The pottery phases were generated from the assemblages recovered from the site, and estimates for them are shown in Table 6.4. The end of Phase 4.1 and start of Phase 4.2 is defined by the appearance of Late Saxon flinty wares. These include MAV, the probably local chalk tempered ware, with some flint. Also present in Phase 4.2 are the more diagnostic Michelmersh ware and Winchester ware. The end of Phase 4.2 and the start of Phase 5 is defined by a number of wares, most diagnostic of which is the Tripod Pitcher ware, but also represented by Newbury/Kennet Valley Fabric B, coarse grey sandy ware (MOE), sandy ware with flint and chalk (MBK), and sandy ware with flint, chalk and 'organic' temper (MAF). In actuality, the calendar dates of these pottery chronologies are relatively poorly understood, with considerable variability in the dating of individual wares, and especial reliance placed on rare finewares (see Cotter, *Digital Section 1.3*). The archaeomagnetic and radiocarbon data provide independent means of estimating the

calendar dates for these phases as described below.

The model shown in Fig. 6.15 is based on the assumption that the ceramic Phases 4.1, 4.2 and 5 are abutting (Buck *et al.* 1992; Naylor and Smith 1988), with the estimated dates of the samples

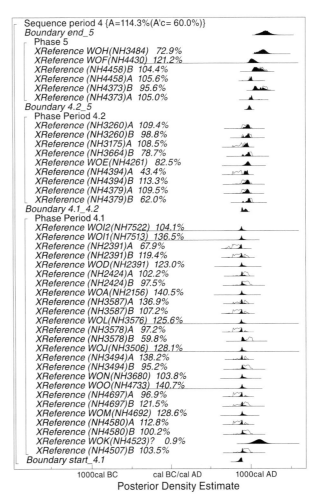

Fig. 6.15 Probability distributions of dates from ceramic phases. Each distribution represents the relative probability that an event occurs at a particular time. Posterior density estimates from the model defined in Figures 6.8–6.13 form the standardised likelihood component of this model.

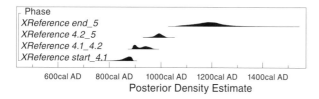

Fig. 6.16 *Probability distributions of dates relating to the beginnings and endings of ceramic phases. The distributions are derived from the model shown in Figures 6.15.*

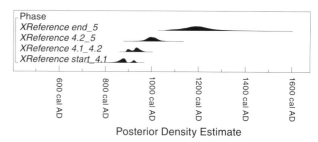

Fig. 6.17 *Probability distributions of dates relating to the beginnings and endings of ceramic phases from the alternative model where calibrated radiocarbon dates form the standardised likelihoods component of the model (see text). Each distribution represents the relative probability that an event occurs at a particular time.*

derived from the model shown in Fig. 6.8. From this, the dates of certain unknown archaeological 'events' (the beginning of ceramic Phase 4.1, the end of ceramic Phase 4.1, start of ceramic Phase 4.2, etc) can be derived as estimates of the dates of transition from one phase to another. The model has good overall agreement (Aoverall=114.3%, A'c=60.0%); estimates for the dates of ceramic phases are given in Table 6.4, and in Fig. 6.16.

Sensitivity analysis

Sensitivity analyses are alternative interpretive models constructed from alternative ways of modelling the information previously presented. By comparing different analyses it is possible to investigate the extent to which the answers are dependent on the radiocarbon measurements, and the stratigraphic sequence. The format of the model is identical to that shown in Fig. 6.15, but this time the radiocarbon and archaeomagentic dates have not been derived from the model shown in Fig. 6.8. This has been undertaken to explore how much the results are influenced by the stratigraphic relationship between samples. The model has good overall agreement (Aoverall=109.4%, A'c=60.0%); estimates for the dates of ceramic phases are given in Table 6.4, and in Fig. 6.17. The results suggest that the use of prior estimates derived from the stratigraphic relationships between samples in Fig. 6.8 included in the model shown in Fig. 6.15 does not strongly affect the outputs of the model.

OTHER ARCHAEOLOGICAL FEATURES

Radiocarbon results were generated from a number of features that were stratigraphically isolated or which contained material culture of uncertain period attribution. The measurements listed below were intended to clarify the phase attribution of these features or material culture. All these contexts were originally recorded as being below the late Roman dark earth and the late prehistoric/early Roman subsoil layers (Steve Teague pers. comm.).

The Northgate House contexts are effectively stratigraphically isolated from the street frontage area. The results from Northgate House (OxA-16757, -16758, -16759, -16775) which proved to

represent further Saxon activity on the site, were not included in the model for the Saxon tenements because the features were not stratigraphically related.

The neonate burial

A single radiocarbon measurement was produced on the neonate burial recovered from context (NH6176) from Northgate House. The result indicates that the individual died in the early first millennium; most probably in the late 1st to early 3rd century cal AD (cal AD 30–210 95.4% confidence; or cal AD 70–130 68.2% confidence; OxA-16713). The collagen from this sample had a $\delta^{13}C$ value of -18.6 ‰, a $\delta^{15}N$ value of 9.8 ‰. and a C/N ratio of 3.2, all of which are within the normal range for human bone. The C:N value of gelatinous extracts of sampled bone is one means to assess collagen preservation, potential diagenesis and to ensure the measurement of in vivo derived carbon isotopes. Ratios between 2.9 and 3.6 are indicative of carbon and nitrogen proportions from unaltered bone (see Hedges and van Klinken 1992).

Northgate House negative features

Four radiocarbon measurements were produced on charred plant remains from two features from Northgate House.

Context NH6177

Two measurements were produced on samples of bread wheat, from the fill (NH6177) of a posthole (NH6178), part of Structure NH8502. The measurements made on these wheat samples are statistically consistent (T'=0.2, T'5%=3.8, v=1; OxA-16757, -16758). The consistency in the measurements could indicate that the dated material derives from the same short-lived phase of archaeological activity, in this case, the harvesting of the cereal grains. This interpretation means it would be appropriate to take a weighted mean prior to calibration; the resultant estimate for the harvesting of the cereal grains is cal 870–975 (95.4% confidence; or cal 890–945 68.2% confidence).

The weighted mean provides an estimate for the presence of the wheat grains on the site in the 9th or 10th century. Bread wheat is considered a staple in the Saxon period in southern England, and its presence during this period is unsurprising. This calibrated range also provides a *terminus post quem* for the infilling of the posthole. If the association of the posthole with the rest of the structure is accurate, this estimate would be applicable for at least a phase of use of the structure. The consistency of the results from this feature provides robust support for the interpretation that the posthole was infilled in the Saxon period, not during an earlier phase of activity on the site.

Context NH6204

Two measurements were produced on charred bread wheat grains recovered from the fill (NH6204) of a shallow pit (NH6203). The measurements made on these wheat grains were statistically consistent (T'=0.3, T'5%=3.8, v=1; OxA-16759, -16775). These results indicate that the wheat grains sampled to produce these data could have been harvested at the same point in time. Because these measurements could be related, it could be more appropriate to take a weighted mean prior to calibration. The estimate for the harvesting of these cereal grains is cal 775–950 (95.4% confidence; or cal 780–895 68.2% confidence). The material was most probably harvested in the 9th century. This mean provides a *terminus post quem* for the infilling of the pit, most probably in the 9th century.

Discussion

All the results on the cereal grains detailed here are statistically consistent, indicating that they all could measure the same point in time, or a short-lived phase of activity. The results from posthole NH6177 are entirely consistent with the results from pit NH6204 (T'=1.4, T'5%=7.8, v=3). If all these measurements were related to the same event, a weighted mean would suggest that this took place cal 780–970 (95.4% probable; or cal 870–950; OxA-16757, -16758, -16759, -16775).

Holloway

Two radiocarbon measurements were produced on material from context (CC3251) recovered from the Holloway in the Discovery Centre (CC3408). The measurements were produced on disarticulated faunal remains. One measurement was produced on a rib from a large mammal, probably cattle (OxA-16793), and one result was produced on a tooth from an ovicaprid (OxA-16794). The two results are not statistically consistent (T'=65.3%, T'5%=3.8, V=1), indicating that the measurements

sampled different archaeological events. Neither of the results are thought to include offsets (neither *in vivo* dietary offsets, nor post-mortem contamination). The inconsistency of the results could indicate that the Holloway was open for a considerable period of time, from 40 cal BC–cal AD 90 (95.4% confidence, or cal AD 1–70 (68.2% confidence; OxA-16793) to cal AD 260–430 (95.4% confidence, or cal AD 340–420 68.2% confidence; OxA-16794). The interpretation of a long-lived landscape feature is, however, problematic because of the uncertain taphonomies of the dated skeletal material.

There are a number of issues concerning the taphonomy of both the dated skeletal elements:

- the material is disarticulated;
- the material does not derive from a context which indicates a functional association between the skeletal material and the depositional environment;
- the material is not of the same radiocarbon age;
- the feature does not represent a 'sealed' context, one which demonstrably can be shown to have been infilled rapidly, or one which contains a range of material culture derived from a limited phase of activity.

Both these results provide poorly understood *termini post quos* for the infilling of the Holloway. It is possible that both these results were produced on redeposited material derived from other primary depositional contexts; neither of these results should be used as robust basis for the phasing of the feature or its use. Both these results could provide mistakenly early estimates. The date of establishment of the Holloway certainly cannot be estimated from these results. The later result should be seen as the most accurate *terminus post quem* for the infilling of the feature of cal AD 260–430 (95.4% confidence; or cal AD 340–420 68.2% confidence; OxA-16794).

SUMMARY OF SIGNIFICANT FINDINGS

- The Saxon occupation of these tenements began in cal 810–890 (*88% probability; start Saxon*; Fig. 6.8) or cal 910–940 (*7% probability*) and probably cal 840–890 (*68% probability*).

- It is *86.3% probable* that these tenements were established before the 880s, which according to the Burghal Hidage, is regarded as the foundation date of the Alfredian *burh*.

- Properties BW 2, BW 4 and BW 5 appear to have been established in the second half of the 9th century.

- It is possible that Properties BW 3 and BW 6 were established slightly later, in the first half of the 10th century. However, Properties BW 3 and BW 6 are more poorly dated for the earlier parts of their sequences than the other properties, meaning the models for these properties are slightly less robust than the others.

- The establishment of Properties BW 2, 4 and 5 might therefore have formed part of a planned development, and it is possible that the other two properties were also established as part of this initial phase.

- It is possible that the properties could have been built up over a few decades rather than all being established at exactly the same time.

- It is likely that the first inhabitants of each tenement knew each other, and that the earliest Saxon occupation sampled here was directly related to the development of Brudene Street.

- Four pottery site phases were established at Winchester Northgate House, and estimates for the transition between these pottery typologies (as presented in the Bayesian model Fig. 6.15) are shown in Table 6.4, and in Fig. 6.16.

- On present understanding, the Holloway cannot be demonstrably phased to any period by the chronometric results alone.

Chapter 7
Overview of the Finds Assemblages

POTTERY

Prehistoric Pottery *by Lisa Brown*

A total of 105 sherds (1462 g) of later prehistoric pottery were recovered from the Northgate House (NH) and Discovery Centre (CC) sites (Fig. 7.1). Of this total, 94 sherds (1293 g) came from NH and 10 sherds (131 g) from the CC site. The pottery possibly dates from as early as the late Bronze Age/early Iron Age transition (c 8th century BC) to the late Iron Age. This report is derived from a more detailed digital report (see *Digital Section 1.1*).

Six fabric groups incorporating 13 varieties were identified (Table 7.1), all previously recorded at other sites in the vicinity.

Fabric A: Sandy fabric with variety of coarse inclusions, flint, shell, chalk. (1 variety)

Fabric B: Predominantly flint-tempered (4 varieties)

Fabric C: Predominantly shell-tempered (2 varieties)

Fabric D: Predominantly sand-tempered (3 varieties)

Fabric E: Smooth fine clay (2 varieties)

Fabric H: Oolitic limestone-tempered (1 variety)

Fabrics A and B and one of the D varieties are likely to be of relatively local origin, manufactured using raw materials of the chalk downs. The shell-tempered and oolitic limestone fabrics have a Jurassic source. One of the sandy fabrics (D15), which has a high glauconite content, has been sourced to clay outcrops of the Nadder Valley near Salisbury (Williams and Wandibba 1984). Both varieties of fabric E, a brickearth, also have a Wiltshire source in the Salisbury area. A single sherd in a fine sandy fabric with quartzite, chalk and shell

inclusions (fabric E) recovered from a posthole in a Phase 4 tenement may be early Iron Age.

Fabric B1 is a common and well-documented fabric utilised in the manufacture of middle Iron Age pottery of the 'St. Catherine's Hill – Worthy Down' type in Hampshire (Cunliffe 1991). Fabric B12 is a smooth clay with rare flint inclusions, somewhat underfired and highly abraded. It corresponds to early Iron Age fabrics from other sites in the region. Fabric B4 has a notable mica content and is very hard fired, possibly a late Iron Age type.

Only nine sherds were classifiable by vessel form and none was decorated (Table 7.2). Three are early Iron Age situlate jar forms in sandy wares—JB2, JB2/3 and JB3.1 (Fig. 7.1, nos. 1–2). A flattened pedestal base in fine shell-tempered ware may belong to a variety of globular jar form with outcurving rim dated to the early-middle Iron Age at Danebury (Cunliffe 1984, 281 and fig. 4.46), but the latter tend to have a raised rather than flat pedestal base.

The remaining five vessels are middle Iron Age types. Two are ovoid jars with incipient bead-rims (JC2), both in flint-tempered ware B1 (Fig. 7.1, no.

Table 7.1: Prehistoric pottery: quantification of fabrics

Fabric group	CC No.	CC Wt	NH No.	NH Wt	Total No.	Total Wt.
A			1	12g	1	12g
B	10	131g	53	688g	63	819g
C			18	223g	18	223g
D			14	180g	14	142g
E			7	72g	7	72g
H			1	35	1	35g

Table 7.2: Prehistoric pottery: forms

Form	Description	Cxt/phase	Ceramic Date	Vessels	Fabric
JB2	Shouldered jar, upstanding rim	NH1613 PR1: Structure NH8505	EIA	1	D15/18
JB2/3	See JB2/JB3	NH4217 MED	EIA	1	D15/18
JB3.1	Large rounded jar, squared upstanding rim	6200 PR1: Structure NH8502	EIA	1	D0
JC2.3	Ovoid jar with proto bead-rim	NH6169 PR1: Structure NH8503	MIA	1	B1
BS3	Flat pedestal base	NH3186	EMIA	1	C01
PB1.1	Straight-walled 'saucepan pot'	NH7607 PR2 : Structure NH8506			
		NH6165 PR2 : Structure NH8505	MIA	3	B1
JC2	Ovoid jar with proto bead rim	CC1701	MIA	1	B1

4). The others are straight-walled vessels commonly referred to as 'saucepan' pots (Fig. 7.1, nos 5, 6). These are also in fabric B1 and finished with a high burnish.

It is possible that some of the earliest pottery belongs to a late Bronze Age/early Iron transitional period but, in the absence of diagnostic sherds of late Bronze Age type, this remains uncertain. Only just over half of all prehistoric sherds were judged to be contemporary with the deposits from which they were recovered, mostly relating to postholes or gullies associated with roundhouses. The remainder of the prehistoric assemblage was residual in Roman and later contexts. Nonetheless, sufficient numbers of distinctive sherds with early or middle Iron Age characteristics were identified to confirm that the structures represented at least two phases of Iron Age occupation on the site.

Although the prehistoric pottery assemblage from the site and from Cunliffe's excavations in the same area (Cunliffe 1964) is small and fragmentary, it clearly corresponds to larger, well-preserved groups recovered from elsewhere in Winchester, and from the wider Hampshire region, including St. Catherine's Hill (Hawkes 1976), Winnall Down (Fasham 1985), Old Down Farm (Davies 1981) and Danebury and its Environs (Cunliffe 1984; Cunliffe and Poole 1991).

Catalogue of illustrated pottery (Fig. 7.1)

1. Jar with upright rim. Fabric D15. Posthole NH1615 (NH1613), Structure NH8508.
2. Jar with lightly thumbed, upstanding rim. Fabric D0. Posthole NH6199 (NH6200), Structure NH8502
3. Ovoid jar. Fabric B1, burnished. Posthole NH6168 (NH6169), possibly relating to Structure NH8504

4. Saucepan pot or ovoid jar. Fabric B1, burnished. Gully NH6163 (NH6165), Structure NH8505
5. Saucepan pot. Fabric B1, burnished. Pit NH7500 (NH7501). Residual in Property J pit, Phase 5
6. Saucepan pot. Fabric B1, burnished. Gully NH7610 (NH7607), Structure NH8506

Roman Pottery *by Edward Biddulph and Paul Booth*

Just over 10,000 sherds weighing 176 kg were collected from deposits phased to the Roman period. A total of 109 fabrics were identified. Fabric quantifications are provided in Table 7.3. Full fabric descriptions, summarised below, can be found in Matthews and Holmes (forthcoming). Descriptions of traded wares can be found in Tomber and Dore (1998), whose fabric codes are shown against the fabric list below in parentheses. This report is an edited version of a more detailed digital report (see *Digital Section 1.2*).

Fabrics

Samian ware
TCA   Central Gaulish samian ware (LEZ SA 2)
TCB   Central Gaulish samian ware, Les Martres de Veyre (LMV SA)
TCC   Central Gaulish samian ware, 1st-century Lezoux (LEZ SA 1)
TSA   South Gaulish samian ware, La Graufesenque (LGF SA)
TUS   Miscellaneous samian ware
TUS(EG) East Gaulish samian ware, all sources

Fine wares
RF   Orange fabric with dense fine sands and occasional medium quartz grains; common iron oxides and mica plates.
RFB   Pinkish orange fabric with fine sand, iron oxides, grey ware and mica-dusted surfaces

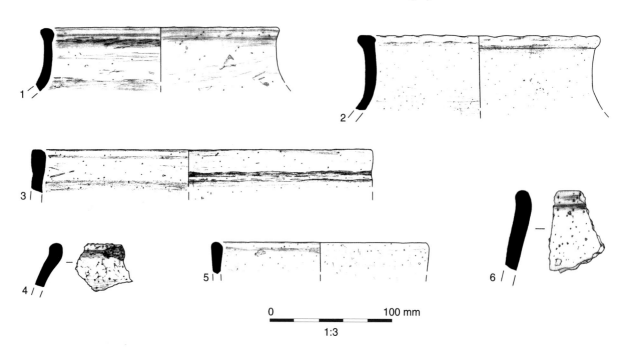

0   100 mm
1:3

Fig. 7.1   Prehistoric pottery (1–6)

T Unsourced or uncertain fine colour-coated fabrics

T(EPO) Céramique à l'éponge (EPO MA)

TBC Central Gaulish black colour-coated ('Rhenish') ware (CNG BS)

TBF Miscellaneous fine wares of uncertain origin

TCR Colchester colour-coated ware (COL CC 2)

TF New Forest colour-coated ware; oxidised iron-rich fabric (Fulford 1975a, 25, fabric 1b; NFO RS 1)

TFC New Forest colour-coated ware, fabric 1c (Fulford 1975a, 25)

TGA Orange-red fine grained micaceous fabric with fine grit and bright red ferrous inclusions

TGC Cologne colour-coated ware (KOL CC)

THT East Gaulish black colour-coated ('Rhenish') ware (MOS BS)

TLA Lyon ware (LYO CC)

TN Terra Nigra (GAB TN 1)

TO/TOR Oxfordshire red/brown colour-coated ware (Young 1977, 123) (OXF RS)

TR New Forest colour-coated ware; reduced iron-rich fabric (Fulford 1975a, 24-5, fabric 1a)

Amphorae

A Unsourced or uncertain amphora fabric

A(LIP) Liparian amphorae, Richborough 527 fabric (LIP AM)

ACE Camulodunum 186 fabric (Peacock and Williams 1986, 120-123)

ADA Dressel 20 fabric (Peacock and Williams 1986, 139-140 (BAT AM 1)

ADAR ?Late version of Dressel 20 fabric with red/brown core

ADB Dressel 2-4 fabric (Peacock and Williams 1986, 105-106)

AFN African cylindrical amphora fabrics (Peacock and Williams 1986, 158-165) (NAF AM 1/2)

AMB ?Eastern Mediterranean amphora fabric. Hard micaceous fabric with brown outer surface and light orange inner surface and core.

APA Gauloise 4 fabric (Peacock and Williams 1986, 142-143)

APB Gallic amphora fabric, probably belonging to the Gauloise series

ASS Southern Spanish amphora fabric, usually Dressel 20 and Dressel 23

Mortaria

J Unsourced or uncertain mortarium fabric

JHA Hard, granular, greyish-cream fabric. A Hampshire product.

JHC Hard fabric, too fine to be considered granular. A Hampshire product.

JHD Similar to JHC, but pale brown to orange-brown in colour. A Hampshire product.

JMA Oxfordshire white ware (Young 1977, 56) (OXF WH)

JMI Rhineland. Hard cream fabric with pale pinkish-orange core

JMU Oxfordshire white-slipped oxidised ware (Young 1977, 117) (OXF WS)

JMV New Forest red-slipped ware (Fulford 1975a, 25; fabric 1b)

JMW Oxfordshire red colour-coated ware (Young 1977, 123) (OXF RS)

JMY New Forest parchment ware (Fulford 1975a, 26; fabric 2a)

JPR Uncertain origin. Soft cream fabric

JRB Rhineland. Self-coloured, smooth, hard and slightly micaceous cream fabric, sometimes with pink core. (RHL WH)

White wares

U Unsourced or uncertain white ware fabrics

UF Fine white ware, occasional iron oxides

UF(NOG) North Gaulish fine white ware (NOG WH 1/2)

UFA Fine white fabric with internal colour-coat; possibly identical to Cirencester fabric 21 (Rigby 1982, 156) and Exeter fabric 105 (Holbrook and Bidwell 1991, 139).

UFN New Forest parchment ware (fine), fabric 2b (Fulford 1975a, 26) (NFO WH 2)

UM White ware with medium sands and common iron oxides

UMP New Forest parchment ware (sandy), fabric 2a (Fulford 1975a, 26) (NFA PA)

Oxidised wares

Red wares

NF Micaceous fabric with moderate fine sand and iron oxides

NFA Micaceous fabric with fine sand; possibly originally mica-dusted

NFB Red fabric with fine sand and iron oxides

NM Micaceous fabric with medium sand and occasional iron oxides

Pink wares

V Unsourced or uncertain pink fabrics

VF Fine pink ware with common iron oxides

VMB Pink ware with medium sands and iron oxides with a yellow or buff slip

Orange wares

WAA Orange fabric with dense fine transparent sands, scattered medium sand, common iron oxides and white slip

WC Orange fabric with medium and coarse sand

WF Dense fine transparent sands and common iron oxides

WFA Orange fabric with sparse fine sand and iron oxides

WFB Orange fabric with fine sand, iron oxides and white slip

WFC Micaceous orange fabric with fine sand, iron oxides and white slip

WFF Orange fabric with fine sand and small soft limestone fragments

WFJ Orange fabric with fine sand, iron oxides and black or grey exterior slip

WM Orange fabric with medium sand and iron oxides

WMA Dense medium sands, transparent, clear or iron-stained red; common iron oxides and white slip

WMG Moderately micaceous orange fabric with medium sand, iron oxides and grey core

WMN Orange fabric with medium sand, iron oxides, grey core and external slip

WO Oxfordshire oxidised ware, fabric 1 (Young 1977, 185)

Buff wares

Y Unsourced or uncertain buff wares

Y(PNKGT) Pink grogged ware (PNK GT)

Table 7.3: Roman pottery: quantification of fabrics (+ = less than 0.5%)

Fabric	Sherds	% sherds	Weight (g)	% weight	MV	% MV	EVE	% EVE
Samian ware								
TCA	204	2.0	2309	1.3	63	4.1	3.91	2.7
TCB	1	+	15	+				
TCC	1	+	5	+				
TSA	65	0.6	515	0.3	24	1.6	1.71	1.2
TUS	6	0.1	60	+	1	0.1	0.18	0.1
TUS(EG)	39	0.4	410	0.2	11	0.7	0.69	0.5
Subtotal	316	3.1	3314	1.9	99	6.5	6.49	4.4
Fine wares								
RF	2	+	6	+				
RFB	6	0.1	34	+				
T	1	+	2	+				
T(EPO)	2	+	20	+	1	0.1	0.06	+
TBC	4	+	14	+	1	0.1	0.10	0.1
TBF	7	0.1	28	+	2	0.1	0.18	0.1
TCR	2	+	12	+	1	0.1	0.18	0.1
TF	182	1.8	2300	1.3	48	3.1	3.69	2.5
TFC	1	+	7	+	1	0.1	0.03	+
TGA	1	+	3	+				
TGC	7	0.1	20	+	1	0.1	0.03	+
THT	11	0.1	41	+	4	0.3	0.96	0.7
TLA	1	+	1	+				
TN	4	+	35	+	1	0.1	0.03	+
TO/TOR	124	1.2	1714	1.0	32	2.1	2.32	1.6
TR	835	8.3	9113	5.2	83	5.4	15.86	10.8
Subtotal	1190	11.8	13350	7.6	175	11.5	23.44	16.0
Amphorae								
A	25	0.2	1204	0.7				
A(LIP)	2	+	143	0.1	1	0.1	0.09	0.1
ACE	5	+	475	0.3				
ADA	64	0.6	9108	5.2	1	0.1	0.33	0.2
ADA R	26	0.3	2677	1.5				
ADB	1	+	14	+				
AFN	4	+	397	0.2				
AMB	2	+	107	0.1				
APA	4	+	93	0.1				
APB	21	0.2	1647	0.9				
ASS	96	1.0	7253	4.1				
Subtotal	250	2.5	23118	13.1	2	0.1	0.42	0.3
Mortaria								
J	1	+	7	+				
JHA	6	0.1	233	0.1	4	0.3	0.35	0.2
JHC	1	+	58	+	1	0.1	0.05	+
JHD	2	+	221	0.1	2	0.1	0.23	0.2
JMA	11	0.1	339	0.2	4	0.3	0.33	0.2
JMI	1	+	36	+	1	0.1	0.05	+
JMU	11	0.1	347	0.2	3	0.2	0.31	0.2
JMV	14	0.1	229	0.1	5	0.3	0.26	0.2
JMW	31	0.3	812	0.5	10	0.7	0.92	0.6
JMY	19	0.2	862	0.5	9	0.6	0.78	0.5
JPR	1	+	91	0.1	1	0.1	0.06	+
JRB	1	+	174	0.1	1	0.1	0.10	0.1
Subtotal	99	1.0	3409	1.9	41	2.7	344	2.3

Table 7.3: Roman pottery: quantification of fabrics (+ = less than 0.5%) (continued)

Fabric	Sherds	% sherds	Weight (g)	% weight	MV	% MV	EVE	% EVE
White wares								
U	1	+	4	+				
UF	18	0.2	111	0.1	2	0.1	0.36	0.2
UF(NOG)	1	+	3	+				
UFA	1	+	5	+				
UFN	33	0.3	973	0.6	10	0.7	1.07	0.7
UM	14	0.1	136	0.1	3	0.2	0.24	0.2
UMP	71	0.7	2303	1.3	13	0.9	1.21	0.8
Subtotal	139	1.4	3535	2.0	28	1.8	2.88	2.0
Oxidised wares								
NF	1	+	2	+				
NFA	5	+	31	+	1	0.1	0.13	0.1
NFB	2	+	5	+				
NM	1	+	5	+				
V	2	+	34	+				
VF	6	0.1	4	+				
VMB	1	+	22	+				
WAA	1	+	15	+				
WC	14	0.1	289	0.2	1	0.1	0.09	0.1
WF	51	0.5	548	0.3	4	0.3	0.51	0.3
WFA	3	+	20	+				
WFB	5	+	36	+	1	0.1	0.23	0.2
WFC	1	+	14	+				
WFF	1	+	2	+				
WFJ	1	+	2	+				
WM	51	0.5	554	0.3	7	0.5	1.46	1.0
WMA	3	+	64	+	1	0.1	0.50	0.3
WMG	1	+	26	+				
WMN	1	+	2	+				
WO	2	+	78	+	1	0.1	0.16	0.1
Y	1	+	13	+				
Y(PNKGT)	1	+	58	+	1	0.1	0.12	0.1
YC	224	2.2	6936	3.9	2	0.1	0.24	0.2
YF	36	0.3	228	0.1	1	0.1	0.25	0.2
YFA	1	+	5	+				
YFD	3	+	37	+				
YFP	2	+	6	+				
YM	35	0.3	439	0.2	4	0.3	0.16	0.1
YM(OVW)	11	0.1	129	0.1	4	0.3	0.30	0.2
YMD	1	+	4	+				
YMZ	1	+	12	+	1	0.1	0.02	+
Subtotal	469	4.7	9620	5.5	29	1.9	4.17	2.8
Reduced wares								
Z	1	+	16	+				
ZC	210	2.1	4039	2.3	22	1.4	1.33	0.9
ZC(MAY)	1	+	61	+	1	0.1	0.19	0.1
ZCZ	10	0.1	386	0.2	2	0.1	0.08	0.1
ZF	621	6.2	7998	4.5	113	7.4	12.60	8.6
ZFB	6	0.1	42	+				
ZFE	2	+	44	+				
ZFG	1	+	1	+				
ZFZ	356	3.5	5088	2.9	66	4.3	9.39	6.4
ZH/ZHA	10	0.1	123	0.1	1	0.1	0.10	0.1
ZM	2875	28.6	33192	18.9	371	24.3	31.78	21.7
ZM+	8	0.1	244	0.1	3	0.2	0.31	0.2

continued overleaf

Table 7.3: Roman pottery: quantification of fabrics (+ = less than 0.5%) (continued)

Fabric	Sherds	% sherds	Weight (g)	% weight	MV	% MV	EVE	% EVE
ZME	11	0.1	169	0.1	1	0.1	0.23	0.2
ZMF	20	0.2	743	0.4	6	0.4	0.42	0.3
ZMJ	96	1.0	1178	0.7	16	1.0	0.97	0.7
ZMO	1	+	7	+	1	0.1	0.05	+
ZMR	2	+	21	+	1	0.1	0.05	+
ZMT	1	+	38	+				
ZMU	1	+	33	+				
ZMZ	1750	17.4	32466	18.4	271	17.7	25.65	17.5
Subtotal	5983	59.5	85889	48.8	875	57.3	83.15	56.7
Black-burnished ware								
ZMA	257	2.6	4392	2.5	69	4.5	5.28	3.6
Grog-tempered wares								
SG	1184	11.8	24306	13.8	205	13.4	17.21	11.7
SGA	124	1.2	4263	2.4	2	0.1	0.11	0.1
SGD	2	+	54	+				
Subtotal	1310	13.0	28623	16.3	207	13.5	17.32	11.8
'Iron Age' wares								
XF	2	+	22	+				
XM	37	0.4	718	0.4	3	0.2	0.14	0.1
Subtotal	39	0.4	740	0.4	3	0.2	0.14	0.1
TOTAL	10052		175990		1528		146.73	

YC   Buff fabric with medium to coarse sand and iron oxides

YF   Buff fabric with fine sand

YFA   Micaceous pinkish buff fabric with sparse fine and medium sands and iron oxides

YFD   Buff fabric with fine sand, iron oxides and grey core

YFP   Buff fabric with fine sand and distinctive pink internal surface

YM   Buff fabric with dense medium sands and common iron oxides

YM(OVW)   Overwey ware (OVW WH)

YMD   Buff fabric with medium sand, iron oxides and grey core

YMZ   As YM, but with additional iron oxides

Reduced (grey and black) wares

Z   Unsourced or uncertain grey wares

ZC   Coarse sandy grey ware

ZC(MAY)   Mayen ware (MAY CO)

ZCZ   As ZC, but with additional iron oxides

ZF   Fine grey ware

ZFB   Very pale greyish white fabric with grey/white slipped surfaces; sparse fine sands

ZFE   Fine grained micaceous fabric with oxidised internal surface

ZFG   Grey fabric with fine sands, iron oxides, grog and oxidised slip

ZFZ   As ZF, but with additional iron oxides

ZH/ZHA Shell-tempered ware

ZM   Medium sandy grey ware

ZM+   Fabric ZM with additional sparse/moderate large sub-rounded pale grey inclusions

ZME   Medium-grained grey ware with common chalk inclusions

ZMF   Buff fabric with pinkish surfaces, commonly finger-wiped; dense sands and common iron oxides. Storage jar fabric.

ZMJ   Medium-grained grey ware with scattered grog-tempering

ZMO   Medium-grained moderately micaceous fabric

ZMR   Medium-grained fabric with scattered flint and grog

ZMT   Medium-grained fabric with dark grey core, oxidised surfaces and margins, and occasional grog

ZMU   Slightly micaceous medium-grained buff fabric with scattered flint and grog. Storage jar fabric.

ZMZ   As ZM, but with additional iron oxides

Black-burnished ware

ZMA   Black-burnished ware, category 1 (DOR BB 1)

Grog-tempered wares

SG   Dark grey fabric with abundant fine sand and common grog and iron oxides (includes Tomber and Dore 1998, 139; HAM GT)

Table 7.4: *Roman pottery: list of key ceramic groups*

Stratigraphic phase	Ceramic phase	Context groups
2.1	AD 55–70	CC1661, CC1740, CC1772, CC2370, CC3272, CC3345
2.1	AD 70–130	CC1738, CC1739, CC1754, CC1781, CC1804, CC1805, CC1858, CC2080, CC2158, CC2365, CC3269, CC3345, CC3459
2.2	AD 130–260	CC1702, CC3418, NH6194, NH7612
2.3	AD 260–330	CC1637, CC1697, CC3331, NH1263, NH1380, NH7517, NH7575
2.4	AD 350–410	CC1579, CC1630, CC2185, NH1398, NH3745, NH4718, NH5059

Table 7.5: *Roman pottery: list of forms represented in key groups*

Form code	Description
Amphorae	
A	Amphorae
Flagons/jugs	
B	Flagons/jugs, general
BA	Small flagons (up to 60 mm rim diameter)
BB	Larger flagons
Jars	
C	Jars, general
CB	Barrel shaped jars
CC	Narrow mouthed jars (rim diameter less than 2/3 girth)
CD	Medium mouthed jars, usually oval-bodied necked jars
CE	High shouldered necked jars
CG	Globular jars
CH	Bead rim jars
CI	Angled everted rim jars
CJ	Lid seated jars
CK	'Cooking pot type' jars
CM	Wide mouthed jars
CN	Storage jars
Jars or bowls	
D	Jar or bowl (a category for types where insufficient survives to allow an estimate of the height:diameter ratio)
DC	Necked jar/bowl
Beakers	
E	Beakers
EA	Butt beakers
EC	Bag shaped beakers
ED	Globular/bulbous beakers
EE	Indented beakers
EF	Poppyhead beakers
EH	'Jar' beaker, usually small examples of cooking-pot jar types
Cups	
F	Cups, general
FA	Hemispherical cups

Form code	Description
FB	Campanulate cups
FC	Conical cups
Mugs/tankards	
GB	Handled mugs/bowls
Bowls	
H	Bowls, general
HA	Carinated bowls
HB	Straight sided (usually flat-based bead and flange-rimmed) bowls
HC	Curving sided bowls
HD	Necked bowls
HG	Globular (not necked) bowls
Bowls or dishes	
I	Bowls/dishes. An indeterminate category, accommodating vessels where insufficient survives to be reasonably sure about the rim diameter:height ratio
IA	Straight sided bowls/dishes
IB	Curving sided bowls/dishes
Dishes	
J	Dishes and platters, general
JA	Straight sided dishes (plain-, bead-, and flange-rimmed)
JB	Curving sided dishes (plain-, bead-, and flange-rimmed)
JC	Platters
JD	Fish dishes
Mortaria	
K	Mortaria, general
KC	Hammer-headed mortaria
KD	Wall-sided mortaria
KE	Tall bead/stubby flanged mortaria
Lids	
L	Lids, general
Miscellaneous	
MB	Candlestick
MG	Strainer

SGA Moderately to heavily grog-tempered fabric with iron oxides and a sandy texture. Reserved for storage jars.

SGD Moderately grog-tempered fabric with iron oxides and fine to medium sands

Wares in the Iron Age tradition

XF Handmade fabric with fine sand and common flint

XM Handmade fabric with medium sand and common flint

Key ceramic groups

A number of key ceramic groups were selected from the entire Roman-period assemblage to provide a picture of the changing pattern of pottery supply to Northgate House and the Discovery Centre sites. The selected context groups generally contained a wide range of forms and fabrics and were well-dated to one of the four stratigraphic phases (Phases 2.1–4); occasionally it was possible to sub-divide these periods into narrower ceramic phases (Table 7.4). Summary descriptions of the vessel type codes used in the quantified tables are given in Table 7.5.

Phase 2.1: Ceramic phase AD 55–70 (Table 7.6)

A total of six ceramic groups, each containing an average of 0.42 EVEs, were assigned a pre-Flavian date (Table 7.6); all were from the Discovery Centre site. Little of this material is likely to date before AD 50 or 60. Good indicators included a *terra nigra Cam* 52 carinated bowl, a type that generally reached Britain after *c* AD 55 (Greene 1979, 111), and the so-called 'Atrebatic' curving-sided bowl that was attested at Alice Holt after AD 60 (Lyne and Jefferies 1979, 30). At the same time, butt-beakers and body sherds from a Drag. 15/17 South Gaulish samian platter suggest an upper date for the key-group assemblage of *c* AD 70/80. Overall, the assemblage was dominated by grey wares, which took an 82% share of the key-group assemblage by EVE. Medium-sandy grey ware without iron oxides were commonest, but that with iron oxides also made a significant contribution. Fine grey wares were less important; curiously, fine fabrics with iron oxides were better represented than those without. Oxidised wares enjoyed a 14% share of the assemblage by EVE. Vessels were identified in buff and red wares, but a greater range of white ware fabrics, including imported North Gaulish pottery, was evident (the New Forest parchment ware is intrusive). In terms of forms, jars were predominant, accounting for 64%; globular, bead-rimmed, and storage jars were the most important categories; high-shouldered necked jars were present, but in small numbers. Table or dining forms were well-represented too; adding the carinated and Atrebatic bowls to the platters and beakers, these took a share of over 30%.

Table 7.6: Roman pottery: key groups, Phase 2.1 (AD 55–70). Quantification by eve. Fabrics totalling 0 are present, but no rim survives.

Fabric	C	CE	Jar CG	CH	CN	Beaker EA	H	Bowl HA	HC	Dish JC	Lid L	Total	% total
ASS												0	0%
NFA						13						13	5%
TN								3				3	1%
TSA												0	0%
UF												0	0%
UF(NOG)												0	0%
UFA												0	0%
UM												0	0%
UMP							8					8	3%
WF												0	0%
WFA												0	0%
XM					6							6	2%
YC					14							14	6%
YF												0	0%
ZC					23							23	9%
ZF						6						6	2%
ZFZ				18								18	7%
ZM	18	5	34	4					8	28	7	104	41%
ZMR										5		5	2%
ZMZ	7		19	14				4		9		53	21%
Total	25	5	53	36	43	19	8	7	8	42	7	253	-
% total	10%	2%	21%	14%	17%	8%	3%	3%	3%	17%	3%	-	-

Phase 2.1: Ceramic phase AD 70–130
(Table 7.7; Fig. 7.2)

The amount of pottery being deposited at the Discovery Centre site increased between the late 1st and early 2nd century. Thirteen groups, averaging 0.52 EVEs each, were assigned to this period, although most groups did not extend beyond AD 100. The proportion of grey wares, which continued to dominate the assemblage, was little changed at 85% by EVE. Medium sandy grey ware without iron oxides remained more important than those with. Fine grey wares and coarse grey wares had reduced proportions. Oxidised wares also experienced a drop and only one form based on rims, a fine white butt-beaker, was identified. Surprisingly, given this apparent reduction in finer pottery, samian ware was better represented than in the mid 1st century, though this is part due to the fact that much more samian was reaching Britain after AD 70, and regions across southern Britain saw South Gaulish samian importation peak around AD 75/80 (eg Dannell 1999, fig. 2.1). Samian from South Gaul was joined by micaceous samian from Lezoux. South Spanish amphorae now arrived alongside containers from southern Gaul. As for forms, jars remained the most important category, though at a slightly lower proportion of 55% by EVE. Globular and bead-rimmed jars continued to be used, but a new type, the oval-bodied necked jar, was emerging as the standard vessel. Curving-sided 'Atrebatic' bowls became more important in the late 1st

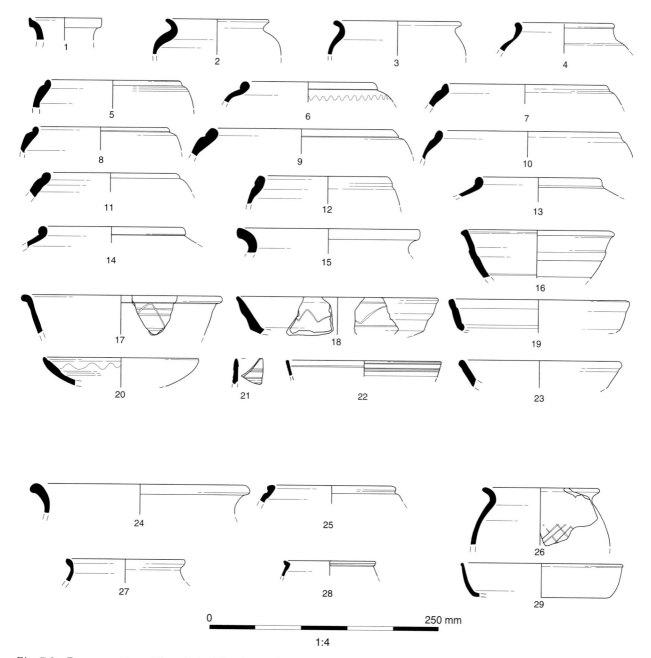

Fig. 7.2 Roman pottery: Phase 2.1, AD 70–130 (1–29)

Table 7.7: Roman pottery: key groups, Phase 2.1 (AD 70–130). Quantification by eve. Fabrics totalling 0 are present, but no rim survives.

Fabric	C	CC	CD	CE	CG	CH	CM	CN	Beaker EA	Bowl HA	HC	Platter JC	Lid L	Total	% total
APB														0	0%
ASS														0	0%
NFA														0	0%
NFB														0	0%
RFB														0	0%
TBF														0	0%
TCA														0	0%
TCC														0	0%
TGA														0	0%
TN														0	0%
TSA										5		81		86	13%
TUS														0	0%
UF									18					18	3%
UM														0	0%
WFA														0	0%
WFB														0	0%
XM														0	0%
YFA														0	0%
YFD														0	0%
YFP														0	0%
YM														0	0%
ZC								7						7	1%
ZCZ								5						5	1%
ZF														0	0%
ZFB														0	0%
ZM	76	28	107	13	68	9	11	4		3	59	80	5	463	69%
ZMR														0	0%
ZMZ				15	15	13		7				44		94	14%
Total	76	28	107	28	83	22	11	23	18	8	59	205	5	673	-
% total	11%	4%	16%	4%	12%	3%	2%	3%	3%	1%	9%	30%	1%	-	-

century, as did platters, which were boosted by samian platters Drag. 15/17, Drag. 18, and Drag. 18/31. Other samian forms—Drag. 29 decorated bowls and Drag. 27 cups—were represented by body sherds only. Beakers saw no change from the mid 1st century and still occurred as (probably residual) butt-beakers in the late 1st century.

Phase 2.2: Ceramic phase AD 130–260 (Table 7.8)

Just four ceramic groups, each containing on average 0.27 EVEs, were assigned to the mid Roman period. Phase 2.2 saw a drop in the amount of pottery being deposited at the Discovery Centre site and the first appearance of groups, albeit on a very small scale, at the Northgate House site. Its size means that the phase assemblage is unlikely to be fully representative of pottery supply and use during this time, but it provides pointers to some of the key changes from the early to mid Roman periods. Grey wares formed a larger proportion of the assemblage (now 75%) compared with the late 1st/early 2nd century. Medium sandy grey wares

without iron oxides were less important as those with iron oxides became predominant, presumably reflecting changes in principal sources. Dorset black-burnished ware, arriving during the mid 2nd century, provided more competition for traditional grey ware producers.

Fine and coarse grey wares were present only as body sherds. Oxidised wares were barely represented; only fine buff ware was recorded. Fine wares increased their proportion to 25% by EVE. Much of this included residual South Gaulish samian, but the assemblage clearly shows the emergence of Central Gaul as the main source for samian in this phase. Some fine wares reached the site from Colchester, but the source was a very minor supplier. South Spain and south Gaul continued to supply amphorae. The assemblage became less jar-orientated in this period (reducing to a 25% share) as dishes made a more significant contribution. This was due mainly to the Dorset potters, who supplied bead- or flange-rimmed dishes; these, along with plain-rimmed dishes, were

Table 7.8: Roman pottery: key groups, Phase 2.2 (AD 130–260). Quantification by eve. Fabrics totalling 0 are present, but no rim survives.

Fabric	Jar			Beaker	Cup	Bowl	Dish - bead/flanged			Dish - plain	Platter	Total	% total
	C	CC	CK	EF	FC	HC	J	JA	JB	JB	JC		
APB												0	0%
ASS												0	0%
TBF												0	0%
TCA					13							13	12%
TCR												0	0%
TSA					9						5	14	13%
WM												0	0%
XM												0	0%
YF												0	0%
ZCZ												0	0%
ZFB												0	0%
ZFE												0	0%
ZM						8			6			14	13%
ZMA								22				22	21%
ZMO	5											5	5%
ZMZ		12	10	9			4			4		39	36%
Total	5	12	10	9	22	8	4	22	6	4	5	107	-
% total	5%	11%	9%	8%	21%	7%	4%	21%	6%	4%	5%	-	-

also adopted by the local grey ware producers. Cups were better represented, while the proportion of platters had fallen sharply. Beakers still made little impact, although poppy-headed beakers had replaced butt-beakers. The small size of the group makes the significance of some of these developments doubtful.

Phase 2.3: Ceramic phase AD 260–350
(Table 7.9; Fig. 7.3)

The relative invisibility of specifically early 4th century ceramic groups at the Northgate House and the Discovery Centre sites—a phenomenon recognised elsewhere in Roman Britain (Going 1992, 101)—means that it is more useful to present data from a larger assemblage spanning the late 3rd to mid 4th centuries. Seven context groups were assigned to this period; these were generally large (averaging 2.00 EVEs), indicating that much more pottery was being used and deposited compared with previous phases. The proportion of grey wares had fallen a little to 68% by EVE. Medium sandy grey wares with iron oxides were again dominant; the proportion of those without had fallen further from its already low mid Roman level. The amount of Dorset black-burnished ware was also reduced, resulting no doubt from competition from local potters who had responded to the arrival of BB1 and adopted a range of BB1-style forms. Some of these forms were also taken up by potters making grog-tempered wares in several small-scale centres in Hampshire. Oxidised wares were better represented than they had been in the mid Roman period. This

was due almost exclusively to the arrival of white ware flagons—possibly local—and New Forest parchment wares. The New Forest industry was responsible too for the increase in fine wares (now 18%), chiefly in the reduced or dark-slipped colour-coated ware, though the red-slipped oxidised fabric was also available. Oxford red colour-coated ware was recorded in this phase, though as body sherds only. Rhenish ware from Central Gaul appears in this phase, but must be residual, since importation of the ware into Britain probably ceased by the mid 3rd century (Greene 1978, 19). Samian ware in this assemblage now included products from East Gaulish factories, which had replaced the Central Gaulish industry as the principal exporter to Britain after AD 200. East Gaulish vessels began to reach Britain by AD 140, but they appear to have been little seen in Winchester until the early 3rd century, and then in small amounts (Lyne, forthcoming). In any case, both East and South Gaulish samian, like the Rhenish ware, was residual by AD 260—or, at least, no new samian reached the town at this time—though the latest products may well have remained in use. The range of amphorae expanded in this phase; South Spanish amphorae and the now residual Gallic amphorae were joined by containers from Mediterranean and north African sources.

Jars had a larger share of the assemblage compared with the mid Roman period, although the proportion of 43% by EVE remains lower than seen in the early Roman period, suggesting that the figure seen in the previous phase was anomalous; still, the general trend was for a reduction of the proportion of jars through time. Narrow-necked jars—including jars of a type produced at Alice Holt (Lyne and Jefferies 1979, class 1A)—and cooking-pot type jars were the most prolific jar forms; the latter was especially important for potters working in grog-tempered and sandy grey wares. Flagons and beakers had a more significant place in this assemblage compared with previous phases, thanks mainly to the New Forest industry. Mortaria made their first significant appearance during this time. Simple bead- or flange-rimmed dishes continued to be deposited in the late 3rd century, but were replaced by dropped flanged dishes and bowls by the early 4th century; the intermediate incipient bead-and-flanged dishes and bowls were evident after AD 270. Plain-rimmed dishes were current throughout the phase. The dishes with plain or dropped-flange rims were based on BB1 prototypes but were more usually available in local grey ware fabrics. This was due in part to the response of local potters accommodating new forms, but it must also signal the rapid decline of supply from Dorset.

Table 7.9: Roman pottery: key groups, Phase 2.3 (AD260–350). Quantification by eve. Fabrics totalling 0 are present, but no rim survives. (Dish/bowl rim types: bead = simple bead or flanged rim; incip. b&f = incipient bead-and-flanged rim; b&f = bead-and-flanged rim or dropped flange rim.)

| Fabric | Flagon | | C | CC | CD | Jar | | | | | E | Beaker | EH | Cup |
	BA	BB				CG	CH	CK	CM	CN		EE		FC
ADA														
AFN														
AMB														
APB														
ASS														
JHA														
JHD														
JMV														
JMY														
JPR														
NFB														
RF														
SG								17		25				
TBC														
TCA														5
TF														
TGC														
TO/TOR														
TR	100										27	86		
TUS(EG)														
UFN														
UMP														
WC														
WF														
WM														
WMA		50												
XM														
YF														
ZC														
ZF					12			69						
ZFZ				40				20					16	
ZM			64		5				26					
ZMA														
ZMJ														
ZMZ			93	110		3	36	43	30	3				
Total	100	50	157	150	17	3	36	149	56	28	27	86	16	5
% total	7%	4%	11%	11%	1%	0%	3%	11%	4%	2%	2%	6%	1%	0%

Based on the key ceramic groups, it is revealing that no new BB1 is certain to have reached the Northgate House or Discovery Centre sites in the 4th century. This is consistent with the situation at other sites from the town, which saw no significant supplies after the early 4th century (Matthews and Holmes, forthcoming).

Phase 2.4: Ceramic phase AD 350–400
(Table 7.10; Figs 7.4–7.7)

The latest pottery groups had date ranges that began towards the end of Phase 2.3, but belonged to contexts assigned to stratigraphic Phase 2.4 (*c* AD 350/75–400/50). In terms of the ceramic chronology,

the groups were broadly dated to the second half of the 4th century, with certain fabrics suggesting deposition after AD 370. Taken together, the groups contained elements that suggest that they are coherent as an assemblage and representative of pottery supply during the final decades of Roman period occupation at the excavated sites. The seven groups selected each on average totalled 3.17 EVEs, suggesting that the amount of pottery available for deposition after AD 350 had increased since the first half of the 4th century.

The proportion of grey wares continued to fall and now stood at 46% by EVE. Compared with the previous ceramic phase, there was little change in

| Bowl | | J/JA incip b&f | D ish/bowl | | | K | Mortarium | | | Lid | Total | % total |
H	HC		JA/JB bead	JA/JB plain	JA/HB b&f		KC	KD	KE	L		
											0	0%
											0	0%
											0	0%
											0	0%
											0	0%
							8	5			13	1%
								21			21	1%
									3		3	0%
						11					11	1%
							6				6	0%
											0	0%
											0	0%
				7							49	3%
											0	0%
			19								24	2%
	5										5	0%
											0	0%
											0	0%
											213	15%
			19								19	1%
											0	0%
	16										16	1%
											0	0%
	14										14	1%
											0	0%
											50	4%
											0	0%
											0	0%
											0	0%
					90						171	12%
					124						200	14%
			8	16	16					7	142	10%
		13		22	19						54	4%
											0	0%
4		7	33	10						22	394	28%
4	35	20	79	55	249	11	14	26	3	29	1405	-
0%	2%	1%	6%	4%	18%	1%	1%	2%	0%	2%	-	-

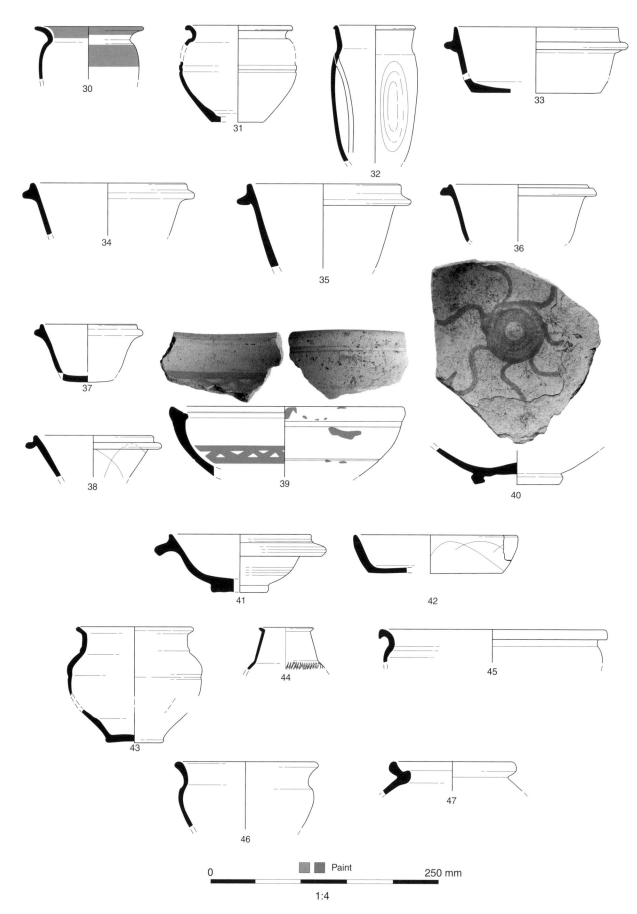

Fig. 7.3   Roman pottery: Phase 2.3, AD 260–350/400 (30–47)

the relationship between medium-sandy grey wares with and without iron oxides (those with oxides still dominating). Black-burnished ware category 1 made a token, if not residual, appearance, supporting the view that new supplies of the fabric had ceased some considerable time before the mid 4th century. Fine grey wares were similarly reduced in quantity, while coarse grey wares were unchanged. Despite the general decline of grey wares, a few new fabrics were introduced, notably storage jar fabric ZMF and shell-tempered ware ZH/ZHA. Part of the market share previously taken by sandy grey wares had been taken by Hampshire grog-tempered wares, which, since forming a minor part of the assemblage in AD 270–350, had become more important after 350, its repertoire becoming more diverse in the process.

Oxidised wares accounted for 5% of the assemblage. This was down from the previous phase, although new fabrics like Overwey ware were present, and the proportion of New Forest parchment wares remained steady. Fine wares enjoyed increased use during the second half of the 4th century, their share of the assemblage almost doubling since the first half of the century. Oxford red colour-coated ware was better represented in this phase. Data from other Winchester sites suggest

that importation of Oxford wares was reaching a peak by the middle of the 4th century (Matthews and Holmes, forthcoming). Still, the proportion of New Forest colour-coated ware beakers and flagons was not significantly different from that of the previous phase, and it appears that consumers avoided closed forms from Oxford, instead preferring New Forest products. H Rees (forthcoming) sees this relationship as complementary, though it is important to note that New Forest dishes and bowls were more plentiful than they had been during the late 3rd century and first half of the 4th century, pointing to direct competition for certain classes of vessels, especially those deriving from samian prototypes. The New Forest and Oxford industries also competed on even terms for the market in mortaria. Samian ware from Central, Eastern and Southern Gaul was recorded in the assemblage, but all occurrences must be residual, as was the East Gaulish Rhenish ware. Other imports reached the site in the form of amphorae; Gallic and South Spanish Dressel 20 amphorae were residual, but southern Spanish potters were also responsible for late Roman olive oil containers, which joined vessels from north Africa. *Céramique à l'éponge* was among the latest imports to arrive; the fabric was otherwise absent from the town, and its occurrence

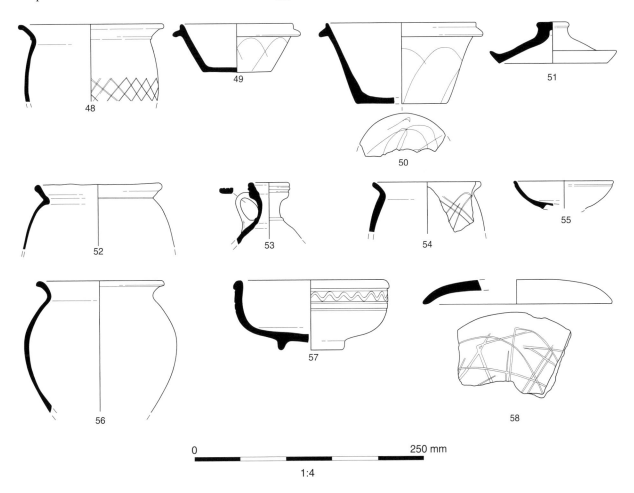

0   250 mm

1:4

Fig. 7.4   Roman pottery: Phase 2.4, AD 350–400 (48–58)

Table 7.10: Roman pottery: key groups, Phase 2.4 (AD 350–400). *Quantification by eve. Fabrics totalling 0 are present, but no rim survives. (Dish/bowl rim types: bead = simple bead or flanged rim; incip. b&f = incipient bead-and-flanged rim; b&f = bead-and-flanged rim or dropped flange rim.)*

| Fabric | Flagon | | | | | Jar | | | | | Beaker | Cup | |
	B	BA	BB	C	CC	CD	CJ	CK	CN	E	EE	FC	H
A													
ADA													
ADA R													
AFN													
APA													
APB													
ASS													
JMU													
JMV													
JMW													
JMY													
SG				97				107	6				
SGA													
T(EPO)													
TCA												19	
TF													8
THT										17	43		
TO/TOR										3			17
TR	30	100								155	100		
TSA													
TUS(EG)													
UF													
UFN													
UM													
UMP													
WC													
WF													
WFB													
WFC													
WM				6									7
XF													
YF													
YM													
YM(OVW)				11		8							
ZC				4	13								
ZF				83									
ZFZ				47						47			
ZH/ZHA													
ZM				87		34	2						
ZMA									10				
ZMF				11									
ZMJ				6									
ZMZ		30	13	87	138	83		110	8				
Total	30	130	13	439	151	125	2	227	14	222	143	19	32
% total	1%	6%	1%	20%	7%	6%	0%	10%	1%	10%	6%	1%	1%

HA	Bowl HC	HD	HG	J/JA incip b&f	Dish/bowl J/JA/JB plain	J/JA/JB/HB b&f	J/JB/HB bead	K	Mortarium KC	KD	KE	Lid L	Total	% total
													0	0%
													0	0%
													0	0%
													0	0%
													0	0%
													0	0%
													0	0%
													0	0%
								4			19		23	1%
								6		26	12		44	2%
								6	5		8		19	1%
					50	48							308	14%
													0	0%
	6												6	0%
							7						26	1%
17	59						2						86	4%
													60	3%
21	46	10					5						102	5%
													385	17%
													0	0%
3													3	0%
	18												18	1%
9	13												22	1%
													0	0%
						7						8	15	1%
													0	0%
													0	0%
													0	0%
	5												18	1%
													0	0%
													0	0%
													0	0%
													19	1%
													17	1%
				6		15	12						116	5%
					4								98	4%
													0	0%
			31		52	38							244	11%
													10	0%
					21								32	1%
						5							11	0%
	6	7		6	24	20	6						538	24%
50	153	17	31	12	151	133	32	16	5	26	39	8	2220	-
2%	7%	1%	1%	1%	7%	6%	1%	1%	0%	1%	2%	0%	-	-

at the Northgate House site may represent a chance arrival and secondary distribution from sites where the fabric is better known, such as Bitterne in Southampton (Fulford 1977, 46; Matthews and Holmes forthcoming).

Jars remained the single most important category of vessel, taking a share of 44% by EVE, little different from the previous phase. Cooking-pot jars continued to be the best-represented form—it was the principal form of grog-tempered ware—but these were joined by oval-bodied necked jars, which re-emerged in Overwey ware and medium sandy grey ware after disappearing in the mid 2nd century. Narrow-necked jars, including those from Alice Holt, were also recorded, as were storage jars. Dishes and bowls made an important contribution, though the proportion was reduced from the previous phase. Simple bead-rimmed dishes were represented by residual samian fabrics and New Forest and Oxford forms copying samian forms. Incipient bead-and-flanged dishes had almost disappeared, with occurrences probably being residual. Plain-rimmed and bead-and-flanged or dropped flange dishes and bowls were predominant and available largely in grog-tempered wares and medium sandy grey wares that had replaced Dorset black-burnished ware. Some of the market share previously enjoyed by dishes had been taken by deep New Forest or Oxford bowls. These included some of the latest products of those industries, notably stamped bowls (Fulford 1975a, type 75; Young 1977, type C78) that were produced from *c* AD 340 onwards. Beakers and flagons were also better represented, again thanks largely to New Forest potters. Vessels were confined to folded beakers—available in the standard New Forest colour-coated ware and also in stoneware—and jug-like containers that were recorded in the colour-coated fabric and probable New Forest grey ware.

Evidence of pottery use

Secondary use of pottery

Eighteen pieces of pot exhibited evidence to suggest that they were being used for purposes different from their original function. Almost half of this group was amphorae and almost exclusively south Spanish vessels (Dressel 20 olive oil containers or late Roman versions). All amphorae sherds had been trimmed to produce tesserae (two examples; a third tessera-sized (22 mm x 22 mm) sherd was in grey fabric ZF) or other useful fragments or, from a number of trimmed shoulder sherds, to give presumably complete vessels a new rim with a wider diameter. This last category may have been required if the amphora was still intended to be used as a container. Similar evidence from the Netherlands points to urinals, tubs, or storage vessels for grain and other dry goods (van der Werff 2003). Elaine Morris (pers.

comm.) notes that amphorae trimmed at the shoulder were found at the salt-production site at Lizard, Cornwall (McAvoy *et al.* 1980), and possibly used as saltwater or brine containers. An exact parallel to the largest Winchester example has been recovered very recently during excavations at Dorchester-on-Thames (P Booth pers. comm..), where a Dressel 20, complete except for the neck and rim, had been set in a pit. The trimmed neck had been carefully smoothed and the handles cut off and smoothed just above their stumps. Three other similarly cut-down Dressel 20 amphorae have been recovered in recent work at Springhead, Kent (Seager Smith *et al.* forthcoming). Whatever its contents, the round and open shape of the Dressel 20 body made the type ideal for storage (in addition to transportation) in a way that the similarly common Gauloise amphorae did not appear to be. Other trimmed sherds were recorded in sandy grey wares and oxidised wares and, more rarely, New Forest colour-coated ware. The function of these adapted pieces cannot be determined, but a sherd of Central Gaulish samian ware had been cut into a circular piece suitable for a counter. Two sherds, in fabrics YC and YM, had post-firing holes of uncertain purpose but not apparently for riveted repairs (see below).

Wear and repair

Wear, usually internal, provides evidence of vessel use, with the patterns helping to suggest possible functions. Wear data tend to be skewed towards colour-coated pottery, which, compared with unslipped uniformly-coloured coarse ware, better displays eroded surfaces as the slip is worn away to exposed the underlying fabric (it should be noted that the sherds of this assemblage were generally in good condition, allowing reliable identification of wear as opposed to abrasion and attrition of surfaces caused by redeposition or other non-use related factors). Consequently, most examples of wear from the Northgate House and Discovery Centre sites were found on colour-coated fine wares. Six of the twelve worn vessels were in samian ware. Of the two Drag. 33 cups from Central Gaul recorded, the wear pattern on one cup was unspecified, but the other cup had a ring of wear around the junction of the base and wall that is characteristic of the form and may be related to its use as a mixing vessel in which honey was stirred into wine or for a sauce prepared at the table (Biddulph 2008, 98); interestingly a grey ware bead-and-flanged bowl was also worn around the edge of the base internally, though this was more likely to be through cooking than dining. The bases of two central Gaulish Drag. 45 mortaria were also heavily worn. Three other worn sherds were observed, but could not be identified to form, though one was almost certainly part of a bowl. Overall, the proportion of worn samian seems low; the two cups represent 13% of the total number of Drag. 33s (including vessels without rims), while the two worn mortaria stand against a further five unworn vessels (being a type designed as a heavy-duty mixing bowl). But while the figures suggest that samian tended to be used intermittently or delicately, perhaps because of a perceived prestige value or vagaries of supply, it was clearly used robustly for food preparation on occasion. However, the significance of these observations is uncertain, since useful comparative information is not available. More quantified data are required from a range of other sites to determine normal levels of samian use (at Northfleet villa in Kent, for example, 6% of Drag. 33 cups were worn). Of the other worn vessels, three were bowls in New Forest and Oxford red colour-coated wares, and the base of a New Forest mortarium was eroded.

Some 12 sherds had evidence of repairs. Three of these were Central Gaulish samian, including two fragments from a Drag 37 bowl with a label stamp of DIVIX[TUS], which may well have been regarded as a special piece. The remaining sherds, remarkably, were all from amphorae, having rivet holes with, in two cases, lead rivets still extant. The sherds in question seemed to be predominantly in the later, thinner walled 'Dressel 20' fabric.

Burnt vessels

Pottery function was also determined by evidence of burning. Some 34 vessels (quantification based on rims) were sooted on their external surfaces, presumably after being placed on the hearth. Twenty-three of these were jars, mostly vessels not

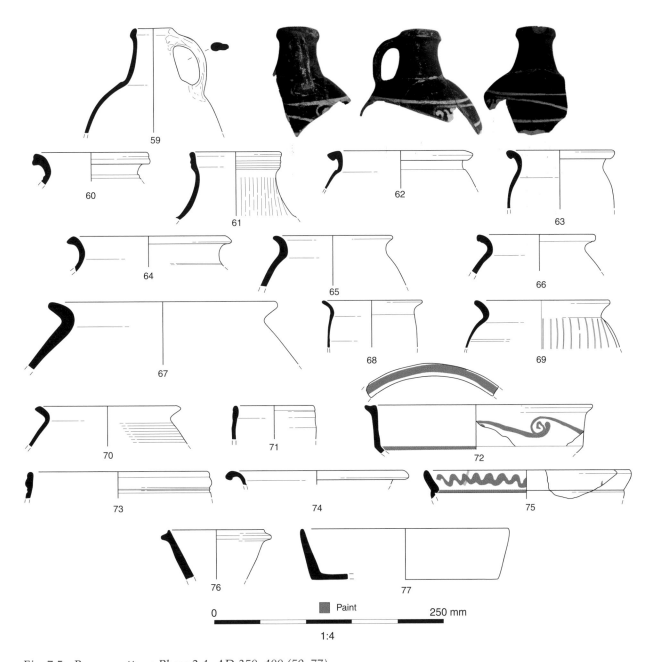

Fig. 7.5 Roman pottery: Phase 2.4, AD 350–400 (59–77)

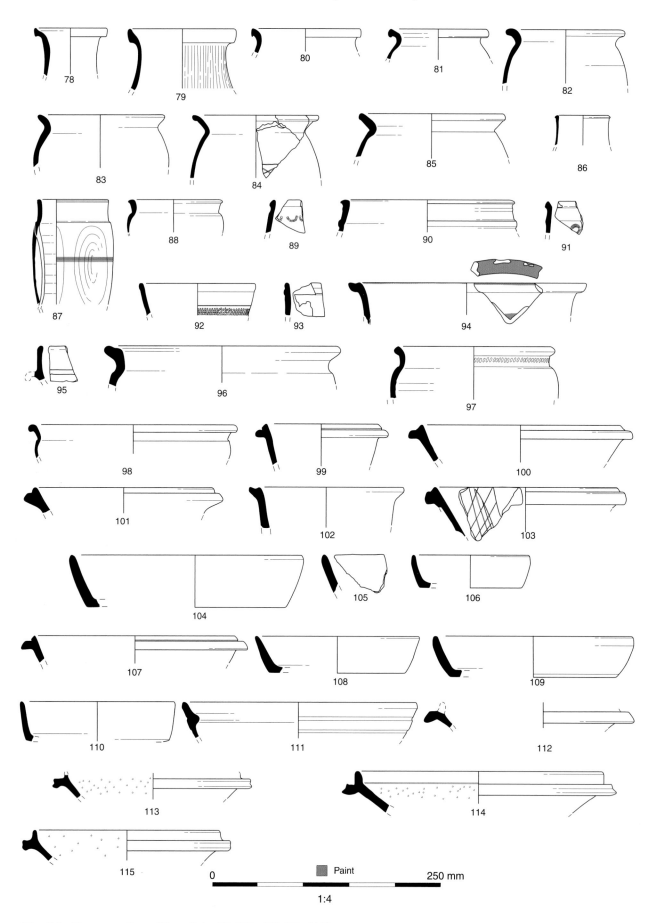

Fig. 7.6   *Roman pottery: Phase 2.4, AD 350–400 (78–115)*

identified to a specific form but including eight cooking-pot jars, seven of which were in late Roman grog-tempered ware. Nine vessels were bowls and dishes, and included seven in grog-tempered ware, sandy grey wares and black-burnished ware. Internal burnt food residues and limescale were limited to eight vessels, almost exclusively cooking-pot type jars in the same sandy or groggy reduced fabrics. The evidence forms a small dataset, but nevertheless points strongly to the use of certain jars and flat-based dishes and bowls with flanged or bead-rims, plain rims and dropped flanges —in black-burnished ware or derived from prototypes in that fabric—as cooking vessels. The use of mortaria could also involve the heat of a hearth or the application of heat to ingredients inside them. Three vessels (in Oxford white ware, Oxford red colour-coated ware, and a Hampshire white ware) were burnt internally on the base; in addition one of these was burnt on its external surface and the top of the rim. A flanged bowl in New Forest parchment ware was similarly burnt, suggesting that it served the same function as mortaria. Unsurprisingly, all the candlestick fragments noted (see above) had evidence of burning.

Graffiti

Graffiti were recorded on ten vessels. These are described in the catalogue of illustrated pottery (below), but it is useful here to consider two that point to a good degree of literacy among some of the town's inhabitants. A New Forest colour-coated beaker was marked [...]AF in good letters (Fig. 7.7, no. 134), while a black-burnished ware vessel was inscribed, in rather cursive lettering, with [...]VE RN or A[...] (the E appearing to be separated from the R by two points) (Fig. 7.7, no. 128). Both are incomplete, but appear to represent personal names. The former is especially interesting; while it is difficult to expand the inscription any further, it is possible that the F, which is the final letter, stands for *'feliciter'*, urging good luck for the user (cf. RIB 2503.352). If so, this recalls the exhortations on so-called motto beakers in Rhenish ware that wish good luck or demand that the user takes drink. The New Forest beaker already in part owed its development to those fine ware products of central and eastern Gaul (cf. Fulford 1975a, 27-8), but the graffito potentially makes that link more explicit.

The pottery in its urban context

The Discovery Centre site produced 19 groups that belonged to the early Roman period. These correspond with the early phase of the earlier Roman key-group assemblage from the northern suburbs at Victoria Road and assemblages from the city defences—Flavian rampart, Jewry Street and Henly's Garage sites (Holmes *et al.*, forthcoming, tables 2.2.7, 2.2.25, 2.4.2, 2.4.3, 2.4.5, 2.4.13, and 2.4.14). Comparing broad ware groups, there is little obvious difference between the areas. Reduced

wares dominate and are accompanied by much smaller proportions of other ware types. Samian is better represented at Victoria Road and the defences than it is at the Discovery Centre, however, and this, along with higher proportions of fine ware and amphorae (especially at the defences), hints at a pattern of supply to parts of the city away from the Discovery Centre area that included higher proportions of continentally-derived or inspired pottery. It is notable that early Roman Gallo-Belgic mortaria, absent from the Discovery Centre, were also recovered from the Victoria Road site and defences. Such differences would be expected to be mirrored in the range of forms present, although this is not easy to confirm, since a complete breakdown of form composition at Victoria Road is not available in the report of that site. However, data are available for grey wares. Compared with the Discovery Centre site, jars are less well-represented and beakers, cups and lids better represented in the northern suburbs. The relatively small number of platters seems at odds with the continental emphasis suggested by other pottery in the group, although there may have been little requirement to supply grey ware platters if the class was preferred in samian ware.

The late Roman dataset from the site is rather larger and stands more comfortably alongside other late Roman assemblages from the city. Much quantified material derives from deposits associated with the city defences, in particular from Henly's Garage and Jewry Street (Holmes *et al.*, forthcoming, tables 2.2.36, 2.4.11–13). Comparing the proportions of fabrics from the various sites, assemblages from the defences contained higher proportions of amphorae and samian and, conversely, lower proportions of fine wares and late Roman handmade grog-tempered wares. This striking difference points to the two assemblage groups (Discovery Centre/ Northgate House sites on the one hand and the defences on the other) deriving, in statistical terms, from separate vessel populations. The reason for the difference could well be chronological and relate to the range of activity along the ramparts.

The late Roman occupation at Jewry Street comprised a succession of timber buildings constructed in an area that had been cultivated from *c* AD 200 (which in turn replaced 2nd-century structures). Late Roman buildings were also recorded at Henly's Garage (Rees, forthcoming). Despite this late Roman activity, the defence deposits appear to have contained higher amounts of residual material than might be expected and received relatively small amounts of new pottery, at least compared with the current site assemblages. The samian and much of the amphorae must be residual, but the small proportion of grog-tempered ware—normally an important fabric in late Roman assemblages—is also notable. Moreover, late Roman Oxford and New Forest fine wares took a smaller share of the defence assemblage compared with the Discovery Centre/Northgate House: some 6% by sherd count against 14%. These observations seem to point to more intensive occupation at the current site. In contrast, occupation along the ramparts may have been less dense, or pottery supply intermittent. It is also possible that older pottery used during previous occupation there or incorporated in manuring spreads for cultivation had not been removed when the late Roman occupation began. While different than assemblages from the city wall, the composition of the late Roman pottery from the site appears to be more comparable to assemblages recovered from The Brooks, a site nearer to the city centre, with reasonably similar proportions of ware groups across the sites (Lyne, forthcoming, tables A2.4.2–5). The exception is black-burnished ware, which is substantially better-represented at The Brooks.

A number of points emerge from these inter-site comparisons. Occupation in the northern suburbs during the later 1st and 2nd centuries admitted a greater amount and range of fine and specialist wares—samian, amphorae, mortaria and fine wares—compared with the current site and so appears to have been different in character. While richly-adorned town houses are known in the suburbs during the late Roman period (Wacher 1995, 301), the excavations from which the pottery was recovered revealed no grand structures but miscellaneous roadside features instead (Rees, forthcoming). However, it is possible that such residences are located close by. Late Roman occupation along the defences was less dense than that nearer the city centre, and its assemblage derived in part from earlier activity. Within the walls, the same range of pottery was reaching the Discovery Centre/Northgate House sites and The Brooks in the late Roman period, suggesting that these sites acquired pottery in a similar way and that they were broadly similar in terms of status and ceramic use.

Catalogue of illustrated pottery (Figs 7.2–7.7)

The following ceramic groups and individual pieces illustrate the typological and chronological range of the assemblage. Graffiti and potters' marks and pieces of intrinsic interest are also shown. The dates given refer to context-group dates (not necessarily identical to stratigraphic phasing), and the catalogue is ordered by this chronology.

Occupation layer CC1754, group CC7002. AD 70–95
1. Jar CC, fabric ZM. Burnished on external surface
2. Jar CD, fabric ZM
3. Jar CD, fabric ZM
4. Jar CE, fabric ZM
5. Jar CG, fabric ZMZ
6. Jar CG, fabric ZMZ
7. Jar CG, fabric ZM
8. Jar CG, fabric ZM. Burnt internally

9. Jar CG, fabric ZM. Burnished on external surface
10. Jar CG, fabric ZM
11. Jar CG, fabric ZM
12. Jar CG, fabric ZM
13. Jar CG, fabric ZM. Burnished on external surface
14. Jar CH, fabric ZM. Burnt externally on shoulder and rim
15. Jar CN, fabric ZMZ
16. Bowl HC, fabric ZM
17. Bowl HC, fabric ZM. Burnt internally
18. Platter JC, fabric ZM. Wavy line decoration on external and internal surfaces
19. Platter JC, fabric ZM
20. Platter JC, fabric ZMZ. Burnished on external surface
21. Platter JC (Drag. 15/17), fabric TSA
22. Platter JC (Drag. 15/17), fabric TSA
23. Lid L, fabric ZMZ

Levelling layer NH7014, group NH8523. AD 120–130
24. Jar C, fabric ZMZ. Burnished on top of rim
25. Jar CG, fabric ZM
26. Jar CK, fabric ZM. Sooting underneath rim
27. Beaker EA, fabric ZMZ
28. Beaker EC, fabric TBF. Black-slipped on rim and shoulder
29. Platter JC (Drag. 18), fabric TSA

Occupation layer NH1263, group NH8512. AD 270–350
30. Jar CK, fabric ZF (black-slipped). Bands of slip on internal surface of rim, lower part of external surface of rim, and shoulder; slip appears striated through wear
31. Jar CM, fabric ZM. Cordoned shoulder
32. Beaker EE, fabric TR. Near-complete vessel
33. Bowl HB, fabric ZF
34. Bowl HB, fabric ZFZ. Burnished on upper surface of flange
35. Bowl HB, fabric ZFZ
36. Bowl HB, fabric ZFZ
37. Bowl HB, fabric ZFZ. Burnished on internal surface of base
38. Bowl HB, fabric ZMA. Faintly-incised arcs on external surface
39. Bowl HC (Fulford 1975a, type 89), fabric UMP. Patches of paint on external surface
40. Bowl H, fabric UMP
41. Bowl HC, fabric WF. Burnt on rim and flange and in patches on external and internal surfaces, possibly through firing rather than use
42. Dish JA, fabric ZMA. Burnished arcs on external surface

'Dark earth' NH4412, group NH8500. AD 270–400
43. Jar CD, fabric ZME

Pit fill NH2623, group NH8524. AD 270–400
44. Beaker E, fabric TCR

Pit fill NH1412, group NH1642. AD 270–400
45. Jar CM (Young 1977, type O27), fabric WO.

Demolition layer NH1328, group NH8516. AD 270–400
46. Jar CM, fabric Y(PNKGT)

Fig. 7.7 (facing page) Roman pottery: Phase 2.4, AD 350–400 (116–123) and pottery of intrinsic interest, graffiti and potter's stamps and marks (124–138)

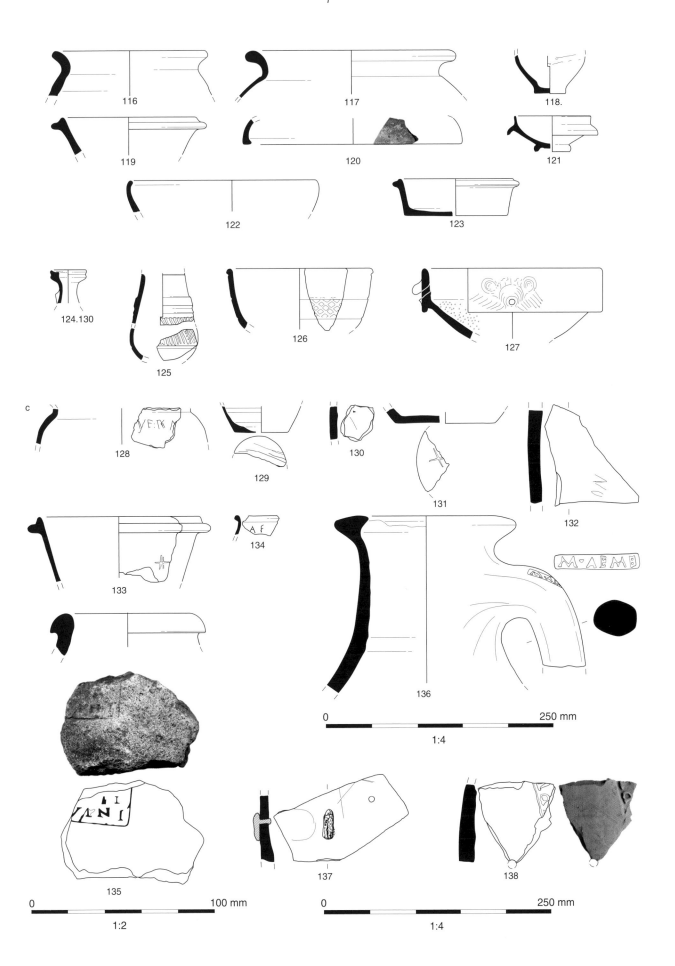

259

Floor NH2510, group NH8523. AD 270–400
47. Jar CJ, fabric ZC(MAY), apparently overfired

Pit fill NH2239, group NH8524. AD 300–400
48. Jar CK, fabric ZF. Burnished zone above lattice
49. Bowl HB, fabric ZMA. Decorated with burnished arcs. Traces of soot on external surface
50. Bowl HB, fabric ZFZ. Worn around edge of base internally
51. Lid L, fabric ZM

Pit fill NH2369, group NH8524. AD 325–400
52. Jar CD, fabric ZF (black-slipped). The vessel is overfired and its rim distorted; a manufacturing second

Pit fill NH2300, group NH8524. AD 325–400
53. Flagon, fabric ZF (black-slipped)
54. Jar CK, fabric SG
55. Cup FA, fabric TF. Footring has broken off

Pit fill NH1395, group NH8516. AD 340–400
56. Jar CK, fabric SG. Tooled burnishing on external surface
57. Bowl HC (Fulford 1975a, type 70), fabric TF
58. Lid L, fabric SG. Burnished decoration on internal surface

'Dark earth' CC1629, group CC7005. AD 340–350
59. Flagon BA, fabric TR. White-painted decoration on shoulder
60. Jar CC, fabric WF, micaceous surfaces
61. Jar CC, fabric ZMZ. White-slipped external surface; burnished neck
62. Jar CD, fabric ZM. Burnished on shoulder and top of rim
63. Jar CD, fabric ZM
64. Jar CD, fabric ZMZ
65. Jar CK, fabric CG
66. Jar CK, fabric CG
67. Jar CK, fabric CG
68. Jar CK, fabric ZF
69. Jar CK, fabric ZM. Burnished lines on shoulder
70. Jar CK, fabric ZM
71. Beaker E, fabric TR
72. Bowl HA, fabric UMS
73. Bowl HC, fabric TF
74. Bowl HC, fabric TO/TOR
75. Bowl HC, fabric UMS
76. Dish JA, fabric ZM
77. Dish JA, fabric ZM

'Dark earth' CC1579, group CC7005. AD 350–370
78. Jar CC, fabric ZMZ
79. Jar CC, fabric ZMZ. White-slipped external surface; shallow ?combing on neck
80. Jar CD, fabric YM(OVW)
81. Jar CD, fabric ZM
82. Jar CK, fabric SK
83. Jar CK, fabric SK
84. Jar CK, fabric ZMA
85. Jar CK, fabric ZMZ. Limescale deposit on internal surface
86. Beaker E, fabric THT
87. Beaker EE, fabric TR
88. Beaker EE, fabric TR
89. Bowl HA, fabric TF. Half-rosette-stamped
90. Bowl HA, fabric TF

91. Bowl HA, fabric TF. Rosette-stamped
92. Bowl HA, fabric TO/TOR. Rouletted below plain zone
93. Bowl HB, fabric TF
94. Bowl HB, fabric UMS
95. Bowl HC, fabric TO/TOR
96. Bowl HC, fabric ZMZ
97. Bowl HD, fabric TO/TOR
98. Bowl HD, fabric ZMZ
99. Dish JA, fabric SG
100. Dish JA, fabric SG
101. Dish JA, fabric SG
102. Dish JA, fabric SG
103. Dish JA, fabric ZMZ. Burnished arcs on external surface and lattice on internal surface
104. Dish JB, fabric SG
105. Dish JB, fabric SG
106. Dish JB, fabric SG
107. Dish JB, fabric SG. Burnished on external surface
108. Dish JB, fabric ZM
109. Dish JB, fabric ZM. Burnished on internal surface
110. Dish JB, fabric ZMZ. Burnished on internal surface
111. Mortarium KC, fabric JMY
112. Mortarium KE (Fulford 1975a, type 81), fabric JMV
113. Mortarium KE (Fulford 1975a, type 81), fabric JMV
114. Mortarium KE (Young 1977, type C100), fabric JMW
115. Mortarium KE (Fulford 1975a, type 102), fabric JMY

'Dark earth' NH5059, group NH8500. AD 350–400
116. Jar C, fabric SG
117. Jar CD, fabric ZM (white-slipped)
118. Beaker E, fabric TR
119. Bowl HB, fabric SG
120. Bowl HC, fabric T(EPO). Flange only
121. Bowl HC (Fulford 1975a, type 63), fabric TF
122. Dish JA, fabric SG
123. Dish JA, fabric ZM (burnished)

Additional pottery of intrinsic interest
124. 'Pulley-rim' flagon B, fabric WM. Orange slip, especially around rim. Context NH1428. AD 270–400
125. Beaker E (Fulford 1975a, grey ware type 1), fabric ZF (black-slipped). Context NH5197. AD 300–400
126. Bowl HC, fabric WF. Imitation of samian Drag. 37 bowl. Incised lattice below plain zone. Context NH2239. AD 300–400
127. Mortarium KD, fabric JMW. 'Bat-head' spout. Internal surface below collar is worn through use. Context NH1398. AD 350–400

Graffiti and potters' marks and stamps
128. Body sherd, fabric ZMA. Context NH7014. AD 120–130. Graffito incised after firing. ?[...]VE:RN or A[...]. Finger-sized dent in body under the final letter; manufacturing flaw
129. Body sherd, fabric ZFE. Context CC1702. AD 120–150. Lines scored after firing, possibly accidentally
130. Base, fabric SG. Context NH1595. AD 270-400. Post-firing
131. Base, fabric SG. Context NH9716. AD 270-400. Small x-graffito made after firing
132. Body sherd, unidentified amphora fabric. Context NH2239. AD 300-400. Possible post-firing graffito
133. Bowl HB, fabric ZFZ. Context NH1231. AD 300-400. Post-firing graffito
134. Beaker E, fabric TF. Context NH2344. AD 325-400. Graffito made after firing: [...]AF

135. Amphora (Richborough 527), fabric A(LIP). Context NH3681. AD 300-400. Potter's stamp, probably HEL VINI
136. Amphora (Dressel 20), fabric ADA. Context NH4435. AD 270-400. Potter's stamp: M AEME
137. Body sherd, fabric ADA. Context NH4754. AD 270-400. Lead rivet, rivet hole and graffito [...]OX incised before firing
138. Body sherd, fabric ADA R. Context NH2344. AD 325-400. Fragmentary stamp

Post-Roman pottery *by John Cotter*

The Northgate House (NH) and Discovery Centre (CC) sites produced a combined total of 21,222 sherds of post-Roman pottery; 14,516 sherds came from NH and 6706 from CC. All this material was briefly examined, spot-dated and recorded to assessment level. A sampling strategy of the most secure deposits was implemented and this resulted in a detailed catalogue of 14,792 sherds weighing 252.356 kg, with a total estimated vessel equivalent (EVE) value of 159.35. It is this sample that forms the statistical basis of this pottery report. A more detailed report can be found in *Digital Section 1.3*.

Pottery of the 9th to 14th centuries, and particularly the 9th to 12th centuries, dominates the excavated assemblage. A single sherd of early-mid Saxon organic-tempered pottery hints at earlier though superficial post-Roman activity in the area, but it is unlikely on the basis of pottery types present that significant occupation of the site commenced much before *c* 850. The marked tail-off of pottery during the later 13th and 14th centuries is almost certainly due to the conversion of most of the site to gardens, certainly by the 15th century, and its survival in this state almost untouched until the 19th and 20th centuries. Post-medieval pottery (16th–20th century), for example, comprises only a tiny fraction of the assemblage recovered from NH (along with only 12 pieces of clay tobacco pipe) and this must reflect a dearth of later activity. The adjacent CC site presents a similar picture apart from a small early 19th-century pottery group sealed by the building of the new library in the 1830s. Details of the small post-medieval pottery collection remain in archive and are not treated in any significant way in this report.

The state of preservation is variable, ranging from small worn sherds in many cases right up to several complete vessel profiles and a few dozen almost complete profiles. Only a half a dozen or so small robust vessel forms, such as oil lamps and crucibles, survived as complete unbroken profiles. Large thin-walled forms such as glazed tripod pitchers and medieval fineware jugs were particularly susceptible to breakage, whereas robust handmade late Saxon cooking pots often survived as large substantial pieces.

Pottery fabrics were recorded using the official codes of the Winchester Museums Service. Wherever possible vessels have been described following the nationally recommended nomencla-

ture and minimum standards of the Medieval Pottery Research Group (MPRG 1998; 2001). The main form of quantification employed in this text is the sherd count, which is supported by EVEs or weight data. The original aim was to record a 50–60% sample of the post-Roman pottery from the site. Attention was initially focussed on recording contexts dated to the late Saxon and Norman periods (Phases 4 and 5) as this, the largest and best-preserved element of the assemblage, clearly had the greater archaeological value and the best potential to address the project research objectives.

Ceramic phasing

In the forthcoming Winchester pottery monograph (Holmes and Matthews, forthcoming), a system of ceramic phasing was established for the city, based mainly on extramural sites excavated by the Winchester Museums Service. The late Saxon phases are referred to as the Late Saxon sandy ware phase, the Michelmersh ware phase and the Winchester ware phase. These are followed by the Tripod Pitcher phase (also known as the Saxo-Norman group). These phases, spanning the period *c* 850–1200, are well-represented on the current site, but in practice the established traditional ceramic phasing is of limited use, as the main signifiers are quite rare (and possibly sometimes residual), and can only be assigned to the contexts which contain them. Consequently, a simpler and more comprehensive phasing system was devised to deal with the site assemblages. This is closely based on the traditional ceramic phasing, but is more flexible in that it can be applied to whole sequences rather than selective contexts. Although largely dependent on established pottery dating it also incorporates the relative dating provided by the site stratigraphy and is supported, in places, by dating from other object categories and by association with a sequence of independent scientific (archaeomagnetic and radiocarbon) dates (see Chapter 6). The latter, except in a few possibly anomalous cases, are in fairly broad agreement with the ceramic dates for these contexts.

Initial site phasing (and much of the final phasing) mirrored the time divisions established in the traditional ceramic phasing, but was somewhat broader; for example Late Saxon (Phase 4, *c* 850–1066) covered the three late Saxon ceramic phases (Late Saxon sandy ware, Michelmersh and Winchester ware phases), but was somewhat closer as far as the post-Saxon phases were concerned (Anglo-Norman, Phase 5, *c* 1050–1225 matching almost exactly the Tripod pitcher phase). Fine tuning the initial phasing gave the two-century block of the 'Late Saxon' phase (a significant 40% of the pottery sample) a simpler two-fold subdivision rather than the threefold subdivision provided by traditional ceramic phasing. This was largely based on the assumption of a *c* 950 introduction date for the common chalky-flinty fabric MAV (see below and *Digital Section 1.3*). Subsequent phases are a little more straightforward but these too rely on the presence of main or secondary ceramic indicators. The Anglo-Norman phase (Phase 5, *c* 1050–1225), for example, is largely defined by the presence of glazed tripod pitchers, but also by the presence of local coarsewares with 'scratch-marked' decoration—a decorative style widely accepted to be post-Conquest in origin. The medieval phase (Phase 6, *c* 1225–1550) is largely defined by the presence of glazed wheel-thrown jugs, mainly those in South Hampshire redware. Although the excavator, out of convention, has Phase 6 ending *c* 1550, it should be borne in mind that the amount of pottery on the site datable after *c* 1400 is remarkably little as most of the site was under cultivation by this time.

Fabrics (Tables 7.11–14)

More detailed descriptions of fabrics and vessel typologies, along with full references, can be found in *Digital Section 1.3*. The shortened fabric descriptions below are listed in alphabetical order.

Fabric MAB. Flint-tempered ware. Possibly from *c* 850 but rare, mainly *c* 1000–1250. Probably local. Fairly rare. Fabric Group 3 (see below for explanation of fabric groups).

Fabric MAD. Tripod Pitcher ware. Date *c* 1050–1225. Possibly local, but recent comparison shows the fabric is visually very similar to tripod pitchers in South-east Wiltshire coarseware (MADW, see below). More than one source may therefore be represented although both are almost certainly products of the same regional tradition. Fairly common. Fabric Group 5.

Fabric MADW. South-east Wiltshire coarseware. Present as tripod pitchers. A few pieces in this fabric were originally identified but in the light of recent comparisons with fabric samples from Wiltshire it may be that this fabric is much commoner in Winchester than was originally thought and perhaps represents the coarser end of the MAD fabric range (see MAD, above). Date *c* 1075–1250. Rare. Fabric Group 5.

Fabric MAF. Fine sandy ware with flint, chalk and 'organic' temper (actually selenite). Possibly from *c* 950, mainly *c* 1050–1150. See variant Fabric MBK. Probably local. Fairly common. Fabric Group 3.

Fabric MAQ. Coarse grained sandy ware with flint. Possibly from *c* 850 but rare, mainly *c* 1000–1250. Probably local and regional. Common. Fabric Group 3.

Fabric MAV. Chalk tempered ware with some flint. Date *c* 850–1200, mainly *c* 1000–1200? Probably local. Very common. Fabric Group 1.

Fabric MBEAU. Beauvais-type ware. Date *c* 900–1100. North-west France. Very rare. Fabric Group 8.

Fabric MBK. Fine sandy ware with flint and chalk. Possibly from *c* 950, mainly *c* 1050–1150. Probably fairly local. Very common. Fabric Group 3.

Fabric MBN. Portchester ware. A wheel-thrown late Saxon coarseware. Date perhaps *c* 925(?)–1050. Source possibly the Portchester area, south Hampshire. Rare. Fabric Group 2.

Table 7.11: Post-Roman pottery: quantification of catalogued sample by fabric

Fabric	Sherds	%	Weight (g)	%	EVE	%
MAB	36	0.24%	674	0.27%	0.53	0.33%
MAD	163	1.10%	3,297	1.31%	0.65	0.41%
MADW	9	0.06%	248	0.10%	0.11	0.07%
MAF	321	2.17%	3,541	1.40%	1.95	1.22%
MAQ	590	3.99%	10,566	4.19%	10.69	6.71%
MAV	3,034	20.51%	68,114	26.99%	33.06	20.75%
MBEAU	2	0.01%	36	0.01%	0	0.00%
MBK	1,324	8.95%	17,520	6.94%	13.2	8.28%
MBN	19	0.13%	268	0.11%	0.18	0.11%
MBX	6,253	42.27%	99,945	39.60%	65.74	41.26%
MCK	6	0.04%	26	0.01%	0	0.00%
MDF	581	3.93%	7,388	2.93%	5.64	3.54%
MDG	9	0.06%	166	0.07%	0.04	0.03%
MDL	94	0.64%	410	0.16%	2.63	1.65%
MFGY	2	0.01%	91	0.04%	0	0.00%
MFI	1	0.01%	130	0.05%	0	0.00%
MMG	16	0.11%	273	0.11%	0.45	0.28%
MMH	62	0.42%	582	0.23%	0.2	0.13%
MMI	223	1.51%	3,530	1.40%	1.95	1.22%
MMK	1	0.01%	18	0.01%	0.06	0.04%
MMQ	12	0.08%	116	0.05%	0	0.00%
MMR	7	0.05%	131	0.05%	0.05	0.03%
MMU	205	1.39%	3,556	1.41%	2.65	1.66%
MNG	80	0.54%	1,282	0.51%	0.5	0.31%
MNV	3	0.02%	2	0.00%	0	0.00%
MNVY	1	0.01%	8	0.00%	0	0.00%
MNX	19	0.13%	317	0.13%	0.08	0.05%
MOE	567	3.83%	10,917	4.33%	5.4	3.39%
MPIN	4	0.03%	59	0.02%	0	0.00%
MSH	165	1.12%	3,472	1.38%	2.67	1.68%
MTE	578	3.91%	8,788	3.48%	4.78	3.00%
MWW	133	0.90%	2,003	0.79%	2.48	1.56%
MZM	138	0.93%	2,458	0.97%	2.57	1.61%
PMED	16	0.11%	302	0.12%	0.18	0.11%
UNID	77	0.52%	1,028	0.41%	0.91	0.57%
WWX	41	0.28%	1,094	0.43%	0	0.00%
Total	14,792	100.00%	252,356	100.00%	159.35	100.00%

Fabric MBX. Chalk-tempered ware. The dominant fabric in late Saxon assemblages. Date *c* 850–1150, mainly perhaps *c* 850–1050? See also MAV, the flintier variant. Probably local. Very common. Fabric Group 1.

Fabric MCK. Kingston-type whiteware. One of the medieval Surrey whitewares. Usually green glazed. Date *c* 1240–1400. Surrey and Surrey/Hampshire border. Rare. Fabric Group 6.

Fabric MDF. Medium grained sandy ware. Common medieval sandy ware (mainly wheel-thrown jars/cooking pots). Date said to be from *c* 1000, mainly *c* 1050–1350. On the site mainly perhaps *c* 1150–1350. Local or regional. Common. Fabric Group 6.

Fabric MDG. Late medieval red ware. Date *c* 1350–1500? Fabric MGR (see below) is a later development of this and is often white painted. Local or regional. Rare. Fabric Group 6.

Table 7.12: Post-Roman pottery: fabrics by phase. Quantification by sherd count.

Fabric	4		4.1		4.2		5		6		Total	Total %
	Sherds	%	Sherds	%	Sherds	%	Sherds	%	Sherds	%		
MAB	1	3.85%		0.00%	4	0.09%	24	0.37%	7	0.30%	36	0.24%
MAD		0.00%		0.00%	4	0.09%	115	1.75%	44	1.91%	163	1.10%
MADW		0.00%		0.00%		0.00%	4	0.06%	5	0.22%	9	0.06%
MAF		0.00%		0.00%	10	0.22%	260	3.96%	51	2.22%	321	2.17%
MAQ		0.00%	17	1.32%	170	3.69%	353	5.38%	50	2.17%	590	3.99%
MAV	11	42.31%	22	1.70%	1150	24.96%	1736	26.44%	115	5.00%	3034	20.51%
MBEAU		0.00%		0.00%		0.00%	2	0.03%		0.00%	2	0.01%
MBK	1	3.85%	4	0.31%	69	1.50%	1086	16.54%	164	7.13%	1324	8.95%
MBN		0.00%		0.00%	15	0.33%	4	0.06%		0.00%	19	0.13%
MBX	12	46.15%	1179	91.25%	2754	59.78%	1792	27.29%	516	22.43%	6253	42.27%
MCK		0.00%		0.00%		0.00%		0.00%	6	0.26%	6	0.04%
MDF		0.00%	2	0.15%	9	0.20%	161	2.45%	409	17.78%	581	3.93%
MDG		0.00%		0.00%		0.00%		0.00%	9	0.39%	9	0.06%
MDL		0.00%	12	0.93%	40	0.87%	33	0.50%	9	0.39%	94	0.64%
MFGY		0.00%		0.00%	2	0.04%		0.00%		0.00%	2	0.01%
MFI		0.00%		0.00%		0.00%	1	0.02%		0.00%	1	0.01%
MMG		0.00%		0.00%	1	0.02%		0.00%	15	0.65%	16	0.11%
MMH		0.00%		0.00%		0.00%	2	0.03%	60	2.61%	62	0.42%
MMI		0.00%		0.00%	1	0.02%	9	0.14%	213	9.26%	223	1.51%
MMK		0.00%		0.00%		0.00%		0.00%	1	0.04%	1	0.01%
MMQ		0.00%		0.00%	1	0.02%		0.00%	11	0.48%	12	0.08%
MMR		0.00%		0.00%		0.00%		0.00%	7	0.30%	7	0.05%
MMU		0.00%	13	1.01%	91	1.98%	89	1.36%	12	0.52%	205	1.39%
MNG		0.00%		0.00%	1	0.02%	49	0.75%	30	1.30%	80	0.54%
MNV		0.00%		0.00%		0.00%		0.00%	3	0.13%	3	0.02%
MNVY		0.00%		0.00%		0.00%		0.00%	1	0.04%	1	0.01%
MNX		0.00%		0.00%		0.00%	4	0.06%	15	0.65%	19	0.13%
MOE		0.00%	5	0.39%	19	0.41%	229	3.49%	314	13.65%	567	3.83%
MPIN		0.00%		0.00%		0.00%	4	0.06%		0.00%	4	0.03%
MSH		0.00%	34	2.63%	91	1.98%	35	0.53%	5	0.22%	165	1.12%
MTE	1	3.85%	1	0.08%	5	0.11%	381	5.80%	190	8.26%	578	3.91%
MWW		0.00%		0.00%	77	1.67%	54	0.82%	2	0.09%	133	0.90%
MZM		0.00%	1	0.08%	60	1.30%	63	0.96%	14	0.61%	138	0.93%
PMED		0.00%		0.00%	3	0.07%	8	0.12%	5	0.22%	16	0.11%
UNID		0.00%	2	0.15%	17	0.37%	44	0.67%	14	0.61%	77	0.52%
WWX		0.00%		0.00%	13	0.28%	25	0.38%	3	0.13%	41	0.28%
Total	26	100.00%	1292	100.00%	4607	100.00%	6567	100.00%	2300	100.00%	14792	100.00%

Fabric MDL. Medium grained sandy crucible fabric. Date *c* 850–1200. Local? Fairly rare. Fabric Group 7.

Fabric MFGY. North French greyware. Date *c* 875–1000. Pas-de-Calais/Flanders. Very rare. Fabric Group 8.

Fabric MFI. Normandy gritty white ware. Date *c* 1070–1250. Normandy. Very rare—a single piece only. Fabric Group 8.

Fabric MFS. Saintonge polychrome ware. Date *c* 1280–1350. South-west France. Very rare—a single piece identified (unsampled context). Fabric Group 8.

Fabric MGR. Late medieval red ware. Date *c* 1475–1550. Possibly West Sussex or east Hampshire. Includes 'black and white painted' wares. Very rare—a single piece identified (unsampled context). Fabric Group 6.

Fabric MGV. Anglo-Saxon organic-tempered ware. Date early to mid Saxon *c* 400–800. Probably local. Very rare—a single piece identified (unsampled context). Fabric Group 7.

Fabric MMG. Pink quartz-tempered ware. A high medieval glazed ware. Date *c* 1225–1400. Rare. Hampshire. Fabric Group 6.

Fabric MMH. Common white ware. A high medieval glazed ware. Date *c* 1225–1400. Rare. Hampshire. Fabric Group 6.

Fabric MMI. South Hampshire red ware. A high medieval glazed ware and the commonest of the several, quite similar, South Hampshire red ware fabrics. Probably from *c* 1175, mainly *c* 1225–1400. Fairly common. South Hampshire. Fabric Group 6.

Fabric MMK. Glazed sandy ware with flint inclusions. A high medieval glazed ware. Date *c* 1225–1400. Hampshire or Sussex? Very rare—a single piece only. Fabric Group 6.

Table 7.13: Post-Roman pottery: fabrics by phase. Quantification by weight (g).

Fabric	4		4.1		4.2		5		6		Total	Total %
	Weight	%	Weight	%	Weight	%	Weight	%	Weight	%		
MAB	56	12.04%		0.00%	38	0.05%	481	0.44%	99	0.27%	674	0.27%
MAD		0.00%		0.00%	68	0.08%	2,098	1.90%	1,131	3.10%	3,297	1.31%
MADW		0.00%		0.00%		0.00%	110	0.10%	138	0.38%	248	0.10%
MAF		0.00%		0.00%	140	0.17%	2,837	2.57%	564	1.55%	3,541	1.40%
MAQ		0.00%	316	1.51%	2,973	3.54%	6,253	5.66%	1,024	2.81%	10,566	4.19%
MAV	179	38.49%	802	3.82%	26,837	31.98%	38,093	34.47%	2,203	6.04%	68,114	26.99%
MBEAU		0.00%		0.00%		0.00%	36	0.03%		0.00%	36	0.01%
MBK	2	0.43%	15	0.07%	780	0.93%	14,810	13.40%	1,913	5.24%	17,520	6.94%
MBN		0.00%		0.00%	184	0.22%	84	0.08%		0.00%	268	0.11%
MBX	223	47.96%	18,705	89.19%	45,258	53.92%	26,973	24.41%	8,786	24.08%	99,945	39.60%
MCK		0.00%		0.00%		0.00%		0.00%	26	0.07%	26	0.01%
MDF		0.00%	16	0.08%	165	0.20%	2,178	1.97%	5,029	13.78%	7,388	2.93%
MDG		0.00%		0.00%		0.00%		0.00%	166	0.46%	166	0.07%
MDL		0.00%	44	0.21%	90	0.11%	198	0.18%	78	0.21%	410	0.16%
MFGY		0.00%		0.00%	91	0.11%		0.00%		0.00%	91	0.04%
MFI		0.00%		0.00%		0.00%	130	0.12%		0.00%	130	0.05%
MMG		0.00%		0.00%	4	0.00%		0.00%	269	0.74%	273	0.11%
MMH		0.00%		0.00%		0.00%	17	0.02%	565	1.55%	582	0.23%
MMI		0.00%		0.00%	1	0.00%	103	0.09%	3,426	9.39%	3,530	1.40%
MMK		0.00%		0.00%		0.00%		0.00%	18	0.05%	18	0.01%
MMQ		0.00%		0.00%	11	0.01%		0.00%	105	0.29%	116	0.05%
MMR		0.00%		0.00%		0.00%		0.00%	131	0.36%	131	0.05%
MMU		0.00%	134	0.64%	1,794	2.14%	1,381	1.25%	247	0.68%	3,556	1.41%
MNG		0.00%		0.00%	6	0.01%	897	0.81%	379	1.04%	1,282	0.51%
MNV		0.00%		0.00%		0.00%		0.00%	2	0.01%	2	0.00%
MNVY		0.00%		0.00%		0.00%		0.00%	8	0.02%	8	0.00%
MNX		0.00%		0.00%		0.00%	47	0.04%	270	0.74%	317	0.13%
MOE		0.00%	193	0.92%	327	0.39%	4,424	4.00%	5,973	16.37%	10,917	4.33%
MPIN		0.00%		0.00%		0.00%	59	0.05%		0.00%	59	0.02%
MSH		0.00%	689	3.29%	2,147	2.56%	522	0.47%	114	0.31%	3,472	1.38%
MTE	5	1.08%	16	0.08%	98	0.12%	5,488	4.97%	3,181	8.72%	8,788	3.48%
MWW		0.00%		0.00%	1,255	1.50%	742	0.67%	6	0.02%	2,003	0.79%
MZM		0.00%	8	0.04%	1,225	1.46%	915	0.83%	310	0.85%	2,458	0.97%
PMED		0.00%		0.00%	98	0.12%	170	0.15%	34	0.09%	302	0.12%
UNID		0.00%	35	0.17%	192	0.23%	538	0.49%	263	0.72%	1,028	0.41%
WWX		0.00%		0.00%	149	0.18%	920	0.83%	25	0.07%	1,094	0.43%
Total	465	100.00%	20,973	100.00%	83,931	100.00%	110,504	100.00%	36,483	100.00%	252,356	100.00%

Fabric MMQ. Pink quartz-tempered ware. A high medieval glazed ware and a finer variant of MMG. Date *c* 1225–1400. Rare. Hampshire. Fabric Group 6.

Fabric MMR. Glazed buff sandy ware. A high medieval glazed ware. Date possibly from *c* 1175, mainly *c* 1225–1400. Hampshire. Rare. Fabric Group 6.

Fabric MMU. Michelmersh-type ware. A late Saxon wheel-thown sandy ware. Date *c* 925(?)–1050. Only known production site Michelmersh, Hampshire. Fairly common. Fabric Group 2.

Fabric MNG. Early South Hampshire red ware. Date *c* 1175–1250. Probably Hampshire. Fairly common. Fabric Group 5.

Fabric MNV. Northern French green glazed white ware. Date *c* 1150–1300. North-west France. Very rare—three pieces only identified. Fabric Group 8.

Fabric MNVY. Northern French yellow glazed white ware. Date *c* 1150–1300. North-west France. Very rare—a single piece only identified. Fabric Group 8.

Fabric MNX. Laverstock-type ware. A high medieval glazed ware. *c* 1230–1270. Source Laverstock kilns, Wiltshire. Rare. Fabric Group 6.

Fabric MOE. Coarse grained sandy ware. Coarse gritty texture. Date *c* 1070–1225. Probably local. Common. Fabric Group 4.

Fabric MPAF. Paffrath-type ware. Date *c* 1075–1225. Rhineland. Very rare—a single piece identified (unsampled context). Fabric Group 8.

Fabric MPIN. Pingsdorf-type ware. Date *c* 925–1250 but commonest *c* 1075–1225. Rhineland. Very rare – five sherds only identified. Fabric Group 8.

Fabric MSH. Late Saxon Sandy ware. A late Saxon wheel-thrown sandy ware. Date *c* 850–950 (–1000?).

Table 7.14: Post-Roman pottery: fabrics by phase. Quantification by EVEs.

Fabric	4		4.1		4.2		5		6		Total	Total %
	EVE	%	EVE	%	EVE	%	EVE	%	EVE	%		
MAB	0.09	24.32%		0.00%		0.00%	0.34	0.52%	0.1	0.45%	0.53	0.33%
MAD		0.00%		0.00%		0.00%	0.4	0.61%	0.25	1.12%	0.65	0.41%
MADW		0.00%		0.00%		0.00%	0.11	0.17%		0.00%	0.11	0.07%
MAF		0.00%		0.00%		0.00%	1.72	2.61%	0.23	1.03%	1.95	1.22%
MAQ		0.00%		0.00%	4.49	7.89%	5.53	8.39%	0.67	3.00%	10.69	6.71%
MAV		0.00%	0.53	3.85%	13.7	24.08%	18.11	27.46%	0.72	3.22%	33.06	20.75%
MBEAU		0.00%		0.00%		0.00%		0.00%		0.00%		0.00%
MBK		0.00%		0.00%	0.98	1.72%	10.77	16.33%	1.45	6.48%	13.2	8.28%
MBN		0.00%		0.00%	0.12	0.21%	0.06	0.09%		0.00%	0.18	0.11%
MBX	0.28	75.68%	11.75	85.27%	30.22	53.11%	17.18	26.05%	6.31	28.22%	65.74	41.26%
MCK		0.00%		0.00%		0.00%		0.00%		0.00%		0.00%
MDF		0.00%		0.00%	0.18	0.32%	1.41	2.14%	4.05	18.11%	5.64	3.54%
MDG		0.00%		0.00%		0.00%		0.00%	0.04	0.18%	0.04	0.03%
MDL		0.00%	0.5	3.63%	1	1.76%	0.97	1.47%	0.16	0.72%	2.63	1.65%
MFGY		0.00%		0.00%		0.00%		0.00%		0.00%		0.00%
MFI		0.00%		0.00%		0.00%		0.00%		0.00%		0.00%
MMG		0.00%		0.00%		0.00%		0.00%	0.45	2.01%	0.45	0.28%
MMH		0.00%		0.00%		0.00%		0.00%	0.2	0.89%	0.2	0.13%
MMI		0.00%		0.00%		0.00%		0.00%	1.95	8.72%	1.95	1.22%
MMK		0.00%		0.00%		0.00%		0.00%	0.06	0.27%	0.06	0.04%
MMQ		0.00%		0.00%		0.00%		0.00%		0.00%		0.00%
MMR		0.00%		0.00%		0.00%		0.00%	0.05	0.22%	0.05	0.03%
MMU		0.00%	0.14	1.02%	0.97	1.70%	1.22	1.85%	0.32	1.43%	2.65	1.66%
MNG		0.00%		0.00%		0.00%	0.46	0.70%	0.04	0.18%	0.5	0.31%
MNV		0.00%		0.00%		0.00%		0.00%		0.00%		0.00%
MNVY		0.00%		0.00%		0.00%		0.00%		0.00%		0.00%
MNX		0.00%		0.00%		0.00%	0.08	0.12%		0.00%	0.08	0.05%
MOE		0.00%	0.33	2.39%	0.07	0.12%	1.93	2.93%	3.07	13.73%	5.4	3.39%
MPIN		0.00%		0.00%		0.00%		0.00%		0.00%		0.00%
MSH		0.00%	0.53	3.85%	1.45	2.55%	0.58	0.88%	0.11	0.49%	2.67	1.68%
MTE		0.00%		0.00%	0.1	0.18%	3.33	5.05%	1.35	6.04%	4.78	3.00%
MWW		0.00%		0.00%	2.06	3.62%	0.42	0.64%		0.00%	2.48	1.56%
MZM		0.00%		0.00%	1.41	2.48%	0.86	1.30%	0.3	1.34%	2.57	1.61%
PMED		0.00%		0.00%	0.05	0.09%	0.09	0.14%	0.04	0.18%	0.18	0.11%
UNID		0.00%		0.00%	0.1	0.18%	0.37	0.56%	0.44	1.97%	0.91	0.57%
WWX		0.00%		0.00%		0.00%		0.00%		0.00%		0.00%
Total	0.37	100.00%	13.78	100.00%	56.9	100.00%	65.94	100.00%	22.36	100.00%	159.35	100.00%

Probably an earlier product of the Michelmersh kilns, Hampshire. Fairly common. Fabric Group 2.

Fabric MTE. Newbury B-style ware. Mainly flint-tempered. Named after the type-site at Newbury in Berkshire. Kilns also known near Newbury. Recent research however suggests the fabric found in Winchester may be a local copy. Date *c* 1050–1200. Probably local. Common. Fabric Group 3.

Fabric MWW. Winchester ware. A late Saxon high quality wheel-thrown glazed tableware. Date *c* 950–1100. Production site unknown but probably local. Fairly common. Fabric Group 2.

Fabric MZM. Sandy grey ware. A late Saxon wheel-thrown sandy ware. Date *c* 950–1050? Either an import or possibly a reduced Michelmersh product? Fairly common. Fabric Group 2.

Fabric PMED. Post-medieval wares. Umbrella code for post-medieval wares *c* 1550–1900. Rare from the site. Fabric Group 7.

Fabric UNID. All unidentified wares. Late Saxon to medieval. Rare. Fabric Group 7.

Fabric WWX. Winchester-style ware. A glazed late Saxon sandy ware. Possibly a variant of Winchester ware (MWW). Date *c* 950–1100. Possibly local. Fairly rare. Fabric Group 2.

Pottery fabrics by property and phase

The quantity of each fabric recovered, by sherd count, weight and EVEs, as well as the percentage of each in phased deposits, is shown in Tables 7.12–14. The 36 fabric codes present from sampled contexts are too numerous to lend themselves to easy graphic representation in the form of pie-charts and the like. These, however, can be ordered into fabric groups based on a range of criteria including physical and/or technological similarity, presumed date or presumed source etc. All of these criteria overlap to varying extents but the following groupings—some more arbitrary than others—have been defined in order that the main trends within the assemblage can be seen more clearly whether spatially or chronologically. Some groupings (eg chalk-tempered wares) are more obvious than others. The justification for other less obvious groupings is expanded upon below.

Group 1. Local chalk-tempered wares (*c* 850–1200). MBX, MAV. The latter fabric (MAV chalk and flint) overlaps with some Group 3 fabrics below (MAQ, MTE). Group 1 vessel forms almost exclusively have sagging bases as opposed to round ones. Not surprisingly this is the largest fabric group from the excavations here comprising 62.74% by sherds (or 61.9% by EVEs; see Table 7.15).

Group 2. Late Saxon wheel-thrown wares (*c* 850–1100). All probably Hampshire products, all basically sandy wares. Includes glazed Winchester ware (MWW) and Winchester-style ware (WWX). Also unglazed Late Saxon sandy ware (MSH), Michelmersh ware (MMU), Portchester ware (MBN, sand and flint), and the unsourced grey ware (MZM) which may be a reduced variant of Michelmersh ware. This small group comprises 4.75% (by sherds) of the site assemblage (or 6.64% by EVEs and 5.10% by weight).

Group 3. Local sand and flint-tempered coarsewares (*c* 850–1250, mostly *c* 1050–1225). MBK, MAF, MAQ, MTE. These all also have some chalk content but usually as a sparse to moderate component. The fine sandy wares MBK and MAF ('organic'-tempered) are clearly related by fabric and manufacturing technique (possibly 'paddle and anvil' technique, both with round-bottomed jars). MBK and occasionally MAF are sometimes decorated with scratch-marked decoration which is apparently a post-conquest phenomenon. MAQ (flint-tempered sandy ware) is also related to these by fabric and can sometimes be seen to share the same distinctive manufacturing technique as well as the common round-bottomed jar form. It does, however, overlap in character with MAV (chalk and flint-tempered) if the chalk content in both is high and the quartz sand content coarser than usual (usually in late examples). MTE, the local Newbury B style of pottery, is placed in Group 3 on the basis of its fabric character, which contains coarse quartz, flint and chalk and appears quite late in the Winchester sequence. However MTE is thin-walled, certainly wheel-thrown in many cases, and normally occurs as jars with pronounced sagging bases. In this latter respect, and in terms of fabric similarity, it could be grouped with MAV in Group 1 but the pronounced flint content aligns it perhaps more properly with Group 3 fabrics. This group comprises 19.27% (by sherds) of the site assemblage (or 19.54% by EVEs).

Group 4. Local coarse quartz-tempered ware, MOE (*c* 1050–1225). Mainly coarse quartz-tempered but often with small amounts of flint and chalk. Usually occurs as large round-bottomed jars frequently with scratch-marked decoration. These features, including shared

rim forms, align MOE most closely with MBK in Group 3 but MOE seems texturally distinct enough to form a separate group. This group comprises 3.84% (by sherds) of the site assemblage (or 3.40% by EVEs).

Group 5. Local glazed quartz-tempered tripod pitcher wares (*c* 1050–1225). MAD, MADW, MNG. Although MAD is technically a fabric and not a form it does seem to occur almost exclusively as tripod pitchers or large jugs. It may be a glazed version of MOE above. MNG, though finer and possibly later (from *c* 1175?), also frequently occurs in these forms and is included here for convenience. This group comprises 1.71% (by sherds) of the site assemblage (or 0.79% by EVEs).

Group 6. High medieval wares (*c* 1225–1450). This mainly comprises glazed and often decorated fine sandy ware jugs of local or presumed Hampshire origin—primarily South Hampshire red ware (MMI) and a range of rarer but apparently related pink, buff or white wares including MDG, MMG, MMH, MMK, MMQ, MMR. However it also includes the rare regional glazed imports Laverstock ware (MNX) and Kingston-type ware (MCK) as well as the predominant unglazed common medieval coarseware or greyware (MDF) which, chronologically and technologically, belongs in this group despite evidence of earlier origins. Apart from the commonest of these two (MMI and MDF) all other high medieval wares are rare from the site as this period is not very well represented here. It therefore seems convenient to lump all high medieval wares together. This group comprises 6.34% (by sherds) of the site assemblage (or 5.33% by EVEs).

Group 7. Miscellaneous, or other wares (Saxon to 19th century). Includes crucibles in the common local crucible fabric (MDL), but not the few other possible crucibles in rarer fabrics (see crucibles elsewhere). Also post-medieval wares (PMED) and unidentified wares (UNID). This group comprises 1.27% (by sherds) of the site assemblage (or 2.34% by EVEs).

Group 8. Continental imports (*c* 850–1350). All rare in Winchester. Includes Beauvais-type ware (MBEAU), Pingsdorf-type ware (MPIN), North French grey ware (MFGY), Normandy Gritty ware (MFI), Northern French green glazed white ware (MNV) and Northern French yellow glazed white ware (MNV). This group comprises only 13 sherds from sampled contexts (plus 3 more from unsampled contexts). The sampled group comprises 0.09% (by sherds) of the site assemblage (or 0% by EVEs and 0.13% by weight).

The quantity of each fabric group and the proportion it forms in each phase is presented in Table 7.15. This shows, among other things, the gradual decline of the major Group 1 local chalky wares from nearly 93% (by sherds) in Phase 4.1 (*c* 850–950) to a little under 54% in Phase 5 (*c* 1050–1225) to only 27% in Phase 6 (*c* 1225–1550), by which time they were almost certainly residual. The virtual monopoly which the chalky wares held in the late Saxon phases gradually yielded to the Group 3 'local' sand- and flint-tempered wares which, by Phase 5, comprised 32% of the phase assemblage, with Group 2 and 4 sandy wares and the Group 5 and 6 glazed sandy wares also encroaching on the declining chalky ware monopoly. Some very early

Table 7.15: Post-Roman pottery: fabric groups by phase. Quantification by sherd count.

Fabric group	4.1		4.2		5		6		Total	Total %
	Sherds	%	Sherds	%	Sherds	%	Sherds	%		
1	1201	92.96%	3904	84.74%	3528	53.72%	631	27.43%	9264	62.74%
2	48	3.72%	347	7.53%	270	4.11%	36	1.57%	701	4.75%
3	22	1.70%	258	5.60%	2104	32.04%	462	20.09%	2846	19.27%
4	5	0.39%	19	0.41%	229	3.49%	314	13.65%	567	3.84%
5		0.00%	5	0.11%	168	2.56%	79	3.43%	252	1.71%
6	2	0.15%	12	0.26%	176	2.68%	746	32.43%	936	6.34%
7	14	1.08%	60	1.30%	85	1.29%	28	1.22%	187	1.27%
8		0.00%	2	0.04%	7	0.11%	4	0.17%	13	0.09%
Total	1292	100.00%	4607	100.00%	6567	100.00%	2300	100.00%	14766	100.00%

but very low sherd count occurrences in Phase 4.1 such as Group 4 coarse quartz-tempered ware (MOE, 5 sherds) and the Group 6 high medieval wares (2 sherds) can almost certainly be discounted as intrusive or misidentified examples. The Group 5 glazed tripod pitcher wares are, appropriately, absent from Phase 4.1 (*c* 850–950) but present in very low quantity (5 sherds) in Phase 4.2 (*c* 950–1050), but even here they may be intrusive, otherwise they are exceptionally early examples of this group. Continental imports, which are very rare anyhow, are not present until Phase 4.2 where they comprise only two sherds of North French grey ware (fabric MFGY), both from Brudene Street East properties (BE2 and BE4). Seven sherds occur in Phase 5 where they occur in a wider range of fabrics and on each of the three frontages, but again mainly from the BE frontage. The four continental sherds from Phase 6 are North French glazed wares of late 12th- or 13th-century date (MNV, MNVY from BE5 and BW3 respectively).

Inter-frontage and inter-property comparisons are rather harder to evaluate in terms of fabric groups because of the variables affecting the quantities of pottery recovered from each property/frontage/phase. The phased quantified data for the eight fabric groups from the three street frontages—SE (Snitheling Street East), BW (Brudene Street West) and BE (Brudene Street East)—are presented in Table 7.16. Without further manipulation of the data, which space does not permit here, there is a fairly high degree of uniformity and predictability in the fabrics groups data. To make a few broad comparisons between the frontages (by sherd count), there is, for example, a much higher chalky ware Group 1 reading for the BE frontage (71.25% of all pottery on that frontage) compared to the BW and SE frontages (around 62% and 54% respectively). This is due, in part, to the relatively low percentage of Group 3 sandy-flinty wares on BE (12%). These make up a much higher percentage on BW and SE (18% and 32% respectively), where they occupy their normal second place after the chalky wares, whereas on BE they are closely followed in third place by the (later) Group 6 high medieval

glazed wares (10.5% of BE) which are not so common on the other two frontages. This is partly the result of the selection procedure to include the high medieval (Phase 6) BE5 assemblage in the detailed catalogue, although it is also, to some extent, a reflection of the fact that high medieval glazed pottery was genuinely common on the BE frontage. In the less common fabric groups, however (excluding G1, G3 and G6), there is some evidence from the BW and SE frontages for a higher proportion of these wares than that found on BE and this fabric diversity may be a reflection of slightly greater prosperity (expressed through G5 glazed wares and late Saxon G2 wheel-thrown wares) and industrial activity (expressed through G7 crucibles, and dyepots). These slightly elevated percentages for BW and SE may in part be a reflection of the unequal size of the three frontage assemblages (mainly for the larger BW assemblage), but as the SE assemblage (*c* 3000 sherds) is smaller than the BE assemblage (4000 sherds) this cannot entirely be the case. The northern end of the BE frontage is reasonably represented in terms of industrial wares (crucibles and dyepots on BE5 and BE4 respectively), except for the central property (BE2), but they all have a relatively low proportion of Phase 4.2 and 5 glazed wares (see below) suggesting, perhaps, that the BE frontage was somewhat less well-to-do than the other two frontages. The only contradiction here is that the BE frontage has most of the imported G8 continental wares (7 sherds, compared to 5 on BW and 1 on SE) but these form only a very small proportion of the sherds on this frontage (0.18%) and one might question whether these few largely unglazed imports (including cooking wares) were really more of an expression of status than glazed Winchester ware vessels.

Glazed wares: Chronological development and distribution on the site

Glazed wares can also be viewed as a fabric group in their own right—although for chronological and cultural purposes they have been accommodated under more than one fabric group in the discussion above (mainly G2, G5 and G6). Just as crucibles and

Table 7.16: Post-Roman pottery: fabric groups by street frontage and phase. Quantification by sherd count.

Fabric group	Frontage	4.1 Sherds	4.1 %	4.2 Sherds	4.2 %	5 Sherds	5 %	6 Sherds	6 %	Total	Total %
1	BE	23	85.19%	1598	89.47%	1170	70.31%	59	11.28%	2850	71.25%
2	BE	4	14.81%	95	5.32%	48	2.88%	4	0.76%	151	3.78%
3	BE		0.00%	81	4.54%	367	22.06%	37	7.07%	485	12.13%
4	BE		0.00%	4	0.22%	30	1.80%	6	1.15%	40	1.00%
5	BE		0.00%	1	0.06%	18	1.08%	1	0.19%	20	0.50%
6	BE		0.00%	1	0.06%	18	1.08%	401	76.67%	420	10.50%
7	BE		0.00%	4	0.22%	11	0.66%	12	2.29%	27	0.68%
8	BE		0.00%	2	0.11%	2	0.12%	3	0.57%	7	0.18%
Sub-total		27	100.00%	1786	100.00%	1664	100.00%	523	100.00%	4000	100.00%
1	BW	1134	93.03%	1555	80.28%	1639	52.92%	547	33.33%	4875	61.76%
2	BW	42	3.45%	165	8.52%	139	4.49%	24	1.46%	370	4.69%
3	BW	22	1.80%	135	6.97%	951	30.71%	339	20.66%	1447	18.33%
4	BW	5	0.41%	15	0.77%	114	3.68%	308	18.77%	442	5.60%
5	BW		0.00%	4	0.21%	83	2.68%	68	4.14%	155	1.96%
6	BW	2	0.16%	10	0.52%	114	3.68%	340	20.72%	466	5.90%
7	BW	14	1.15%	53	2.74%	53	1.71%	14	0.85%	134	1.70%
8	BW		0.00%		0.00%	4	0.13%	1	0.06%	5	0.06%
Sub-total		1219	100.00%	1937	100.00%	3097	100.00%	1641	100.00%	7894	100.00%
1	SE	44	95.65%	751	84.95%	719	39.81%	25	18.38%	1539	53.59%
2	SE	2	4.35%	87	9.84%	83	4.60%	8	5.88%	180	6.27%
3	SE		0.00%	42	4.75%	786	43.52%	86	63.24%	914	31.82%
4	SE		0.00%		0.00%	85	4.71%		0.00%	85	2.96%
5	SE		0.00%		0.00%	67	3.71%	10	7.35%	77	2.68%
6	SE		0.00%	1	0.11%	44	2.44%	5	3.68%	50	1.74%
7	SE		0.00%	3	0.34%	21	1.16%	2	1.47%	26	0.91%
8	SE		0.00%		0.00%	1	0.06%		0.00%	1	0.03%
Sub-total		46	100.00%	884	100.00%	1806	100.00%	136	100.00%	2872	100.00%
TOTAL		1292		4607		6567		2300		14,766	

dyepots can occur in several fabrics but can still be viewed as indicators of industrial activity, so glazed pottery can occur in many fabrics but can be viewed collectively as an important technological development or cultural phenomenon within English medieval pottery. In the general late Saxon to early medieval pottery assemblage here there are relatively few indicators of social stratification—the assemblage is clearly dominated by coarse local cooking wares which, being the functional objects that they are, provide precious few indications of anything but cooking and storage. Glazed wares, in medieval England, as in many cases elsewhere, tended to be used for table wares, mainly jugs for the serving of wine and other beverages. They were more attractive and showy than coarsewares and, in certain social contexts, can be taken as a minor indicator of moderate prosperity and perhaps higher social status. The connection between glazed wares, increased prosperity and social drinking is a reasonably well accepted phenomenon in medieval archaeology although the very richest in society probably expressed their wealth though glass or metalware drinking vessels.

In the context of everyday late Saxon and early medieval Winchester it seems reasonable to assume that the presence of glazed tablewares (spouted pitchers, tripod pitchers and jugs) can be taken as an indicator of greater prosperity—though perhaps only slightly greater prosperity. In some cases, however, the presence or absence of glazed wares may be due to functional differences between areas (eg. kitchen and dining areas) but there seems to be little clear evidence for this from this site—partly because no complete building plan was recovered. Winchester was one of those few places in late Saxon England where glazed pottery, in the form of glazed and decorated Winchester ware, was available as early as *c* 950. Many areas of England had no regular supply of glazed wares until the late 12th

aTable 7.17 Post-Roman pottery: quantities of glazed wares on each of the phased properties as percentage of total phased pottery assemblage (Phases 4.2, 5 and 6)

| Property | Sherds | Phase 4.2 | | | | Sherds | Phase 5 | | | | Sherds | Phase 6 | | |
		sherds % all prop	Wgt	Wgt % all prop			sherds % all prop	Wgt	Wgt % all prop			sherds % all prop	Wgt	Wgt % all prop
BE 2	23	2.93%	221	1.41%		14	3.14%	425	4.96%			0.00%		0.00%
BE 4	12	1.62%	72	0.49%		24	3.59%	424	2.90%			0.00%		0.00%
BE 5	8	3.09%	113	2.73%		18	3.27%	166	1.72%		241	46.17%	3725	44.87%
BW 1		0.00%		0.00%		6	3.64%	53	2.07%		5	8.47%	30	4.57%
BW 2	29	3.60%	583	4.82%		14	6.73%	223	7.52%		18	14.40%	559	20.80%
BW 3	2	0.69%	35	0.69%		13	1.08%	140	0.82%		142	9.75%	2095	9.05%
BW 4	5	1.08%	120	1.41%		81	7.79%	1323	8.20%			0.00%		0.00%
BW 5	16	4.49%	294	4.20%		29	6.09%	953	8.58%			0.00%		0.00%
SE 1		0.00%		0.00%		73	5.08%	1597	6.94%		5	62.50%	138	66.67%
SE 2	4	1.04%	49	0.81%		5	1.35%	61	1.25%		7	5.47%	61	4.51%
Grand Total	99	2.15%	1,487	1.77%		277	4.22%	5365	4.86%		418	18.17%	6608	18.11%

century. Glazed pottery was still comparatively rare during the 10th–12th centuries and it was probably more an indicator or higher social status then than it was later on from the 13th century onwards when glazed wares were more commonplace. For these reasons a detailed discussion of the high medieval (Phase 6) glazed wares is largely excluded here as the inclusion of this obscures to some extent the picture of what was going on here in the 10th–12th centuries.

The 795 sherds of glazed pottery from the catalogued properties (Phases 4.1 to 6) comprise 5.38% (by sherds) of the entire assemblage (or 5.35% by weight) (Table 7.17). Discounting the single (unidentified) sherd in Phase 4.1 as intrusive, the 99 sherds in Phase 4.2 (c 950–1050) comprise 2.15% of all pottery in that phase. This proportionately more than doubles in Phase 5 (c 1050–1225) where the 277 glazed sherds comprise 4.22% of that phase, and in Phase 6 (c 1225–1550) the 418 glazed sherds comprise an impressive 18.17% of the phase assemblage.

To bring out any trends in the late Saxon to early medieval phased assemblage each of the ten catalogued properties was considered in turn and the combined sherd total of its Phase 4.2 and 5 glazed pottery was calculated as a proportion of all its pottery in those combined phases. The proportion varies from Property BW 3 in lowest (10th) position with 15 sherds comprising just 1%, to adjacent Property BW 4 in first place with 86 sherds comprising 5.73% of the total from that property (though nearly all from Phase 5). The Brudene Street West (BW) frontage holds the three highest consumers of glazed wares in this time period with Property BW 4, as mentioned, in first place, adjacent Property BW 5 in second place with 5.40% and Property BW 2 in third place with 4.24% (but in first place in Phase 4.2 with 3.6% of that phase). In fourth place is Property SE 1 with 3.77% of the combined phase (but in this case all from Phase 5) and

Property BE 5 occupies fifth place, with a total of 26 glazed sherds comprising 3.21% (the others in descending order are: BW 1, 6th with 3.14%; BE 2, 7th with 3%; BE 4, 8th with 2.55%; SE2, 9th with 1.19% and BW 3, 10th, already mentioned).

It should be noted that these figures are percentages of the combined phase total for each site and, for the lower counts, do not always reflect the actual number of sherds of glazed pottery. The lowest number of sherds (6 sherds) was actually from Property BW 1 although proportionately this occupies 6th position whereas Property BW 3 with 15 sherds is only in 10th. Of these Property BW 1 is the least excavated property and the validity of its glazed ware rating may well be diminished by this. The contiguous block of Properties BW 1–6 all rate highly as glazed ware consumers in the combined phase except, surprisingly, Property BW 3, which is right in the middle. Why this should be is unclear as the phase sample is reasonably large and in the following high medieval phase (Phase 6) Property BW 3 was one of the highest consumers of glazed wares on the site (9.7% of its Phase 6 assemblage— mostly from the backfill of a large well). Property BW 4 was among the lowest consumers of glazed wares in Phase 4.2 (5 sherds or 1.08% of its phase assemblage) but rose to be the largest consumer in Phase 5. Why it produced so few glazed wares in the earlier phase is puzzling but these few pieces are quite large and possibly represent five separate Winchester ware spouted pitchers. The Phase 4.2 assemblage on this property also produced the most highly decorated (coarseware) spouted pitcher from the whole site (fabric MAV, Fig. 7.11, no. 38), so perhaps it was not so impoverished as first appears. Property SE 1, with its abundant evidence for textile dyeing in Phase 4.2 (see dyepots, *Digital Section 1.3, Appendix 2*) curiously produced not a single sherd of glazed pottery in this phase and Property SE 2 produced only four sherds in this phase (1% of all its phase assemblage). In the following Phase 5 (c

1050–1225) Property SE 2 remained glaze impoverished but Property SE 1 became the fourth largest consumer of glazed pottery on the site (73 sherds), mostly large tripod pitchers/jugs (fabric MAD and MNG), a few Winchester ware vessels (in lower grade fabric) and a ?jug base in Normandy Gritty ware—the only one from this site. This coincides with the animal bone evidence for this phase which suggests the property was occupied by a furrier and therefore probably by a person of some wealth.

For Phase 4.2 alone, although the total of glazed sherds is smaller (99 sherds), Property BW 5 is proportionately the highest consumer of glazed wares which comprise 4.5% of its total assemblage for this phase. In second place is Property BW 2 with 3.6% and in third place Property BE 2 with 2.93%. Glazed Winchester ware occurs as 133 sherds in the sampled contexts. The highest sherd counts (Phases 4.2 to 6) were from Property BW 2 with 25 sherds, BW 5 had 20 sherds and BW 4 had 17 sherds. Other properties with high Winchester ware counts were BE 2 and BE 4 with 20 sherds each and BE 5 with 13 sherds.

From a broader perspective, considering the frontages rather than individual properties, in the combined Phase 4.2 and 5 assemblages from each frontage the differences between each of them in terms of glazed ware 'enrichment' is not strikingly different. Brudene Street West (BW) is in first place with glazed wares (195 sherds) forming 3.87% of its combined phase assemblage, Snitheling Street East (SE) is in second place with 82 glazed sherds forming 3.05% of its assemblage and Brudene Street East (BE) is in third place with 99 sherds though forming only 2.87% of its assemblage. If the presence of glazed wares can be taken as an indicator of relative wealth (though not necessarily great wealth) then the properties on BW seem always to have been somewhat more prosperous during the 10th–12th centuries than the other two frontages, with BE perhaps being perhaps the least prosperous—a suggestion also hinted at in the fabric groups data above. The glazed ware data for Phase 6 (c 1225–1550) is of somewhat less value and reliability as the Phase 6 deposits were only catalogued from six properties (BE 5, BW 1, BW 2, BW 3, SE 1 and SE 2). These show quite low glazed ware sherd counts for most of the properties but very high counts for Property BW 3 and especially BE 5. Those from Property BW 3, as mentioned above, are mostly from the backfill of a high status stone well house possibly belonging to the residence of the Archdeacon of Winchester. This appears to have been rapidly back-filled in the early 13th century. The highest glazed ware sherd count for this phase (and any phase) is from Property BE 5 with 241 glazed sherds, which comprise an impressive 46% of all Phase 6 pottery from that property. These came from a truncated chalk-built medieval cellar and a flint-lined well which suggests the owners of this property were people of some wealth. The pottery included small sherds

from the only North French green-glazed ware jug from the entire site. Elsewhere on the same frontage, on Property BE 2, a high quality Saintonge polychrome ware jug rim was recovered (from unsampled contexts), the only example from the excavations. Apart from these very rare instances of imported high quality pottery, most of the glazed wares during this period were regionally sourced jugs in South Hampshire red wares.

Vessel forms by property and phase

The quantity of each type of vessel form recovered from sampled contexts on the site is shown in Table 7.18. This shows what might have been predicted for the vessel composition of a site dominated by late Saxon and early medieval pottery. The assemblage is dominated by the jar form (83.34% by EVEs). The presence of sooting on a great many of these confirms their use as cooking pots although some unsooted examples were probably multi-purpose jars for storage, etc. Lack of vessel form diversity is a characteristic of Saxon and early medieval pottery assemblages, with the jar usually dominating—sometimes exclusively. A few bowls and spouted pitchers or jugs complete the picture along with rare forms such as lamps or crucibles. Vessel form diversity, reflecting the wider range of uses to which pottery was put, is more a feature of high medieval and post-medieval pottery. In a mainly domestic and mainly early pottery assemblage such as this where cooking is almost exclusively the main activity reflected in the pottery, this rather limits the extent to which pottery can inform us of any other functions to which it might have been put. Other functions can of course be inferred from the non-cooking pot forms (eg jugs for serving liquids, etc.) but unless these other forms occur in unusually high quantities, suggesting more of one type of activity than another in a certain area, then

Table 7.18: Post-Roman pottery: quantification of vessel form by EVEs. (See Digital Section 1.3 for vessel codes)

Vessel	EVE	%
BOWL	4.45	2.79%
CIST		0.00%
COST	0.1	0.06%
CRUC	3.22	2.02%
CUP	0.04	0.03%
CURF	0.04	0.03%
FPOT	0.14	0.09%
JAR	132.8	83.34%
JUG	3.27	2.05%
LAMP	10.19	6.39%
MISC	0.17	0.11%
SPP	4.06	2.55%
TPTCH	0.87	0.55%
Total	159.35	100.00%

it is difficult to know if slight variations in the pottery data from different areas (or properties as here) carry much significance. Ultimately the main reason for comparing the vessel form assemblages from the three different street frontages here and the ten catalogued properties is to see if these reflect any differences in the activities going on within each frontage and property. Except perhaps for the industrial pottery forms such as metallurgical crucibles and dyepots, which are relatively rare, and a few function-specific vessel forms such as lamps and curfews, which are equally rare, the pottery assemblages from these properties and frontages exhibit a high degree of similarity with little marked evidence for specific activities other than food preparation, the serving of beverages and storage.

Some variations within the quantified form data can of course be observed—just as the data for glazed ware occurrence across the site has already been analysed as a possible indicator of the relative prosperity of contemporary properties (see above), and with some degree of success. The distribution of glazed tableware forms (spouted pitchers, tripod pitchers and jugs) also bears-out these findings to a large degree so there is little point in revisiting the distribution of these forms in great detail. These would, most likely, only tell us where and when beverages were served and consumed in higher than usual quantities—thus, so the reasoning goes, showing us which areas were relatively wealthier than others. There is certainly a predictable degree of chronological variation from phase to phase as certain vessels forms (and fabrics) became more popular or fell out of use but the variations between individual properties are not very marked (even for glazed wares) and thus difficult to interpret in terms of function or area specialisation. For the most part, it would seem the same sorts of activity were taking place in each of the ten catalogued properties but

here and there to a slightly differing degree.

Some of these typological and hence functional differences can be highlighted and summarised here without the degree of data manipulation employed for the analysis of the glazed wares (see above). Doubtless further manipulation of the data would probably reveal further minor variations across the site but, for the present, do not permit every possible variation to be explored. The relative proportions of different vessel forms in each phase for the whole site are presented in Table 7.19. Notable trends here include the almost total domination of the jar form in the earliest phase, Phase 4.1, where it comprises 92.24% (by EVEs) of all identifiable forms in the phase assemblage whereas in the latest phase, Phase 6, this figure had dropped to 79.20% as a result of gradual form diversification. Other than jars the range of vessel forms available in Phase 4.1 was limited to a few spouted pitchers, a single lamp, a miscellaneous form (?costrel) and a few crucibles.

Bowls do not appear in the Phase 4.1 data—they probably existed but were very rare. Bowls were never very common on this site. They appear in Phase 4.2 and reached their peak in the following Phase 5 where they comprised only 3.70% of the phase assemblage. Many of these seem to have been of the socket-handled kind with a wide diameter and the evidence from sooting suggests these were mainly used for cooking—like an early form of saucepan. Elsewhere the presence of bowls in large quantities on medieval sites (mainly rural ones) has sometimes been taken as evidence for their use in dairying practices (Brown 1997, 92–3), so their relative scarcity in this corner of urban Winchester may be an indication that dairying activities were of low priority here. Spouted pitchers, for serving beverages, were never very common either. They reached their peak in Phase 4.2 where comprised 5.25% of the vessel assemblage

Table 7.19: Post-Roman pottery: vessel form by phase. Quantification by EVEs.

Vessel	4.1 EVE	4.1 %	4.2 EVE	4.2 %	5 EVE	5 %	6 EVE	6 %	EVE	Total %
BOWL		0.00%	1.26	2.21%	2.44	3.70%	0.75	3.35%	4.45	2.80%
CIST		0.00%		0.00%		0.00%		0.00%		0.00%
COST		0.00%	0.1	0.18%		0.00%		0.00%	0.1	0.06%
CRUC	0.6	4.35%	1	1.76%	1.12	1.70%	0.5	2.24%	3.22	2.03%
CUP		0.00%		0.00%		0.00%	0.04	0.18%	0.04	0.03%
CURF		0.00%		0.00%	0.04	0.06%		0.00%	0.04	0.03%
FPOT		0.00%	0.05	0.09%	0.09	0.14%		0.00%	0.14	0.09%
JAR	12.71	92.24%	46.2	81.20%	55.81	84.64%	17.71	79.20%	132.43	83.30%
JUG		0.00%		0.00%	0.5	0.76%	2.77	12.39%	3.27	2.06%
LAMP	0.1	0.73%	5.27	9.26%	4.72	7.16%	0.1	0.45%	10.19	6.41%
MISC		0.00%	0.03	0.05%	0.14	0.21%		0.00%	0.17	0.11%
SPP	0.37	2.69%	2.99	5.25%	0.5	0.76%	0.2	0.89%	4.06	2.55%
TPTCH		0.00%		0.00%	0.58	0.88%	0.29	1.30%	0.87	0.55%
Total	13.78	100.00%	56.9	100.00%	65.94	100.00%	22.36	100.00%	158.98	100.00%

(although the weight percentage is higher at 13.15%). Tripod pitchers were also relatively scarce. They were apparently present in Phase 4.2 (*c* 950–1050, but probably at the very end of this phase), relatively common in Phase 5, and reached their peak in Phase 6 (presumably early in the phase, unless they were residual?) where they comprised 1.30% of the vessel assemblage. Jugs (or undiagnostic tripod pitchers) were present but fairly rare in Phases 4.2 and 5 but the high medieval form of glazed jug is well-represented in Phase 6 where it comprised 12.39% of the assemblage.

Cresset oil lamps were present but rare in Phase 4.1 but fairly common in the following Phase 4.2 where they comprised 9.26% of the assemblage and in Phase 5 where they comprised 7.16%, but these robust little forms usually survive in the ground quite well which gives them a slightly higher EVEs reading—the figure for weight in Phase 4.2, for instance, is only 2.92%. Crucibles, being smallish too, are also subject to slight EVEs over-representation. They are present, but fairly rare in all phases (perhaps mainly residual in Phase 6 at 2.24% by EVEs); their true peak was in Phases 4.2 and 5

Table 7.20: Post-Roman pottery: vessel form by street frontage and phase. Quantification by EVEs.

Vessel	Frontage	4.1		4.2		5		6		Total EVE	Total %
		EVE	%	EVE	%	EVE	%	EVE	%		
BOWL	BE		0.00%	0.23	1.20%	0.24	1.45%	0.17	2.97%	0.64	1.54%
CRUC	BE		0.00%		0.00%	0.29	1.75%		0.00%	0.29	0.70%
CURF	BE		0.00%		0.00%		0.00%		0.00%		
JAR	BE	0.16	100.00%	16.79	87.45%	13	78.55%	3.46	60.38%	33.41	80.24%
JUG	BE		0.00%		0.00%		0.00%	1.82	31.76%	1.82	4.37%
LAMP	BE		0.00%	1.85	9.64%	2.57	15.53%		0.00%	4.42	10.61%
MISC	BE		0.00%	0.03	0.16%		0.00%		0.00%	0.03	0.07%
SPP	BE		0.00%	0.3	1.56%	0.34	2.05%	0.2	3.49%	0.84	2.02%
TPTCH	BE		0.00%		0.00%	0.11	0.66%	0.08	1.40%	0.19	0.46%
Sub-total		0.16	100.00%	19.2	100.00%	16.55	100.00%	5.73	100.00%	41.64	100.00%
BOWL	BW		0.00%	0.69	2.69%	1.6	5.43%	0.52	3.27%	2.81	3.33%
CIST	BW		0.00%		0.00%		0.00%		0.00%		
CRUC	BW	0.6	4.49%	1	3.90%	0.43	1.46%	0.5	3.14%	2.53	3.00%
CUP	BW		0.00%		0.00%		0.00%	0.04	0.25%	0.04	0.05%
CURF	BW		0.00%		0.00%		0.00%		0.00%		
FPOT	BW		0.00%	0.05	0.20%		0.00%		0.00%	0.05	0.06%
JAR	BW	12.3	92.00%	18.84	73.51%	24.96	84.67%	13.58	85.41%	69.68	82.58%
JUG	BW		0.00%		0.00%	0.29	0.98%	0.95	5.97%	1.24	1.47%
LAMP	BW	0.1	0.75%	3.42	13.34%	1.95	6.61%	0.1	0.63%	5.57	6.60%
MISC	BW		0.00%		0.00%	0.1	0.34%		0.00%	0.1	0.12%
SPP	BW	0.37	2.77%	1.63	6.36%	0.08	0.27%		0.00%	2.08	2.47%
TPTCH	BW		0.00%		0.00%	0.07	0.24%	0.21	1.32%	0.28	0.33%
Sub-total		13.37	100.00%	25.63	100.00%	29.48	100.00%	15.9	100.00%	84.38	100.00%
BOWL	SE		0.00%	0.34	2.82%	0.6	3.01%	0.06	8.22%	1	3.03%
COST	SE		0.00%	0.1	0.83%		0.00%		0.00%	0.1	0.30%
CRUC	SE		0.00%		0.00%	0.4	2.01%		0.00%	0.4	1.21%
CURF	SE		0.00%		0.00%	0.04	0.20%		0.00%	0.04	0.12%
FPOT	SE		0.00%		0.00%	0.09	0.45%		0.00%	0.09	0.27%
JAR	SE	0.25	100.00%	10.57	87.57%	17.85	89.65%	0.67	91.78%	29.34	89.02%
JUG	SE		0.00%		0.00%	0.21	1.05%		0.00%	0.21	0.64%
LAMP	SE		0.00%		0.00%	0.2	1.00%		0.00%	0.2	0.61%
MISC	SE		0.00%		0.00%	0.04	0.20%		0.00%	0.04	0.12%
SPP	SE		0.00%	1.06	8.78%	0.08	0.40%		0.00%	1.14	3.46%
TPTCH	SE		0.00%		0.00%	0.4	2.01%		0.00%	0.4	1.21%
Sub-total		0.25	100.00%	12.07	100.00%	19.91	100.00%	0.73	100.00%	32.96	100.00%
TOTAL		13.78		56.9		65.94		22.36		158.98	

where they comprised 1.76% and 1.70% respectively. The rarest vessel forms in these tables are nearly always present by just one or two vessels including a few curfew sherds in Phases 5 and 6 and a single cup in Phase 6 from Property BW 3 (probably in Tudor Green ware, *c* 1375–1500, but catalogued as fabric PMED). The latter is the latest type of medieval pottery identified from the site apart from a handful of much later intrusive post-medieval sherds.

The quantity and distribution of vessel forms across each of the three street frontages and through each phase is presented in Table 7.20, but the value of the latter varies according to the size of each property assemblage. The table shows, among other things, slighter higher values for bowls on the BW frontage for Phase 5 particularly (discounting the high Phase 6 EVEs value for SE as only 2 sherds were present). This probably just represents a slighter wider range of kitchenware forms on this possibly wealthier frontage and possibly a wider range of foodstuffs being prepared. It is less likely to represent an increased concern with dairying practices as most of the bowls had clearly been used for cooking. These figures are slightly biased towards Property BW 5 which produced an almost complete socket-handled bowl (Fig. 7.11, no. 42). Property BW 5, however, also holds the second highest glazed ware count for Phase 4.2 to 5 indicating moderate wealth.

Oil lamps: their possible significance

The distribution data for oil lamps is a little ambiguous and capable of a number of possible interpretations depending on whether they are viewed as an indicator of slightly higher or lower status dwellings, or neither. The lamps here are mainly in local 10th–12th century coarsewares at a time when most domestic lighting was probably in the form of rush lamps. Tallow or wax candles were not widely used in domestic contexts in Winchester (and elsewhere) until after *c* 1200 (Barclay and Biddle 1990, fig. 307). The possession of ceramic lamps then might be seen as either as an indication of slightly greater wealth, or as an accessory to certain activities or trades (textile working, writing etc.), or both. A very high number of ceramic lamps (105) were recovered from two medieval houses in Lower Brook Street, Winchester, and their distribution here has been interpreted as perhaps a reflection of the use of these buildings for light industry (requiring long hours of indoor work) as well as density of occupation along the street (ibid., 986). Abundant evidence for tanning pits from the site might imply that leather working and similar activities took place there. Elsewhere in the city the lack of ceramic lamps from the Castle, the Bishop's palace and the domestic buildings of the cathedral imply that only the wealthiest tier of society could afford candles at this time and thus had little need for ceramic lamps (ibid.). The wealthiest occupants of the site might have used stone cressets or even

glass hanging lamps—in which case ceramic lamps would be fairly low in this hierarchy—but still probably well above rush lamps. Lamps are present on all the catalogued properties except SE 2. In terms of the three street frontages, the BE frontage has the highest percentage of lamps at 10.61% (EVEs) of the identified forms from the whole frontage (or 3.44% weight), and most of these were from Phase 5 (15.53% of that phase). Of these, Property BE 4 has the highest percentage of lamps on the site (19 sherds, 14.76% EVEs, 5.84% weight). Adjacent Property BE 5 also has a moderate amount (3.88% EVEs). This is at slight odds though with the relatively low glazed ware count for this frontage (see above) which suggested that the occupants of BE (in Phases 4.2 and 5) might be somewhat poorer than those of the other two frontages (see also fabric groups data above). However, Property BE 4 did have quite a high Winchester ware sherd count (20 sherds) so perhaps it was slightly better-off than its BE neighbours at this time?

The BW frontage is also quite well-endowed with oil lamps at this time too—particularly the two northernmost Properties BW 4 and BW 5. Property BW 4 has the highest percentage of lamps on this frontage (7 sherds, 12.02% EVEs, 2.18% weight) and this property also has the highest number of glazed sherds (in Phases 4.2 and 5) than any property on the site (see above). Adjacent Property BW 5 also has quite a high percentage of lamps (10 sherds, 5.32% EVEs, 3.34% weight) and the second highest number of glazed sherds on the site. In the case of Properties BW 4 and BW 5 the high percentage of lamps and glazed wares (mainly tripod pitchers) may be a genuine reflection of somewhat greater wealth but this correlation does not seem to hold true for Property BE 4 across the road which has many lamps but not much glazed ware. The Snitheling Street frontage (SE) has the lowest percentage of lamps (0.61% EVEs, 0.17% weight) and these come from Property SE 1 alone (2 sherds, 0.80% EVEs, 0.22% weight) yet SE 1 has a high glazed ware count for these phases (fourth highest on the site)—again mostly tripod pitchers—which suggests comparative wealth. In Phase 5 this property was a possible furrier's residence (see above and bone report, below) and in Phase 4.2 this property produced the highest number of dyepots from the whole site (see dyepots *Digital Section 1.3*, *Appendix 2*), both facts suggesting a connection with the textile industry and the origin of the late Saxon 'Street of the Tailors' (Snitheling Street).

The very low presence of oil lamps from the SE frontage might appear to rule out any significant connection between oil lamp usage and the textile industry and also perhaps between oil lamps and high glazed ware counts? There may, however, be other factors at play here which are not reflected in the ceramic evidence and which we do not fully understand. It may be that the excavated Snitheling Street properties provide too small a sample of pottery compared to the other two frontages and perhaps there are dumps of ceramic lamps that have not yet been discovered? Or it may be that the tailors and furriers on SE were content to use rush lamps or some other type of non-ceramic lighting accessory (a furrier potentially could produce his own tallow—animal fat—candles)? In the case of the BE frontage there may be a special explanation for the high concentration of oil lamps and the low presence of early glazed wares. Rather than simply signifying that its occupants were somewhat poorer than those of the wealthier BW frontages (which still might be the case), the concentration of lamps here might suggest that the function of this area was different from BW and SE. Like SE, with its tailors and furriers, it may have had an artisanal function but perhaps a more heavy duty one, such as tanning and leather working (as at the Lower Brooks Street sites above)? And perhaps these related industries required increased illumination (lamps) but being perhaps primarily workshops they had little need for glazed wares or ceramic fripperies? Whatever its exact nature there seems to have been some sort of craft activity going on in the BE frontage that required a high number of oil lamps and perhaps these were primarily workshops rather than private residences (as on the BW frontage?) or combined residence/workshops (as on Property SE 1?). Ceramic lamps, in this case, may not therefore be a reliable indicator of greater wealth but rather of craft specialisation, at least when found in quantity. On the possibly wealthier BW properties (BW 4 and 5) the relatively high number of lamps there may just be reflection of the fact that they could easily afford them anyhow, and perhaps social entertaining and/or more lightweight trades did not require quite so much illumination.

Other vessel forms

The jug/tripod pitcher form has a fairly low presence in Phases 4.2 and 5 but the increased incidences of the glazed tripod pitcher (mainly Phase 5) have been noted above (eg Properties SE 1, BW 4). The jug form does not become really common until the high medieval period and is best represented on the BE frontage (mainly Property BE 5) where very high glazed ware sherd counts (see above) have already revealed its presence. In Phase 6, on BE frontage, the form reached its peak where it comprised 31.76% by EVEs (or 59% by weight) challenging the long-established monopoly of the jar/cooking pot. The spouted pitcher form, glazed or unglazed, also has a fairly low presence across the site (mostly under 5% EVEs) but there are two instances where two almost complete highly decorated chalky-flinty ware examples of this form result in an unusually high percentage of the property assemblages, namely Property SE 2 (11.38% EVEs, 20.05% weight caused by Fig. 7.10, no. 31) and Property BW 4 (3.97% EVEs, 14.67% weight caused by Fig. 7.11, no. 38).

The distribution of crucibles across the site has been considered at length elsewhere (see fabric MDL, *Digital Section 1.3*). This identified Property BW 2 as having the highest quantity of crucibles on the site, followed by Properties BE 5 and SE 2. They were never very common however and clearly the copper-working industry they represent was widely dispersed across the site. The distribution of dyepots likewise has identified Property SE 1 as having the highest quantity of these, followed by Properties BW 4 and BW 3 (see dyepots *Digital Section 1.3, Appendix 2*).

The rarest vessel forms here are usually represented by just a few examples and these are not always from sampled contexts. High medieval (Phase 6) vessel forms, other than jugs and jars, are rare from this site but common on other sites in Winchester where this period is better represented. One or two possible costrels (flasks) in late Saxon sandy ware have been identified including an example from Property SE 1 (see fabric MSH), and a possible high medieval example was identified from BW 3 (see fabric MDG). Dripping pans—a mainly high medieval ceramic form for collecting fat from spit roasts—occur as one definite example from an unsampled context on Property BW 5, Phase 6 (see fabric MDF). This example is of semicircular form which might imply the presence of a proper fireplace on Property BW 5 by this date. There is one definite example of a high medieval cistern or bunghole jar, most likely for brewing or storing ale (see fabric MDG). This occurs on Property BW 3 (Phase 6) the possible residence of the Archdeacon. Ceramic curfews (firecovers) reflecting a concern with fire prevention are rare but represented by at least four separate examples from Properties BE 2 and BE 5 (both Phase 6) and from Properties BW 2 and SE 2 (both Phase 5). Chimney pots, also perhaps reflecting a concern with fire prevention and ventilation, are not represented in the quantified tables here as the three examples recovered come from unsampled contexts. These are probably of 13th-century date and also perhaps reflect buildings of a fairly substantial nature. One example comes from Property BE 3 (Phase 5), another from adjacent Property BE 2 (Phase 6), the third example is from a modern context on the Northgate House site.

Vessel forms analysis: General conclusions

The data on fabric groups, glazed ware distribution and vessel form distribution have been examined in a number of ways to bring out any trends that might exist. For the overwhelming bulk of the assemblage—mainly represented by the ubiquitous jar/cooking pot—there is undoubtedly a high degree of similarity between the assemblages from the ten catalogued properties and three street frontages. This is taken to mean that the overall differences in social status between these properties and their occupants was not particularly marked and the general utilitarian nature of most of the pottery suggests a fairly low to middling class of occupant with occasional hints, here and there and from time to time, of moderate wealth reflected by the increased concentrations of glazed tablewares or decorated spouted pitchers, implying social dining and entertaining. The distribution of industrial vessels, mainly metallurgical crucibles and dyepots, also highlights a few properties where the high concentration of these suggests craft specialisation. This is more likely to be so in the case of crucibles, as copper metallurgy (clearly their main use) is likely to have been a specialist trade. This highlights Property BW 2 (in Phase 4.2) as a likely copper-smith's workshop at some point in time, and also perhaps Properties BE 4 and SE 2 but perhaps not to the same degree. As a few crucible sherds occur on almost every property it is difficult to know if these represent sporadic and short-lived metallurgy workshops on almost every property, or just rubbish present as a background scatter across the whole site, or even perhaps, in some cases, unused crucibles used as oil lamps.

The same is true, to some extent, for the many jar sherds showing evidence of purplish internal madder-staining implying use as dyepots and thus related to the textile industry (see *Digital Section 1.3, Appendix 2*). These occur on almost every property in varying numbers and probably imply small-scale domestic textile dyeing on almost every property between the 10th and 12th centuries. The marked concentration of these on Property SE 1, however, (mainly in Phase 4.2), is suggestive of craft speciali-sation and quite possibly linked to the origin of the name Snitheling Street—the 'Street of the Tailors'. The higher than usual concentration of ceramic oil lamps on the Brudene Street East (BE) frontage (BE4 particularly) is also possibly an indication of craft specialisation rather than an indication of wealth. These properties were relatively poor in glazed tablewares and this fact, plus the high number of lamps could imply they were primarily workshops of some kind (tanning/leather working?) rather than private residences or social areas.

The ceramic evidence suggests that the central area of the excavations—the Brudene Street West frontage—was perhaps a few degrees more prosperous than the other two street frontages. To some extent, however, the data are biased here because of the better level of layer preservation and deeper stratigraphy yielding a larger and more varied assemblage of pottery. Nevertheless, a proportionate analysis of early (ie 10th to early 13th century) glazed wares from the site indicates that the Brudene Street West frontage had a higher concentration of these (including glazed Winchester ware) than the other two properties and this is inter-preted here as evidence of somewhat greater prosperity at this time. The adjacent Properties BW 4 and BW 5 had the highest concentrations of early glazed wares from the whole site (mainly Phase 5). Property BW 4 also had the largest and most highly decorated local coarseware spouted pitcher from the whole site. This may originally have had three spouts (like a similar example from Chichester) and

might have had a special ceremonial significance. Coincidentally, or perhaps not, Property BW 4 also had the second highest concentration of madder-stained sherds from the site (after Property SE1). Properties BW 4 and BW 5 also had a high concen-tration of ceramic oil lamps, but unlike those across the road in BE 4 these were possibly intended to illuminate private residences and social gathering rather than a common workshop. Like other types of evidence from this site the pottery assemblage, for a variety of reasons, is patchy and incomplete. It is highly possible over the centuries of occupation that the function and status of any given property could have changed even within a single lifetime but evidence for this will not always survive.

Brown has published a useful summary of pottery types from The Brooks site in Winchester comparing this quantified assemblage with three other properties of similar date in both urban and rural Hampshire and Wiltshire (Brown 1997). However, all of these sites are of high medieval date (late 13th–14th century) and thus slightly too late to allow direct comparison with the site here. The Brooks site, furthermore, was a wealthy town house by this date, which does not seem to have been the case for most of the earlier properties here. The greater variety of vessel forms and imported wares at The Brooks is a reflection both of the wealth of its merchant owners and of the increasing diversity of ceramic forms available by the 14th century. There are one or two points of overlap, however, between The Brooks and the two properties here where high medieval pottery is best represented—BE 5 and BW 3. Brudene Street East Property BE 5 is the only property on the site with evidence of a high medieval (Phase 6) chalk-built cellar and a flint-lined well, both features suggesting occupation by someone of some wealth. The property produced a much larger assemblage of high medieval glazed jug sherds than any other on the site (16.44% by EVEs of all identifiable forms from the property, or 37.83% by weight, or 48.37% by sherd count) including one or two imported North French jugs, which are very rarely found in Winchester. In this sense Property BE 5 compares reasonably well with data from The Brooks where jugs were very abundant (Brown 1997, table 6). The Brooks data, however has to be adjusted to make direct compar-isons with the data here as 'unidentified' body sherds have been treated as a vessel form in their own right whereas they are completely excluded from this sort of data in the present report (eg the 50% jug EVEs, or rim percent, from The Brooks adjusts to 53% here).

The 13th–14th century occupants of Property BE 5 may therefore have been reasonably prosperous merchants with a wine cellar and perhaps a direct connection with markets in Winchester or Southampton from which imported pottery could be acquired, perhaps as an accessory of the wine trade. However, most of his glazed jugs were in relatively local but still decorative South Hampshire red wares and pink wares and these would easily have been available in local Winchester markets. Similarly Property BW 3, with its high status stone well-house backfilled with the second highest assemblage of high medieval glazed wares from the site, has tentatively been identified as the likely residence of the Archdeacons of Winchester. The large assemblage of (highly fragmentary) glazed jugs from here also hints at increased wine consumption and social entertainment as befits a person of this status. In addition, a possible glazed costrel (flask) and a ceramic cistern for ale-brewing from this site point to wine or ale consumption and a degree of self-sufficiency, as do a couple of small sherds from a Tudor Green ware cup (*c* 1375–1500), the latest type of medieval pottery recovered from the site (PMED).

General conclusions

It is difficult to assess to what extent the study of the pottery assemblage from these excavations has advanced our knowledge of late Saxon and medieval pottery from Winchester. The quantified data and computerised records certainly constitute a significant resource in their own right whose full potential has by no means been fully exploited. Each of the separate accounts of the forty or so pottery fabrics from the site has in its own way widened or deepened our knowledge of these types and this perhaps is the report's strongest contribution. This is truer for the late Saxon and early medieval (Saxo-Norman) wares than for the high medieval wares—the latter, poorly preserved in any case, have been adequately dealt with in other reports. The lack of scientific fabric characterisation means, unfortunately, that our knowledge of exactly where most of this pottery was produced remains one of the biggest outstanding obstacles in the study of Winchester's medieval pottery. To date the only definite late Saxon production site identified in the region is at Michelmersh, about 8 miles west of Winchester, where wheel-thrown Michelmersh ware was produced *c* 925/50–1050. However, recent scientific analysis now suggests that Late Saxon sandy ware, an even earlier wheel-thrown ware, may have been produced in the same Michelmersh area from as early as *c* 850 (Mepham and Brown 2007). Chalk-tempered wares, the dominant pottery tradition in Winchester *c* 850-1150, remain unsourced but must have been fairly locally produced. These were also common in mid Saxon Southampton (Timby 1988, 80–2) and comparisons with the typology and fabric descriptions of the Southampton examples that are not local to Southampton suggest that the same source or sources supplying Winchester from *c* 850 may have been the same as those supplying Southampton *c* 750–850. This source, thought to have been located around 15 miles north of Southampton where the Reading Beds outcrop immediately south of the chalk escarpment, is

therefore more likely to have been closer to Winchester than Southampton, perhaps to the south of the city. If such an industry (perhaps dispersed along the chalk valleys) was that much closer to Winchester then perhaps the dating of chalk-tempered ware (MBX) in the city could be even earlier than the local *c* 850 start-date traditionally accepted? The simplicity of this ware type and the inability to date it very closely could mean that its earliest occurrences in the city might have been overlooked.

The exact source of the remarkable late Saxon glazed Winchester ware industry (*c* 950–1100) is still unknown but presumed to be fairly local. A few defectively glazed and flawed 'seconds' vessels from the site here would seem to support this notion. These have been scientifically examined by Alan Vince (see *Digital Section 1.3, Appendix 3*) and the results support the suggestion of a fairly local origin.

Some late Saxon or Saxo-Norman sandy and flinty coarsewares in the city (MBK, MOE) have recently been suggested to be from the London Clay area east of the city in the area of Alton and Petersfield perhaps (Blackmore 2007, and this report). These round-bottomed more archaic-looking jar forms are completely different in style to the more robust sagging based jars of the dominant local chalky ware tradition (MBX, MAV) and it is difficult to see why they should have become popular in the city and why chalky wares should simultaneously have been in decline. They may perhaps represent potters or pottery merchants from east of the city travelling to markets in Winchester to peddle their wares, or possibly Winchester folk travelling to markets in those areas during the 11th and 12th centuries. Whatever the case, chalky wares fell out of fashion and were effectively gone by *c* 1200 when the region was swamped by sandy ware cooking pots (also perhaps from the east) and increasingly by glazed jugs from sources in south Hampshire. Microscopic analysis of late Saxon 'organic-tempered' sandy ware sherds, in this report (MAF *c* 950–1150), has also demonstrated that this is not true organic tempering (chaff etc.), in the early Anglo-Saxon sense, but that these are actually voids caused by the dissolution of needle-like crystals of the mineral selenite (gypsum)—another mineral commonly found in the London Clay to the south and east of the city. Examination of identical sherd samples from Southampton also suggests this to be the case. It always seemed rather incongruous that a basically early-mid Anglo-Saxon pottery tempering tradition could have persisted in the region as late as *c* 1150 and it now seems this notion can be dispelled.

The number of imported continental wares recovered from the site—fifteen or so sherds covering the period *c* 900–1250—is remarkably low, but consistent with the established view that imported wares were very rare in inland Winchester and somehow never made it up the twelve miles of river connecting the city with the port of South-ampton where imported pottery was relatively abundant. One rare imported type known from earlier excavations in the Staple Gardens area is Badorf-type ware, a 9th–10th century Rhenish ware often imported as large relief-band amphoras (Helen Rees pers. comm; Hodges 1981, 37). This type has not been identified from the present excavations. A sherd of early 15th-century Valencian lustreware from Staple Gardens has also been published (Hurst 1964, fig. 63.12). The only new type of imported pottery identified from the present excavations that does not seem to have been previously noted in Winchester is a Rhenish Paffrath-type ware 'ladle', probably of 11th–12th century date. By and large, Winchester citizens did not express their wealth and status through imported continental pottery. Why should they need to when they had attractive yellow-glazed Winchester ware in the late Saxon period and regionally-sourced glazed tripod pitchers and highly decorated South Hampshire red ware jugs in the early and high medieval periods?

Overall the pottery from the site suggests occupation of low to middling status with occasional hints of relative wealth. The distribution of certain classes of pottery across the site, particularly the industrial wares and the glazed wares, has identified areas of more intense industrial activity or relative wealth against a general background of fairly monotonous local coarsewares, primarily cooking pots. Study of the crucible fabrics confirms earlier studies suggesting that (true) organic-tempered crucibles are primarily late Saxon in date, and that post-conquest examples are mainly in sandy wares and are generally larger.

The distribution of crucible sherds has also highlighted one or two properties (mainly BW2) where copper-working metallurgy was relatively intense, suggesting the presence of workshops here. The identification of over 300 purplish-red madder-stained sherds from pots used as dyepots—the largest collection from an English excavation—would appear to support earlier suggestions that Winchester was heavily involved with the textile industry in the late Saxon and early medieval periods. The distribution of dyepot sherds across the site has also highlighted a few properties where this activity was most intense, in particular Property SE1 during the period *c* 950–1050, and it hardly seems a coincidence that the location of this property was on Snitheling Street—the 'Street of the Tailors'. These sherds are also the only hard archae-ological evidence for the likely importation of the commodity dyestuff madder, probably from France, during this period.

The distribution of glazed wares may have highlighted areas of relative wealth, mainly the Brudene Street West properties, whereas an unusual concentration of ceramic oil lamps in the northern properties of the Brudene Street East frontage (BE4

and BE5), coupled with a general poverty in glazed wares, has suggested this area may have been an area of workshops for some craft specialisation requiring a fair degree of illumination, possibly leather working or textile production etc.

Catalogue of illustrated pottery (Figs 7.8-7.17)

1. Fabric MAB, Jar with thumbed rim. Very coarse flint temper. Di 280 mm., Group NH8550, Context NH3580, Phase 5
2. Fabric MAD, Tripod pitcher with combed dec and applied thumbed strips. Dark greenish-brown glaze (reconstruction drawing). Di 150 mm., Group NH8543, Context NH3286, Phase 6
3. Fabric MAD, Tripod pitcher rim with complex rouletted dec on top, inside and outside. Greenish-brown glaze. Di 190 mm., Group DC7021, Context DC3126, Phase 5
4. Fabric MAD, Wide tripod pitcher rim with circular gridiron stamps on top. Combed dec and traces of applied thumbed strips on the outside. Decayed greenish-brown glaze. Di 220 mm., Group DC7024, Context DC2114, Phase 6
5. Fabric MAD, Unglazed MAD (or fine brown MOE). Probable tripod pitcher sherd with applied strips or cordons and traces of combed and possible rouletted dec, Group DC7021, Context DC3126, Phase 5
6. Fabric MAD, Tripod pitcher base with applied foot with deep circular indent. Grey-green glaze, Group NH8612, Context NH5128, Phase 5
7. Fabric MAF, ?Cresset lamp rim. Possibly with notch or perforation cut through rim. Unsooted. Di 80 mm., Group DC7031, Context DC3021, Phase 5
8. Fabric MAQ, Jar with simple A2P-type rim. MAQ/MBK hybrid. 12-13C ctx. Di 140 mm., Group DC7039, Context DC6043, Phase 5
9. Fabric MAQ, Small jar rim. Di 120 mm., Group NH8530, Context NH4130, Phase 4.2
10. Fabric MAQ, Jar rim. Cavetto neck. Grooved rim. MAQ/MBK. Di 180 mm., Group DC7019, Context DC2077, Phase 5
11. Fabric MAQ, Jar profile. Bag-shaped with rounded base. Weak shoulder carination. Di 240 mm., Group NH8636, Context NH1391, Phase 5
12. Fabric MAQ, Jar profile with rounded base. Finer MAQ/MBK fabric. Di 210 mm., Group DC7007, Context DC1381, Phase 4.2
13. Fabric MAQ, Hammerhead bowl rim. Oxid. Di. 270 mm., Group DC7031/DC7043, Context DC3013, 2212, Phase 5/6
14. Fabric MAQ, Profile small chalice-shaped cresset lamp with pedestal base. Heavily sooted internally. Di 80 mm., Group DC7023, Context DC2027, Phase 5
15. Fabric MAQ, Complete small chalice-shaped cresset lamp with pedestal base. Only slight traces sooting. Very coarse fabric. SF220. Di 87 mm., Group DC7019, Context DC2077, Phase 5
16. Fabric MAQ, Cresset lamp profile. Possibly with plain flat base or damaged short pedestal-type base? Heavily sooted internally. Di 125 mm., Group NH8594, Context NH2462, 2461, Phase 4.2
17. Fabric MAQ, Chimney pot rim. Unsooted. Di 160 mm., Group DC7051, Context DC1160, Phase 6

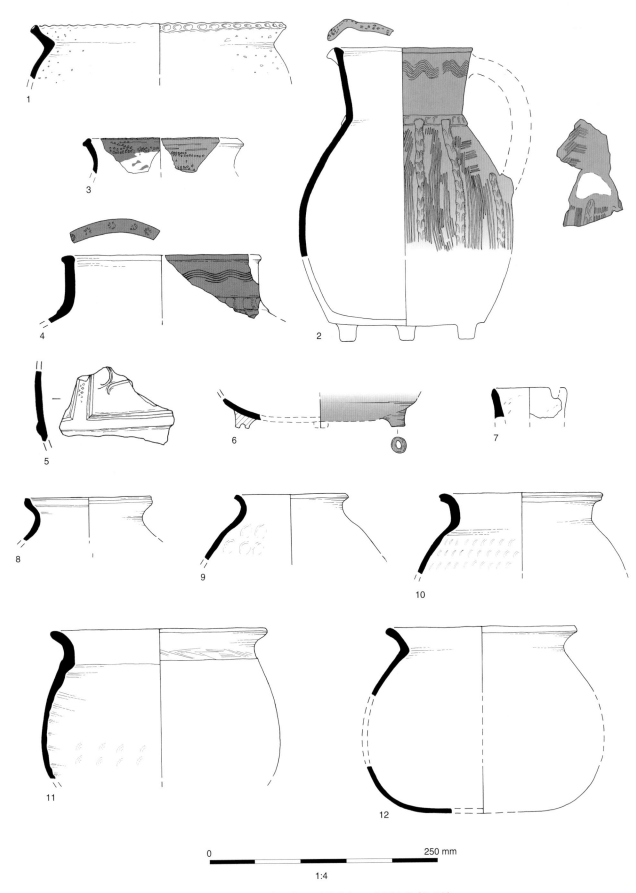

Fig. 7.8 Post-Roman pottery: MAB (1), MAD (2–6), MAF (7), and MAQ (8–12)

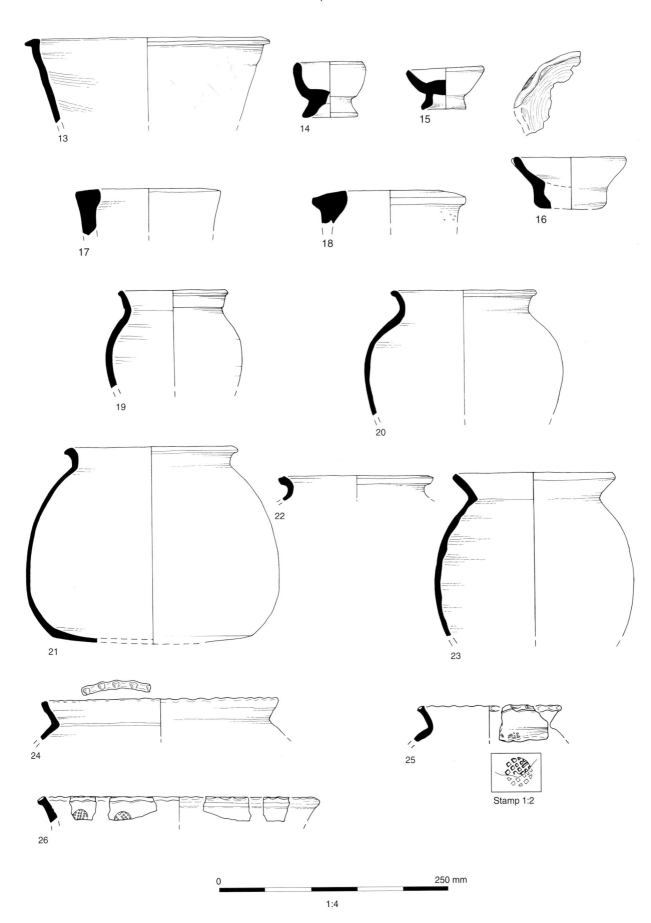

Fig. 7.9   Post-Roman pottery: MAQ (13–19) and MAV (20–26)

18. Fabric MAQ, Chimney pot rim. Unsooted. Very coarse fabric. Di 160 mm., Group DC7051, Context DC1109, Phase 5

19. Fabric MAV, Near-profile smallish globular jar. Upright rim. Di 120 mm., Group DC7031, Context DC3018, Phase 5

20. Fabric MAV, Jar profile. A1C-type rim form. Di 160 mm., Group DC7019, Context DC2036, Phase 5

21. Fabric MAV, Profile globular jar. Short near-upright rim. Di 190 mm., Group NH8612, Context NH5202, Phase 5

22. Fabric MAV, Jar. Unusually squared rim. Di 170 mm., Group , Context NH1070, Phase 8

23. Fabric MAV, Near-profile jar. A3B-type flaring rim form. Di 180 mm., Group DC7017, Context DC1618, Phase 5

24. Fabric MAV, Jar rim with spaced thumbing. Oxid. Di 260 mm., Group NH8542, Context NH4177, Phase 5

25. Fabric MAV, Jar with thumbed rim and circular gridiron stamps on shoulder. Oxid. Di 160 mm., Group NH8500, Context NH1215, Phase 2.4

26. Fabric MAV, Jar with thumbed rim and circular gridiron stamps inside rim. Di 310 mm., Group DC7014, Context DC1360, 1361, Phase 4.2

27. Fabric MAV, Large jar rim with shoulder carination. B2-type rim form. Di 340 mm., Group DC7008, Context DC1398, Phase 5

28. Fabric MAV, Near-profile large jar. Di 330 mm, Group DC7007, Context DC1381, Phase 4.2

29. Fabric MAV, Jar with horizontal rim. Late? Di 280 mm., Group DC7051, Context DC1517, Phase 5

30. Fabric MAV, Jar base/body profile. Oxid. Base Di 160 mm., Group NH8554, Context NH3546, Phase 5

31. Fabric MAV, Spouted pitcher with thumbed rim and impressed dimple dec on body. Di 180 mm., Group NH8621, Context NH1589, Phase 4.2

32. Fabric MAV, Spouted pitcher with combed dec on shoulder. Oxid. Di 120 mm., Group DC7019, Context DC2078, 2094, Phase 5

33. Fabric MAV, Spouted pitcher with incised oblique stroke dec on rim. Di 170 mm., Group DC7015, Context DC1663, Phase 5

34. Fabric MAV, Large spouted pitcher with incised oblique stroke dec on rim. Oxid. Di 280 mm., Group NH8531, Context NH4562, Phase 4.1

35. Fabric MAV, Large jar rim with incised oblique stroke dec on rim and incised/combed dec on shoulder. Oxid. Di 280 mm., Context DC3176, Phase 4.2

36. Fabric MAV, Jar shoulder with incised/combed dec. Oxid, Group NH8633, Context NH1022, Phase 5

37. Fabric MAV, Jar shoulder with incised/combed dec (interlaced chevrons). Oxid, Group NH8636, Context NH1362, Phase 5

38. Fabric MAV, Large, highly dec spouted pitcher with thumbed rim and incised and stabbed dec on body. Oxid. Di 300 mm., Group NH8567, Context NH3389, Phase 4.2

39. Fabric MAV, Spouted pitcher rim (evidence of spout) with stabbed pit dec. Di 240 mm., Group NH8593, Context NH9767, Phase 5

40. Fabric MAV, Jar shoulder with carination and unusual incised diagonal line and dot dec. Di at girth c. 210 mm., Context NH5022, Phase 6

41. Fabric MAV, ?Jar body sherd with incised ?vertical line dec. Oxid, Group DC7021, Context DC3235, Phase 6

42. Fabric MAV, Unusual deep bowl profile with tubular socket handle. Di 270 mm., Group NH8593, Context NH9666, Phase 5

43. Fabric MAV, Bowl, or jar, with slightly inturned rim. Di 280 mm., Group NH8603, Context NH7600, Phase 4

44. Fabric MAV, Bowl with near-vertical rim (rim added on as separate coil). Di 290 mm., Group NH8596, Context NH2411, Phase 4.2

45. Fabric MAV, Bowl (or curfew?). Flaring walls. Di 400 mm., Group NH8620, Context NH6051, Phase 5

46. Fabric MAV, Shallow bowl with curved sides. Di 250 mm., Group DC7056, Context DC1254, Phase 4

47. Fabric MAV, Profile small spiked cresset lamp. Heavily sooted internally. Di 64 mm., Group DC7050, Context DC1315, Phase 5

48. Fabric MAV, Profile spiked cresset lamp. Heavily sooted internally. Di 84 mm. SF1255, Group NH8530, Context NH4130, Phase 4.2

49. Fabric MAV, Profile cresset lamp with pedestal base. Heavily sooted internally. Di 83 mm. SF268, Group , Context DC2277, Phase 6

50. Fabric MAV, Cresset lamp rim. Unusual deep form. Sooted internally. Di 120 mm., Group DC7039, Context DC3029, Phase 5

51. Fabric MAV, Bowl, probably used as lamp. Has oxidised 'tide marks' internally and some sooting on rim. Di 240 mm, Group DC7023, Context DC2027, Phase 5

52. Fabric MAV, Curfew rim. Di 450 mm., Group DC7051, Context DC1160, Phase 6

53. Fabric MAV, Chimney pot rim. Slight sooting internally. MAV/MAQ fabric. Di 150 mm., Context NH2251, Phase 8

54. Fabric MBEAU, Beauvais-type ware. Jar base with red painted vertical lines externally and continuing under base. Base Di c. 180 mm., Group DC7058, Context DC1022, Phase 4

55. Fabric MBEAU, Beauvais-type ware.?Jar sherd with red painted lattice decoration, Group DC7015, Context DC1292, Phase 6

56. Fabric MBK, Jar rim. Silty, early-looking MBK/MAQ fabric. 10C ctx? Di 130 mm, Group NH8619, Context NH6116, Phase 4.2

57. Fabric MBK, Jar rim. MBK/MDF hybrid? 13C? Di. 200 mm., Group NH8514, Context NH8020, Phase 6

58. Fabric MBK, Jar rim with cavetto neck and slight shoulder carination. Di 220 mm., Group NH8593, Context NH9666, Phase 5

59. Fabric MBK, Jar with thumbed rim and scratch-marked dec. Di 220 mm., Group NH8612, Context NH5128, Phase 5

60. Fabric MBK, Large jar rim with scratch-marked dec. Di 340 mm., Group NH8612, Context NH5128, Phase 5

61. Fabric MBK, Jar shoulder. Unusual incised vertical line dec., Group NH8623, Context NH1029, Phase 5

62. Fabric MBN, Jar with rouletted rim. Di. 120 mm., Group NH8596, Context NH2422, Phase 4.2

63. Fabric MBN, Jar body with rouletted dec, Group NH8554, Context NH3491, Phase 5

64. Fabric MBN, Jar body with rouletted dec and prominent rilling or ribbing, Group DC7009, Context DC1408, Phase 4.2

65. Fabric MBX, Small jar. Di 70 mm., Group NH8622, Context NH1180, Phase 4.2

66. Fabric MBX, Small jar. Near profile. Di 85 mm. 10C pit group, Group NH8531, Context NH4232, Phase 4.1

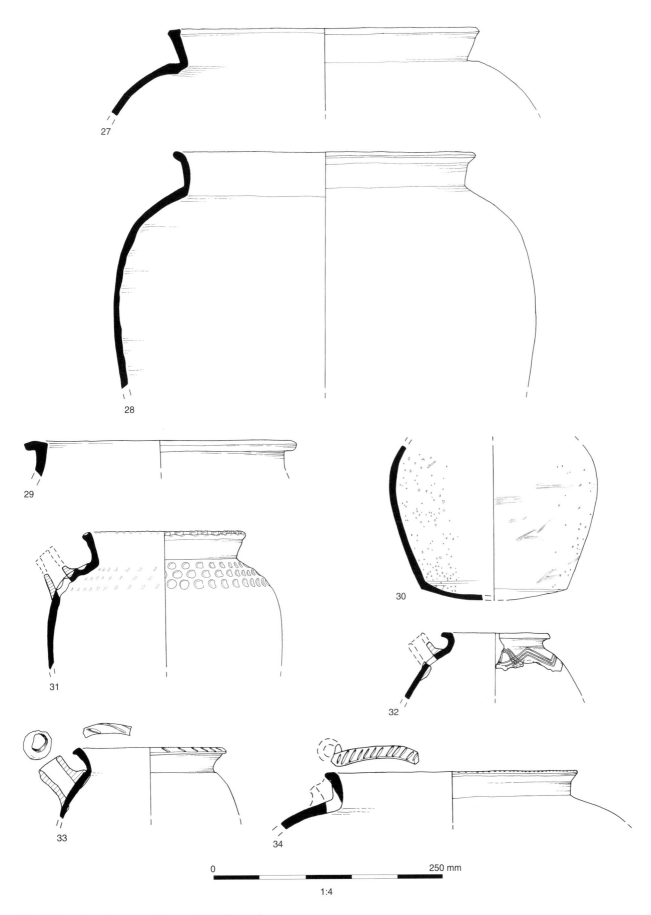

Fig. 7.10   Post-Roman pottery: MAV (27–34)

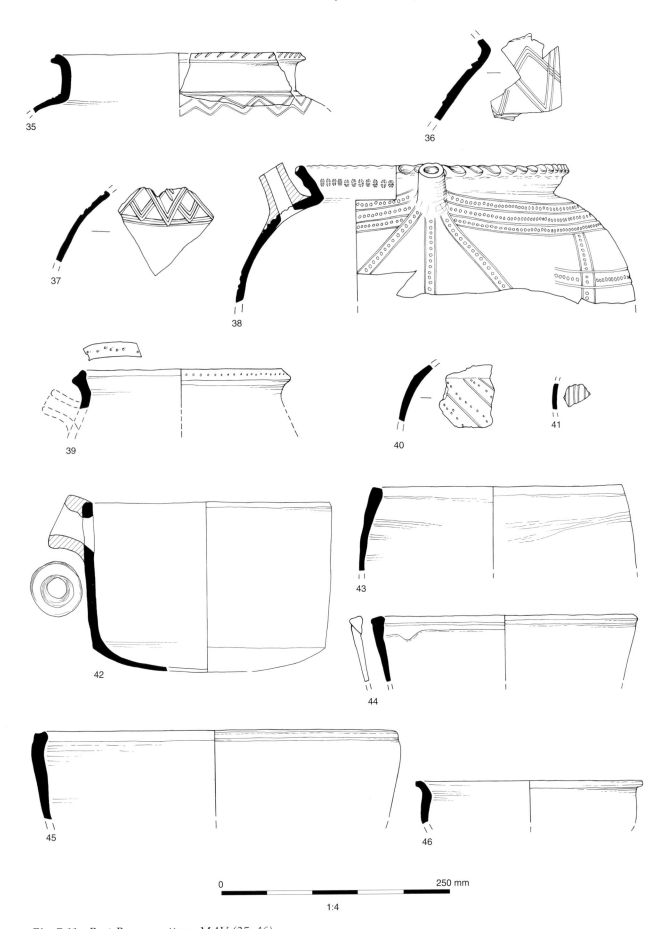

Fig. 7.11   Post-Roman pottery: MAV (35–46)

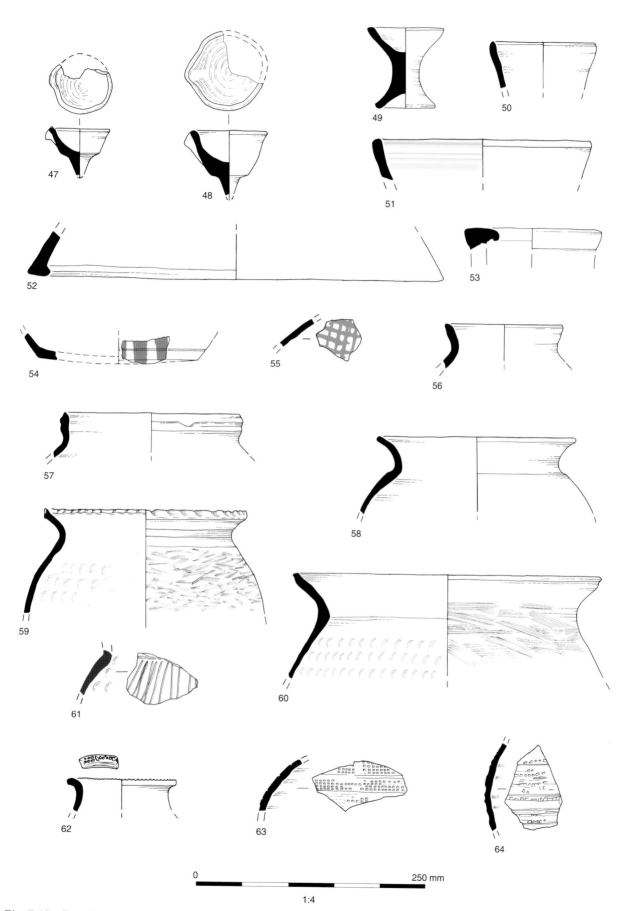

Fig. 7.12   Post-Roman pottery: MAV (47–53), MBEAU (54–5), MBK (56–61) and MBN (62–4)

67. Fabric MBX, Small jar with thumbed rim. Di 100 mm., Group NH8578, Context NH3400, Phase 4.1

68. Fabric MBX, Small jar with prominent shoulder carination. Di 110 mm., Group NH8550, Context NH3699, Phase 5

69. Fabric MBX, Jar with cavetto neck. Bevelled A2 rim form. 10C ctx. Di 160 mm., Group NH8619, Context NH6116, Phase 4.2

70. Fabric MBX, Jar with spaced groups of thumbing on rim. L11-12C ctx? Di 180 mm., Group NH8538, Context NH4223, Phase 4.2

71. Fabric MBX, Jar with cavetto neck. Incipient bead rim form A1C. Shoulder carination. 10C ctx. Di 160 mm., Group NH8619, Context NH6116, Phase 4.2

72. Fabric MBX, Jar rim with prominent shoulder carination. Late? Di 210 mm., Group NH8609, Context NH4623, 4624, Phase 4.1

73. Fabric MBX, Jar rim with prominent shoulder carination. Di 270 mm., Group NH8556, Context NH3669, Phase 4.2

74. Fabric MBX, Slack-sided jar or bowl. Di 210 mm., Group NH8592, Context NH2044, Phase 5

75. Fabric MBX, Jar rim. Dec int with band of stabbed pits. Di 140 mm., Group DC7018, Context DC2288, Phase 4.2

76. Fabric MBX, Sherd with multiple circular gridiron stamps. Residual in 13-14C ctx., Group DC7042, Context DC2107, Phase 6

77. Fabric MBX, Sherd with small circular gridiron stamps (stamps Di 11 mm.), Group NH8558, Context NH3416, Phase 4.2

78. Fabric MBX, Sherd with all over sunburst stamps, Group NH8543, Context NH3282, Phase 6

79. Fabric MBX, Sherd with cross-in-circle stamps, Group NH8620, Context NH6148, Phase 5

80. Fabric MBX, Jar or deep bowl rim with upright pierced lug handle. 8-9C? Residual. Di c. 240 mm?, Group NH8576, Context NH3496, Phase 5

81. Fabric MBX, Spouted pitcher with thumbed rim and complete stubby tubular spout. Di 240 mm., Group NH8528, Context NH4592, Phase 4.1

82. Fabric MBX, Spouted pitcher with handle. 10C ctx. Di. 190 mm., Group NH8619, Context NH6116, Phase 4.2

83. Fabric MBX, Bowl. Di 220 mm. 9-10C context. Assoc with madder-stained vessels, Group NH8619, Context NH6161, Phase 4.2

84. Fabric MBX, Bowl profile with socket handle. 10-11C ctx? Di 220 mm., Group NH8530, Context NH4277, Phase 4.2

85. Fabric MBX, Cresset lamp. Possibly pedestal-type? Di 140 mm., Group NH8632, Context NH1145, Phase 4

86. Fabric MBX, Cresset lamp. Possibly pedestal-type? Di 150 mm., Context NH2097, Phase 4.2

87. Fabric MDF, Jar with brushed decoration. Di 260 mm., Context NH805, Phase EVAL

88. Fabric MDL, Crucible rim with pouring lip. Vitreous external coating with reddish copper staining plus a few specks of greenish copper internally. Some organic inclusions in fabric. Di c. 60 mm., Group NH8529, Context NH4394, Phase 4.2

89. Fabric MDL, Crucible rim with thick external vitreous coating, extending partly internally, with reddish copper staining and slag-like debris plus a few specks of greenish copper embedded internally. Organic inclusions in fabric. Di c. 40 mm., Group NH8633, Context NH1022, Phase 5

90. Fabric MDL, Crucible profile with pouring lip. Fine cream sandy fabric. Probably unused. Di 80 mm., Group NH8602, Context NH7616, Phase 5

91. Fabric MDL, Crucible rim. Trace of spout. Fine brown sandy fabric like MMU. Sooted externally. Di 120 mm., Group NH8633, Context NH1027, Phase 5

92. Fabric MFI, Normandy gritty white ware. Jar/jug base with single speck of clear yellow glaze externally. Base Di 81 mm., Group NH8620, Context NH6101, Phase 5

93. Fabric MMU, Jar rim. Di 200 mm., Group NH8622, Context NH1155, Phase 4.2

94. Fabric MMU, Jar in oxid Michelmersh fabric but handmade rather than wheel-thrown. Di 210 mm., Group NH8633, Context NH1022, 1030, Phase 5

95. Fabric MMU, Jar rim with incised wavy line dec on rim. Di 140 mm., Group NH8628, Context NH1085, Phase 5

96. Fabric MMU, Jar with thumbed rim (or possibly MSH?). Probably residual in 10-12C ctx. Di 180 mm., Group NH8576, Context NH2229, Phase 5

97. Fabric MMU, Spouted pitcher with inturned rim and notched shoulder cordon. Di 160 mm., Group NH8615, Context NH5046, Phase 6

98. Fabric MMU, Spouted pitcher with inturned rim and stamped strip decoration. Di 160 mm., Group DC7027, Context DC2312, Phase 6

99. Fabric MMU, Small jar base. Base Di 54 mm., Group NH8567, Context NH3466, Phase 5

100. Fabric MMU, Shallow dish profile. Di 310 mm., Group NH8622, Context NH1155, Phase 4.2

101. Fabric MMU, Crucible rim. Sooted externally. Di 100 mm., Group NH8609, Context NH4623, Phase 4.1

102. Fabric MNG, Tripod pitcher rim and handle. Highly dec with applied strip and roulette dec. Yellow-brown glaze (fabric related to Winchester ware?). Di 190 mm., Context NH303, 305, Phase EVAL

103. Fabric MOE, Unusual jar rim form. Pale br-buff. Di. 310 mm., Group DC7042, Context DC2203, Phase 6

104. Fabric MOE, Jar rim with scratch-marked dec. Di 195 mm., Group DC7024, Context DC2113, Phase 6

105. Fabric MOE, Large jar rim. B2-related rim form. Di 320 mm., Group NH8632, Context NH1293, Phase 5

106. Fabric MPAF, Paffrath-type ware. 'Ladle' rim with attached handle fragment. Di 90 mm., Group DC7059, Context DC1131, Phase 6

107. Fabric MPIN, Pingsdorf-type ware. Jar/beaker body with red painted dec. probably 'commas', Group NH8575, Context NH2038, Phase 5

108. Fabric MSH, Unusually simple handmade jar rim (?or MMU/MZM). Di 140 mm., Group , Context DC3276, Phase 6

109. Fabric MSH, Simple jar rim with lightly combed wavy band on shoulder. Di 130 mm., Group NH8632, Context NH1146, Phase 4

110. Fabric MSH, Jar rim. Di 120 mm., Group NH8607, Context NH4695, Phase 4.1

111. Fabric MSH, Jar profile. 10C ctx. Di 150 mm., Group NH8619, Context NH6116, Phase 4.2

112. Fabric MSH, Jar rim. Internally hollowed. Di 160 mm., Group NH8559, Context NH3069, Phase 5

113. Fabric MSH, Rim from narrow-necked ?costrel. Di 75 mm., Group NH8619, Context NH6116, Phase 4.2

114. Fabric MSH, Sherd from odd vessel form with scar of applied spout or tubular handle. Possibly a costrel?, Group NH8607, Context NH4689, Phase 4.1

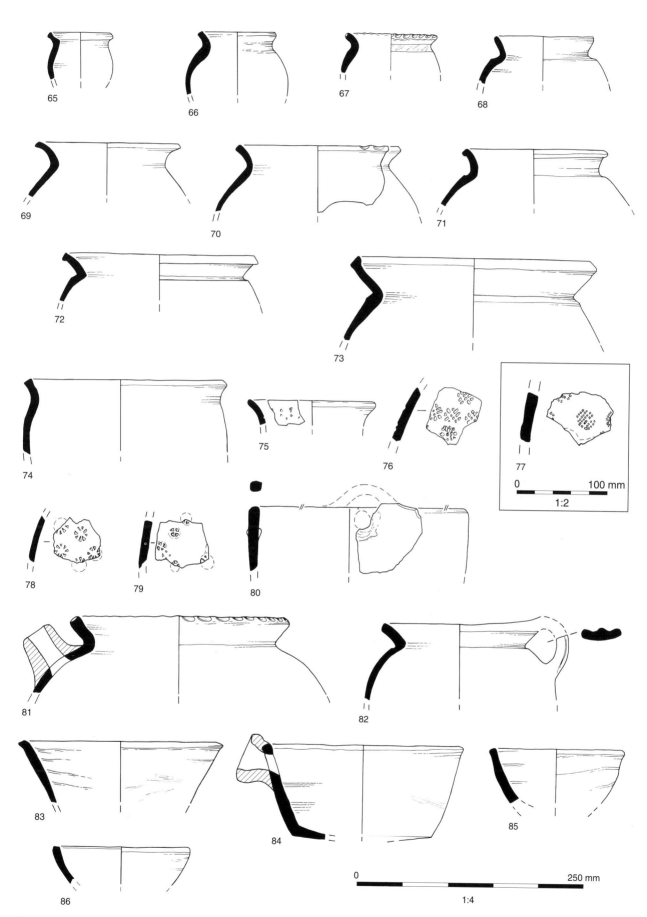

Fig. 7.13   Post-Roman pottery: MBX (65–86)

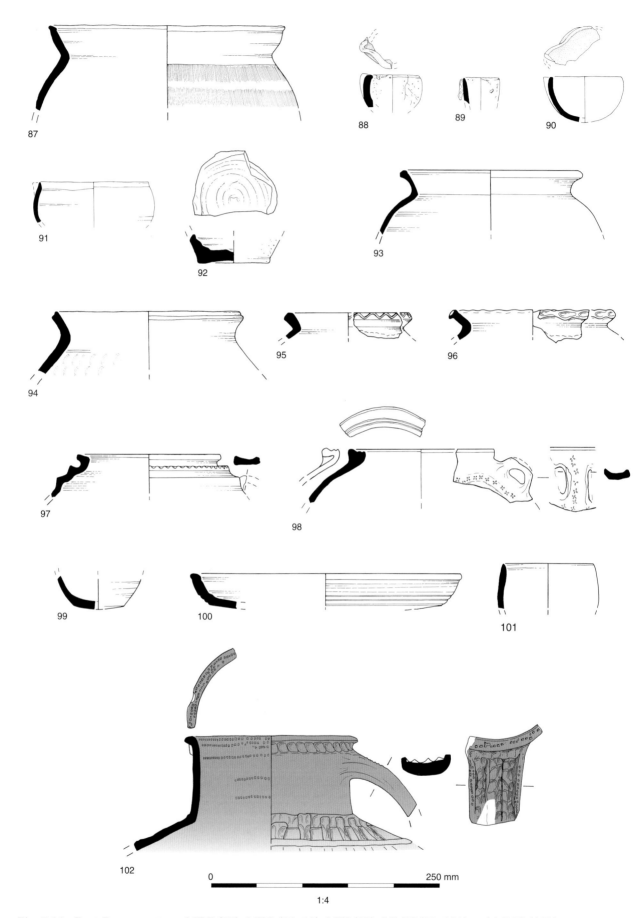

Fig. 7.14   Post-Roman pottery: MDF (87), MDL (88–91), MFI (92), MMU (93–101) and MNG (102)

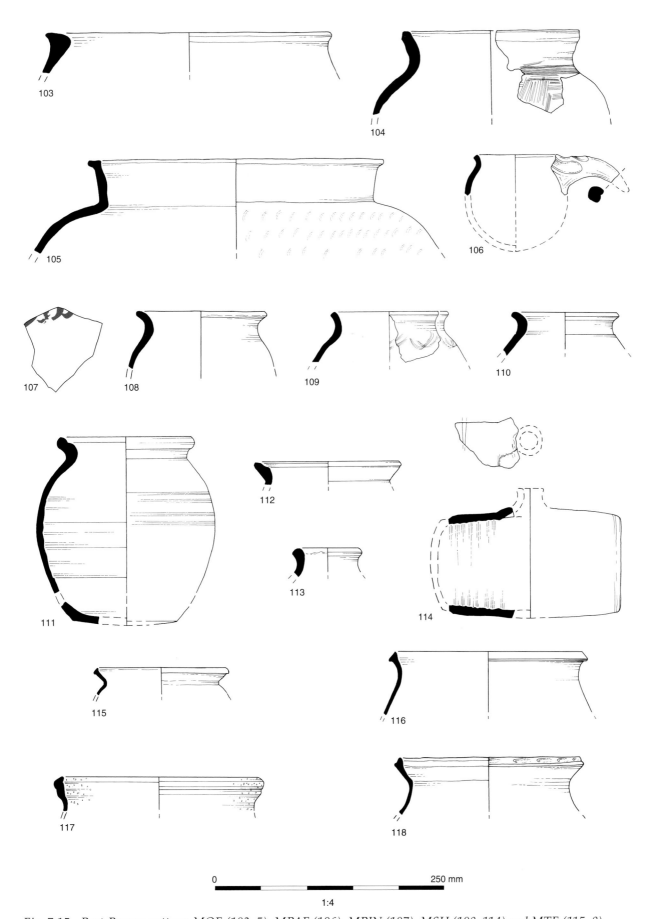

0   250 mm

1:4

Fig. 7.15   Post-Roman pottery: MOE (103–5), MPAF (106), MPIN (107), MSH (108–114) and MTE (115–8)

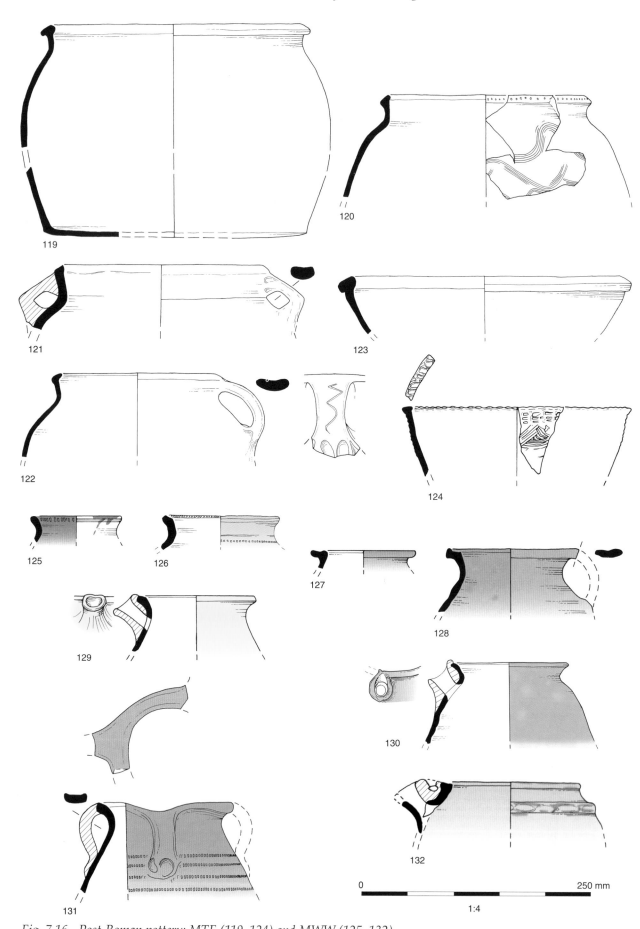

Fig. 7.16   Post-Roman pottery: MTE (119–124) and MWW (125–132)

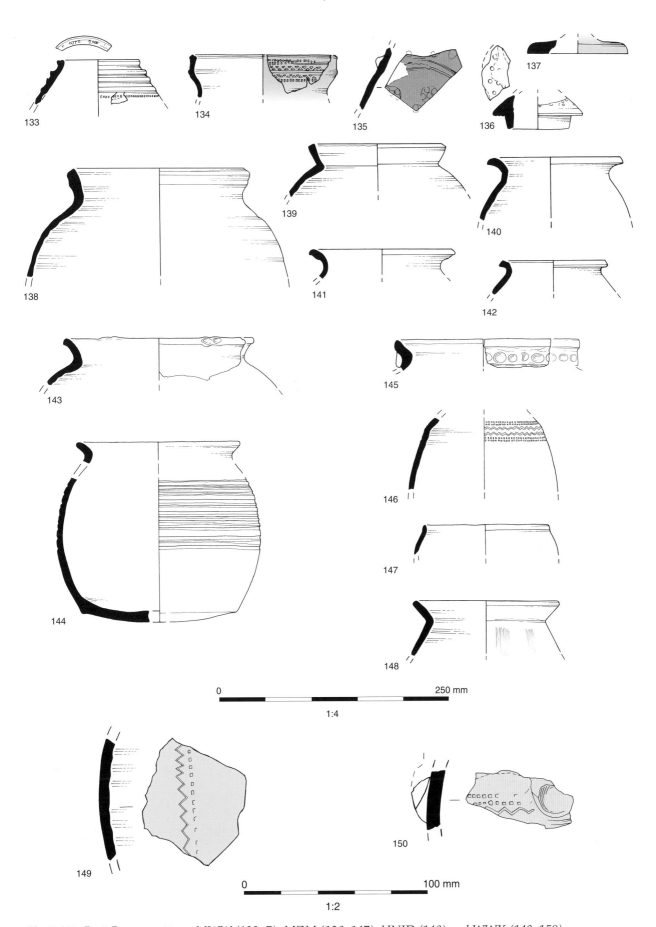

Fig. 7.17   Post-Roman pottery: MWW (133–7), MZM (138–147), UNID (148) and WWX (149–150)

115. Fabric MTE, Small delicate jar rim. Di 150 mm., Group NH8539, Context NH4186, Phase 5
116. Fabric MTE, Jar with triangular rim. Di 220 mm., Group NH8632, Context NH1364, Phase 5
117. Fabric MTE, Sub-collared jar rim. Wheel-turned? V coarse flint. Di 230 mm., Group NH8537, Context NH4170, Phase 6
118. Fabric MTE, Jar with thumbed rim. Elongated thumbing style. Di 200 mm., Group NH8542, Context NH4294, Phase 5
119. Fabric MTE, Jar profile with beaded/clubbed rim. Di 290 mm., Group NH8632, Context NH1364, Phase 5
120. Fabric MTE, Jar with stabbed dec on rim and combed dec on body. (Or possibly MAQ?). Di 230 mm., Group NH8576, Context NH2174, Phase 5
121. Fabric MTE, Cauldron (jar) rim with elbow handle. Di 220 mm., Group NH8620, Context NH6036, Phase 5
122. Fabric MTE, Cauldron (jar) with incised dec on handle and body. Di 190 mm., Group NH8575, Context NH2356, Phase 5
123. Fabric MTE, Bowl rim. Di 320 mm., Group DC7050, Context DC1095, Phase 5
124. Fabric MTE, Bowl with thumbed rim and combed dec on body. Di 250 mm., Group NH8633, Context NH1007, Phase 6
125. Fabric MWW, ?Spouted pitcher with crude rouletted dec on rim. Coarser orange-buff fabric. Unusually unglazed save for band of patchy greenish glaze along top of rim. Di 100 mm., Group NH8620, Context NH6051, Phase 5
126. Fabric MWW, ?Spouted pitcher with rouletted dec on rim and on body. Partially glazed over break – possibly a waster? Di 130 mm., Group NH8530, Context NH4328, Phase 4.2
127. Fabric MWW, Jar rim. Gr-yell glz. (just possibly N. French?). Di 114 mm., Group NH8556, Context NH3669, Phase 4.2
128. Fabric MWW, Spouted pitcher with flanged rim. Di 140 mm., Group DC7050, Context DC1448, Phase 5
129. Fabric MWW, Spouted pitcher. Simple everted rim. Complete spout. Di 130 mm., Group NH8538, Context NH4223, Phase 4.2
130. Fabric MWW, Spouted pitcher. Possible second or ?waster with glaze over broken spout. Di 130 mm., Group DC7050, Context DC1274, Phase 5
131. Fabric MWW, Spouted pitcher with rouletted dec and probably 3 handles. Di 150 mm., Group NH8596, Context NH2411, Phase 4.2
132. Fabric MWW, Spouted pitcher with inturned rim and external cordon (notched?) on shoulder. Thick yell-brown glaze all over. Di 150 mm., Group NH8530, Context NH4270, 4271, Phase 4.2
133. Fabric MWW, Spouted pitcher with inturned rim. Multiple shoulder cordons and crude rouletted dec on top of rim. Trace of applied spout/handle. Coarser orange-brown fabric with marl streaks. Di 90 mm., Group NH8530, Context NH4163, Phase 4.2
134. Fabric MWW, Unusual sub-collared jar rim with complex rouletted decoration. Di 160 mm., Group NH8596, Context NH2426, Phase 5
135. Fabric MWW, Sherd with curved applied strip and cinquefoil stamps, Group NH8560/NH8583, Context NH3090, 3532, Phase 5
136. Fabric MWW, Locking lid with stamped circles dec. Unglazed. Max Di 100 mm., Context DC1051, Phase 6

137. Fabric MWW, ?Lid or ?pedestal base fragment. Glazed on upper surface only. Di 110 mm., Group NH8596, Context NH2390, Phase 5
138. Fabric MZM, Jar rim. A3B rim form. Di 200 mm., Group DC7019, Context DC2004, Phase 4.2
139. Fabric MZM, Jar rim. A3B rim form. Di 150 mm., Group DC7050, Context DC1274, Phase 5
140. Fabric MZM, Jar. Simple everted rim. Di 150 mm., Group NH8543, Context NH3286, Phase 6
141. Fabric MZM, Jar rim. Thin-walled. Di 160 mm., Group NH8619, Context NH6155, Phase 5
142. Fabric MZM, Small jar with squared rim. Di 120 mm., Group NH8530, Context NH4381, Phase 4.2
143. Fabric MZM, Jar rim with grouped thumbing. Or reduced MMU? Di 210 mm., Group NH8530, Context NH4130, Phase 4.2
144. Fabric MZM, Jar profile with horizontal grooved dec. Fine-medium sandy pale grey fabric. Or MMU/import? Di 180 mm., Group NH8542, Context NH4177, Phase 5
145. Fabric MZM, Jar rim with applied thumbed strip on neck. Fine-medium sandy pale grey fabric. Or MMU/import? Di 190 mm., Group DC7023, Context DC2027, Phase 5
146. Fabric MZM, ?Jar or pitcher body with complex rouletted dec. Trace of applied feature. Or MMU?, Group DC7023, Context DC2027, Phase 5
147. Fabric MZM, ?Crucible or 'ginger jar' rim. Sooted internally. Di 140 mm., Group , Context DC2171, Phase 5
148. Fabric UNID, Unidentified jar. Probably a late Saxon regional or Continental greyware import. Vertical knife-trimming externally. Di 160 mm., Group NH8554, Context NH3491, Phase 5
149. Fabric WWX, Winchester-style ware. White-slipped sherd with rouletted dec., Group DC7007, Context DC1376, Phase 4.2
150. Fabric WWX, Winchester-style ware. White-slipped sherd with rouletted dec. and handle stub, Group DC7007, Context DC1376, Phase 4.2

BUILDING MATERIALS

Roman ceramic building material *by Cynthia Poole and Ruth Shaffrey*

The assemblage of 6788 fragments of Roman tile (806 kg) is dominated by brick and undiagnostic flat tile (Table 7.21; Fig. 7.18). Brick, flat tile, tegulae, imbrices, box flue and tesserae were identified but only a single probable voussoir. No complete example of any type was found and complete lengths or widths were rare. The fabric series established for the site was linked to the Winchester type series devised by Foot (1994). The digital report (*Digital Section 7*) includes full descriptions of the fabrics and tile forms.

The bricks include a complete bessalis and evidence of pedalis, lydion, sequipedalis and possibly bipedalis bricks. One brick with considerable variation in thickness may be a solid voussoir. A few tegulae mammatae were also identified. Roofing included tegulae with standard flange and cutaway forms, rectangular flanges being most common and with two or three finger grooves alongside the flange, a common feature on

Winchester tiles. The imbrices included a small number of thicker fragments, which may indicate the use of ridge tiles.

Flue tile consisted predominantly of box flue with typical combed keying, whilst one of the two with knife scoring was a half box flue tile (Fig. 7.18, no. 4). A single possible voussoir with combing on adjacent surfaces was identified (Fig. 7.18, no. 5). Tesserae mostly measured between 20 and 30 mm suggesting they derived from plain tessellated pavements.

Markings on the tiles include in addition to the keying on the flue tiles, a small number of tally marks, animal imprints (mostly dog) and a range of signature marks. The latter include both combed and finger marks, mostly forming simple arcs together with a number of less common patterns (Fig. 7.18, nos 1–3). Similar signatures have been found at The Brooks (Foot 1994), Brading villa, Isle of Wight (Tomlin 1987, 99) and at the villas of Houghton Down, Grateley and Dunkirt Barn (Cunliffe and Poole 2008) to the north-west of Winchester.

Production and distribution

The tile fabrics and characteristics have much in common with the ceramic building material found in Winchester at The Brooks site, which has been analysed in detail by Foot (1994) in relation to patterns of production and distribution. Although the fabrics were not recorded in the same detail, they support the differences in early and late varieties consistent with those from The Brooks site.

Foot (1994) concluded that the source area for tile reaching Winchester was to the south or south-east on the Tertiary clays of the Hampshire Basin. He places the source of his group 1 (equivalent to much

of Group E) in the area of Bishop's Waltham close to the Roman road from Chichester to Winchester. The tiles in this group were of much better finish and quality than later phase material with knife trimmed edges a notable feature. His group 2 tiles (equivalent to many of the Group E subtypes and fabric B) are linked to the kiln at Braxells Farm, which lies about 4 km from the Group 1 tilery. The combed signatures on bricks are exclusively associated by Foot with this group and at NH/CC have been found in fabrics E1 and E2 and in deposits of Phase 2.4 or later. Foot has linked the micaceous group to the Alton/Farnham area, but only a very small quantity (fabric D1) of this was identified from the site all in Phases 2.3 and 2.4 or later.

The assemblage broadly supports Foot's conclusions but the preservation is much poorer and varieties more limited than The Brooks material, and as a result comparison of characteristics cannot be made for all forms or fabrics.

The stratified groups

The character of the assemblage shows little change either spatially or temporally. Brick remains dominant throughout with smaller quantities of roofing and occasional tesserae and flue tile. The flue tile must certainly have been brought in from buildings outside the area of the excavation, as no buildings had any form of heating system or evidence of baths. Nor was any evidence of tessellated pavements found within any of the structures, suggesting these too derived from outside the area. There is no reason why one or more of the structures identified on site should not have been roofed with tile, but no one building appears to form a focus. All groups appear to be mixed dumps used as make-up or infill for levelling and yard surfaces brought in from several sources, including buildings that had heating systems and baths. Some such as the tegula mammata and knife scored flue tiles are early forms generally of 1st to early 2nd century date.

Although the assemblage is quite substantial, the quantity does not compare with the 3.7 tons from The Brooks site, where well preserved Roman town houses were found. Though it is tempting to try and assign material to individual buildings on site, the proportions of different forms both within the whole assemblage and individual groups do not conform with ones associated with definite buildings such as Northfleet Villa (Poole forthcoming) or Beauport Park (Brodribb 1979) where brick formed about a third of both assemblages, tegula *c* 35–40% and imbrex *c* 12%. The dominance of brick on this site has more in common with rural agricultural sites, often of low status, where brick or tegula tends to be recycled in hearths, ovens or similar structures. The brick hearth CC1567 and the burnt tile associated with Structure NH8516 suggest similar factors may have been at play on this site. The overall impression is of a very mixed assemblage derived from numerous sources, though the

Table 7.21: Roman ceramic building material quantified by weight and fragment count

Form	Weight (g)	% of assemblage by wt	Fragment count	% of assemblage by count
Flue incl. voussoir	7619	0.9	90	1.3
Imbrex	47649	2.5	529	7.8
Tegula	90025	0.8	599	8.8
Flat tile	62759	11.2	942	13.9
Flat/indet	19943	7.8	362	5.3
Brick and brick/flat	531925	66.0	2487	36.6
Wall	4448	0.1	20	0.3
Tegula mammata	6553	0.4	14	0.2
Tessera	3223	3.9	92	1.4
Chipped disc	472	0.6	6	0.1
Indeterminate	31312	5.9	1647	24.3
Grand Total	805928	100.0	6788	100.0

Fig. 7.18   Illustrated Roman tile (1–5)

possibility that the brick does derive from the lining or cover of the channel CC1642 has been considered. However, Roman aqueducts are normally lined with mortar and the character of the assemblage in the channel is the same as that in the dark earth indicative of dumping of tile from buildings outside the excavation area.

Phase 2.1 (c AD 43–130/50)

All material assigned to this phase was found adjacent to the Roman street (Street CC1703) and apart from one structure formed a low density scatter across the area of fragments, which included tegula, imbrex and brick. The majority of the tile formed part of hearth CC1567. This was constructed of bricks made in fabrics C, E1, E2 and E3, three with signature marks and probably all pedales from their size.

A key research question is whether the conduit (CC1642) was lined with brick to form a covered culvert. The conduit construction (CC1850) consisted of flints set in mortar and its fill consisted of a robbing layer with mortar fragments (CC1642), overlain by dark earth deposits (CC7005). No tile was found in the construction levels nor in the primary fill. The material in the robbing deposits consisted of a variety of forms including tegula, imbrex, flue and voussoir, though dominated by brick. Some brick had mortar on the surfaces, or was burnt and some had a heavily worn surface or edge. Burning and heavy wear was also found on some of the other tiles. It is pertinent to note that one of the lower layers (CC1611) of the secondary fill is described as ashy silt with demolition debris. The assemblage found in the dark earth deposits forming the upper fill was similar to that in the underlying layers. The mix and character of forms, and the condition of the tile is not consistent with its use as the structure of a culvert.

One may conclude that a brick lining is unlikely, though some form of cover would be a reasonable supposition where the channel cuts across Street CC1703. No form of voussoir or vaulting tiles have been identified and if tile was used, it must be assumed that any covering arch was constructed of bricks set in mortar. This could certainly account for the exceptionally large quantity of brick surviving in Phase 2.4, but a timber or opus signinum cover are alternatives, though the evidence for opus signinum is lacking. Any additional height resulting from a vaulted cover needs to be considered in relation to road levels and the impact this would have where they cross.

The character of the tile in the channel does not stand out as significantly different to that in the other areas of the dark earth. Evidence of burning and ashy deposits in the channel suggest at least some of this material was brought in and dumped from elsewhere. This together with the preponderance of brick and reused tegula may suggest demolition debris from a hypocaust.

Phase 2.2 (c AD 130/50–270)

The burnt Structure NH8522 produced small quantities of brick, tegula and tesserae, with greater quantities in the overlying levelling deposits (NH8523) comprising brick, tegula, imbrex and tesserae. However, whether these represent demolition debris from the burnt building or material brought in from outside to level the area is uncertain, though there is nothing to distinguish this from all the other groups of tile.

Phase 2.3 (c AD 270–350/75)

Street deposits were a complete contrast in that Street CC1703 produced only two tiny fragments whilst Street NH8511/8513 produced 14.5 kg of brick and tile. This reflects the materials used for construction of the road surfaces, with clean flint gravel and pebbles used exclusively for the main Street CC1703, and more mixed materials used for the side Street NH8511/8513 which included tile mixed in with the metalling as well as in the interleaving accumulations of soil, where it may have been used to firm up more muddy hollows.

Many of the individual structures had relatively small quantities of tile associated with them all consisting of various combinations of brick, roofing, flue tile and tesserae. These groups do not indicate any constructional significance in relation to Structures CC7003, NH8521 and NH8517/8. Much of the tile associated with Structure NH8516 had been reused as posthole packing, whilst a large group from pit NH1413 contained heavily fired tegulae and brick, suggesting it derived from a demolished oven or flue.

The largest group came from Pit Group NH8524, which comprised dumps of varying size in pit and well fills, as well as an associated surface layer. There was seemingly little difference between material deposited in each pit with all containing a predominance of brick, together with smaller amounts of tegula and imbrex, a few tesserae and occasionally flue tile.

Illustration catalogue (Fig. 7.18)

1. Context NH1239: Signature mark: type 6. Tegula.
2. Context NH5182: Signature mark: type 10. Brick.
3. Context NH4718: part of signature on tile deliberately chipped to triangle (probably from tegula) for use as flooring or wall inlay.
4. Context NH1321: flue tile with knife scored keying
5. Context CC3368: voussoir with combed keying design – 'union jack' saltire in frame and small area of combing on adjacent side.

Post-Roman ceramic building material *by Cynthia Poole*

The assemblage of ceramic building material found in post-Roman contexts amounts to 4881 fragments (551,842 g), of which 792 fragments (79,305 g) are medieval, post-medieval or modern, the remainder being residual Roman (4089 fragments, 472,537 g). The mean fragment weight (MFW) of the post-Roman tile is 100 g.

Ceramic building material was recovered from 94 features or layers, with pits producing two thirds of the assemblage. All material was recovered from secondary deposits with no direct relationship to primary structural features apart from some roof tile reused in a modern wall and in an Anglo-Norman foundation trench. The assemblage comprises predominantly roofing, brick and flooring of medieval date, together with small quantities of more modern material including brick, roofing, floor paviours and drainpipe. The forms are fully quantified by phase in Table 7.22. Nearly 50% by weight was found in modern (Phase 8) contexts, mainly layers rather than features. A small quantity (1%) found in prehistoric and Roman contexts is undoubtedly intrusive.

Several fabrics are the same or very similar to tile fabrics found at Southampton French Quarter (Poole in prep.). These resemble some of the contemporary pottery fabrics and complement the evidence from kiln sites such as Laverstock, which indicates that ridge tile and roof furniture was produced by potters. Coarse flint gritted fabrics used for producing chimney pots in Sussex (Dunning 1961) was most common at both Winchester and Southampton in the Anglo-Norman phase.

Roofing

A small quantity of curved and flanged tile was identified from Anglo-Norman and medieval deposits. These are similar to Roman tegula and imbrex in design and it is thought they were introduced by the Normans. The flat tile comprises plain fragments, of which a small number could be positively identified as peg tile by the presence of square and circular peg holes. One very crude example is of Anglo-Norman date. Some of the flat tile had splashes of glaze but all those with extensive areas of glazing are thought to be pieces of crested ridge tile (Fig. 7.19, nos 6–12). The ridge tile was glazed in shades of green, amber or brown. The crest was either triangular or pyramidal in form and included both cut and thumb pressed. It survived to some extent on 16 examples and as a scar sometimes with associated stab marks on a few.

Brick

Only a small amount of the brick has been definitely identified as of medieval origin. Much of it is post-medieval or modern. The only near complete brick came from Phase 5 well CC2049, which also produced the largest group of brick in a dump of post-medieval building rubble used as levelling during Phase 8.

Table 7.22: Quantification and forms of medieval and post-medieval tile by phase

Type	Phase	PH 1.3	LRB 2.3	LRB (LC4) 2.4	LSAX 4	LSAX 4.1	LSAX 4.2	AN 5	Med 6	Mod 8	Unphased U	Grand Total
Brick	Nos		1		2		4	23	9	70	2	111
	Wt (g)		92		178		469	5623	1603	17768	68	25801
Drainpipe	Nos							2		2	1	5
	Wt (g)							31		102	97	230
Floor	Nos				7	1	2	5	15	6		36
	Wt (g)				832	95	335	525	2012	2515		6314
Roof: curving	Nos							2				2
	Wt (g)							89				89
Roof: flanged	Nos							2	7			9
	Wt (g)							175	310			485
Roof: flat	Nos		1		3	2	16	19	110	67	2	220
	Wt (g)		18		192	56	422	826	4032	4582	66	10194
Roof: peg	Nos			5	1		3	5	126	92		232
	Wt (g)			650	72		105	772	10146	13655		25400
Roof: ridge	Nos	1					1	2	55	2		61
	Wt (g)	19					24	66	3203	96		3408
Roof: ridge crested	Nos			1			2		69			72
	Wt (g)			31			160		6067			6258
Indet	Nos		2		4	1	4	19	6	7	1	44
	Wt (g)		68		124	20	42	511	104	262	8	1139
Total Sum of Nos		1	4	6	17	4	32	79	397	246	6	792
Total Sum of Wt (g)		19	178	681	1398	171	1557	8618	27477	38980	239	79318

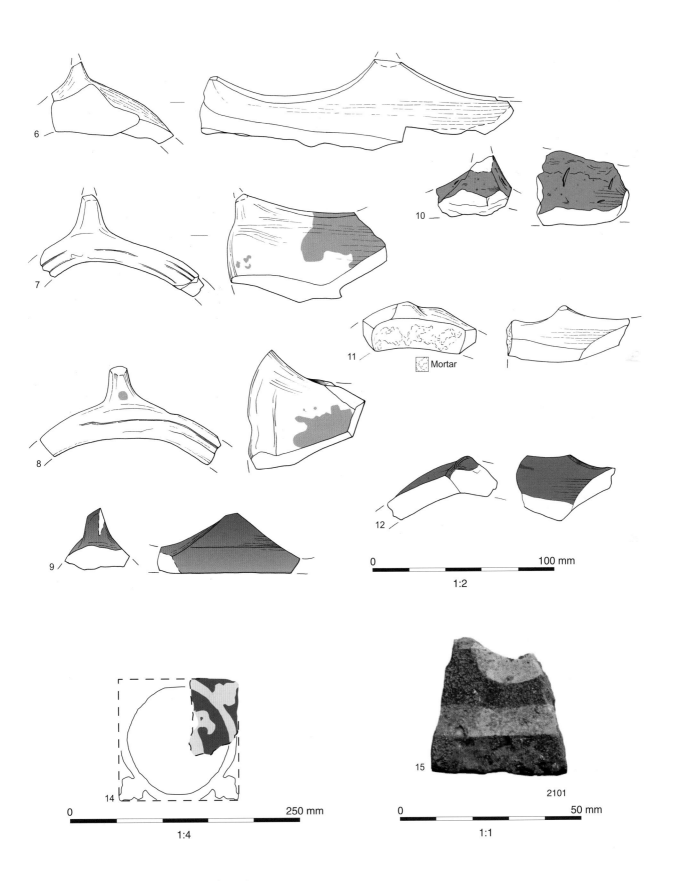

Fig. 7.19   Illustrated medieval tile (6–15)

Floor

Floor tile formed only 8% of the assemblage. Most of the medieval floor tile was plain glazed green or brown or unglazed and heavily worn, some from Anglo-Norman contexts but most from phase 6. Three fragmentary decorated bichrome tiles were found (Fig. 7.19, nos 13–14). One had a scoop cut in the base for keying. This had a pattern consisting of the head (facing R) of a spread eagle within a circle with trefoil at the angle. The position of the head suggests a double headed eagle, rather than a single headed eagle found on a very similar tile from the St George's street excavations in Winchester (Cunliffe 1964, fig. 56. 2). The decorated tiles normally date from the 12th–14th century and were often used by religious establishments, and are still visible in the floors of Winchester cathedral and the Hospital of St Cross.

Discussion

Medieval building material occurred in low density and was poorly preserved, perhaps reflecting the level of use of ceramic materials for building, roofing and floors, though other factors such as truncation of the excavation levels may have distorted the overall distribution observed. Brick is very poorly represented, suggesting buildings used timber as their main component. Where brick was present it was used in limited ways to provide greater strength or durability, or where fireproof materials were needed such as in fireplaces, hearths or ovens. Roofing is the most common material, comprising peg tiles and crested ridge tiles. An increase in the use of ceramic roofing to decrease fire risk was encouraged by most city authorities during the medieval period, but it is clear from the quantity found that only a limited number of buildings in the area used roof tile. The pattern needs to be viewed in conjunction with other building materials as documentary sources indicate slate from Devon and Cornwall was more prevalent in Winchester than roof tile (Hare 1991). There is also a notable absence of chimneys, louvers and finials, normally associated with higher status buildings, suggesting that those structures that did utilise tile did not house the most wealthy merchants of the city. Floor tile is sparse and was used in only a few residences. However, the decorated floor tiles appear to relate to specific plots utilising more tile, and so may indicate that the owners of certain properties were successful people wishing to display their wealth. It could also be argued that they derived from the Archdeacon's residence.

The distribution of tile across the site when related to individual properties suggests few properties used tile, as several produced none or only a few fragments. A number of properties which stand out as producing relatively more material in Phases 5 and 6 are BE 2, BE 5, and BW 3/BW 4. It is also noteworthy that those properties producing most ceramic building material also produced most stone flooring and roofing, indicating the more prestigious buildings were utilising a variety of materials.

Ceramic brick and tile was not normally in use before the Conquest, unless re-using Roman materials. Although some high status sites associated with the church or nobility may have had early access to these materials, it is unlikely that ordinary domestic properties were sufficiently wealthy to utilise ceramic tile. There were two possible establishments which, during the Anglo-Norman period, may have been the first to start using tile on any scale. These were centred on Properties BE 2–BE 3 and BW 3–BW 4. The evidence suggests the buildings were initially roofed with Anglo-Norman curved and flanged tiles, and some rooms were floored with plain floor tiles, probably during the 11th–12th century. Subsequently the roofs were refurbished during the 12–13th centuries with peg tiles and glazed crested tiles and some floors retiled with decorated encaustic tiles. At this stage a third property, BE 5, started using ceramic roofing and glazed, decorated floor tile.

Illustration catalogue (Fig. 7.19)

6. Context NH3234: medieval crested ridge tile: crest type 1
7. Context NH3234: medieval crested ridge tile: crest type 1c
8. Context NH3234: medieval crested ridge tile: crest type 1c
9. Context NH3234: medieval crested ridge tile: crest type 1c – applied crest spur
10. Context NH3234: medieval crested ridge tile: crest with stab marks at base (?type 5 or 6)
11. Context NH3234: medieval crested ridge tile: crest type 11
12. Context CC6013: medieval crested ridge tile: crest type 11c
13. Context NH3236: floor tile encaustic tile with bichrome decoration : head (facing R) of a spread eagle (probably double-headed) within a circle with trefoil at the angle. 13th-14th century.
14. Context CC2101 floor tile encaustic tile with bichrome decoration

Structural clay, fired clay and mortar
by Cynthia Poole

Structural and fired clay comprising 3261 fragments (37,366 g) with an overall mean fragment weight (MFW) of 11.5 g was recovered from 262 contexts; 1877 fragments (4986 g) were recovered from sieved samples. A third of the assemblage was recovered from Roman deposits, just under half from late Saxon contexts and about a fifth from medieval and later deposits. Minimal quantities were found in prehistoric contexts and amounts decreased after the Saxon period. The largest proportion (40%) was found in pit fills and the remainder was distributed through a wide range of other features and layers.

This report is derived from the detailed digital report (*Digital Section 5*).

Fabrics

Nine provisional fabrics were allocated during the assessment, of which one (H) is a pottery fabric. The remainder were placed in two broad groups: a sandy group (fabrics A, B and F) and a calcareous group (fabrics C, D, E and G). Pieces of mortar, cement and concrete were also noted. The fabrics are described in detail in *Digital Section 5*.

Forms

Oven and hearths

Oven and hearth fragments dominated the assemblage. Most probably represent domestic structures. Oven wall fragments supported on a wattle framework were most common and other less diagnostic structural elements may include perforated oven plate and hearth.

Industrial

A range of material representing industrial activity, probably bronze working, comprises furnace wall or lining (Fig. 7.20, no. 1), mould fragments (Fig. 7.20, nos 2–3) and possible crucible. The largest groups come from late Saxon and Anglo-Norman phases, indicating more intensive activity than in the Iron Age and Roman periods.

Wall/Structural

A few pieces may relate to building structure, although little constructional detail survives for any period. A few formless mortar fragments were found in late Saxon, Anglo-Norman and medieval contexts. Mortar/plaster characterised by a very flat smooth surface, occasionally with evidence of whitewash, is interpreted as wall render. One piece had a *c* 28 mm circular perforation, probably to hold a wooden dowel for the attachment of a fixture or fitting. The painted Roman wall plaster has been reported separately (see Biddulph, below).

Examples of wall daub or render in fabrics C, E and F, usually 30–40 mm thick, was identified from Roman, Saxon and medieval contexts. Some was thick render having flat surfaces both sides. A fragment of Roman daub with a combed surface was probably the impression of a combed tile rather than keying on the daub surface. The few, small fired clay fragments associated with burnt building Structure NH8522 were indistinct, with two surfaces at right angles, possibly the top or base of a wall panel. Surprisingly little wall daub was present, and this material may have been cleared and dumped elsewhere. The plaster from the burnt building has been reported separately and was not seen by the author. However, one fragment of fired clay in fabric C from Structure NH8522 was 22 mm thick and had two interwoven lath impressions,

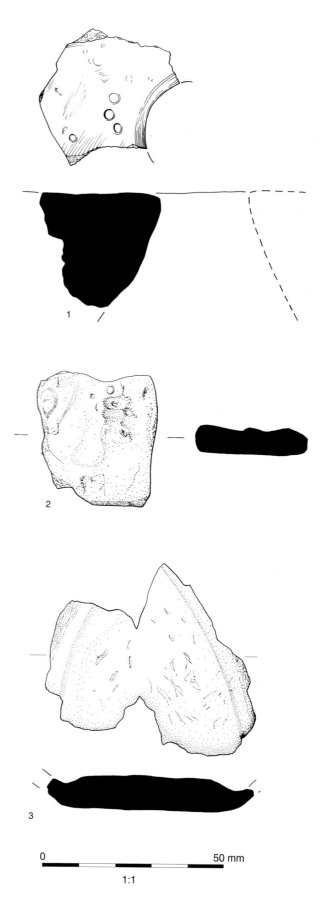

Fig. 7.20 Illustrated Fired clay (1–3)

both over 22 mm wide by *c* 6–7 mm thick, suggesting it derived from a ceiling or thin internal partition walls.

The medieval wall daub contained a very high density of coarse straw or hay added as a strengthening agent, typical of daub found in standing buildings (Graham 2004), but had no withy or lath impressions. Similar daub was found at in medieval levels at Southampton French Quarter (Poole http://library.thehumanjourney.net/44/1/SOU_13 82_Specialist_report_download_F4.pdf).

Discussion

The Iron Age and Roman assemblage

The only significant pieces of fired clay from the Iron Age were a heavily fired small brick and a small vitrified fragment of furnace lining from postholes of Structure NH8502. These may indicate industrial activity, perhaps bronze-working, in the vicinity. The brick is unusual and its deposition in a posthole may reflect similar motivation to deliberate placing of pottery sherds, frequently refired, in the postholes of early Iron Age structures (Brown 2000).

The nature of Roman fired clay was consistent through all phases. Most from Phases 2.1 and 2.2 was non-diagnostic, probably derived from ovens or hearths. A few fragments of wall daub occurred in the area of Structures CC7003 and CC7006 and burnt building Structure NH8522. The group centred on Phase 2.3 Structure NH8521 was interpreted as wall daub representing material cleared and dumped from Phase 2.2 Structure NH8522. A little furnace lining associated with pit CC1556 occurred in Phase 2.3. Only in the later Roman period (Phases 2.3 and 2.4) did oven wall appear and dominate the assemblage. The majority is in sandy fabric F, with lesser quantities in fabric A and calcareous groups C and E. One large deposit in fabric C was associated with Structure CC7003.

During recording it was noted that much of the oven wall in fabric F, though from several contexts, had very similar characteristics: consistency of firing, wattles commonly stripped of bark and with diameters commonly larger than average and external thick white lime plaster wash. This almost certainly derives from a single building, centred on Structure NH8521. Groups of the same type were found in late Saxon deposits in the area of Properties BW 2 and BW 3, which overlie Structure NH8521, suggesting the later deposits were residual.

A similar pattern appears with oven structure in fabric A, which concentrated in the Roman period in the area of Structure NH8516, suggesting that the similar oven debris in fabric A found in features on Property SE2 was residual Roman. The limited spatial distribution of fabric A suggests it all derived from a single structure.

The Saxon-medieval assemblage

A comparison of Roman and post-Roman fabrics and forms produces a number of broad distinctions. Pieces indicative of industrial activity, including furnace structure, moulds and crucible are more prevalent in the post-Roman group. Most of the structural material related to buildings was also found in these later periods. The calcareous fabrics are more common compared to the Roman period, especially that used for oven wall.

Fired clay is sparse in late Saxon Phase 4.1, with small amounts of furnace and wall daub. In Phase 4.2 increasing quantities of industrial material appear, including furnace lining and wall and crucible, together with oven structure and some wall daub. Metalworking moulds were the only new form found in the Anglo-Norman phase. The association of furnace debris with oven wall at some properties suggests these are from related structures. The exterior surfaces of furnace walls would not be vitrified and could not be separated from structures used for lower temperature activities. This pattern continues into the Anglo-Norman and high medieval periods, though quantities noticeably decrease in the later phase. The similarity of assemblages from late Saxon to Anglo-Norman on many properties may indicate that much of the Anglo-Norman and medieval fired clay was residual Saxon. The general decline in quantities of fired clay through the medieval period certainly reflects changes in materials used for ovens, hearths or similar structures, with brick, tile and stone increasingly used, as well as a decrease in construction at surface or sub-surface levels. The fired clay from the individual properties is summarised below:

Property BE 1: Virtually all fired clay occurred in late Saxon (Phase 4) contexts. Diagnostic elements were oven structure and wall in fabric C and E and furnace lining.

Property BE 2: Most fired clay from Phases 4.2, 5 and 6 was indeterminate, apart from a little wall daub and render in Phase 4.2 and perforated furnace wall/lining in Phase 5.

Property BE 3: The only diagnostic material was furnace and crucible fragments from Phase 4 pit CC1063.

Property BE 4: Furnace lining occurred in Phases 4.1, 4.2 and 6. A group of mould fragments was discarded in pit CC2043 during Phase 5.

Property BE 5: Fragments of oven wall, furnace and crucible were found in Phase 4.2 in pits (CC6028, CC3184) and a posthole (CC6030).

Property BW 1: A few insignificant fragments of non-diagnostic fired clay occurred in Phases 4.2 and 5.

Property BW 2: Little material derived from the use of this property.

Property BW 3: Most structural clay was found in

Phase 5 with a small amount from Phase 6. Recognisable forms included wall daub, render and a substantial dump of oven wall in layer NH3098.

Property BW 4: A moderate density of fired clay—oven wall, a little furnace lining and wall daub—was found in late Saxon (Phase 4) and Anglo-Norman (Phase 5) phases

Property BW 5: A low density scatter of small mainly indeterminate fragments was found in Phase 4 and 5 contexts.

Property SE 1: Furnace lining, fuel ash slag and oven wall and possible oven plate predominantly occurred in Phase 5, though a small quantity was found in Phase 4.

Property SE 2: A moderate scatter of fired clay, mainly furnace lining, was found in Phase 4.2, and a few further pieces of furnace in Phase 5.

Property SE 3: Furnace lining dominates the assemblage in the late Saxon and Anglo-Norman period. One piece of furnace wall had a tuyère perforation (Fig. 7.20, no. 1). A hearth tile or large block of hearth floor occurred in Phase 5.

Catalogue of illustrated fired clay (Fig. 7.20)

1. Context CC1085: fired clay: fragment of vitrified furnace wall with perforation for tuyère.
2. Context CC2237: fired clay: fragment of metal-working mould
3. Context CC2115: fired clay: fragment of metal-working mould

Structural stone *by Ruth Shaffrey*

Phase 1: Prehistoric

A fragment of possible wall veneer of Paludina limestone, the only piece of structural worked stone recovered from a Phase 1 context (NH6507), was probably intrusive.

Phase 2: Roman

The wide variety of stone types represented in the small Roman assemblage includes both local and imported materials. Slabs of various types of shelly limestone, mainly from the Purbeck beds, were probably used for roofing, as evidenced by examples retaining original edges and perforation (eg NH4742, a soil above Structure NH8521). Other slabs were probably used as wall courses or in flooring, although none has significant wear except one roughly trapezoidal slab of Purbeck limestone (NH2619). Tooled fragments of shelly limestone and locally available chalk indicate that stone structures were located nearby.

More exotic imported stone took the form of thin slabs, probably best interpreted as wall veneer. One fragment of dark green and white marble is probably Campan Vert from the Hautes Pyrenees (fill CC2251 of pit CC2249). A pinkish variety of

Yellow Lez Breccia from Lez, Haute Garonne, France (NH6160) came from a late Saxon pit NH6158 but is almost certainly residual from Roman activity. Although French marbles are generally less common than those from eastern Mediterranean areas, Campan Vert has been found at Silchester and Dorchester (Pritchard 1986, 187) and both varieties were found at Fishbourne palace (Cunliffe, 1971, 17). These marbles suggest that a high status Roman building with ornamental marble inlay, probably wall veneer, was located nearby. Both pieces were identified by Monica Price of Oxford University Museum.

Phase 4: Late Saxon

Most of the stone from late Saxon contexts is limestone slabbing, used either for roofing, (at least 3 kg) flooring (at least 1 kg) or as wall courses, although few (11 kg) retain distinguishing features. Deposits of this phase also produced four pieces of neat triangular limestone shapes with one worn face (eg NH1262). These may be the reused ends of pointed roof-stones, although similar shaped pieces of ceramic building material also occur. These triangular pieces may also have been used as large tesserae.

In addition, Late Saxon deposits produced a Purbeck marble slab, probably wall veneer, smoothed but not polished on both faces (NH4365). As there is currently no evidence for the use of Purbeck marble between AD 400 and 1100 (Blair 1991, 47), this presumably dates to the later part of the period or is residual Roman. Another fragment of wall veneer, an exotic piece of Yellow Lez Breccia from Lez, Haute Garonne, France (NH6160), is almost certainly residual from Roman activity (see Phase 2).

Saxon contexts produced very little imported stone, the structural stone being mainly chalk. Context NH3346 produced 17 blocks of soft chalk, most retaining tool marks on at least one face, and several are slightly curved. The predominance of chalk suggests the presence of mostly domestic structures nearby, as previous excavations highlighted a clear difference between the use of imported stone, such as Bath stone and Quarr, for large scale building projects and local sources of chalk and flint for domestic buildings (Biddle 1990, 318).

Phase 5: Anglo-Norman

Anglo-Norman contexts produced large quantities of structural material. The blocks and architectural fragments are mainly chalk, most of it quite soft. Many of the blocks have one or more dressed faces (NH3128) and two pieces of chalk voussoir were used to line well CC3043 (CC3044). The softer pieces were clearly from nearby outcrops, but some of the harder chalk (NH3236) was probably been imported and may be Beer stone from Devon, a hard chalk used in the cathedral (Anderson 1990, 309).

A number of other lithologies previously identified in Winchester were present, including Quarr stone (NH2107, NH2606, NH4447), a creamy coloured shelly limestone consisting of dissolved clam moulds surrounded by a strong calcite cement (Bishop 2001, 34). This was exploited until the main deposit was exhausted by the end of the 12th century (ibid., 167), and so the recovery of six fragments from Anglo-Norman and medieval contexts here is appropriate. It adds to at least 578 other pieces recorded in Winchester (Anderson 1990, table 52). In addition to Quarr stone there are other imported limestones, including a few blocks of Oolitic limestone, probably Bath or Portland stone. Neither limestone is common in Hampshire but both are known from Cathedral Green and Wolvesey Palace in Winchester (ibid., 311). Various other shelly limestones were also recovered. The structural stone includes some moulded architectural pieces that may be fragments of columns (NH3083 and NH3399).

The presence of imported building stone in Anglo-Norman contexts is in keeping with the major building projects which took place during that phase. Stone masons are known to have been more numerous in the 12th century than in later medieval Winchester (Keene 1985, 283) and, as a result, more private houses were built of stone than at a later date (ibid.).

A diamond-shaped white limestone fragment (NH2278, SF 959) and a fragment of Purbeck marble slab (NH5183) are both wall veneer. Purbeck marble was most intensively worked between 1250 and 1350 but was popular from about 1170 to 1550 (Blair 1991, 41) and is thought to have been worked on site at the Cathedral from the 13th century (Anderson 1990, 313).

As with Phase 4, a number of slabs were recovered. Some have only worked edges, suggesting they were utilised as courses in wall construction (NH3356), and one (NH4728) has mortar adhering. Others have worn surfaces, suggesting they were used as flooring, including some large stone tesserae in neat triangular shapes, each with one worn face (eg NH1194). Approximately 2.5 kg of these slabs are roof-stones (eg NH1395 reused as a whetstone and NH4742) while a further considerable number (7.7 kg) retain no evidence of working but are likely to have been used or intended for one of these functions. Most are limestone, probably Purbeck and one is a fragment of a moulded architectural piece (NH1155), probably from the top of a column.

In addition there are two pieces of more exotic stones. One thick slab of marble may be Campan Vert as seen in earlier phases and a second piece of probable wall veneer is of Sussex 'marble'. Both of these may be residual from Roman phases or may have come from Wolvesey Palace which has produced more fragments of exotic imported stone than other excavated sites in Winchester (Biddle 1990, table 54).

Phase 6: medieval

Medieval contexts produced a number of chalk and limestone blocks retaining tool marks, including several blocks of Quarr stone and Bembridge limestone (presumably brought in association with the Quarr stone), as well as oolitic limestone. As Quarr stone cannot have been obtained in any quantity from the quarry after the 12th century (see Phase 5), it must date to earlier activity and indeed one of the pieces was found in demolition layer NH4102. This context also produced a hard chalk hood mould. This use of stone probably relates to earlier larger scale building projects somewhere rather than the 13th- and 14th-century extensions made to the archdeacon's house.

Medieval contexts produced the bulk of the stone roofing material—15 kg in total. Most of the medieval stone roofing is slate (11 kg), probably imported from Devon or Cornwall. Slate was being shipped from the Devon ports to Southampton as early as the 12th century and over 800,000 slates were imported for the king's buildings at Winchester between 1171 and 1186 (Wood 1983, 295).

Other roof-stones, mainly Purbeck limestone and Pennant sandstone, were used. Tilers and slaters were quite common in Winchester (Keene 1985, 283) and slated roofs not out of the ordinary. Many properties produced some stone roofing material, but Properties BW 3 and BW 5 produced significantly more slates than other properties (6.6 kg and 4.5 kg respectively), suggesting that slate was used for roofing there.

Painted wall plaster *by Edward Biddulph*

A total of 251 fragments of Roman-period wall plaster were recovered. Three plaster fabrics were identified. Fabric 1 had a soft yellow-brown matrix filled with moderate to frequent chalk fragments, sand grains of varying size and straw or grass impressions. Fabric 2 had a white matrix, but was essentially similar to fabric 1 and should perhaps be regarded as a variant of it. Fabric 3 was a hard yellow-brown matrix filled with moderate chalk fragments, quartz pieces, smaller sand grains, crushed flint, and occasional black or red iron-rich grains.

Fabric 1 was commonest, followed by fabric 3, then fabric 2. The backs of some pieces had the impressions of reed or wattle rods, indicating that the plaster had been applied to reed bundles fixed to roof timbers or wattle and daub walls. The plaster generally survived on its mortar backing up to a thickness of 25 mm. A large fragment appeared to comprise two layers of plaster, each with an application of red-brown paint, suggesting that the room from which the fragment derived was re-plastered at least once. Different types of surface treatment were recognised. In some cases, the plaster was simply skimmed to form a surface. A thin coat of white or colour paint could be applied directly to this surface for further refinement. Other pieces saw an application of colour paint on top of a white base paint.

Coloured washes or painted geometric or figurative designs were recorded on plaster from three groups. Traces of colour and patterning, usually applied on a white base, were seen on a few pieces from Structure NH8522 (Phase 2.3). Red- or orange-brown washes were recorded on some 25 fragments (three being on a fabric 3 mortar). Dark grey paint was seen on a further 17 pieces, one of these a little more decorative, featuring a light grey stripe sandwiched between darker grey stripes or panels. Group NH8523 (Phase 2.3), levelling over Structure NH8522, contained a single fragment, which had traces of a red-brown painted surface above a white undercoat on a fabric 1 mortar.

Pit Group NH8524 (Phase 2.3) contained plaster fragments that had a relatively wide range of decorative schemes, all on fabric 1 mortar. A small fragment of plaster was painted turquoise. No edges were seen, but the fragment may be part of a border. Another fragment was decorated with a red-brown stripe or panel and a sphere-like motif on a white background. Traces of a red-brown wash bordered by a dark grey stripe or panel were seen on other pieces.

The fragments do not allow decorative schemes to be fully reconstructed, but the evidence points to panels painted orange- and red-brown and grey bordered by light grey stripes in Structure NH8522, and red-brown panels in Group NH8523. The scheme was more complex in Pit Group NH8524, involving red-brown, grey and turquoise borders and perhaps a floral or rounded pattern. The decoration on the plaster from groups NH8522, NH8523 and NH8524 suggests that the buildings they belonged to served a domestic function. Wall paintings would be appropriately placed in areas used for social gatherings and entertaining, for example, a dining room, bath suite or reception area. The plain walls of groups NH8516 and NH8521 might indicate lower status, although given the very small amount recovered from those groups, it is uncertain to what extent the plaster is representative of the overall decoration.

TOOLS, EQUIPMENT, PRODUCTS AND EVERYDAY OBJECTS

Iron Age coin *by Philip de Jersey*

A single Iron Age coin (SF NH1263) was recovered from Phase 1.3 subsoil deposit NH4390. This is a base silver unit attributed to the Cotswolds tribe of the Dobunni. Although in relatively poor condition, enough of the reverse design is visible to confirm its identification. The weight, the presence of some silver and the relatively unstylized cock's head below the horse all suggest a date early in the

Dobunnic uninscribed series, perhaps *c* 40 BC. The class A silver units stand at the head of a long series of silver coinage, probably beginning *c* 50 BC; this coin is thus likely to date between *c* 50–40 BC. Coins of the Dobunni are relatively rare finds in Hampshire, with only 15 examples recorded in the Celtic Coin Index. Of these nine were recovered in excavations at Hayling Island temple, including three silver units also of class A. This coin is therefore a somewhat unusual find from Winchester.

Roman coins *by Paul Booth*

Some 305 Roman coins were recovered from the site, most dating to the late 3rd and 4th centuries. The assemblages are summarised in Table 7.23 using the revised period numbering scheme of Reece (eg 1991) and then grouped into four wider coin loss phases (A to D, Reece 1973, 230–1). A fuller report and detailed identifications are presented in the digital report (*Digital Section 2*).

The earliest coin is a Claudian copy *as* of Minerva type (SF417). This is not particularly well preserved, but is clearly a 'clumsy copy' in the terms of Kenyon's recent discussion of other examples from Winchester (2008, 120), equivalent to grade C in his discussion of the material from Colchester (Kenyon 1987, 27). Another *as* is almost certainly of Domitian, while other early Roman coins include a *sestertius* of Trajan.

An *as* of later 1st-century date (SF1517b) was fused to a *sestertius* of Faustina II, one of five coins dated to the reign of Marcus Aurelius. Three of the four late 2nd-early 3rd century coins were *denarii*, two of them plated, one (SF1762) probably of Geta, the other (SF1135) not closely identified. The unplated *denarius* was of Julia Mamaea. The fourth coin in this group was a *sestertius* of Severus Alexander (SF1820).

Regular issues of period 13 include one of Gallienus (Dianae Cons Aug) and one of Tetricus I (Hilaritas Augg). Regular *antoniniani* were relatively scarce, though corrosion made some attributions questionable. Single issues of Salonina (uncertain reverse type), Postumus (Laetitia), Gallienus (Apolloni Cons Aug) and Claudius (Pax Aug), and two of Victorinus (Pietas Aug), fall into this category. Twelve or thirteen coins of the Tetrici, however, were all assigned to the 'irregular radiate' group, along with three further coins each of Claudius and Victorinus. These were placed in period 14. Other (mostly regular) issues of this period include an *antoninianus* of Carausius (Laeti Ti Aug), a *quinarius* of Allectus (Virtus Aug, galley type), one of Probus (Spes Aug), eight of Carausius and three of Allectus. The irregular coins assigned to this period include two based on Consecratio types of Claudius II and one of Tetricus II (?Pax Aug).

Early 4th century coins were fairly well-represented, though at least two were assigned to this period on their general characteristics rather than specifically identifiable features. One coin of AD 326 (SF1340), has an unusual variant on the reverse legend, which reads CONSTAN/TINAS/ANG below the wreath, rather than CONSTAN/TINUS/AUG. The more numerous coins of AD 330–348 are mostly unremarkable. A minimum of 12 of these 51 coins are probably irregular issues, amongst which a small mule (SF1759a) of a standard obverse right-facing imperial head (otherwise illegible) with a victory reverse of Constantinopolis type is notable. The other irregular types of this period were Urbs Roma, Gloria Exercitus 2 standards (3), Gloria Exercitus 1 standard (6) and an uncertain reverse type. Other coins of this period single examples of Pax Publica and Victoriae dd Augg q NN.

A FEL TEMP REPARATIO (Phoenix on globe) coin of AD 348–350 is the only regular issue from period 18 (AD 348–364). All but one of the other 11 coins assigned to this period are small pieces dominated by Fel Temp Reparatio fallen horseman types, the remaining coin, also irregular, being of Victoriae DD NN Aug et Cae(s) type. Another group of four small coins from a Phase 2.3 deposit (NH2290) might also have been minims of this period on the basis of their size (8–11 mm) and general character, but had no other identifiable features and were assigned to a general late 3rd–4th century category.

Issues of the House of Valentinian (period 19) were relatively numerous and divided between the principal common types of this period, Securitas Reipublicae (13), Gloria Romanorum (8) and Gloria Novi Saeculi (1). Two coins of period 20 are also present, both Vot XV Mult XX issues of Gratian. Ten coins are assigned with varying degrees of confidence to the final period (21), including coins of Victoria Auggg type, one being attributable to Arcadius.

Table 7.23: Quantification of Roman coins by issue period and phase

Date	Reece Period	Northgate House (NH)			Discovery Centre (CC)		
		Total coins	Phase total	% of coins assigned to phase	Total coins	Phase total	% of coins assigned to phase
-41	1						
41–68	2/3				1		
69–96	4				1		
41–96	2-4	1					
96–117	5	1					
117–138	6						
138–161	7						
161–180	8	5					
180–192	9						
193–222	10	1					
222–238	11	2					
193–238	10/11	1					
238–260	12						
Other Phase A		4	15	6.4	2	4	8.5
260–275	13	21			4		
275–296	14	80 (59)			14 (10)		
Phase B			101	43.2		18	38.3
296–317	15	8					
317–330	16	8			4		
Other Phase C		2	18	7.7		4	8.5
330–348	17	51			8		
348–364	18	12					
364–378	19	22			8		
378–388	20	2					
388–402	21	7			3		
Other Phase D		7	101	43.2	2	21	44.7
3-4C		20			2		
uncertain		1					
TOTAL		256	235		49	47	

Mints

Too few of the 3rd century coins could be attributed to mints to make discussion worthwhile. The 4th-century coins (including probable as well as certain attributions) are quantified by mint in Table 7.24.

These present a fairly typical pattern of mint distribution, comparable to recent analyses of material from the northern suburbs and sites on the defences of Winchester (Davies 2008, 132, 134). The same range of mints is represented (with the exception of Amiens, missing from the present sites), and in broadly similar proportions and with broadly similar principal trends, in line with fairly well-established patterns. The main trend is the decline in the importance of Trier after the middle of the 4th century. In the present sites, in slight contradiction to the pattern shown by Davies, there are no identified Trier coins at all after AD 348, though this may be exaggerated by the paucity of mintmarks identified on the coins of period 21. Only one such coin was attributed to a mint, in this case Lyons, which also produced one of the two period 20 coins (the other was not attributed).

Chronology, context and residuality

The Discovery Centre site had the longer Roman occupation sequence, starting at least in the 2nd century, whereas the Northgate House site appears to have seen little activity before the middle of the 3rd century. This is reflected in the coin list from that site, although the Discovery Centre, with the longer sequence, does not have a significantly higher representation of early Roman coins. The significance of the single Claudian copy at this site is uncertain, but the relative proximity of this findspot to the small concentration of these coins at Victoria Road (Kenyon 2008) may be relevant, although it should also be noted that the Discovery Centre piece was clearly redeposited as it occurred in a late Roman context. Indeed only one of the four 1st–2nd century coins from this site was in a remotely contemporary context (SF500 from context 1667). The situation at Northgate House was broadly similar, with two early coins occurring in contexts of Phase 2.2, though it is likely that the individual context dates were later than those of the coins themselves

At Northgate House some 11 late Roman coins were recorded from the top of the natural subsoil, presumably deriving from later deposits which interfaced directly with that layer, while the 1st–2nd century *as* from the Discovery Centre and an *as* and *sestertius* from Northgate House, mentioned above, were the only coins from either site in contexts of Phase 2.1 and Phase 2.2 respectively. The broad phasing scheme employed for the Roman period makes meaningful discussion of coin loss in relation to it rather difficult, particularly for Phase 2.3, which spans a hundred years from the beginning of the last third of the 3rd century. Deposits of this

Table 7.24: Numbers of 4th-century coins attributed to mints

| Mint | Northgate House | | Discovery Centre | | |
	300–364	364–402	300–364	364–402	Total
London	2		1		3
Trier	23		5		28
Lyons	9	6	1	1	17
Arles	2	5		3	10
Rome	1				1
Aquileia		1		1	2
Siscia	1	1		1	3
Thessalonica	1				1
Total	39	13	7	6	65

phase produced 54 Roman coins, while those of the final Roman Phase, 2.4, contained 100 coins.

A broad range of coins was present in these deposits, including two presumably intrusive coins of AD 364–378 in Phase 2.3. These apart, the relative scarcity of coins of period 17 in this phase is notable. By contrast, these coins made up a large proportion of the assemblage in Phase 2.4 contexts, while coins of subsequent periods demonstrate that the sequence did indeed run right to the end of the 4th century if not beyond. A large proportion of the Phase 2.4 assemblage, however, was still composed of later 3rd century coins. It is not possible to determine if the range of earlier coins in these latest contexts simply reflects a substantial degree of redeposition or if some of this material remained in circulation. Reece (2002, 57) has argued, for example, that some 'barbarous radiates' remained in use until AD 330, but this would not explain their frequency in later contexts. The character of these contexts, with a high proportion of 'dark earth' deposits, might be a better explanation for the mixed groups of coins, with a high likelihood that they will contain residual material. A recently examined sequence of dark earth deposits associated with the forum at Cirencester, however, contained only 10 coins (out of a total of 193) which were of later 3rd century date, all the rest being certainly or probably dated after AD 330 (Booth 2008), so this suggests a rather different pattern of deposition compared to that in the present sites. All the latest (ie period 21) coins stratified in 'contemporary' deposits were from Northgate House. The 56 coins from the six contexts concerned (2034, 4428, 4688, 4696, 4718 and 6059) were grouped together to see if they demonstrated a pattern of loss any different from that already discussed. The figures suggest that a slightly higher proportion of the later coins, from period 18 onwards, occurred in these contexts in comparison to the generalised Phase 2.4 group, but this would be expected and there was still a fairly broad spread of earlier material with no suggestion of the presence of a 'tight' late 4th century assemblage in these contexts.

General discussion

In total, the Northgate House/Discovery Centre assemblage forms a good group which can be compared with other evidence from Winchester. This comparison is based on the very useful discussion of the coin evidence from sites in the extramural areas and on the defences of Roman Winchester recently published by Davies (2008), set alongside the summary totals for three main groups of coins from other Winchester sites published by Reece (1991, 20).

The principal conclusion of Davies' analysis concerned the ratio of coins of Reece's Phases B and D. The occurrence of a high proportion of coins of Phase D is generally considered to be a 'rural' characteristic, while a high proportion of Phase B coins is typical of the larger urban centres of Roman Britain. As would be expected, therefore, most of the Winchester groups considered by Davies fell into the latter category. Nevertheless it was notable that while the material from the northern suburb was grouped in this way, the assemblages from the eastern and western suburbs were both distinctly 'rural' in character (Davies 2008, 132). The group from the eastern suburbs, however, was small (only 35 coins) and the extent to which it can be regarded as representative is unclear. Overall, the coins from the north-west quarter of the walled town are consistent with the urban trend and although the Phase B:D ratio differs slightly between Northgate House and the Discovery Centre, being more weighted in favour of Phase D in the latter site, both fall firmly in this group.

These comparisons are expressed graphically in Figure 7.21, which draws on data presented by Davies (2008) in his figure 73 and listed by Reece (1991, sites 20–22). This shows clearly the slightly unusual (but small) group from the town defences (Davies 2008, 128) and the 'rural' (but also small) groups from the eastern and western suburbs. Lankhills has been added to underline the extreme contrast provided by a late Roman cemetery group. This collection combines the material from the 1967–72 excavations (Reece 1979) and that from work carried out by OA from 2000–2005 (Booth 2010).

Post-Roman coins *by Martin Allen*

Identifications

SF 1211: coin 1 Anglo-Saxon 'sceat', ?Series K (Type 32a), North 1994, 63, no. 89, 0.06 g (fragment).

This fragment can be tentatively identified as a Series K sceat on the basis of the long cross on the obverse, which is similar to the cross before the bust in Series K, and the faint traces of a beaded arc on the reverse, which might be the arc of the 'wolf-headed serpent' of Type 32a. Series K has been dated *c* 720–730/740, but use of such secondary sceattas continued until the introduction of broad pennies into southern England in the 760s and 770s (Grierson and Blackburn 1986, 184–9, discusses the chronology of sceattas). A probable *terminus post quem* for this coin is *c* 770.

SF 223 Alfred (871–899) to Eadgar (957/9–975), round halfpenny. ?Winchester mint; three fragments (0.13 g, 0.02 g and 0.01 g).

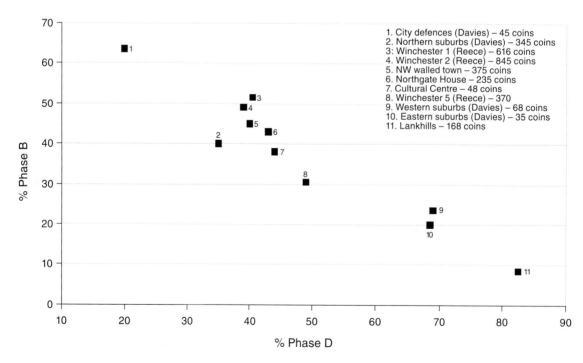

1. City defences (Davies) – 45 coins
2. Northern suburbs (Davies) – 345 coins
3: Winchester 1 (Reece) – 616 coins
4: Winchester 2 (Reece) – 845 coins
5. NW walled town – 375 coins
6. Northgate House – 235 coins
7. Cultural Centre – 48 coins
8. Winchester 5 (Reece) – 370
9. Western suburbs (Davies) – 68 coins
10. Eastern suburbs (Davies) – 35 coins
11. Lankhills – 168 coins

Fig. 7.21   The proportions of coins in Reece's phases B and D (after Davies 2008, fig. 73, with additions)

These fragments seem to be from a previously unrecorded type of halfpenny struck between the 880s and Eadgar's reform of the coinage in *c* 973. The obverse of this new type has a normal Circumscription Cross design of an inscription in an outer circle around a central small cross. The letter X of REX is visible on the obverse of the largest of the three fragments. The design on the reverse seems to have four limbs of a cross radiating from a central pellet, with a small cross pattée at the end of each limb of the cross (visible on one terminal on the largest fragment and on another terminal on the second fragment). One limb of the cross without its terminal is visible on the smallest fragment. In one angle of the cross (on the second fragment) is the letter I, and in another angle (on the largest fragment) is T. The reverse inscription might be tentatively reconstructed as WINT or PINT, referring to Winchester (*Winton*).

The closest comparison for this new type on previously recorded halfpennies is a type showing two vertical limbs radiating from a central pellet, with a small cross pattée at the end of each limb and WIN horizontally across the field. This type is known from a coin of Eadwig (955–959) in the Fitzwilliam Museum (North 1994, 146, no. 740/3, Pl. 12, 11) and a coin of Eadgar found in London no later than 1842, which is now lost (Blunt 1961, 44, 46–7, Pl. III, 14–15; Blunt *et al.* 1989, 204, 206, Pl. 25, 395). Halfpennies of the mid 10th century are often copied from or were inspired by earlier issues of Alfred and Edward the Elder (899–924) (Blunt *et al.* 1989, 202–4), and it is possible that this Winchester find is a new type from the reign of Alfred or Edward the Elder, analogous to Alfred's pennies of Winchester with PIN in a vertical line on the reverse (North 1994, 126, no. 647).

SF 1211: coin 2 Athelstan (924–939), penny, Circumscription Cross type (*c* 928–939), North 1994, 134, nos 671–2, uncertain mint and moneyer, 0.49 g (eleven fragments).

Most of these fragments do not have a legible inscription, but three of the largest fragments have visible portions of an obverse inscription of Athelstan's Circumscription Cross type (E_, EL and X TOT respectively), and the full inscription can be reconstructed as E_EL[STAN RE]X TOT [BRIT].

Hoard evidence indicates that coins of Athelstan survived in circulation in relatively large numbers until Eadgar's reform of the coinage in *c* 973 (Blunt 1974, 51–5). A probable *terminus ante quem* for the deposition of this coin is the end of Eadgar's reign in 975, when it may be assumed that the recoinage of pre-reform coins was effectively complete.

SF 1055 Cnut (1016–1035), Pointed Helmet type, *BMC* xiv, Hildebrand G, North 1994, 168, no. 787, London, moneyer Edric, 0.79 g (broken into two pieces). The inscription on the obverse is +CNVT RECX:· and on the reverse is +EDRIC ON LVNDEN [N and D ligated].

Cnut's Pointed Helmet type is conventionally dated to *c* 1023–1029, although the precise chronology of the coinage of Cnut is uncertain. The Pointed Helmet type was replaced by the Short Cross type of *c* 1029–1035, and 1035 can be suggested as a probable *terminus post quem* of this coin. A date later than 1035 cannot be entirely ruled out however, as the Pointed Helmet type occurs in some English hoards after 1035 (Allen 2006, 515–17). Pointed Helmet is the second most numerous type in the Wedmore hoard (deposited *c* 1043), which contained large numbers of obsolete coins apparently retained as savings, and it last appears as a very minor residual element in English hoards in the 1060s and 1070s. Thus a date as late as the 1070s is possible, although unlikely.

Significance

Coin 223, which is probably a new type of halfpenny from the Winchester mint in the late 9th or 10th century, is an important discovery for the study of Anglo-Saxon numismatics and the history of Winchester. The datings of coins 223 and 1055 do not conflict with the suggested datings of their contexts (3466 and 3364) to the 9th–12th centuries, but they might provide more precise chronologies of the contexts.

The two coins from context 4095 (1211: coins 1 and 2) are significantly earlier than their context, which is the upper fill of a small pit of the 11th–12th centuries, and they may be not be primary deposits.

Objects of metal, glass, shale and worked bone
by H E M Cool, with a contribution by Paul Booth

The excavations at Northgate House and the Discovery Centre produced just under 1500 items of metalwork, glass, worked bone and other skeletal material. This is a substantial body of material which can throw light on both the occupation on the site and on Winchester more generally. The city has been well-served by small finds' publication which allows this group to be put in context. In 1990 the late Saxon and later finds from the 1961 to 1971 excavations were published (Biddle 1990), and the small finds from all the excavations in the suburbs and defences between 1972 and 1986 were published whilst this material was being worked on (Rees *et al.* 2008). Whilst these are very valuable and informative works, the lack of any site narratives or information on other categories of finds for these sites makes full evaluation of them difficult. Northgate House and the Discovery Centre provide the first opportunity to set a large small finds assemblage from Winchester within its full context. This obviously enables a better appreciation of them to be gained, but it has also meant that for the first time that we are probably seeing the full range of items such as worked bone and antler from the city. This category of material was heavily exploited to make objects during the late Saxon and Anglo-

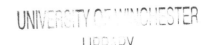

Norman periods, and some of them are easy to confuse with unworked animal bone. It is only after that category of material has been fully examined, as here, that one can be sure that all the items have been made available to the small finds specialist.

A large body of material such as this naturally leads to a large report and so the presentation of this has been split into two parts. This section in the printed volume provides a brief overview of the assemblage and draws attention to some of the more important items that have been recovered. The full report including the catalogue entries, typological discussion and many of the tables summarising certain aspects of the data are available in the digital files (*Digital Section 3*). The parts should be seen as complementary and full supporting evidence for points made here is presented in the digital report.

The independently-dated finds reflect occupation in two main periods. The Roman period is well represented with material ranging in date from the mid 1st century into the 5th century. There is then a gap of several centuries with nothing in the assemblage suggesting early to mid Saxon occupation. Late Saxon and Anglo-Norman activity of the 10th to 12th century is strongly represented but items belonging to the 13th century or later are rare. Table 7.25 compares the independently dated Roman and later assemblages by function excluding items such as hobnails for which there is no later equivalent, vessel glass and nails.

The smaller size of the Roman assemblage is almost certainly the result of the nature of the excavations and the mitigation strategies that were followed. In the Roman vessel glass assemblage, for example, one of the earliest fragments (no. 40) was found in a late Saxon context probably because it is

a fragment from a robust pillar moulded bowl and is precisely the sort of item that survives in a recognisable form in a residual context. An urban site that has deep blue pillar moulded bowls might be expected to have a range of other mid 1st century vessels but only one is represented (no. 42), presumably because the early contexts that might have produced them were not excavated. Certainly late Roman material is much better represented than that of the 1st and 2nd centuries. The Roman finds thus only provide a partial picture of the nature of the activity in this area at that time. For the late Saxon and Anglo-Norman periods, by contrast, a much fuller and more richly textured picture emerges.

The Roman period

The Roman finds assemblage is a fairly typical one for an urban site but a particularly interesting aspect is the evidence indicating a military presence in the vicinity in the later 2nd to 3rd centuries. The items that suggest this are two very similar divided bow brooches from Phase 2.3 contexts (nos 3 and 4) and the strap fitting no. 97. The brooches belong to a type (Hull Type 189; see Bayley and Butcher 2004) in use at the end of the 2nd century and into the 3rd century. By that time the majority of the population of southern Britain had stopped wearing bow brooches. This is well demonstrated by looking at the brooch assemblage from the Winchester suburb and defences sites which only produced a single later 2nd to 3rd century knee brooch compared with 41 1st to 2nd century forms (Rees *et al.* 2008, 38 no. 42). Bow brooch wearing continued within military communities, which is why the presence of these two brooches alone would have been sufficient to raise the possibility of a military involvement. This is supported by the strap mount no. 97 from a Phase 2.4 context in the Discovery Centre area. The combination of asymmetrical openwork decoration with the integral rivet and washer is typical of the sort of strap fitting used in the 3rd century by the military (Bishop and Coulston 2006, 182, 190).

These are not the only pieces of evidence for the military at Winchester during the late 2nd and 3rd centuries. At Victoria Road a strap-end was found in an early to mid 3rd century context and a brass inlaid iron scabbard slide of 3rd century form was also recovered (Rees *et al.* 2008, 173 nos 934, 939). In discussing the latter a very similar slide was noted as having come from the unpublished Biddle excavations at Ashley Terrace in 1964. It is also known that there is another divided bow brooch from one of the Biddle excavations, as Webster cited it as comparanda when publishing a brooch from Caerleon (Webster 1992, 112). This body of military material is probably best interpreted as indicating the presence of detachments of the army on policing duties.

A find worthy of special comment is the set of bone weaving tablets (no. 37) found in a floor level

Table 7.25: Small finds: A comparison of the Roman and later assemblage by function. The items are assigned by typological date. Nails, hobnails and vessel glass are excluded.

Function	Roman	Late Saxon to Medieval	Total
Personal	30	33	63
Toilet	3	3	6
Textiles	7	31	38
Household	-	12	12
Recreation	2	3	5
Weighing	1	7	8
Writing	-	3	3
Transport	-	22	22
Structural	7	14	21
Tools	6	44	50
Fasteners	24	72	96
Agricultural	-	2	2
Military	4	2	6
Religion	1	2	3
Industrial	4	19	23
Total	89	269	358

of Structure NH8520 which was constructed after the late 3rd century. This consisted of four square tablets, each with six holes and a triangular multi-perforated plate. In Roman Britain, triangular tablets are the most common form. Square ones appear to be a later introduction with the earliest securely dated example being one from Wroxeter in a 3rd century context (Mould 2000, 131 no. 172). The context of this set supports a late date as does the example from Victoria Road found in a mid to late 4th century well fill (Rees *et al.* 2008, 76 no. 363). The fifth element of the set, the triangular plate, is a particularly welcome addition. These have occasionally been found before but their function has been uncertain. The plate shows the typical wear patterns that weaving tablets acquire around their perforations. This feature, together with the association of the plate with the set of four tablets, indicates that such items can now be seen as part of a specialised weaving apparatus.

Weaving tablets were used to produce narrow bands of densely woven fabric which had a variety of uses. These bands formed the starting point for lengths of fabrics woven on a warp-weighted loom (Walton Rogers 2007, 27–8), and richly decorated examples could be used as decorative edging sewn onto garments whose cloth had been woven on a larger loom (see Walton Rogers 2007, 89–97 for examples). Weaving tablets were also used to form the selvedges (finished edges of fabric) on lengths of fabric woven on larger looms where the weft threads were those used on the larger loom with the small tablets governing the warp threads (Wild 1970, 74). In Britain when sets are found, they regularly consist of four plates, and it may be significant that Wild (ibid.) has hypothesised that some tubular selvedges that were tablet woven may have needed four tablets to create. The association of the triangular plate with the four weaving tablets here might, however, suggest that this set was not being used in this way. The fact that the tablets have six holes, rather than the more normal four, also places this set apart.

The mention in the *Notitia Dignitatum* of a state weaving works at *Venta* in Britain (Rivet and Smith 1979, 492) has often led in the past to a link being made between any textile equipment found in Winchester and this establishment (see for example Clarke 1979, 369). So it is perhaps worth drawing attention to the paucity of textile working equipment that has been recovered from both these excavations and the ones on the suburb and defences sites (Rees *et al.* 2008, 75–6). The amount recovered is even smaller if Stephens (2008) is correct and bone needles are in fact hairdressing aids. A set of weaving tablets is an item that would have been as much at home in a domestic work basket as the industrial confines of a state weaving works. There is some evidence that attitudes towards the production of textiles may have been changing in the 4th century. Certainly implements associated with weaving start to be deposited in female graves in a way that had not been seen before, and the shale industries of Dorset started producing lathe-turned spindle whorls (eg Lankhills: Booth *et al.* 2010). Where found in graves, these whorls tend to be associated with women of high status judged from their grave furnishings. The late square weaving tablets should probably be seen against this domestic background, and the presence of this set need have no connection with any industrial establishment.

The 4th century finds from the site have several features that are worthy of special note. Amongst the vessel glass assemblage there is a fragment (no. 57) that comes from a vessel with indented and trailed decoration. This is rarely observed in Romano-British 4th century assemblages but is one that has been noted as being characteristic of contemporary glass in the north of Gaul (Arveiller-Dulong *et al.* 2003, 156). This is not the only possible import from that area in the glassware of 4th-century Winchester. The Brooks produced one certain example of an indented truncated conical beaker and the body fragment no. 58 from these excavations might possibly be from another. This is another late 4th to 5th century form, uncommon in Britain but present in the cemetery at Épiais-Rhus (Vanpeene 1993, 50 no. 81, pl XVIII). A late-4th century grave at the Lankhills School cemetery also produced an indented beaker, this time additionally decorated with spiral trails (Harden 1979, 215 no. 51, fig. 27). This is a rare form everywhere, but might be another candidate to be an import. Excavations by Oxford Archaeology at Lankhills produced a glass tettine (Booth *et al.* 2010), another form that is regularly found in 4th-century cemeteries in north Gaul but which otherwise is unknown from 4th-century Britain. A pattern is thus starting to emerge from the Winchester sites that suggests in the late 4th century part of Winchester's glass was being supplied from the glass-houses in northern Gaul.

Another welcome aspect of the assemblage is the presence of several items that indicate occupation during the late 4th century and into the 5th century. These include the fastener of a bone bracelet (no. 28), a polychrome glass counter (no. 60) and a terminal of a spur (no. 98). All of these items can be paralleled amongst the grave goods at the Lankhills School cemetery (Clarke 1979, Booth *et al.* 2010), and Northgate House/Discovery Centre area may well be one of the areas where the people buried there lived.

Finally one context, the fill of pit CC3330, is of special interest. As well as the shale table leg (see below), it contained one of the substantially complete divided bow brooches (no. 4), a very unusual figured mount (no. 94) and a large number of hobnails indicative of at least one shoe. Whilst this could be casual rubbish disposal, it is an unusual group and it might be possible that some element of structured deposition was taking place. Shoes were sometimes used in these rituals.

Shale table leg fragment by Paul Booth

Cess pit CC3330, phased to the late Roman period, produced part of a shale table leg (SF322). The fragment is *c* 215 m long including a tenon 23 mm high and represents between approximately one third and one half of the length of the original object. The surviving piece is split approximately up the middle of the leg but is otherwise in good condition. The upper part of the leg has a marked internal concavity while the outer face is more gently bowed out and then in. There is linear moulding on the side of the leg on the lower part of the fragment, but there is no indication of the animal head decoration typical of the better known examples of this type. The concavity on the inner face is more normally seen about halfway up table legs with the animal head feature, rather than at the top, as here. An almost identical table leg was found in the centre of Winchester in a demoltion deposit associated with the forum, dated to the 4th century or later (Denford 1988). The exact form of these legs seems a little unusual in comparison with the examples discussed by Liversidge (eg 1955, 37–47) and further finds listed by Lawson (1975, 268).

The late Saxon to medieval finds

As noted in the introduction there is a clear absence of material belonging to the early to mid Saxon period followed by an explosion of material that can be dated to the 10th to 12th centuries. The paucity of material belonging to the 13th century and later is very well demonstrated by the incidence of 'sewing' pins and lace tags. Had there been considerable occupation on the site in the high medieval period, it could have been expected that these would be common especially on sites excavated under modern conditions with sieving taking place. 'Sewing' pins were in use from the 13th century onwards in Winchester (Biddle and Barclay in Biddle 1990, 560–71), and were clearly being used in very large quantities as dress accessories by the 14th century. Lace tags were also an important part of dress from the 14th century onwards. Only two 'sewing pins' (nos 132–3) and one lace tag (no. 150) were recovered from Northgate House and the Discovery Centre, graphically illustrating the change of occupation type after the 12th century. It is noticeable that the items that can be assigned later dates are dress fittings, precisely the sort of item that can be expected to be the subject of casual loss rather than formal rubbish disposal. There are, for example, a buckle (no. 139) and strap ends and mounts (nos 145, 147) of 14th-century date and two examples of the fine wire accessories common in the 16th and 17th centuries.

The 10th to 12th century assemblage of small finds is divided between a large number of functions (see Table 7.25). Some categories of finds are very well represented such as equipment for manufacturing textiles (nos 157–88), items related to

weighing items (nos 211–7) and those connected with transport (nos 221–39). The fasteners section includes numerous items connected with security (nos 297–310) as well as a large number of the somewhat enigmatic riveted mounts whose precise function is unknown (nos 311–33). The personal ornaments include a wide range of items including simple utilitarian iron buckles (nos 135–8), the pin of a silver annular brooch (no. 122) and two hooked tags (nos 139–40). There are also items such as a chess piece (no. 208), styli (nos 218–20) and arrow-heads (nos 371–2) which point to quite specialised activities taking place. A notable find was a bone spatula with a very distinctive style of figurative incised decoration (no. 198) which is the seventh example to have been found in Winchester (Collis and Kjølbye-Biddle 1979). From a typological point of view many of these items provide valuable insights into categories of finds they belong to. These aspects are considered at length in the digital report (*Digital Section 3*).

Many of the objects recovered came from pit fills and so it seems reasonable to assume that they may have been in use in the properties on which they were found rather than representing brought-in rubbish or levelling material. The finds thus also provide an opportunity to explore whether the different properties were being used for different functions, and it is this aspect that will be explored here. It can be achieved more easily for some properties than others as, to a certain extent, the number of finds reflects the footprint of the excavation. Properties BE 1–3, for example, produce approximately half the number of finds that Properties BW 2–5 do, reflecting the different areas dug. The total numbers of objects from the different properties can be seen in *Digital Section 3, Table 7*.

Naturally, residuality needs to be taken into consideration given the underlying Roman occupation and the fact that pit digging is likely to have disturbed the early layers. It is possible, though, to assess the proportion of securely identified Roman finds in the assemblages belonging to Phase 4 and later on each property. The figures are given *Digital Section 3, Table 8* and from that it is clear that it is not a uniform problem. Both Properties BW 1 and BW 6 have no identifiable Roman items. In Properties BW 2, BW 4, SE 2 and SE 3, the level of residuality is between 3% and 5%. In Properties BE 4, BW 3 and SE 1 the level is between 11% and 16%. In Properties BE 2, BE 5 and BW 5 it is between 20% and 24%. The highest amount of residuality is in Properties BE 3 (33%) and BE 1 (36%). As noted, the number of items associated with each property varies. Of the properties least affected by residuality from the Roman period (16% or less), BE 4, BW 2, BW 3, BW 4 and SE 1 have large assemblages of more than 50 items, SE 2 and SE 3 have 20 and 32 items respectively, and BW 1 and BW 6 have less than 10 items each. In what follows these figures have to be kept in mind, but certainly in the case of Properties BE 4, BW 2, BW 3, BW 4 and SE 1 where there are large assemblages with relatively little residuality, the assemblages should be reflecting the activities going on in them.

The relatively large numbers of items that have quite specific functions (tools associated with the manufacture of textiles, padlocks, balances, horseshoes) can be used to structure the enquiry. The relatively homogeneous date range of the finds makes it moderately easy to extract assemblages from the different properties which exclude most of the residual Roman material and the items that clearly belong to the 13th century and later. We also have the advantage that during the 10th to 12th centuries the use of the area appears to be domestic and secular. The dataset is thus much simpler with regard to both chronology and site type than the one relating to the 1961–71 excavations which Barclay, Biddle and Orton explored in their pioneering work on assemblage composition (Biddle 1990, 42–73). It might also be suspected that the assemblages considered there may have included a component of residual material that has been excluded here.

Table 7.26 shows the incidence of selected items with specific functions. These are shown as both absolute numbers and percentage of the property total once allowance has been made for residual material. Percentages on such small numbers can be misleading but here it allows a rapid comparison across properties. To aid interpretation the properties identified as originally having relatively large assemblages with low levels of residuality are shown in red.

The textile equipment can be divided into a variety of different categories. There are fibre preparation tools such as the teeth from wool combs and flax heckles (nos 157–8); a large number of spindle whorls of different forms (nos 159–73); tools used in weaving such as pin beaters (no. 174), picker-cum-beaters (nos 175–6) and eyed weaving tools (nos

177–84) and miscellaneous other items of which the tenterhook no. 185 is the most notable. The distribution is summarised in *Digital Section 3, Tables 10 and 11*. As can be seen from Table 7.26 here, tools for the production of cloth occur on all of the ten properties with more than ten items and on one of the properties with less than that. Excluding the last mentioned property, they form between 6% and 27% of the total. It is noticeable that the properties at the lower end of the range (BE 1, SE 1) have only spindle whorls whilst that at the top (Property BW 4) has tools for the whole range of production (fibre preparation, yarn spinning, cloth weaving). The size of the assemblage does not necessarily influence this. Property BE 4, the most prolific one, has only two categories of these tools (yarn spinning, cloth weaving). Both of these were properties with a low level of residuality where it seems reasonable to assume the pit contents are reflecting the activities in them. So the pattern suggests there might have been a degree of specialisation and localisation in the process. Spinning would have been a regular task which could be carried out everywhere as a woman can easily carry a spindle around with her. Fibre preparation and weaving are more static tasks and would appear here to have been carried out on a smaller number of properties.

The presence of shod horses appears to be a regular feature of the properties, so the absence of any on Property BW 4 is noteworthy. There is clear evidence of a blacksmith at work on this property as evidenced by a tanged punch (no. 274) and a rotary whetstone (see Shaffrey below and Starley below). Presumably this is a smith making items such as knives. Certainly this property had the highest incidence of iron blade fragments of all the properties. The presence of blacksmithing and cloth manufacture on this property would have made it a hive of industry, if the activities were taking place at the same time.

Table 7.26: Selected categories of finds from the different properties. Figures in red reflect properties with relatively low levels of residuality. The total figure reflects the assemblage once probable residual material has been removed.

| Property | Cloth production | | Horseshoes | | Padlocks | | Balances | | Total |
	No.	%	No.	%	No.	%	No.	%	No. Finds
BE1	1	8	-	-	-	-	-	-	12
BE2	2	15	1	8	1	8	2	15	13
BE3	2	18	1	9	-	-	-	-	11
BE4	5	11	3	7	4	9	1	2	44
BE5	2	29	-	-	-	-	-	-	7
BW1	-	-	-	-	-	-	-	-	1
BW2	5	22	2	8	1	4	-	-	23
BW3	4	19	1	5	2	10	-	-	21
BW4	6	27	-	-	2	9	-	-	22
BW5	2	10	4	19	1	5	1	5	21
BW6	-	-	-	-	-	-	-	-	1
SE1	1	7	2	14	-	-	2	14	14
SE2	-	-	-	-	-	-	-	-	4
SE3	1	16	-	-	-	-	-	-	17

An interesting feature of the assemblage was the large quantify of security fittings. These consisted primarily of barrel padlocks and their keys, but there were also two keys for fixed locks, one of the latter (no. 307) being an example of a rare form that appears to be a local development. Security fittings were also a regular find during the 1961–71 excavations in the city centre (summarised in *Digital Section 3 Table 19*). It might be tempting to think that properties where there are relatively large numbers of them might have had some special concerns over security. Inspection of Table 7.26 though suggests that security was a widespread concern in late Saxon Winchester. The high number in Property BE 4 falls into a regular pattern when considered against the background of all finds from all properties. There are ten properties with more than ten items and padlocks and their fitting occur on six of these, with the BE 4 pattern being proportionately the same as that on Properties BE 2, BW 3 and BW 4.

Balances were also relatively common. There were four equal-armed balances with fixed arms (nos 211–3, 216) as well as a suspension fork (no. 217) that might have come from a balance of that type or from a folding balance. Balances such as these are a common feature of late Saxon and Anglo-Norman assemblages. At Winchester there is the opportunity to consider the numbers recovered across a relatively large number of sites where occupation of this date occurs, and this is done in *Digital Section 3 Table 12*. When this is done it can be seen that these balances have been found regularly, but interrogation of the data does suggest that the number found during these excavations might be somewhat exceptional. An interesting question arises as to what these little balances were used to measure. Presumably they were common because people had a need to weigh small items regularly. Possibly they distrusted the coinage of the period as it may be doubted that many people would have needed to measure small quantities of other expensive items such as spices or precious or semi-precious metals and stones. An interesting feature of Table 7.26 here is that there is not a close association between the padlocks and their fittings and the balances. Whatever was being weighed was not felt to be in great need of security.

Something similar could be seen in the contemporary houses at Brook Street. Padlocks occurred regularly and, especially in the case of Building XII, in some numbers (see *Digital Section 3, Table 19*). Balances in contrast were restricted to Building IX/X (Biddle 1990, 922–4). From these excavations it is also noticeable that no weighing equipment was found on Property BW 4. Does this indicate that the industrial activities there did not need the ability to weigh small items such as coinage? Though the textile production might have been for domestic use, one would have thought a smith making items such as knives would have been likely to engage in commercial transactions. If the balances were used to check coinage, their absence from this property is interesting given the numbers from the others. Whether their principal use was to check coinage seems open to question. Certainly there is no obvious link between the incidence of coinage and the incidence of balances on any of the Winchester sites. So, at present, we are no closer to knowing quite why so many balances were needed.

Several of the less common items recovered from the excavations can also be put in context by reference to Table 7.26. The presence of two arrowheads (nos 371–2) from Property BW 2 is noteworthy as arrowheads were not particularly common finds in 10th to 12th century contexts within the 1961–71 excavations. In the city centre there was one from the castle bailey in a late 11th century context, three from scattered properties in Brook Street and a large one thought to be appropriate for large game from a mid 12th-century context at Wolvesey Palace (Goodall in Biddle 1971, nos 3990–91, 3995A, 396–7). Those from the castle and Wolvesey Palace clearly indicate a use amongst military and aristocratic milieus in the Anglo-Norman period, and so the recovery of two from this property, one of them in an Anglo-Norman context, is of some interest. The other finds include spindle whorls for the preparation of yarn but no other textile equipment. Shod horses were present and there was a concern for security, but there were no balances. It has to be said, therefore, that nothing else from the property suggested that its inhabitants were any more socially elevated than those in neighbouring properties.

Property BE 2 where the decorated scoop no. 189 was found had a well furnished assemblage where balances were well represented, but again nothing else that marks it as particularly out of the ordinary. It has been suggested that they might have had a liturgical function (Kjølbye-Biddle in Biddle 1990, 830), though when they were first discussed it was noted that all but one came from a domestic context and a household function was preferred (Collis and Kjølbye-Biddle 1979, 382–3). The context of no. 189 would suggest that a domestic use was likely, as would the wear patterns that can be seen on it.

The excavations have also produced a small number of what might be considered within this assemblage to be, if not luxury items, then things that are a little out of the normal pattern, possibly indicative of a more leisured existence. There is a small concentration of these on Property BE 3 during Phase 6 which produced both the chess piece no. 208 and the mount from a more elaborate casket than normal (no. 200). Possibly by chance the same property produced one of the only two vessel glass fragments found (no. 195) from a Phase 5 context. In some circumstances vessel glass can be taken as indicative of a high-status site. The chess piece could have been contemporary with the Phase 5 occupation as could the mount. The only items of semi-precious metal, the silver brooch pin no. 122, came from Property SE1 in a Phase 6 context. Another elaborate casket fitting (no. 203) had come from the same property in a Phase 5 context.

Summary catalogue of small finds (Figs 7.22–7.32)

A full catalogue is presented in the digital report (*Digital Section 3*).

Roman

Personal Ornaments

Brooches

1   **Strip bow brooch**; bow and foot fragment. Copper alloy. Ctx CC1383. SF CC196. (ID 1342) Phase 5 BE3.
2   **Trumpet brooch (Fig. 7.22)**; complete apart from tip of pin. Copper alloy. Ctx NH6507. SF NH1650. (ID 591) Phase 1.3.
3   **Divided bow brooch (Fig. 7.22)**; in two fragments, parts missing. Copper alloy with white metal coating. Ctx NH1353. SF NH924. (ID 807).
4   **Divided bow brooch (Fig. 7.22)**; in two pieces, missing pin. Copper alloy. Ctx CC3331. SF CC331. (ID 1344) Phase 2.3.
5   **Penannular brooch (Fig. 7.22)**; complete. Copper alloy. Ctx CC2325. SF CC281. (ID 1528) Phase 4.2 BE 4.

Hair pins

6   **Hair pin**. Bone. Ctx NH1428. NH SF156. (ID1560). Phase 2.3.
7   **Hair pin (Fig. 7.22)**. Bone. Ctx NH2619. SF NH998. (ID 183) Phase 2.3.
8   **Hair pin**. Bone. Ctx NH1385. Sf NH133. (ID 1564) Phase 2.3.

Beads

9   **Bead**. Translucent deep blue glass. Ctx CC1762. (ID1581). Phase 2.1.
10   **Bead**. Translucent emerald green glass. Ctx NH4718, SF NH1358.(ID 570) Phase 2.4.
11   **Bead**. Green/blue cloudy glass. Ctx NH1270. (ID1578). Phase 2.4.
12   **Bead**. Jet. Ctx NH7589. (ID 1582). Phase 4 BW5.

Bracelets

13   **Bracelet**; fragment. Copper alloy. Ctx NH3236. (ID 534). Phase BW 3.
14   **Bracelet (Fig. 7.22)**; fragment. Copper alloy. Ctx CC1680. SF CC498 (ID 1355) unphased.
15   **Bracelet**; fragment. Copper alloy. Ctx CC1579. SF CC478. (ID 1374) Phase 2.4.
16   **Bracelet**; three fragments. Copper alloy. Ctx CC109. SF CC7. (ID 1521) Unphased.
17   **Bracelet**; three fragments. Copper alloy. Ctx NH1260. SF NH104. (ID 801) Phase 2.3.
18   **Bracelet**; three fragments. Copper alloy. Ctx NH5059. SF NH1438. (ID 126) Phase 2.4.
19   **Bracelet**; fragment. Copper alloy. Ctx NH2208, SF NH832. (ID 585) Phase 4.1 BW5.
20   **Bracelet**; fragment. Copper alloy. Ctx NH3539. (ID 116) Phase 5.
21   **Bracelet**; fragment. Copper alloy. Ctx U/S. SF NH1410 (ID 146).
22   **Bracelet**; fragment. Copper alloy. Ctx NH u/s. SF NH1439. (ID 536).
23   **Bracelet**; fragment. Copper alloy. Ctx NH4694. SF NH1324. (ID 524) Phase 2.4.
24   **Bracelet**; fragment. Copper alloy. Ctx NH1204, SF NH76. (ID 802) Phase 4.2 SE2.
25   **Bracelet**; two fragments. Copper alloy. Ctx CC1435. SF CC427. (ID 1373) Phase 5 BE2.
26   **Bracelet (Fig. 7.22)**; fragment. Lead or other white metal alloy. Ctx NH3587. Sample NH234. (ID 363) Phase 4.1 BW4.
27   **Bracelet (Fig. 7.22)**; fragment. Copper alloy. Ctx NH4696. SF NH1330. (ID 148) Phase 2.4.
28   **Bracelet fastener (Fig. 7.22)**, chipped at one end. Copper alloy. Ctx CC1459. Sf CC441. (ID 1359) Phase 5 BE3.

Finger ring

29   **Finger ring**. Copper alloy. Ctx NH7517. SF NH1782.(ID 565) Phase 2.3.

Ear ring

30   **Ear ring**. Copper alloy. Ctx NH4394, sample NH266. (ID 561) Phase 4.2 BW2.
31   **Ear ring (Fig. 7.22)**. Copper alloy. Ctx CC408, SF CC5. (ID 1520) Unphased.

Hobnails

32   **Hobnails** (28). Iron. Ctx CC3331, SF CC395, Sample CC328. (ID 1533) Phase 2.3.
33   **Hobnails** (95). Iron. Ctx CC3331, SF CC1113, Sample CC328. (ID 1305) Phase 2.3.

Toilet equipment

34   **Chatelaine tool (Fig. 7.22)**; complete. Copper alloy. Ctx NH3314. SF NH1026. (ID 579) Phase 5 BW3.
35   **Nail cleaner**; complete but broken in two. Copper alloy. Ctx NH2228. NH253. (ID 1527) Phase 4.2.
36   **Unguent bottle**; cylindrical neck fragment. Blue/green glass. Ctx CC1762, SF CC869. (ID 1399) Phase 2.1.

Textile equipment

37   **Set of weaving tablets (Fig. 7.23)**. Bone. Ctx NH5208. SF NH1493. (ID 178) Phase 2.3.
38   **Needle**. Bone. Ctx NH3371. (ID 1503) Phase 6.
39   **Needle**. Bone. Ctx NH1398. SF NH154. (ID 1565) Phase 2.4.

Household equipment

40   **Pillar moulded bowl**. Ctx CC469, SF CC203. (ID 1419) Phase 4.2 BE4.
41   **Pillar moulded bowl**. Ctx CC1740, SF CC862. (ID 1389) Phase 2.1
42   **Body fragment**. Ctx CC3160, SF CC389. (ID 1393) Phase 2.4.
43   **Bowl**; rim fragment. Ctx NH2444, SF NH1508. (ID 172) Phase 2.4.
44   **Cylindrical cup**; rim fragment. Ctx NH6061, SF NH1645. (ID 168) Phase 1.3.
45   **Bowl or jar**; rim fragment. Ctx CC1580, SF CC460. (ID 1403) Phase 2.4.
46   **Jug** (?); body fragments. Ctx CC2193, SF CC682. (ID 1391) Phase 2.1.
47   **Base fragment**. Ctx CC1611, SF CC466. (ID 1394) Phase 2.3.
48   **Base fragment**. Ctx CC1459, SF CC1459. (ID 1413) Phase 5 BE3.
49   **Bottle**. Ctx NH2384, SF NH909. (ID 161) Phase 4.2 BW5.
50   **Bottle**. Ctx NH6151, SF NH1677. (ID 159) Phase 5 SE1.
51   **Prismatic bottle**. Ctx NH6059. SF NH1666. (ID 164) Phase 2.4.
52   **Prismatic bottle**. Ctx CC1689, SF CC476. (ID 1390) Phase 2.2.
53   **Hemispherical cup**. Ctx CC1579, SF CC457. (ID 1398) Phase 2.4.

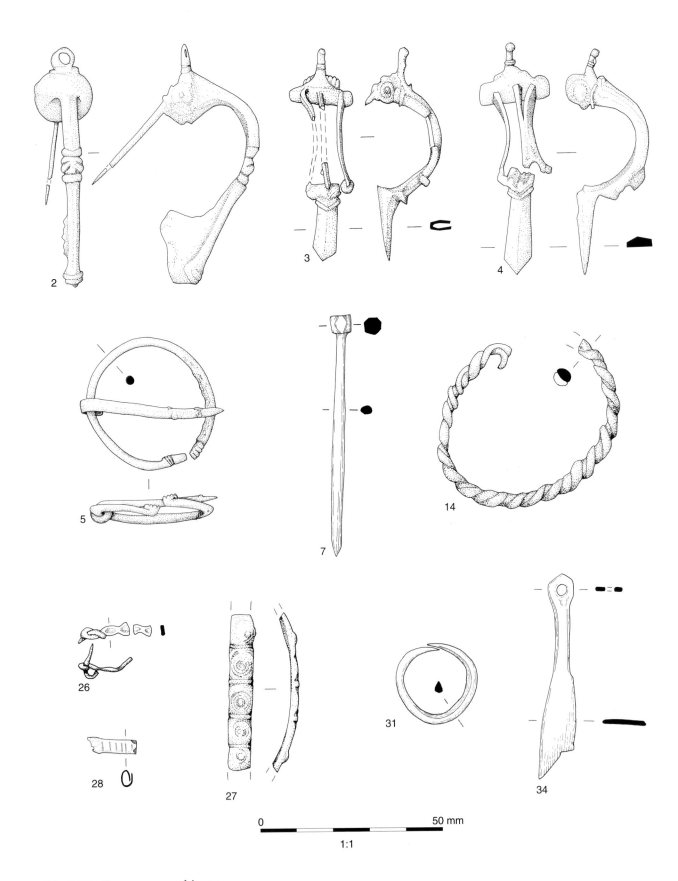

Fig. 7.22   *Roman personal items*

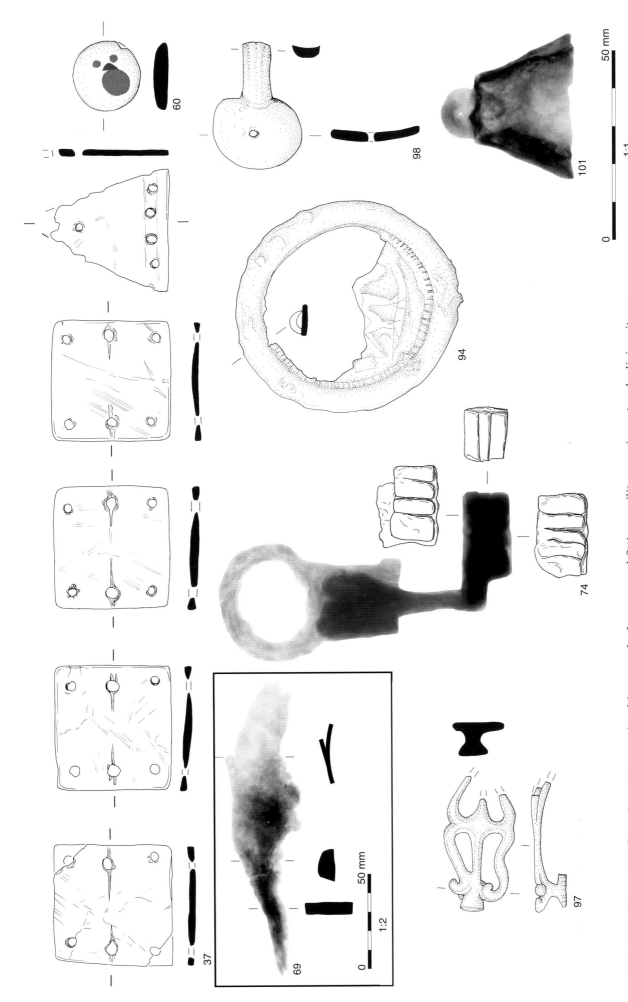

Fig. 7.23   Roman textile equipment, recreational items, tools, fasteners and fittings, military equipment and religious items

313

54 **Truncated conical beaker**, rim fragment. Ctx NH2216, SF NH916. (ID 169) Phase 4.2.

55 **Beaker**; base fragment. Ctx NH4282, SF NH1254. (ID 163) Phase 2.4.

56 **Base fragment**. Ctx NH5108, SF NH1456. (ID 171) Phase 5 SE1.

57 **Body fragment**. Ctx NH2398, SF NH913. (ID 155).

58 **Body fragment**. Ctx NH5094, SF NH1435. (ID 167) Phase 6.

Recreation items

59 **Counter**. Bone. Ctx NH1566. SF NH237. (ID 1566) Phase 2.3.

60 **Counter (Fig. 7.23)**. Glass. Ctx CC2315. CC NH294. (ID 1433) Phase 6.

Weighing equipment

61 **Weight?** Lead alloy. Ctx NH4390. (ID 961) Phase 1.3.

Structural finds

62 **Hinge pivot?.** Iron. Ctx NH2000, SF NH801. (ID 223) Phase 2.3.

63 **Strap hinge**; fragment. Iron. Ctx NH7521, SF NH1822. (ID 417) Phase 2.3.

64 **Window glass**. Ctx CC1405. SF CC859. (ID 1410) Phase 4.2 BE2..

65 **Window glass**, 2 fragments. Ctx CC1277. SF CC163. (ID 1425) Phase 6 BE3.

66 **Egyptian blue**. Ctx CC1579. SF CC504. (ID 1432) Phase 2.4.

Tools

67 **Trowel**; fragment. Iron. Ctx NH7018, SF NH1702. (ID 415) Phase 2.3.

68 **Spoon bit (?).** Iron. Ctx NH1383, SF NH177. (ID 940) Phase 2.3.

69 **Tool ? (Fig. 7.23)** Ctx NH2622, SF NH1505. (ID 301) Phase 2.3.

70 **Utilised tine**. Antler. Ctx CC1611. SF CC554. (ID 1436) Phase 2.3.

71 **Handle**. Bone. Ctx CC1579. SF CC564. (ID 1438) Phase 2.4.

72 **Handle**. Bone. Ctx NH1395; SF NH208. (ID 1576) Phase 2.3.

73 **Handle (?).** Bone. Ctx CC1630. (ID1568), Phase 2.4.

Fasteners and fittings

74 **Slide key (Fig. 7.23)**. Iron. Ctx NH1265, SF NH110 (ID 800) Phase 4 SE3.

75 **Conical-headed studs** (2). Copper alloy. Ctx NH2589. SF NH1510. (ID 562). Phase 2.2.

76 **Conical-headed stud**. Copper alloy. Ctx NH2589. SF NH989. (ID 129) Phase 2.2.

77 **Conical-headed stud**. Copper alloy. Ctx NH2589. SF NH1511 Ctx NH2589 SF NH1511 (ID 551). Phase 2.2.

78 **Conical-headed stud**. Copper alloy. Ctx CC1410. SF CC428. (ID 1372) Phase 2.3.

79 **Dome-headed stud**. Ctx NH2562. SF NH983. (ID 543) Phase 2.3.

80 **Dome-headed (?) stud**. Copper alloy. Ctx NH2589. SF NH1523. (ID 560) Phase 2.2.

81 **Dome-headed stud**. Copper alloy. Ctx NH1410. SF NH430. (ID 1375) Phase 2.3.

82 **Flat-headed stud**. Copper alloy. Ctx NH4767. SF NH1371. (ID 569) Phase 2.3.

83 **Flat-headed stud**. Ctx NH7418. SF NH1773. (ID 564) Phase 2.3.

84 **Hollow-headed stud**; head fragment. Copper alloy. Ctx NH u/s. SF NH68 (ID 815).

85 **Stud**. Copper alloy. Ctx NH2589. SF NH1513. (ID 124) Phase 2.2.

86 **Stud**. Copper alloy. Ctx NH2034. SF NH954. (ID 133) Phase 2.4.

87 **Stud**. Copper alloy. Ctx NH2034. SF NH960. (ID 130) Phase 2.4.

88 **Pottery repair**. Lead alloy. Ctx NH6059, SF NH1662. (ID 960) Phase 2.4.

89 **Pottery repair?** Lead alloy. Ctx NH6059, SF NH1664. (ID 959) Phase 2.4.

90 **Ferrule**. Iron. Ctx NH5186, SF NH1479. (ID 311) Phase 2.3.

91 **Loop-headed spike**. Iron. Ctx NH1413 SF NH136. (ID 797) Phase 2.3.

92 **Split pin**. Iron. Ctx NH3745. (ID 449) Phase 2.4.

93 **Staple**. Iron. Ctx NH1313, SF NH115. (ID 770) Phase 2.3.

94 **Mount (Fig. 7.23)**. Copper alloy and iron. Ctx CC3331, SF CC323. (ID 1522) Phase 2.3.

95 **Openwork mount**; nine fragments. Copper alloy. Ctx CC3331 SF CC332. (ID 1350) Phase 2.3.

96 **Mount**. Copper alloy. Ctx NH1486 SF NH155. (ID 812) Phase 2.3.

Military equipment

97 **Strap mount (Fig. 7.23)**; one end missing. Copper alloy. Ctx CC1579. SF CC473. (ID 1381) Phase 2.4.

98 **Spur (Fig. 7.23)**; one arm. Copper alloy. Ctx NH2221 SF NH829. (ID 546) Phase 5 BW5.

99 **Buckle plate**. Copper alloy. Ctx CC1592, SF CC446. (ID 1363) Phase 2.3.

100 **Buckle plate or strap end**. Copper alloy. Ctx NH6061, Sf NH1645. (ID 144) Phase 1.3.

Religious items

101 **Bell (Fig. 7.23)**. Iron. Ctx NH1175, SF NH166. (ID 925) Phase 2.3.

Industrial by-products

102 **Sprue? (Fig. 7.24)** Copper alloy. Ctx NH2444. SF NH957. (ID 544) Phase 2.4.

103 **Cylindrical moile**, fragment. Ctx NH6061, SF NH1614. (ID 154) Phase 1.3.

Miscellaneous

104 **Shank**; fragment. Bone. Ctx CC3371. SF CC336. (ID 1448) Phase 2.1.

105 **Shank**; fragment. Bone. Ctx NH1415. NH sf139. (ID1562). Phase 2.3.

106 **Shank**; fragment. Bone. Ctx NH9543. (ID1563). Phase 2.3.

107 **Shank**; fragment. Bone. Ctx NH1426. SF NH153 (ID1574). Phase 2.3

108 **Shank**; fragment. Bone. Ctx NH2239. SF NH839. (ID 1500) Phase 2.3.

109 **Shank**. Bone. Ctx NH1316. NH sf119. (ID1561). Phase 2.4.

110 **Shank**; fragment. Bone. Ctx NH2269. (ID1571). NH2269. (ID1571). Phase 5 BW4.

111 **Shank**; fragment. Bone. Ctx NH3286 : SF NH1021. (ID 184) Phase 6 BW3.

112 **Shank**; fragment. Bone. Ctx NH2129. SF NH827. (ID 1501) Phase 6 BE5

113 **Spike**. Iron. Ctx NH6061, SF NH1613. (ID 439) Phase 1.3.

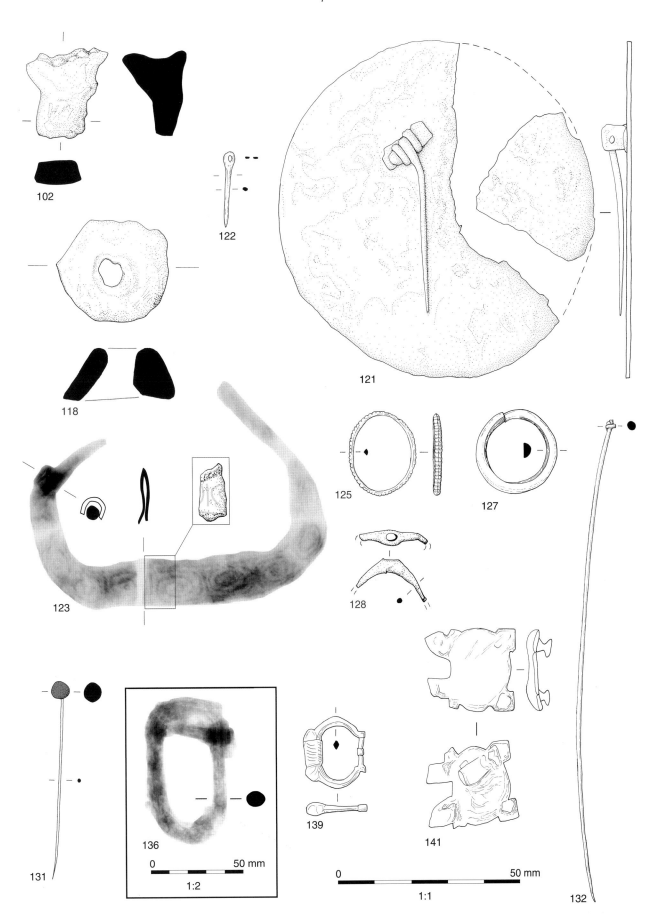

Fig. 7.24   *Roman industrial by-products and miscellaneous items, and post-Roman personal equipment*

114 **Spike**. Iron. Ctx CC1687 SF CC566 (ID 1116) Phase 2.3.
115 **Spike**. Iron. Ctx CC1630 SF CC491. (ID 1204) Phase 2.4.
116 **Ring**. Iron. Ctx NH6061. (ID 486) Phase 1.3.
117 **Ring**. Iron. Ctx NH6059, SF NH1603. (ID 39) Phase 2.4.
118 **Weight (Fig. 7.24)**. Lead alloy. Ctx NH2039, SF NH936. (ID 963). Phase 2.4.
119 **Bar**. Bone. Ctx NH1522. SF NH142. (ID 1567) Phase 2.1.
120 **Fragment**. Bone. Ctx CC1630. (ID1568), Phase 2.4.

Late Anglo-Saxon to Medieval

Personal equipment

Brooch
121 **Disc brooch (Fig. 7.24)**. Copper alloy. Ctx NH4398, SF NH1267. (ID 825) Phase 4.2 BW1.
122 **Brooch or buckle pin**. Silver. Ctx NH5095, SF NH1448. (ID 567) Phase 6 SE1
123 **Brooch? (Fig. 7.24)** Iron. Ctx NH7667, SF NH1803. (ID 402) Phase 4 BW6.
124 **Brooch?** Iron. Ctx NH1109, SF NH197. (ID 779) Phase 4.2 SE2.

Rings
125 **Finger ring (Fig. 7.24)**. Copper alloy. Ctx NH1210. SF NH72 (ID 816) Phase 4.2 SE2.
126 **Ring**, Bone. Ctx NH4369. (ID1573). Phase 4.2 BW2.
127 **Ring (Fig. 7.24)**. Bone. Ctx CC1357. SF CC936. Sample CC137. (ID 1468) Phase 4.2 BE2.
128 **Finger ring (Fig. 7.24)**. Gilded copper alloy. Ctx NH3224. SF NH1013. (ID 581) Phase 6 BW3.

Hooked tags
129 **Hooked tag**. Iron. Ctx CC2290, SF CC1013, Sample CC251. (ID 1289) Phase 4.2 BE4.
130 **Hooked tag**. Copper alloy. Ctx CC3084, SF CC392, sample CC309. (ID 1387) Phase 5 BE5.

Pins
131 **Dress pin (Fig. 7.24)**. Copper alloy broken wire shank, globular dark green spherical glass head. Ctx NH2027, SF NH809. (ID 141) Phase 5 BW4.
132 **'Sewing pin'**. Copper alloy. Ctx NH3234. SF NH1059. (ID 588) Phase 6 BW3
133 **'Sewing pin'**. Copper alloy. Ctx CC1296. SF CC169. (ID 1334) Phase 6 BE3.

Beads
134 **Bead**. glass. Ctx CC3050, SF CC1115. (ID 1463) Phase 5 BE5.

Buckles and strap fittings
135 **Buckle**; complete. Iron. Ctx CC1022, SF CC114. (ID 1121) Phase 4 BE1.
136 **Buckle (Fig. 7.24)**; complete. Iron. Ctx CC2256, SF CC260 (ID 1088) Phase 4.2 BE4.
137 **Buckle frame?** Iron. Ctx NH2534, SF NH965. (ID 286) Phase 4.2. BW5.
138 **Buckle**. Iron. Ctx CC2051, SF CC612. (ID 1111) Phase 5 BE4.
139 **Buckle frame (Fig. 7.24)**. Copper alloy. Ctx CC u/s, SF CC311 (ID 1345)
140 **Buckle plate**. Copper alloy. Ctx NH6081, SF NH1623. (ID 121) Phase 5 SE1.

141 **Buckle plate (Fig. 7.24)**. Copper alloy. Ctx CC2172, SF CC687, Sample CC216. (ID 1388) Phase 5 BE4.
142 **Buckle pin**. Copper alloy. Ctx NH1148, SF NH60 (ID 804) Phase 4 SE3.
143 **Buckle pin**. Copper alloy. Ctx CC3118, SF CC309. (ID 1348) Phase 4.2 BE5.
144 **Buckle pin**; fragment. Iron. Ctx CC2142, SF CC642. (ID 1266) Phase 6 BE4.
145 **Strap end**. Copper alloy. Ctx NH4102, SF NH1215 (ID 587) Phase 6 BW2.
146 **Bar mount**. Copper alloy. Ctx NH2374. SF NH958. (ID 131) Phase 4.2.
147 **Bar mount**. Copper alloy. Ctx NH3236. SF NH1014. (ID 589) Phase 6 BW3
148 **Mount**. Copper alloy. Ctx CC3178, SF CC312. (ID 1346) Phase 6 BE4.
149 **Strap guide**. Copper alloy. Ctx NH4297. (ID 115) Phase 4.2. BW2.

Other dress fittings
150 **Lace chape**. Copper alloy. (ID 810) Phase 6 SE3.
151 **Wire fastener**. Copper alloy. Ctx CC3183. SF CC314. (ID 1349) Phase 6 BE4.
152 **Wire accessory (Fig. 7.25)**. Copper alloy. Ctx CC3276. SF CC1116. Sample CC325. (ID 1471) Phase 6 BE5
153 **Pendant**. Copper alloy. Ctx CC2235; CC259. (ID 1526) Phase 6 BE 4

Toilet equipment
154 **Single-sided composite comb (Fig. 7.25)**. Antler. Ctx NH3433, SF NH1079. (ID 177) Phase 4.2 BW4.
155 **Single-sided composite comb**. Antler. Ctx NH4174. SF NH1225. (ID 187) Phase 4.2 BW2.
156 **Tweezers (Fig. 7.25)**; complete. Copper alloy. Ctx NH2276. SF NH866 (ID 676) Phase 5 BW5.

Textile equipment
157 **Comb tooth (Fig. 7.25)**. Iron. Ctx NH3225, SF NH1018. (ID 513) Phase 4.2 BW 4.
158 **Heckle or comb tooth (Fig. 7.25)**. Iron. Ctx NH2516, SF NH963. (ID 522) Phase 4.1 BW 5.

Spindle whorls
159 **Spindle whorl**. Bone. Ctx NH4535. SF NH1292. (ID 174) Phase 4.1 BW2.
160 **Spindle whorl**. Bone. Ctx NH4148. SF NH1223. (ID 179) Phase 4.2 BW2.
161 **Spindle whorl**. Bone. Ctx NH4146. SF NH1238. (ID 173) Phase 4.2 BW2.
162 **Spindle whorl**. Bone. Ctx NH 4034. (ID 423) Phase 4.2 BW2.
163 **Spindle whorl**. Bone. Ctx NH4322. SF NH1288. (ID 180) Phase 4.2 BW2
164 **Spindle whorl**. Bone. Ctx NH4584. SF NH1295 (ID 181) Phase 5 BW3.
165 **Spindle whorl**. Bone. Ctx NH3222. (ID 418) Phase 5 BW4
166 **Spindle whorl**. Bone. Ctx NH2575. (ID 424) Phase 4.2 BW 4.
167 **Spindle whorl**. Bone. Ctx NH2577. SF NH975. (ID 175) Phase 6 BW4.
168 **Spindle whorl**. Bone. Ctx CC1354. SF CC567. Sample CC134. (ID 1442) Phase 4.2 BE2.
169 **Spindle whorl**. Bone. Ctx CC2247. (ID1558). Phase 4.2 BE4
170 **Spindle whorl**. Bone. Ctx CC2247. SF CC270. (ID 1451) Phase 4.2 BE4.

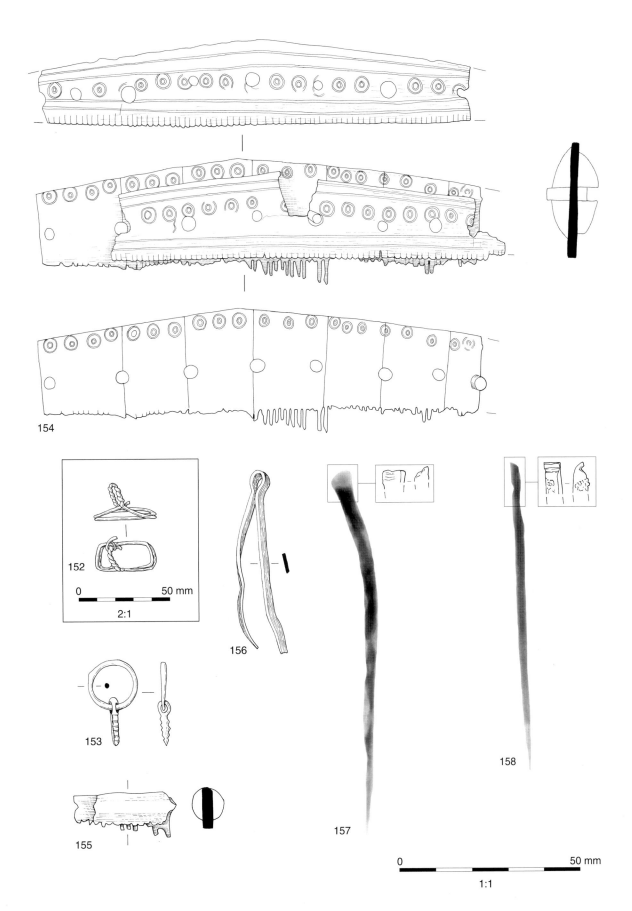

Fig. 7.25   *Post-Roman personal items and textile equipment*

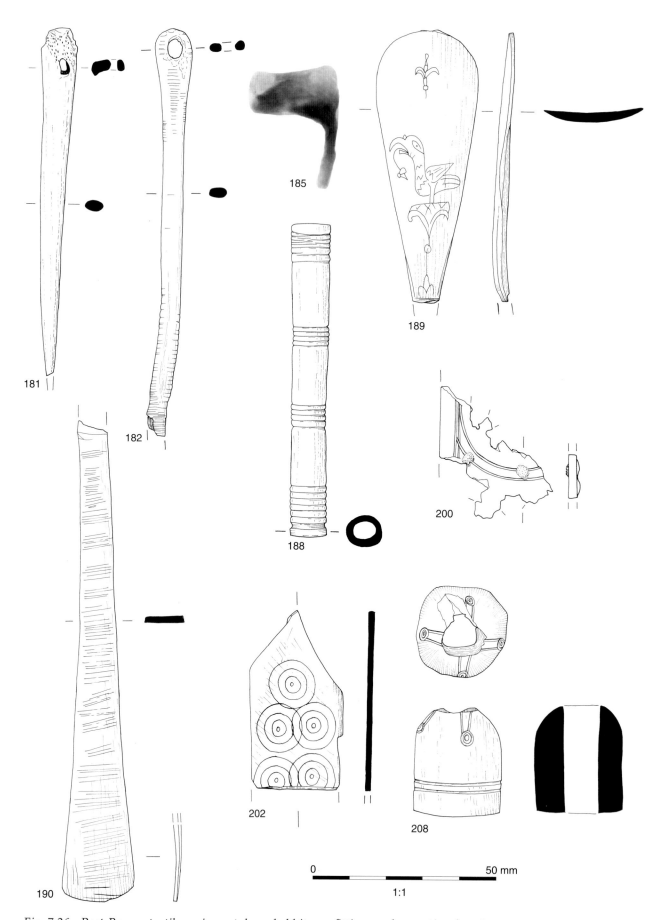

Fig. 7.26   Post-Roman textile equipment, household items, fittings and recreational equipment

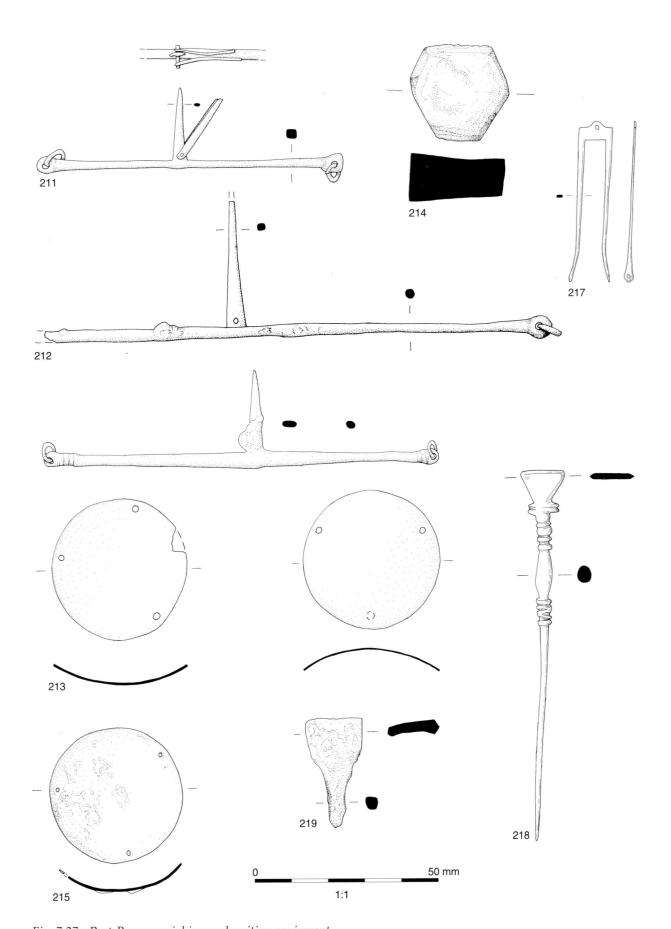

Fig. 7.27   Post-Roman weighing and writing equipment

171 **Spindle whorl**. Bone. Ctx CC2004. SF CC204. (ID 1452). Phase 4.2 BE4.

172 **Spindle whorl**. Bone. Ctx NH4697. SF NH1327. (ID 421) Phase 4.1 SE3

173 **Spindle whorl**. Bone. Ctx NH2577. SF NH975. (ID 175) Phase 6 BW4.

Weaving tools

174 **Pin beater**. Bone (? Ivory). Ctx CC2228. SF CC606. (ID 1449) Phase 4.2 BE4.

175 **Picker-cum-beater**. Bone. Ctx NH3314. SF NH1034. (ID 1502) Phase 5 BW3.

176 **Picker-cum-beater?** Bone. Ctx NH8001. SF NH1900. (ID 185). Phase 8.

177 **Eyed weaving implement**. Bone. Ctx NH3532. SF NH1098. (ID 1505) Phase 5 BW4.

178 **Eyed weaving implement**. Bone. Ctx CC1535. SF CC444. (ID 1439) Phase 5 BE3.

179 **Eyed weaving implement**. Bone (? Fibula). Bone. Ctx CC2157. SF CC243. (ID 1435) Phase 5 BE3.

180 **Eyed weaving implement**. Bone. Ctx CC2288, SF CC275. (ID 1434) Phase 4.2 BE4.

181 **Eyed weaving implement (Fig. 7.26)**. Bone. Ctx CC2157. SF CC243. (ID 1447) Phase 5 BE4.

182 **Eyed weaving implement** (?) **(Fig. 7.26)**. Bone. Ctx CC3021. SF CC304. (ID 1453) Phase 5 BE5.

183 **Eyed weaving implement**. Bone. Ctx CC3276, SF CC339. (ID 1441) Phase 6 BE5

184 **Eyed weaving implement**. Bone. Ctx NH u/s. SF NH1360. (ID 1504) Unphased.

Other

185 **Tenter-hook**(?) **(Fig. 7.26)**, fragment. Iron. Ctx NH2044, SF NH828. (ID 278) Phase 5 BW5.

186 **Needle**. Iron. Ctx NH3126, SF NH1004. (ID 495) Phase 6 BW3.

187 **Bobbin**. Bone. Ctx NH1364. SF NH124. (ID1577). Phase 5 SE3.

188 **Bobbin (Fig. 7.26)**. Bone. Ctx NH3286. (ID 425) Phase 6 BW3

Household items

189 **Spatula/spoon (Fig. 7.26)**. Bone. Ctx CC1354. SF CC568. (ID 1459) Phase 4.2 BE2.

190 **Spatula (Fig. 7.26)**. Bone. Ctx CC1577. SF CC447. (ID 1461) Phase 4 BE3.

191 **Spatula**. Iron. Ctx NH3068. (ID 681) Phase 6 BW3.

192 **Flesh hook**. Iron Ctx NH2570, SF NH974. (ID 519) Phase 5 BW4

193 **Flesh hook**; fragment. Iron. Ctx CC2328, SF CC623. (ID 1242) Phase 6 BE4.

194 **Vessel**; 5 broken fragments very heavily corroded. Copper alloy. Ctx NH3561. SF NH1117. (ID 593) Phase 5 BW4.

195 **Body fragment**. Potash glass. Ctx CC1345, SF CC418.(ID 1412) Phase 5 BE3.

196 **Body fragment**; potash glass now reduced to dust. Ctx CC1307. SF CC867. (ID 1405) Phase 6 BE2.

Box and furniture fittings

197 **Mount**. Ctx NH3094. (ID 182) Phase 5 BW4.

198 **Mount**. Bone. Ctx NH2250. (ID1572). Phase 5 BW5.

199 **Mount** ?. Bone. Ctx CC1345, SF CC420. (ID 1443) Phase 5 BE3.

200 **Mount (Fig. 7.26)**. Bone. Ctx CC1281. SF CC508. (ID 1462) Phase 6 BE3.

201 **Mount**. Bone. Ctx CC1281. SF CC507. (ID 1444) Phase 6 BE3.

202 **Mount (Fig. 7.26)**. Bone. Ctx CC2328, SF CC608. (ID 1507) Phase 6 BE4.

203 **Mount**. Antler. Ctx NH5128. (ID 189). Phase 5 SE1

204 **Mount**. Bone. Ctx NH5168. (ID 1570) Phase 5 SE1.

205 **Box fitting**. Iron. Ctx NH2243, SF NH848. (ID 237) Phase 5 BW4.

206 **Chest mount**; fragment. Iron. Ctx NH2353, SF NH9000. (ID 87) Phase 5 BW5

207 **Box mount** (?). Copper alloy. Ctx NH3539. SF NH1112. (ID 577) Phase 5 BW4.

Recreational equipment

208 **Chess piece (Fig. 7.26)**. Bone. Ctx NH4046. Sf NH1207. (ID 186) Phase 6 BW3.

209 **Skate**. Bone. Ctx NH9666 (ID1557). Phase 5 BW5.

210 **Skate**. Bone. Ctx NH5044. (ID1552). Phase 6 SE1

Weighing equipment

211 **Equal-armed balance (Fig. 7.27)**. Copper alloy. Ctx CC1525. SF CC439. (ID 1354) Phase 4.2 BE2.

212 **Equal-armed balance (Fig. 7.27)**. Copper alloy. Ctx CC1138. SF CC149. (ID 1523) Phase 6 BE2.

213 **Equal-armed balance (Fig. 7.27)**. Ctx CC2126. SF CC2250. (ID 1524) Phase 4.2 BE 4.

214 **Weight**. Lead alloy. Ctx NH3340. SF NH1045. (ID 964) Phase 4.2 BW3.

215 **Scale pan (Fig. 7.27)**. Copper alloy sheet. Ctx NH2099. SF NH819. (ID 592) Phase 6. BW5

216 **Equal-armed balance**. Copper alloy. Ctx NH5132. SF NH1462. (ID 568) Phase 5 SE1.

217 **Balance fork (Fig. 7.27)**. Copper alloy. Ctx NH5120. SF NH1469. (ID 674) Phase 5 SE1.

Writing equipment

218 **Stylus (Fig. 7.27)**; in three fragments. Copper alloy. Ctx NH2071. SF NH814 (ID 590). Phase 5 BW5.

219 **Stylus (Fig. 7.27)**; head only. Copper alloy. Ctx CC1261. SF CC162 (ID1336). Phase 4 BE3.

220 **Stylus (Fig. 7.28)**. Iron. Ctx NH6061, SF NH1644. (ID 42) Phase 1.3.

Transport equipment

Horseshoes

221 **Horseshoe (Clark Type 1)**; Iron. Ctx NH6061, SF NH1636. (ID 40) Phase 1.3.

222 **Horseshoe (Clark Type 1)**; fragment. Iron. Ctx NH4281, SF NH1244. (ID 314) Phase 5 BW2

223 **Horseshoe (Clark Type 2)**; fragment. Iron. Ctx NH4181. SF NH1227. (ID 55) Phase 5 BW2.

224 **Horseshoe (Clark Type 1)**; complete. Iron. Ctx NH3167, SF NH1006. (ID 736) Phase 6 BW3.

225 **Horseshoe (Clark Type 1)**; fragment. Iron. Ctx NH2292, SF NH879. (ID 282) Phase 4.1 BW5.

226 **Horseshoe (Clark Type 1)**; fragment. Iron. Ctx NH2208, SF NH831. (ID 241) Phase 4.1 BW5

227 **Horseshoe (Clark Type 2)**; arm fragment. Iron. Ctx NH2070. (ID 639) Phase 5 BW5,

228 **Horseshoe (Clark Type 2)**; arm fragment. Iron. Ctx NH2107. (ID 463) Phase 5 BW5

229 **Horseshoe (Clark Type 1) (Fig. 7.28)**; half extant. Iron. Ctx NH5054, SF NH1453. (ID 290) Phase 4.2 SE 1.

230 **Horseshoe (Clark Type 2) (Fig. 7.28)**; half. Iron. NH5046, SF NH1441. (ID 302) Phase 6. SE1

231 **Horseshoe (Clark Type 2)**; fragment of arm. Iron. Ctx CC1464, SF CC431. (ID 1207) Phase 5 E2.

232 **Horseshoe**; arm fragment. Iron. Ctx CC1384, SFCC415. (ID 1210) Phase 5 BE3.

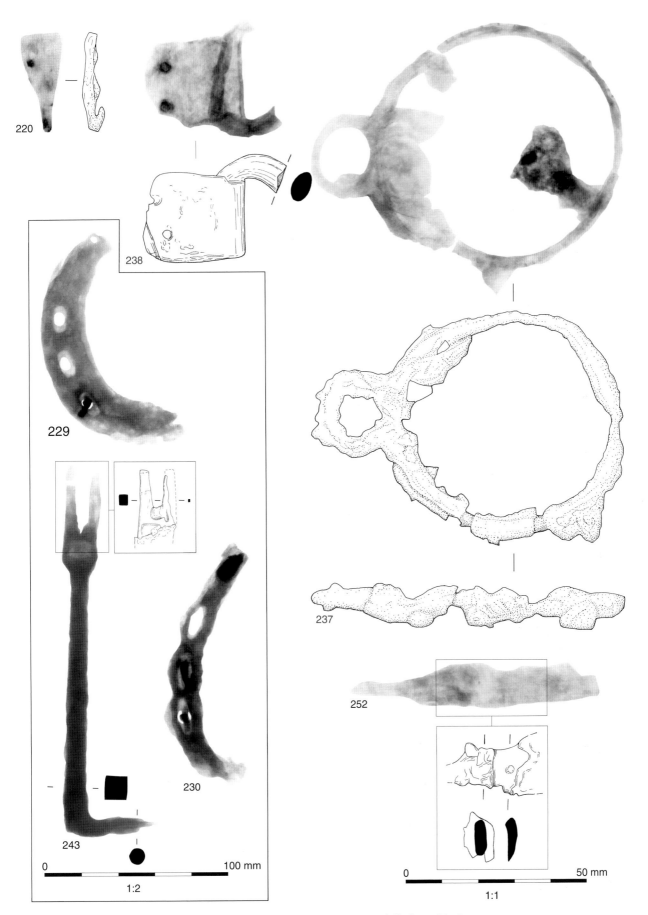

Fig. 7.28   Post-Roman writing equipment, transport items, structural finds and knives

233 **Horseshoe**; arm fragment. Iron. Ctx CC3254, SF CC318. (ID 1136) Phase 4.2 BE4.

234 **Horseshoe** (Clark Type 3); arm fragment. Iron. Ctx CC2132, SF CC235. (ID 972) Phase 5 BE4.

235 **Horseshoe**; arm fragment. Iron. Ctx CC2061, SF CC2061. (ID 1104) Phase 5 BE4.

236 **Horseshoe nails** (3); Iron. Ctx CC1096, SF CC808. (ID 1531) Phase 5 BE 1.

Other fittings

237 **Bridle fitting? (Fig. 7.28)** Iron. Ctx NH3301, SF NH 1036. (ID 499) Phase 4.2 BW4

238 **Strap junction (Fig. 7.28)**. Iron. Ctx NH3395, SF NH1069. (ID 746) Phase 5 BW3.

239 **Prick spur?**; fragment. Iron. Ctx CC2382 SF CC293. (ID 1156) Phase 4.2 BE4

Structural finds

240 **Double spiked loop**. Iron. Ctx CC2289, SF CC276. (ID 1160) Phase 4.2 BE4.

241 **T Clamp**. Iron. Ctx CC2265. SF CC277. (ID 1154) Phase 6 BE4.

242 **Hinge pivot**. Iron. Ctx NH5094. (ID 103) Phase 6 SE1.

243 **Hinge pivot (Fig. 7.28)**. Iron. Ctx NH1057 SF NH191. (ID 888) Phase 4.2 SE2.

242 **Hinge pivot**. Iron. Ctx NH1257, SF NH232. (ID 884) Phase 4.2 SE2.

243 **Structural fitting**. Iron. Ctx NH1007, SF NH50. (ID 877) Phase 6 SE2.

244 **Hinge pivot?**. Iron. Ctx NH8020. (ID 709) Phase 6 BW1.

245 **Masonry clamp**. Ctx NH4124 SF NH1217. (ID 208) Phase 6 BW 1.

246 **Staple?**. Iron. Ctx NH 4020, SF NH1200. (ID 191) Phase 6 BW2.

247 **Split pin**. Iron. Ctx NH4130. Ctx NH 4130. (ID 215) Phase 4.2 BW2.

Knives and tools

248 **Blade**; fragment. Iron. Ctx NH4094, SF NH1214. (ID 216) Phase 4.2 BW2.

249 **Blade**; fragment. Iron. Ctx NH4164, SF NH1237. (ID 315) Phase 4.2. BW 2.

250 **Blade**; fragment. Iron. Ctx NH4130. SF NH1293. (ID 62) Phase 4.2 BW2

251 **Knife**; complete. Iron. Ctx NH3363, SF NH1063. (ID 487) Phase 4.2 BW 3.

252 **Knife (Fig. 7.28)**; fragment. Iron. Ctx NH3356, SF NH1057. (ID 492) Phase 5 BW 3.

253 **Blade**; fragment. Iron. Ctx NH3476, SF NH1088. (ID 740) Phase 4.1 BW3.

254 **Blade**; fragment. Iron. Ctx NH3105, SF NH1121. (ID 68) Phase 5 BW3

255 **Blade**; fragment. Iron. Ctx NH3033. (ID 111) Phase 5 BW3.

256 **Knife (Fig. 7.29)**; fragment. Iron. Ctx NH3236. (ID 483) Phase 6 BW3

257 **Knife**; fragment. Iron. Ctx NH3672, SF NH1130. (ID 193) Phase 4.1 BW4

258 **Blade**; fragment. Iron. Ctx NH3672, SF NH1131. (ID 201) Phase 4.1 BW4

259 **Blade**; fragment. Iron. Ctx NH2026, SF NH808. (ID 271) Phase 6 BW 4.

260 **Knife**; complete. Iron. Ctx NH2366; SF NH901. (ID 824) Phase 4.2 BW5.

261 **Knife**; fragment. Iron. Ctx NH2208, SF NH831. (ID 240) Phase 4.1 BW5.

262 **Blade**; fragment. Iron. Ctx NH7506, SF NH1800. (ID 464) Phase 5 BW5.

263 **Blade**; fragment. Iron. Ctx CC1154, SF CC576, sample CC111. (ID 994) Phase 4 BE1.

264 **Knife**; complete. Iron. Ctx CC1354, SF CC807. (ID 1236) Phase 4.2 BE2.

265 **Handle**; fragment. Bone. Ctx CC1144. SF CC157 (ID 1437). Phase 6 BE2.

266 **Knife (Fig. 7.29)**; fragment. Iron. Ctx CC2003, SF CC202. (ID 1070) Phase 4.2 BE4.

267 **Knife**; fragment. Iron. Ctx CC2126, SF CC229. (ID 1095) Phase 4.2 BE4.

268 **Knife**. Iron. Ctx NH2278, SF NH871. (ID 114) Phase 5 BE4

269 **Blade**; fragment. Iron. Ctx CC2288, SF CC280. (ID 1155) Phase 4.2 BE4.

270 **Blade**, fragment. Iron. Ctx CC2246, SF CC269. (ID 1105) Phase 4.2 BE4.

271 **Knife**, fragment. Iron. Ctx CC3013, SF CC303. (ID 1145) Phase 5 BE5.

272 **Knife**; complete. Iron. Ctx NH5107, SF NH1454. (ID 285) Phase 5 SE 1.

Iron tools

273 **Auger(?) (Fig. 7.29)**; fragment. Iron. Ctx NH4052; SF NH1208. (ID 207) BW3.

274 **Tanged punch (Fig. 7.29)**. Iron. Ctx NH2106, SF NH823. (ID 247) Phase 4.2 BW4.

275 **Tanged knife?** Ctx NH7506. (ID 404) Phase 5 BW 5.

276 **Socketed axe-head**; complete. Iron. Ctx CC2380, SF CC291. (ID 1151). Phase 4.2 BE4.

277 **Bladed tool (Fig. 7.29)**; fragment. Ctx CC2458, SF CC602. (ID 979) Phase 4.2 BE4.

278 **Tanged implement**. Ctx CC2310 SF CC274. (ID 1157) Phase 5 BE4.

288 **Chisel edged tool**. Iron. Ctx NH6161. SF NH1680. (ID 7). Phase 4.2. SE1

Modified bone tools

289 **Socketed point**. Bone metapodia. Ctx NH1126. (ID 1551). Phase 4.2 SE2.

290 **Socketed point**. Bone – sheep/goat tibia. Ctx CC2027. (ID1556). Phase 5 BE4

291 **Socketed point**. Bovine metatarsal? Ctx NH7510. (ID 427) Phase 5 BW5.

292 **'Lucet'**. Bone. Ctx CC1064 SF CC475. (ID 1454) Phase 4 BE 3.

293 **Utilised bone**. Cattle metatarsal. Ctx NH1450. SF NH188. (ID1555). Phase 5 SE3

294 **Utilised bone**. Cattle metatarsal. Ctx NH1450. SF NH188. (ID1554). Phase 5 SE3

295 **Utilised bone**. Bone, metatarsal ? Ctx NH1407 (ID 1553). Phase 5 SE3.

296 **Modified proximal end of metatarsal?** Bone. Ctx CC2256. SF CC605. (ID 1450) Phase 4.2 BE4.

Fasteners and fittings

Locks and keys

297 **Padlock bolt (Fig. 7.29)**. Iron. Ctx NH4281, SF NH1245. (ID 304) Phase 5 BW2.

298 **Padlock case ?** Ctx NH3325. SF NH1044. (ID 728) Phase 5 BW3.

299 **Padlock bolt**. Iron. Ctx NH3016. (ID 100) Phase 5 BW3.

300 **Barrel padlock (Fig. 7.30)**. Iron. Ctx NH3094. (ID 52) Phase 5 BW4.

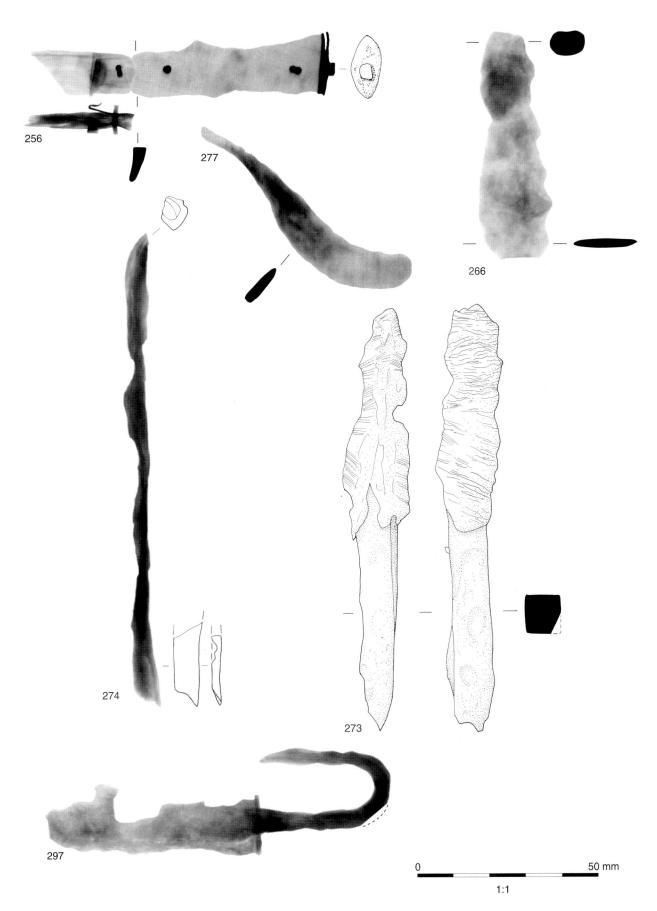

Fig. 7.29   Post-Roman knives, tools, fasteners and fittings

301 **Padlock key**. Iron. Ctx NH2534. SF NH964. (ID 92) Phase 4.2 BW5.

302 **Padlock bolt** ? Iron. Ctx NH2243, SF NH848. (ID 238) Phase 5 BW4.

303 **Padlock key (Fig. 7.30)**. Iron. Ctx CC1525, SF CC443. (ID 1211) Phase 4.2 BE2.

304 **Barrel padlock**. Ctx CC2161, SF CC244. (ID 971) Phase 4.2 BE4.

305 **Barrel padlock casing (Fig. 7.30)**. Iron. Ctx CC3254, SF CC319. (ID 1128) Phase 4.2 BE4.

306 **Lock fitting?** Iron. Ctx CC2003, SF CC200 (ID 1075) Phase 4.2 BE4

307 **Key**. Iron. Ctx CC3389, SF CC356. (ID 1182) Phase 4.2 BE4

308 **Padlock bolt**. Iron. Ctx CC2238, SF CC262. (ID 1093) Phase 5 BE4.

309 **Padlock key (Fig. 7.30)**. Iron. Ctx CC2027, SF CC271. (ID 1107) Phase 5 BE4.

310 **Key (Fig. 7.30)**. Iron. Ctx CC3237, SF CC347. (ID 1133) Phase 4.2 BE5.

Riveted bone mounts

311 **Riveted mount (Fig. 7.30)**. Bone. Ctx CC1022, SF CC154. (ID 1455) Phase 4 BE1.

312 **Riveted mount**. Bone. Ctx CC1354. SFCC483. (ID 1457) Phase 4.2 BE 2.

313 **Riveted mount**. Bone. Ctx CC1365, SF CC551. (ID 1458) Phase 4.2 BE 2.

314 **Riveted mount (Fig. 7.30)**. Bone. Ctx CC2004. SF SF CC223. (ID 1456) Phase 4.2 BE4.

315 **Riveted mount**. Bone. Ctx CC2171, SF CC607. (ID 1460) Phase 5 BE4.

316 **Mount**? Bone. Ctx CC2163. (ID 1569) Phase 4.2 BE4

317 **Riveted mount**. Bone. Ctx NH4322. (ID 1547) Phase 4.2 BW2.

318 **Riveted mount**. Bone. Ctx NH4322. (ID 1546) Phase 4.2 BW2

319 **Mount or roughout**. Bone. Ctx NH4322. (ID 1548) Phase 4.2 BW2

320 **Riveted mount**. Bone. Ctx NH1365, (ID1534) Phase 4.2. BW3

321 **Riveted mount**. Bone. Ctx NH4594, SF NH1299. (ID 176) Phase 5 BW3.

322 **Riveted mount**. Bone. Ctx NH 2399, Sample NH173. (ID 431) Phase 4.2 BW 5.

323 **Mount**. Bone (large mammal rib). Ctx NH1156; SF NH65. (ID1536). Phase 4.2. SE 2.

324 **Riveted mount**. Bone. Ctx NH1450. SF NH188. (ID1540). Phase 5 SE3.

325 **Riveted mount**. Bone. Ctx NH1407. SF NH184. (ID1542). Phase 5 SE3.

326 **Riveted mount**. Bone (large mammal rib). Ctx NH1340. (ID 1544). Phase 5 SE3.

327 **Riveted mount**. Bone (large mammal rib). Ctx NH1407. (ID1541). Phase 5 SE3.

328 **Riveted mount**. Bone. Ctx NH1340. (ID1545). Phase 5 SE3.

329 **Riveted mount**. Bone. Ctx NH1342, (ID1538) Phase 5, SE 3.

330 **Mount**. Bone (large mammal rib). Ctx NH1340. (ID 1543). Phase 5 SE3

331 **Mount**. Bone. Ctx NH1450; SF NH188. (ID1536). Phase 5. SE 3.

332 **Riveted mount (Fig. 7.31)**. Bone. Ctx NH3159. SF NH1005. (ID 422) Phase 8

333 **Riveted mount**. Bone. Ctx NH7593, (ID1535) Phase 8.

Studs

334 **Flat-headed stud**. Copper alloy. Ctx NH3103. SF NH1040. (ID 578) Phase 5 BW3

335 **Flat-headed stud**; head only. Copper alloy. Ctx NH3236. SF NH1016. (ID 580) Phase 6 BW3.

336 **Conical-headed stud**. Copper alloy. Ctx NH2263. SF NH849. (ID 140) Phase 5 BW4

337 **Stud**; fragmented. Copper alloy. Ctx NH2353, SF NH907. (ID 553) Phase 5 BW5

338 **Flat-headed stud**. Copper alloy. Ctx CC1218. SF CC158. (ID 1337) Phase 5 BE2.

339 **Flat-headed stud**. Iron. Ctx CC2467 SF CC1030 (ID 1300) Phase 5 BE4.

340 **Rivet**. Copper alloy. Ctx NH1222. SF NH87. (ID 819) Phase 4.2 SE2

Other items

341 **Mount (Fig. 7.31)**. Copper alloy. Ctx CC1303, SF CC189. (ID 1331) Phase 4 BE1.

342 **Angle bracket**. Iron. Ctx CC1349, SF CC409. (ID 1205) Phase 4 BE1.

343 **Staple**; 2 examples. IronCtx CC1027, SF CC104. (ID 1039) Phase 4 BE1.

344 **Split pin**. Iron. Ctx CC1254, SF CC185. (ID 1027) Phase 5 BE1.

345 **Mount**. Copper alloy. Ctx CC1090. SF CC142. (ID 1338) Phase 5 BE3.

346 **Mount**. Copper alloy. Ctx CC2095 SF CC665. (ID 1370) Phase 5 BE4.

347 **Chain loop?** Iron. Ctx CC2178 SF CC1004. (ID 1324) Phase 4.2 BE4.

348 **Staple**. Iron. Ctx NH2278, SF NH868. (ID 228) Phase 5 BE4

349 **Hook fragment**. Iron. Ctx CC2097, SF CC217. (ID 1089) Phase 6 BE4.

350 **Finial (Fig. 7.31)**. Iron. Ctx NH8049. (ID 112) Phase 6 BW1.

351 **Angle binding**. Ctx NH4328, SF NH1247 (ID 206). Phase 4.2 BW2.

352 **Staple**. Iron. Ctx NH4085, SF NH 1233. (ID 73) Phase 4.2 BW2.

353 **Split pin and loop (Fig. 7.31)**. Iron. Ctx NH4025, SF NH1202. (ID 65) Phase 6 BW2.

354 **Chain**, broken link. Iron. Ctx NH4369, SF NH261. (ID 359) Phase 4.2 BW2.

355 **Staple**. Iron. Ctx NH3507, SF NH1109. (ID 197) Phase 4.1 BW 3.

356 **Staple**. Iron. NH3354, SF NH1065. (ID 502) Phase 5 BW3.

357 **Staple**. Iron. Ctx NH3105, SF NH1122. (ID 328) Phase 5 BW3.

358 **Staple**. Iron. Ctx NH3105, SF NH1122. (ID 328) Phase 5 BW3.

359 **Looped pin**. Iron. Ctx NH3105, SF NH1119. (ID 321) Phase 5 BW 3.

360 **Mount**. Copper alloy. Ctx NH2106. SF NH821. (ID 545) Phase 4.2 BW 4.

361 **Chain (Fig. 7.31)**. Iron. Ctx NH2241, SF NH 850. (ID 259) Phase 5 BW 4.

362 **Washer; fragment**. Iron. Ctx NH6204, sample NH374. (ID 625) Phase 4 SE1.

363 **Stapled hasp**. Iron. Ctx NH5114, SF NH1458. (ID 313) Phase 5 SE1.

364 **Suspension hook**. Iron. Ctx NH5046, SF NH1428. (ID 337) Phase 6 SE1

365 **Openwork mount; fragment**. Copper alloy. Ctx NH6095, SF NH1651. (ID 143) Phase 5 SE1.

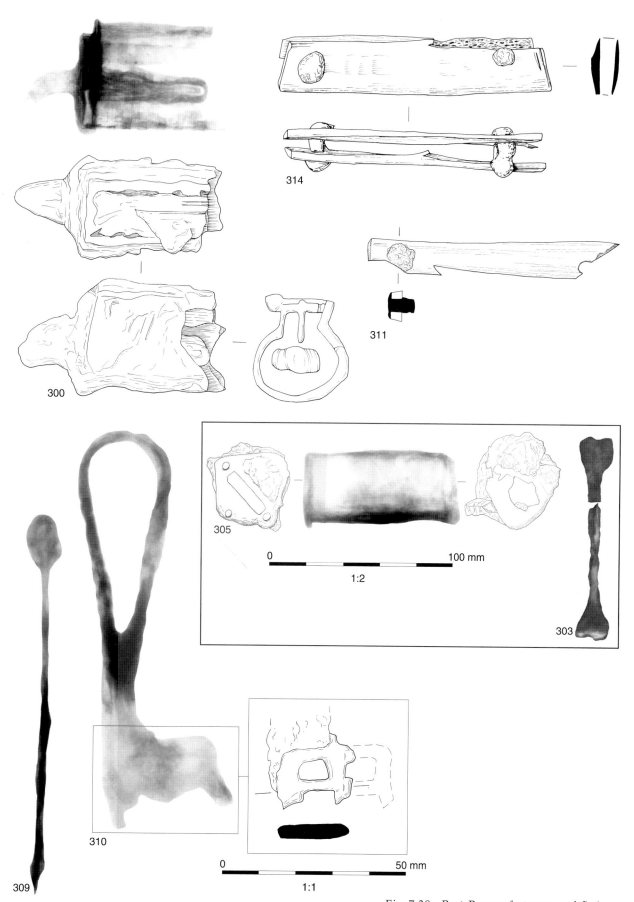

Fig. 7.30   Post-Roman fasteners and fittings

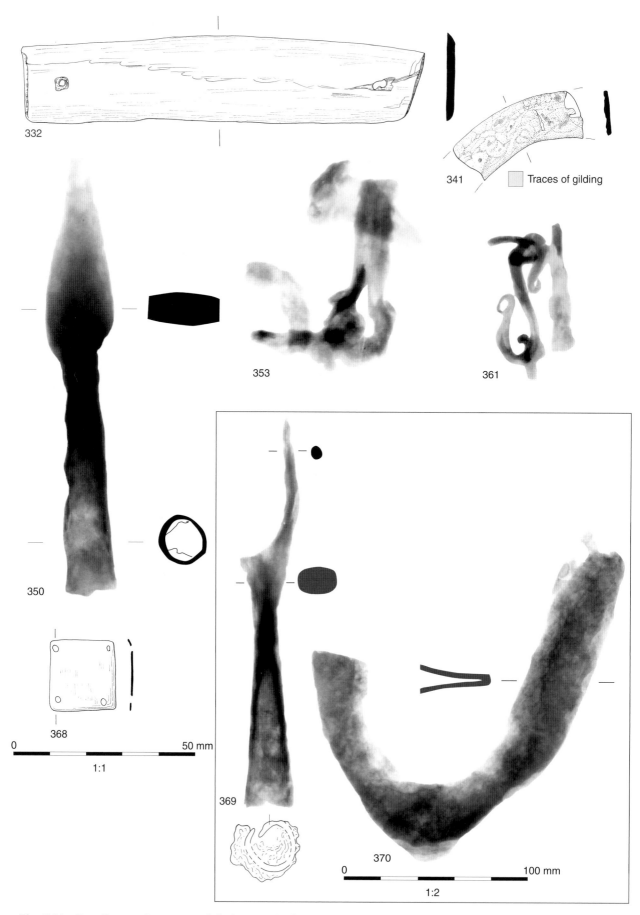

Fig. 7.31   Post-Roman fasteners and fittings, agricultural and horticultural equipment

366 **Binding; fragment**. Iron. Ctx NH1264, SF NH99. (ID 883) Phase 4 SE3.

367 **Suspension fitting**. Iron. Ctx NH8027. (ID 106) Phase 5.

368 **Mount (Fig. 7.31)**. Copper alloy. Ctx NH8044. SF NH1901. (ID 120) Phase 6.

Agricultural and horticultural equipment

369 **Fork (Fig. 7.31)**. Iron. Ctx NH9554. (ID 113) Phase 4 BW5.

370 **Spade shoe (Fig. 7.31)**. Iron. Ctx CC2265 SF CC279, (ID 1162) Phase 6 BE4.

Hunting and Military Equipment

371 **Arrowhead (Fig. 7.32)**. Iron. Ctx NH4095, SF NH1213. (ID 196) Phase 4.2 BW 2.

372 **Arrowhead (Fig. 7.32)**. Iron. Ctx NH4186, SF NH1248. (ID 198) Phase 5 BW2.

Religious items

373 **Figurine (Fig. 7.32)**; fragment. Copper alloy. Ctx NH1062 SF NH193. (ID 805) Phase 5 SE2.

374 **Bell clapper (Fig. 7.32)**. Iron. Ctx NH2027. (ID 721) Phase 5 BW4.

Industrial and craft by products

375 **Working waste**. Antler. Ctx NH4714. SF NH1338. (ID 428) Phase 4.1 BW2.

376 **Rough-outs**. Bone. Ctx NH4322. (ID1549) Phase 4.2 BW2

377 **Rough-out**. Bone. Ctx NH4425. SF NH1283. (ID 1506) Phase 4.2 BW2.

378 **Working waste**. Bone. Ctx NH3286. SF NH1023. (ID 426) Phase 6 BW 3.

379 **Working waste**. Bone. Ctx NH2114. (ID 188) Phase 4.2 BW4.

380 **Rough-out**. Bone. Ctx NH3168. (ID1558). Phase 4.2. BW4

381 **Working waste**. Bone. Ctx NH2323. (ID 1550). Phase 5 BW5.

382 **Rough-out**. Bone. Ctx NH1513. SF NH163. (ID1575) Phase 4 SE3.

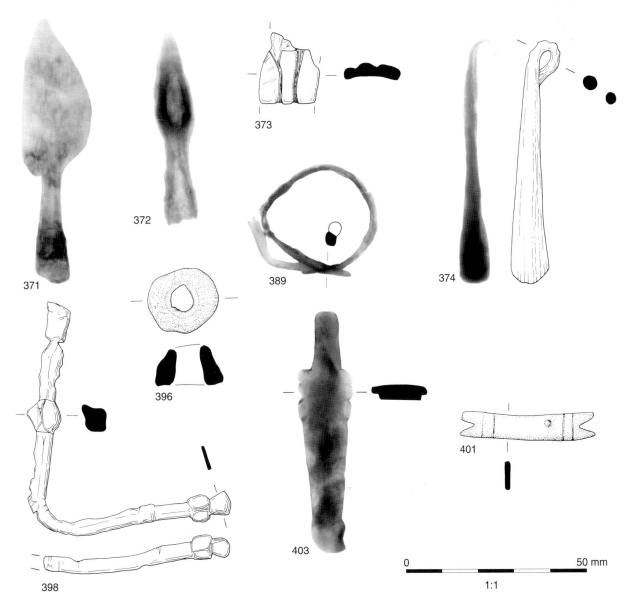

Fig. 7.32   Post-Roman hunting and military equipment, religious items and miscellaneous items

383 **Rough-out**. Ctx CC1362. SF CC555. (ID 1446) Phase 4.2 BE2

384 **Working waste**. Antler tine. Ctx CC3219, SF CC340. (ID 1440) Phase 6 BE5.

385 **Working waste**. Bone. Ctx CC3277. (ID1539) Phase 6 BE5

Miscellaneous

386 **Ring**. Iron. Ctx 2116. (ID 723) Phase 4.2 BW4

387 **Penannular ring**. Copper alloy. Ctx NH4085. SF NH1231. (ID 528). Phase 4.2 BW2.

388 **Ring**. Copper alloy. Ctx NH4075. SF NH1209. (ID 575) Phase 6 BW2

389 **Ring (Fig. 7.32)**. Iron. Ctx NH3353, SF NH1054. (ID 743) Phase 5 BW3.

390 **Ring**. Copper alloy. Ctx NH3286. SF NH1029. (ID 128) Phase 6 BW3.

391 **Spiral ring**. Iron. Ctx NH3467, SF NH1089. (ID 303) Phase 5 BW4.

392 **Ring; fragment**. Iron. Ctx NH2023 SF NH962. (ID 83) Phase 4.2 BW5.

393 **Ring; segment**. Copper alloy. Ctx NH5051. SF NH1421. (ID 539) Phase 6. SE1.

394 **Ring**. Iron. Ctx CC2003, SF CC201. (ID 1072) Phase 4.2 BE4.

395 **Weight**. Lead alloy and stone. Ctx NH4425, SFNH1281. (ID 968) Phase 4.2 BW2.

396 **Weight (Fig. 7.32)**. Lead alloy. Ctx NH4133, SF NH1221 (ID 826) Phase 4.2 BW2.

397 **Spike**. Iron. Ctx NH3354, SF NH1048. (ID 742) Phase 5 BW3.

398 **Implement (Fig. 7.32)**. Lead alloy. Ctx NH3246, SF NH1015. (ID 970) Phase 5 BW4.

399 **Antler beam**. Ctx NH2628. (ID 429) Phase 4.2 BW4.

400 **Point**. Iron. Ctx NH2241, SF NH847. (ID 232) Phase 5 BW4.

401 **Notched bar (Fig. 7.32)**. Copper alloy. Ctx NH7606, SF NH1766. (ID 563) Phase 5 BW6.

402 **Cast plate fragment**. Copper alloy. Ctx CC3029, SF CC366. (ID 1352) Phase 5 BE5.

403 **'Blade' (Fig. 7.32)**. Iron. Ctx NH1014. SF NH169. Phase 6 SE2.

Worked stone objects *by Ruth Shaffrey*

Prehistoric (Phase 1)

A single large saddle quern of Lodsworth Greensand was recovered from early Iron Age pit fill NH6183. It is quite worn with only one surviving original edge. Lodsworth Greensand saddle querns of early date are relatively uncommon although a late Bronze Age example was found during the Danebury Environs project at Longstock, New Buildings (Cunliffe and Poole 2000, 69). The only other stone item from the prehistoric phase is an unworked but possibly utilised flint sphere.

Roman (Phase 2)

A single whetstone was recovered from Roman Phase 2.3 context NH2608; it is a typical slab of probable Pennant sandstone. Approximately five querns were recovered from Roman contexts, including three examples of Lodsworth Greensand plus numerous small weathered Lava quern

fragments. Both Lava and Lodsworth Greensand rotary querns are typical of Roman assemblages in this region. A single probable millstone fragment of Lodsworth Greensand was found in an Anglo-Norman context but is almost certain to be evidence of Roman milling because the main focus of Lodsworth Greensand quern production is early Roman (Peacock 1987). A number of quern fragments deposited in Saxon contexts may also be residual Roman material. Lodsworth Greensand rotary querns consistently measure between 300 and 450 mm diameter and millstones are rare with only four known examples, including this one. Winchester is located towards the western edge of the Lodsworth Greensand distribution and is the only known millstone in that area (Peacock 1987).

Roman contexts produced an assortment of other worked stone including a single undecorated shale bracelet fragment, a small flint sphere, and a fragment of Purbeck marble mortar. A single object found in dark earth is made of Cornish Greenstone (Fig. 7.34, no. 7). It is quite small and resembles a mace head but has been much altered; the edges are facetted and the item has been well used. It is similar to, though smaller than, known cushion stones (eg Butler and van der Waals 1966) but may have been used as a metal smithing tool (Roe pers. comm.).

Two processors include a pebble with extensive wear on one side, suggesting it was used as a rubber (SF 505). The second is an extremely well used mixing slab/mortar (Fig. 7.36, no. 13) with both faces worn very smooth and highly concave.

Late Saxon (Phase 4)

Eleven whetstones were recovered from late Saxon contexts in Properties BE 1, BE 2, BE 4, BW 1, BW 2, BW 4 and BW 6. Four are primary whetstones, three are rotating and four are hones. The primary whetstones utilise the greatest variety of lithologies including quartzite, possible Kentish Rag and sandstone. The rotating whetstones are made only of Pennant sandstone while the hones utilise Pennant and other sandstones.

The non-rotating whetstones and hones vary in design, some being small neat hand held items, occasionally with extensive use wear. These small varieties include SF 230, which is unusually tapered and heavily worn on all sides with the end also worn through use (Fig. 7.35, no. 10). Both faces of one Pennant sandstone slab shaped hone are worn concave through extensive use and are encrusted with iron deposits.

Late Saxon contexts produced single examples each of quern fragments of Lodsworth Greensand, Millstone Grit and sandstone, plus five contexts containing lava quern fragments. There were no spatial patterns to the quern distribution, with single quern fragments from inside the boundaries of Properties BE 2, BE 4, BE 5, BW 2 and SE 1 and two inside Property BE 1.

Saxon contexts also produced a plain bun-shaped chalk spindle whorl (Fig. 7.33, no. 4) and a chalk vessel, probably a lamp. The lamp is flat bottomed with curved but almost vertical sides and flat but crudely shaped inside.

Anglo-Norman (Phase 5)

Twelve whetstones were recovered from Anglo-Norman contexts in Properties BE 1–3, BW 3–5 and SE 1. Of these, four are primary whetstones, two rotating, and the remainder are hones. Of two fragments of Norwegian Ragstone (micaceous schist), one is a primary whetstone (Fig. 7.34, no. 8) and the other an unfashioned but utilised piece of the same stone. The rotating whetstones and the remaining primary whetstones are sandstone, probably Pennant sandstone and Kentish Rag. One of the rotating whetstones has wear on both circumference and main faces indicating it was used for more than one purpose.

A number of quern fragments were recovered from Anglo-Norman contexts but, as with earlier phases, no patterning of quern fragment deposition was observed. Five contexts produced lava quern fragments, all weathered and mostly very small. Two sandstone quern fragments were also recovered. A millstone fragment of Lodsworth Greensand came from Property BE 3 (NH1150, SF 58). The presence of a millstone fragment in pit NH1149 is an indication of a mill somewhere in the vicinity, although probably not on the actual site, and almost certainly relating to the Roman occupation.

Ten other items of worked stone were recovered from Anglo-Norman contexts. These mainly represent either industrial or domestic activity. A single mudstone counter in Property SE 1 is a recreational object. This property also produced a single crudely-made chalk lamp (Fig. 7.33, no. 1). Stone lamps are not common and, although its presence is noteable, it is made of chalk, a locally available material and is not of good quality, which suggests domestic rather than high status use.

All the stone spindle whorls in Properties BW 3, BW 4 and SE 1 are made of chalk, but they do vary in design. A whorl from BW 3 is plain, two from BW

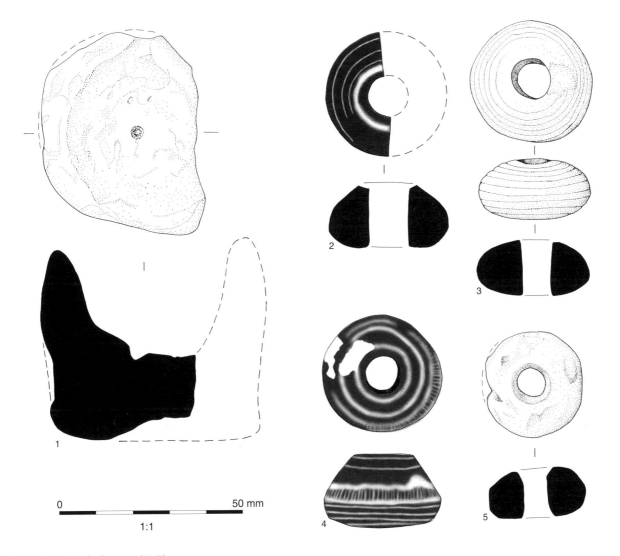

0   50 mm

1:1

Fig. 7.33 Worked stone (1–5)

0   100 mm

1:2

0   50 mm

1:1

Fig. 7.34 Worked stone (6–8)

4 and SE 1 are incised with rings around the circumference, and the fourth (BW 3) is incised with short vertical lines around the circumference (Fig. 7.33, no. 4). As with earlier excavations, there are more spindle whorls from Anglo-Norman contexts than medieval, a decline probably related to the introduction of the spinning wheel (Keene 1985, 300). A single chalk loom weight is evidence for weaving.

Medieval (Phase 6)

Eight whetstones were recovered from medieval contexts in properties BE 3–5, BW 2 and BW 3. Three of these are primary types, one is a rotating whetstone and four are hones. The primary whetstones are made of Norwegian Ragstone, Kentish Ragstone and quartzite and all the other hones are made of sandstone, including Pennant sandstone. The whetstones vary in shape but mostly seem to represent personal and domestic use and continue the theme of tools being well used (eg SF 1060, worn on all sides and now quite bulbous (Fig. 7.35, no. 11).

Three other pieces of worked stone recovered from medieval contexts include a chalk spindle whorl, a possible marble and a disc fragment which may be part of a floor stone. The spindle whorl, in keeping with those from Anglo-Norman contexts, is made of chalk and has linear decoration around the circumference.

Discussion

The Pennant sandstone, Kentish Rag and other sandstones used for the non-rotating whetstones and hones are typical of urban assemblages of Roman-medieval date. Twelve properties in total produced whetstones or hones but no one property produced numbers high enough to indicate the presence of a workshop.

The small numbers of Norwegian Ragstone whetstones reflects the generally early date of the excavated archaeology as this material became popular from the later 13th century and was not common during the Saxon period (Moore 1978, 70, Ellis and Moore 1990, 283). Of the three Norwegian Ragstone whetstones from these excavations two have not been neatly shaped but show evidence of extensive use. They may have resulted from breakage or are left over fragments from production of larger items (Ellis and Moore 1990, 280). They support the idea that the raw material was brought to Winchester and further production happened within the town (Ellis and Moore 1990, 280, quoting Falck-Muus 1922). The evidence from these excavations also continues to show that, despite the apparent commonness of the material, it was highly valued as a resource and was used in whatever state was available. It may also indicate that these whetstones were not readily available or cheap to replace, hence their continued use.

Although some Norwegian Ragstone may have been brought into Winchester from London (Ellis and Moore 1990, 280), a large rod of 550 mm long recently found at Southampton, albeit of a slightly later 13th–14th century date (Shaffrey in prep), suggests this port as another, closer and more likely source. Whetstones could easily have been added to the large loads of wine which were brought to Winchester from Southampton during the medieval period, the port being the main source for Winchester's wine (Keene 1985, 272).

In contrast to other whetstones and hones, rotating whetstones were found only in small numbers in Saxon and Anglo-Norman phases of Properties BW 2–4. The four fragments with measurable diameters are comparable to the rotating whetstones at early medieval Dorestad, which measured between 210 and 400 mm diameter (Kars 1983, 4). Two are of comparable thickness to the Dorestad examples at around 70 mm thick but the remainder are much thinner at between 20–30 mm thick. The centre of none of the examples survived so it is not possible to determine if they were perforated. The thinner examples seem likely to have been used for sharpening small blades. The limited focus of distribution indicates the presence of a smith's workshop somewhere within the boundaries of one of these properties, possibly Property BW 3, which has the highest number of whetstone fragments of any single property (five), or BW 4 which has the most rotating whetstone fragments. How these whetstones were powered is not clear, although water-driven whetstones are known to have been operating outside East Gate on the bridge (Keene, 1985, 279).

Quern numbers are fairly low and many of them are likely to be residual. The lack of evidence probably reflects the city's large number of water powered mills (Keene 1985, 254) and supports the documentary evidence that only small numbers of people would have owned and used their own rotary quern (ibid.).

The assemblage of other items of worked stone includes a broad range of things largely representing domestic or small scale industrial activity. There are no patterns of distribution of particular artefact types, except the whetstones which might indicate the presence of a smith's workshop. Most items, notably the spindle whorls, made use of locally available materials such as chalk.

Catalogue of illustrated stone objects (Figs 7.33–6)

1   **Lamp.** Chalk. Crudely made with hole in centre perhaps for fixing ceramic lamp. Has slight rim around base. Blackened by burning along one internal top edge. Ctx NH 6039. Ph 5

2   **Spindle whorl.** Chalk. Broken almost exactly in half. Burnt and blackened with prominent white circles near the base and top and fainter ones in between. Perforation measures 11 mm diameter. Measures 33 mm diameter x 17 mm high. Ctx NH 2577. Ph 5. SF 976

3   **Spindle whorl.** Chalk. With wide perforation, 11-13

mm diameter. Decorated with nine evenly spaced rings around the circumference 1.5 mm apart. Burnt. Measures 31.5-32 mm diameter x 15.5 mm high. Ctx NH 5161. Ph 5. SF 1470

4   **Spindle whorl.** Chalk. Bun shaped with flat base but which curves up slightly to the edges. Perforation is 10 mm diameter. Dark with four paler rings. Measures 34 mm diameter x 19 mm high. Ctx NH 4593. Ph 5. SF 1297

5   **Spindle whorl, complete.** Small complete. Flattened bun shaped whorl. Not decorated and with slightly biconical perforation. Ctx NH 1323. Ph 4. SF 114

6   **Pivot stone and secondary whetstone, including rotating.** Pennant sandstone. Thick and flat with circular edge worn very smooth and with smoothed dips on both faces. On one face there are two extremely worn sockets caused either through tertiary use as pivot sockets or as deep shallow

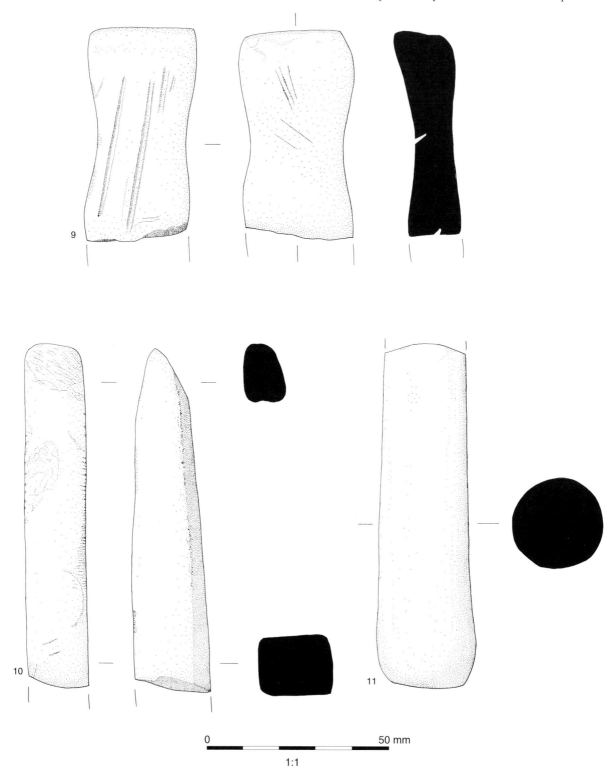

Fig. 7.35   Worked stone (9–11)

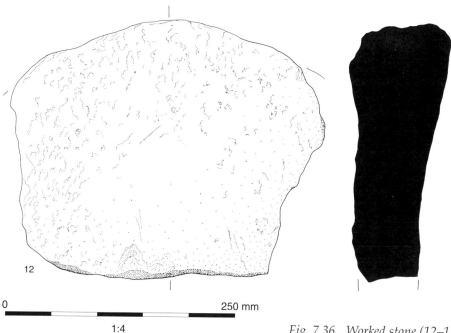

0   250 mm

1:4

Fig. 7.36 Worked stone (12–13)

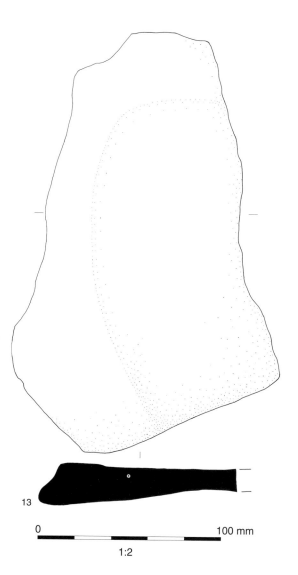

0   100 mm

1:2

mortars. Measures 290 mm diameter x 68 mm thick. Ctx NH 3221. Ph 4.1

7   **Metal smithing tool.** Cornish Greenstone. Heavily reused as the profile has been changed on two sides. One side has been broken and then partly worn smooth. Measures >40 x max 44 x max 24. Ctx NH 4718. Ph 2.4. SF 1341

8   **Whetstone.** Grey schist, Norwegian Rag. Elongate with flattened oval cross section. Unevenly utilised and heavily worn on both major faces including one large groove and polish. Measures 85 x 42 x 14 mm. Ctx NH 6053. Ph 5

9   **Whetstone, probably primary.** Probable Kentish Rag. Very well used cigar shaped whetstone with rectilinear cross section. There are also two straight narrow fairly deep grooves suggesting the sharpening of fine points on one of the main faces. Measures > 55 mm long x 27-31 mm wide x 11-16 mm thick. Ctx NH 1222. Ph 5

10   **Whetstone, primary.** Fine grained micaceous dark grey sandstone. Heavily tapered so is almost pointed at one end. Heavily used so all the faces (and the wide end) are smooth, flat and polished. Measures 92 mm long x 15 x 21 at the wide end. Ctx CC 2126. Ph 4.2. SF 230

11   **Elongate, rounded primary whetstone.** Fine-grained grey sandstone, possible Kentish Rag. Incomplete with sub-square section. Is slightly bulbous at the complete end. Appears to have been generally used over all the surfaces and possibly across the end as well. Measures >90 mm length x 24-27 mm x 23-26 mm. Ctx NH 3286. Ph 6. SF 1060

12   **Saddle quern.** Lodsworth Greensand. Large saddle quern with three broken edges. Worn and concave grinding surface. The one surviving edge is curved. Measures 310 x 270 mm diameter x 100 mm thick. Ctx NH 6184. Ph 1.1. SF 1685

13   **Possible grinding or mixing slab.** Slab with no original edges but worn very smooth and concave on both faces so that very thin in the centre. Measures 180 x 130 x 8 mm. Ctx NH 2619. Ph 2.3

Struck flint *by Hugo Lamdin-Whymark*

In total, 362 struck flints were recovered, including 129 chips measuring below 10 mm, retrieved from sieved residues (Table 7.27). Flint was recovered from 157 contexts across the excavated areas. Most was clearly redeposited from Roman and later contexts. The raw material is of local origin; cortical pieces exhibit either a thick white cortex from sources in the chalkland landscape, or a thin and abraded cortex typical of flint from the local river gravels. A small number of Mesolithic or early Neolithic flints indicates an early presence in the landscape typical of the chalklands of southern England. The blades and bladelets present exhibit dorsal blade scars and platform edge abrasion characteristic of this period. In contrast, the unspecialised flakes which dominate the assemblage appear to have been struck from irregular and unprepared cores, predominately using a hard hammer percussor, such as a hammerstone, without preparation of the platform edge. This reduction strategy is typical of middle to late Bronze Age industries, although comparable flintwork is known in the Iron Age (Ford *et al.* 1984; Humphrey 2003). The artefacts form a relatively low density spread, but nevertheless reflect a period of activity in the local landscape. Due to the limited number of diagnostic flint artefacts and the lack of contextual associations it was not possible to precisely characterise the nature of this activity. The Roman and later activity may have augmented the prehistoric assemblage with additional flakes and chips, some from construction in flint, the majority representing accidental debitage created whilst cutting pits and foundations.

METALWORKING

Surface X-ray fluorescence (XRF) analysis of non-ferrous metalworking debris *by Cath Mortimer*

Surface X-ray fluorescence (XRF) analysis was used to determine the metals present within visible metallic droplets on the surfaces of 17 crucibles, and hence suggest which types of alloy were being melted and cast at site. Four other samples were also analysed (Table 7.28).

Metals from the melting process are present within vitrified areas where they have combined with other elements from the hearth and from the crucible fabric itself, but the relationship between the elements found in vitrified layers and those of the original metal load is even more complex than that between the metallic deposits and the metal load. Analysis was carried out on those samples where metallic deposits could be clearly seen. Occasionally vitrification with copper alloy deposits becomes detached from the crucible, and one sample (NH4491) is probably an example of this. Another fragment seems be from a large, thick-walled crucible (NH4694); although there are

Table 7.27: The worked flint assemblage by category type

Category Type	NH	CC	Grand Total
Flake	96	104	200
Blade	3	1	4
Bladelet	1	4	5
Blade-like	2	1	3
Irregular waste	8	4	12
Sieved chips 10-4 mm	19	110	129
Tested nodule/bashed lump		2	2
Multiplatform flake core	1		1
Scraper on a non-flake blank		1	1
Other scraper	1		1
Awl		1	1
Spurred piece		1	1
Denticulate		1	1
Retouched flake	1		1
Grand total	132	230	362

Table 7.28: XRF analyses of crucibles and other metalworking debris. Only non-ferrous metals are noted, except where iron alone was detected. Bold type is used where the metal is particularly abundant and brackets where there is only a trace.

Context	SF	Phase	Property	Sample ID	XRF
CC1519	541	6	BE 2	CA waste	**Cu Sn** Pb Zn
CC3151	338	6	BE5	crucible	Cu Zn Pb
NH1022		5	SE2	crucible	Cu Zn Pb Sn
NH2240		5	BW4	crucible	**Zn** Cu Pb (Sn)
NH2356		5	BW4	crucible	Cu Zn Pb
NH2444		2.4		crucible	Cu Zn Pb
NH2459		5	BW4	crucible	Cu Pb Sn(Zn)
NH2577		5	BW4	crucible	**Zn** Cu Pb
NH2583		5	BW4	crucible	**Zn** Cu Pb
NH3528		5	BW4	crucible	Cu Pb Sn (Zn)
NH3558		5	BW4	crucible and ?crucible	Cu Pb (Zn)
NH3571		5	BW3	ceramic	only Fe
NH3669		4.2	BW3	crucible	Cu Zn Pb (Sn)
NH4085		4.2	BW2	crucible	Cu Pb Sn (Zn)
NH4394		4.2	BW2	crucible	Cu Pb Sn (Zn)
NH4394	266	4.2	BW2	crucible	**Zn** Cu Pb Sn
NH4401		4.2	BW2	crucible	Cu Zn Pb Sn
NH4464	279	4.1	BW2	crucible and vitrification	**Zn Pb** Sn Cu
NH4491	281	4.1	BW2	vitrification	Cu Zn Pb Sn
NH4535		4.1	BW2	crucible	**Zn** Cu Pb Sn
NH4623		4.1		crucible?	only Fe
NH4694		2.4		crucible	Pb, Zn (Cu)

no metallic droplets, the inner surface was analysed. Two other samples were analysed, one (NH4623) has a crucible form, but with oxidised surfaces, and the other (NH3571) is a piece of shaped, fired clay, also oxidised, with possible metallurgical connections. Lastly, although there is only a small amount of copper alloy waste at the site, one large irregular mass (small find 541, CC1519) was selected for analysis. A full report can be found in *Digital Section 4*.

Results

All the analyses on metallic droplets showed that copper alloys were being melted and cast at the site. Copper, zinc and lead were detected in each case, and tin was detected in the majority of cases. Iron was also detected in each analysis because iron is present in most early copper alloys, as well as in the crucible fabric and because it is easily detectable by surface XRF. Other relevant elements (eg nickel, arsenic, antimony, silver) were sought but not detected.

Many of the copper alloys can be characterised as either zinc-rich or tin-rich. Five samples (NH2356, 2444, 2577, 2583 and CC3151) are amongst those with the highest levels of detectable zinc, and revealed no tin at all. Two samples (NH2240, 3669) had significant amounts of zinc and only very low levels of tin. These seven samples can be characterised as being brass-like. Conversely, four samples showed only very small traces of zinc (NH2459, 3528, 4085, 4394) but plenty of tin, more characteristic of bronzes. Seven analyses (NH1022, 4394, 4401, 4464, 4491, 4535 and CC1519) showed all four major elements clearly present, although zinc was more prominent than tin in three of these (NH4394, 4464 and 4535). These probably reflect quaternary copper alloy, where zinc, tin and lead were all important alloying elements; this includes NH4491, the sample of copper-alloy debris within vitrification and CC1519, the copper alloy waste. One sample (NH3558) showed copper, lead and only a tiny trace of zinc, so is only classifiable as a copper alloy.

Amongst the other samples selected for analysis, only iron was detected on both NH4623 (a crucible form, but with oxidised surfaces) and NH3571 (shaped, fired clay, oxidised). There is therefore no clear analytical evidence that these were used for metalworking although, according to specialist opinion (see Cotter above), the 'unused crucible' samples are unlikely to have been designed as lamps. NH3571 may be considered with the other fired clay material at the site (see Poole above). Analysis confirmed that the large possible crucible (NH4694; Phase 2.4) was probably in contact with a copper alloy at high temperatures, since large zinc and lead peaks and a small copper peak were observed.

Discussion

The site provides only limited evidence for copper alloy casting, probably of small decorative objects, and no evidence of precious metalworking. The analysed crucibles come from Phases 2.4 to 6, with a concentration in Phases 4.1, 4.2 and 5. They come from five properties BW 2, BW 3, BW 4, SE 2 and BE 5, with seven examples from BW 2 and seven from BW 4. It is difficult to see any clear patterns within these phases and properties, but notably five of the six quaternary alloys are from BW 2, and four of the brass alloys from BW 4. However, the four brass alloys from Property BW4 were all found on fragments with walls that were distinctly thinner than those of the average crucibles, about 4.9 mm, compared with averages between 6 and 7 mm. This suggests that these four samples originated from a single crucible, broken and scattered over several contexts within the same property. The wall thicknesses of the other analysed crucibles are more typical of those found across the site, so the same situation may not have applied elsewhere. This example serves to warn against over-interpretation of numbers of crucibles present, and hence the intensity of production.

Soil analysis (see MacPhail and Crowther, Chapter 8) showed industrial-related dumped soils in Property BW 5 had elevated levels of the heavy metals Pb, Zn and Cu, but these were not at levels that would have been 'sufficient in themselves to provide unequivocal evidence of non-ferrous metalworking.' Only a small amount of copper alloy waste was found, including a little spillage, and some traces of copper alloy within non-diagnostic slags (see Starley below). It should be noted that the small size of crucibles would have meant only small amounts of metal would be melted, hence only minor quantities of metal were available to be lost or discarded during working. Furthermore, it seems likely that small artefacts would be cast at a workbench rather than on the workshop floor (as for late medieval cauldrons), which would allow a 'cleaner' operation with less metal loss. Of the small amount of mould evidence at the site (see Poole above), an example of a mould for a decorative fitting (CC2237; Property BE 4, Phase 5) would fit with this type of working.

The metalworking debris *by David Starley*

The excavation produced a quantity of ferrous metalworking debris. This material was assessed by Lynne Keys (Keys 2006) prior to joint re-examination resulting in this report. The total 70 kg of debris retained was re-examined, classified, categorised into the main functional categories of smithing, smelting and undiagnostic ironworking (Table 7.29), and the results considered in the light of contextual information, phasing and the research aims of the project. This report is abstracted from a detailed digital report that accompanies this volume (*Digital Section 4*). Digital Appendix 1 presents the complete data from the 4.65 kg of sieved residues. The full data for the examination of bulk debris is presented in Digital Appendix 2.

Table 7.29: Breakdown of metalworking activity by debris

Activity	Classification	Weight (g)
Smelting	possible ore	6
Smithing	smithing hearth bottoms	20721
	hammerscale	25
Non-ferrous metalworking	copper alloy debris	189
Non diagnostic metalworking	undiagnostic ironworking slag	35849
	iron lumps	900
	fayalitic runs	130
	slagged pot	26
	iron-rich cinder	3
Possible metalworking or other high-temp process	vitrified hearth/furnace lining	3101
	cinder	2060
	fuel ash slag	517
	fired clay	80
Fuel	burnt coal	38
	charcoal	3
Non-slag	ferruginous concretion	884
	burnt stone	855
	concrete	115
	stone	15
	bone	7
Total		65,524

Functional categories

Iron smithing

Evidence for iron smithing was recovered in two forms—bulk slags and micro slags. Of the bulk slags, the most easily recognisable are normally the smithing hearth bottoms. In addition to bulk slags, iron smithing also produces micro slag of two types (Starley 1995). Flake hammerscale consists of fish-scale like fragments of the oxide/silicate skin of the iron dislodged during working. Spheroidal hammerscale results from the solidification of small droplets of liquid slag expelled during hot working, particularly when two objects are being fire-welded together or when the slag-rich bloom of iron is first worked into a billet or bar. Hammerscale is important in interpretation of activity on sites, not only because it is highly diagnostic of smithing, but, because it tends to build up in the immediate vicinity of the smithing hearth and anvil, it may give a more precise location of the activity than the bulk slags, which may be transported elsewhere for disposal (Mills and McDonnell 1992).

Undiagnostic ferrous metalworking

The largest category of material was undiagnostic ironworking slag. Such irregularly-shaped fayalitic slags can be produced by both iron smelting and iron smithing processes, but it is not possible to determine which by visual examination. A very small quantity of iron-rich cinder was recognised by its significant content of iron not chemically combined as silicates, but visible as rust-orange coloured hydrated iron oxides and iron hydroxides.

Non-ferrous metalworking

The presence of green copper alloy corrosion products led to a number of fragments being classified as copper alloy debris (see Mortimer above). These might relate to specialised copper alloy working. However, they may also be associated with ironworking, in which copper coatings or inlays are applied to iron objects or components are brazed together, or possibly with the recycling of such composite artefacts.

Undiagnostic – metalworking or other high temperature process

Several categories of the material recovered can be produced by a wide range of high temperature activities and are of little help in distinguishing between these processes. Material listed as vitrified hearth/furnace lining may derive from either ironworking or, particularly with fragments showing brightly coloured glazes, from non-ferrous metalworking. A material closely associated with vitrified hearth/furnace lining, but separately classed as cinder, comprises only the lighter portion of this—a porous, hard and brittle slag formed by the reaction between alkali fuel ash and fragments of clay that had spalled away from the heath/furnace lining, or another source of silica, such as the sand sometimes used as a flux during smithing. The small amount of fired clay without any surface vitrification could have derived from structures associated with metallurgical purposes, or from those used for other high temperature activities. Fuel ash slag is a very lightweight, light coloured, porous material which results from the reaction between alkaline fuel ash and silicates from the soil, sand or clay at elevated temperatures.

Fuel

Very little charcoal was identified, although many pieces of slag retained the impressions, if not actual fragments, of charcoal. A number of fragments of burnt coal were identified, together with very occasional undiagnosnic slag which either contained burnt coal inclusions or was of a clinkery nature, suggesting coal-fuelled smithing.

Discussion

The analytical examination of metalworking debris from the site re-examined a total of 70 kg of metallurgical debris. The bulk slag, as assessed by Lynne Keys (2006), showed the dominant activity to be iron smithing. In addition, a few fragments from non-ferrous metalworking were identified (see

Mortimer above). A couple of fragments which might have been indicative of smelting were carefully considered, but rejected as providing insufficient proof of primary metal production. The fuel for the iron smithing was, for all periods except the post-1750 phase, charcoal. Although very occasional fragments of coal, or partially burnt coal were also identified in Roman, late Saxon and medieval contexts these were not directly associated with the metalworking debris.

The most significant findings of the post-assessment analysis derive from the quantification of the hammerscale in the 4.65 kg of magnetic material extracted from the sieved residues of soil samples. Whereas the total mass of bulk slags could have been the product of only a few weeks' work by a single smith, the hammerscale provided evidence of much more sustained activity. More importantly, the hammerscale was often found in its primary contexts, such as occupation layers, giving far more precise indications of the locations and date of the iron smithing. It would appear, not untypically, that bulk slag was being almost entirely removed from the site of smithing and only occasionally remained in the vicinity of the ironworking, notably in the fill of pits used primarily for disposal of cess and other non-industrial waste.

The evidence for metalworking activity was restricted to some degree both as a result of the mitigation strategy and, more significantly, by truncation of earlier horizontal stratigraphy by later activity. Under these circumstances, the survival of an even poorly preserved metalworking workshop would be unexpected. Although some hearths survive and some may be linked to ironworking, it should be borne in mind that, traditionally, smithing is carried out using raised hearths and that, after demolition, their positions may be difficult to recognise. More likely to survive are the recesses for anvil blocks and quenching pits and further detailed study of the environs of occupation layers containing hammerscale may allow such features to be recognised. A possible example of one of these is oval feature NH2209 in Phase 4.1 of Property BW 5, which was recorded as a posthole, but might otherwise be the socket for an anvil base.

There is plenty of evidence that smithing was a significant activity through most of the Roman period, but little to show the exact position of any workshop. The first clear evidence of iron smithing comes early in the Roman settlement, in Phase 2.1, immediately adjacent to the Roman street (Street CC1703). Here a yard area (Group CC7002) associated with Structure CC7049 on the street frontage had bulk slag added to its surface, whilst hammerscale was found in several pits. Phase 2.2 provided little evidence of smithing, but there is much stronger evidence in Phase 2.3, again largely from pits. Continuation into Phase 2.4 is apparent with smithing debris within various dark earth deposits.

During the late Saxon period (Phase 4), there is a good deal of evidence for metalworking debris, particularly in the form of hammerscale, including some in the occupation levels where they provide the most precise location of the activity. Property BW4 provides some of the strongest evidence with hammerscale *in situ* within a structure's occupation layers. The location within a building is important; smithing relies on accurate judgement of temperature, as this is achieved by observing the colour of the metal which cannot be easily carried out in full daylight conditions. This group was also associated with charcoal spreads and a hearth, though it may not have had a metalworking function. Ironworking within this property appears to show considerable continuity, with evidence through to the Anglo-Norman phase (Phase 5).

Other foci of iron smithing appear to have been Properties BE 2, BW 2 and BW 3 in Phase 4.2, with BW 2 continuing through to Phase 5 if not 6. If the identification of an anvil base is correct then BW 5 may also have once housed a smithy. Beyond these foci occasional deposits of slag are found across the site, particularly in pits. Such distribution appears to show that the property boundaries did not prevent the linear transport of debris, though it may be that iron smithing was more widely distributed than the surviving layers suggest. There was a relative paucity of slag from the SE properties but one large pit in Property SE 3 produced evidence of smithing in the form of hammerscale which spans Phases 4 and 5. This might provide supporting evidence for the interpretation of the published Winton Domesday evidence, which appears to show that a named blacksmith, Richard, may have inhabited this property (Teague pers. comm.), in addition to continuity of craft specialism before and after the Norman Conquest. Unfortunately, no more than small quantities of undiagnostic slag were recovered to support similar documentary evidence for a smith named Harding on the adjacent Property SE 2.

Across the site, there was evidence of extensive pit digging and it may be prudent to consider to what extent this activity accounts for the concentrations of slag found in their lower levels. This may be residual material transferred from disturbed and now lost layers.

Apart from the waste debris, the intended products of the smithing activity are not easily identified. It is not known to the specialist whether the ferrous finds included any unfinished artefacts or stock material. As mentioned in the classification, it is generally held that a lower ratio of flake to spheroidal hammerscale indicates either primary consolidation of iron blooms, or the welding together of separately made parts. The percentages recorded from these samples were biased by their collection from wet sieved soil samples; there is a tendency for spheroidal hammerscale to float off during wet sieving. In the absence of smelting debris it would seem unlikely that bloom smithing was taking place. However, whilst some samples recorded a third as much spheroidal as flake, others revealed none, it could therefore be suggested that there was a range of types of work being undertaken.

The economic importance of the industry is difficult to judge. Calculating from the surviving mass of hammerscale is likely to considerably underestimate the amount originally produced, given the limits on excavation, truncation of site and the partial sampling strategy. The quantity of evidence in the Roman period is fairly restricted, but from late Saxon to Anglo-Norman there appears to have been fairly intensive activity over an extensive area. In terms of demands on local resources, with the exception of the probable re-cycling of old ferrous artefacts there would have been a need for a trade in bar iron. For the Roman period, very large scale iron production sites are known, such as those in the Sussex Weald (Cleere and Crossley 1983), which would undoubtedly have been able to serve a wide area. On the other hand smaller sites, many yet to be discovered, might have provided more local sources. The finding of small quantities of smelting slag within Winchester on The Brooks site (Starley 1993) suggests that such sources might be very close at hand indeed.

Nationally, iron production in the post-Roman periods appears less impressive in scale. However, the corpus of information from the examination of artefacts suggests much higher quality, not least in the choice of specific iron alloys, with presumably well developed trade networks. The possibility of specialist steel production in mid Saxon Southampton has been raised by Mack *et al.* (2000), which would have provided easy river transport to Winchester. Beyond the requirements for iron the main resource would have been charcoal to fuel the hearths. Given the fragile nature of the material such a resource would have been probably gathered locally, but as recorded for historic iron smelting (Hildebrand 1992), the possibility of water borne transport might have considerably extended the distance from which it was worth supplying.

Chapter 8
Overview of the Environmental Evidence

MAMMAL AND BIRD BONE *by Lena Strid*

Although a large number of excavations have taken place in Winchester, very few reports from intra-mural sites have been published. Most comparative material comes from sites in the northern, western and eastern suburbs (Maltby 2010; Serjeantson and Rees 2009).

An assemblage of almost 61,000 fragments (47 kg) was recorded from Northgate House and the Discovery Centre. The bones were recovered by hand and from wet sieving of bulk samples to 0.5 mm. The sieved fragments constituted 50% of the total assemblage by numbers, but only 4.2% of the total fragment weight. A full record of the assemblage, together with a methodology, metrical analyses, full details of pathologies and non-metrical traits, and a longer discussion, can be found in the digital report (*Digital Section 11*) and in the site archive.

The bones were identified using the Oxford Archaeology comparative skeletal collection in addition to standard osteological identification manuals (see *Digital Section 11*).

The presence of residual artefacts and ecofacts is a feature of most urban sites that span centuries of occupation. Many stratigraphically secure post-Roman contexts on the site contained varying amounts of residual Roman pottery. If all contexts containing residual pottery were omitted, many significant deposits would have been excluded. To provide large enough groups to validate statistical analyses, while making a reasonable effort to exclude residual bones, the following strategy was adopted: all contexts containing 10% or fewer sherds of residual pottery would be analysed, as well as contexts containing fewer than 5 sherds of pottery and stratigraphically secure contexts with no pottery. Exceptions were made for two contexts (NH5168, NH5202), which comprised the base and third fills of pit NH5169, as the three other fills from this pit contained several foot bones of squirrel, suggesting furrier activity.

All medieval contexts from the Discovery Centre were analysed according to the above strategy, but only partial analysis of the assessed medieval context groups from Northgate House was undertaken.

The assemblage

Bones were recorded from four main phases: Phase 2 (Roman), Phase 4 (late Saxon), Phase 5 (Anglo-Norman) and Phase 6 (medieval). The late Saxon and Anglo-Norman assemblages were by far the most numerous (Table 8.1).

Preservation ranged generally from good to fair, providing ample opportunities for observation of butchering marks and pathologies. Burnt bones were generally scarce. Gnawed bones were slightly more common in the Roman assemblage, although not very numerous. The majority of the bones were gnawed by carnivores, probably dog. Probable cat gnawing marks were seen on a few bones from Phases 4 and 5. Rodent gnawing was observed on a small number of bones in each phase.

Bones from both meat-rich and meat-poor body parts of cattle, sheep/goat and pig were present in every phase group. Specific butchers' streets are documented for Winchester from the 10th century (Hagen 2002, 315). As these streets are not within the excavated site, the inclusion of meat-poor body parts in the assemblages suggests that body parts such as cattle and sheep/goat metapodials and phalanges were either useful in other ways, such as marrow extraction or glue making, or were included in the portioned carcass.

The bird assemblage comprised around 4% of the total 60,595 recorded faunal fragments. About 51% of the bird bones were identified to species/family. Domestic fowl (*Gallus gallus*) is the most common bird, followed by duck (*Anatinae / Aythyinae / Tadorninae / Merginae*) and then goose (*Anser anser / Anser domesticus*). Altogether, 16 species/families are represented: Domestic fowl, goose, brent goose (*Branta bernicla*), duck, mallard (*Anas platyrhynchos*), teal (*Anas crecca*), grey partridge (*Perdix perdix*), pigeon (*Columba* sp.), woodcock (*Scolopax rusticola*), lapwing (*Vanellus vanellus*), snipe (*Gallinago gallinago*), kittiwake (*Rissa tridactyla*), cormorant (*Phalacrocorax carbo*), jackdaw (*Corvus monedula*), crane (*Grus grus*) and buzzard (*Buteo buteo*).

The Roman assemblage

The recorded Roman assemblage consisted of 8016 fragments, of which 1755 (21.9%) were identified to taxon. Viewing the Roman mammal assemblage as a whole, the most numerous species, based on the number of identified fragments per species (NISP) is cattle, whereas sheep/goat has the largest number of individuals, based on the calculation of minimum number of individuals (MNI)

Table 8.1. Number of identified bones (NISP) /taxon by chronological phase in the Northgate House and Discovery Centre assemblage

	Phase 1	Phase 2	Phase 2.1	Phase 2.2	Phase 2.3	Phase 2.4	Phase 4	Phase 4.1	Phase 4.2	Phase 5	Phase 6	TOTAL
Cattle	9	754	96	15	385	268	914	226	688	1420	223	3330
Sheep/goat	28	593	140	5	253	195	1230	214	1016	2248	358	4457
Sheep	1	43	11		18	14	149	43	106	595	45	833
Goat		3			3		37	6	31	91	6	137
Pig	8	250	25	3	144	78	592	139	453	719	155	1724
Horse	1	26	3	2	8	13	41	12	29	133	6	207
Red deer		6			2	4	2		2	4		12
Roe deer							2		2	5		7
Deer sp.		2			2		7	2	5	7	2	18
Dog		16			14	2	17	1	16	23	3	59
Cat							14		14	498	7	519
Hare							2		2	6	9	17
Lagomorph										1		1
Fox										8		8
Badger							1		1			1
Pine marten?							1		1			1
Stoat										6		6
Ferret/Polecat										9		9
Small mustelid										3		3
Squirrel										308	1	309
Rat		1			1		6		6	5		12
House mouse		1			1							1
Wood mouse		1			1							1
Mouse sp.		6			6		2		2	3		11
Bank/field vole	1	3			2	1				4	2	10
Shrew		1			1							1
Rodent		2	1		1		3	1	2	5	1	11
Frog	7	2			1	1	20		20	10	4	43
Toad							26		26	1	1	28
Amphibian	1	8	2		5	1	31		31	19	5	64
Fowl	9	33		3	16	14	384	38	346	317	64	807
Goose		1			1		9	3	6	44	18	72
Brent goose										1		1
Duck		9			6	3	22	1	21	36	5	72
Domestic duck										1		1
Mallard		1				1	2		2			3
Teal							1	1		3		4
Pigeon		1			1					5	1	7
Partridge										1		1
Crane										1		1
Snipe										1	2	3
Woodcock							1		1	1	1	2
Wader										2		2
Kittiwake							2		2			2
Comorant		1				1						1
Buzzard										1		1
Jackdaw										5		5
Corvid										2		2
Passerine							4		4	16	5	25
Bird sp.	5	28	3		14	11	325	37	288	574	340	1272
Microfauna							2		2	3		5
Micromammal		26			26		3	2	1	44	3	76
Small mammal		14	6	1	1	6	55	9	46	428	18	515
Medium mammal	29	709	210	10	306	183	2100	371	1729	2821	447	6106
Large mammal	26	1501	555	15	511	420	1619	414	1205	2857	381	6384
Indeterminate	226	3964	1153	47	1286	1478	9530	2716	6814	11892	3517	29138
TOTAL	351	8016	2205	101	3016	2694	17157	4237	12920	25187	5630	56339
Weight (g)	1446	90171	10820	1106	48148	30097	128148	28408	99740	198737	28499	447001

Note: Totals presented in this table exclude general Phase 4 animal bone assemblage, which was excluded from the detailed analysis

Table 8.2. Roman assemblage, Phase 2: Anatomical distribution of all species, including NISP, MNI and weight.
Skeletal element used for MNI is marked with an asterisk.

	Cattle	Sheep/goat	Sheep	Goat	Pig	Horse	Deer sp.	Red deer	Dog
Antler							2	6	
Horn core	9		4	3					
Skull	55	26	12		29				2
Mandible	73	80	12		36	3			1
Loose teeth	92	102	2		39	6			
Hyoid	4	7							
Atlas	8	1							
Axis	4	1							1
Vertebrae									4
Ribs						2			2
Sternum									
Sacrum	1	1							
Scapula	29	17			17	1			1
Humerus	66	38			13				1
Radius	51	52			13				2
Ulna	27	14			18*				
Carpals	2	3							
Metacarpal	60*	41	7		12	2			
Pelvis	27	36			15	2			
Femur	54	21			9	2			
Patella		1							
Tibia	39	51*			10	1			
Fibula					10				
Calcaneus	25	4			6	1			
Astragalus	19	3			3				
Tarsals	5	1			1	1			
Metatarsal	45	67	6		11	1			
Phalanx 1	37	11			3	1			
Phalanx 2	8	4			2	1			
Phalanx 3	4	6			1	1			
Lateral metapodial					1				
Indet. metapodial	9	5			1	1			2
Carpal/tarsal									
Sesamoid									
Long bone									
Indeterminate	1								
Total (NISP)	754	593	43	3	250	26	2	6	16
MNI	18	22			7	1		1	1
Weight (g)	43645	5481	942	252	4080	1604	35	129	72

(Table 8.2). When examining the Roman subphases, regardless of method, sheep/goat dominate in Phase 2.1 while cattle are dominant in Phases 2.3 and 2.4. Phase 2.2 contained too few bones to carry out such an analysis. This provides some, albeit it fairly limited, evidence suggesting a change in the focus of animal husbandry in the region as a consequence of Romanisation. Although sheep/goat dominated during the foundation of *Venta Belgarum*, cattle, which the Romans favoured over sheep/goat, became more prominent as Roman influence took hold. In the later periods sheep/goat consistently outnumber cattle (Table 8.1), probably because the nearby downs were more suitable for sheep.

Meat-providing domestic mammals

Cattle

Few ageable and sexable cattle bones were recovered from individual sub-phases, so the Roman cattle assemblage was analysed as a unit. Adult cattle dominated the assemblage by all ageing methods; the mandibular wear stages (MWS) correspond closely to those from the Winchester Northern suburbs and the nearby rural settlement Owslebury. The focus on adult cattle as opposed to young adults particularly reflects the importance of cattle as providers of traction for agriculture. If cattle were mainly raised for meat, they would have been slaughtered at a younger age. While a peak of young cattle (MWS:21–25) was observed in the assemblage, this is probably due to the small sample size. There were somewhat fewer senile cattle at Winchester than at Owslebury, which may indicate that older cattle were less attractive for the meat market.

Of the twelve measureable metacarpals (late Roman phase), five were found to be within the range of cows and seven within the range of bulls and oxen (Mennerich 1968, 11f, 35, in Vretemark 1997, 48). This is in contrast to the pelves, where a majority were female.

Several cattle bones in all four sub-phases had been butchered. Cut marks resulting from skinning occurred on five first phalanges and around one horn core. Several long bones were axially split, presumably for marrow extraction. Chop marks associated with dismemberment were also recorded. These occurred proximally, mid-shaft and distally on long bones, as well as on pelvis (ilium), axis and the articular process of the mandible. Knife cuts suggesting dismemberment were found distally on the humerus and metacarpal, and proximally on the femur. Filleting cuts occurred on the pelvis (ilium), femur, scapula, hyoid, mandibular ramus and the skull (zygomatic).

Pathological conditions were found on 16 cattle bones, mostly on bones from the lower legs and feet. Details of these, and of non-metrical traits, are provided in the digital report (*Digital Section 11*).

Sheep/goat
Of the 639 sheep/goat bones, 43 could be identified as sheep and three (horn cores from Phase 2.3) as goat, so it is likely that the majority of the sheep/goat bones in the assemblage were sheep (cf. Maltby 1981, 159–160).

The sheep/goats appear to have been steadily culled throughout the first few years, with a small peak in culling at 1–2 years . When dividing the assemblage into sub-phases, the slaughter pattern shows a focus on 4–6 year olds in Phase 2.3 and 1–2 year olds in Phase 2.4. Almost 55% of the late fusing bones are unfused, so representing sheep/goats of less than 3–3.5 years of age. This slaughter age pattern is similar to that at Owslebury and the Roman suburbs (Maltby 1994; Maltby 2010) showing a cull of young sheep for meat, probably in their second autumn, and a later cull of adult sheep after they had yielded a few years' worth of milk, wool, dung and offspring.

The sheep/goat remains which could be attributed to males or females included pelves and horn cores. The derived ratio of males to females varied, however, depending on which element was used for the sex estimation: the pelves were mainly female, while the horn cores were mainly male. While skulls of hornless ewes can skew a horn core assemblage towards a male majority, no hornless skulls were found in the assemblage. The measurable sheep bones are within the same size range as sheep bones from other Roman sites in Britain (ABMAP).

Butchery marks were observed on 31 sheep/goat bones. Cut-marks associated with skinning were found at the proximal end of eight metapodials and the distal end of two metapodials. Limb bone butchery was limited to one radius, two pelves, two femora and 13 metapodials. The radii, femora and pelves had cut marks indicative of filleting. The butchery marks on the metapodials were more varied. These included skinning cut marks at the proximal and distal ends and axial splitting for marrow extraction. Cut-marks on skulls, mandibles and hyoid resulted from severing the head, disarticulating the mandible from the skull and possibly removal of the tongue. Both sheep and goat horn cores had been chopped from the skulls, suggesting the inclusion of tanners' or horn workers' waste. The contexts containing goat horn cores (NH2610, NH9543, CC1697) consist of mixed butchery and kitchen waste, which would suggest that the horn cores represent small scale craft activity rather than intensive industrial waste.

Six sheep/goat bones displayed pathological conditions. Congenital traits were found on 19 mandibles and two skulls.

Pig
The pig dental eruption and attrition data show that juvenile, immature and sub-adult pigs were slaughtered. The bone fusion is consistent with the dental age estimation and with the data from the Northern Suburbs (Maltby 2010). A pig's only economic value lies in their meat and fat, so there is no reason to keep more than the necessary breeding animals alive once they have reached their full growth. Their high fecundity and growth rate enables routine slaughter of immature individuals.

There was a considerable bias in favour of boars. A predominance of boar is common in most Roman assemblages in Britain and north-western continental Europe (Luff 1982, 263) and has been interpreted as the slaughter of surplus young boars (Johnstone and Albarella 2002, 31). Bengt Wigh (2001, 80) further extrapolates, writing that as sows yield less meat than boars, surplus sows would be slaughtered early, before the eruption of the permanent canines at 6–9 months.

The axial splitting of long bones, which is very common for Roman cattle butchery, was virtually non-existent for pig. Pig butchery was mainly carried out with cleavers, dismembering the carcass at the joints. Evidence for portioning was found on three pelves, where the ilium had been chopped away. Filleting cut marks occurred on a mandible indicating the utilisation of cheek meat, whereas cut marks indicating filleting or dismemberment were observed on a distal fibula and on a metatarsal. Instead of being split axially, a tibia had been broken open mid-shaft for marrow extraction.

The only pig bone with a pathology in the assemblage was a maxillary canine, whose root was deformed by exostoses. This is believed to be a result of a chronic infection (Baker and Brothwell 1980, 150–1).

Other domestic mammals

Horse

The majority of the horse bones are from adult horses, which is consistent with other Romano-British sites (Locker 1990, 208; Johnstone and Albarella 2002, 34; Maltby 1993, 329–30; Luff 1999, 205). In contrast to the northern suburbs, no articulated remains were found. This may be related to regulations concerning the disposal of horse carcasses in intra-mural and extra-mural areas (Maltby 2010). The proximal end of one tibia from Phase 2.3 was unfused, indicating a horse of less than 3.5 years of age at death. Due to fragmentation, withers' heights could not be calculated. Butchering marks were not observed.

Dog

The dog remains comprise one semi-articulated puppy in Phase 2.3. and two disarticulated sub-adult or adult bones each from Phases 2.3 and 2.4. As the bones were fragmented, withers' heights could not be calculated. While dogs have been used in ritual deposits in wells and other features on Roman sites (Maltby 2010; Fulford 2001, 215), the puppy's placement in a secondary fill of a cess pit may suggest deliberate killing in order to control the dog population.

Wild mammals

Wild mammals in the Roman assemblage include deer, rodents, insectivores and amphibians. The deer remains (Phase 2.3) consisted of two antler tine fragments from either red deer or fallow deer. While the Romans introduced a small number of fallow deer to Britain, they were kept in game parks or similar enclosures, probably near the owners' villas (Sykes *et al.* 2006, 953–4). The two fragments of deer antler are therefore likely to be from the native red deer. The scarcity of wild fauna in the assemblage is consistent with contemporary sites in Britain and continental Europe (Luff 1982, 268–83), indicating that hunted game provided an insignificant part of the diet.

The presence of amphibians and voles suggest that areas adjacent to that excavated included wetlands and open grassland. The voles and wood mice may have been killed by cats and transported some distance. House mice on the other hand are a commensal species and would have lived in close contact with people.

Birds

Relatively few bird bones were recovered. Fowl dominate, with duck (*Anatidae, Anas plathyrhynchos*) the second most common bird. The dominance of duck over goose has been observed at other Roman sites. However, archaeological, documentary and pictorial evidence suggest that duck and goose husbandry in Britain was not fully developed during the Roman period (Albarella 2005) so the majority of the ducks and geese in the Winchester assemblage were probably wild birds; all the ducks

and geese were adult. Despite the absence of butchering marks, it is assumed that they were eaten. Secondary products such as eggs and feathers were undoubtedly also utilised.

The number of fowl remains is very low when compared to data from other Romano-British towns, although at a similar level to suburban Winchester sites (Maltby 2010). While retrieval methods and taphonomic differences may play a part, it suggests that poultry were not commonly kept in the town, and those which were kept may have been primarily valued for their eggs. Most fowl were adults, or subadults; only a few juveniles were present. One tibiotarsus had cut marks on the distal condyles, indicating disarticulation of the foot prior to cooking.

Pigeon is found on many Roman sites, although normally only present in small numbers. It is uncertain whether the pigeon bone recovered from Phase 2.3 was from the stock dove (*Columba oenas*) or rock pigeon (*Columba livia*) as these species are of similar size. Dovecotes were usually placed on the roof, according to Roman authors (Rivet 1982, 207), and would thus elude archaeological discovery.

Cormorant bones, as well as bones from other sea birds, are very rare on Romano-British sites, so the carpometacarpus from late Roman Dark Earth context NH4718 is an unusual find. No sea birds are mentioned in Parker's 1988 study of birds from Romano-British sites (Parker 1988, 210–3), although one cormorant bone was retrieved from the Roman settlement Halangy Down at the Scilly Isles (Locker 1996). Cormorants are normally associated with coastal areas, but may live at inland marshes and lakes, and often move inland in winter (Cramp 1980, 202). The paucity of cormorant and other sea birds suggests that they were generally not considered suitable for eating by the Romano-British population.

The late Saxon assemblage

The late Saxon assemblage could be divided into two sub-phases: Phase 4.1 and Phase 4.2, comprising a total of 4237 and 12920 fragments respectively. A further 4597 animal remains derived from contexts that could not be dated to either phase, and were therefore excluded from the detailed analysis. However, noteworthy bones from contexts dated only to Phase 4 have been included for discussion where appropriate.

Approximately 16% and 22% of the late Saxon faunal remains in the two sub-phases could be identified to species (see Table 8.1). Of the 1230 sheep/goat bones, 149 could be identified as sheep and 37 as goat. The goat remains comprise horn cores and a few metapodials. They are found in a variety of properties, and since only five of the horn cores have butchery marks it suggests that horn working was a small-scale craft in this part of the town.

In both Phases 4.1 and 4.2 sheep/goat is the most numerous taxa regardless of quantification method (Tables 8.3 and 8.4). This contrasts both with other

Table 8.3. Late Saxon assemblage, Phase 4.1: Anatomical distribution of all species, including NISP, MNI and weight. Skeletal element used for MNI is marked with an asterisk

	Cattle	Sheep/goat	Sheep	Goat	Pig	Horse	Deer sp.	Red deer	Roe deer	Dog
Antler							2	1		
Horn core	25	8	22	25						
Skull	66	79	39	3	58	1				2
Mandible	54	120	6		38	5				4
Loose teeth	58	92	1		36	7				
Hyoid	1	2								
Atlas	12	8			11					1
Axis	9	20			1				1	1
Vertebrae		1								
Pygostyle										
Urostyle										
Ribs										
Sternum										
Neck cartilage										
Sacrum	5									
Synsacrum										
Furcula										
Coracoid										
Scapula	23	41			11	3*	2*			
Humerus	54*	57			23	1			1	2*
Radius	45	90			24*	1				1
Ulna	23	33			25	1	1			1
Radioulna										
Carpals	15	6			1					
Metacarpal	29	82	15	3	38	2		1		
Carpometacarpus										
Pelvis	46	61			28	1				
Femur	45	24			22	1				1
Patella		2								
Tibia	38	112*	1		32					
Fibula					11					
Tibiotarsus										
Tibiofibula										
Calcaneus	15	14			6	1				
Astragalus	11	6			1	1				
Tarsals	9	6			2					
Metatarsal	45	70	21		42	1				3
Tarsometatarsus										
Phalanx 1	26	35			16	2				
Phalanx 2	17	18			7					
Phalanx 3	14	11			6	1				
Indet. Phalanx		1								
Lateral metapodial					8					
Indet. metapodial	3	17	1		6					
Sesamoid										
Indet. lateral phalanx										
Carpal/tarsal										
Long bone										
Indeterminate										
Total (NISP)	688	1016	106	31	453	29	5	2	2	16
MNI	18	49			16	2	2	1	1	2
Weight (g)	39387	11505	2952	2525	5976	2472	149	136	44	127

Table 8.4. Late Saxon assemblage, Phase 4.2: Anatomical distribution of all species, including NISP, MNI and weight.
Skeletal element used for MNI is marked with an asterisk

	Cattle	Sheep/ goat	Sheep	Goat	Pig	Horse	Deer sp.	Red deer	Roe deer	Dog	Cat	Hare	Badger	Pine marten?
Antler							2	1						
Horn core	25	8	22	25										
Skull	66	79	39	3	58	1				2				
Mandible	54	120	6		38	5				4				
Loose teeth	58	92	1		36	7					1			
Hyoid	1	2												
Atlas	12	8			11					1				
Axis	9	20			1				1	1				
Vertebrae		1												
Pygostyle														
Urostyle														
Ribs														
Sternum														
Neck cartilage														
Sacrum	5													
Synsacrum														
Furcula														
Coracoid														
Scapula	23	41			11	3*	2*							
Humerus	54*	57			23	1		1		2*	1	1	1	
Radius	45	90			24*	1				1				
Ulna	23	33			25	1	1			1	1			
Radioulna														
Carpals	15	6			1									
Metacarpal	29	82	15	3	38	2		1						
Carpometacarpus														
Pelvis	46	61			28	1					3*			
Femur	45	24			22	1				1				
Patella		2												
Tibia	38	112*	1		32						1	1		
Fibula					11									
Tibiotarsus														
Tibiofibula														
Calcaneus	15	14			6	1								
Astragalus	11	6			1	1								
Tarsals	9	6			2									
Metatarsal	45	70	21		42	1				3	2			1
Tarsometatarsus														
Phalanx 1	26	35			16	2					1			
Phalanx 2	17	18			7									
Phalanx 3	14	11			6	1					4			
Indet. Phalanx		1												
Lateral metapodial					8									
Indet. metapodial	3	17	1		6									
Sesamoid														
Indet. lateral phalanx														
Carpal/tarsal														
Long bone														
Indeterminate														
Total (NISP)	688	1016	106	31	453	29	5	2	2	16	14	2	1	1
MNI	18	49			16	2	2	1	1	2	2	1	1	1
Weight (g)	39387	11505	2952	2525	5976	2472	149	136	44	127	19	7	6	< 0

late Saxon assemblages from Winchester (Bourdillon 2009; Coy 2009) and with mid Saxon assemblages from Southampton (Bourdillon and Coy 1980; Bourdillon and Andrews 1997), where cattle were the most numerous domesticate. Although the relative proportion of sheep/goat bones can be artificially skewed by the recovery of either large craft waste deposits of metapodials and horn cores, or of articulated skeletons, neither of these deposit types were encountered in this assemblage. Hence the dominance of sheep/goat probably relates to socio-economic dietary variations between different parts of the town.

When comparing the NISP between the two subphases, the proportion of sheep/goat increases in Phase 4.2 at the expense of cattle and to some extent, pig; however the MNI values are too small to be reliable (Hambleton 1999, 40). Despite its relatively large size, the assemblage from Phase 4.1 also had too few ageable, sexable and measureable bones to facilitate comparisons with Phase 4.2.

Meat providing domestic mammals

Cattle

Two peaks of culling were evident from the dental data from both Phases 4.1 and 4.2: at 18–30 months old and when senile. This suggests that the bovine part of the diet consisted of young cattle raised for meat and old breeding cows or draught oxen past their prime. The age estimation is consistent with the contemporary suburban Winchester assemblages (Bourdillon 2009; Coy 2009), but while the 46+ MWS predominate in the Northgate House/Discovery Centre assemblage, in the Western suburbs the 41–45 MWS dominate. If this is a true difference, and not skewed by the small sample, it may point towards socio-economic differences between the western suburbs and the north-east intramural area. The peak of sub-adult cattle is confirmed by the fusion data and by horn core age estimation, which, while not a very large sample, is dominated by 2–3 year old cattle.

All lines of evidence (pelvic morphology and metacarpal metrical analysis) from Phase 4.2 indicate that females dominate the assemblage. A predominance of cows is consistent with Maltby's interpretation of Roman rural livestock trade (see discussion above). The dominance of cows is less clear for Phase 4.1, but relatively few pelves were present.

Almost 12% of the cattle bones had been butchered. The tradition of axial splitting of long bones continues in the late Saxon period. A similar frequency of chop marks indicative of dismembering was observed on long bones as well as on mandible and pelvis. Dismembering cut marks were more frequent than in the Roman period, and are rather common on long bone joints, as well as on calcaneus, astragalus and the mandible. Fine cut marks were found on a number of long bones, scapulae and hyoids probably indicative of filleting and tongue removal. Skinning cut marks occurred on the phalanges and at the base of horn cores.

Twenty seven cattle bones (1.3%) displayed evidence of some kind of pathology. The majority were affected by thin bone growth on the surface of the bone, indicating infection. Congenital conditions occurred on one mandibular M3, where the third posterior cusp was missing.

Sheep/goat

The slaughter pattern for sheep/goat in Phase 4.2 is one focussed on 2–6 year old sheep/goats, with a small secondary peak in the 3–4 year range. An apparent preference for older sheep/goats in Phase 4.1 is based on a small number of mandibles and is therefore unreliable. As before, this implies a mixed sheep economy, where some sheep were slaughtered early for meat, whereas others were kept longer for wool, dairy products and breeding. This is very similar to the assemblages from the Northern and Eastern suburbs and the City Defences at Winchester (Serjeantson and Smith 2009, 230–1).

Most sheep were horned: three displayed tiny or rudimentary horn cores, and one sheep in a Phase 4 late Saxon context (NH11559) was hornless. This is consistent with the other Winchester assemblages, where a minority of the sheep were hornless (Bourdillon 2009; Coy 2009) and has been connected to an influence of imported continental hornless breeds in the Roman period, as both sexes in the native British sheep breeds were horned (Maltby 1994, 94). Male sheep/goats dominated the late Saxon assemblages. This may reflect a preference for wool husbandry, since wethers yield better quality wool than ewes and rams. The larger horn cores of rams would have been more suitable for horn working than the smaller, or non-existing, horn cores of ewes.

Evidence for skinning was found on a first phalanx, which had cut marks mid-shaft. Skulls were severed from the rest of the carcass at the axis, and in many cases horn cores were chopped off the skulls. Cut marks for disarticulation occurred on the elbow joint, hip joint and the tarsal joint. Disarticulation/portioning chop marks were found not only at the joints of long bones but also mid-shaft. Other evidence for portioning occurred on a scapula, which was chopped in two mid-blade. Filleting cut marks occurred on the mandible, axis, scapula, humerus, radius, pelvis, femur and tibia. Axial splitting of long bones, in order to extract marrow, only occurred on metapodials. Cut marks on the distal metapodials could either be from skinning or foot removal, possibly in order to boil hooves for glue or rendering them for oil (Serjeantson 1989, 141).

Pathological conditions were recorded on 40 bones, less than 4% of the late Saxon sheep/goat assemblage.

Pig

As for other sites of this period in Winchester, the pig dental age estimation shows a wide distribution of slaughter ages, ranging from juvenile to adult.

This is confirmed by the epiphyseal fusion data: high fecundity enables a quick turnover in livestock. There were no major differences in fusion between Phase 4.1 (n:67) and Phase 4.2 (n:219). A small number of neonatal pig bones were present, which suggests some local pig rearing, probably in backyards. The number of teeth from boars and sows are roughly equivalent, however, suggesting a pig husbandry that was not focussed on optimum meat yields.

Butchery marks indicate that pig carcasses were suspended: both atlas, skull, mandible and pelvis show signs of sagittal splitting. With the exception of the sagittal splits, butchery marks on pig are overwhelmingly carried out with knives rather than cleavers. Nevertheless, a few chop marks (most likely by cleavers) were noted on a distal humerus. Disarticulation by knives was recorded on atlas, distal humerus, proximal radius, proximal ulna and proximal metapodials. Filleting marks were evident to the mandible, scapula, ulna, pelvis, femur and metapodials. This indicates that in addition to the utilisation of the larger muscle masses of the body for meat, the flesh on head and feet were also eaten.

Pathologies were observed on four pig bones from Phase 4.2.

Other domestic mammals

Horse

Consistent with other sites in Winchester, with the exception of the western suburbs (Bourdillon 2009), all horse bones which could be aged belonged to full-grown adult horses. A paucity of young horse bones is typical for urban Saxon assemblages, suggesting that horse breeding would have occurred in the countryside rather than in the cities. Withers' heights of 1.28 m and 1.43 m respectively were calculated from a metacarpal and a metarsal from deposits in Phase 4.1.

Butchery marks occurred on three horse bones from Phase 4.2. Cut marks observed on the mid-shaft of a femur and a pelvis (ischium) are typical of filleting. A radius displayed chop marks on the distal half of the bone, suggesting disarticulation, or possibly rough filleting. While horse was not normally eaten in late Saxon England, horse flesh may have been fed to dogs, a practice which is known from post-medieval sources (Thomas and Locock 2000).

An unarticulated second and third phalanx from Phase 4.2 had ossified muscle attachments, so called enthesophytes, near the joint surfaces. This condition is connected to muscular stress (Roberts and Manchester 1999, 110) and may be related to the use of horses for traction or heavy load-carrying.

Dog

Semi-articulated remains from four dogs were recovered from Phase 4.2: one neck from Property BW 4, one skull from Property BW 5 and one articulated hind foot from Property BE 4, which displayed exostoses on metatarsal 4 and 5, probably connected to a healed mid-shaft fracture. Since they were found in different properties, it is unlikely that they come from the same dog. A further five disarticulated dog bones were also found in this phase.

Cat

There were fourteen disarticulated bones from both adult and sub-adult cats, all from Phase 4.2. Interestingly, one humerus has a cut mark anteriorly mid-shaft. This butchery pattern most likely indicates the utilisation of cat for meat. Cat meat was not considered part of the normal Saxon diet, but could be eaten during desperate times, such as long sieges or starvation periods. Another possibility is the use of cat meat for medicinal/magical purposes (Doll 2003, 267).

Wild mammals

The scarcity of wild mammals is consistent with other late Saxon sites in Britain (Sykes 2006b, 164).

Deer

Red deer and roe deer were identified in the assemblage, along with three unspeciated antler fragments and three limb bone fragments. Since fallow deer is unlikely to be present in the vicinity of late Saxon Winchester (see above), it is probable that the unidentified deer fragments are from red deer. The red deer remains consisted of antler and non-meat bearing lower leg bones. The roe deer remains consisted of a neck vertebra and two bones from the shoulder. Three antler fragments, one of red deer (Phase 4.2) and two of unidentified deer (Phase 4.1 and 4.2), were sawn off, which strongly suggests antler working. Until the late 18th century, sawing only occurred for bone working, not butchery (MacGregor 1985, 55).

Hare

The three hare bones were recovered from three different properties (BE 1, BE 5 and BW 4). All bones are long bones, which would suggest that they represent kitchen waste. Juvenile, sub-adult and adult hares were identified.

Mustelids

Mustelids (ie badger, otter, stoat, polecat, weasel, pine marten and stone marten) are generally rare in the archaeological record and when they occur it is usually in small numbers. Eva Fairnell's (2003) survey of fur animal bones on archaeological sites in Britain yielded 43 records for badger and 10 for pine marten. Despite mustelid fur having been utilised since the Palaeolithic, actual evidence for skinning is rare: in the survey only two badger and two pine marten bones show cut marks indicating skinning (ibid., 36–41).

A badger humerus in Property BE 4 displayed horizontal cut marks supradistally on the anterior and lateral sides, such as would be found after disarticulation of the elbow joint. Historically, badgers have occasionally been utilised for meat and fat

(Griffiths 1993, 341; Neal and Cheeseman 1996, 221). It has been estimated that in autumn, approximately 30% of the badger's body weight is fat (During 1986, 141). Archaeological examples of badger bones with cut marks indicating dismemberment include bones from a Roman fort and 17th century deposits at Carrick Castle (Harman 1993, 232; Thomas 1998, 987).

Comparison of a mustelid metatarsal from Property BE 5 with modern comparatives in both the Oxford Archaeology and the English Heritage reference collections established that the Winchester metatarsal is larger than a male Welsh ferret and a male polecat, but smaller than a male Scandinavian pine marten. As a result, it has been tentatively identified as a female pine marten. Deposits of mustelid metapodials and phalanges, combined with an absence of other skeletal elements, usually are considered an indication of fur processing (Fairnell 2003, 10-11).

Birds

Domestic fowl was the most common bird in both Phase 4.1 and 4.2, comprising over 90% of the identified avian remains. While most recovered bones were long bones, pelves and sterna, it is likely that entire carcasses were disposed of. Spurs occurred on three tarsometatarsals. Another tarsometatarsal displayed woven bone growth where the spur should have been, probably a reaction to the removal of a spur. Spur removal seem to have had two purposes: either for castration, or to facilitate tied-on metal spurs on fighting cocks (West 1982). Medullary bone was present in seven long bones, indicating egg-laying hens.

The fowl remains also contained two articulated adult skeletons (including one hen), both from pit CC2225, Phase 4.2. Cut marks were absent, which suggests they may have been diseased or died of natural causes and subsequently were judged unfit for consumption. Pathological conditions were recorded on 19 of their bones: full details are available in *Digital Section 11*.

Butchery marks on fowl bones consisted of knife cuts from filleting and disarticulation, and were mostly midshaft and at the joints of longbones. A goose radius and ulna displayed cut marks at the joints, associated with disarticulation. A cooked bird is rather easy to disarticulate without tools, which may explain the relative scarcity of butchery marks on bird bones in archaeological assemblages.

Mallard and teal were the only identified duck species. As domestic ducks were bred from mallards, some of these ducks may have been domestic, although Albarella argues that domestic ducks were very rare in England until the late medieval period (Albarella 2005, 255–6). Most parts of the duck skeleton are present, which suggests that they represent remains of meals. Butchering marks from disarticulation occurred on three bones.

The other birds include goose, woodcock and kittiwake as well as unidentified passerine. Seabirds have been eaten in historical times in communities around the North Sea (Serjeantson 1988), but kittiwake is an unusual find for an inland site. Birds from late Saxon contexts not phased to either Phase 4.1 and Phase 4.2 include teal (one carpometacarpus), lapwing (two coracoids), woodcock (two humeri, one ulna), unidentified wader (one humerus, two tarsometatarsi) and blackbird-sized passerine (one humerus, one tarsometatarsus).

The Anglo-Norman assemblage

The recorded Anglo-Norman assemblage comprises 25187 bone fragments, of which 6525 (25.9%) were determined to taxon (Table 8.1). Sheep/goat is the most common animal in the assemblage, regardless of method used (Table 8.5). Similar NISP proportions have been recorded for Winchester's western suburban assemblages (Coy 2009).

Meat providing domestic mammals
Cattle
In contrast to the late Saxon period, the tooth wear analysis of the Anglo-Norman cattle indicates almost no young animals. Regardless of the method used, the sex estimation shows a consistent predominance of female cattle. Taken together, this suggests that dairy products increased in importance in the Winchester region in this period, but there may also have been a greater focus on the use of animals for traction. Based on an analysis of 110 horncores, most belonged to 3–7 year old cattle. The slaughter pattern in the western suburbs is strongly focussed on adult or old adult cattle with a MWS of 41–45. The scarcity of younger animals is unsurprising: they would have had smaller horn cores which may have been considered less valuable as a raw material than the larger adult horn cores. It would therefore seem that there was a limited trade in surplus young adults, probably male, for meat, whereas most cattle brought into Winchester for slaughter were adult. These would have been fully grown cattle, which would have yielded milk and calves for a few years before they were fattened for the market. The draught and breeding animals were killed at a later age, when they were past their prime.

When compared to measurement data from other Anglo-Norman sites in Britain (ABMAP), the cattle bones from the site are at the upper end of the size range. The exception is the radius, although the small number of measured radii may bias the comparison.

Almost 13% of the cattle bones exhibited evidence of butchery. Fifty of these, mostly from Property SE 3, had butchery marks characteristic of horn working, where horn cores had been chopped off the skull and horn sheaths had been removed from the horn core. Skinning cut marks occurred on phalanges and around the base of horn cores. Chop marks and cut marks on atlas and axis indicate axial splitting of the carcass, head removal and filleting. Evidence of disarticulation were found at several

Table 8.5. Anglo-Norman assemblage, Phase 5: Anatomical distribution, including NISP, MNI and weight for all major mammals. Skeletal element used for MNI is marked with an asterisk

	Cattle	Sheep/goat	Sheep	Goat	Pig	Horse	Deer sp.	Red deer	Roe deer	Dog	Cat	Lago-morph	Hare	Fox	Small mustelid	Stoat	Ferret	Squirrel
Antler							3	2										
Horn core	285	135	364	86														
Skull	86	200	77		66	14				3	6							
Mandible	104	290	19	1	60	9				3	8	1						
Loose teeth	72	220	3		59	43				2	1							
Hyoid	5	11			2													
Atlas	21	30			4	3					3							
Axis	14	19			7	5				1	2							
Vertebrae						7					76							
Ribs		1									90							
Sternum											1							
Sacrum	4					4					2							
Scapula	52	90			42	5	1			1	10		1					
Humerus	74	95		1	51	2	1			1	19							
Radius	68	182			36	3			1	5*	12		1					3
Ulna	47	61			51	2				1	9		1					
Carpals	7	5			4						1							
Metacarpal	88	155	62	1	53	1		1	3*		43				3	3	6	18
Pelvis	90	133			43	7				1	12		1					1
Femur	60	58			30	8*				3	22							
Patella	5																	
Tibia	67	204			53*	2	2*	1	1	1	21		1					3
Fibula					23						15							
Calcaneus	38	18			13						3							2
Astragalus	27	12			2	1					2							2
Tarsals	10	10			3						3							
Metatarsal	94*	181*	66	2	49	4				1	53*		1			3	3	49*
Phalanx 1	49	64			18	3					29	1						100
Phalanx 2	13	31			18	1					20							75
Phalanx 3	21	12			14	3					17			7				
Indet. Phalanx		1																
Lateral metapodial					10	3												
Indet. metapodial	8	24	4		8						16							55
Sesamoid	10				1													
Indet. lateral phalanx		2			2													
Carpal/tarsal											2							
Long bone																		
Indeterminate																		
Total (NISP)	1419	2248	595	91	719	133	7	4	5	23	498	1	6	8	3	6	9	308
MNI	31	88			28	5	2	1	1	3	13	1	1			1	1	11
Weight (g)	69777	21820	23723	3173	9803	7792	526	291	99	119	391	4	14	<0	<0	<0	<0	<0

limb bone joints and on the mandible. Occasionally, disarticulation at the joints had been carried out by chopping. One femur had been chopped in two at mid-shaft, for portioning or to extract the marrow. Two humeri, three radii and ten metapodials had been split axially, presumably for marrow extraction. Fine cut marks, mostly related to filleting, were found on a number of bones including the mandible, hyoid, scapula, humerus and pelvis.

Several cattle bones displayed pathological conditions, the majority of which were connected to infections or joint disorders; some are linked to the use of cattle for traction.

Sheep/goat
Of the 2934 sheep/goat bones, 595 could be identified as sheep and 91 as goat. Most of the goat fragments were horn cores and were largely from deposits interpreted as horn/bone working waste dumps. A predominance of goat horn cores over post-cranial elements has been observed on many British and European sites and may to some extent

be caused by identification bias, since horn cores are very easy to speciate. It has been argued that the over-representation of goat horn cores could be due to goat skins being imported with the horn cores attached (see below). However, post-cranial goat remains are rarely found in large quantities, and the origin of these hypothetical skins remains unknown (Albarella 2003, 80–1).

The fusion data suggest that the sheep/goats were primarily slaughtered as sub-adults or adults. However, while only eight bones in the early fusing category were unfused, over 240 bones show surface porosity, indicating they were foetal or neonatal at the time of death. The foetal/neonatal bones are present at almost every Anglo-Norman property. However, over a third of those identified were associated with Property SE 3. This area was known as Snidelingsestret, or Snitherlingastret— The Tailor's street, in the Anglo-Saxon period (S Teague pers. comm.) and the property has been interpreted as a furrier's workshop (see discussion below). In addition to squirrel, lamb skin, so-called budge, may also have been prepared there. Almost half of the foetal/neonatal remains are metapodials, suggesting that they may have arrived at the property as part of uncured skins (cf Serjeantson 1989).

The mandibular age estimation shows that half of the Anglo-Norman caprines were slaughtered at 2–4 years of age; few very young mandibles were retrieved. This slaughter age pattern is consistent with that from the western suburbs and suggests that the local sheep husbandry had a mixed strategy, rearing sheep for meat, wool and dairy products. Sheep were slaughtered at a relatively young age for meat, and the young adults of 3–4 years of age would have yielded a few wool clips and offspring before being killed. The older animals represent sheep kept for wool and breeding purposes.

Males dominated according to the sex estimation based on pelvis morphology, although horn core evidence suggests females were more frequent among the goats, and males among the sheep. A large number (179) of sheep and goat horn cores, the majority from Property SE 3, had been removed from the skull by chopping; some horn cores also showed signs of horn sheath removal. These horn cores almost certainly relate to craft working, a topic discussed further below.

Apart from horn removal, thirteen skulls had been split sagitally in order to extract the brain, which would have been eaten. Sagittal splits also occurred on atlas and axis, showing that the carcass was suspended during the butchering process. A heavy cleaver severed the skull from the rest of the carcass. Further disarticulation by cleavers took place at the scapula, distal radius, proximal and distal femur and distal tibia. Several cut marks were observed at the neck, mandible, elbow, carpal and tarsal joints, suggesting that some disarticulation was carried out by knives. Evidence of

portioning was found on the pelvis (ilium) and mid-blade on the scapula. Filleting marks were recorded on scapula, radius, pelvis and tibia. Cut marks also occur on a skull and on several hyoids, suggesting removal of cheek meat as well as utilisation of the tongue. A small perforation on one scapula suggests the shoulder being hung for smoking or for ageing the meat. Several metapodials had been split longitudinally to extract the marrow. Skinning marks were found on at the metapodial joints.

The 46 sheep/goat bones that displayed pathological conditions only amounted to 1.6% of the total sheep/goat bones in the Anglo-Norman phase, suggesting that animals were generally well looked after. Congenital conditions were found primarily on the mandibles, 52 of which had an extra foramen on the buccal side, beneath the premolars.

Pig
Many pig long bones were unfused, indicating the slaughter of mostly juvenile and sub-adult animals. The mandibular age estimation displays a peak in the immature and sub-adult age groups, which equates to a preferred slaughter age of 0.5–1.5 years (Habermehl 1975, 147). Since the younger pigs are slaughtered before they were fully grown, pork production was suboptimal. A premature slaughter of young pigs could be a sign of limitations of space or fodder; it is likely that as in the late Saxon period, pigs were kept in the backyards. The piglet remains from the site are disarticulated and display no butchering marks, which makes any further interpretation difficult. Of the 26 pig mandibular canines that could be sexed, 69% were from boars.

Thirty pig bones were butchered. Paramedial and axial splitting occurred on two axis vertebrae, indicating suspension of the carcass during the butchery process. Chop marks derive mostly from portioning rather than from disarticulation. They occurred on the scapula, ulna, pelvis, femur and tibia. Knives were generally used for disarticulation: cut marks were recorded on the scapula, humerus, radius and calcaneus. Filleting cut marks were found on the atlas, scapula, humerus, pelvis, femur, tibia and metatarsal.

Nine bones exhibited pathological conditions, most of which were associated with inactive infections.

Other domestic mammals
Horse
The paucity of horse bones is expected for an intermural urban assemblage, since horses were not food animals. Judging by epiphyseal fusion and tooth wear, most horses were adult. Immature horse remains consisted of three deciduous molars and one ulna. The ulna was unfused proximally, indicating an age at death of less than 3.5 years. Horse remains in urban sites normally consists of adult or old adult horses (Rackham 1995, 173–4).

The few measurable horse bones from the site are all within the same size range as metacarpals from other Anglo-Norman sites in Britain. Withers' heights of 1.231 m and 1.372 m respectively were calculated from the metatarsal and the tibia. Butchery marks were absent, which is in line with the Church's prohibition of eating horse meat (Egardt 1962, 77–8). Horse bones with butchery marks of any kind are rare, but there are a few examples from medieval suburban Winchester, although most are associated with skinning or feet removal rather than butchering for food (Serjeantson and Smith 2009, 153).

The only pathological conditions on the horse bones are enthesophytes, indicating muscle strains (Roberts and Manchester 1999, 110). They were found on the dorsal/lateral edge of the ilium/ischium border on a pelvis and on the glenoid process on a scapula and, as for the pathologies exhibited by some of the cattle, suggest that the animals were used to pull or carry heavy loads.

Dog
The dog remains consist of one semi-articulated juvenile dog skeleton from Property BE 4 and ten disarticulated bones from a range of properties. With the exception of a neonatal radius from

Plate 8.1 Fractured dog femur (unhealed) with extensive bone growth at the fracture. Normal dog femur to the left. Anterior view

Property SE 1, all other dog bones were adult. Withers' heights could be calculated on two radii from dogs of small and medium size. Three of the disarticulated bones displayed pathologies. A pelvis had a healed fracture on the ischium and a radius had some exostoses at the distal joint surface. These may be due to muscle strains. A femur had an unhealed fracture on the supradistal part of the shaft, which had lead to an infection. The infection had subsequently caused large exostoses and smooth bone growth on the shaft (Plate 8.1).

Cat
An overwhelming majority of the 498 cat bones were retrieved from Property SE 1, mostly associated with the pits NH5169 and NH5175; ten semi-articulated individuals were recovered. With the exception of one neonatal kitten, all articulated cats were *c* 8.5–11.5 months of age at death. Similarly large quantities of articulated cat skeletons in this age group have been found at several Scandinavian sites (see below). Cut marks on mandibles, skulls and paws suggest that the Scandinavian cats were utilised for their fur. The cat remains in Property SE 1 include three bones with cut marks: typical skinning cut marks were observed on the frontal bone of a skull and on the horizontal ramus of a mandible from the same individual. A femur displayed a diagonal cut mark on the anterior side, just below the (unfused) trochanter major. This type of cut mark is associated with butchery, which is unusual to find on cat bones. Although cats were normally not eaten, medieval sources mention the use of cat meat and fat for medicinal purposes (Doll 2003, 267). Butchering marks on cat bones have been recorded from Haithabu, Germany (Johansson and Hüster 1987, 40–4).

Wild mammals

The wild mammals signify craft activity as well as dietary habits. As is common for the Anglo-Norman period, game is rare outside ecclesiastical and high-status sites (Sykes 2006b, 164) and would have contributed very little to the average person's diet.

Deer
Apart from three antler fragments, the deer remains include bones from meat-rich body parts, such as shoulder and shank, and meat-poor metapodials. It has been argued that metapodials may have been included in skins sold to tanners (Serjeantson 1989) or been sold as raw material to bone workers (MacGregor 1985, 30) but it could also be argued that the metapodials were included in the portion of venison that was sold by the butchers.

Hare
The hare remains primarily derive from meat-rich parts of the front and hind limbs, which suggests they were kitchen waste. A single phalanx from Property BE 3 may signify butchery waste or furrier's waste.

Fox, mustelids and squirrel

All but two of the fox, mustelid and squirrel bones derive from pit NH5169 in Property SE 1 (Table 8.6). Due to the large concentration of bones from the lower limbs and the absence of other skeletal elements from these taxa, the bones are believed to be waste from a furrier's workshop (see discussion below). Squirrel was the most numerous of the fur animal species. This is not surprising, as squirrel fur was highly popular, and very desirable, during the Anglo-Norman period.

The mustelid remains included stoat and polecat/ferret together with three metacarpals from small mustelids of stoat/ferret size. Ferret is the domesticated form of polecat, and was used in the Middle Ages for hunting rabbits, by releasing the ferrets into the warrens in order to flush the rabbits out and be netted. As polecat and ferret can only be

distinguished on the skull (Bond and O'Connor 1999, 362), speciation was not possible. The earliest written records of ferret in north-western Europe date to the early 13th century (Van Damme and Ervynck 1988, 281). Securely identified ferret bones are extremely rare archaeologically, most likely due to the limited ways of distinguish them from the native polecats (Van Damme and Ervynck 1988, 278–9).

Birds

Over 70% of the identified avian remains are domestic fowl and most parts of the skeleton are present. Unfused or fusing bones comprised 12% of the bones with fusion indicators present, indicating the killing of immature birds. Of the 36 tarso-metatarsi with the prerequisite zone intact, 11 had spurs, indicating males. On two of these, the spurs

Table 8.6. Phase 5 pit NH5169: Anatomical distribution of all fur bearing species and neonatal caprines, including NISP, MNI and weight

	Sheep/goat (juvenile)	Dog	Cat	Lagomorph	Hare	Fox	Small mustelid	Stoat	Ferret/ Polecat	Squirrel	Small mammal
Skull	5		4								
Mandible	5		8	1							
Atlas			2								
Axis			2								
Vertebrae			45								57
Ribs			69								44
Sternum			1								1
Scapula	3		7								
Humerus	2		12								
Radius	6		9		1					3	
Ulna	3		8		1						3
Carpals			1								
Metacarpal	10		39				3	3	6	18	5
Pelvis	2		5								
Femur	4		11								
Tibia	5		13							3	1
Fibula			12								
Calcaneus			3							2	1
Astragalus			2							2	
Tarsals			3								
Metatarsal	12*	1	47*					3	2	49*	
Phalanx 1			27							100	64
Phalanx 2			20							75	38
Phalanx 3			17			7					73
Indet. metapodial	1		16							55	23
Carpal/tarsal			2								7
Long bone											3
Indeterminate											3
Total (NISP)	58	1	393	1	2	7	3	6	8	307	323
MNI	5	1	12		1	1		1	1	11	
Weight (g)	204	< 0	240	4	2	< 0	< 0	< 0	< 0	1	18

* - where samples contained many tiny dermal denticles, teeth or scales these items have been scored as 0 or (if no other remains) 1 per sample. Only a proportion of the fine residues were sorted.

Nfi - not further identified to genus or species

were sawn off or broken off, which suggests castration or cock-fighting (see above). Medullary bone, indicating egg-laying hens, occurred on seven long bones. Butchery marks are somewhat rare, occurring on 24 fowl bones. The most common form of butchery was disarticulation of tibiotarsus and tarsometatarsus. Other butchery marks consist of cut marks associated with filleting and disjointing, which were found on femora, coracoids and a scapula. Pathological conditions were found on four fowl bones.

Two duck species could be identified: mallard or domestic duck and teal. Domestic duck is on average larger than mallard (Woelfle 1967, 81) and as one humerus was particularly large it is probably from a domestic bird. Many of the duck bones were from the wing. It has been argued that a disproportionate amount of wing bones may be a natural phenomenon, due to decomposition factors, rather than human intervention (Bovy 2002). However, in this case three humeri and two ulnae display cut marks associated with disarticulation. One of the humeri also displayed cut marks on its shaft from filleting.

Most goose bones were from either greylags or domestic geese, although one carpometacarpus could be identified as the smaller Brent goose. Only one immature bone was found, which is in contrast to the fowl. This difference may relate to fowl being raised within the town, and geese outside, being driven into the town for slaughter. According to medieval sources, geese were slaughtered in May at 12–16 weeks as 'green geese' and in late autumn as 'stubble geese' (Serjeantson 2002, 42). These two groups can be difficult to detect in the archaeological material, since geese are skeletally mature at 16 weeks (ibid., 45–6). Eleven goose bones had been butchered; most cuts were from filleting and disarticulation. There was also evidence for portioning on the sternum and synsacrum.

The pigeons may have been wild or domestic. While doves were kept in continental Europe during the Roman period, it is thought that domestic dove keeping was introduced by the Normans (Hansell and Hansell 1988, 59). However, the absence of juvenile remains suggests that dovecotes were absent (Serjeantson 2006, 141). This in itself is no indication that the bones are from wild pigeon, since domestic birds kept elsewhere may also have been eaten.

A relatively large variety of wild birds were present. It is assumed that most remains are from kitchen waste. Snipe and woodcock were the only identified waders. Waders occur fairly frequently in Anglo-Norman assemblages, but only constituted a small part of the diet. Grey partridge is less common in urban sites than waders, such as woodcock. Grey partridge is associated with the elite diet, through falconry and game parks (Sykes 2004, 96–7). Its presence in Property BW 3 opens up the suggestion of higher status inhabitants, or the sale of poached birds on the urban markets. Crane is a relatively commonly occurring bird in Anglo-Norman sites, and would only become a high-status food in the later medieval period. It is present in small numbers on most sites of this date (Sykes 2004, 98).

The opportunistic and scavenging corvids are common on urban sites. Jackdaw and crow/rook are the only corvids present. While young rooks are commonly eaten, their scavenging nature makes mature corvids less appetising. Intriguingly, the jackdaw bones in pit NH5175 consist of four complete tarsometatarsi: three right and one left. A single buzzard humerus may represent utilisation of wing feathers, or merely the remains of a deliberate killing in order to protect the domestic chicken flocks.

Both medium-sized passerines (blackbird size) and small passerines (house sparrow size) are present. Passerines were common food birds in medieval and post-medieval England (Serjeantson 2001; Serjeantson 2006, 142), and despite the lack of cut marks on the bones, it would seem likely that they were eaten.

The medieval assemblage

A total of 5630 bone fragments were recorded, of which 918 (16.3%) were identified to taxon (Tables 8.1 and 8.7). The trend of sheep/goat numerical predominance, seen in the previous phases, continues in the medieval period. This is consistent with the suburban Winchester assemblages (Serjeantson and Smith 2009, 126) but is in contrast to Southampton, where the French Quarter assemblage shows a reversed pattern for cattle and sheep/goat when compared to Winchester (Bates forthcoming). The different species ratio between Winchester and Southampton probably reflects the surrounding landscape; Southampton is closer to the sea, and its nearby wetlands would thus be more suitable for cattle grazing.

The meat providing domestic mammals
Cattle
Very few cattle bones could be aged or sexed. The three ageable mandibles had teeth wear patterns indicative of adult and senile cattle, which was consistent with the age ranges derived from horn cores. Although based on a relatively small data set, the slaughter age pattern for the northern and eastern suburban sites shows that adult cattle were primarily butchered. Among the horn cores from the suburban sites, 3–7 year old cattle were slightly more common than those of 7–10 years (Serjeantson and Smith 2009). The relatively advanced age of cattle suggests that they continued to be important for dairy or traction purposes, rather than reared just for meat.

Butchery marks were present on 24 bones. Four horn cores had cut marks or chop marks at their bases, indicating removal of horn sheath for horn working. One skull had its snout chopped off, but

Table 8.7 Medieval assemblage, Phase 6: Anatomical distribution, including NISP, MNI and weight for all major mammals. Skeletal element used for MNI is marked with an asterisk

	Cattle	Sheep/goat	Sheep	Goat	Pig	Horse	Deer sp.	Dog	Cat	Hare	Squirrel
Antler											
Horn core	10	5	16	5							
Skull	12	20	8	1	18	1					
Mandible	14	50	3		13				1		
Loose teeth	21	27	2		19	1		1			
Hyoid	1	4									
Atlas	5	1			3						
Axis	2	3			1						
Vertebrae											
Ribs											
Sternum											
Sacrum	1										
Scapula	18*	14			10			1	1		
Humerus	8	21			9*			1		2	
Radius	18	36			7	1				3	
Ulna	8	14			9					1	
Carpals	3	3									
Metacarpal	11	29	8		11	1					
Carpometacarpus											
Pelvis	13	24			11				1		
Femur	12	11			5	1			3*		
Patella											
Tibia	9	50*			12				1		
Fibula					1						
Calcaneus	11	7									
Astragalus	6	5			2					1	
Tarsals					1						
Metatarsal	20	25	8		10		2				1
Phalanx 1	14	2			4					1	
Phalanx 2	3	2			2						
Phalanx 3	3	2			3					1	
Indet. Phalanx											
Lateral metapodial					1						
Indet. metapodial		3			3						
Sesamoid											
Carpal/tarsal											
Long bone											
Indeterminate											
Total (NISP)	223	358	45	6	155	6	2	3	7	9	1
MNI	10	20			6	1		1	2	1	1
Weight (g)	9849	3937	1256	129	2364	791	104	27	17	15	< 0

otherwise the skulls and mandibles displayed no butchering marks. Two atlas vertebrae showed signs of sagittal splitting as well as disarticulation from the skull. Sagittal splitting of the axial skeleton is generally considered a sign of suspension of the carcass during the butchery process (O'Connor 1982, 16). Knives were used for most of the disarticulation. Cut marks were observed on calcaneus, distal humerus, proximal radius and proximal metapodials. Evidence of portioning of the carcass was only found on three scapulae, which had been split through the glenoid surface. One metatarsal had been split longitudinally, most likely in order to

extract the marrow. Pathological conditions occurred on six cattle bones.

Sheep/goat
Of the 409 sheep/goat bones, 45 were identified as sheep and six to goat. The goat fragments are all horn cores, three of which display butchering marks indicating horn working, so most of the sheep/goat bones are probably from sheep.

The mandibular tooth wear data show three peaks for age at death: at 2–6 months, at 2–3 years and then at 4–6 years, although the number of ageable mandibles is low: the three peaks only comprise 7, 7 and 5 mandibles each. The sheep assemblage from the northern and eastern suburbs show a single peak of 4–6 year old sheep which is in line with the focus on wool production that took place during the middle ages. However, the Northgate House/Discovery Centre assemblage is by no means unique in displaying a wide range of slaughter ages: on a countrywide basis, most sheep in both rural and urban settlements were slaughtered at a range of ages between 1 and 6 years, representing animals killed when they had just reached full size, presumably for meat, with others retained until they had produced a few clips of wool, lambs and possibly also milk.

When viewing the assemblage as a whole, male sheep/goats dominated. While the pelves showed similar proportions of males and females, the horn cores were mostly from male animals. This discrepancy between the two sexing methods is probably due to the presence of hornless ewes. Interestingly, there are no horned ewes depicted in medieval English manuscript illuminations (Armitage and Goodall 1977).

Butchery marks occurred on 38 sheep/goat bones. Chopped off sheep and goat horn cores, probably for use in horn working, were recovered from four different properties (BE 2, BE 4, BW 2 and BW 5) but the bone assemblage provides no evidence for large-scale horn working in this period. Cut marks indicative of skinning were only found on a sheep/goat first phalanx, while cut marks on the proximal ends of two metapodials may have resulted from either skinning or disarticulation. One sheep/goat axis and 15 vertebrae from medium mammals (probably sheep/goat) had been split axially, which is considered typical of the practice of suspending the carcass while butchering. Paramedial and sagittal splitting occurred in almost equal numbers. Disarticulation of limb bones took place at the joints of long bones and mandibles, by using heavy cleavers. Cut marks at joints, suggesting disarticulation using knives, were observed on mandible, calcaneus, distal humerus, proximal radius and proximal metapodials. Filleting cut marks were found on the hyoid, radius and tibia. An ilium being severed from the rest of the pelvis was the only indication of portioning in the assemblage. Two metapodials and one radius had been split longitudinally in order to extract marrow.

Pathological conditions were observed only on horn cores and metapodials. Twelve sheep/goat mandibles displayed an extra foramen on the buccal side of the horizontal ramus. This non-metric trait has been used to distinguish sheep and goats (Halstead and Collins 2002, 548–9).

Pig
Only a few pig bones could be aged and the results are is consistent with previous periods at the site: most pigs are immature or sub-adult at death and few bones belong to pigs older than 3.5 years. All

mandibular canines recovered were male, although, considering the small number of sexable teeth at the site this result must be viewed with caution.

Butchery marks on pig bones primarily consisted of disarticulating cut marks which occurred on three distal humeri and on the neck region of two skulls; one metatarsal had been disarticulated by chopping through the proximal joint. Cut marks on a scapula neck suggest filleting or disarticulation while a pelvis, a mandible and a skull had been chopped through, the latter suggesting extraction of the brain.

Other domestic mammals
Horse
Only five horse bones were retrieved from the medieval phase. Judging by the surface structure, all were adult. One skull had a canine, suggesting it was male. This is, however, not a secure sex determination, as mares with canines occur occasionally (Habermehl 1975, 54; Pieper *et al.* 1995, 135). Due to fragmentation, no bones could be measured. Butchering marks and pathologies were absent. The anterior part of a metacarpal was flattened and smooth, suggesting it was used as a skate (see below and Cool, Chapter 7)

Dog
Only three adult dog bones were recovered. A withers' height of 0.35 m was calculated from measurement of one humerus.

Cat
A small number of cat bones were found in four different properties. Juvenile, sub-adult and adult cats were present and none of the bones displayed cut marks.

Wild mammals
Deer, hare and squirrel were identified. The deer remains comprised two metatarsals from either red or fallow deer which may have been transported to the site as part of a deer hide, although venison may have been eaten. The hare bones were from the front limb and the paws. A single squirrel metatarsal in Property BE 4 may indicate that a small amount of furrier activity took place at the site; this property also contained a few cattle and sheep/goat horn cores. It is not clear whether this indicates a diversification of the craft activity at the property, or whether the squirrel bone is an accidental inclusion. The guild structure was rather strict in the Middle Ages, specifically in terms of who was allowed to carry out which tasks within a craft (Shaw 1996, 116–7).

Birds
Domestic fowl is by far the most frequent bird, followed by goose; this pattern is common in medieval bone assemblages (Serjeantson 2006, 134). No wild geese were positively identified and all the goose remains were from adults. Geese moult twice

a year, and feathers and down can then be collected. There is documentary evidence of plumers, that is people who dealt in feathers, from 15th century Winchester (Serjeantson and Smith 2009). They would have provided, among others, the large monastic community with feathers for quills and down for bedding. Three bones bear butchering marks indicating disarticulation and portioning of long bones.

Almost one fifth of the fowl remains were from juveniles, which is consistent with other contemporary Winchester sites (Serjeantson and Smith 2009) and suggests eggs were more important than meat. Butchering marks were found on three fowl bones: a coracoid, humerus and tibiotarsus, indicating portioning, filleting and disarticulation respectively.

Duck, pigeon, woodcock and snipe are represented by small numbers of bones. The duck bones are all in the mallard/domestic duck size range. The small number of duck bones is consistent with other medieval Winchester sites (Serjeantson and Smith 2009). Skeletal abnormalities suggesting infection or possibly muscle strains, were present on a tarsometatarsus, which displayed bone growths, or exostoses, on the mid-shaft as well as on the 'shaft' of the trochlea for the second metatarsal. The single adult pigeon bone in the assemblage may have been either from a wild or a domestic bird.

Worked bone and other crafts using animal remains

Four properties (BE 3, BE 4, SE 1, SE 3) from Phase 5 contained waste indicative of bone and horn workshops. Small quantities of worked bone and antler have been found all over the excavation area, in contexts dating to the Roman period and onwards. Previous excavations in Winchester have also revealed a scattered background of bone and antler work waste on almost all sites and phases. This is consistent with many contemporary sites in north-western Europe. Bone, antler and horn working do not require large structural investments and can therefore take place anywhere, in contrast to tanners, whose work requires long term planning and access to water. The larger deposits of bone and horn work waste, such as found in Properties BE 3, SE 1 and SE 3, are fairly straightforward to interpret. But what of the scattered work waste that is found in small numbers around the city? Even assuming the same level of taphonomic loss that has affected the non-worked bones, there are too few waste fragments to account for the craft being full-time occupation (Mainman and Rogers 2000, 2535–6).

Ailsa Mainman argues that the making of non-complicated products may have been sporadic activities, carried out on a household production level (Mainman 1999, 1872). An alternative view has been put forward by Kristina Ambrosiani and Axel Christophersen, who argue that comb making (and other crafts) was carried out by itinerant craftsmen (Ambrosiani 1982; Christophersen 1980, 217). In the

second half of the 11th century, specialist areas became more common in urban centres (Henry 2005), and *Tannerestret* (Tanner's Street) and *Flescmangerstret* (Butcher's Street) are known from the 10th century in Winchester (Biddle and Keene 1990, 245; Hagen 2002, 15 (in Sykes 2006a, 69)). The archaeological finds indicate that bone, antler and horn craftsmen did not restrict their location until later.

The larger work waste deposits that are occasionally found would probably have originated from specialised production. Depending on the finished products, this would fall into 'attached specialist production' or 'workshop production for trade'. These categories, coined by Eva Andersson (2003, 47) identify four different levels of production which should be viewed as a general trend, rather than absolute stages. Two or more categories may have existed side by side on the same street, or indeed, in the same property. The extensive urban nature of Winchester makes it highly likely that attached specialist production occurred within its walls. With the exception of squirrel (see above, Anglo-Norman period), none of the bone or antler finds show signs of high status production.

Horn working

Horn cores from cattle, sheep and goat, many of them bearing evidence of having been chopped from the skull, occurred in Property BE 3 (pit CC1268), Property BE 4 (pits CC2035, CC2043) and Property SE 3 (pit NH1598), all dating to the Anglo-Norman phase. Curiously, the very old cattle that are rather common in the whole Anglo-Norman assemblage are almost entirely absent from these deposits. Instead the cattle horn cores are mainly from 3–7 year old cattle and, in fewer numbers, from 2–3 year old cattle. All horn cores in the above-mentioned pits were short horned according to Armitage's and Clutton-Brock's (1976, 331) definition. The horn cores in the entire Anglo-Norman assemblage follow this trend, with almost 90% being short horned (n:19). One small horned and one long horned animal were also identified.

Sixteenth century artworks indicate that hides were delivered to the tanning yards with the horns and feet intact. The tanners removed feet and horns, which they would sell on to other craftsmen: one crafts' waste being another craft's raw material (Serjeantson 1989, 136–8). Sometimes large deposits of horn cores and foot bones are found in excavated tanning yards, and it has been suggested that these were disposed of because decomposition had progressed too far, and/or because no sale could be made (O'Connor pers. comm.). In Winchester, the tanners' yards were situated on what was then *Tannerestret*, and is now Lower Brook Street, in the low-lying eastern part of the town. The horn core deposits in Properties BE 3 and SE 3 are therefore more likely to indicate horn workers' yards than tanning yards.

In order to remove the horn sheath from the horn core, the horn must either be soaked or laid in the open for the soft tissues to decompose to such an extent that the horn sheath can be twisted loose (Albarella 2003, 74). The horn sheath was then heated, cut open and pressed flat. This procedure yields a flat sheet of horn, which can then be used to make objects such as lantern panes and combs (MacGregor 1985, 66–7). Slightly over half of the horn cores in Properties BE 3, BE 4 and SE 3 displayed butchering marks. The relative scarcity of marks mid-horn core and at the tip indicates that most horn sheaths were removed entirely from the horn core. Albarella (2003, 74) posits that tips were sawn or chopped off in order to facilitate the removal of the horn sheath or to use the solid tip as a raw material.

Bone and antler working

Pit NH1598 in Property SE 3 contained 589 fragments of large mammal ribs, in various stages of production. The ribs had been sawn off transversally and split down the mid-line. In many cases the inner bone surface had been smoothed and some pieces had holes for rivets drilled in the midline of the fragments. None were decorated. Such fragments were used as mounts, for example on caskets, but also as strengthening plates for double sided horn combs (MacGregor 1985, 95). Similar work waste fragments are known from several sites in north-western Europe, such as 13th–14th century Winchester western suburbs, 10th–11th century York and 11th–14th century Schleswig (Rees *et al.* 2008, 361; MacGregor *et al.* 1999, 1952–9; Ulbricht 1984, 37–8). The presence of plain fragments suggests some utilitarian purpose, possibly industrial (MacGregor *et al.* 1999, 1952).

Occasional bone and antler working took place in all phases and at most properties. The Roman finds included two fragments of chopped off antler pieces and one half-finished mount made of a large mammal rib. Mount production continued in the late Saxon phase, where 11 half-finished rib fragments were found in Property SE 3, six in Property BW 2 and one each in Properties SE 2, BE 4 and BW 5. There was no evidence for mount production in the Anglo-Norman phase. Half-finished bone objects include two spindle whorls made from cattle femoral heads (Properties BE 4, BW 4; late Saxon) and a skate made from a horse metacarpal (Property SE 1; medieval). Three Anglo-Norman sheep metapodials had holes drilled into the proximal joint surface. This procedure can be used for marrow extraction, but since it was more common to split the bones open in order to extract marrow, it is more likely that the metapodials are crude implement handles. Late Saxon and Anglo-Norman antler working took place in Properties SE 2, BW 4, BW 6 and BE 4. Most antler fragments comprised tines and offcuts of the main branch. Two antlers from the Anglo-Norman phase were shed. There is no evidence for antlers being removed from deer carcasses, although the considerable fragmentation of the antler makes it difficult to be certain.

Furrier

Pit NH5169 in Property SE 1 contained the most interesting evidence for craft activity: 745 bones of cat, fox, squirrel, ferret/polecat, stoat and unidentified small mammals were recovered (Table 8.6) The remains of fox, squirrel, polecat/ferret and stoat are exclusively from the feet and the lower legs, whereas most elements of the cat skeleton are represented. While cut marks were only observed on two individual cats, the composition of the assemblage suggests craft waste from furriers.

Furs from squirrels and mustelids formed a very extensive trade in early medieval Europe. Squirrel in particular was a high-status fur, which would have been appropriate for garments for many of Winchester's inhabitants, bearing in mind that Winchester was the capital of Wessex at the time. The grey winter fur of the European red squirrel was considered very attractive, and a large-scale long-distance trade in squirrel pelts took place from Scandinavia and Russia to Western Europe (Veale 2003, 63–5). The foot bones were often left on the fur, and were later removed by furriers at their final destination. Similar deposits of foot bones are known from the Bedern site in York (14th century), St Denis, France (12th century) and Birka, Sweden (8th–10th century) (Bond and O'Connor 1999, 365–6; L'Unité d'archéologie 2008; Wigh 2001, 121–3).

Over 95% of this deposit came from sieved samples; another indication of the importance of sieving, as well as a possible explanation of the rarity of these finds, despite the extensiveness of the medieval fur trade (cf. Veale 2003).

In contrast to squirrel, fox and mustelids, the cat remains comprised semi-articulated skeletons. While these may represent natural deaths or disposal of unwanted animals, their presence in deposits full of animal bones used for fur suggests otherwise. Deposits of large number of articulated and semi-articulated cat skeletons interpreted as remains of furrier activity have been found in Cambridge (Luff and Moreno 1995) and in several 9th–11th century Scandinavian sites, such as Birka, Odense, Lund, Viborg and Lödöse (Wigh 2001; Hatting 1990; Magnell 2006; Enghoff 2007; Vretemark 2000). In all these cases, including Winchester, the majority of the cat bones were unfused or fusing, suggesting juvenile and sub-adult animals. This is not a natural mortality curve, but has been interpreted as the deliberate slaughter of almost fully grown cats, in order to utilise their fur. This is further emphasised by the presence of cutmarks from skinning on skulls and mandibles.

Tawying, furrying or parchment making?

Pit NH5169 also contained bones from neonatal lambs/kids. Due to the lack of cut marks it is difficult to tell whether they represent the remains of meals or tawying waste. There is a slight over-representation of metapodials, which is usually seen as an indication of leatherworking waste (Serjeantson 1989). Furriers and tawyers were separate professions according to medieval guild structures. However, evidence of blurred lines between the various crafts preparing skins and hides are known from other sites, such as Northampton, where the guild structure was weak (Shaw 1996, 116–7). Since the guild system was less developed in the Anglo-Norman period, it is plausible that workshops could carry out several adjacent crafts.

A similar combination of sub-adult cat bones and neonatal/juvenile lamb bones were found in 14th century Cambridge (Luff 1996, 120) and in 11th–12th century Lund, Sweden (Magnell 2006, 24–9), possibly signifying a specialisation of furrier work. Cat and lamb skins were considered low status furs in medieval England, suitable for nuns, monks, craftsmen, servants and farmers (Newton 1980, 66–8; Veale 2003, 5). Despite the high status nature of Winchester in the Anglo-Norman period, there would have been plenty of inhabitants whose purse stretched more towards cat and lamb pelts.

Another, less likely, possibility is that the lamb remains are waste from small scale parchment production. The monasteries and court officials would have required large amounts of parchment, so there clearly was a local demand for it. To make parchment, the hides of young lambs, kids and calves were de-haired, and placed in a lime solution for a few days. They were then shaved thin, rubbed with pumice and dried on a stretch-frame (Reed 1975, 74). In order to avoid cuts in the skin, small pebbles were put at the edges of the skin and the thongs were tied around them, and elaborate structures were not needed for this process. The skins are small, and a medium-sized barrel might be enough for soaking. On the other hand, the absence of pumice stones and pebbles argues against parchment production taking place at Property SE 1 (Shaffrey pers. comm.), although pumice and pebbles may not have been recognised as significant finds during excavation.

FISH REMAINS *by Rebecca Nicholson*

This report summarises the analysis of over 10,000 fish bones identified to taxon. All tables and a fuller methodology and discussion are available in the accompanying digital report (*Digital Section 12*), and the raw data can be found in archive.

The assemblage

From over 10,000 identified bones, only 67 were retrieved by hand, a stark indication of the problems encountered when comparing bones from sites where different collection methods were used. Unsurprisingly, at Northgate House and the Discovery Centre the volumes of processed soil varied significantly between the different periods of activity, reflecting in part changes in density of occupation over time. Changes in the abundance of fish remains reflect to some degree these variations in the volumes of sieved soil (further details in *Digital Section 12*), but the overall trend is for the concentration of fish remains to increase over time. Phase 4.2 stands out as having a greater concentration of identified fish bones per litre of soil than Phase 5, but this may be due to the excellent preservation of organic materials within some of the late Saxon cess pits. The increase in fish bone concentration between Phases 4.1 and 4.2 may, however, be real since pits with mineralised fills were present throughout Phase 4. Taken together with the increasing complexity in social organisation manifest in developing towns, it is clear that while broadly speaking the late Saxon material may reflect the fish generally available to the local population, the deposits from later periods are more likely to reflect social demographics.

Using any means of quantification has inevitable limitations, and in this report only numbers of identified specimens (NISP) have been tabulated (Tables 8.8 and 8.9).

Of the few bones recovered by hand collection on site, most were, unsurprisingly, from large fish including cod, flatfishes (especially large plaice) and conger eel, the last often from fish of >1 m long. Occasional bones from bass, sea bream(s), gurnard, scad and eel were also collected, but the most significant find was a very large sturgeon scute from NH5185.

Iron Age and Roman deposits

A very small number of fish bones were recovered from these phases, perhaps not surprising given the types of deposits encountered. Those Phase 1 deposits which produced fish remains (only eleven bones, from herring, eel and flatfish) included posthole fills, subsoil layers and gully fills, none of which are promising repositories for general rubbish, and the possibility that these bones are intrusive can not be ruled out. Fish remains were found in pit fills from Phase 2, but were also found in trample layers and dumps. The fish represented most frequently, albeit by small numbers of bones, were eel and herring. Small flatfishes, mainly or exclusively from the plaice/flounder dab family Pleuronectidae, were also represented in a number of samples. Sea bream, including black sea bream, was identified in Phases 2.2 and 2.3, while salmonids were present in three Roman samples and one sample from late Roman Phase 2.4 (Dark Earth). Three of these bones were vertebrae from large fish, probably salmon while the fourth, a single tiny vertebra from context NH1739, was

Table 8.8. Numbers of identified fish remains recovered from bulk-sieved samples, by phase.

Species	1	1.1	1.2	1.3	2.1	2.2	2.3	2.4	4	4.1	4.2	5	6	Total
Elasmobranchii (elasmobranchs)									3	1	4	29	6	43
Rajidae (rays)										1	10	7	1	19
Raja clavata (thornback)									8	3	8	22	17	58
Conger conger (conger)											1	15	21	37
Anguilla anguilla (eel)		1			7		5	19	202	36	1063	230	267	1830
Clupeidae (herring family)							2	5	79	150	76	355	297	964
Clupea harengus (herring)			4	5	3		4	3	348	64	2251	2473	770	5925
Sardina pilchardus (pilchard)												3		3
Salmonidae (salmon family)				1				1	2		4	3	8	19
Salmo salar (salmon)				1	1									2
Salmo trutta (trout)									2	4	4	3	6	19
cf. Salmo trutta											2			2
cf. Osmerus eperlanus (smelt)													3	3
Esox lucius (pike)									4				3	7
Cyprinidae (carp family)									1		8	14	2	25
cf. Cyprinidae													1	1
Leuciscus leuciscus (dace)										1	5	2		8
Leuciscus/Gobio (dace/chub/gudgeon)											1			1
Rutilus rutilus (roach)													1	1
Gobio gobio (gudgeon)											2			2
Gadidae (cod family)									13		21	35	244	313
Gadus morhua (cod)											21	11	30	62
Pollachius pollachius (pollack)												1	9	10
Gadus/Merlangius (cod/whiting)											17		36	53
Merlangius merlangus (whiting)											12	12	200	224
Melanogrammus aeglefinus (haddock)												1	19	20
Molva molva (ling)												1		1
Merluccius merluccius (hake)												1		1
Trisopterus sp. (bib/poor cod/pout)												1		1
Belone belone (garfish)											1	18	48	67
Antherina presbyter (sand smelt)									1					1
Gasterosteus aculeatus (3-spined stickleback)									1	4	7			12
Triglidae (gurnard family)												1	9	10
Trigla lucerna (tub gurnard									1				6	7
Cottidae (cottid family)									3		3	4		10
Dicentrarchus labrax (sea bass)											2	1	6	9
Perca fluviatilis (perch)													1	1
Trachurus trachurus (scad)											4	5		9
cf. Trachurus trachurus											1			1
Sparidae (sea breams)					1				1		1	6	19	28
cf. Sparidae										1			1	2
Sparus sp. (gilthead/Couch's bream)													2	2
Pagellus boragaveo (red sea bream)													3	3
Spondyliosoma cantharus (black sea bream)							1							1 2
Mugilidae (grey mullet)												1	1	2
cf. Mugilidae									1					1
Liza sp. (thin-lipped/golden grey mullet)										1				1 2
Scombridae (mackerels)									1		8	3	2	14
cf. Scombridae									2					2
Scomber scombrus (mackerel)									3	8	66	23	26	126
Flatfishes nfi			1		1		1		6	7	33	54	18	121
Scophthalmidae (turbot/brill/megim)												3	1	4
cf. Scophthalmidae												3		3
Pleuronectidae (right-eyed flatfishes)					7			2	20	17	76	149	51	322
Pleuronectes platessa (plaice)									39	1	18	31	5	94
Platychthys flesus (flounder)											2	2		4
Limanda limanda (dab)					2						2			4
Limanda/Platychthys (dab/flounder)											1	1		2
Glyptocephalus cynoglossus (witch sole)									1					1
Hippoglossus hippoglossus (halibut)											1	2		3
Solidae (soles)									2		1		6	9
Solea solea (dover sole)												5	8	13
Unidentified	5		2	8	26	1	3	4	148	299	956	1269	6841	9562
Grand Total	5	1	7	13	48	2	17	34	893	597	4693	4800	8997	20107

Table 8.9. Numbers of hand collected fish bones, by phase

Species	1.3	2.3	2.4	4	4.1	4.2	5	6	Total
Accipenser sturio (sturgeon)							1		1
Raja clavata (thornback)					1				1
Anguilla anguilla (eel)							1		1
Conger conger (conger)						4	7	4	15
Gadidae (cod family)							5	2	7
Gadus morhua (cod)						1	4	4	9
Belone belone (garfish)							2		2
Triglidae (gurnards)							1		1
Dicentrarchus labrax (sea bass)							1		1
Trachurus trachurus (scad)							1		1
Sparidae (sea breams)							1		1
Scomber scombrus (mackerel)							1		1
Flatfish						1	4		5
Pleuronectidae (right-eyed flatfish)				3		2	10		15
Pleuronectes platessa (plaice)				1		2	3		6
Unidentified	1	8	1	3		10	41	7	71
Grand Total	1	8	1	7	1	20	83	17	138

probably from brown trout. While salmon, trout and eels may have come from local rivers and streams, and flounders can be found in fresh water as far up the Itchen as Winchester, the herrings and sea bream, and probably also the flatfish, must have been imported, possibly pickled, smoked or salted at least in the case of herrings, which deteriorate rapidly once caught. Cess pit sample NH554 in Phase 2.4 mainly produced bones from eel (including elver) but also included an anal ptery-giophore from a small flatfish.

Late Saxon, 850–1050

Deposits from Phase 4 produced over 4800 identified bones, almost all from cess pit fills, pit fills and occupation deposits most of which were dated to the later part of this period (Phase 4.2).

Herring, followed by eel, were the most frequent fish most commonly represented both by numbers of bones and the proportion of samples containing these taxa. Herring represent around 60% and eel around 30% of the recorded assemblage in Phase 4.2. Some of these bones were concreted in cess and some were corroded and deformed in a manner consistent with chewing and passage through the gut (Jones 1986; Nicholson 1993). Considerable numbers of bones from tiny, juvenile fishes were intact, which given the aggressive nature of digestive juices indicates that these were not from cess. It would seem likely that the cess pits also incorporated some spoilt or undersized fish or possibly guts from larger fish. Smaller flatfishes (particularly plaice) mackerel and thornback ray were also relatively common, but their remains were never nearly as numerous as those from herring and eel. Gadids were rare, and generally small: cod, whiting and hake were all identified. The larger bones must have been

discarded together with other general kitchen waste.

Other fish represented included garfish, scad, sea bream(s), tub gurnard, bass, grey mullet, conger eel, small cottid(s), salmonids including trout and probably salmon, pike, cyprinids including dace and gudgeon, and even 3-spined stickleback. A single vertebra was identified as sand smelt. All of the freshwater fishes were small individuals. Where eel cleithra were measureable, all came from fish of less than 400 mm, and usually between 250 and 350 mm long. Although pike can grow to over 1 m the individuals represented here were only around 300 mm or less. The cyprinids were even smaller—most were under 150 mm while the majority of the salmonid bones were from small brown trout.

Anglo-Norman, 1050–1225

Fish remains from the Anglo-Norman period in Properties BE 3–5 and BW 1–6 largely came from pit fills, but within this category pits positively identified as cess pits were rare. The assemblage was dominated by clupeids, notably herring (80% of the recorded assemblage). Eel was much less frequently recorded than in samples dating to the preceding centuries (6.5%). Gadids continued to be relatively rare and generally small, with bones from cod, whiting, haddock and hake identified. Flatfishes, particularly plaice/flounder/dab were particularly common in this period, overtaking eel by numbers of identified bones. Elasmobranchs, including rays, were again represented in many samples. Taxa represented by one or several bones were extremely similar to those identified in Phase 4 deposits.

Almost all of the identified bones from Property SE 1 came from the fills of pits within Pit Group NH8612, especially the fills of pit NH5045. Herring was again common, but sea bream(s), scad, trout, garfish, cottid(s) and cyprinid(s) were recovered in addition to mackerel, rays, flatfishes and eel. Several gadid bones were also recovered, including a fragment from a large ling dentary. Together with cod, ling were widely traded as dried stockfish in the middle ages. The presence of a dentary suggests that this fish was fresh, since stored ling would have lacked the head. Hand collected bone included head bones from large (1 m) cod, large eel (at least 700 mm), large plaice (600 mm), conger eel, gurnard, garfish and notably scute fragments from at least one large sturgeon. This scute, together with other fish bones, was recovered from NH5185, a fill of pit NH5169 from Pit Group NH8612 in Property SE 1. This property was located to the south of the archdeacon's residence, in an area known to be wealthy by and possibly part of a substantial capital tenement owned by Silvester in 1249 (Keen 1985 and Teague, pers. comm.).

Medieval, 1225–1500

Only a selection of samples from deposits assigned to the medieval period were included in this analysis, from Properties BE 1–5. Over 2000 bones were identified to at least family level. Again, most bones were recovered from pit fills. Clupeids, especially herring, were still numerically dominant (around 50% of identified bones) gadids were evidently much more common in the medieval deposits than previously, representing around 25% of bones in the sieved assemblage. Whiting, averaging around 400–450 mm was particularly common, with cod, haddock and pollack also present. Pit fill CC3276 in Property BE 5 contained a large number of whiting bones from at least nine complete fish, ranging in size from 250 mm to well over 500 mm but averaging 350–450 mm. Eel accounted for 12% of identified bones and flatfishes just 2.5%. Measurements on the cleithrum indicated eels of 350–420 mm. Elasmobranchs, garfish, conger eel, bass, tub gurnard, mackerel, grey mullet and sea bream(s) were all identified. Freshwater fish were scarce but included occasional bones from small perch, pike, trout and cyprinids including roach.

Discussion and conclusions

The fish assemblage from Northgate House and the Discovery Centre is the largest yet recorded in Winchester. Previous work has concentrated on the suburbs, while little bone has been recorded from intramural areas. The assemblage includes fish remains dating from the Iron Age to the medieval period. While marine fish were present in all periods, the increase in the concentration of fish in soil samples from the late Saxon period (Phase 4.2) onwards appears to support the model proposed by Barrett *et al.* (2004) for significant expansion of fishing in the decades either side of AD 1000, at least for herring. Gadids only really appear to form a

significant part of the fish assemblage in Phase 6, and there was no clear evidence for the dried and salted stockfish which were extensively traded from the 11th century and throughout the medieval centuries. While it is not yet possible to identify preserved fish from the condition of individual bones alone, it is likely that both fresh and preserved fish were eaten regularly. Documentary records from Southampton indicate that pickled, salted and smoked (red) herrings were traded, and eel and stockfish were also sent to Winchester. The similarity in fish assemblages from the sites in Winchester and published assemblages from contemporary sites in Southampton also provides support for the suggestion that the primary source of sea fish available in Winchester, probably from the time of Roman settlement, was Southampton Water and the Solent. While freshwater fish were obviously eaten, apart from the migratory eel, their dietary significance never appears more than minor. These findings are in keeping with the results from other sites in Winchester, suggesting that a similar range of fish was eaten by many of the Winchester townsfolk, at least from the late Saxon to the mid 13th century. While sturgeon, found in Property SE 1 (Phase 5), demonstrates that some very expensive fish were available to the most affluent, there is very little else in the assemblage from these Winchester sites to suggest the high status which could be expected given the significance of Winchester throughout these periods of its history.

MARINE MOLLUSCS *by Greg Campbell*

Sea-shell must have been imported to Winchester from the coast, and at some speed, since they have a limited 'shelf-life'. Shellfish at inland sites are, therefore, good indicators of variation in long-distance transport efficiency between periods. Also, shellfish in the shell are a luxury food inland, since a better yield of protein and animal calories is achieved by consuming almost any other locally available animal (even one with little flesh), or by importing marine animals with a better proportion of flesh to waste (such as sea fish, or preserved shellfish flesh). So marine shells are not simply another component of the diet, they are the main, and usually the sole, means of studying perishable luxury imports at past inland sites.

An assemblage of approximately 21,000 marine shells was recovered from 1050 contexts, the greater part by hand, but some 3600 shells were retrieved by wet-sieving of bulk soil samples for recovery of charred plant remains by flotation. For all these 260 samples (almost all of which were of 40 litres excavated volume), shells over 10 mm were recovered by wet-sieving during the initial processing, and the fraction sized between 10 and 4 mm were examined, and retained and sorted if more than a dozen or so shell fragments were noted.

A fuller treatment of the analysis is available on the accompanying digital report (*Digital Section*

13), and in the archive. Hand-retrieved material greatly predominated over sieved shellfish. Analysis of the difference showed hand-retrieval significantly over-estimated oysters compared to other edible shellfish. It also seriously over-estimated the edible shellfish compared to the non-edible species, which are the better indicators of habitat exploited. Conclusions are therefore broad; robust comparisons and contrasts between phases or with other excavations or sites must wait for larger numbers of samples of larger volume from future excavations.

There was no convincing evidence for prehistoric marine shellfish. Convincing shellfish consumption began early in the Roman occupation (Phase 2.1), peaked in the late 3rd–mid 4th centuries (Phase 2.3), and continued into the late Roman period (Phase 2.4). Overall, the Roman level of shellfish consumption was low compared to later periods. Oysters were the most common shellfish consumed, with some mussels and periwinkles. Oystering appeared to be based on fast-growing near-shore and embayment oysters to produce large shells, with some use of cultch to ensure supply, and with negligible harvesting of reefs.

Shellfish were relatively common in the late Saxon period (Phase 4), and a wide range of species were consumed. Oysters continued to be the most common, but carpet shells were more common than cockles and mussels were less common than in Roman phases. The general Phase 4 shells were different from more closely datable shells from sub-Phases 4.1 and 4.2, possibly because 'kitchen-waste' was more often discarded on waste ground, and 'table-waste' was more often discarded or lost near habitations.

The Anglo-Norman period (Phase 5) saw the highest consumption of shellfish in this part of the town, with a very wide range of types, implying the residents' status and income had improved from the preceding phase. Mussels were as popular as they had been in Roman times. Periwinkles were very popular, so much so that they were discarded in masses; all were harvested for their large size from almost identical habitats. In the later medieval period (Phase 6), shellfish seem to have fallen off, giving the impression that the status and income of the residents had diminished. Mussels and carpet-shells became less popular, and periwinkles and cockles more popular, perhaps because of increased

silting near the shore (inter-tidal mussels favour solid areas and carpet-shells favour coarse gravels, not muds).

Most oysters came from the late Saxon and medieval phases. Typical growth seemed similar to present-day oysters, making it likely that sea conditions were quite changed from the Roman period. Both natural reefs and more dispersed beds were being harvested, mainly sub-tidal beds by dredging. Dredging probably slowly depleted the reefs, moving dredging effort somewhat more towards bays and harbours. There seems to have been some intentional management of the oyster beds, such as the spreading of cultch (mainly mussel shells).

HUMAN SKELETAL REMAINS *by Helen Webb*

This report details the findings of the analysis of four Roman neonate skeletons (NH1528, NH4768, NH6176 and NH8510) and a single deposit (NH6236) of cremated bone of medieval date, excavated from Northgate House. It does not include NH1395, a single skull fragment (of about 25–35 years old) recovered from a Roman pit, and NH2426, three neonate vertebral arches, recovered from a medieval pit. These were assessed (Geber 2005) but did not warrant further analysis.

The remains were examined in accordance with standard osteological practice (Brickley and McKinley 2004). Methodological details are given in the full report available in the digital report (*Digital Section 10*) and archive.

Neonate burials

Neonate skeletons NH1528 and NH4768 were recovered from north-south orientated earth-cut graves (Table 8.10). Skeleton NH1528 was laid in a supine position, with the head to the north, and the arms and legs flexed. The head was probably facing west, with the mandible recovered from over the right shoulder. The arms were bent so that the hands lay over the pelvic area, and the right leg was flexed with the knee at a right angle. The position of the left leg was difficult to ascertain as only the lower parts of it (distal femur, tibia and fibula) were present, probably due to post-mortem disturbance. The grave itself was closely associated with a mid 3rd to mid 4th century (Phase 2.3) building

Table 8.10 Archaeological and osteological inventory of the four neonate skeletons and cremated bone NH6236

Skeleton No.	Context	Date	Preservation	Completeness	Age	Pathology
NH1528	Grave	Mid 2nd–mid 3rd C	Good	50 - 75 %	36 - 38 weeks	-
NH4768	Grave	Mid 3rd–mid 4th C	Good	>75 %	37 - 39 weeks	Endocranial lesions
NH6176	Posthole	Mid 2nd–mid 3rd C	Good	>75 %	40 - 42 weeks	-
NH8510	?Grave	Not dated	Good	50 - 75%	39 - 40 weeks	-
NH6236	Base of cesspit	11th-12th C	Good	-	Adult (>18 years)	-

(Structure NH8518). A bone fragment was radiocarbon dated to 50–176 cal AD (OxA-16713). Skeleton NH4768 was lying in a crouched position with the hands and feet close together, facing west with the head at the south end of the grave. The grave of NH4768 was immediately adjacent to, or possibly even within, timber Structure NH8521, dated to the mid 3rd to mid 4th century (Phase 2.3).

Skeleton NH6176 was not identified on site as a burial; the bones were recovered post-excavation during sieving of the fill from a posthole adjacent to a Roman timber Structure NH8520, dated to the mid 3rd to mid 4th century (Phase 2.3). Skeleton NH8510 was not identified during the excavation and was originally assigned the same context number as NH4768, although the exact location of this burial remains unclear.

All skeletons were fairly complete (50-75% or >75%), with low to medium fragmentation, indicating limited or no post depositional disturbance. They ranged in age from between 37–39 weeks old to 40–42 weeks old (see Table 8.10). In a modern clinical setting, full term is calculated to be about 40 weeks (280 days/10 lunar months) (Scheuer and Black 2000, 6), so whilst skeleton NH6176 and probably NH8510 may have been born at full term, or *possibly* overdue in the case of NH6176, it would appear that skeletons NH1528 and NH4768 may have been born up to four and three weeks prematurely (respectively). It was not possible to say whether any of these skeletons represent live or still births.

Neonate NH4768 displayed areas of new bone growth on the endocranial surface of the occipital bone. Porous, woven bone was present on the cruciform eminence and along the occipital (sagittal) sulcus. A study of endocranial lesions in non-adult skeletons by Lewis (2004), found that in individuals under six months of age, all cases (in her study) of endocranial lesions were porous or immature new bone lesions, and most (82%) occurred on the cruciate eminence of the occipital bone, as was the case here (ibid., 91–93). It is also suggested, however, that many of the lesions in such young individuals (0–0.5 years) were probably non-pathological in origin, and the result of the normal rapid bone growth in that part of the skeleton (ibid., 94). That being said, intra-cranial haemorrhage, as a result of mineral deficiency during a rapid growth period, can occur in pre-term infants (Seow 1992, cited in Lewis 2004, 94), and indeed, the age estimate of skeleton NH4768 was 37–39 weeks.

The fact that the three Roman burials were recovered from contexts associated with structures is typical of this period when infants were rarely buried in formal adult cemeteries (Philpott 1991, 97; Esmonde Cleary 2000, 133). The practice of infant burial in association with buildings may have been more common at rural and small town sites, although it is also frequently found in major urban centres (Philpott 1991, 97).

Cremated bone

The cremated bone (NH6236) was recovered from the basal deposit of an 11th–12th century (Phase 5) cesspit, found during environmental processing (Table 8.10). It comprised a total weight of 74.4 g. At least one adult was present; there were no fragments of bone indicative of a more precise age or sex and no pathology was noted. The fragments were predominantly buff/white in colour, indicating that oxidation had taken place, but there were also occasional light bluish grey fragments (< 5%), indicative of incomplete oxidation. The majority of fragments were less than 10 mm in size, with the majority measuring 2–5 mm. The maximum fragment size was 22 mm by 11 mm. In general the bone was in good condition. Fragments of trabecular bone were present, as were occasional fragments of articular surface. Most parts of the body were represented, including the skull, the long bones of the arms and legs, ribs and pelvis. Two teeth were represented, a mandibular premolar and the roots of a molar.

CHARRED AND MINERALISED PLANT REMAINS *by Wendy Carruthers*

The 140 samples discussed in this report (Table 8.11) were selected following assessments of 357 flots. Pits producing frequent charred and mineralised plant macrofossils were abundant at Northgate House and the Discovery Centre and as widespread a sampling regime as possible was adopted so as to overcome the problems of 'patchy data' highlighted by Frank Green (cited in Serjeantson and Rees 2009).

Methods

Samples were processed using standard methods of floatation in a Siraf-type tank. Meshes of 500 microns were used to retain the residues and flots. Further methodological details, together with the full discussion of results are provided in the digital report (*Digital Section 15*) and archive.

Notes on preservation

Charred plant remains were variable in their state of preservation, with soil layers such as the Phase 1.3 'subsoil' and Phase 2.4 Dark Earth producing a higher percentage of unidentified grain, as might be expected for a ploughsoil.

The sites examined for this report were typical of many sites in Winchester in producing plant remains that were preserved both by charring and mineralisation. Concentrated cess was obvious in many of the late Saxon features, since amber-coloured seeds, arthropod remains and fine bran fragments were visible in the flots. In addition, residues were large and large clinker-like concretions—some with matted straw, bran fragments and seed impressions—could be seen in the best preserved deposits (eg Plate 8.2). Apart from 19 samples specifically examined for mineralised remains, a few other features (eg CC2177, NH2619, NH2134, NH2237) contained reasonable quantities of material but these were not analysed in detail.

Period summaries and comparisons with contemporary sites in the area

Pre-Roman (Phase 1)

Charred plant remains were frequent (average density = 7.8 fragments per litre of soil processed (fpl) for Phases 1.1 and 1.2) and reasonably well preserved. The general character of the whole Phase 1 assemblage was one of burnt domestic waste, most of which probably derived from the piecemeal processing of hulled wheats (primarily spelt but with some emmer) and hulled barley over domestic hearths (see Fig. 8.1). Barley may have been more important in Phase 1.1, or the differences seen between roundhouses NH8508 and NH8502 could indicate different uses, eg. stock rearing versus human habitation. Bread-type wheat, oats, Celtic beans and black mustard may have been more important than their charred record suggests (although it is possible that some of the bread-type wheat at least was intrusive). This is because they do not need to come into contact with heat during their initial processing, although drying prior to grinding, storage or oil extraction would involve contact with fire.

Wild foods were being gathered from woodland margins and hedgerows, including hazelnuts and

Plate 8.2   Concreted bran fragments

sloes. The range of weed seeds was typical of an Iron Age charred cereal assemblage, including indicators of winter sowing such as cleavers (*Galium aparine*), some indicators of nutrient-rich soils (eg henbane (*Hyoscyamus niger*)) and others of nutrient-poor soils (eg small-seeded weed vetches (*Vicia/Lathyrus* sp.)). The fairly high rate of recovery of charred material from this phase could in part be due to contamination, although hulled wheat remains were also relatively frequent for the period. The evidence suggests that the level of arable activity on the site was fairly high, but was probably not taking place on such a scale to produce accumulations of cereal processing waste. No storage pits

Table 8.11: Numbers of samples analysed for plant remains, by phase and property

Each * represents a sample residue sorted for mineralised remains (total sorted residues = 19 samples)

Property/ phase	Pre-Roman 1 & 1.1	1.2	1.3	Roman 2.1	2.2	2.3	Post-Roman Dark Earth 2.4	4	Late Saxon 4.1	4.2	Anglo-Norman 1050-1225 5	Medieval 1225-1550 6	Total/ per property
BE1								3**					3**
BE2										2	1*		3*
BE3								1					1
BE4										7*****	2**	2*	11********
BE5											3	1	4
BW1											2		2
BW2									10	5	2		17
BW3										2	9*	3	14*
BW4									4	6*	2		12*
BW5								1	1*	4*	1		7**
BW6								1					1
SE1									1	4**	7*		12***
SE2										3		1	4
SE3								4			4		8
No property	16	7	3	3	1	11	6*						47*
Total no. samples per phase	16	7	3	3	1	11	6*	10**	16*	35*********	31*****	7*	146 (19*)

were encountered in this area of the enclosure, probably because the gravel/clay soils would not have been very suitable.

Earlier excavations within the Oram's Arbour enclosure (Biddle 2005) produced sparse charred plant assemblages dating from the Beaker period. The middle Iron Age defensive ditch and a few middle Iron Age features from Sussex Street produced small numbers of spelt wheat, hulled barley and oat remains. Apart from the absence of bread-type wheat grains, these findings fit in with the site's results. They lend some support to the suggestion that the bread-type wheat at Northgate House may be intrusive.

The presence of a concentration of black mustard seeds in posthole NH6210 (Structure NH8502) is of particular interest, as several late Bronze Age and Iron Age sites have now produced evidence for oil-seed crops such as brassicas. Campbell and Straker (2003) list a number of Bronze Age and Iron Age sites that have produced large assemblages of brassica seeds, including a large deposit recovered from an Iron Age pot sherd at Old Down Farm.

The Phase 1.3 subsoil sealing these features showed signs of being manured with burnt household waste (frequent abraded cereal grains), with the appearance of corn cockle suggesting that cultivation had taken place in the Roman period. If animal waste was also used, it may not have contained much burnt material as there was little evidence of fodder. The soil micromorphology results (see Mcphail and Crowther below) also

produced evidence for cultivation, and the presence of Roman artefacts indicated that this probably continued into the Roman period (Steve Teague, pers. comm.).

Roman and Dark Earth (Phase 2)

Bread-type wheat and hulled wheat (predominantly spelt) were the main cereals being consumed, and there is evidence that spelt was being used for malting in Phase 2.1 (c AD 43–130/50) (see Fig. 8.1). Barley was still an important crop, but the recovery of a predominantly barley sample from a layer of trample, CC1762, suggests that, as in later phases, it may have been primarily used for fodder. Oats and rye were minor crops, or perhaps their use for fodder meant that they rarely became charred. Hazelnut shell was present in some samples indicating a low but common use of wild food resources. The arable weed assemblage was similar to Phase 1, but corn cockle and rye grass started to become more common, being present in low numbers in six of the fifteen samples. Chess seeds were roughly twice as frequent as in Phase 1. Perhaps large grasses such as chess and rye grass were tolerated as weeds, since they were edible and could only be eradicated by hand weeding the crop in the field. This can do more damage than good to a crop sown by broadcasting the seed.

Apart from the malting deposit, the general character of the charred assemblages was one of domestic waste, probably originating from hearths

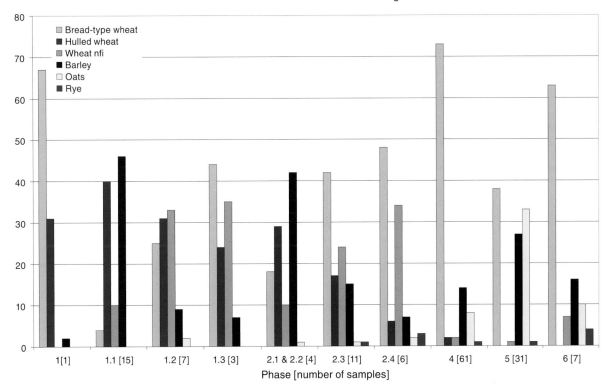

Fig. 8.1 Cereals as percentage of identified grain, by phase

over which piecemeal crop processing of hulled cereals and hand cleaning had been carried out. The large deposit of bread-type wheat in midden NH1346 (presuming contamination was not a major factor) probably represented stored grain that had been burnt to eliminate storage pests, since almost half of the grains showed signs of pest damage. The few large deposits of bread-type wheat that have been found in the Roman period in Britain have primarily been from storage contexts, such as South Shields granary (van der Veen 1994).

Charred cereal remains were frequent in the samples (average density = 14.1 fpl) suggesting that the arable economy was well-established. Although negative data should be viewed with caution (as crop processing could have removed some weed seeds), the low occurrence of leguminous weed seeds and absence of weeds of acidic or clay soils, such as sheep's sorrel and stinking chamomile, suggest that cultivation was taking place on the local, fertile calcareous soils and that the intensity was not excessive, unlike sites such as Stansted (Carruthers 2008) which showed signs of stress due to intensive cropping of spelt wheat.

Additional evidence of diet was recovered from cess pit NH4744, a small Phase 2.4 pit possibly associated with Roman Structure NH8521. Unfortunately preservation conditions were not as good as in the later phases, but mineralised remains indicated that in addition to foods made from flour (eg bread), peas and sloes or cherries were being consumed. This is very similar to the simple diet revealed in the late Saxon to medieval cess pits, being rural rather than urban in character with no evidence of imported foods (although the information was limited).

The five Dark Earth (Phase 2.4) samples produced relatively high numbers of charred cereal grains (Fig. 8.1) with some signs of erosion and fragmentation possibly due to plough damage, but perhaps not as much as might be expected if the soil had been worked for a long period. The 'lower Dark Earth' sample showed no obvious difference to the others in this respect. The charred remains appear to represent burnt domestic waste that had been used to fertilise the soil. The occurrences of the different cereals were intermediate between the Roman and late Saxon periods, with bread-type wheat being dominant and hulled wheat dropping off sharply. Although barley was not particularly frequent to indicate the use of animal waste, oats and rye were a little more frequent. Of course, most of the dung and stable waste used for manuring would probably not be burnt or contain burnt material, so it would leave few traces. The presence of a mineralised field bean hilum and a brassica seed could indicate the use of some material cleaned out of cess pits.

Late Saxon to medieval phases (Phases 4–6)

Cereals

By this period bread-type wheat was the main crop being consumed by the occupants, although barley, oats and rye were also present in varying quantities (Fig. 8.1; Table 8.12). The almost complete absence of cereal chaff fragments and very low incidence of weed seeds in the Phase 4 to 6 samples demonstrated that cereals being brought to these plots had already been fully processed. Unprocessed oats and barley may have been brought in to be used for fodder, and this would be less likely to become

Table 8.12: Distribution of major crops in different types of context during Phases 4 to 6 (charred remains only).

Numbers shown are 'numbers of samples where the crop is dominant' (but occurrence of peas/beans recorded rather than dominance).

Number of samples where charred cereal is dominant	Phase	Wheat	Barley	Barley/ oats dredge	Oats	Total no. samples examined for each feature type	Occurrence of Charred Peas and field beans (no. of items including uncertain IDs)
Floor/occupation layers + 'garden soil'	4	2			2	25	12
	5		3	2	3	13	8
	6	2				3	
Pits	4	13				31	15
	5	3	2		1	13	2
	6					3	
Hearths & rakeout	4				2	3	5
	5					2	
Postholes	4	2				2	1
	5	1			1	2	1
	6	1				1	

charred. However, charred assemblages containing this type of waste, including hay, oats, dredge (a barley and oats mixed crop) and cultivated vetch were recovered from many of the occupation layers, and these also produced very little chaff and weed seeds. The only sample to produce more than one or two rachis fragments was sample 214, from layer NH3240, Property BW 3 (46 wheat, barley and rye rachis fragments), and the hay meadow taxa in this sample suggested burnt fodder or dung was probably represented.

Free-threshing bread-type wheat was the principal cereal grown for human consumption by this time, and this falls from the ear when ripe so must be processed on the farm. Rye is also a free-threshing cereal, but there was only a small increase in this cereal in the Winchester samples from the Roman period onwards (Fig. 8.1), and Green (2009) noted how rare it was in samples from Winchester. It may have been purchased more often as mixed wheat/rye flour to make bread, leaving little trace in the fossil record, or it may have been eaten green in the field by livestock. Rye may have been avoided to some extent because it is very susceptible to ergot infection, and possible outbreaks of ergotism or 'St Anthony's Fire' (which can lead to abortions, convulsions and gangrene) are chronicled in the 6th and 8th centuries (Hagen 1992, 116). Barley and oats require additional stages of processing to remove the husks, which may be one reason why they were considered best suited for fodder. It is uncertain whether small amounts of hulled wheat (probably spelt) continued to be grown into the Saxon period, as has been found on some sites in southern Britain (eg late Saxon Stansted; Carruthers 2008). The fact that 39 definite and possible hulled wheat grains were found in the Phase 4 samples but only three cf. hulled wheat grains were found in the Phase 5 samples suggests that this did not represent residual material, but a crop that was being 'phased out'. Spelt is a hardy crop that produces good yields and stores well in the husk, so it may have continued to be grown for fodder by some farmsteads. If so, its presence in grain brought into town could be as occasional contaminants, or it may have been purchased to feed livestock being kept in back yards.

Whilst most cereals may have been purchased as flour and so leave traces in the mineralised cess but not charred assemblages, small amounts of cereals may have been used whole in broths and cereal pottages, or used to make groats and frumenty (Hagen 1992). Hagen (ibid., 59) mentions a range of Anglo-Saxon recipes that could well have produced the type of food remains found in many of the cess pits, such as bean soup (beonbrod), pea soup (pysena brod) and cereal pottages containing oil seeds such as flax (linseed). The remains from other foods such as carrots and mallow leaf broth are unlikely to be identifiable, although a few seeds of each taxon were found (perhaps having been used as flavourings, see below).

As indicated by the dominance of cereal bran in faecal concretions in the cess pit fills, bread was the staple food of the late Saxon and Anglo-Norman periods (Hagen 1992, 19). Hagen (ibid., 20) states that wheaten bread was considered to be far superior to other breads such as barley bread. She also notes that on special occasions such as feast days loaves were sprinkled with seeds such as poppy and fennel, both of which were recovered from cess pits in Properties BE 2, BE 4, BW 2, BW 4 and SE 1. Pit NH6138 produced abundant mineralised poppy seeds and a fennel seed. Mustard seeds (*Brassica/Sinapis* sp.), which were common in many features, may also have been used in this way or for seasoning dishes.

Comparisons of the cereal assemblages from Winchester with those from mid Saxon to medieval Southampton (Hunter 2005, Wendy Smith, pers. comm.) and late Saxon to medieval Oxford (Pelling 2006 and pers. comm.) show that scarcity of chaff and weed seeds in urban settings is a common phenomenon. Late Saxon cess pits in Oxford (Ruth Pelling pers. comm.), however, produced some samples that contained reasonable quantities of chaff and weed seeds, suggesting semi-processed grain or grain plus processing waste were being brought into the burh at this time. A sample from mid Saxon Southampton contained charred oats still enclosed in chaff (Hunter 2005, 164), suggesting that oats were being brought into Hamwic for fodder. Green (2009) gives details of two large late Saxon grain deposits from Winchester including a possible deposit of malted barley from Sussex Street and a large deposit of rye from Trafalgar House. These types of rich samples, however, are unusual and they are often the result of accidents or deliberate burning of contaminated grain. The overall picture from urban sites was that bread-type wheat (and in Oxford, rivet-type wheat) and barley were the dominant cereals being deposited as burnt waste in town, with lesser quantities of oats and rye. This was also the impression gained by Green (2009) in his study of sites in the western and northern suburbs of Winchester, with large deposits of bread-type wheat or barley sometimes being present. Barley appears to have been more frequent in Southampton in the mid and late Saxon periods, and rye may also have been a little more common, but, as Table 8.13 shows, caution must be taken when making these sorts of comparisons. Comparing the waste from different types of feature between different sites may not be valid. Green (ibid.) also points out that cereals being consumed as flour will leave little trace (or at least traces that can be identified to cereal type). Therefore, a large amount of data, together with documentary sources, must be examined before an overall, reliable picture can be obtained. If changes through the phases are to be fully understood at Winchester, not only would sufficient charred and mineralised

Table 8.13: Main economic plants by phase and property

Property / Economic Plants	Pre-Roman 1	Pre-Roman 2	Roman	BE 1	BE 2	BE 3	BE 4	BE 5
main cereal (charred)	Hulled barley, Spelt wheat	Spelt wheat, hulled barley	Spelt wheat, bread-type wheat	Bread-type wheat	Hulled barley bread-type wheat	Bread-type wheat	Bread-type wheat, hulled barley	HULLED BARLEY & OATS (DREDGE?), BREAD-TYPE WHEAT
other cereals & fodder crops (charred)	emmer wheat, oats, rye (bread-type wheat?)	Oats, (bread-type wheat?)	Hulled barley, oats, rye	Hulled barley, oats, rye	Oats, rye	Barley, oats, rye	Oats, rye, Cultivated vetch	Rye, cultivated vetch, hay?
cereal bran			+	++++	+++		++++	
pulses (pea) (bean)		[cf.B]	P	BP++++	B++		BP+++	[P]
hedgerow fruits & nuts	HNS	HNS, [cf.sloe]	HNS+	HNS++ Elderberry	HNS+++	HNS	HNS++ Blackberry Bird cherry	HNS+++, [blackberry], [hawthorn]
orchard fruits ?			Sloe/ cherry+++	Plum ++ bullace / damson/ greengage++ sloe/ cherry +++Apple+			Plum++ Sloe/ cherry+++ Apple+++ Apple/pear+++	
flavourings/ oilseeds	Brassica (cf. black mustard)+++				Brassica carrot poppy	brassica	Opium poppy	Brassica+++
fibre and possible dye plants				flax	Flax		bird cherry, blackberry,	Blackberry,
imported foods								
number of samples / mineralised samples examined	16 / 0	7 / 0	15 / 1	3 / 2	3 / 1	1 / 0	11 / 8	4 / 0

KEY : HNS = hazelnut shell fragments; B = field bean; P = pea; occasional = no symbol; several = ++; frequent = +++; abundant = ++++;

CAPITALS = some large charred cereal deposits present >100 grains; [ ] = charred pulses & fruits, all cereals charred

samples from each phase have to be examined, but also context types would have to be taken into consideration (see Table 8.12).

Pulses

In addition to bread, pulses were clearly a very important component of the diet. Peas and beans could be grown on a garden scale or as part of a crop rotation system on farmsteads. In addition to being an easily dried and stored source of protein, they can help to restore fertility to poor soils (due to nitrogen-fixing bacteria in their root nodules). Pulses can be ground into flour and added to bread, they can be added whole to soups and pottages, and they can be fed to livestock. A total of 75% of the charred pulses came from Phase 4 samples, and

there were far fewer mineralised pulse remains in the Phase 5 samples than in Phase 4. The consumption of pulses, therefore, appears to have decreased from Phase 4 to Phase 5 (the Phase 6 data was too limited). It is uncertain what replaced this relatively cheap source of protein, but examples of changes in the diet at Sedgeford, Norfolk, during the medieval period cited by Woolgar *et al.* (2006, 91) showed a change from a mainly bread and dairy based diet in the 13th century to a heavily meat and fish based diet by the early 15th century. Perhaps, at this early date in Winchester, dairy products were increasing in importance and beginning to replace pulses, or maybe a wider variety of cereal based dishes were being consumed, as oats and rye became more readily available.

BW 1	BW 2	BW 3	BW 4	BW 5	SE 1	SE 2	SE 3
Bread-type wheat, oats	Bread-type wheat	oats	BREAD-TYPE WHEAT, oats	BREAD-TYPE WHEAT	BREAD-TYPE WHEAT	Bread-type wheat	BREAD-TYPE WHEAT
hulled barley	Hulled barley, oats	Hulled barley, bread-type wheat	Hulled barley, rye	Hulled barley, oats	Hulled barley, oats	Hulled barley, oats, rye	Hulled barley, oats, rye
			++++	++++	+++		
	[BP]	[BP]	BP ++	BP++	BP++		
HNS+++	HNS++++, elderberry	HNS++++,	HNS+++	HNS++	HNS++,	HNS++ elderberry+++	HNS++
	bullace/ damson/ greengage		[Bullace/ damson/ greengage], [sloe] ++, [apple]	Sloe/ cherry Apple, apple/pear	Sloe/ cherry, apple	Sloe/ cherry++, Apple +++, apple/pear+++	
	Poppy, brassica	brassica	Opium poppy, brassica++		Opium poppy+++ brassica		
	Flax, elderberry, cf. dyers greenweed	cf. dyers greenweed	cf. Flax	flax	Elderberry?, bryony, sloes		
				cf. fig	Grape, Fennel , cf. peach		
2 / 0	17 / 0	14 / 0	12 / 1	7 / 2	12 / 3	4 / 0	8 / 0

Comparisons with the mid Saxon cess pits at Hamwic (Carruthers 2005b; Hunter 2005) suggest that pulses were possibly even more important components of the diet earlier in the Saxon period, so perhaps the decline seen in Winchester between Phases 4 and 5 was part of a larger trend.

Using the mineralised cess pit data from Winchester as the most accurate indication of importance of pulses, therefore, of the 17 Phase 4 to 6 cesspit samples examined only the two poorest samples produced no evidence for eating pulses (BE 4-CC2120; BW 3- NH3438; both <1% faecal concretions) and these were from Phases 5 and 6. The only reasonably well preserved samples to produce low concentrations of pulse remains were SE 1-NH5175 and BE 4-CC2305, (both Phase 5, both 50% faecal concretions; 2 hilums and 3 pulse testa fragments only). Since a grape pip was recovered from a Phase 5 pit on Property SE 1, this could be another indication that the occupants enjoyed a slightly higher standard of living than the occupants of some of the other properties. Perhaps they had an alternative source of protein to pulses, such as greater quantities of meat or fish. All of the Phase 4 cess pit samples produced high or medium concentrations of pulses, suggesting that not only were pulses as much a part of the staple diet as cereal-based foods such as bread, but they were also probably being consumed all year round, even when other foods such as fresh leaf vegetables were available. Pulses were, therefore, being eaten on a daily basis either because they were cheap and 'filling', or possibly for cultural reasons.

Nuts, fruits, vegetables and flavourings

Charred hazelnut shell (HNS) fragments were remarkably frequent and widespread, particularly in samples from layers in all phases. This suggests that, rather than eating hazelnuts piecemeal around the fire and throwing the shells into the household fire (from where it became thrown into cess pits with human food waste), HNS was more closely associated with burnt animal fodder and bedding, and general waste from occupation layers. Whether this suggests that some sort of large scale drying was taking place prior to grinding the nuts into flour or storage requires further investigation. Perhaps the shells were collected over time to be used for kindling for smithing hearths and kilns. Some, but not all, of the hearth and rakeout samples examined for this report produced large numbers of HNS fragments, eg rakeout NH4226 = 482 fragments; hearth NH3782 = 777 fragments.

A few charred and frequent mineralised *Prunus* sp. (plums, cherries, sloes etc.) stones and kernels were recovered from all phases. Unfortunately because mineralisation mainly preserves soft tissues, most of the remains consisted only of the seed kernel, so identification was based on size and shape. This meant that distinction between the small round stones of cherries and sloes could not be made. Because the fruits of sloes are astringent to taste and they are rarely eaten today, it might be thought that most of the sloe/cherry kernels were from more palatable cherries. However, amongst the charred whole stones, only sloe was identified. When preserved by drying and rehydrated, the astringent taste of sloes is lost (Wiltshire 1995). Cooking can also improve flavour. Because sloes are much more likely to be growing wild in the hedgerows, being a particularly useful thorny shrub for hedging (also called blackthorn), sloes would have been much easier to gather for free, or cheaper to buy from market than cherries (which in the authors experience are heavily predated by birds). Other members of this genus are more likely to have been growing as orchard fruits, such as bullace/damson/greengage and plum. These were less common in the cess pits, but found in all three periods. Where the same fruits were found in successive phases, eg plums in Properties BE 4, Phases 4.2 and 5, it is possible that a fruit tree was growing on the plot (NB. the life of an apple tree is usually about 70–100 years).

The mineralised seeds of apples/pears are fortunately often preserved with their seed coats and on these occasions they can be identified as apple. Where seed coats were not preserved the identification had to be left at apple/pear, although no pear seeds were positively identified. It is impossible to tell from the seeds whether the apples were wild crab apples or a cultivated orchard variety. Apple pips were present in Phase 4 and 5 samples.

In view of the frequency of other possibly hedgerow fruits and nuts it is surprising that blackberry seeds were so rare. They were common in samples from the middle Saxon cess pits at Hamwic (Carruthers 2005a). No wild strawberry seeds were found, and this is another native hedgerow fruit

that is often common in faecal deposits. It is unlikely that this is because of seasonal availability, since fruits can readily be preserved by boiling them down to a thickened pulp, particularly if honey is added to raise the sugar content (Hagen 1992). Also, because a reasonable number of cess pit samples was examined it is likely that cess from all seasons was represented. The absence may indicate that ungrazed open areas of scrub were not common in the vicinity of the town, or that such resources were jealously guarded by land owners.

Seeds that may have been used to add flavour to food include native plants such as mustard seed (*Brassica/Sinapis* sp.), carrot seed and poppy seed. Non-native flavourings include opium poppy, a plant that has a long history of use, dating back to the Iron Age. These seeds can also be used to provide oil, as can flax (linseed). Fennel, a herb originating in the Mediterranean, was tentatively identified in a Phase 4 cess pit fill. All of these taxa were recovered from mid Saxon Hamwic cess pits, along with several additional taxa that were not present in Winchester, such as coriander, caraway, lovage and dill. Herbs such as these could be grown in back yards as pot herbs, although fennel would probably have been bought as imported seed since it does not set seed well in the British climate.

Imported fruits and flavourings were notably scarce in the Winchester samples, presumably indicating a fairly low status. A single possible fig seed was present in a Phase 4.1 pit fill NH2451, Property BW 5. The remaining imported taxa were found in Property SE 1, with the fennel seed coming from a Phase 4.2 pit fill and the grape pip coming from a Phase 5 pit fill. A small mineralised fragment of a deeply ridged, thick walled stone, probably peach (*Prunus persica*), was recovered from pit NH6231, Phase 4.2. If this identification is correct it would be the earliest post-Roman record of peach for the British Isles. Peaches originate from China: they were grown or imported into many regions by the Romans, including Britain since it was recorded from 1st/2nd century AD New Fresh Warf, London (Willcox 1977). No early medieval records for this soft fruit exist for Great Britain to the author's knowledge. Being perishable, they would probably have been very expensive to import. Peaches can be grown in this country, but are more likely to fruit well against a wall or under glass. With increasing climatic warming that began in the 11th century AD, it is possible that peaches were successfully grown outdoors in milder parts of the British Isles such as Winchester.

Many other plants may have been consumed but they do not leave an identifiable trace in mineralised pit fills, such as leafy vegetables, leeks, onions and root vegetables. Some of the plants growing as common weeds of disturbed ground, such as fat hen and mallow, can be used as leaf vegetables. Possible wild turnip (cf. *Brassica rapa*) seeds were common in samples from all phases, and even wild plants of this species can be used as a root or a leaf vegetable (Mabey 1972, 166). Leaves from the common hedgerow herb, garlic mustard (*Alliaria petiolata*), can be used as a flavouring, as the name suggests, and has an alternative name of 'poor man's mustard'.

Possible medicinal plants

Many of the native plants present in the samples can be used for a variety of medicinal purposes, including poisonous weeds such as henbane and corn cockle. One theory as to why corn cockle was so frequent in Saxon cess pits is that the seeds can help to remove worms (Hagen 1992, 116). However, precise dosing would be important as eating them can prove fatal. Unless large concentrations of seeds occur it would be impossible to differentiate the seeds of native medicinal and vegetable plants from the seeds of ruderal weeds growing close to the features. Amongst the plants listed in old herbals such as Culpepper (1826) and Grieve (1931), the following were present as mineralised fruits/seeds and so may well have been consumed for medicinal purposes;

Opium poppy – seeds are not effective but crushed capsules were used internally and externally for pain relief
Figs – laxative
Corn cockle seed – to cure dropsy and jaundice, and remove worms (poison!)
Hemp agrimony – astringent, tonic, diuretic (roots and leaves), tanning leather
Carrot seed – carminative, stimulant and useful with flatulence
Fennel seed – carminative, for coughs, dispels fleas
Henbane seeds – antispasmodic, hypnotic, mild diuretic, mainly external use (poison!)
Black nightshade and woody nightshade seeds – externally to relive inflammation and internally as a mouthwash (poison!)
White bryony seed – emetic, tanning leather (poison!)
Fairy flax – purgative

Fibre crops and possible dyeplants

Cultivated flax seeds are commonly found in Saxon charred samples despite the fact that the oily seeds do not preserve well by charring. Both charred and mineralised seeds were recovered in small numbers in seven Phase 4 and 5 samples. These may have been a useful by-product of flax plants being grown for fibre, but no flax processing waste was found (although it is more likely to survive in waterlogged deposits). The identification of dyeplants is more problematic, as many of the edible fruits with coloured berries can be used to provide a range of colours. Several seeds were tentatively identified as *Genista* sp., a genus that includes dyers greenweed (*G. tinctoria*). Dyers greenweed is one of the dyeplants recovered from Viking York (Tomlinson 1985). All parts of the plant produce a green/yellow

dye. Although many potsherds stained with madder were recovered from the plots, preservation of the root by mineralisation or charring in a recognisable form is unlikely. Unfortunately no waterlogged deposits were found; Tomlinson recovered most of her dye remains from waterlogged deposits. The following plant remains could have been used for dyeing;

Sloes, plums, elderberries – blue/black
Bird cherry – dark grey to green
Bracken – brown/green
Dyers greenweed – green/yellow
White bryony – red
Blackberry – purple
Black and woody nightshade – red

In addition to fruits and seeds, other parts of plants like the leaves of carrot and bark of apple trees could have been used. The root of white bryony, for example, produces a red dye like madder. The presence of seeds could indicate that plants were being brought onto the property for dyeing purposes. This is particularly likely for plants like white bryony, which is unlikely to be growing locally as it is a twining plant of woods and hedgerows. It may have served a dual purpose, with the berries being used medicinally and the roots being used for dyeing.

Differences in waste deposition and the occurrence of fodder crops

From Table 8.12 it can be seen that most of the large deposits of charred bread-type wheat were recovered from the Phase 4 pits, mixed in with mineralised faecal waste. These large deposits are likely to mainly represent stored grain that was deliberately burnt in order to destroy pest infestations. They may have been primarily deposited in cess pits because they were located close-by, or perhaps to ensure that the pests and diseases were well and truly buried and could not re-infect the stored crop. It is notable that all of the cess pit samples contained reasonable quantities of charred cereal remains, suggesting that this was not just a casual occasional deposit of hearth sweepings, but a more deliberate, regular activity carried out on every property. Similarly, mineralised straw and, sometimes, rush fragments were present in every cess pit. In some cases concretions of matted straw were present. It is likely that these remains represent material swept up from floors, into which charred grain was mixed, having been burnt during preparations for cooking. No charred grain was observed concreted in with the straw, however, so perhaps the deposition of separate hearth sweepings and floor sweepings was more common. Charred material and straw would have been thrown into cess pits in order to reduce smells and soak up liquids. Straw and rushes may also have been used for toilet paper. Occasional moss fragments were mineralised, but not sufficient to suggest it had been regularly used as toilet paper, as has been found in some medieval cess pits (Greig 1981).

The Phase 5 cereal assemblages were more varied in composition and fewer large deposits of bread-type wheat were recovered. This could suggest that storage conditions had improved over time, since fewer large deposits of stored grain were being destroyed. Alternatively it could indicate a wider range of cereals were being eaten by humans, or a different type of waste was being thrown into the cess pits. Most of the deposits of oats, barley and dredge present in samples from layers appear to represent fodder and stable waste, since they are mixed with hay grown on damp meadows and cultivated vetch.

Where sufficient comparable contexts have been examined, eg Phases 4 and 5 pits and layers, changes can be seen as follows. In Phase 4 oats were the main fodder crop being spread around the layers as waste, whilst in Phase 5 a wider variety of fodder crops were being used, including barley, barley/oat dredge, oats and cultivated vetch. Of the four samples to produce confirmed cultivated vetch seeds, all were from Phase 5 (2 pits, 2 layers), so it appears that this fodder crop (which has been eaten by humans in times of famine) was introduced in the Anglo-Norman period. No clear conclusions can be drawn for Phase 6 because too few samples were suitable, but there may have been a reduction in keeping livestock in the town, since fewer fodder-type deposits were found. Bread-type wheat was much more dominant, although there was a small increase in rye.

Charred pulses were also commonly present in samples from layers and it is possible that some peas and beans were used to feed livestock being kept in back yards.

Arable crop quality over time and corn cockle contamination

The late Saxon to Anglo-Norman arable fields must have been a riot of colour, with weeds such as corn cockle (large dark pink flowers), stinking chamomile (white, daisy-like flowers) and corn marigold (yellow) growing as major crop contaminants. Corn cockle in particular was rife throughout Phases 4 and 5, despite the fact that these large, black seeds could easily be picked out of the flour prior to milling. Clearly, where cereals were purchased already ground into flour, quality control was more difficult, although the fragments of black seed coats of corn cockle can be spotted amongst the flour if contamination is particularly bad.

Corn cockle seeds can have deleterious effects on people and livestock if present in high numbers, because they have a high saponin content. Wilson (1975) mentions a figure of > 0.5% in bread or gruel causing ill effects. Silverside (1977) suggests that crop rotations involving root crops could help to eradicate this harmful weed, because it cannot lie dormant for long periods and its germination is

suppressed by root crops. Therefore, changes to the crop rotation system later in the medieval period may be at least part of the reason why later medieval sites usually produce fewer charred seeds than were found in these samples.

It is difficult to compare Phases 4 and 5 with Phase 6 as only one mineralised sample and seven charred samples were examined from the latest phase. One Phase 5 cess pit, NH3438 on Property BW 3, contained abundant mineralised whole corn cockle seeds but no evidence of impressions. It is possible that this household was careful to remove contaminants prior to milling, although bran-rich faecal concretions were also rare in this deposit, so the pit may have contained another type of waste rather than cess. Grieve (1931) notes that the seeds have been used to cure dropsy and jaundice in the past, and, as noted above, they can be used for their anti-helminthic effect. The fact remains, however, that 82 corn cockle seeds were recovered from a relatively small amount of residue, so this must indicate hand-cleaning unless medicinal use is suggested. Since many more charred and mineralised samples were examined from Phase 4 it appears that hand-cleaning was much more common in the Anglo-Norman phase than the late Saxon phase. This would improve the quality and taste of the flour and reduce the ill effects of this noxious weed.

Since corn cockle flowers are bright pink and showy, it is perhaps surprising that it became such a problem in Saxon and Anglo-Norman times, as this weed in particular would have been easy to remove in the field. It would appear that the quality of grain and flour being sold at market in towns such as Winchester was not always of a very high quality. On the other hand, impurities such as chaff were very rare in samples from Phases 4 to 6 and small-seeded weeds were low in number. Crop processing, in particular winnowing, appears to have been effective enough to have removed all but the larger, heavier weed seeds of a similar size and density to grain. Indications of crop quality from cereal grain size also suggest that the quality was generally good, with most of the wheat grains being large and plump, and the oats and barley grains being well-formed and often notably large. Variations in wheat grain shape, from very square grains to more elongated or pear-shaped grains suggest that a wide variety of land-races were being cultivated, and that grain was being brought into the town from a wide area. This suggestion is also supported by the range of soil preferences represented in the arable weed assemblage (see below).

Weed ecology

Although it is not always possible to be sure that the weed seeds present in the charred assemblage represent arable weeds (rather than another type of burnt waste) some taxa that were consistently present, and are also often found on other sites, can be useful in providing ecological information. One arable weed indicative of damp clay soils, stinking chamomile, increased significantly in the Phase 5 samples which may indicate that grain was being brought in to town from a different source during this phase, perhaps from further afield to supply the growing population. Corn chamomile is often associated with wheat, because wheat prefers heavier soils.

Corn marigold, a weed of sandy acidic soils was scarce in Phase 4 but increased from Phase 5 to Phase 6. In all cases, the samples where corn marigold seeds were present produced notably high levels of oats or rye. The sample from Phase 6 that produced the highest number of seeds (14 seeds; sample 214) was the only sample to produce rye rachis fragments, although no rye grains were recovered. These statistics confirm that oats and rye were being grown on poorer, sandy soils. It also suggests that rye may have been more common in Phase 6 than the charred plant record suggests, perhaps being used as an early bite fodder which is cut before it sets seeds.

Charred seeds from plants of wet ground and marsh, such as spike-rush and sedges (*Carex* spp.), greatly increased over time. Because these wet ground taxa can become charred either amongst hay or as arable weeds growing along field margins next to ditches, these figures are difficult to interpret. Samples that contained burnt hay such as sample 214 in Property BW 1, produced large numbers of seeds from wetland taxa. The results may reflect increased amounts of fodder including hay being burnt on the properties rather than the movement of arable onto wetter soils, or they could suggest that hay meadows were becoming damper.

Conclusions

The charred and mineralised assemblages from Winchester have helped to draw together and clarify previous evidence for agriculture and diet summarised by Green (2009). Unfortunately the pre-Roman (Phase 1) and Roman (Phase 2) assemblages were difficult to interpret because of concerns about possible contamination. Apart from the surprisingly frequent bread-type wheat found in both periods, the spelt, emmer and hulled barley frequencies were similar to many sites in southern Britain. There was evidence for malting spelt wheat in Phase 2.1.

The late Saxon (Phase 4) and Anglo-Norman (Phase 5) samples provided detailed evidence of diet, which was fairly simple in nature, based on cereals and pulses with hedgerow and orchard fruits and nuts. The trace of imported fruits and spices mainly came from Property SE 1. Several properties produced evidence to suggest that livestock was being kept in the backyards. Flax and possible dyeplant remains were present on some properties, providing evidence for craft working.

Bearing in mind differences in preservation, diet in late Saxon Winchester was more similar to late Saxon Oxford than Southampton, although the cereal evidence was similar.

THE WOOD CHARCOAL *by Dana Challinor*

This report presents the results of the analysis of 20 samples. The aims of the charcoal analysis were to provide evidence for the type and character of fuelwood used, the exploitation of woodland resources and managed woodland and any temporal changes over the phases represented.

Twenty fragments from each sample were selected for identification, ten from the >4 mm fraction and ten from the >2 mm fraction. Classification and nomenclature follow Stace (1997). All of the specimens were consistent with native taxa and the taxonomic level of identification varies according to the anatomical similarity between genera. Most of those given to species level are based upon the likely provenance and period, ie where a genus is represented by a single species. Fuller details are available in the digital report (*Digital Section 16*), and in archive

Late Saxon (Phase 4.1)

Property BW 2

Two samples were examined. Context NH4712 came from a pit with metalworking evidence (kiln fragments and hammerscale) and produced an assemblage dominated by oak (*Quercus*), with a fair amount of heartwood present. A few pieces of hazel (*Corylus avellana*), including roundwood fragments were also recorded. Sample NH551, context NH4711, from the same feature was also dominated by oak, but the charcoal was more fragmented. The processes of iron smelting and smithing would both have required charcoal as fuel (Edlin 1949, 160; Cleere and Crossley 1985, 37) and oak would have provided good quality charcoal, capable of achieving the high temperatures necessary.

In contrast the burnt layer NH4556, which came from a charcoal spread related to a hearth and from probable domestic waste, produced a more mixed assemblage of oak, alder (*Alnus glutinosa*), hazel, willow/poplar (*Salix/Populus*), hawthorn group (Maloideae) and holly (*Ilex aquifolium*), indicating less focused selection of wood for fuel.

Property BW 4

An occupation layer (NH3494) with evidence of domestic burning was examined from BW 4. This sample produced a mixed assemblage, with lots of oak and hazel, and a few fragments of hawthorn group, field maple (*Acer campestre*) and ash (*Fraxinus excelsior*).

Property BW 5

A lens of charcoal in an occupation deposit at the south end of the tenement, NH2424, may represent mixed domestic and metalworking debris, since a large fragment of a smithing hearth was found in an associated deposit. The charcoal comprised mixed taxa, with oak, hazel, hawthorn group, field maple and ash. All of the hazel came from small diameter roundwood. In contrast to the smithing associated deposit in Property BW 2 (NH4712), oak was not dominant.

Late Saxon (Phase 4.2)

Property BW 2

An assemblage from occupation layer (NH4217) overlying floor surface NH4225 appeared to comprise mostly oak, but several other taxa were identified, including hazel, hawthorn group and ash. Fragments of oak and ash sapwood were noted and the hazel came from small diameter roundwood.

Property BW 4

A sample of domestic debris from an occupation layer (NH3186) associated with substantial chalk floors in BW 4 produced a mixed assemblage with beech, oak, hazel, hawthorn group, blackthorn (*Prunus spinosa*) and ash. The blackthorn and hazel came from roundwood. This was the only Saxon sample to contain beech charcoal.

Property BW 5

Context NH2377 came from one of the large sub-rectangular 'cess' pits in Pit Group NH8598. Some of these pits contained fragments of smithing hearths so the origin of the charcoal may have been from metalworking, mixed with domestic debris. The charcoal assemblage appeared to be mainly oak, including some very large fragments, with heartwood, sapwood and small branchwood represented. Three other species, mostly from roundwood, were noted—hazel, hawthorn group and field maple. The dominance of oak in this sample may relate to metalworking activities, but large oak fragments have been recovered from other Saxon cess pits, where it has been suggested that the charcoal may have been deliberately deposited to help mask odours (Gale 2005).

Property BE 2

Two samples from a probable structure in this property were from slumped floor/occupation deposits. Context CC1354 was thought to belong to layers of slumped floors (Group CC7014) over the top of pit CC1352. Scorching evidence indicates that the deposits were associated with a hearth and represent domestic activity. The sample from context CC1420 came from a similar deposit (Group CC7009) slumped over pit CC1397. The taxonomic composition of these samples was extremely similar—both produced oak, hazel, alder, hawthorn group field maple and ash, with a significant component of roundwood fragments.

Property BE 4

The two samples from BE 4 dating to Phase 4.2 derived from domestic activities associated with pits in Pit Group CC7018. Context CC2360 was directly associated with hearth debris and the assemblage contained a significant component of oak, whilst CC2290 was more mixed. Both samples contained hazel, alder, hawthorn group and ash. Context CC2360 also produced two small round-wood fragments of spindle tree (*Euonymus europaeus*) and blackthorn.

Anglo-Norman (Phase 5)

Property BW 2

Two samples (contexts NH4186 and NH4189) from Group NH8539 were from floor debris of probable hearth rake-outs, and presumably represent domestic waste. The assemblages were similar in composition, dominated by beech (*Fagus*) and containing oak, hazel and hawthorn group, including many roundwood fragments.

Property SE 1

Pit NH5192 was part of a group of postholes\small pits (Pit Group NH8612) which may have been part of a structure associated with metalworking. The sample was notable for its abundance of very large fragments of charcoal, many of which were from hazel stems. Several pieces were 12 years old, as was one of the cherry (*Prunus avium*) stems. A few fragments of oak, alder and hawthorn group were also identified.

Property SE 3

The two samples from SE 3 came from large rectangular pits, one of which was a possible cellar (NH8635) containing dumps of cess and domestic waste. The other pit (NH8636) also contained backfill layers of cess and was in addition associated with smithing waste. The assemblages were notably contrasting, with NH8635 apparently dominated by beech, and NH8636 dominated by oak. Small quantities of other, but different, species were present in both, including hazel and blackthorn in NH8635 and birch (*Betula* sp.), alder and field maple in NH8636.

Property BE 5

Contexts CC3034 and CC3083 came from pit

CC3010 which contained slumped floors interspersed with domestic occupation deposits, many with a high charcoal content indicating sweepings from hearths. Both assemblages were mixed in character; with significant components of oak and beech and a range of other species, including hazel, alder, hawthorn group and field maple.

Medieval (Phase 6)

Property SE 2

A single sample dating to this phase came from the fills of a rubbish pit (NH1005). The assemblage was primarily composed of oak and beech, with a few fragments of hazel, blackthorn and hawthorn group.

Property BE 4

Context 2092 came from an occupation deposit which was interspersed with several slumped floor layers, representing domestic debris. The assemblage contained a diverse range of taxa, with mixed hazel and alder and oak, and single fragments of willow/poplar, hawthorn group and ash.

Discussion: changes over time and supplies of firewood

On first examination, the charcoal assemblages exhibit a reasonable degree of similarity across the areas and throughout the phases represented (Fig. 8.2). This indicates some consistency in the selection of firewood and possibly methods of procuring firewood. However, there are a few significant changes over time. Firstly, and most importantly, there is an apparent rise in the use of beech (*Fagus sylvatica*). No beech charcoal was identified from the Phase 4.1 samples, and only one of the seven Phase 4.2 samples contained beech. Almost all of the later Phase 5 and 6 samples produced beech, which formed a significant component or was dominant in five of the assemblages. Oak continued to be used and was present in all of the later samples, but the rise in the use of beech wood may account for small decreases in the occurrence of taxa such as hawthorn group and hazel, and field maple.

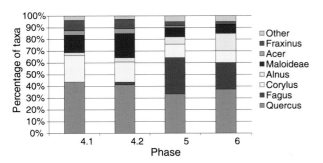

Fig. 8.2   Taxonomic composition of charcoal by phase

This shift in the charcoal record indicates a change in the source of firewood resources, or a change in the management regime. Supplies of firewood would have been provided from locally managed woodlands (Rackham 2006), and any charcoal fuel (such as required for metalworking or for odour disposal) would certainly not have travelled any great distance. It is interesting that a similar shift in the utilisation of beech is mirrored at other urban sites such as Oxford (Challinor 2002) and Southampton (Challinor forthcoming). The evidence from Southampton is particularly interesting given its proximity to Winchester, although the charcoal record is slightly later there, with beech not recorded as significant until the high medieval period, rather than the Anglo-Norman period. Changes in the local woodlands around Winchester may have preceded those around Southampton.

One final possibility should be mentioned—that the increase in beech may relate to the use of charcoal as fuel. Beech makes a good charcoal, as does alder, which also appears in greater quantity in the later samples. Whilst the evidence for smithing is not securely linked to specific buildings, there does seem to be a lot of residual evidence for it in the samples and the charcoal may have derived from it. Moreover, charcoal may have been used for other purposes, such as being deliberately deposited into cess pits to absorb odours (Gale 2005). Nonetheless, the comparable evidence from Southampton and Oxford suggests that a more widespread change may be occurring in Anglo-Norman and medieval fuel use.

ANALYSIS OF SAMPLES FOR EGGS OF INTESTINAL PARASITES AND OTHER MICROFOSSILS *by Andrew K G Jones*

The presence of ancient human faecal material in medieval deposits in Winchester was first reported by Taylor (1955) who found three kinds of intestinal parasites in well stratified peat like samples associated with a timber tank structure. The samples in the present study contrasted markedly with those described by Taylor: they varied considerably in colour, texture and moisture. None were highly organic peat like material with visible straw-like structured peats of the first Winchester find. A few resembled coprolites and on closer inspection contained inclusions, notably small splinters of large mammal bones, indicating they were canine (probably dog) droppings. The remaining soil/earth samples also varied, ranging from dark grey brown clay with low organic content, to friable very dark grey organic silt. A methodology for the concreted samples and the unconsolidated earth samples can be found in *Digital Section 14*.

The concreted samples, although most unpromising at first sight, proved to be the most productive with two samples yielding parasite ova. The presence of eight ova in context CC2177 (a Phase 4.2 pit) is convincing evidence for the presence of significant amounts of faeces, probably of human origin. The other sample (CC2010 – a Phase 4.2 pit) yielded a single trichurid ovum and while this too may be interpreted as evidence for the presence of faecal matter, low concentrations of parasite ova have relatively little interpretive value. Only one of the earth samples (NH2399 – a Phase 4.2 pit/well) produced a single trichurid ovum.

Measurements taken on ancient trichurid ova from a sample of concreted material recovered by wet sieving earth samples has provided good evidence that the worms responsible for the eggs were the human whipworm, *Trichuris trichiura*.

SOIL MICROMORPHOLOGY, CHEMISTRY AND MAGNETIC SUSCEPTIBILITY *by Richard Macphail and John Crowther with a contribution by Gill Cruise*

Selected monoliths employed in the assessment of Northgate House and the Discovery Centre were subsampled for bulk analyses (chemistry and magnetic susceptibility) and thin sections (see Tables 1 and 2 in *Digital Section 17*). In all, 17 bulk samples and 21 thin sections were analysed. Pollen assessment data also contributed to the investigation. A summary is provided here, while the full report, including all tables, thin section scans, photomicrographs and SEM-EDAX images, is provided in the archive and is available in *Digital Section 17*.

A total of 34 contexts and sub-units were identified and described and of these, 26 were specifically counted employing some 34 identified characteristics (Tables 4–5 in *Digital Section 17*).

Winchester Discovery Centre context DC3409 is clearly a middle Iron Age holloway accumulation which shows the effects of trampling, including the inclusion of dung residues. Context DC6001 records a probable pre-Roman arable soil, developed over the local natural Eb horizon of typical palaeoargillic brown earth soil (Carstens soil series). Contexts

DC1356, DC1357 and DC1358 are late Saxon (Phase 4.2) domestic floor deposits (eg DC1357), and dumps/spreads rich in ash and phosphate-rich materials such as bone and coprolites, and include much burned food/kitchen waste.

Northgate House contexts NH4436/NH4393 are typical decalcifying weakly humic and biologically worked Dark Earth that originated from soil formation in 'urban' middens on waste(?) ground, and includes coarse resistant relict Roman material (coprolites, bone, burned daub and iron slag, for example). In contrast, the overlying late Roman Dark Earth (NH4412) records both middening (including domestic ash waste) and inputs of probable dung residues. Context NH5059 seems to have been influenced by in situ animal pounding— such 'rural' signatures in NH4412 and NH5059 are recorded elsewhere in late Roman deposits and Dark Earth.

The Phase 5 sequence recorded in Monolith NH226 reveals a sequence of floor and occupation deposits associated with industrial/craft activity, with very strongly burned hearth and furnace/ Crucible debris indicating temperatures of 1000–1200°C being employed, and enrichment in lead and some enrichment in copper and zinc, also being recorded. In contrast, the Phase 4.2–5 sequence sampled in Monolith NH253 found multiple floors and associated domestic/kitchen hearths; these were probably regularly renewed/ reconstructed because they became eroded when ashes were raked out.

Occasionally, the balance of floor deposit sources varied from dominantly domestic kitchen hearth rakeout, to mixed deposits containing industrial and stable waste. At both NH226 and NH253, material included from outside space was recorded. A poorly preserved sample from Monolith NH559 indicates mainly domestic (kitchen hearth?) use of space. Similarly, Monolith NH187 records a pit containing intercalated cess and domestic floor sweepings.

Bibliography

Addyman, P V, Hopkins, B G, and Norton, G T, 1972 A Saxo-Norman pottery kiln producing stamped wares at Michelmersh, Hampshire, *Medieval Archaeol* **16**, 127-30

Albarella, U, 1995 Depressions on sheep horncores, *J Archaeol Sci* **22**, 699-704

Albarella, U, 2003 Tawyers, tanners, horn trade and the mystery of the missing goat, in P Murphy and P E J Wiltshire (eds), *The environmental archaeology of industry, Symposia of the Association for Environmental Archaeology* **20**, Oxford, 71-86

Albarella, U, 2005 The role of domestic ducks and geese from Roman to medieval times in Britain, in G Grupe and J Peters (eds), *Feathers, grit and symbolism: Birds and humans in the ancient old and new worlds*, Oxford, 249-258

Allason-Jones, L, 1989 *Ear-rings in Roman Britain*, BAR Brit Ser **201**, Oxford

Allen, D, 2001 Glass, in Booth and Evans 2001, 255-9

Allen, M, 2006 The volume of the English currency, *c* 973-1158, in G Williams and B J Cook (eds), *Coinage and history in the North Sea World, c AD 500-1200*, Brill, Leiden, 487-523

Ambrosiani, K, 1982 Vikingatida kammar i öst och väst. Ett diskussionsinlägg, *Fornvännen* **72**, 180-183

Anderson, F W, 1990 Provenance of building stone, in Biddle (ed.) 1990, 306-14

Andersson, E, 2003 Textile production in Scandinavia during the Viking Age, in L B Jørgensen, J Banck-Burgess and A Rast-Eicher (eds), *Textilien aus Archäologie und Geschichte. Festschrift für Klaus*, Neumünster, 46-62

Andrews, P, 1997 *Excavations at Hamwic: volume 2: excavations at Six Dials*, CBA Res Rep **109**

Armitage, P, 1982 A system for ageing and sexing the horncores of cattle from British postmedieval sites (with special reference to unimproved British longhorn cattle), in B Wilson, C Grigson and S Payne (eds), *Ageing and sexing animal bones from archaeological sites*, BAR Brit Ser **109**, Oxford, 37-54

Armitage, P, and Clutton-Brock, J, 1976 A system for classification and description of the horncores of cattle from archaeological sites, *J Archaeol Sci* **3**, 329-48

Armitage, P, and Goodall, J, 1977 Medieval horned and polled sheep: The archaeological and iconographic evidence, *Antiq J* **57**, 73-89

Arthur, P, 1978 The lead glazed wares of Roman Britain, in Arthur and Marsh (eds) 1978, 293-355

Arthur, P, and Marsh, G (eds), 1978 *Early fine wares in Roman Britain*, BAR Brit Ser **57**, Oxford

Arveiller-Dulong, V, Sennequier, G, and Vanpeen, N, 2003 Verreries du Nord-Ouest de la Gaule: productions et importations, in Foy and Nenna 2003, 147-60

Ashmore, P, 1999 Radiocarbon dating: avoiding errors by avoiding mixed samples, *Antiquity* **73**, 124-30

Astill, G, 2000 General survey 600-1300, in Palliser (ed.) 2000, 27-50

Bacher, A, 1967 *Vergleichend morphologische Untersuchungen an Einzelknochen des postcranialen Skeletts in Mitteleuropa vorkommender Schwäne und Gänse*, Inaugural-Dissertation, Ludwig-Maximilians-Universität, München

Baker, D, Baker, E, Hassall, J, and Simco, A, 1979 Excavations in Bedford 1967 – 1977 *Beds Archaeol J* **13**, 1-232

Baker, J, and Brothwell, D, 1980 *Animal diseases in archaeology*, Academic Press, London

Barbet, A, Tuffreau-Libre, M, and Coupry, C, 1999 Un ensemble de pots à peinture à Pompéi, *Rivista di Studi Pompeiana* **10**, 71-81

Barclay, K, and Biddle, M, 1990 Stone and pottery lamps, in Biddle 1990 (ed.), 983-99

Barfield, L H, 2006 Bone inlay, in Hurst 2006, 214-6

Barrett, J, 1995 'Few know an earl in fishing clothes'. Fish middens and the economy of Viking Age and late Norse earldoms of Orkney, Caithness and Shetland, unpubl PhD Thesis, Univ. Glasgow

Barrett, J H, Locker, A M, and Roberts, C M, 2004 Dark Age economics revisited – the English fish bone evidence, AD 600-1600, *Antiquity* **78**, 618-636

Barry, M, 2001 Population biology and shell characteristics of Littorina littorea on three Yorkshire shores, unpubl MSc thesis, University of Leeds

Bates, A, forthcoming The animal and bird bone, in Brown and Hardy forthcoming

Bayley, J, 1992 Metalworking ceramics, *Medieval Ceramics* **16**, 3-10

Bayley, J and Barclay, K, 1990 The crucibles, heating trays, parting sherds and related material, in Biddle 1990 (ed.), 175-97

Bayley, J, and Butcher, S, 2004 *Roman brooches in Britain: a technological and typological study based on the Richborough collection*, London

Bayley, J, and Doonan, R, 2000 Glass manufacturing evidence, in Mainman and Rogers 2000, 2519-28

Bayliss, A, 2007 Bayesian buildings: an introduction for the numerically challenged, *Vernacular Architect* **38**, 76-87

Bayliss, A, Bronk Ramsey, C, van der Plicht, J, and Whittle, A, 2007 Bradshaw and Bayes: towards a timetable for the Neolithic, *Cambridge Archaeol J* **17(1) suppl**, 1-28

Beedham, G E, 1972 *Identification of the British mollusca*, Hulton, Amersham

Beer, R J S, 1976 The relationship between Trichuris trichiura (Linnaeus 1758) of man and Trichuris suis (Schrank 1788) of the pig, *Research in Veterinary Science* **20**, 40-54

Beresford G, 1974 The Medieval Manor of Penhallam, Jacobstow, Cornwall, *Medieval Archaeol* **18**, 90-145

Biddle, B, 2005 Staple Gardens, in Whinney 2005, 75-8

Biddle, M, 1964. Excavations at Winchester in 1962-3; Second interim report, *Antiq J* **44**, 188-219

Biddle, M, 1965 Excavations at Winchester 1964; Third interim report, *Antiq J* **45**, 230-64

Biddle, M, 1967a Excavations at Winchester 1966; Fourth interim report, *Antiq J* **47**, 251-79

Biddle, M, 1967b Two Flavian burials from Grange Road, Winchester, *Antiq J* **47**, 224-50

Biddle, M, 1968 Excavations at Winchester 1967; Sixth interim Report, *Antiq J* **48**, 250-84

Biddle, M, 1970 Excavations at Winchester, 1969; Eighth interim report, *Antiq J* **50,** 277-326

Biddle, M, 1972 Excavations at Winchester, 1970; Ninth interim report, *Antiq J* **52**, 93-131

Biddle, M, 1973 Winchester: the development of an early capital, in H Jankuhn, W Schlesinger and H Steuer (eds), *Vor- und Frühformen der europaischen Stadtim Mittelalter*, 229-61

Biddle, M, 1975a Excavations at Winchester, 1971; Tenth and final interim report: part 1, *Antiq J* **55**, 96-126

Biddle, M, 1975b Excavations at Winchester, 1971; Tenth and final interim report: part 2, *Antiq J* **55**, 295-337

Biddle, M, 1975c Felix Urbs Winthonia: Winchester in the age of monastic reform, in D Parsons (ed.), *Tenth Century Studies*, London, 123-40

Biddle, M, 1975d The evolution of towns: Planned towns before 1066, in M W Barley (ed.), *The plans and topography of medieval towns in England and Wales*, CBA Res Rep **14**, 19-31

Biddle, M (ed.), 1976 *Winchester in the early Middle Ages: an edition and discussion of the Winton Domesday*, Winchester Studies **1**, Oxford

Biddle, M, 1983 The study of Winchester: archaeology and history in a British town, *Proc Brit Acad* **69**, 93-135

Biddle, M (ed.), 1990 *Object and economy in medieval Winchester*, Winchester Studies **7**, Oxford

Biddle, M, and Barclay, K, 1974 Winchester Ware, in V I Evision, H Hodges and J G Hurst (eds), *Medieval pottery from excavations: Studies presented to Gerald Dunning*, London, 133-5

Biddle, M, and Hill, D, 1971 Late Saxon planned towns, *Antiq J* **51(1)**, 70-85

Biddle, M, and Keene, S, 1990 Leather working, in Biddle (ed.) 1990, 245-47

Biddle, M, and Kjølbye-Biddle, B, 2007 Winchester: from Venta to Wintancaestir, in L Gilmour (ed.), *Pagans and Christians – from Antiquity to the Middle Ages. Papers in honour of Martin Henig, presented on the occasion of his 65th birthday*, BAR Int Ser **1610**, 189-214

Biddle, M, and Quirk, R N, 1964 Excavations near Winchester Cathedral, 1961, *Archaeol J* **119,** 150-94

Biddulph, E, 2005 Last orders: choosing pottery for funerals in Roman Essex, *Oxford J Archaeol* **24** (1), 23-45

Biddulph, E, 2006 The Roman pottery from Pepper Hill, Southfleet, Kent (ARC PHL97, ARC NBR98), *CTRL specialist report series*, ADS, http://archaeologydataservice.ac.uk/catalogue/adsdata/arch-335-1/dissemination/pdf/PT2_Spec_Reps/01_Ceramics/CER_research_reports/CER_RomanPot/CER_RomanPot_Text/CER_ROM_PHL_text.pdf?CFID=45&CFTOKEN=454ECBCD-4089-404A-BD2E40E91FF417B6

Biddulph, E, 2008 Form and function: the experimental use of samian ware cups, *Oxford J Archaeol* **27 (1)**, 91-100

Birbeck, V with Smith, R, Andrews, P, and Stoodley, N, 2005 *The origins of mid-Saxon Southampton: excavations at the Friends Provident St Mary's Stadium 1998-2000*, Wessex Archaeology, Salisbury

Bishop, C M, 2001 Quarr stone: an archaeological and petrological study in relation to the Roman, Anglo-Saxon and medieval stone building industries of southern Britain, unpubl PhD thesis, University of Reading

Bishop, M C, and Coulston, J C N, 2006 *Roman military equipment from the Punic Wars to the fall of Rome*, 2 edn, Oxbow, Oxford

Blackmore, L, 2007 Publication report on the post-Roman pottery from Granville House, St Peter Street, Winchester, unpubl report, WINCM AY256, Museum of London ref: AOC/WINCM-AY256

Blades, N, 1995 Copper alloys from English archaeological sites 400-1600: an analytical study using ICP-AES, unpubl PhD thesis, Royal Holloway and Bedford New College, University of London

Blair, J, 1991 Purbeck Marble, in J Blair and N Ramsay (eds), *English medieval industries: craftsmen, techniques, products*, Hambledon and London, London, 40-56

Blair, J, 1993 Hall and chamber: English domestic planning 1000-1250, in G. Meirion-Jones and M Jones, *Manorial Domestic buildings in England and Northern France*, Soc Antiq Occ Paper **15**, London, 159-72

Blair, J, 2005 *The Church in Anglo-Saxon Society*, Oxford

Blanchard, I, 2007 The twelfth-century: A neglected epoch in British economic and social history, Chapter 8: Burhs and Borough, http://www.ianblanchard.com

Blunt, C E, 1962 Two Anglo-Saxon notes, *Brit Numis J* **31**, 44-8

Blunt, C E, 1974 The coinage of Athelstan, 924-939: a survey, *Brit Numis J* **42**, 35-158

Blunt, C E, Stewart, B H I H, and Lyon, C S S, 1989 *Coinage in tenth-century England from Edward the Elder to Edgar's reform*, British Academy, London

Boessneck, J, Müller, H H, and Teichert, M, 1964 Osteologische Unterscheidungsmerkmale zwischen Schaf (Ovis aries Linné) und Ziege (Capra hircus Linné), *Kühn-Archiv* **78**, 331-58

Bond, J M, and O'Connor, T P, 1999 Bones from medieval deposits at 16-22 Coppergate and other sites in York, *The archaeology of York* **15/5**, York

Booth, K, Farrant, A, Hopson, P, Woods, M, Evans, D, and Wilkinson, I, 2008 *Geology of the Winchester district: sheet description of the British Geological Survey 1:50 000 Series Sheet 299 Winchester (England and Wales)*, British Geological Survey

Booth, P, 2007 Oxford Archaeology Roman pottery recording system: an introduction, Oxford Archaeology unpubl guidelines, revised

Booth, P, 2008 Coins, in A Simmonds and A Smith, Excavations on the site of the Roman forum at Cirencester, in Holbrook 2008, 56-8

Booth, P, 2010 The coins, in Booth *et al.* 2010

Booth, P, and Evans, J, 2001 *Roman Alcester: Northern extramural area*, CBA Res Rep **127**, York

Booth, P, Simmonds, A, Boyle, A, Clough, S, Cool, H E M, and Poore, D, 2010 *The late Roman cemetery at Lankhills, Winchester, excavations 2000-2005*, Oxford Archaeology Monograph **10**, Oxford

Borgard, P, and Cavalier, M, 2003 The Lipari origin of the 'Richborough 527', *J Roman Pottery Stud* **10**, 96-107

Bourdillon, J, 2009 Late Saxon animal bone from the northern and eastern suburbs and the city defences, in Serjeantson and Rees 2009, 55-81

Bourdillon, J, and Andrews, P, 1997, The animal bone, in P Andrews, *Excavations at Hamwic, volume 2: excavations at Six Dials*, CBA Res Rep **109**, York, 242-45

Bourdillon, J, and Coy, J, 1980 The animal bones, in P Holdsworth, *Excavations at Melbourne Street, Southampton 1971-76*, CBA Res Rep **33**, 79-121

Bovy, K M, 2002 Differential avian skeletal part distribution: explaining the abundance of wings, *J Archaeol Sci* **29**, 965-78

Box, G E P, 1979 Robustness in scientific model building, in R L Launer and G N Wilkinson (eds), *Robustness in Statistics,* Academic Press, New York, 201-36

Branigan, K, 1977 *Gatcombe Roman Villa*, BAR Brit Ser **44**, Oxford

Brewer, R J, 1986 Other objects of bronze, in Zienkiewicz 1986, 172-89

Brewer, R J, 1986 The beads and glass counters, in Zienkiewicz 1986, 146-56

Brickley, M, and McKinley, J (eds), 2004 *Guidance to Standards for Recording Human Skeletal Remains Institute of Field Archaeologists / British Association of Biological Anthropology and Osteoarchaeology,* University of Reading

Brisbane, M, 1988 Hamwic (Saxon Southampton): an 8th century port and production centre, in R Hodges and B Hobley (eds), *The rebirth of towns in the west AD 700-1050*, CBA Res Rep **68,** London, 101-8

British Geological Survey, 2002 1:50,000 Map Series, Winchester Sheet 299, NERC

Brodribb, G 1979 A survey of tile from the Roman bath house at Beauport Park, Battle, E Sussex *Britannia* **10**, 139-56

Bronk R C, 1995 Radiocarbon calibration and analysis of stratigraphy: the OxCal program, *Radiocarbon* **36**, 425-306

Bronk R C, 1998 Probability and dating, *Radiocarbon* **40**, 461-74

Bronk R C, 2000 Comment on 'The use of Bayesian statistics for C14 dates of chronologically ordered samples: a critical analysis', *Radiocarbon* **42**, 199-202.

Bronk R C, 2001 Development of the radiocarbon calibration program OxCal, *Radiocarbon* **43**, 355-63

Bronk R C, Higham, T, and Leach, P, 2004 Towards high precision AMS: progress and limitations, *Radiocarbon* **46**, 17-24

Brooks, N, 1964 The unidentified forts of the Burghal Hidage, *Medieval Archaeol* **8**, 74-90

Brothwell, D, Dobney, K, and Jaques, D, 2005 Abnormal sheep metatarsals: a problem in aetiology and historical geography, in J Davies, M Fabiš, I Mainland, M Richards and R Thomas (eds), *Diet and health in past animal populations: current research and future direction*, Oxbow books, Oxford, 75-79

Brown, A, 1994 A Romano-British shell-gritted pottery and tile manufacturing site at Harrold, Beds, *Bedfordshire Archaeol J* **21**, 19-107

Brown, D H, 1994 Pottery and late Saxon Southampton, *Proc Hampshire Fld Club Archaeol Soc* **50**, 127-52

Brown, D H, 1997 Pots from Houses, *Medieval Ceramics* **21**, 83-94

Brown, D H, 2002 *Pottery in Medieval Southampton, c. 1066-1510*, CBA Res Rep **133**

Brown, D H, forthcoming Pottery, in Brown and Hardy forthcoming

Brown, L, 2000 The pottery, in B Cunliffe and C Poole, The Danebury Environs programme: *The prehistory of a Wessex landscape. Volume 2 – Part 6: Houghton Down, Stockbridge, Hants 1994*, English Heritage and OUCA Monograph **49**, Oxford, 75-102

Brown, R and Hardy, A, forthcoming Trade and prosperity – war and poverty, an archaeological and historical investigation into Southampton's

French Quarter, Oxford Archaeology monograph

Browne, S, Ottaway, P J, Qualmann, K E, Rees, H, Scobie, G D, Teague, S, and Whinney, R, forthcoming *Roman Cemeteries and Suburbs of Winchester: Excavations 1971-85*, Winchester Museum Service/English Heritage Reports

Buck, C E, Cavanagh, W G and Litton, C D, 1996 *Bayesian Approach to Interpreting Archaeological Data*, Chichester

Buck, C E, Litton, C D, and Smith, A F M, 1992 Calibration of radiocarbon results pertaining to related archaeological events, *J Archaeol Sci* **19**, 497-512

Buschbaum, C, and Saier, B, 2001 Growth of the mussel Mytilus edulis L. affected by tidal emergence and barnacle epibionts, *Journal of Sea Research* **45**, 27-36

Butler, J J, and van der Waals, J D, 1966 Bell beakers and early metalworking in the Netherlands, *Palaeohistoria* **12**, 41-139

Campbell, G, and Straker, V, 2003 Prehistoric crop husbandry and plant use in southern England: development and regionality, in K A Robson Brown (ed.) *Archaeological Sciences 1999: Proceedings of the Archaeological Science Conference, University of Bristol*, BAR Int Ser **1111**, Oxford, 14-30

Carreras Monfort, C, and Williams, D, 2003 Spanish olive-oil trade in late Roman Britain: Dressel 23 amphorae from Winchester, *J Roman Pottery Stud* **10**, 64-8

Carrott, J, Hall, A, Issitt, M, Kenward, H, and Large, F, 1996 Medieval plant and invertebrate remains principally preserved by anoxic waterlogging at The Brooks, Winchester, Hampshire (site code: BRI and BRII): Technical Report. Reports from the Environmental Archaeology Unit, York 96/20, 32

Carruthers, W J, 1988 Mystery object no. 2 – animal, mineral or vegetable?, *Circaea* **6(1)**, 20

Carruthers, W J, 1989 The carbonised plant remains, in Fasham *et al.* 1989, 131-4

Carruthers, W J, 2000a The mineralised plant remains, in Lawson and Gingell 2000, 72-84, 91-95

Carruthers, W J, 2005a Mineralised plant remains, in Birbeck *et al.* 2005, 157-73

Carruthers, W J, 2005b The plant remains: comparing and contrasting the assemblages, in Birbeck *et al.* 2005, 183–5

Carruthers, W J, 2008 Charred, mineralised and waterlogged plant remains, in Cooke *et al.* 2008, CD-Rom chapters 29 and 34

Catchpole, T, 2007 Excavation at the Sewage Treatment Works, Dymock, Gloucestershire, 1995, *Trans Bristol Gloucestershire Archaol Soc* **125**, 137-219

Challinor, D, 2002 The charcoal, in Z Kamash, D R P Wilkinson, B M Ford and J Hiller, Late Saxon and medieval occupation: evidence from excavations at Lincoln College, Oxford 1997-2000, *Oxoniensia* **67**, 199-287

Challinor, D, forthcoming, Charcoal, in Brown and Hardy, forthcoming

Christophersen, A, 1980 *Håndverket i forandring. Studier i horn og bein håndverkets utvikling i Lund ca 1000-1350, Acta Archaeologica Lundensia, series in 4o* **13**, Lund

City of Winchester, http://www.cityofwinchester.co.uk/history/html/streetnames.html, (accessed 25 August 2008)

Clark, J (ed.), 2004 *The medieval horse and its equipment c 1150-1450*, Medieval finds from excavations in London **5**, new edn, London and Woodbridge

Clark, A J, Tarling, D J, and Noël, M, 1988 Developments in archaeomagnetic dating in Britain, *J Archaeol Sci*, **15**, 645-67

Clarke, A, and Fulford, M, 2002 The excavation of Insula IX, Silchester: the first five years of the 'Town Life' project, 1997-2001, *Britannia* **33**, 129-166

Clarke, G, 1979 *The Roman cemetery at Lankhills*, Winchester Studies **3**: Pre-Roman and Roman Winchester. Part 2, Oxford University Press, Oxford

Clarke, H, 1984 *The archaeology of medieval England*, British Museum Press, London

Cleere, H, and Crossley, D, 1985 *The iron industry of the Weald*, Leicester University Press, Leicester

Coe, D, and Newman, R, 1993 Excavations of an early Iron Age building and Romano-British enclosure at Brighton Hill South, Hampshire, *Proc. Hampshire Fld Club Archaeol Soc* **48**, 5-26

Cohen, A, and Serjeantson, D, 1996 *A manual for the identification of bird bones from archaeological sites*, Archetype Press, London

Cole, M, 1994 *Merdon Castle, Hursley, Hants: report on geophysical survey*, AML Report **26/94**

Collis, J, 1970 Excavations at Owslebury, Hants: second interim report, *Antiq J* **50**, 246-61

Collis, J, 1978 Winchester *Excavations 1949-1960, Vol 2: Excavations in the suburbs and Western parts of the town*, Winchester Museums and Libraries Committee

Collis, J, and Kjølbye-Biddle, B, 1979 Early medieval bone spoons from Winchester, *Antiq J* **59**, 375-91

Cooke, N, Brown, F, and Phillpotts, C, 2008 *From hunter gatherers to huntsmen: A history of the Stansted landscape*, Framework Archaeology Monograph. **2**, Salisbury and Oxford

Cool, H E M, 1983 Roman personal ornaments made of metal, excluding brooches from southern England, unpubl PhD thesis, Univ Wales

Cool, H E M, 1990 Roman metal hair pins from southern Britain, *Archaeol J* **147**, 148-82

Cool, H E M, 2000 The parts left over: material culture into the fifth century, in T Wilmott and P Wilson (eds) *The late Roman Transition in the North*, BAR Brit. Ser. **299**, Oxford, 47-65

Cool, H E M, 2002 An overview of the small finds from Catterick, in Wilson 2002, 24-43

Cool, H E M, 2003 Local production and trade in glass vessels in the British Isles in the first to seventh centuries AD, in Foy and Nenna 2003, 139-43

Cool, H E M, 2007a Metal and glass, in Catchpole 2007, 171-83

Cool, H E M, 2007b Small finds, in Miles *et al.* 2007, 249-60

Cool, H E M, 2008a Glass vessels, in Rees *et al.* 2008, 78-98

Cool, H E M, 2008b Copper alloy, in Garner 2008, 307-17

Cool, H E M, 2008c Glass and frit beads and ornaments, in Garner 2008, 302-3

Cool, H E M, Lloyd-Morgan, G, and Hooley, A D, 1995 *Finds from the Fortress*, Archaeology of York **17/10**, York

Cool, H E M, and Philo, C (eds), 1998 *Roman Castleford: excavations 1974-85. Volume I: the small finds*, Yorkshire Archaeology **4**, Wakefield

Cool, H E M, and Price, J, 1987 The glass, in Meates 1987, 110-42

Cool, H E M, and Price, J, 1995 *Roman vessel glass from excavations in Colchester 1971-85*, Colchester Archaeol Rep **8**, Colchester

Cool, H E M, and Price, J, 2002 Glass from Prof. Wachers excavations, in Wilson 2002, 213-43

Cotter, J, 1997 *A Twelfth-Century Pottery Kiln at Pound Lane, Canterbury*, Canterbury Archaeological Trust

Coy, J, 1989 The provision of fowls and fish for towns, in D Serjeantson and T Waldron (eds), *Diet and crafts in towns: the evidence of animal remains from the Roman to the post-medieval periods*, BAR Brit Ser **199**, Oxford, 25-40

Coy, J, 1996 Medieval records versus excavation results: examples from southern England, *Archaeofauna* **5**, 55-63

Coy, J, 2009 Late Saxon and medieval animal bone from the western suburb, in Serjeantson and Rees 2008, 27-54

Crabtree, P, 1996 Production and consumption in an early complex society: animal use in middle Saxon East Anglia, *World Archaeol* **28 (1)**, 58-75

Cramp, S (ed.), 1980 *Birds of the Western Palearctic. Volume I: ostrich to ducks*, Oxford University Press, Oxford

Crook, J, 1985 Winchester's cleansing streams – Part 2: The Lockburn, *Winchester Cathedral Record* **54**, 15-24

Crothers, J H, 1992 Shell size and shape variation in Littorina littorea (L.) from west Somerset, in J Grahame, P J Mill and D G Reid (eds), *Proceedings of the Third International Symposium on Littorinid Biology*, Malacological Society of London, London, 91-7

Crowfoot, E, Pritchard, F, and Staniland, K, 2006 Textiles and clothing, c.1150-c.1450, *Medieval finds from excavations in London* **4**, Museum of London

Crummy, N, 1983 *The Roman small finds from excavations in Colchester, 1971-9*, Colchester

Archaeol Rep **2**, Colchester

Crummy, N, 1992 The Roman small finds from the Culver Street site, in P Crummy 1992, 140-205

Crummy, P, 1979 The system of measurement used in town planning from the 9th to the 13th centuries, *Anglo-Saxon Studies in Archaeology and History*, BAR Brit Ser **72**, 149-64

Crummy, P, 1981 *Aspects of Anglo-Saxon and Norman Colchester* CBA Res Rep **39**

Crummy, P, 1992 *Excavations at Culver Street, the Gilberd School, and other sites in Colchester 1971-85*, Colchester Archaeol Rep **6**, Colchester

Culpepper, N, 1826 *Culpepper's complete herbal*, 1979 facsimile edn, Gareth Powell Ltd, Hong Kong

Cummins, V, Coughlan, S, McClean, O, Conelly, J M, and Burnell, G, 2002 *An assessment of the potential for the sustainable development of the edible periwinkle* (Littorina littorea), *Industry in Ireland*, Marine Resource Series **22**, Dublin

Cunliffe, B, 1962 The Winchester City Wall, *Proc Hampshire Fld Club Archaeol Soc* 22(2), 51-81

Cunliffe, B, 1964 *Winchester excavations, 1949-1960, volume 1*, Winchester Museums and Libraries Committee, Winchester

Cunliffe, B, 1971 *Excavations at Fishbourne, 1961-1969. Volume 2: the finds*, Society of Antiquaries Report **27**, London

Cunliffe, B, 1975 *Excavations at Portchester Castle, Volume 1*, Society of Antiquaries Report **32**, London

Cunliffe, B, 1984 *Danebury: an Iron Age hillfort in Hampshire. Volume 2. The excavations, 1969-1978: the finds*, CBA Res Rep **52**, London

Cunliffe, B, 1985 Building Materials, in B Cunliffe and J Munby, *Excavations at Portchester Castle Vol. 4: Medieval, the Inner Bailey*, Soc of Antiq London, London

Cunliffe, B, 1996 The Iron Age of Hampshire: an assessment, in D Hinton, and M Hughes (eds), *Archaeology in Hampshire: a framework for the future*, Hampshire County Council, 26-30

Cunliffe, B, 2005 *Iron Age communities in Britain*, 4 edn, Routledge, London

Cunliffe, B, and Poole, C, 1991 *Danebury: an Iron Age hillfort in Hampshire; Volume 4: The excavations 1979-1988*, CBA Res Rep **73**

Cunliffe, B, and Poole, C, 2000 *The Danebury Environs programme: the prehistory of a Wessex landscape, vol. 2*, English Heritage and OUCA Monograph **49**, Oxford

Cunliffe, B, and Poole, C, 2008 *The Danebury Environs Roman programme: A Wessex landscape during the Roman era. Vol. 2: The sites*, OUCA Monograph **71**, Oxford

Cutting, C L, 1955 *Fish saving: a history of fish processing from ancient to modern times*, Leonard Hill, London

d'Ambrosio, A, Guzzo, P G, and Mastroberto, M, 2003 *Storie da un'eruzione: Pompei, Ercolano, Oplontis*, Electa, Milan

Dainton, M, 1992 A quick, semi-quantitative method for recording nematode gut parasite eggs from archaeological deposits, *Circaea* **9**, 58-63

Dannell, G, 1999 Decorated South Gaulish samian, in R P Symonds and S Wade, *Roman pottery from excavations at Colchester, 1971-86*, Colchester Archaeol Rep **10**, Colchester, 13-74

Darby, H C, 1976 *A new historical geography of England before 1600*, Cambridge University Press, Cambridge

Dark, P, 2004 New evidence for the antiquity of the intestinal parasite *Trichuris* (whipworm) in Europe, *Antiquity* **78**, 676-681

Davidson, A, 1999 The Oxford companion to food, Oxford University Press, Oxford

Davies, J, 2008 The other Roman coins, in Rees *et al.* 2008, 123-37

Davies, S M, 1981 Excavations at Old Down Farm, Andover. Part 2: prehistoric and Roman, *Proc Hants Field Club Archaeol Soc* **37**, 81-163

Denford, G D, 1988 Roman furniture from Market Street, *Winchester Museums Service Newsletter* **2**, 5

Dineley, M, 2004 *Barley, malt and ale in the Neolithic*, BAR Int Ser **1213**, Oxford

Dobney, K, 2001 A place at the table: the role of vertebrate zooarchaeology within a Roman research agenda, in James and Millett (eds) 2001, 36-45

Dobney, K, Jaques, D, and Irving, B, 1995 *Of butchers and breeds: report on vertebrate remains from various sites in the city of Lincoln*, Lincoln Archaeological Studies **5**, Lincoln

Dobney, K, Jaques, D, Johnstone, C, Hall, A, La Ferla, B, and Haynes, S, 2007 The agricultural economy, in K Dobney, D Jaques, J Barrett and C Johnstone, *Farmers, monks and aristocrats: the environmental archaeology of Anglo-Saxon Flixborough*, Excavations at Flixborough **3**, Oxford, 116-89

DoE, 1990a Planning and Policy Guidance (PPG) note 16: Archaeology and Planning, HMSO, London

DoE, 1990b Planning and Policy Guidance (PPG) note 15: Planning and the Historic Environment. HMSO, London

Doll, M, 2003 *Haustierhaltung und Schlachtsitten des Mittelalters unter der Neuzeit. Eine Synthese aus archäologischen, bildlichen und schriftlichen Quellen Mitteleuropas*, Internationale Archäologie **78**, Verlag Marie Leidorf GmbH

Draper, J C, 1966 Mesolithic distribution in southeast Hampshire, *Proc Hants Field Club Archaeol Soc* **23**, 110-19

Duncan, H, 2002 Domestic metalwork, in Roberts 2002, 249-80

Dunning, G C, 1961 Medieval chimney-pots, in E M Jope, *Studies in building history*, Odhams, London, 78-93

Dunning, G C, Hooley, W, and Tildesley, M L, 1929 Excavations of an early Iron Age village on Worthy Down, Winchester, *Proc Hants Fld Club Archaeol Soc* **10**, 178-92

Dunning, G C, Hurst, J G, Myres, J N L, and

Tischler, F, 1959 Anglo-Saxon pottery: a symposium *Medieval Archaeol*, **3**, 1-78

Dunning, G C, and Wilson, A E, 1953 Late Saxon and early medieval pottery from selected sites in Chichester, *Sussex Archaeol Collect* **91**, 140-150

During, E, 1986 *The fauna of Alvastra. An osteological analysis of animal bones from a Neolithic pile dwelling*, Stockholm studies in archaeology **6**, University of Stockholm, Stockholm

Dyer, C, 1988 The consumption of freshwater fish in medieval England, in M Aston (ed.), *Medieval fish, fisheries and fishponds in England*, BAR Brit Ser **182**, Oxford, 27-38

Eckardt, H, and Crummy, N, 2008 *Styling the body in late Iron Age and Roman Britain*, Monographies Instrumentum **36**, Montagnac

Edlin, H L, 1949 *Woodland crafts in Britain: an account of the traditional uses of trees and timbers in the British countryside*, Batsford, London

Egan, G, 1991 Industry and economics on the medieval and later London waterfront, in G L Good, R H Jones and M W Ponsford (eds), *Waterfront archaeology: Proceedings of the third International Conference*, CBA Res Rep **74**, 9-12

Egan, G, 1998 *The medieval household: daily living c 1150-c 1450*, Medieval finds from excavations in London **6**, London

Egan, G, 2005 *Material culture in London in an age of transition*, MoLAS Monograph **19**, London

Egan, G, and Pritchard, F, 2002 *Dress accessories c 1150-c 1450*, Medieval finds from excavations in London **3**, London

Egardt, Brita, 1962 *Hästslakt och rackarskam: en etnologisk undersökning av folkliga fördomar*, Nordiska museet

Ellis, P, (ed.), 2000 *The Roman baths and macellum at Wroxeter*, English Heritage Archaeol Rep **9**, London

Ellis, P, and White, R, 2006 *Wroxeter archaeology: excavations and research on the defences and in the town, 1968-1992*, Shropshire Archaeological and Historical Society, Shrewsbury

Ellis, S E, and Moore, D T, 1990 The hones, in Biddle (ed) 1990, 868-81

Elmehaisi, F O M, 1987 Biometrical investigations of archaeological *Trichuris* (whipworm) eggs, unpubl MSc dissertation, University of York

Emberley, J V, 1998 *Venus and furs: the cultural politics of fur*, London

Enghoff, I B, 2000 Fishing in the southern North Sea region from the 1st to the 16th century AD: evidence from fish bones, *Archaeofauna* **9**, 59-132

Enghoff, I B, 2007 Dyreknogler fra vikingetidens Viborg, in M Iversen, D E Robinson, J Hjermind and C Christensen (eds), *Viborg Søndersø 1018-1030. Arkæologi og naturvidenskab i et værkstedsomrade fra vikingetid*, Viborgs stiftsmuseum, Jysk Arkæologisk Selskab, 239-268

English Heritage, Wolvesey Castle (Old Bishop's Palace), web link: http://www.english-heritage.org.uk/server/show/nav.19864 (accessed on 24 Nov 2009)

Erblersdobler, K, 1968 *Vergleichend morphologische Untersuchungen an Einzelknochen des postcranialen Skeletts in Mitteleuropa vorkommender mittelgroßer Hühnervögel*, Inaugural-Dissertation, Ludwig-Maximilians-Universität, München

Esmonde Cleary, S, 2000 Putting the dead in their place: burial location in Roman Britain, in J Pearce, M Millett M and M Struck, *Burial, society and context in the Roman world*, Oxbow Books, Oxford, 127-42

Evans, D, 2008 The Foresters Arms, Queen Street, 2003-4, in Holbrook (ed) 2008, 40-3

Evans, D R, and Metcalf, V M, 1992 *Roman gates, Caerleon*, Oxbow Monograph 15, Oxford

Evans, J, 1989 *A history of jewellery, 1100-1870*, 2 edn reprint 1970, New York

Evans, J, 2001 Material approaches to the identification of different Romano-British site types, in James and Millett (eds) 2001, 26-35

Fagan, B, 2006 *Fish on Friday: feasting, fasting and the discovery of the New World*, Basic Books, New York

Fairnell, E, 2003 The utilisation of fur-bearing animals in the British Isles: A zooarchaeological hunt for data, unpubl MSc thesis, University of York

Farmer, D, 2000 *A brief history of Oliver's Battery* (pamphlet)

Fasham, P J, 1980 Excavations on Bridgett's and Burntwood Farms, Itchen Valley parish, Hampshire 1974, Proc *Hampshire Fld Club Archaeol Soc* 36, 37-86

Fasham, P J, 1982 The excavation of four ring-ditches in Central Hampshire (MARC3 Sites R17, Feature 1972; R7; R30; and R 363) *Proc Hampshire Fld Club Archaeol Soc* 38, 19-56

Fasham, P J, 1985 *The prehistoric settlement at Winnall Down, Winchester: excavations of MARC3 Site R17 in 1976 and 1977*, Hampshire Field Club Monograph 2, Winchester

Fasham, P J, Farwell, D E, and Whinney, R J B, 1989 *The archaeological site at Easton Lane, Winchester*, Hampshire Field Club Monograph 6, Winchester

Fasham, P J, and Whinney, R J B, 1991 *Archaeology and the M3*, Hampshire Field Club Monograph 7, Winchester

Faulkner, P, A, 1958 Domestic planning from the twelfth to the fourteenth centuries, *Arch J* 115, 150-83

Foot, R, 1994 Report on the brick and tile from The Brooks excavation, Winchester Museum Service unpubl report

Ford, S, Bradley, R, Hawkes, J, and Fisher, P, 1984 Flint-working in the metal age, *Oxford J Archaeol* 3(2), 157-173

Fowler, E, 1960 The origin and development of the penannular brooch in Europe, *Proc Prehist Soc* 26, 149-77

Foy, D, and Nenna M D (eds), 2003 *Échanges et commerce du verre dans le monde antique*, Monographies Instrumentum 24, Montagnac

Freeman, R, 1991 *The art and architecture of Owen Browne Carter 1806-1859*, Hampshire Papers 1, Hampshire County Council

Frere, S S, 1972 *Verulamium excavations volume 1*, Rep Res Comm Soc Ant London 28, London

Fulford, M, 1975a *New Forest Roman pottery*, BAR Brit Ser 17, Oxford

Fulford, M, 1975b The pottery, in Cunliffe 1975, 270-367

Fulford, M, 1977 Pottery and Britain's trade in the later Roman period, in D P S Peacock (ed.), *Pottery and early commerce: characterisation and trade in Roman and later ceramics*, London, 35-84

Fulford, M, 1979 Late Roman pottery, in G Clarke, *Pre-Roman and Roman Winchester. Part 2: the Roman cemetery at Lankhills*, Winchester Studies 3, Oxford, 221-37

Fulford, M, 2001 Links with the past: pervasive 'ritual' behaviour in Roman Britain, *Britannia* 32, 199-218

Gahan, A, and McCutcheon, C, 1997 Medieval pottery, in M F Hurley and O M B Scully, *Late Viking age and medieval Waterford: Excavations 1986-1992*, Waterford, 285-336

Gaimster, D R M, Margeson, S, and Hurley, M, 1990 Medieval Britain and Ireland in 1989, *Medieval Archaeol* 34, 162-252

Gale, R, 2005 Charcoal, in Birbeck *et al.* 2005, 154-56

Garner, D, 2008 *Excavations at Chester: 25 Bridge Street, 2001*, Archaeological Service Excavation and Survey Report 14, Chester

Gaspar, M B, Santos, M N, Vasconcelos, P, and Montiero, C C, 2002 Shell morphometric relationships of the most common bivalve species (Mollusca: Bivalvia) of the Algarve coast (southern Portugal), *Hydrobiologia* 477, 73-80

Geber, J, 2005, The human skeletal remains from Northgate House, Staple Gardens, Winchester WINCM: AY93, in Teague and Ford 2006

Giertz, W, 1996 Middle Meuse Valley ceramics of Huy-type: a preliminary analysis, *Medieval Ceramics* 20, 33-64

Gifford, 2004a Northgate House site, Staple Gardens, Winchester. Archaeological desk-based assessment (Report No. 10911.R01)

Gifford, 2004b Northgate House, Winchester. Results of the archaeological evaluation. (Report No. 10911.R03)

Gifford, 2004c Northgate House, Winchester. Results of the 2004 archaeological evaluation. (Report No. 10911.R04)

Gifford, 2004d Archaeological mitigation strategy (Report No. 10911.R05. rev E)

Gifford, 2005 Rationale for archaeological mitigation and backfilling report including drawing No. 10911-2100 Rev T (Report No. 10911-Arch-R06)

Gillam, J P, 1976 Coarse fumed ware in North Britain and beyond, *Glasgow Archaeol J* 4, 57-80

Gingell, C J, and Morris, E L, 2000 Pottery, in Lawson and Gingell 2000, 136-78

Going, C J, 1992 Economic 'long waves' in the Roman period? A reconnaissance of the Romano-British ceramic evidence, *Oxford J Archaeol* **11(1)**, 93-117

Graham, A, 2004 *Wattle and daub: craft, conservation and Wiltshire case study*, http://www.tonygrah am.co.uk/house_repair/wattle_daub/WD.html

Grant, A, 1982 The use of toothwear as a guide to the age of domestic ungulates, in B Wilson, C Grigson and S Payne (eds), *Ageing and sexing animal bones from archaeological sites*, BAR Brit Ser **109**, Oxford, 91-108

Green, F J, 1979 Phosphate mineralisation of seeds from archaeological sites, *J Archaeol Sci* **6**, 279-284

Green, F J, 2005 Sites in the western suburbs, in Qualmann *et al.* 2005, 75-78

Green, F J, 2009 Late Saxon, medieval and post-medieval plant remains, in Serjeantson and Rees 2009, 14-26

Green, M, 2000 *A Landscape revealed, 10,000 Years on a Chalkland Farm*, Tempus Publishing Ltd

Greene, K, 1978 Imported fine wares in Britain to AD 250: a guide to identification, in Arthur and Marsh (eds) 1978, 15-30

Greene, K, 1979 *The pre-Flavian fine wares: report on the excavations at Usk 1965-1976*, Univ. of Wales Press, Cardiff

Greep, S J, 1986 The objects of worked bone, in Zienkiewicz 1986, 197-216

Greep, S J, 1996 Objects of worked bone and antler, in Jackson and Potter 1996, 525-38

Greep, S J, 1997 Objects of bone, antler and ivory, in Wenham and Heywood 1997, 144-8

Greig, J, 1981 The investigation of a medieval Barrel-latrine from Worcester, *J Archaeol Sci* **8**, 265-82

Grierson, P, and Blackburn, M, 1986 *Medieval European coinage with a catalogue of the coins in the Fitzwilliam Museum, Cambridge. Vol 1: The Early Middle Ages (5th-10th centuries)*, Cambridge University Press, Cambridge

Grieve, M, 1931 *A modern herbal*, revised edn 1992, Tiger Books International, London

Griffith, H I, 1993 The Eurasian badger, Meles meles (L. 1758) as a commodity species, *J of Zoology* **230**, 340-42

Habermehl, K H, 1975 *Die Altersbestimmung bei Haus- und Labortieren*, 2nd ed, Verlag Paul Parey, Berlin, Hamburg

Hagen, A, 1992 *A handbook of Anglo-Saxon food processing and consumption*, Anglo-Saxon Books

Hagen, A, 2002 *A handbook of Anglo-Saxon food and drink: Processing and distribution*, Anglo-Saxon Books, Frithgarth

Halstead, P, 1985 A study of mandibular teeth from Romano-British contexts at Maxey, in F Pryor, *Archaeology and environment in the Lower Welland Valley*, East Anglian Archaeology Report **27**, 219-24

Halstead, P, and Collins, P, 2002 Sorting the sheep from the goats: Morphological distinctions between the mandibles and mandibular teeth of adult Ovis and Capra, *J Archaeol Sci* **29**, 545-53

Hambleton, E, 1999 *Animal husbandry regimes in Iron Age Britain. A comparative study of faunal assemblages from British Iron Age sites*, BAR Brit Ser, **282**, Archaeopress, Oxford

Hamerow, H, 1993 *Excavations at Mucking Vol 2: The Anglo-Saxon settlement*, English Heritage Archaeol rep **23**, English Heritage

Hamilton, S, and Manley, J 1997 Points of view: prominent enclosures in 1st millennium BC Sussex, *Sussex Archaeol Collections* **135**, 93-112

Hamilton-Dyer, S 1986 A note on the sieved material from the garderobe layers A296-8, in J Oxley (ed.), *Excavations at Southampton Castle*, Southampton City Museums, Southampton, 37-8

Hamilton-Dyer, S 1993 Fish remains, in Woodward *et al.* 1993, 345-46

Hamilton-Dyer, S 1997 Bone report for the Lower High Street project, Southampton. Saxon and early Post-Conquest, and High Medieval/early Post-Medieval, unpubl document

Hamilton-Dyer, S 2000 The fish remains, in M Fulford and J Timby (eds), 2000, *Late Iron Age and Roman Silchester: excavations on the site of the Forum-Basilica 1977, 1980-86*, Britannia Monograph Ser **15**, 482-84

Hamilton-Dyer, S 2004 Fish bone from Staple Gardens, in K E Qualmann *et al.* 2004, 75

Hansell, P, and Hansell, J, 1988 *Doves and dovecotes*, Millstream Books, Bath

Harcourt, R A, 1974 The dog in prehistoric and early historic Britain, *J Archaeol Sci* **1**, 151-75

Harden, D B, 1979 Glass vessels, in Clarke 1979, 209-20

Hardy, A, Charles, B M, and Williams R J, 2007 *Death and taxes: The archaeology of a Middle Saxon estate centre at Higham Ferrers, Northamptonshire*, Oxford Archaeology Monograph **4**, Oxford

Hare, J N, 1991 The growth of the roof-tile industry in later medieval Wessex, *Medieval Archaeol* **35**, 86-103

Harman, M, 1993 The animal bone, in M J Darling and D Gurney, *Caister-on-Sea excavations by Charles Green, 1951-55*, East Anglian Archaeology **60**, 223-38

Harrison, L, 1995 The environmental remains. Invertebrate remains, in K J Matthews, *Excavations at Chester: The evolution of the heart of the city. Investigations at 3-15 Eastgate Street 1990/1*, Chester City Council Archaeological Service Excavation and Survey Reports **8**, Chester

Harrison, P, 1989 Union Street, *Winchester Museums Service Newsletter* **4**, 8-10

Hartley, E, Hawkes, J, Henig, M, and Mee, F (eds), 2006 *Constantine the Great: Yorks Roman Emperor*, York and Aldershot

Hartley, K F, and Tomber, R, 2006 A mortarium bibliography for Roman Britain, *J Roman Pottery Stud* **13**

Harvey, B, 1993 *Living and dying in England 1100-1540: the monastic experience*, Clarendon Press, Oxford

Harvey, J, 1981 *Medieval gardens*, London

Haslam, J (ed.), 1984 *Anglo-Saxon towns in southern England*, Phillimore Chichester **18**

Hather, J G, 2000 *The identification of northern European woods; a guide for archaeologists and conservators*, Archetype, London

Hattatt, R, 1987 *Brooches of antiquity*, Oxford

Hatting, T, 1983 Osteological investigations on Ovis aries L., *Videnskablige meddelelser fra dansk naturhistorisk forening* **144**, 115-135

Hatting, T, 1990 Cats from Viking Age Odense, *J Danish Archaeol* **9**, 179-93

Havard, T, and Watts, M, 2008 Bingham Hall, King Street, 2002, in Holbrook (ed.) 2008, 33-40

Hawkes C F C, Myres J N L, Stevens C G, 1930 Saint Catherine's Hill, Winchester, *Proc Hampshire Fld Club Archaeol Soc* 11, 1-286

Hawkes, C F C, 1976 St. Catherine's Hill, Winchester: the report of 1930 re-assessed, in D W Harding, (ed.), *Hillforts: Later Prehistoric Earthworks in Britain and Ireland*, Academic Press, London

Hawkes, S C, 1994 Longbridge Deverill Cow Down, Wiltshire, House 3: a major round house of the Early Iron Age, *Oxford J Archaeol* **13(1)**, 49-69

Hayward, P, Nelson-Smith, T, and Shields, C, 1996 *Sea-Shore of Britain and Europe*, London

Hedges, J W 1978 The loomweights, in Collis 1978, 33-9

Hedges, R E M, Bronk, C R, and Housley, R A 1989 The Oxford Accelerator Mass Spectrometry facility: technical developments in routine dating, *Archaeometry*, **31**, 99-113

Hedges, R E M, and van Klinken, G J, 1992 A review of current approaches in the pre-treatment of bone for radiocarbon dating by AMS, *Radiocarbon* **34(3)**, 279-91

Henry, P, 2005 Who produced the textiles? Changing gender roles in Late Saxon textile production: the archaeological and documentary evidence, in F Pritchard and J P Wild (eds) *Northern archaeological textiles. NESAT VII. Textile symposium in Edinburgh, 5th-7th May 1999*, Oxbow Books, Oxford, 51-7

Hildebrand, K, 1992 *Swedish iron in the seventeenth and eighteenth centuries, export industry before industrialization*, Jernkontorets Bergshistoriska Skriftserie **29**, Oslo

Hillam, J, 1991 *Tree ring analysis of timbers from The Brooks, Winchester, Hampshire*, Ancient Monuments Laboratory Report **69/92**, London

Hillson, S, 1992 *Mammal bones and teeth. An introductory guide to methods of identification*, Institute of Archaeology, University of London

Hinton, D A, 1982 *Medieval jewellery: from the eleventh to the fifteenth century*, Shire Archaeology **21**

Hinton, D A, Keene, S, and Qualmann, K E, 1981 The Winchester Reliquary, *Med Arch* **25**, 45-77

HMSO, 1990a *Planning policy guidance 16: Archaeology and planning*, London

HMSO, 1990b *Planning policy guidance 15: Planning and the historic environment*, London

Hobbs, R 1996 *British Iron Age coins in the British Museum*, London

Hodges, R A 1981, *The Hamwih pottery: the local and imported wares from 30 years' excavations at Middle Saxon Southampton and their European context*, CBA Res Rep, **37**

Holbrook, N (ed.), 1998 *Cirencester: the Roman town defences, public buildings and shops*, Cirencester Excavations **5**, Cirencester

Holbrook, N (ed.), 2008 *Excavations and observations in Roman Cirencester, 1998-2007*, Cirencester Excavations **6**, Cirencester

Holbrook, N, and Bidwell, P T, 1991 *Roman finds from Exeter*, Exeter Archaeol Rep **4**, Exeter

Holmes, K, Matthews, C, and Rees, H, 2004 Iron Age Pottery, in Qualmann *et al.* 2004

Holmes, K, Turner, A, Matthews, C, King A C, Ball R, and Rees, H, forthcoming The suburbs, in Holmes *et al.* forthcoming

Holmes, K, and Matthews, C (ed. H Rees), forthcoming All this of pot and potter: 1500 years of Winchester pottery, excavations 1971-86, English Heritage/Winchester Museums Service

Holt, T J, Rees, E I, Hawkins, S J, and Seed, R, 1998 *Biogenic Reefs: An overview of dynamic and sensitivity characteristics for conservation management of marine SACs*, UK Marine SACs Project **9**, Oban

Howel, I (ed.), 2005 *Prehistoric landscape to Roman villa: excavations at Beddington, Surrey 1981-7*, MoLAS Monograph **26**, MoLAS/English Heritage, London

Hughes, M K, and Diaz, H F, 1994 *The Medieval warm period*, The Netherlands

Humphrey, J, 2003 The use of flint in the British Iron Age, in J Humphrey (ed.), *Researching the Iron Age: selected papers from the proceedings of the Iron Age Research Students Seminars 1999 – 2000*, Leicester Archaeology Monograph **11**, Leicester

Hunter, K, 2005 Charred plant remains, in Birbeck *et al.* 2005, 163-73

Hurst, D, (ed.) 2006 *Roman Droitwich: Dodderhill fort, Bays Meadow villa and roadside settlement*, CBA Res Rep **146**, York

Hurst J G, 1976 The pottery, in D M Wilson (ed.) *The Archaeology of Anglo-Saxon England*, 283-348

Hurst, J G, and Keene, C H, 1961 The kitchen area of Northolt Manor, Middlesex *Medieval Archaeol* 5, 211-99

Jackson, R P J, and Potter, T W, 1996 *Excavations at Stonea, Cambridgeshire 1980-85*, London

Jacomet, S, 1987 *Prähistorische GetreideFunde*, Botanisches Institut der Universität Abteilung Pflanzen Systematik und Geobotanik, Basel

James, S, 1999 An early medieval building tradition, in C E Karkov (ed.) *The archaeology of Anglo-Saxon England: basic readings*

James, S, and Millett, M (eds), 2001 *Britons and Romans: advancing an archaeological agenda*, CBA Res Rep **125**, York

James, T B, 1988 *Newsletter Hampshire Fld Club Archaeol Soc*, New Series **9**

James, T B, 1997 *English Heritage book of Winchester.* London, Batsford, 1st Edition

James, T B, 2007 *English Heritage book of Winchester.* London, Batsford, 2nd enlarged edition

James, T B, and Roberts, E, 2000 From palace to Pentice: Winchester and late-medieval urban development *Medieval Archaeol* **44**, 181-200

Johansson, F, and Hüster, H, 1987 *Untersuchungen an Skelettresten von Katzen aus Haithabu (Ausgrabung 1966-1969)*, Berichte über die Ausgrabungen in Haithabu, Bericht **24**, Karl Wachholtz Verlag, Neumünster

Johnstone, C, 2004 A biometric study of equids in the Roman World, unpubl Ph.D thesis, University of York, (http://www.york.ac.uk/depts/arch/pgstudents/Johnstone.html)

Johnstone, C, and Albarella, U, 2002 *The Late Iron Age and Romano-British mammal and bird bone assemblage from Elms Farm, Heybridge, Essex (site code: HYEF93-95)*, Centre for Archaeology Report **45**, English Heritage, Portsmouth

Jones, A K G, 1982 Human parasite remains: prospects for a quantitative approach, in A R Hall and H K Kenward (eds), *Environmental archaeology in the urban context*, London, CBA Res Rep **43**, 66-70

Jones, A K G, 1986 Fish bone survival in the digestive system of pig, dog and man: some experiments, in D C Bruinkhuisen and A T Clason (eds), *Fish and Archaeology*, BAR Int Ser **294**, Oxford, 53-61

Jones, A K G, 1988 Fish bone from excavations in the cemetery of St. Mary Bishophill Junior, in T P O'Connor, *Bones from the General Accident site, Tanner Row*, The Archaeology of York **15/2**, CBA, London, 126-31

Jones, A K G, 2008 Analysis of earth samples from excavations at Southampton French Quarter (SOU1382) for eggs of intestinal parasites and other microfossils, Unpubl report submitted to Oxford Archaeology, Division of Archaeological, Geographical and Environmental Sciences, University of Bradford

Jones, V, and Dickinson, B, forthcoming Samian ware, in Holmes *et al.* forthcoming

Jordanova N, Jordanova J, and Karloukovski, V, 1996 Magnetic fabric of Bulgarian loess sediments derived by using various sampling techniques, *Studia geophyisca et geodetica* **40**, 36-49

Karloukovski, V, and Hounslow, M W, 2005 Report on the archaeomagnetic dating of seventeen hearths from Northgate, Winchester, Lancaster University (report for Oxford Archaeology)

Kars, H 1983 Early-medieval Dorestad, an archaeo-petrological study, part 5: The whetstones and the touchstones, *Berichten van de Rijksdienst voor het Oudheidkundig Bodemonderzoek* **33**, 1-37

Keene, D J, 1985 *Survey of Medieval Winchester*, Winchester Studies **2**, Oxford

Keene, D J, 1990a Shingles, in M Biddle (ed.) 1990, 320-26

Keene, D J, 1990b The textile industry, in M Biddle (ed.) 1990, 200-13

Keene, D J, 1990c Wooden Vessels, in M Biddle (ed.) 1990, 959-68

Keller, C, 1995, Pingsdorf-type ware: an introduction, *Medieval ceramics* **19**, 19-28

Kemp, P, and Bertness, M D, 1984 Snail shape and growth rates: evidence for plastic shell allometry in Littorina littorea, *Proceedings of the National Academy of Science of the United States of America* **81**, 811-13

Kent, B W 1992 *Making dead oysters talk: Techniques for analyzing oysters from archaeological sites*, Crownsville, Maryland

Kent, J T, Briden, J C, and Mardia, K V, 1983 Linear and planar structure in ordered mulivariatem data as applied to progressive demagnetisation of palaeomagnetic remanence, *Geophys J Royal Astro Soc* **81**, 75-87

Kenward, H K, and Hall, A R, 1995 *Biological evidence from Anglo-Scandinavian deposits at 16-22 Coppergate*, The archaeology of York **14/7**, CBA, York

Kenyon, R, 1987 The Claudian coinage, in N Crummy (ed.), *The coins from excavations in Colchester 1971-9*, Colchester Archaeological Report **4**, Colchester, 24-41

Kenyon, R, 2008 The copper coins of Gaius and Claudius from Victoria Road, in Rees *et al.* 2008, 118-23

Keys, L, 2006a The slag, in Teague and Ford 2006

Keys, L, 2006b The slag, in Teague 2006

Kilmurry, K 1980 *The pottery industry of Stamford, Lincolnshire, c. AD 850-1250*, BAR **84**, Oxford

King, A, 1991 Food production and consumption – meat, in R F J. Jones (ed.), *Britain in the Roman period: Recent trends*, J R Collins Publications, Department of Archaeology and Prehistory, University of Sheffield, 15-20

Kipling, R, and Scobie, G, 1990 Staple Gardens 1989 *Winchester Museums Service Newsletter* **6**, 8-9

Koch, W, 1954 *Lehrbuch der allgemeinen Tierzucht*, Stuttgart

L'Unité d'archéologie, Saint Denis, http://www.saint-denis.culture.fr/en/3_2a_pelletier.htm (accessed 31 July 2008)

Larsen, C S, 1997 *Bioarchaeology: Interpreting behavior from the human skeleton*, Cambridge University Press, Cambridge

Lawson, A J, 1975 Shale and jet objects from Silchester, *Archaeologia* **105**, 241-75

Lawson, A J, and Gingell, C J, 2000 *Potterne 1982-5: animal husbandry in later prehistoric Wiltshire*, Wessex Archaeology Rep **17**, Salisbury

Lewis M, 2004 Endocranial lesions in non-adult skeletons: understanding their aetiology, *Int J*

Osteoarchaeology **14**, 82-97

Littler, A S 1979 Fish in English economy and society down to the Reformation, unpubl PhD thesis, Univ Swansea

Liversidge, J, 1955 *Furniture in Roman Britain*, Alec Tiranti, London

Lloyd-Morgan, G. 2006 Small copper alloy ornaments other than ornaments, in Hurst (ed.) 2006, 196-200

Locker, A, 1990 The mammal, bird and fish bones, in D S Neal, A Wardle and J Hunn, *Excavation of the Iron Age, Roman and medieval settlement at Gorambury, St Albans*, English Heritage rep **14**, 205-10

Locker, A, 1996 The bird bones, in P Ashbee, Halangy Down, St Mary's Isles of Scilly, excavations 1964-1977, *Cornish Archaeol* **35**, 113-15

Locker, A 1997 The fish bones from excavations at The Brooks, Winchester, unpubl manuscript

Locker, A 2001 *The role of stored fish in England 900-1750 AD: the evidence from historical and archaeological data*, Publishing Group Ltd, Univ Southampton

Longin, R, 1971 New method of collagen extraction for radiocarbon dating, *Nature* **230**, 241-2

Luff, R M, 1982 *A zooarchaeological study of the Roman North-western provinces*, BAR Int Ser **137**

Luff, R M, 1996 Bene't Court: A preliminary assessment of the animal bones, in D N Edwards, Excavations at Bene't Court, Cambridge, Cambridge Archaeological Unit, Cambridge, unpubl archive report

Luff, R M, 1999 Animal and human bones, in Turner, R, *Excavations of an Iron Age settlement and Roman religious complex at Ivy Chimneys, Essex 1978-83*, East Anglian Archaeol Rep **88**, 204-23

Luff, R M, and Moreno Garcia, M, 1995 Killing cats in the medieval period. An unusual episode in the history of Cambridge, England, *Archaeofauna* **4**, 93-114

Lyne, M A B, 1994 Late Roman handmade wares in south-east Britain, unpubl PhD thesis, Univ Reading

Lyne, M A B, forthcoming Appendix 4: The late Roman pottery supply to Winchester: evidence from The Brooks, in Holmes and Matthews forthcoming

Lyne, M A B, and Jefferies, R S, 1979, The Alice Holt/Farnham Roman pottery industry, CBA Res Rep **30**, London

Mabey, R, 1972 *Food for Free*, Collins, London

MacGregor, A, 1985 *Bone, antler, ivory and horn. The technology of skeletal materials since the Roman period*, Croom Helm, London

MacGregor, A, Mainman, A J, and Rogers, N S H (eds), 1999 *Bone, antler, ivory and horn from Anglo-Scandinavian and medieval York*, The archaeology of York **17/12**, York Archaeological Trust/CBA, York

Mack, I, McDonnell, G, Murphy, S, Andrews, P, and Wardle, K, 2000 Liquid steel in Anglo-Saxon England, *Historical Metallurgy* **34 (2)**, 87-96

Mackenzie, D, 1980 *Goat husbandry*, 4th ed, Faber and Faber; London, Boston

Macphail, R I, 1981 Soil and botanical studies of the 'Dark Earth', in M Jones and G. W Dimbleby (eds), *The environment of man: the Iron Age to the Anglo-Saxon period*, BAR Brit Ser **87**, Oxford, 309-31

Magnell, O, 2006 *Att befolka en stadsdel – Pälsare i det medeltida kvarteret Blekhagen, Lund*, META medeltidsarkeologisk tidskrift, **4**, 2006

Mainman, A J, 1999 Past research, in MacGregor, *et al.* 1999

Mainman, A J, and Rogers, N S H, 2000 *Craft, industry and everyday life: Finds from Anglo-Scandinavian York*, The archaeology of York **17/14**, York Archaeological Trust/CBA, York

Maltby, M, 1981 Iron Age, Romano-British and Anglo-Saxon animal husbandry – a review of the faunal evidence, in M Jones and G. Dimbleby (eds), *The environment of man: the Iron Age to the Anglo-Saxon period*, BAR Brit Ser **87**, 155-203

Maltby, M, 1987 *The animal bones from the excavations at Owlesbury, Hants. An Iron Age and Early Romano-British settlement*, AML Rep **6/87**, English Heritage

Maltby, M, 1993 Animal bones, in Woodward *et al*, 315-40

Maltby, M, 1994 The meat supply in Roman Dorchester and Winchester, in A R Hall and H K Kenward (eds), *Urban-rural connexions: perspectives from environmental archaeology*, Oxbow Books, Oxford, 85-102

Maltby, M, 2007 Chop and change: Specialist cattle carcass processing in Roman Britain, in B Croxford, N Ray, R Roth and N White (eds), *TRAC 2006. Proceedings of the sixteenth annual Theoretical Roman Archaeology Conference*, Oxbow Books, Oxford, 59-76

Maltby, M, 2010 Feeding a Roman town. Environmental evidence from excavations in Winchester, 1972-1985, Winchester Museums and English Heritage

Mann, J E, 1982 *Early medieval finds from Flaxengate. Vol 1: Objects of antler, bone, stone, horn, ivory, amber and jet*, Archaeology of Lincoln **14.1**, London

Manning, W H, 1976 *Catalogue of Romano-British ironwork in the Museum of Antiquities, Newcastle upon Tyne*, Newcastle upon Tyne

Manning, W H, 1985 Catalogue of the Romano-British iron tools, fittings and weapons in the British Museum, London

Manning, W H, Price, J, and Webster, J, 1995 *Report on the excavations at Usk 1965-1976: The Roman Small Finds*, Cardiff

Matthews, C, and Holmes, K, forthcoming Fabric list and descriptions, in Holmes and Matthews forthcoming

Matthews, C, forthcoming Pottery from the later cemeteries, in Holmes and Matthews forthcoming

May, E, 1985 Widerristhöhe und Langknochen-masse bei Pferd – ein immer noch aktuelles problem, *Zeitschrift für Säugertierkunde* 50, 368-82

Mays, S, 1998 *The archaeology of human bones*, London

McAvoy, F, with Morris, E L, and Smith G, 1980 The excavation of a muliti-period site at Carngoon Bank, Lizard, Cornwall, 1979, *Cornish Archaeol* 19, 31-62

McCann, J, and McCann, P, 2004 *The Dovecotes of Historical Somerset*, Somerset Vernacular Building Research Group

McCobb, L M E, Briggs, D E G, Carruthers, W J, and Evershed, R P, 2003 Phosphatisation of seeds and roots in a Late Bronze Age deposit at Potterne, Wiltshire, UK, *J Archaeol Sci* 30, 1269-81

McNeil, I, 1990 *An Encyclopaedia of the history of technology*, Routledge

Meates, G W, 1979 *The Roman villa at Lullingstone, Kent. Volume 1 – the site*, Kent Archaeol Soc. Monograph 1, Maidstone

Meates, G W, 1987 *The Roman villa at Lullingstone, Kent. Volume 2 – the wall paintings and finds*, Kent Archaeol Soc Monograph 3, Maidstone

Mellor, M, 2003 The Saxon and medieval ceramic finds from the town sites, in A Dodd (ed.) *Oxford before the University*, Oxford Archaeol Unit Thames Valley Landscapes Monograph 17, Oxford 326-45

Mennerich, G, *1968 Römerzeitliche Tierknochen aus drei Fundorten des Niederrheingebiets*, unpubl dissertation, München

Mepham, L, 2000 pottery, in Birbeck V, *Archaeological Investigations on the A34 Newbury Bypass, Berkshire/Hampshire, 1991-7*, Trust for Wessex Archaeology Ltd

Mepham, L, and Brown L, 2007 The Broughton to Timsbury pipline, Part 1: A Late Saxon pottery kiln and the production centre at Michelmersh, Hampshire, *Proc Hampshire Fld Club Archaeol Soc* 62, 25-68

Message on the ZooArch discussion list, 24 Aug 2007, http://www.jiscmail.ac.uk/cgi-bin/webadmin?A0=ZOOARCH

Miles, D, Palmer, S, Smith, A, Jones, G P, 2007 *Iron Age and Roman settlement in the Upper Thames Valley*, Thames Valley Landscapes Monograph 26, Oxford

Millett, M, 1987 An early Roman burial tradition in central southern England, *Oxford J Archaeol* 6(1), 63-6

Mills, A, and McDonnell, J G, 1992 *The identification and analysis of the hammerscale from Burton Dassett, Warwickshire*, AML Report 47/92

Ministry of Agriculture, Fisheries and Food Agricultural Development and Advisory Service, *1977 Manual of veterinary parasitological laboratory techniques*, Technical Bulletin 18, HMSO, London

Monk, M A, 1985 The plant economy, in Fasham 1985

Mook, W G, 1986 Business meeting: Recom-mendations/resolutions adopted by the Twelfth International Radiocarbon Conference, *Radiocarbon* 28, 799

Moore, D T, 1978 The petrography and archaeology of English honestones, *J Archaeol Sci* 5, 61-73

Moore, H, and Preston, S, 2008 Late Saxon and early medieval occupation at 26-7 Staple Gardens, Winchester, *Proc Hampshire Fld Club Archaeol Soc* 63, 135-78

Morales A, and Rosenlund K, 1979 *Fish bone measurements*, Steenstrupia, Copenhagen

Palliser, D M (ed.), 2000 *The Cambridge Urban History of Britain, Volume 1 600-1540*, Cambridge

Morton, A D (ed.), 1992 *Excavations at Hamwic: Volume 1*, CBA Res Rep 84

Mould, Q, 2000 The small finds, in Ellis (ed.) 2000, 108-44

MPRG 1998, *A Guide to the classification of medieval ceramic forms*, Medieval Pottery Research Group Occasional Paper 1

MPRG 2001, *Minimum standards for the processing, recording, analysis and publication of Post-Roman ceramics*, Medieval Pottery Research Group Occasional Paper 2

Munby, J, 1987 Medieval domestic buildings, in J Schofield and R Leech (eds) *Urban archaeology in Britain*, 156-66

Musty, J, Algar, D J, and Ewence, P F, 1969 The medieval pottery kilns at Laverstock, near Salisbury, Wiltshire, *Archaeologia* 102, 83-150

NASA-IGRF Geomagnetic Field Model, 2005 http://nssdc.gsfc.nasa.gov/space/model/models/igrf.html

Naylor, J C, and Smith, A F M, 1988 An archaeolog-ical inference problem, *J American Statistical Association* 83, 588-95

Neal, D S, 1996 *Excavations on the Roman Villa at Beadlam, Yorkshire*, Yorkshire Archaeological Report 2, Leeds

Neal, E, and Cheeseman, C, 1996 *Badgers*, T & AD Poyser Natural History, London

Nenk, B S, Margeson, S, and Hurley, M, 1995 Medieval Britain and Ireland in 1994, *Medieval Archaeol* 39

Newman, P B, 2001 *Daily life in the Middle Ages*, McFarland

Newton, S M, 1980 *Fashion in the age of the Black Prince*, Boydell & Brewer Ltd

Nicholson, R A, 1993 An investigation into the effects on fish bone of passage through the human gut: some experiments and comparisons with archaeological material, *Circaea* 10, 38-51

Nicholson, R A, forthcoming Fish remains, in Brown and Hardy forthcoming

Noe-Nygaard, N, 1974 Mesolithic hunting in Denmark illustrated by bone injuries caused by human weapons, *J Archaeol Sci*, 1, 217-48

Noel M, and Batt C M, 1990, A method for correcting geographically separated remanence directions for the purpose of archaeomagnetic dating, *Geophys J. Int*, 102, 753-56

North J J, 1994 *English Hammered Coinage. Volume I. Early Anglo-Saxon to Henry III c. 600-1272*, 3rd ed. London

OA, 2004 Northgate House, Winchester: Research design. (client report)

OA, 2005a Northgate House, Staple Gardens, Winchester, Hampshire, NGR SU 479 297: Written scheme of investigation for archaeological excavation of Areas 3a and 3b. Rev. 4 (client report)

OA, 2005b Winchester Cultural Centre, Winchester Library, Jewry Street, Winchester, Hampshire, NGR SU 480 297: Written scheme of investigation for an archaeological evaluation and watching brief (client report)

OA, 2005c Winchester Cultural Resource Centre Winchester Library, Jewry Street, Winchester: Archaeological evaluation and watching brief report (client report)

OA, 2005d Cultural Discovery Centre, Winchester Library, Jewry Street, Winchester, Hampshire, NGR SU 480 297: Written scheme of investigation for archaeological excavation and watching brief (client report)

OA, 2005e World War 2 air raid shelter graffiti, Jewry Street, Winchester: Written scheme of investigation for archaeological recording (client report)

OA, 2005f Winchester Library, Winchester: Written scheme of investigation for archaeological recording (building recording) (client report)

OA, 2006 Two World War 2 air raid shelters Jewry Street, Winchester: Graffiti: Historic building recording (client report)

OA, 2007a Winchester Joint Publication, Winchester, Hampshire, NGR SU 479 297: Revised research aims (client report)

OA, 2007b Winchester Library (Former Corn Exchange) Jewry Street, Winchester: Historic building investigation and recording (client report)

OA, 2007c Winchester Joint Publication, Winchester, Hampshire: Updated project design (client Report)

O'Connor, S, 1999 The preservation, identification and preservation of the finds, in MacGregor *et al.*, 1898-901

O'Connor, T P, 1982 *Animal bones from Flaxengate, Lincoln, c 870-1500*, The archaeology of Lincoln **18-1**, Lincoln Archaeological Trust, Lincoln

O'Connor, T P, 1988 *Bones from the General Accident site, Tanner Row*, The archaeology of York: The animal bones **15/2**, York Archaeological Trust/CBA

Ottaway, P, 1992 *Anglo-Scandinavian Ironwork from Coppergate*, The archaeology of York **17/6**, London

Ottaway, P J, 2001 Excavations on the site of the Roman signal station at Carr Naze, Filey, 1993-94, *Archaeol J* **157**, 79-199

Owens, E J, 1992 *The city in the Greek and Roman world*, Routledge

Page, P, Atherton, K, and Hardy, A, 2005 *Barentin's Manor: excavations of the moated manor at Harding's Field, Chalgrove, Oxfordshire 1976-9*, Oxford Archaeology Thames Valley Landscapes Monograph **24**, Oxford

Pantin, W A, 1962-3 Medieval English town-house plans, *Medieval Archaeol* **6-7**, 202-39

Parfitt, K, Corke, B, and Cotter, J, 2006 *Townwall Street, Dover: Excavations 1996*, Canterbury Archaeological Trust

Parker, A, 1988 The birds of Roman Britain. *Oxford J Archaeol* **7**, 197-226

Payne, A, Corney, M, and Cunliffe, B, 2007 *The Wessex Hillforts Project: Extensive survey of hillfort interiors in Central Southern England*, English Heritage

Payne, S, 1973 Kill-off patterns in sheep and goats: the mandibles from Aşwan Kale, *Anatolian studies*, **13**, 281-303

Peacock, D P S, 1987 Iron Age and Roman Quern Production at Lodsworth, West Sussex, *Antiq J* **67**, 61-85

Peacock, D P S, and Williams, D F, 1986 *Amphorae and the Roman economy*, London

Pearson, G W, and Stuiver, M, 1986 High precision calibration of the radiocarbon time scale, 500-2500 BC, *Radiocarbon* **28**, 839-62

Peers, C, and Ralegh, C A R, 1943 The Saxon monastery of Whitby, *Archaeologia* **89**, 27-88

Pelling, R, 2002 The charred plant remains, in Z Kamash, D Wilkinson, B Ford and J Hiller, Late Saxon and medieval occupation: Evidence from excavations at Lincoln College, Oxford, 1997-2000, *Oxoniensia* **67**, 199-286

Pelling, R, 2006 The charred and waterlogged plant remains, in D Poore, D Score and A Dodd, No 4A Merton Street, Merton College, Oxford: the evolution of a medieval stone house and tenement and an early college property, *Oxoniensia* **71**, 211-339

Pelling, R, in preparation, Oxford Castle: The charred, mineralised and waterlogged plant remains

Phillipson, D W, 1964 The Roman coins [from Staple Gardens], in Cunliffe 1964, 181-82

Philpott, R, 1991 *Burial practices in Roman Britain*, BAR Brit Ser **219**, Oxford

Pieper, H, Heinrich, D, and Reichstein H, 1995 *Untersuchungen an Skelettresten von Vögeln und Pferden aus dem mitteralterlichen Schleswig. Ausgrabung Schild 1971 – 1975*, Ausgrabungen in Schleswig/ Berichte und Studien **11**, Wachholtz Verlag, Neumunster

Pinhorne C M W, and Cooper J M, 1998 Subterranean Winchester, *Hampshire Field Club Archaeol Soc Newsletter* **30**, 12-14

Platt, C, and Coleman-Smith, R, 1975 *Excavations in Medieval Southampton, 1953-1969*, Leicester University Press, Leicester

Pollard, R J, 1987 The other Roman pottery, in Meates 1987, 164-305

Poole, C, 2000 Structural daub and baked clay, in Cunliffe and Poole 2000

Poole, C, 2008 The wall daub, painted plaster and mortar, in Cunliffe and Pool 2008

Poole, C, forthcoming The fired clay, in P Andrews, E Biddulph, A Hardy and A Smith forthcoming, Settling the Ebbsfleet Valley: CTRL excavations at Springhead and Northfleet, Kent: The late Iron Age, Roman, Saxon and medieval landscape, Oxford Wessex Archaeology

Poole, C, forthcoming The fired clay, in Brown and Hardy forthcoming

Poppe, G T, and Goto, Y, 1991 *European seashells I (Polyplacophora, Caudofoveata, Solenogastra, Gastropoda)*, Hackenheim

Poppe, G T, and Goto, Y, 1993 *European seashells II (Scaphopoda, Bivalvia, Cephalopoda)*, Hackenheim

Pratt, C, and Coleman-Smith, R, 1975 *Excavations in medieval Southampton 1953-1969: Vol 1 the excavation reports*, Leicester University Press

Price, J, 1978 The glass flask, in Collis 1978, 102

Price, J, 2002 Broken bottles and quartz sand: glass production in Yorkshire and the north in the Roman period, in Wilson and Price 2002, 81-93

Price, J, and Cottam, S, 1996 The glass, in D S Neal 1996, 93-108

Price, J, and Cottam, S, 1998 *Romano-British glass vessels: a handbook*, CBA Practical Handbook in Archaeology **14**, York

Price, J, and Worrell, S, 2006 Glass, in Ellis and White 2006, 129-38

Pritchard F A, 1986, Ornamental stonework from Roman London, *Britannia* **17**, 169-90

Pritchard F A, 1991 Dyepots, in Vince and Jenner 1991, 168-9

Prummel, W, and Frisch, H J, 1986 A guide for the distinction of species, sex and body side in bones of sheep and goat, *J Archaeol Sci* **13**, 567-77

Qualmann, K E, 1991 The Winchester evidence, in Fasham and Whinney 1991, 10-11

Qualmann, K E, 1993 Roman Winchester, in S J Greep (ed), *Roman towns: the Wheeler inheritance. A review of 50 years' research*, CBA Res Rep **93**, 66-77

Qualmann, K E, Rees, H, Scobie, G D, and Whinney, R, 2004 *Oram's Arbour – the Iron Age enclosure at Winchester Volume 1: investigations 1950-1999*, Winchester Museum Service, Winchester

Quirk, R N, 1957 Winchester Cathedral in the tenth century, *Archaeol J* **114**, 28-68

Rackham, D J, 1995 Appendix: Skeletal evidence of medieval horses from London sites, in J Clark (ed.), The medieval horse and its equipment c. 1150-c. 1450, *Medieval finds from excavations in London* **5**, Museum of London, London, 169-74

Rackham, O, 2006 *Woodlands*, London

Rahtz, P, 1976 Building and rural settlement, in D M Wilson (ed.), *The archaeology Anglo-Saxon England*, Cambridge University, 49-98

Redknap, M, 1986 The wall plaster, in M Millett and D Graham, *Excavations on the Romano-British small town at Neatham, Hampshire, 1969-1979*,

Hampshire Fld Club Archaeol Soc Monograph **3**, Gloucester, 138-9

Redknap, M, 1998 Counters, in Timby 1998, 105

Reece, R, 1973 Roman coinage in the western empire, *Britannia* **4**, 227-51

Reece, R, 1991 *Roman coins from 140 sites in Britain*, Cotswold Studies **4**, Cirencester

Reece, R, 2002 *The coinage of Roman Britain*, Stroud

Reed, R, 1975 *The nature and making of parchment*, Elmete Press, Leeds

Rees, H, forthcoming Summary and overview, in Holmes and Matthews forthcoming

Rees, H, Crummy, N, Ottaway, P J, and Dunn, G, 2008 *Artefacts and society in Roman and medieval Winchester: Small finds from the suburbs and defences, 1971-1986*, Winchester Museums Service, Winchester

Reichstein, H, 1995 *Erste Nachweise zum Vorkommen von Hauseseln im mittelalterlichen Schleswig-Holstein, Ausgrabungen in Schleswig: Berichte und Studien*, **11**, Wachholtz Verlag; Neumünster, 179-87

Reid, D G, 1996 *Systematics and evolution of Littorina*, London

Reimer, P J, Baillie, M G L, Bard, E, Bayliss, A, Beck, J W, Bertrand, C J H, Blackwell, P G, Buck, C E, Burr, G S, Cutler, K B, Damon, P E, Edwards, R L, Fairbanks, R G, Friedrich, M, Guilderson, T P, Hogg, A G, Hughen, K A, Kromer, B, McCormac, F G, Manning, S, Bronk Ramsey, C, Reimer, R W, Remmele, S, Southon, J R, Stuiver, M, Talamo, S, Taylor, F W, van der Plicht, J, and Weyhenmeyer, C E, 2004 IntCal04 terrestrial radiocarbon age calibration, 0-26 cal kyr BP, *Radiocarbon* **46**, 1029-58

Reinhard, K J, and Bryant V M Jr, 1992 Coprolite analysis: a biological perspective on archaeology, *Advances in archaeological method and theory* **4**, 245-88

Reynolds, P J, and Langley, J K, 1979 Romano-British corn-drying ovens: an experiment, *Archaeol J* **136**, 27-42

Richards, J D, 1991 *Viking Age England*, English Heritage

Richards, J D, 1999 The Scandinavian presence, in J Hunter and I Ralston (eds), *The archaeology of Britain*, Routledge, 194-209

Richardson, C A, Collis, S A, Ekaratne, K, Dare, P, and Key, D, 1993 The age determination and growth rate of the European flat oyster, Ostrea edulis, in British waters determined from acetate peels of umbo growth lines, *ICES J Marine Research* **50**, 493-500

Rigby, V, 1982 The coarse pottery, in J S Wacher and A D McWhirr, *Cirencester excavations I: early Roman occupation at Cirencester*, Cirencester, 153-200

Rigold, S E 1978 A medieval coin-balance from Roche Abbey, Yorkshire, *Antiq J* **58**, 371-4

Riley, H T, 1868 *Memorials of London and London life*, London

Rivet, A L F, and Smith, C, 1979 *The place-names of Roman Britain*, London

Rivet, A L F, 1982 Viae aviarae?, *Antiquity* **56**, 206-7

Roberts, C, and Manchester, K 1999 *The archaeology of disease*, 2nd ed, Cornell Press, Ithaka

Roberts, E, 2003 *Hampshire houses 1250-1700: Their dating and development*, Hampshire County Council

Roberts, I, 2002 *Pontefract Castle: Archaeological Excavations 1982-86*, Yorkshire Archaeology **8**, Wakefield

Robinson, M, 2003 Environmental reports, in A Dodd (ed.) *Oxford before the University*, Oxford Archaeol Unit Thames Valley Landscapes Monograph **17**, 365-89

Rogers, N S H, 1993 *Anglian and other finds from Fishergate*, The archaeology of York **17/9**, London

Rogers, W P, 1996 Tests for dye on potsherds from The Brooks, Winchester, unpubl TRA Report on behalf of Winchester Museums Service, 15 February 1996

Rumble, A, 2003 *Property and piety in early medieval Winchester: documents relating to the topography of the Anglo-Saxon and Norman City and its Ministers,* Winchester Studies **4/3**, Oxford

Sadler, P, 1991 The use of tarsometatarsi in sexing and ageing domestic fowl (Gallus gallus L.), and recognising five toed breeds in archaeological material, *Circaea* **8** (1), 41-8

Saier, B, 2000 Age-dependent zonation of the periwinkle Littorina littorea (L.) in the Wadden Sea, Helgoland, *Marine Res* **54**, 224-29

Samuel, A M, 1918 *The herring: its effects on the history of Britain*, London

Scheuer L, and Black S, 2000 *Developmental juvenile osteology*, Elsevier Academic Press, London

Schmid, E, 1972 *Atlas of animal bones for prehistorians, archaeologists and quatrenary geologists*, Elsevier, London

Schofield, J, 1994 *Medieval London Houses*, Yale University Press

Schofield, J, and Vince, A G, 2003 *Medieval towns: the archaeology of British towns in their European setting*, 2nd ed, Continuum

Schweingruber, F H, 1990 *Microscopic wood anatomy*, 3rd Ed, Swiss Federal Institute for Forest, Snow and Landscape Research

Scobie, G, 1994 Staple Gardens 1994, *Winchester Mus Service Newsl* **19**, 4-6

Scobie, G, 1995,, Topography and Development of Winchester (Part 1), *Winchester Mus Service Newsl* **21**, 4-6

Scobie, G, 1995b Topography and development (Part 2): Roman Winchester, *Winchester Mus Service Newsl* **22**, 4-9

Scobie, G, 1996 Topography and development (Part 4): Late Saxon Winchester, *Winchester Mus Service Newsl* **24**, 2-5

Scobie, G, 1997 Views on medieval urban environment – or what a of load of rubbish, *Winchester Mus Service Newsl*, **27**, 2-4

Scobie, G, forthcoming The Brooks, Winchester: The post-Roman remains, Winchester Museums Service

Scobie, G, and Qualmann, K E, 1993 *Nunnaminster: A Saxon and medieval community of nuns,* Winchester Museums Service

Scobie G D, Zant, J M, and Whinney R J B, 1991 *The Brooks, Winchester: a preliminary report on the excavations, 1987-88,* Winchester Museums Service Archaeological Report **1**, Winchester

Scott, E, 1999 *The archaeology of infancy and infant death*, BAR Int Ser **819**, Oxford

Scott, E M (ed.), 2003 The Third International Radiocarbon Intercomparison (TIRI) and the Fourth International Radiocarbon Intercomparison (FIRI) 1990-2002: results, analysis, and conclusions, *Radiocarbon* **45**, 135-408

Seager Smith, R, Brown, K, Mills, J M, and Biddulph, E, forthcoming Late Iron Age and Roman pottery, in P Andrews, E Biddulph, A Hardy and A Smith, Settling the Ebbsfleet Valley: CTRL excavations at Springhead and Northfleet, Kent – the Late Iron Age, Roman, Saxon and medieval, Oxford Wessex monograph

Seed, R, 1980 Shell growth and form in the Bivalvia, in D C Rhoads and R A Lutz (eds), *Skeletal growth of aquatic organisms: biological records of environmental change*, New York

Seeley, F, 1995 Roman doorbells, *Roman Finds Group Newsletter* **9**, 5-6

Seetah, K, 2006 Multidisciplinary approach to Romano-British cattle butchery, in M Maltby (ed.), *Integrating zooarchaeology*, Oxbow books, Oxford, 109-116

Serjeantson, D, 1988 Archaeological and ethno-graphical evidence for seabird exploitation in Scotland, *Archaeozoologia* **2**, 209-24

Serjeantson, D, 1989 Animal remains and the tanning trade, in D Serjeantson and T Waldron (eds), *Diet and crafts in towns: The evidence of animal remains from the Roman to the post-medieval periods*, BAR **199**, Oxford, 129-46

Serjeantson, D, 1996 The animal bones, in S Needham and T Spence, *Refuse and disposal at Area 16 east, Runnymede*, Runnymede Bridge research excavations **2**, British Museum Press, London, 194-253

Serjeantson, D, 2001 A dainty dish: consumption of small birds, in H Buitenhuis and W Prummel (eds), Late Medieval England, in *Animals and man in the past. Essays in honour of Dr. A.T.Clason emeritus professor of archaeozoology Rijksuniversiteit Groningen, the Netherlands*, ARC-Publicatie **41**, 263-73

Serjeantson, D, 2002 Goose husbandry in medieval England, and the problem of ageing goose bones, *Acta Zoologica Cracoviensia* **45** (special issue), 39-54

Serjeantson, D, 2006 Birds: Food and a mark of status, in Woolgar *et al* 2006, 31-147

Serjeantson, D, 2009 Food, craft and status: The Winchester suburbs and defences in a wider context, in Serjeantson and Rees (eds) 2009, 166-83

Serjeantson, D, and Rees, H, (eds) 2009 *Food, craft and status in medieval Winchester: The plant and animal remains from the suburbs and city defences*, Winchester Museums and English Heritage

Serjeantson, D, and Smith, P, 2009, Medieval and post-medieval animal bones from the northern and eastern suburbs and the city defences, in Serjeantson and Rees (eds) 2009, 82-157

Shaffrey, R (forthcoming) The worked stone, in Brown and Hardy forthcoming

Shaw, M, 1996 The excavation of a late 15th- to 17th-century tanning complex at The Green, Northampton, *Post-Medieval Archaeol* 30, 63-127

Shennan, S, 1997 *Quantifying archaeology*, Iowa University Press, Iowa

Silverside, A J, 1977 A phytosociological study of British arable weed and related communities, Univ Durham PhD thesis

Davis, S, Laboratório de Zoo-Arqueologia, Instituto Português de Arqueologia, Portugal (personal communication)

Sjödin, E, 1994 *Får*, LT:s Förlag, Stockholm

Slota Jr, P J, Jull, A J T, Linick, T W, and Toolin, L J, 1987 Preparation of small samples for 14C accelerator targets by catalytic reduction of CO, *Radiocarbon*, 29, 303-6

Smith, J M H, 2005 *Europe after Rome*, Oxford

Smith, J T, 1997 *Roman villas: a study in social structure*, Routledge, London

Smith, W (forthcoming) Charred, mineralised and waterlogged plant remains, in Brown and Hardy forthcoming

Stace, C, 1997 *New flora of the British Isles*, 2nd Ed, Cambridge University Press, Cambridge

Starley, D, 1993 *The assessment of Roman and later slag and other metalworking debris from Winchester, Brooks 1987-8*, AML Report 81/93

Starley, D, 1995 *Hammerscale*, Historical Metallurgy Society Datasheet 10

Steane, J M, 1985 *The archaeology of medieval England and Wales*, London

Stenhouse, M J, and Baxter, M S, 1983 14C dating reproducibility: evidence from routine dating of archaeological samples, *PACT* 8, 147-61

Stephens, J, 2008 Ancient Roman hairdressing: on (hair)pins and needles, *J Roman Archaeol* 21, 111-32

Strid, L, Archive report on the faunal remains from Abingdon Cinema (ABCIN02), unpubl report, Oxford Archaeology

Stuart, J D M, and Birkbeck, J M, 1936 A Celtic village on Twyford Down-excavated 1933-1934, *Proc Hampshire Fld Club Archaeol Soc* 13, 188-212

Stuiver, M, and Kra, R S, 1986 Editorial comment, *Radiocarbon* 28(2B), ii

Stuiver, M, and Polach, H A, 1977 Reporting of 14C data, *Radiocarbon* 19, 355-63

Stuiver, M, and Reimer, P J, 1986 A computer program for radiocarbon age calculation, *Radiocarbon* 28, 1022-30

Stuiver, M, and Reimer, P J, 1993 Extended 14C database and revised CALIB 3.0 14C age calibra-tion program, *Radiocarbon* 35, 215-30

Sykes, N J, 2004 The dynamic of status symbols: wildfowl exploitation in England AD 410-1550, *Antiquity* 161, 82-204

Sykes, N J, 2006a From Cu and Sceap to Beffe and Motton: the management, distribution and consumption of cattle and sheep, AD 410-1550, in Woolgar *et al.* 2006, 56-71

Sykes N J, 2006b The impact of Normans on hunting, in Woolgar *et al.* 2006, 162-75

Sykes, N J, White, J, Hayes, T E, and Palmer, M R, 2006 Tracking animals using strontium isotopes in teeth: the role of fallow deer (Dama dama) in Roman Britain, *Antiquity* 80, 948-59

Symonds, R P, 1992 *Rhenish wares, fine dark coloured pottery from Gaul and Germany*, Oxford Univ Comm for Archaeol Monograph 23

Tait, H (ed.), 1986 *Seven thousand years of jewellery*, London

Talk on bone evidence from tanneries. Archaeological Leather Group, tanning conference 12-13 April 2008

Tatton-Brown, T W T, 1980 The use of Quarr stone in London and East Kent, *Medieval Archaeol* 24, 213-15

Taylor, E L, 1955 Parasitic helminths in mediaeval remains, *The Veterinary Record* 67, 216-18

Taylor, J, 2004 The distribution and exchange of pink, grog-tempered pottery in the East Midlands: an update, *J Roman Pottery Stud* 11, 60-6

Teague, S, 1989a Lower Barracks, Winchester: archaeological evaluation, Winchester Museums Service archive LB 89 (unpubl archive report)

Teague, S, 1989b Excavations at The Square, *Winchester Mus Service Newsl* 3, 3-5

Teague, S, 1990 28-29 Staple Gardens, *Winchester Mus Service Newsl* 6, 6-8

Teague, S, 1991 Excavations at 2 Parchment Street, *Winchester Mus Service Newsl* 9, 3-5

Teague, S, 1998a Excavations at Andover Road 1998, *Winchester Mus Service Newsl* 31, 2-4

Teague, S, 1998b The deposit model, unpubl draft text for the Winchester Urban Archaeological Assessment, Winchester Museums Service/English Heritage

Teague, S, 2002 Dolphin House, St Peter Street, Winchester: Report on an archaeological evaluation, Winchester Museums Service, client report

Teague, S, 2006 Winchester Cultural Discovery Centre, Winchester Library, Jewry Street, Winchester, Hampshire. Post-excavation assessment and updated project design (client report)

Teague, S, and Ford, B, 2006 Northgate House, Staple Gardens, Winchester, Hampshire. Post-excavation assessment and updated project design (client report)

Tebble, N, 1966 *British bivalve seashells: A handbook for identification*, London

Teegen, W R, 2005 Rib and vertebral fractures in medieval dogs from Haithabu, Starigard and Schleswig, in J Davies, M Fabis, I Mainland, M

Richards and R Thomas (eds), *Diet and health in past animal populations. Current research and future directions*, 34-8

Thienpont, D, Rochette, F, and Vanparijs, O F J, 1986 *Diagnosing Helminthiasis by Coprological Examination. Janssen Research Foundation*, Belgium

Thirsk, J, 1967 *The Agrarian history of England and Wales 1500-1640*, Cambridge

Thomas, R N W, 1988 A statistical evaluation of criteria used in sexing cattle metapodials, *Archaeozoologia* **2(2)**, 83-92

Thomas, R, and Locock, M, 2000 Food for the dogs? The consumption of horseflesh at Dudley Castle in the eighteenth century, *Environmental Archaeol* **5**, 83-91

Thorpe, N, and Whinney, R, 2001 Oram's Arbour, Winchester, *Current Archaeol* **176**, 324-6

Ticehurst, N F, 1923 Some birds in the fourteenth century, *British birds* **17(2)**, 29-35

Timby, J, 1988 The Middle Saxon pottery, in P Andrews (ed.), *Southampton finds, volume I: the coins and pottery from Hamwic*, Southampton Archaeology Monograph **4**, 73-125

Timby, J R, 1998 *Excavations at Kingscote and Wycomb, Gloucestershire*, Cotswold Archaeological Trust Monograph, Cotswold Archaeological Trust

Timby, J, Brown, R, Biddulph, E, Hardy, A, and Powell, A, 2007 *A slice of rural Essex: archaeological discoveries between Stansted Airport and Braintree*, Oxford Wessex Archaeology Monograph **1**, Oxford and Salisbury

Tomber, R, 2003 Appendix 3: A Richborough 527 stamp from London, in Borgard and Cavalier 2003, 106

Tomber, R, and Dore, J, 1998 *The national Roman fabric reference collection: a handbook*, Mus of London Archaeol Service Monograph **2**

Tomalin, D J, 1987 *Roman Wight, a guide catalogue to "The island of Vectis, very near to Britannia"* Isle of Wight CC, Newport

Tomlinson, P, 1985 Use of vegetative remains in the identification of dyeplants from waterlogged 9th-10th century AD deposits at York, *J Archaeol Sci* **12**, 269-83

Tuffreau-Libre, M, 1999 Les pots à couleur de Pompéi : premiers résultats, *Rivista di Studi Pompeiana* **10**, 63-70

Tyson, R, 2000 *Medieval glass vessels found in England c. AD 1200-1500*, CBA Res Rep **21**, York

Ulbricht, I, 1984 *Die Verarbeitung von Knochen, Geweih und Horn im mittelalterlichen Schleswig. Ausgrabung Schild 1971-1975*, Ausgrabungen in Schleswig: Berichte und Studien **3**, Wachholtz Verlag, Neumünster

Unger, R W, 2004 *Beer in the Middle Ages and the Renaissance*, University of Pennsylvania Press

van Arsdell, R D, 1989, *Celtic coinage in Britain*, London

van Damme, D, and Ervynck, A 1988 Medieval ferrets and rabbits in the castle of Laarne (East-Flanders, Belgium): A contribution to the history of a predator and its prey, *Helinium* **28 (2)**, 278-84

van der Veen, M, 1994 Reports on the biological remains, in P Bidwell and S Speak, *Excavations at South Shields Roman fort*, Soc Antiq Newcastle upon Tyne Monograph **4**

van der Werff, J H, 2003 The third and second lives of amphoras in Alphen Aan Den Rijn, The Netherlands, *J Roman Pottery Stud* **10**, 109-16

Vandeputte, K, Moens, L, Dams, R, 1996 Improved sealed-tube combustion of organic samples to CO2 for stable isotopic analysis, radiocarbon dating and percent carbon determinations, *Analytical Letters* **29**, 2761-73

Vanpeene, N, 1993 *Verrerie de la Nécropole dÉpiais-Rhus (Val dOise)*, Centre de Recherches Archéologiques du Vexin Français Cahier Archéologique **8**, Guiry-en-Vexin

Vaughan-Williams, A, Austin P, Branch, N P, and Warman, S, 2005 19/20 Staple Gardens, Northgate, Winchester, Hampshire (site code: AY93): Bioarchaeological analysis (unpubl report)

VCH, 1912 Winchester: Fairs and trades, *A history of the county of Hampshire* **5**, 33-44

Veale, E M, 2003 *The English fur trade in the later Middle Ages*, London Record Society **38**, 2nd ed

Vince, A G., and Jenner, A, 1991 The Saxon and early medieval pottery of London, in A G Vince (ed.), *Aspects of Saxon and Norman London 2: finds and environmental evidence*, LAMAS Special Paper, **12**, 19-119

Vince, A G, Lobb, S J, Richards, J C, and Mepham, L, 1997 *Excavations in Newbury, Berkshire, 1979 – 1990*, Wessex Archaeol Rep **13**

Vince, A G., and Steane, K, 2008 The pottery, in Moore and Preston 2008

Viner, L, 1998 The finds evidence from Roman Cirencester, in Holbrook (ed.) 1998, 294-323

von den Driesch, A, 1976 *A guide to the measurement of animal bones from archaeological sites*, Peabody Museum of Archaeology and Ethnology, Harvard University

Vretemark, M, 1997 *Från ben till boskap. Kosthåll och djurhållning med utgångspunkt i medeltida benmaterial från Skara*, Skrifter från Länsmuseet Skara **25**

Vretemark, M, 2000 *Gamla Lödöse – analys av djurbensmaterial*, Riksantikvarieämbetet, Stockholm

WA, 2004 'document 1' Summary of archaeological results in revised Area 1 (formerly Block C Central, North, Link Trench and Lift Pit), unpubl client report

WA, 2008 19-20 Jewry Street, Winchester, Hampshire: Post-excavation assessment report, unpubl client report

Wacher, J S, 1995 *The towns of Roman Britain*, 2nd ed, London

Walker, K E, and Farwell, D E, 2000 *Twyford Down, Hampshire: Archaeological investigations on the M3 motorway from Bar End to Compton, 1990-93*, Hampshire Fld Club Monograph **9**

Walton P, 1989 *Textiles, cordage and raw fibre from 16-22 Coppergate*, The Archaeology of York **17/5**

Walton Rogers, P 1996 Tests for dye on potsherds from The Brooks, Winchester, unpubl TRA Report on behalf of Winchester Museums Service, 15 February 1996

Walton Rogers, P, 1999 Textile making equipment, in MacGregor *et al.* 1999, 1964-71

Walton Rogers, P, 2007 *Cloth and Clothing in Early Anglo-Saxon England*, CBA Res Rep **145**, York

Ward, G K, and Wilson, S R, 1978 Procedures for comparing and combining radiocarbon age determinations: a critique, *Archaeometry* **20**, 19-31

Ward-Perkins, J B, 1940 *London Museum Medieval Catalogue*, London

Ward-Perkins, J, and Claridge, A, 1976 *Pompeii AD 79*, London

Watson, B (ed.), 1998 Roman London: recent archaeological work: including papers given at a seminar held at the Museum of London on 16 November 1996, *J Roman Archaeol: Suppl ser* **24**

Watson, P, 2001 Textiles, in J Blair and N Ramsay (eds), *English medieval industries: craftsmen, techniques, products*, Continuum, 319-54

Watt, J, Pierce, G J, and Boyle, P R, 1997 *Guide to the identification of North Sea fish using premaxilla and vertebra*, ICES Cooperative Res Rep **220**, Denmark

Waugh, H, and Goodburn, R, 1972 The non-ferrous objects, in Frere 1972, 114-62

WCC, 2001 Winchester District Local Plan review, Winchester City Council

WCC, 2005 Hampshire County Library, Jewry Street, Winchester: Brief for archaeological field-work (Planning ref: HCC ref. WRG014), Winchester City Council

Webster, J, 1992 Objects of bronze, in Evans and Metcalf 1992, 103-63

Webster, L E, and Cherry, J (eds), 1979 Medieval Britain in 1978, *Medieval Archaeol* **23**, 234-78

Wenham, L P, and Heywood, B, 1997 *The 1968 to 1970 excavations in the vicus at Malton, North Yorkshire*, Yorkshire Archaeol Rep **3**, Leeds

West, B, 1982 Spur development: recognising caponised fowl in archaeological material, in B Wilson, C Grigson and S Payne (eds), *Ageing and sexing animal bones from archaeological sites*, BAR Brit Ser **109**, Oxford, 255-61

Wheeler, A 1978 *Key to the fishes of Northern Europe*, Frederick Warne, London

Wheeler, A, and Jones, A K G, 1989 *Fishes*, Cambridge Manuals in Archaeology, CUP

Wheeler, R E M, 1930 *London in Roman times*, London Museum Catalogues **3**, London

Whinney, R, 1981 Jack-O-Tooles Row, Boarhunt – a medieval kiln dump, *Proc Hampshire Fld Club Archaeol Soc* **37**, 41-8

Whinney, R, 1989 Lower Barracks – further progress, *Winchester Museums Service Newsletter* **4**, 11

Whinney, R, 1994 Oram's Arbour: the Middle Iron Age enclosure at Winchester, in A P Fitzpatrick and E L Morris (eds), *The Iron Age in Wessex: recent work*, Trust for Wessex Archaeol and Association Française D'Etude de L'Age du Fer, Salisbury

Whitney, E, 2004 *Medieval science and technology*, Greenwood

Wigh, B, 2001 *Animal husbandry in the Viking Age town of Birka and its hinterlands*, Riksantikvarieämbetet, Stockholm

Wild, J P, 1970 *Textile manufacture in the northern Roman provinces*, Cambridge

Wild, J P, 1988 *Textiles in archaeology*, Aylesbury

Wilkinson, M, 1979 The fish remains, in M Maltby, *The animal bones from Exeter 1971-1975*, Exeter Archaeol Reports **2**, 74-89

Willcox, G H, 1977 Exotic plants from Roman waterlogged sites in London, *J Archaeol Sci* **4**, 269-82

Williams, D F, and Wandibba, S, 1984 Petrological examination, in Cunliffe 1984, Mf 8, D13-E3

Willis, S, 1998 Samian pottery in Britain: exploring its distribution and archaeological potential, *Archaeol J* **155**, 82-133

Wilson, D G, 1975 Plant remains from the Graveney Boat and the early history of Humulus lupulus L. in W. Europe, *New Phytologist* **75**, 627-48

Wilson, P R, 2002 *Cataractonium: Roman Catterick and its hinterland. Excavations and research, 1958-1997, part 2*, CBA Res Rep **129**, York

Wilson, R J A, 2006 Urban defences and civic status in early Roman Britain, in R J A Wilson (ed.), *Romanitas: essays on Roman archaeology in honour of Sheppard Frere on the occasion of his ninetieth birthday*, Oxbow Books, Oxford, 1-48

Wilson, P, and Price, J, 2002 *Aspects of industry in Roman Yorkshire and the north*, Oxford

Wiltshire, P E J, 1995 The effect of food processing on the palatability of wild fruits with high tannin content, in H Kroll and R Pasternak (eds), *Res Archaeobotanicae Proc 9th IWGP Symposium, Kiel*, Oetker-Vosges, Kiel, 385-97

Winder, J M, 1980 The marine mollusca, in Holdsworth, P, *Excavations at Melbourne Street, Southampton 1971-76*, CBA Res Rep **33**, London, 121-27

Winder, J M, 1992 The Oysters, in I P Horsey, *Excavations in Poole 1973-1983*, Dorset Nat Hist Archaeol Soc Monograph **10**, Dorchester, 194-200

Woefle, E, 1967 *Vergleichend morphologische Untersuchungen an Einzelknochen des postcranialen Skelettes im Mitteleuropa vorkommender Enten, Halbgänse und Säger*, Inaugural-Dissertation, Ludwig-Maximilians-Universität, München

Wood, M, 1965 *The English medieval house*, London

Woodward, A, and Leach, P, 1993 *The Uley Shrines: excavation of a ritual complex on West Hill, Uley, Gloucestershire: 1978-79*, English Heritage Archaeol Rep **17**, London

Woodward, P J, Davies, S M, and Graham, A H, 1993 *Excavations at the Old Methodist Chapel and Greyhound Yard, Dorchester, 1981-4*, Dorset Nat His Archaeol Soc Monograph **12**, Dorchester

Woolgar, C M, Serjeantson, D, and Waldron, T, 2006 *Food in medieval England: diet and nutrition*, Oxford University Press

Worley, F, forthcoming Animal bones from Northfleet, in P Andrews, E Biddulph, A Hardy and A Smith, Settling the Ebbsfleet valley. CTRL excavations at Springhead and Northfleet, Kent – the late Iron Age, Roman, Anglo-Saxon and medieval landscape. Vol 2: The finds, Oxford Archaeology

WUAD, Winchester Urban Archaeological Database, Winchester Museum Service

Xu, S, Anderson, R, Bryant, C, Cook, G T, Dougans, A, Freeman, S, Naysmith, P, Schnabel, C, and Scott, E M, 2004 Capabilities of the new SUERC 5MV AMS facility for 14C dating, *Radiocarbon* **46**, 59-64

Yorke, B A E, 1982 The foundation of the Old Minster and the status of Winchester in the seventh and eighth centuries, *Proc Hants Field Club Archaeol Soc* **38**, 75-83

Young, C J, 1977 *The Roman pottery industry of the Oxford region*, BAR Brit Ser **43**, Oxford

Yule, B, 1990 The 'dark earth' and late Roman London, *Antiquity* **64**, 620-28

Yule, B, 2005 *A prestigious Roman building complex on the Southwark waterfront: excavations at Winchester Palace, London, 1983-90*, MoLAS Monograph **23**, London

Zananiri, I, Batt, C M, Tarling, D, Lanos, P, and Linford, P, 2007 Archaeomagnetic secular variation in the UK during the past 4000 years and its application to archaeomagnetic dating, *Physics of the Earth and Planetary Interiors* 160, 97-107

Zant, J, 1990 A Saxon 'Sceat' from The Square, *Winchester Mus Service Newsl* **8**, 2-3

Zant, J M, 1993 *The Brooks, Winchester, 1987-88: The Roman structural remains*, Winchester Mus Service Archaeol Rep **2**, Winchester

Zant, J, 2009 *Carlisle Millennium Project – excavations in Carlisle 1998-2001, vol 1: stratigraphy vol 1*, Lancaster imprints **14**, Oxford Archaeol Unit

Zienkiewicz, J D, 1986 *The legionary fortress baths at Caerleon. Vol 2: The finds*, Cardiff

Index